Community care a

third edition

Luke Clements is a consultant solicitor with Scott-Moncrieff, Harbour & Sinclair in London and a recognised authority on community care law. He is a Senior Research Fellow at Cardiff Law School at the University of Wales and a member of the Law Society's Mental Health and Disability Committee. He is a consulting editor to the *Journal of Community Care Law and Practice* and *Social Care Law Today* (Arden Davies Publishing) and an editor of the *Community Care Law Reports* (Legal Action Group). He has written widely and his recent publications include *Disabled Children and the Law* (Jessica Kingsley, 2001) and *Disabled People and European Human Rights* (Policy Press, 2003) – both written with Janet Read.

Luke Clements can be contacted by e-mail at clementslj@cf.ac.uk.

The Legal Action Group is a national, independent charity which campaigns for equal access to justice for all members of society. Legal Action Group:
- provides support to the practice of lawyers and advisers
- inspires developments in that practice
- campaigns for improvements in the law and the administration of justice
- stimulates debate on how services should be delivered.

Community care and the law

THIRD EDITION

Luke Clements

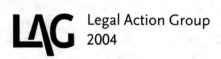 Legal Action Group
2004

Third edition published in Great Britain 2004
by LAG Education and Service Trust Limited
242 Pentonville Road, London N1 9UN
www.lag.org.uk

First published 1996
Reprinted with revisions 1997
Second edition 2000

British Library Cataloguing in Publication Data
a CIP catalogue record for this book is available from the British Library.

Crown copyright material is produced with the permission of the Controller of
HMSO and the Queen's Printer for Scotland.

ISBN-10 1 903307 19 8
ISBN-13 978 1 903307 19 8

Typeset by Regent Typesetting, London
Printed by Antony Rowe Ltd, Chippenham, Wilts

For my mother
for whom, as a nurse and a mother,
a wife, a widow and lover of defenceless animals,
family and community care did not prove to be
an academic subject.

Preface

Community care law results from a hotchpotch of statutes, many of which originated as private members' bills (and all the better for it). Although there are a number of general rules which can be applied to the subject, the most important appears to be that for every general rule there is at least one exception.

As with the previous editions, I have had great difficulty in deciding what to exclude. How can any text do justice to the subject and yet exclude detailed consideration of welfare benefits or special education? And so on. These subjects, however, are not covered in detail. I have tried to keep to the central community care statutes as listed in National Health Service and Community Care Act 1990 s46. Welfare benefits are not covered for two reasons: the first is that they change so frequently and the second is that the Child Poverty Action Group and the Disability Alliance already publish comprehensive and indispensable annual guides. The same can also be said for the excellent Education Law and Practice published by the Legal Action Group (1999).

I have tried to keep to a minimum the use of abbreviations, but have had to shorten references to the commonly used statutes. Likewise I have referred throughout to the early and important general policy guidance, Community Care in the Next Decade and Beyond: policy guidance (1990) as the '1990 Policy Guidance'. In several chapters or sections a particular piece of policy or practice guidance is important and in that section I have given it a shortened title, having of course explained what the shortened title refers to.

In writing this book I have received enormous assistance from count-less kind and wise people. Many important concepts have been explained to me by social workers in particular, and my clients have taught me far more than (I hope) they will ever realise. In preparing this edition, very par-ticular thanks are due to Pauline Thompson of Age Concern England. Special thanks are also due to: John Bangs, Richard Bartholomew, Steve Brett, Camilla Parker, Marion Chester, Jerry Clore, Gareth Cottrell, Phil Fennell, Stephen Knafler, Jenny McGhie, Ed Mitchell, Andrew Powell-Chandler, Michael Power, Janet Read, Adrian Rhead and Liz Wilson.

What is wrong in this text is entirely my own doing and I would wel-come any critical feedback.

Contents

Table of cases

om a hotchpotch of statutes, many of which
s' bills (and all the better for it). Although
ules which can be applied to the subject, the
at for every general rule there is at least one

ns, I have had great difficulty in deciding
ext do justice to the subject and yet exclude
e benefits or special education? And so on.
t covered in detail. I have tried to keep to
tutes as listed in National Health Service
s46. Welfare benefits are not covered for
y change so frequently and the second is
roup and the Disability Alliance already
spensable annual guides. The same can
ation Law and Practice published by the

num the use of abbreviations, but have
ommonly used statutes. Likewise I have
nd important general policy guidance,
ade and Beyond: policy guidance (1990)
several chapters or sections a particular
is important and in that section I have
f course explained what the shortened

ived enormous assistance from count-
portant concepts have been explained
r, and my clients have taught me far
ise. In preparing this edition, very par-
Thompson of Age Concern England.
Bangs, Richard Bartholomew, Steve
er, Jerry Clore, Gareth Cottrell, Phil
Ghie, Ed Mitchell, Andrew Powell-
, Adrian Rhead and Liz Wilson.
ely my own doing and I would wel-

Table of statutes

Table of statutory instruments

Table of circulars and guidance

Table of local government ombudsman complaints

Table of European conventions and treaties

Abbreviations

1990 policy guidance	*Community care in the next decade and beyond: policy guidance* (1990)
AIA 1996	Asylum and Immigration Act 1996
BCHS	'Better Care. Higher Standards' policy
CA 1989	Children Act 1989
CC(DD)A 2003	Community Care (Delayed Discharge, etc) Act 2003
CC(DP)A 1996	Community Care (Direct Payments) Act 1996
CDCA 2000	Carers and Disabled Children Act 2000
CHAI	Commission for Healthcare Audit and Inspection
CI	(Social Services Inspectorate) Chief Inspector's letter
CMHT	Community mental health team
CPA	Care programme approach
CRAG	Charging for residential accommodation guidance
CRB	Criminal records bureau
C(RS)A 1995	Cares (Recognition and Services) Act 1995
CSDPA 1970	Chronically Sick and Disabled Persons Act 1970
CSA 2000	Care Standards Act 2000
CSCI	Commission for Social Care Inspection
CSIW	Care Standards Inspectorate for Wales.
DAT	Drug action team
DETR	Department of the Environment, Transport and the Regions
DFG	Disabled facilities grant
DGM	District General Manager Guidance
DHSS	Department of Health and Social Security
DPA 1998	Data Protection Act 1998
DP(SCR)A 1986	Disabled Persons (Services, Consultation and Representation) Act 1986
DSS	Department for Social Security
ECHR	European Convention on Human Rights
EEA	European Economic Area
EL	Executive letter
EPA	Enduring power of attorney
EPIOC	Electric powered indoor/outdoor wheelchair
EU	European Union
FACS	Fair Access to Care Services 2002 Policy Guidance
FSS	Formula Spending Share
GP	General practitioner
HA	Health authority
HA 1999	Health Act 1999
HASSASSAA 1983	Health and Social Services and Social Security Adjudications Act 1983
HGCRA 1996	Housing Grants, Construction and Regeneration Act 1996
HIMP	Health improvement and modernisation plans *formerly* Health Improvement Programme

HRA 1998	Human Rights Act 1998
HSC	Health service circular
HSCA 2001	Health and Social Care Act 2001
HSC(CHS)A 2003	Health and Social Care (Community Health and Standards) Act 2003
HSG	Health service guidance
HSPHA 1968	Health Services and Public Health Act 1968
IAA 1999	Immigration and Asylum Act 1999
ICAS	Independent Complaints Advocacy Service
ILF	Independent living fund
JIP	Joint investment plan
LA	Local authority
LAC	Local authority circular
LASSA 1970	Local Authority Social Services Act 1970
LASSL	Local authority social services letter
LDP	Local delivery plan
LEA	Local education authority
LGA 1974	Local Government Act 1974
LGA 2000	Local Government Act 2000
LHB	Local health board
LIT	Local implementation team
MHA 1983	Mental Health Act 1983
NAA 1948	National Assistance Act 1948
NAFWC	National Assembly for Wales Circular
NASS	National Asylum Support Service
NCSC	National Care Standards Commission
NHS	National Health Service
NHSA 1977	National Health Service Act 1977
NHSCCA 1990	National Health Service and Community Care Act 1990
NIAA 2002	Nationality, Immigration and Asylum Act 2002
NSF	National Service Framework
NTA	National Treatment Agency for Substance Abuse
OT	Occupational therapist
PALS	Patient Advice and Liaison Service
PCC(S)A 2000	Powers of Criminal Courts (Sentencing) Act 2000
PCT	Primary care trust
PPF	Planning and priorities framework
POVA	Protection of vulnerable adults
RHA 1984	Registered Homes Act 1984
RMO	Responsible medical officer
RNCC	Registered nursing care contribution
RSL	Registered social landlord
SAP	Single assessment process
SHA	Strategic health authority
SSD	Social services department
SSI	Social Services Inspectorate
STBOP	Shifting the balance of power
STG	special transitional grant
UFSAMC	Unified and Fair System for Assessing and Managing Care (in Wales)
WHC	Welsh Health Circular
WOC	Welsh Office Circular

Diagrams contained in this text

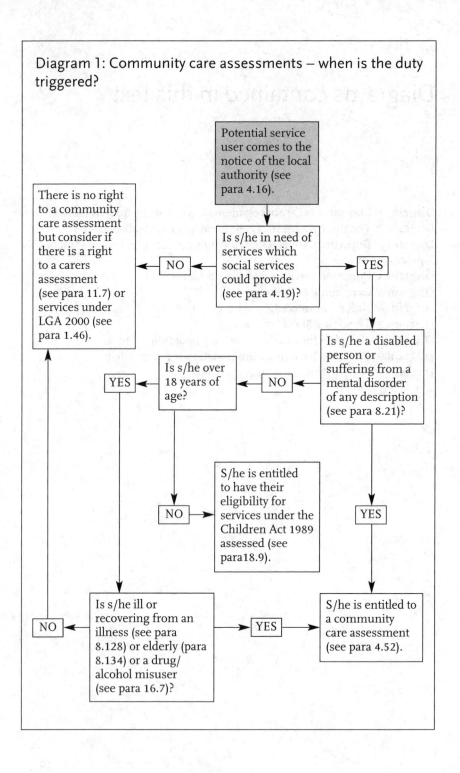

Diagram 1: Community care assessments – when is the duty triggered?

Potential service user comes to the notice of the local authority (see para 4.16).

Is s/he in need of services which social services could provide (see para 4.19)?

There is no right to a community care assessment but consider if there is a right to a carers assessment (see para 11.7) or services under LGA 2000 (see para 1.46).

NO

YES

Is s/he a disabled person or suffering from a mental disorder of any description (see para 8.21)?

Is s/he over 18 years of age?

NO

YES

NO

S/he is entitled to have their eligibility for services under the Children Act 1989 assessed (see para18.9).

YES

NO

Is s/he ill or recovering from an illness (see para 8.128) or elderly (para 8.134) or a drug/ alcohol misuser (see para 16.7)?

YES

S/he is entitled to a community care assessment (see para 4.52).

Diagram 2: The three stages in assessment and care planning

1 Information gathering
The social services department obtain sufficient information in order to make a decision about the most appropriate way of meeting the person's community care needs (see para 4.37).

Note
Depending on the extent of the person's care needs, this may be a brief process, or more complex, potentially requiring input from carers (see para 11.27), and others with relevant information such as health (see para 4.68) and housing (see para 4.68). It may also require consideration of factors such as the person's emotional, cultural and psychological needs and preferences (see para 4.38).

2 Service provision decision
The social services department decides which of the 'needs' and 'requirements' that have been identified in the assessment 'call for the provision of services' (see para 4.72).

Note
The social services department may not consider that it is 'necessary' to provide everything which is identified in the assessment as being of potential benefit to the person. In general it will only provide services which are essential or for which the assessed need meets its 'eligibility criteria' (see para 4.74).

3 Care plan
The social services department now prepares a 'care plan' which explains what 'care needs' must be met and details the services that are to be provided in order to do this (see para 5.2). The care plan also explains what health or housing services are to be provided by the housing or health authority (if any). The plan will take account of the user's preferences and also identify those 'unmet needs' which do not qualify for services (see para 5.38).

Diagram 3: Department of Health Guidance concerning the assessment process

General Assessment Guidance Adults with community care needs	Carers	Disabled children
• Fair Access to Care Services – Policy Guidance (2002) [*FACS (2002) Policy Guidance*] (see para 4.48 • Fair Access to Care Services – Practice Guidance (2003) [*FACS (2003) Practice Guidance*] (see para 4.50) • Community Care in the Next Decade and Beyond: policy guidance (1990) [*the 1990 Policy Guidance*] (see pvii) • Care Management and Assessment: Practitioners' Guide (1991) (see para 4.50)	FACS guidance is not of direct relevance as carer's assessments are not governed by s47 NHSCCA 1990. Guidance on carer's assessments is in *The Carers and Disabled Children Act 2000: a practitioners' guide to carers assessments* (2001) (see para 11.31)	FACS guidance is not of direct relevance. Specific guidance exists as *The Framework for the Assessment of Children in Need and their Families* (2000) Policy and Practice Guidance (see paras 18.12 and 18.14)

Specific user group assessment guidance

Older people	Mental Health Service users	People with learning disabilities
• NSF of Older People (see para 14.2) • Single assessment process (2002) (see para 14.3)	• NSF for Mental Health (1999) (see para 15.2) • Effective Care Co-ordination in Mental Health Services – Modernising the Care Programme Approach (1999) (see para 15.5)	• Valuing people: White Paper (2001) (see para 13.4) • Valuing people: implementation policy guidance LAC(2001)23 (see para 13.6)

For the Welsh Assembly equivalent guidance, see footnotes 55–60 at pp75–76 below.

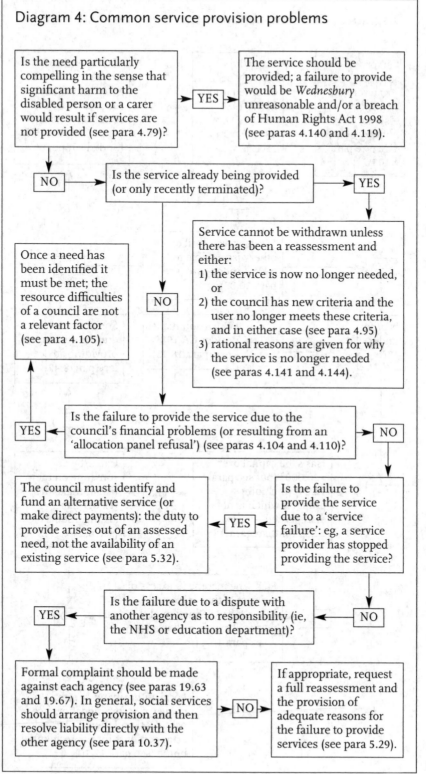

Diagram 4: Common service provision problems

Is the need particularly compelling in the sense that significant harm to the disabled person or a carer would result if services are not provided (see para 4.79)?

→ YES → The service should be provided; a failure to provide would be *Wednesbury* unreasonable and/or a breach of Human Rights Act 1998 (see paras 4.140 and 4.119).

NO →

Is the service already being provided (or only recently terminated)?

→ YES →

Service cannot be withdrawn unless there has been a reassessment and either:
1) the service is now no longer needed, or
2) the council has new criteria and the user no longer meets these criteria, and in either case (see para 4.95)
3) rational reasons are given for why the service is no longer needed (see paras 4.141 and 4.144).

Once a need has been identified it must be met; the resource difficulties of a council are not a relevant factor (see para 4.105).

NO

Is the failure to provide the service due to the council's financial problems (or resulting from an 'allocation panel refusal') (see paras 4.104 and 4.110)?

YES ← → NO

The council must identify and fund an alternative service (or make direct payments): the duty to provide arises out of an assessed need, not the availability of an existing service (see para 5.32).

← YES ← Is the failure to provide the service due to a 'service failure': eg, a service provider has stopped providing the service?

YES ← Is the failure due to a dispute with another agency as to responsibility (ie, the NHS or education department)? ← NO

Formal complaint should be made against each agency (see paras 19.63 and 19.67). In general, social services should arrange provision and then resolve liability directly with the other agency (see para 10.37).

→ NO → If appropriate, request a full reassessment and the provision of adequate reasons for the failure to provide services (see para 5.29).

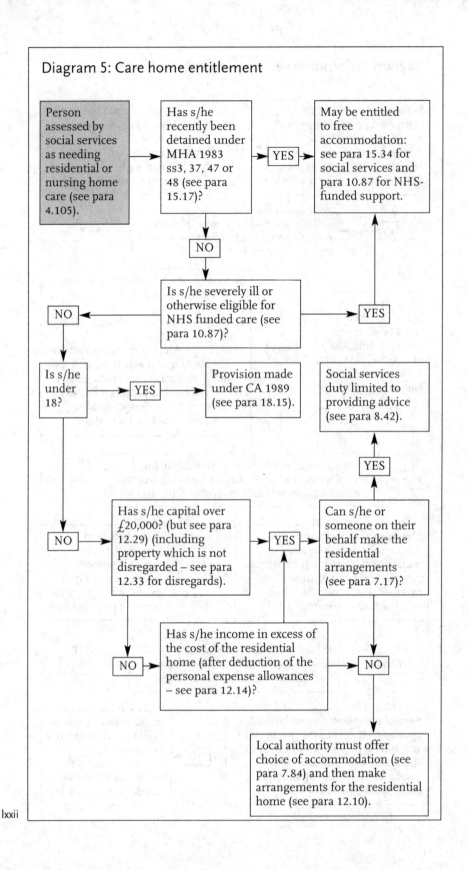

Diagram 5: Care home entitlement

Person assessed by social services as needing residential or nursing home care (see para 4.105).

Has s/he recently been detained under MHA 1983 ss3, 37, 47 or 48 (see para 15.17)?

YES

May be entitled to free accommodation: see para 15.34 for social services and para 10.87 for NHS-funded support.

NO

Is s/he severely ill or otherwise eligible for NHS funded care (see para 10.87)?

NO

YES

Is s/he under 18?

YES

Provision made under CA 1989 (see para 18.15).

Social services duty limited to providing advice (see para 8.42).

YES

NO

Has s/he capital over £20,000? (but see para 12.29) (including property which is not disregarded – see para 12.33 for disregards).

YES

Can s/he or someone on their behalf make the residential arrangements (see para 7.17)?

NO

Has s/he income in excess of the cost of the residential home (after deduction of the personal expense allowances – see para 12.14)?

NO

Local authority must offer choice of accommodation (see para 7.84) and then make arrangements for the residential home (see para 12.10).

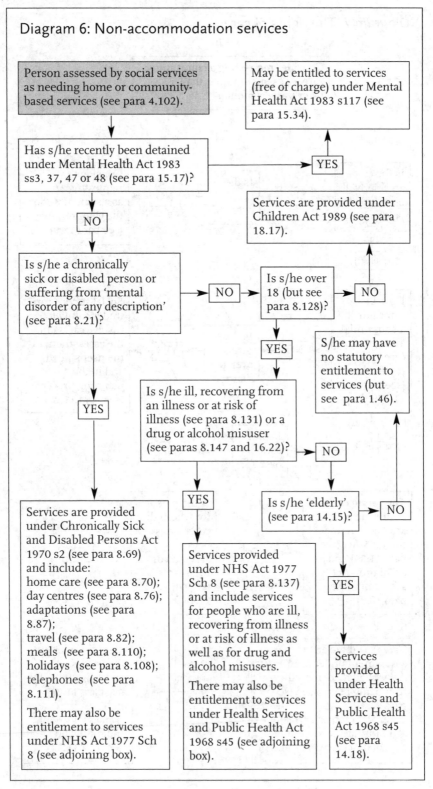

Diagram 6: Non-accommodation services

Person assessed by social services as needing home or community-based services (see para 4.102).

Has s/he recently been detained under Mental Health Act 1983 ss3, 37, 47 or 48 (see para 15.17)?

May be entitled to services (free of charge) under Mental Health Act 1983 s117 (see para 15.34).

YES

NO

Is s/he a chronically sick or disabled person or suffering from 'mental disorder of any description' (see para 8.21)?

NO

Is s/he over 18 (but see para 8.128)?

NO

Services are provided under Children Act 1989 (see para 18.17).

YES

YES

Is s/he ill, recovering from an illness or at risk of illness (see para 8.131) or a drug or alcohol misuser (see paras 8.147 and 16.22)?

NO

S/he may have no statutory entitlement to services (but see para 1.46).

YES

Is s/he 'elderly' (see para 14.15)?

NO

Services are provided under Chronically Sick and Disabled Persons Act 1970 s2 (see para 8.69) and include:
home care (see para 8.70);
day centres (see para 8.76);
adaptations (see para 8.87);
travel (see para 8.82);
meals (see para 8.110);
holidays (see para 8.108);
telephones (see para 8.111).

There may also be entitlement to services under NHS Act 1977 Sch 8 (see adjoining box).

Services provided under NHS Act 1977 Sch 8 (see para 8.137) and include services for people who are ill, recovering from illness or at risk of illness as well as for drug and alcohol misusers.

There may also be entitlement to services under Health Services and Public Health Act 1968 s45 (see adjoining box).

YES

Services provided under Health Services and Public Health Act 1968 s45 (see para 14.18).

lxxiii

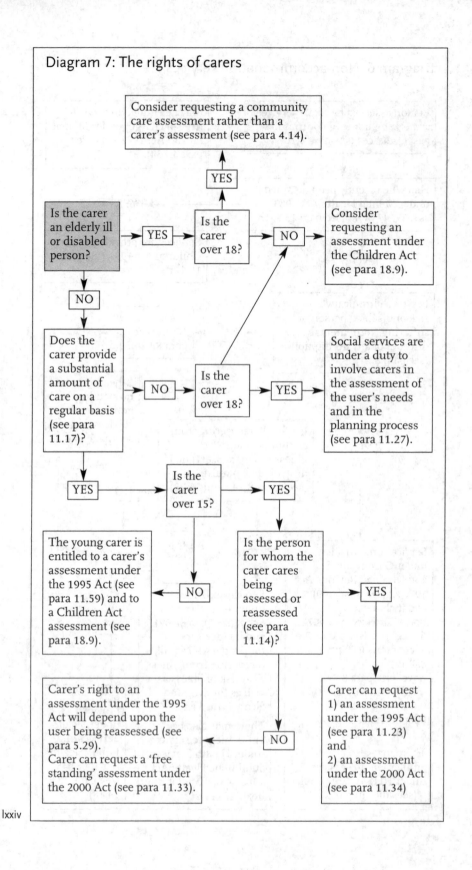

Diagram 7: The rights of carers

Consider requesting a community care assessment rather than a carer's assessment (see para 4.14).

Is the carer an elderly ill or disabled person?

Is the carer over 18?

Consider requesting an assessment under the Children Act (see para 18.9).

Does the carer provide a substantial amount of care on a regular basis (see para 11.17)?

Is the carer over 18?

Social services are under a duty to involve carers in the assessment of the user's needs and in the planning process (see para 11.27).

Is the carer over 15?

The young carer is entitled to a carer's assessment under the 1995 Act (see para 11.59) and to a Children Act assessment (see para 18.9).

Is the person for whom the carer cares being assessed or reassessed (see para 11.14)?

Carer's right to an assessment under the 1995 Act will depend upon the user being reassessed (see para 5.29).
Carer can request a 'free standing' assessment under the 2000 Act (see para 11.33).

Carer can request 1) an assessment under the 1995 Act (see para 11.23) and 2) an assessment under the 2000 Act (see para 11.34)

Diagram 8: Charging for care home accommodation

Is s/he eligible for NHS funded care (see para 10.87) or has s/he recently been detained under Mental Health Act 1983 ss3, 37, 47 or 48 (see para 15.16)?

→ YES → S/he may be entitled to free accommodation under the continuing care provisions (see para 10.87) or under Mental Health Act 1983 s117 (see para 15.34).

↓ NO

Is s/he under 18? → YES → The charges are assessed under Children Act 1989 procedures (see para 18.52).

↓ NO

Does the resident own a property (see para 12.33)? → YES → Is the stay in residential accommodation temporary or is the property occupied by: a partner (see para 12.33c); or a relative (see para 12.33c) who is either
- over 60, or
- the resident's child who is under 16 (see para 12.33c); or
- incapacitated (see para 12.33c)?

↓ NO

Has s/he savings over the upper capital limit (see para 12.29)? ← YES ← [from above box]

NO ← (left)

↓ YES

S/he is liable for the full cost (see para 12.33, but see 12.33a and 12.33e). ← NO ← Will local authority agree to ignore the value of the property (see para 12.33e)?

[Is the stay box] → NO → Is the net value of the property over upper capital limit? (see para 12.29): for valuation process and special rules for jointly owned property see para 12.37.

Will local authority agree to ignore the value of the property (see para 12.33e)? ← YES ← Is the net value of the property over upper capital limit?

Local authority assess income liability (see para 12.14) and any tariff income from savings (see para 12.80). ← YES ← Will local authority agree to ignore the value of the property (see para 12.33e)?

Is the net value of the property... → NO → Local authority assess income liability...

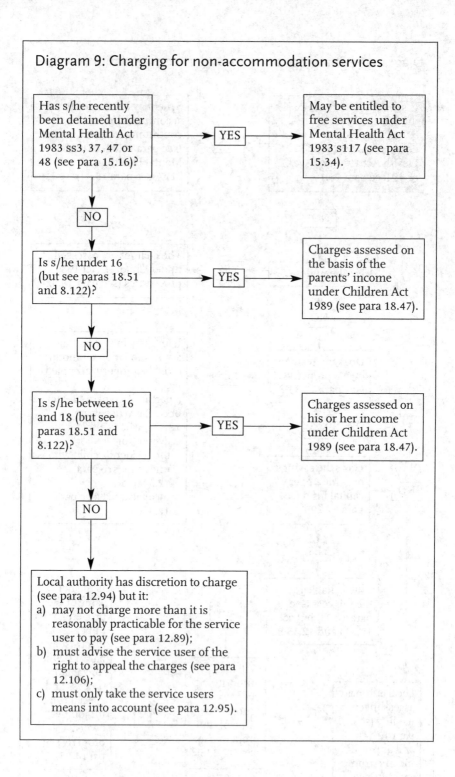

Diagram 9: Charging for non-accommodation services

Has s/he recently been detained under Mental Health Act 1983 ss3, 37, 47 or 48 (see para 15.16)?

YES → May be entitled to free services under Mental Health Act 1983 s117 (see para 15.34).

NO

Is s/he under 16 (but see paras 18.51 and 8.122)?

YES → Charges assessed on the basis of the parents' income under Children Act 1989 (see para 18.47).

NO

Is s/he between 16 and 18 (but see paras 18.51 and 8.122)?

YES → Charges assessed on his or her income under Children Act 1989 (see para 18.47).

NO

Local authority has discretion to charge (see para 12.94) but it:
a) may not charge more than it is reasonably practicable for the service user to pay (see para 12.89);
b) must advise the service user of the right to appeal the charges (see para 12.106);
c) must only take the service users means into account (see para 12.95).

Diagram 10: Complaints flow diagram

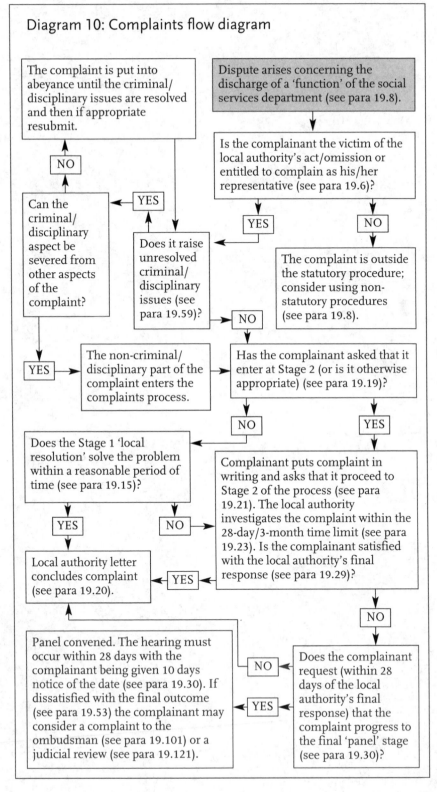

The complaint is put into abeyance until the criminal/disciplinary issues are resolved and then if appropriate resubmit.

Dispute arises concerning the discharge of a 'function' of the social services department (see para 19.8).

Is the complainant the victim of the local authority's act/omission or entitled to complain as his/her representative (see para 19.6)?

Can the criminal/disciplinary aspect be severed from other aspects of the complaint?

Does it raise unresolved criminal/disciplinary issues (see para 19.59)?

The complaint is outside the statutory procedure; consider using non-statutory procedures (see para 19.8).

The non-criminal/disciplinary part of the complaint enters the complaints process.

Has the complainant asked that it enter at Stage 2 (or is it otherwise appropriate) (see para 19.19)?

Does the Stage 1 'local resolution' solve the problem within a reasonable period of time (see para 19.15)?

Complainant puts complaint in writing and asks that it proceed to Stage 2 of the process (see para 19.21). The local authority investigates the complaint within the 28-day/3-month time limit (see para 19.23). Is the complainant satisfied with the local authority's final response (see para 19.29)?

Local authority letter concludes complaint (see para 19.20).

Panel convened. The hearing must occur within 28 days with the complainant being given 10 days notice of the date (see para 19.30). If dissatisfied with the final outcome (see para 19.53) the complainant may consider a complaint to the ombudsman (see para 19.101) or a judicial review (see para 19.121).

Does the complainant request (within 28 days of the local authority's final response) that the complaint progress to the final 'panel' stage (see para 19.30)?

lxxvii

Introduction

1.1　When Sir William Beveridge declared war on the five giant evils in society he had in mind Giant Want; Giant Disease; Giant Ignorance; Giant Squalor and Giant Idleness. At the end of World War II legislation was brought forward with the purpose of slaying some of these monsters: the Education Act 1944, the National Health Service Act 1946 and the National Assistance Act 1948. Giant Squalor was to be slain by a concerted programme of slum clearance and the building, within ten years, of three million new houses.[1]

1.2　The neglect of disabled, elderly and ill people living in the community was in many respects the forgotten sixth Giant. Part III of the National Assistance Act 1948 did however contain the means by which Giant Neglect was to be slain, namely the provision of 'community care services for ill, elderly and disabled people' and indeed for anyone else who was 'in need of care and attention which is not otherwise available'.[2]

1.3　It is difficult to lay down strict rules as to the nature of these 'services'. In general they are provided by social services departments, although the National Health Service (NHS) also has community care responsibilities (see chapter 10); in general they are personal care services although social services departments may now provide the disabled person with cash by a direct payment (see chapter 9). While the service is primarily concerned with personal care rather than health care, on occasions it will involve the provision of general nursing (see para 10.77). Likewise, while community care is not primarily concerned with the provision of housing or education services, at its margins it does embrace obligations in both these areas (see chapter 17 and para 8.79). At its heart community care is about the provision of accommodation in residential care homes and the provision 'in the community' of home helps, adaptations, day centres and meals on wheels. As an arm of the welfare state it commands over £11 billion per annum of public resources.[3]

1.4　The state's assumption of responsibility for the provision of community care services predates Beveridge, however, by almost 400 years and although National Assistance Act 1948 s1 boldly proclaims that the 'Poor Law is abolished', the present scheme bears many traits of its infamous forebear.

1　N Timmins, *The Five Giants* (Fontana, 1996).
2　National Assistance Act 1948 s21.
3　*With Respect to Old Age*. Royal Commission on long term care (Cm 4192-I, TSO, 1999).

I.5   Sir William Holdsworth[4] considered that the poor law system commenced with a Statute of 1535–1536,[5] the preamble to which declared that
the former Acts were defective because no provision was made in them for
providing work for the unemployed. Sir William listed six principles, which
he considered as underlying the early poor law development, namely:

1) the duty to contribute to the support of the poor was a legal duty of the
   state;
2) the parish (via the justices) was the administrative unit for assessing
   need and payments;
3) the impotent poor were to be supported in the places in which they were
   settled (but not necessarily where they were born – previously they
   would have been directed to return to their birth place);
4) the children of people who could not work had to be taught a trade to
   enable them to support themselves;
5) the able bodied vagrant and beggar should be suppressed by criminal
   law;
6) the able bodied should have work provided for them and it be compulsory for them to do that work.

I.6   We see, particularly in (1) to (3) above, signs of this parentage today. The
obligation still rests with local councils (albeit social services authorities
rather than the parish). The concept of ordinary residence persists, as
do the liable relative rules and the importance of the inter-relationship
between community care and education, housing and employment. While
categories (5) and (6) are of relevance to our present welfare benefits system, they too have echoes in the concept of work fare, claimants availability for work and indeed in National Assistance Act (NAA) 1948 s51 under
which it still remains a criminal offence to 'neglect to maintain oneself'.

I.7   With the abolition of the 'Poor Law' by NAA 1948 Pt I local resources (principally the workhouses) had to be redistributed. The best of these were
absorbed into the fledgling NHS and the remainder were put to use in
meeting the new obligations created by NAA 1948 Pt III.[6]

I.8   Part II of the 1948 Act replaced the poor law system with a national
means-tested benefits system known as 'national assistance' administered
by the National Assistance Board, rather than by local councils. In due
course Part II was repealed and national assistance replaced by supplementary benefit, which itself has been replaced by income support.
Income support is, however, based upon essentially the same means-
tested national principles which characterised national assistance.

I.9   Part III of the Act tackled the needs of vulnerable people for residential
accommodation and community or home-based (domiciliary) care services. NAA 1948 s21 obliged authorities to provide residential accommo-

---

4   Sir William Holdsworth in volume IV *A History of English Law* (3rd impression 1977)
    p390 onwards.
5   27 Henry VIII c25.
6   For an excellent account of the evolution of 'community care' see Means and Smith,
    Community Care (Macmillan, 1994).

dation for elderly and disabled people as well as temporary residential accommodation for homeless people where their homelessness had arisen through unforeseen circumstances. The accommodation obligations were met by the use of workhouses: as hostels for the homeless and as 'homes' for the disabled and elderly. The residential accommodation obligations under NAA 1948 s21 have changed little since 1948; it is still the statutory basis for the vast majority of local authority residential accommodation placements. In 1977 the primary duty to accommodate homeless people was transferred to housing authorities via Stephen Ross MP's private member's Bill which became the Housing (Homeless Persons) Act 1977, and with it many of the appalling problems highlighted in the film 'Cathy Come Home'.

I.10 The only other significant change to NAA 1948 s21 resulted from the National Health Service and Community Care Act (NHSCCA)1990. The 1990 Act repealed a provision under National Health Service Act 1977 Sch 8 which enabled social services authorities to provide residential accommodation for people who needed it through illness and by amendment this accommodation obligation was transferred to NAA 1948 s21. The 1990 Act also amended NAA 1948 s21 to enable social services authorities to purchase nursing home accommodation in addition to residential care accommodation.

I.11 Despite the rationing and general shortages present in 1948, NAA 1948 s21 placed a duty on authorities to provide residential accommodation for such persons who were ordinarily resident in their area and who were in need of care and attention which was not otherwise available to them. This obligation, in addition to the other social welfare duties – the house building programme, the creation of the new NHS and the education reforms – represented a huge public spending commitment. Perhaps not surprisingly therefore, when it came to the provision of community or domiciliary care services, authorities were not obliged to provide these services, although they were given discretion to do so if they were able.

I.12 NAA 1948 s29 empowered[7] authorities to provide four general types of service:

- advice and guidance;[8]
- the preparation of a register of disabled people;
- the provision of 'occupational activities' (such as workshops) for disabled people; and
- facilities which assist disabled people to overcome limitations of communication or mobility.

I.13 The power to provide such services was limited to disabled people. This represented the concern in 1948 to ensure that those people who had sacrificed their health for peace be given priority when it came to the provision of

---

7   These discretionary powers were subsequently converted to 'target duties' (see para 8.40) by directions issued as LAC (93)10.

8   It is pursuant to this provision that most social services welfare rights units are provided.

scarce resources.[9] In 1948 there was in relative terms a greater number of younger disabled people – in the form of wounded soldiers returning home and those injured in the bombing at home. This legislative prioritisation of the needs of disabled people (as opposed to those of the temporarily ill or elderly) remains anachronistically today, albeit to a lesser extent.

1.14   Given the enormous obligations placed on authorities in the post-war years of austerity, the community care services provided under NAA 1948 s29 were in general modest. Authorities were not under a statutory duty to provide them and in any event the community care services available under NAA 1948 s29 were vaguely expressed, eg, 'assistance in overcoming limitations of mobility or communication'. What was required therefore was a statutory provision (similar in nature to NAA 1948 s21) which provided, as of right, specific community care services for all those in need.

1.15   Although the post-war austerity years gave way to the increasingly prosperous 1950s and the relatively affluent 1960s, the provision of community care services remained a 'Cinderella' area in social welfare terms. The mid and late 60s were also characterised by a change in social philosophical attitudes – with, for instance, the enactment of the Family Law Reform Act 1969, the Children and Young Persons Act 1969 and the creation of social services departments consequent upon the Seebohm Report. This attitude was at considerable variance with that which promoted NAA 1948 s29; the cross-heading to which section blandly states 'services for blind, deaf, dumb and crippled persons, etc.' While therefore the pressure for a change in the statutory framework of community care services was present by the mid-60s, reform was slow in coming.

1.16   We will never again see major social welfare legislation of the type enacted during the period 1945–1951. Since that time, beneficial social welfare legislation has generally originated from one of two sources. The first is the European Court of Human Rights; into this category one might place the Mental Health Act 1983 and the Children Act 1989. In terms of community care, questions concerning physical or learning difficulties, age and (non-mental) ill health have attracted hardly any complaints to Strasbourg. The second source is Acts of Parliament which started life as private members' Bills, such as the Housing (Homeless Persons) Act 1977.

1.17   On 6 November 1969 it was announced that Alf Morris MP had won first place in the annual ballot for private members' Bills. He chose to promote his own Bill (which he himself drafted), the Chronically Sick and Disabled Persons Bill. The Act received Royal Assent on 29 May 1970, the day that parliament was dissolved for the 1970 general election.[10] The most important section of that Act has proved to be section 2. It is drafted to make the provision of services under NAA 1948 s29 obligatory (rather than discretionary) and in place of section 29's vague wording, to spell out precisely what services are to be provided. The 1970 Act remains the finest

---

9   H Bolderson, *Social Security, Disability and Rehabilitation* (Jessica Kingsley, 1991) at p115.

10   For an account of the passing of the Act, see *Be it enacted* . . . (RADAR 1995).

community care statute, providing disabled people with private law rights to specific services.

I.18   Despite the significance of section 2, however, history has shown it to have three defects. The first is that its services are only available to disabled people (as with NAA 1948 s29). Other statutory provisions are therefore required to cater for people who need such services not because they are 'permanently and substantially handicapped',[11] but because they are either frail elderly or ill (but not permanently ill). The second defect concerns two particular drafting imperfections with this section, which are considered below. The third is that the section has proved to be simply too generous – from the perspective of view of social services authorities. On any reasonable interpretation it entitles disabled people to receive high quality services 'as of right'. In 1970, at the end of the 'Golden Phase' of the twentieth century,[12] such rights were perhaps seen as a logical next step in the development of the welfare state. The subsequent turmoil in the west, precipitated by the oil crisis in the early 1970s, led to a general retreat from such specific and (in budgetary terms) open-ended welfare rights. As a consequence, subsequent community care legislation has been cloth of a duller weave; generally 'resource' rather than 'rights' oriented. Section 2 is, sadly, out of step with all the other community care legislation and this incongruity is becoming ever more obvious.

I.19   Section 2 provided disabled people with the right to good quality community care services. The need for elderly people to have such services (when they were not themselves 'permanently and substantially handicapped') was satisfied by the enactment of Health Services and Public Health Act 1968 s45 which enabled authorities to make similar arrangements for 'promoting the welfare of old people'.[13] Likewise authorities were empowered to provide such services for ill people (ie, those not 'chronically sick') by virtue of NHSA 1977 Sch 8. Thus by 1977 social services authorities were under varying degrees of obligation to provide an array of community care services to the three main client groups: ill, elderly and disabled people.

I.20   During the late 1970s and in the 1980s the closure of long-stay mental hospitals gathered pace, such that community care became linked in the public mind with the care of people with mental health difficulties in the community rather than by incarceration in isolated hospitals. Mental Health Act 1983 s117 accordingly made particular provision for community care services to be provided for certain patients on their discharge from hospital. Section 117 services are only available to a restricted number of people.[14] Most people with a mental health difficulty receive their community care services under Chronically Sick and Disabled Persons Act (CSDPA) 1970 s2.

11 The definition applied under the NAA 1948, see para 8.36.
12 E Hobsbawn, *Age of Extremes* (Michael Joseph, 1994).
13 Sections 2 and 45 came into force on the same date, 29 August 1970.
14 People who are discharged after detention under Mental Health Act 1983 s3 or one of its criminal provisions, see para 15.19.

1.21   When the term 'community care services' is used today in its generic legal sense, it means (as defined by NHSCCA 1990 s46):

> ... services which a local authority may provide or arrange to be provided under any of the following provisions –
> (a) Part III of the National Assistance Act 1948;
> (b) section 45 of the Health Services and Public Health Act 1968;
> (c) section 21 of and Schedule 8 to the National Health Service Act 1977; and
> (d) section 117 of the Mental Health Act 1983.

1.22   Although NHSCCA 1990 s46 does not mention services under CSDPA 1970 s2 as being 'community care services', this is because the Department of Health has always considered section 2 to be part of NAA 1948 s29. This somewhat confusing statement is explained at para 8.112 below. The question of the status of CSDPA 1970 s2 constitutes the first of its two drafting problems. The second concerns the question of when the duty under the Act crystallises in favour of a disabled person. Section 2 services are only owed to an individual when the authority is 'satisfied' that the services are necessary in order to meet his or her needs. What happens if the authority simply fails to decide whether or not it is 'satisfied' as to the person's need? In essence the provision of services requires a collateral duty to 'assess' a person's eligibility for that service. Whilst Tom Clarke MP endeavoured (unsuccessfully) to fill this lacuna via his private member's Bill in 1986,[15] it was only as a result of NHSCCA 1990 s47 that a comprehensive duty to assess potential service users for their possible need for services under the community care statutes was created.

1.23   A significant motivation for the 1990 Act was the soaring social security expenditure on residential care and nursing home accommodation; this had increased from about £10m per annum in 1979 to £2.5 billion per annum in 1993. Hospitals were closing long-stay geriatric and psychiatric wards and discharging the patients into private nursing homes where the cost could be funded by the Department of Health and Social Security (DHSS) (as it then was), essentially, therefore, transferring the cost from one central government department's budget (the NHS) to another (Social Security). At the same time social services authorities were doing much the same, by closing their own funded residential care homes and transferring the residents to independent-sector homes, which again were capable of being funded via the DHSS, thus transferring the cost from local to central government.

1.24   The 1990 Act sought to cap this expenditure by transferring most of the funding responsibility to social services authorities and restricting access to residential and nursing homes if the person was to be supported by public funds. Access in such cases was to be conditional on the authority being satisfied that such a placement was appropriate. Social services authorities were provided with a 'special transitional grant' to compensate them for their extra costs in implementing the community care reforms and in

15   Disabled Persons (Services, Consultation and Representation) Act 1986 s4.

particular for assuming responsibility for funding such accommodation. In the first full year of the reforms (1994–95) the grant amounted to £735.9 million of which 85% was ring-fenced to the extent that it had to be spent on independent sector care services.[16]

I.25   The Act also endeavoured to bring together the disparate statutes which governed individual entitlement to community care services and, by various amendments, create a degree of coherence in this field of law. It was preceded by a white paper, *Caring for People* (Cm 849, 1989), which owed much to a report prepared by Sir Roy Griffiths for the Secretary of State for Social Services, *Community Care: Agenda for Action* (1988). The NHSCCA 1990 does not, however, convert into law many of the themes which infuse the white paper, the Griffiths report and many of the subsequent practice guides issued by the Department of Health. These documents received considerable publicity and a number of myths have arisen therefore about the legal entitlement of service users.

I.26   The white paper set out six key objectives in relation to the community care reforms namely (at para 1.11):

–   **to promote the development of domiciliary, day and respite services to enable people to live in their own homes wherever feasible and sensible.**
    Existing funding structures have worked against the development of such services. In future, the Government will encourage the targeting of home-based services on those people whose need for them is greatest;

–   **to ensure that service providers make practical support for carers a high priority.**
    Assessment of care needs should always take account of the needs of caring family, friends and neighbours;

–   **to make proper assessment of need and good case management the cornerstone of high quality care.**
    Packages of care should then be designed in line with individual needs and preferences;

–   **to promote the development of a flourishing independent sector alongside good quality public services.**
    The Government has endorsed Sir Roy Griffiths' recommendation that social services authorities should be 'enabling' agencies. It will be their responsibility to make maximum possible use of private and voluntary providers, and so increase the available range of options and widen consumer choice;

–   **to clarify the responsibilities of agencies and so make it easier to hold them to account for their performance.**
    The Government recognises that the present confusion has contributed to poor overall performance;

–   **to secure better value for taxpayers' money by introducing a new funding structure for social care.**
    The Government's aim is that social security provisions should not, as they do now, provide any incentive in favour of residential and nursing home care.

16   For further details see Meredith M, *The Community Care Handbook* (ACE 1995) p165.

I.27   The NHSCCA 1990 was however largely silent on these themes. It provided no practical support for carers – this was left to Malcolm Wicks MP and his private member's Bill which became the Carers (Recognition and Services) Act 1995. As to the emphasis on individual choice (or 'preferences'), this concept appears nowhere in any of the legislation, with the exception of the National Assistance Act 1948 (Choice of Accommodation) Directions 1992.

I.28   The reforms of the 1990s coincided with the emergence, at a national political level, of the disability rights movements. Many disabled people viewed the community care regime as disabling and disempowering and sought greater control, by way of direct payments and involvement at a strategic planning level. On the positive side, the Disability Discrimination Act 1995, the Community Care (Direct Payments) Act 1996 and the Human Rights Act 1998 have begun to address – directly or indirectly – some of these issues.

I.29   The last ten years, have not however seen any radical new thinking by the governments in England and Wales – in philosophical or legal terms. The report of the Royal Commission on long term care '*With Respect to old age*' (1999) which recommended fundamental change in the funding arrangements was rejected (or more accurately, in Wales 'not implemented'). Instead the focus has been on structural/administrative reform with the Health and Social Care Act 2001 providing for the effective merger of social and health care bodies. During the period of organisational turbulence and reorganisation, health and social services staff have additionally been subjected to a plethora of targets, performance indicators, auditing regimes, National Service Frameworks and central government microguidance. As Onora O'Neill observed in the 2002 Reith lecture: 'central planning may have failed in the Soviet Union but it is alive and well in Britain today'.

I.30   At the beginning of the 21st century, there appears to be no prospect of a fundamental reappraisal of the role of the law in relation to the provision of community care services. Community care law remains a hotchpotch of conflicting statutes, which have been enacted over a period of 50 years; each statute reflects the different philosophical attitudes of its time. Community care law is in much the same state as was the law relating to children in the 1980s. The law was in a mess; there were no unifying principles underlying the statutes; there were many different procedures for essentially similar problems (for instance, the umpteen different ways a child could end up in local authority care or a custody or maintenance order could be made, and so on). A great deal of this confusion and nonsense was swept away by the Children Act 1989, which repealed many statutes, in full or in part, and replaced them with a unified procedure underscored by a set of widely accepted basic principles. It takes no great genius to realise that community care law is crying out for similar treatment.

CHAPTER 1

Social services function and the regulatory regime

Introduction

1.1   Social services authorities are the creatures of statute, being created by the Local Authority Social Services Act (LASSA) 1970. The statute brought into effect a reorganisation of the various welfare departments recommended by the Seebohm report.[1] The Act remains the primary statute governing such authorities. Being statutory bodies, they are obliged to restrict their activities to actions specifically authorised by statute. These permitted actions (or 'functions') are listed in the first Schedule to LASSA 1970. The list is regularly up dated and comprises the familiar (and long) list of statutory provisions, such as the National Assistance Act 1948, the Children Act 1989, the Carers and Disabled Children Act 2000 and so on.

1.2   Although it is unlawful for a statutory body to act outside its statutory authority, the rigors of this requirement have been significantly relaxed by Local Government Act (LGA) 2000 Pt I – the general effect of which is to empower local authorities to do anything which they consider will promote the economic, social or environmental well-being of their area (see para 1.46 below where Part I of the Act is considered in greater detail).

Statutory duties and powers

1.3   Social services functions are normally expressed as being obligatory (ie, a statutory duty) or discretionary (ie, a statutory power). Accordingly the use of words 'can' and 'may' in a statute are interpreted as conferring a permissive power rather than a duty. Conversely, the appearance of the words 'shall' or 'must' are in general construed as creating a duty – an obligation to do or refrain from doing something. This is not, however, always the case. As de Smith points out[2] a local authority empowered to approve building plans has been held to be obliged to approve plans that were in conformity with its bylaws,[3] whereas a local authority required by statute to provide suitable alternative accommodation for those displaced by a closing order has been held not to be obliged to place them at the top of the housing waiting list.[4]

1.4   Where an authority has a power to act, but not a duty, it must (when the possible use of that power arises) exercise its discretion in each case. Authorities are generally free to refuse to use a power, provided they reach such a decision in accordance with the principles of administrative law (and the refusal does not result in a breach of the European Convention on

---

1   Report of the Committee on Local Authority and Allied Personal Social Services (Cmnd 3703).

2   De Smith, Woolf and Jowell, *Judicial Review of Administrative Action* (5th edn, Sweet & Maxwell, 1995) at p301.

3   *R v Newcastle-upon-Tyne Corporation* (1889) 60 LT 963.

4   *R v Bristol Corporation ex p Hendy* [1974] 1 WLR 498.

Human Rights).[5] A fixed policy of never using a power would constitute a fetter on their discretion and be unlawful (see para 19.151 below).

Specific and target duties

1.5 Statutory duties owed by public bodies can be divided into two categories, general public law duties (known as 'target' duties) and specific duties owed to individuals. Specific duties are worded in precise and personal terms, so that it is clear that they are intended to confer enforceable rights upon individuals, and also clear when these rights arise. Accordingly a failure to comply with a specific law duty may entitle an aggrieved party to a court order compelling the authority to carry out its duty (for instance an order requiring it to provide a specific community care service).

1.6 In *R v Gloucestershire County Council ex p Mahfood*,[6] McCowan LJ held that Chronically Sick and Disabled Persons Act (CSDPA) 1970 s2 created specific public law duties, stating that once an authority had decided that it was under a duty to make arrangements under CSPDA 1970 s2, it was 'under an absolute duty to make them. It is a duty owed to a specific individual and not a target duty':[7] an analysis accepted by Sedley J (as he then was) in *R v Islington LBC ex p Rixon*.[8] The duty under Mental Health Act 1983 s117 has also been held to be capable of being an individual public law duty.[9]

1.7 In contrast, general public law (or 'target') duties are worded in broad and impersonal terms, and contain a 'degree of elasticity'[10] in their interpretation – such that it is generally left to the authority in question to decide when (and to what extent) the duty comes into being. Callaghan[11] argues that target duties are essentially aspirational in nature, requiring an authority to 'do its best';[12] and that 'courts will permit public authorities to take into account practical realities, including budgetary and resource considerations, in determining how best to fulfil the target duty'.

1.8 A notable example of such a general duty is to be found in National Health Service Act (NHSA) 1977 s1[13] which places a duty on the secretary of state 'to continue the promotion in England and Wales of a comprehensive

---

5 See paras 1.49 and 19.172 below, ie, the reference to *R (J) v Enfield LBC and Secretary of State for Health (intervener)* (2002) 5 CCLR 434.

6 (1997) 1 CCLR 7.

7 (1997) 1 CCLR 7 at 16G.

8 (1996) 32 BMLR 136; (1997) 1 CCLR 119, at 125H where he referred to 'the duties brought into being by section 2 of the Chronically Sick and Disabled Persons Act 1970 and owed to the individual'.

9 *R (IH) v Secretary of State for Home Department and others* [2003] UKHL 59; [2003] 3 WLR 1278; (2004) 7 CCLR 147 (see 15.20 below).

10 Per Woolf LJ in *R v Inner London Education Authority ex p Ali* (1990) 2 Admin LR 822, 828D.

11 C Callaghan (2000) *What is a 'Target Duty'?* Judicial Review (2000), 5(3), 184–187.

12 *R v Radio Authority ex p Bull* [1998] QB 294 at 309, CA.

13 See *R v Barnet LBC ex p B* [1994] 1 FLR 592.

health service'. The duty is not expressed as being owed to any specific individual and it is particularly difficult for a court to decide when it has been
breached. To mount a successful action, an aggrieved patient would have to
show, not only that he or she failed to receive a health service due to the service not being 'comprehensive' (whatever that may mean) but also that the
secretary of state had effectively abandoned any intention of 'promoting'
such a service. As the Court of Appeal held in *R v North and East Devon
Health Authority ex p Coughlan*.[14]

> 25. When exercising his judgment [the secretary of state] has to bear in
> mind the comprehensive service which he is under a duty to promote as
> set out in section 1. However, as long as he pays due regard to that duty,
> the fact that the service will not be comprehensive does not mean that he
> is necessarily contravening either section 1 or section 3.

1.9   Even if these formidable hurdles are overcome and the patient succeeds in
such a claim, the final order would merely require the secretary of state to
review his or her actions: it would not result in a mandatory order that the
absent service be provided

1.10   It is not always clear whether a particular obligation falls into the
specific or target category. As Scott Baker J observed in *R (A) v Lambeth
LBC*:[15]

> Community care legislation has grown up piecemeal through numerous
> statutes over the past half century. There are many statutes aimed at
> different targets whose provisions are drawn in differing language.
> Each Act contains its own duties and powers. Specific duties have to be
> distinguished from target or general duties and duties from discretions.
> Sometimes a local authority has several ways in which it can meet an
> obligation. Some provisions overlap with others and the inter-relationship
> is not always easy.

1.11   A number of community care duties can be characterised as hybrid in
nature; that is to say that although drafted in general terms, they can 'crys-
tallise'[16] during the assessment process (see para 4.1) into specific public
law duties owed to individual service users. Thus the general duty under
National Assistance Act (NAA) 1948 s21(1)(a) to provide residential
accommodation for adults in need of care and attention (see para 7.2)
may be converted by a community care assessment into a specific public
law duty.[17]

1.12   Arguments concerning the enforceability of such statutory provisions

---

14 (1999) 2 CCLR 285; [2000] 2 WLR 622; [2000] 51 BMLR 1; [2000] 3 All ER 850.
15 [2001] LGR 513; the quotation also appears in the subsequent Court of Appeal
    judgment *R (A) v Lambeth LBC* (2001) 4 CCLR 486 at 499–450.
16 See the comments of Laws LJ in *R (A) v Lambeth LBC* (2001) 4 CCLR 486 at 499D
    where he adopted Richard Gordon QC's use of this phrasing.
17 See for example *R v Sefton MBC ex p Help the Aged and Blanchard* (1997) 1 CCLR 57;
    [1997] 36 BMLR 110; and *R v Kensington and Chelsea RLBC ex p Kutjim* (1990) 2 CCLR
    340; [1999] 4 All ER 161.

are becoming increasingly rarefied and difficult to follow.[18] In *R (W) v Lambeth LBC*[19] and *R (G) v Barnet LBC*[20] for example, the Court of Appeal and the House of Lords grappled with the differing phrasing of the obligations to provide care services for disabled children and disabled adults. It concluded that although the assessment process for adults (under National Health Service and Community Care Act (NHSCCA) 1990 s47) could result in specific public law duties, this was not the case in relation to children (whose assessments process was governed by Children Act 1989 s17). Not only is it difficult to follow the logic of the Court's analysis in reaching this conclusion – it is particularly difficult to see the sense in (effectively) prioritising the rights of disabled adults to services over the rights of disabled children.

1.13   It has been argued that what we are seeing in such cases is an 'attempt to shore up the increasingly questionable public policy approach towards the state delivery of community care services'.[21] In effect, that the artificial distinction between target and specific public law duties stems from the judiciary's anxiety over the resource implications of their judgments,[22] and that this entirely artificial construct is proving to be insufficiently flexible to mediate between the complexities of state responsibilities (in a post Human Rights Act 1998 era) and individual need. Increasingly the courts appear to be using the imperative (if not the logic) of the European Convention on Human Rights in determining the enforceability of statutory obligations – and this approach is considered in greater detail at para 4.116 below.

Local Authority Social Services Act 1970

1.14   LASSA 1970 sets the general framework of social services authority functions and responsibilities (the material parts of the Act are in appendix A, p560 below). The local authorities concerned are county councils, the London and metropolitan boroughs, other unitary authorities and the City of London (LASSA 1970 s1).

1.15   As a consequence of LGA 2000 s102 social services authorities now have considerable flexibility as to how their elected members supervise the discharge of their social services responsibilities: this may be by way of a

---

18 See for instance the comments of Potter LJ in *R v Kensington and Chelsea RLBC ex p Kutjim* (1990) 2 CCLR 340 at 353J where he admitted to finding difficulty in following the arguments of Sedley J (concerning a parallel set of target duties) in *R v Islington LBC ex p Rixon* (1998) 1 CCLR 119; (1996) 32 BMLR 136.

19 [2002] EWCA Civ 613;(2002) 5 CCLR 203.

20 [2003] UKHL 57; [2003] 3 WLR 1194; (2003) 6 CCLR 500 (see para 18.18 below).

21 L Clements 'The Collapsing Duty: A Sideways Look at Community Care and Public law' in *Judicial Review Journal* [1997]162.

22 Lord Hoffman put the position frankly when delivering the 2001 Commercial Bar Lecture ('The Separation of Powers', London: unpublished transcript) commenting: 'even when a case appears to involve no more than the construction of a statute or interpretation of a common law rule, the courts are very circumspect about giving an answer which would materially affect the distribution of public expenditure'.

traditional social services committee, or by way of the new executive arrangements introduced by the 2000 Act.

1.16   By LASSA 1970 s6(1), every social services authority must have a director of social services – whose roles and responsibilities have been the subject of guidance in CI (2002) 9. By LASSA 1970 s6(6) it is the authority's duty to 'secure the provision of adequate staff[23] for assisting [the director] in the exercise of his functions'.

1.17   While authorities will be given a wide discretion by the courts in deciding what is an 'adequate' staff (for the purposes of s6(6)), the question may be raised in judicial review proceedings, particularly where the applicant is challenging the non-provision of a service dependent upon 'human resources'.[24] In *R v Hereford and Worcester CC ex p Chandler*,[25] for instance, leave to seek judicial review was granted on several grounds, including the argument that the applicant had not received the service he needed (a one-to-one carer) because the authority had inadequate staff, in breach of its statutory duty under LASSA 1970 s6(6). Judicial review is however unlikely to be appropriate where the complaint concerns the interruption of services due to unpredictable staff absences. Thus in *R v Islington LBC ex p McMillan*,[26] the complaint concerned the interruption of home care assistance to the applicant due to (among other things) staff illness. The court did not consider this to be in breach of the duty owed (and in any event not something that would warrant any remedy). Where however the complaint concerns a repeated failure of the service due to predictable interruptions, then this would seem at least a matter of maladministration and amenable to remedy through the complaints system.

1.18   LASSA 1970 (as amended) sets out the broad framework as to how social services departments are to be organised. As with many social welfare statutes, reserve powers were retained by the secretary of state to enable 'orders', 'directions' and 'guidance' to be issued, however in the early years of the Act, central government exercised a lightness of touch over these levers of control:

> . . . there was no notion of a direct line of command from central government dictating either the organisational structure of social work at the local level or the detailed policies to be implemented within and through that structure in response to legislation. Within loose overall financial controls there was room for local authority social services departments to shape structures and policies within the framework of central government's legislation and general policy guidance.[27]

23 As well as the parallel duty, under NHSA 1977 s21 and Sch 8, to provide 'sufficient' approved social workers for the purposes of the Mental Health Act 1983.
24 To establish a case under this ground, useful evidence can be obtained from social services committee minutes; which not infrequently record unsuccessful requests by the director for extra staff.
25 Unreported but see September 1992 *Legal Action* 15: settled on terms that the applicant receive the assessed service.
26 (1997) 1 CCLR 7 at 10.
27 J Harris, *The Social Work Business* (Routledge, 2003) at p18.

1.19 This however is no longer the case. Through the provisions of LASSA 1970 s7, (see below) and an array of performance indicators,[28] performance ratings[29] and inspection regimes, the Department of Health (in England) and the Assembly (in Wales) exercise a degree of control over the actions of social services departments – which is at times best characterised as micro-management.

Regulations

1.20 The responsibilities of social services authorities are, as outlined above, listed in LASSA 1970 Sch 1. Many of these statutes contain provisions which enable the secretary of state to elaborate on the statutory regime by promulgating various forms of delegated legislation – most commonly as regulations, rules and orders. These flesh out the bare bones of the duty or power imposed by the primary statute. In relation to residential accommodation, for instance, National Assistance Act (NAA) 1948 s22(1) requires authorities to charge for such accommodation and NAA 1948 s22(5) authorises the secretary of state to issue regulations detailing how this shall be done. These were subsequently issued as the National Assistance (Assessment of Resources) Regulations 1992.[30]

1.21 Such delegated legislation has the force of law, and the procedure by which it is promulgated is set out in the Statutory Instruments Act 1946, as modified in relation to Wales by the Government of Wales Act 1998. These Acts detail the requirements for publication and the various types of procedures by which the legislation is laid before Parliament/the Assembly and so on. Delegated legislation must not, therefore, stray outside the ambit of its enabling statutory provision. Accordingly, in the example of the NAA 1948 above, the regulations issued under section 22(5) could only lawfully address the question of the assessment of charges for residential accommodation. Judicial review will lie where the statutory instrument exceeds such limits.[31] In similar terms, delegated legislation must not derogate from provisions in the enabling legislation; thus where rights are conferred by a statute, any subsequent regulations must not detract from those rights.[32]

---

28 There being 49 core indicators (in 2003) measuring, for instance, local authority delivery of intensive home care services; the number of adults with learning disabilities helped to live at home; the number of assessments of adults and older people leading to provision of service; the number of carer assessments; the waiting time for care packages; the ethnicity of older people receiving assessment, etc. See www.dh.gov.uk/assetRoot/04/07/03/99/04070399.pdf.

29 See for instance CI (2003) 13.

30 SI No 2977; see para 12.7 below.

31 See, for instance, *Re Ripon* [1939] 2 KB 838 and *Dunkley v Evans* [1981] 1 WLR 1522.

32 See, for instance, *King v Henderson* [1898] AC 720.

Directions and guidance

1.22   LASSA 1970 ss7(1) and 7A require social services authorities to be administered under the general supervision of the secretary of state.[33] The provisions state as follows:

> *Local authorities to exercise social services functions under guidance of Secretary of State*
>
> 7(1)   Local authorities shall, in the exercise of their social services functions, including the exercise of any discretion conferred by any relevant enactment, act under the general guidance of the Secretary of State.
>
> *Directions by the Secretary of State as to exercise of social services functions*
>
> 7A(1)   Without prejudice to section 7 of this Act, every local authority shall exercise their social services functions in accordance with such directions as may be given to them under this section by the Secretary of State.
>
> (2)   Directions under this section –
> (a)   shall be given in writing; and
> (b)   may be given to a particular authority, or to authorities of a particular class, or to authorities generally.

1.23   The distinction between 'directions' and 'guidance' is therefore, a distinction between having to act 'in accordance with' directions as opposed to having to act 'under' guidance.

Directions

1.24   Directions are mandatory, and are phrased as such. The power of the secretary of state to issue directions, contained in LASSA 1970 s7A(1) is replicated in many other statutes, and as noted at para 10.27, such a power also exists in relation to the health service under NHSA 1977 s17. In relation to social services functions, however, examples of such directions include the Complaints Procedure Directions 1990 and the National Assistance Act (Choice of Accommodation) Directions 1992. These have the force of law and are set out as any statutory instrument would be. Directions are nevertheless problematical constitutional instruments; if they were true statutory instruments, they would be laid before parliament in accordance with the constitutional convention that it is parliament which makes law rather than the executive. They would also be published as Statutory Instruments[34] and accessible to the general public, whereas it is often difficult to discover whether a direction has in fact been issued and then equally difficult to discover from whom a copy may be obtained.

1.25   While directions are usually published separately, they may appear as appendices to guidance issued by the Department of Health or Welsh

---

33   That is, the Secretary of State for Health in England and the Assembly in Wales.

34   Directions are only published in the form of a statutory instrument if this requirement is stipulated in the primary Act: see for instance NHSA 1977 s18(1).

Assembly. In this context important directions were issued as appendices to local authority circular LAC(93)10/Welsh Office Circular WOC 35/93 (concerning NAA 1948 Part III and NHSA 1977 Sch 8),[35] and DHSS Circular 19/71 (concerning Health Services and Public Health Act 1968 s45).[36]

1.26   It is difficult to obtain copies of those directions that are not issued as Statutory Instruments (and this includes most directions authorised by the community care legislation). The failure by the Department of Health to make this legislative material available would appear to be unlawful. In *R (Salih) v Home Department*,[37] Stanley Burnton J referred to the 'fundamental requisite of the rule of law that the law should be made known' and held that this requirement extended to certain extra-statutory policy documents issued by the government.

1.27   In *R v North Derbyshire Health Authority ex p Fisher*,[38] the court had to decide whether a circular issued by the secretary of state was 'guidance' or a 'direction'. Dyson J agreed with the respondents proposition that:

> If it is the intention of the Secretary of State to give directions which attract a statutory duty of compliance, then he should make it clear that this is what he is doing. The difference between a policy which provides mere guidance and one which the . . . authority is obliged to implement is critical. Policy which is in the form of guidance can be expressed in strong terms and yet fall short of amounting to directions.

1.28   The judge went on to analyse the particular circular and having regard to its language and substance, the absence of the word 'direction' and the use of the word 'guidance' he concluded that it did not constitute a direction from the secretary of state.

Social services guidance

1.29   There are two basic types of social services guidance:

- *formal guidance* (often referred to as 'policy guidance') issued by the secretary of state specifically declaring that it is issued under LASSA 1970 s7(1) (ie, 'section 7(1) guidance');
- *general guidance* (often called 'practice guidance') of the classic form, ie, advice which an authority should have regard to when reaching a decision, but which it is not required to follow slavishly.

Social services policy guidance

1.30   Policy guidance is a higher-status form of guidance and is thus generally labelled as such and frequently it is then stated 'this guidance is issued under Local Authority Social Services Act 1970 s7(1)'. Examples of such

35 See paras 7.4, 8.18 and 8.129 where these directions are considered in detail.
36 See para 14.14 where this direction is considered in detail.
37 [2003] EWHC 2273 (Admin) at para [45].
38 (1997) 1 CCLR 150 at 154.

guidance include policy guidance issued concerning the Carers (Recognition and Services) Act 1995 as LAC (96)7[39] (see para 11.2); policy guidance concerning the charging for residential accommodation rules, generally known as CRAG, which is composed of many circulars (see para 12.7); and policy guidance concerning the 'Fair Access to Care Services' issued as LAC(2002)13 (see para 4.50). Such guidance covers the breadth of social services responsibilities; thus a series of volumes of LASSA 1970 s7(1) guidance have been issued concerning the implementation of the Children Act 1989.

1.31   In *R v Islington LBC ex p Rixon*,[40] Sedley J held:

> In my judgment Parliament in enacting section 7(1) did not intend local authorities to whom ministerial guidance was given to be free, having considered it, to take it or leave it. Such a construction would put this kind of statutory guidance on a par with the many forms of non-statutory guidance issued by departments of state. While guidance and directions are semantically and legally different things, and while 'guidance does not compel any particular decision' (*Laker Airways Ltd v Department of Trade* [1977] QB 643, 714 per Roskill LJ), especially when prefaced by the word 'general', in my view Parliament by section 7(1) has required local authorities to follow the path charted by the secretary of state's guidance, with liberty to deviate from it where the local authority judges on admissible grounds that there is good reason to do so, but without freedom to take a substantially different course.

1.32   This view was reiterated in *R v Gloucestershire CC ex p Barry and others*,[41] where Hirst LJ contrasted the binding nature of policy guidance with other social services guidance which he considered to be merely of 'persuasive authority on the proper construction of the legislation'.[42]

1.33   Accompanying the enactment of the NHSCCA 1990, the government issued a substantial volume of general policy guidance, entitled *Community Care in the Next Decade and Beyond: policy guidance* (1990).[43] In many publications this is simply referred to as 'the Policy Guidance' (and in this book referred to as the '1990 policy guidance') since it represents the first and still the most definitive general statement of the key policy objectives underpinning the 1990 community care reforms.

1.34   The consequences of failing to take into account LASSA 1970 s7(1) policy guidance were spelt out by Sedley J in *ex p Rixon* (above):

> . . . if this statutory guidance is to be departed from it must be with good reason, articulated in the course of some identifiable decision-making process even if not in the care plan itself. In the absence of any such considered decision, the deviation from statutory guidance is in my judgment a breach of law . . .

39 WOC 16/96 and WHC (96)21 in Wales.
40 (1997) 1 CCLR 119, at 123; (1996) *Times* 17 April.
41 (1997) 1 CCLR 19, at 24; 4 All ER 421, CA
42 Hirst LJ's dissenting opinion was approved by the majority in the House of Lords (1997) 1 CCLR 40.
43 (1990): London, HMSO.

1.35 It follows that if a local authority decides not to follow policy guidance it must give clear and adequate reasons for its decision and its departure from the guidance must be as limited as possible in the particular circumstances.

1.36 Although policy guidance has quasi-legal characteristics, it cannot amend or frustrate primary or subordinate legislation, but can of course be the subject of judicial review if it contains an error of law.[44] It can, in addition be struck down if its purpose is to circumvent or frustrate a statutory provision.[45] In *R v Secretary of State for Health ex p Pfizer Ltd*,[46] Collins J held that HSC 1998/158, which suggested that GP's should not prescribe Viagra, was unlawful in that it (among other things) sought to restrict the GP's statutory duty to provide patients with all necessary and appropriate personal medical services.[47]

Policy guidance and NHSCCA 1990 s47(1)

1.37 In the *R (B and H) v Hackney LBC*,[48] Keith J held that the LASSA 1970 s7(1) policy guidance was not 'strong guidance' in relation to the assessment process under NHSCCA 1990 s47(1). Section 47 is unusual, in that subsection (4) gives to the secretary of state the power to issue directions 'as to the manner in which an assessment . . . is to be carried out' and that in the absence of any such directions, assessments should be carried out 'as the local authority considers appropriate'. In referring to the paragraphs in the 1990 policy guidance that dealt with the assessment process,[49] Keith J said 'I do not think that when local authorities carry out an assessment to which section 47(1) relates, they need do any more than take into account what the [1990 policy guidance] contains'. This finding is considered further at para 4.49 below.

Social services practice guidance

1.38 The majority of guidance issued by the Department of Health/Welsh Assembly concerning community care is not issued under LASSA 1970 s7(1), but is general guidance. Authorities are not therefore required to 'act under' it. Such guidance is advice on how an authority might go about implementing or interpreting a particular statutory responsibility. It is often said that policy guidance tells an authority what it must do, whereas practice guidance suggests how it might go about doing it.

---

44 See for instance *R v North and East Devon Health Authority ex p Coughlan* [2000] 2 WLR 622; (1999) 2 CCLR 285 and *Gillick v West Norfolk Area Health Authority* [1986] AC 112.

45 *R v Secretary of State for Health ex p Pfizer Ltd* (1999) 2 CCLR 270 and *R v Worthing Borough Council ex p Birch* (1985) 50 P&CR 53.

46 (1999) 2 CCLR 270.

47 Under National Health Service (General Medical Services) Regulations 1992 SI No 635 Sch 2 para 12(1).

48 [2003] EWHC 1654 (Admin).

49 1990 policy guidance paras 3.15–3.20.

1.39   Administrative law requires authorities, when reaching a decision, to have regard to all material factors. Relevant practice guidance obviously falls into such a category, and therefore a failure to have regard to it (rather than a failure to follow it) may result in the subsequent decision being quashed. In *ex p Rixon*,[50] Sedley J referred to practice guidance in the following terms:

> While such guidance lacks the status accorded by section 7(1) of Local Authority Social Services Act 1970, it is, as I have said, something to which regard must be had in carrying out the statutory functions. While the occasional lacuna would not furnish evidence of such a disregard, the series of lacunae which I have mentioned does . . .[51]

1.40   Practice guidance takes many forms. It may be by way of a circular, eg, LAC (93)2, which gives advice on alcohol and drug services within community care. It may be way of a department letter to the senior officer of an authority, in which case it is often referred to as a 'local authority social services letter'; thus LASSL (93)6 is the sixth such letter sent in 1993 (and it contained advice on the implementation of the independent living fund). Guidance can also be issued by way of a letter or advice note from the Social Services Inspectorate (SSI).[52] Thus an important early advice letter on the implementation of the community care reforms was sent by Herbert Laming (the then Chief Inspector of the SSI); this is often referred to as the 'Laming Letter', although its official title is CI (92)34, ie, the 34th such letter sent by the Chief Inspector that year.

NHS directions and guidance

1.41   The main types of health circulars which concern community care are detailed at para 1.43 below. While NHSA 1977 s17 empowers the secretary of state to issue directions to NHS bodies in much the same way as he or she can to social services departments under LASSA 1970 s7A, there is no specific provision in the 1977 Act concerning the issuing of guidance (although the Health and Social Care Act 2001 s45(10) makes it clear that care trusts (see para 10.10) are subject to such LASSA 1970 s7 guidance). The nature and relevance of NHS guidance is considered at para 10.26 below.

Accessing guidance

1.42   Guidance can take many forms. Until 2002 health and social services guidance was usually to be found in sequentially numbered lists – each list cor-

---

50   *R v Islington LBC ex p Rixon* (1997) 1 CCLR 119, QBD.

51   (1997) 1CCLR 119 at 131E.

52   The SSI was abolished in April 2004 with its functions being transferred to the Commission for Social Care Inspection (see para 7.70 below).

responding to a particular function area of health or social services. Thus, for example, the most frequent form of social services guidance was to be found as a numbered circular, commonly identified by a reference – such as 'LAC (93)10' – which (in this example) revealed that it was the tenth 'Local Authority Circular' issued by the Department of Health in 1993. Since 2002 the Department of Health has indicated that it intends to 'adopt a less hands-on approach with clear priorities, fewer targets and less guidance and instruction from the centre'[53] and to this end has since 2002 significantly reduced the number of formal circulars it issues (ie, LACs or HSCs – see below).

1.43   The Department of Health and Welsh Assembly issue a large amount of guidance to health and social services authorities relevant to community care. Where these appear as sequentially numbered circulars, the most common are as follows:

Department of Health – social services

LAC   Local Authority Circular: the most important social services guidance.

LASSL   Local Authority Social Services Letter: guidance of lesser importance and issued by the Chief Inspector of the Social Services Inspectorate (or deputy).[54]

CI   A Chief Inspectors letter: again, this is guidance of lesser importance issued by the Chief Inspector of the Social Services Inspectorate.

Department of Health – health

HSG   Health Service Guidelines: the most important health guidance. Since 1998 this guidance has been discontinued and is now issued under the label 'HSC' (see below).

HSC   Health Service Circular: since 1998 the most important health guidance (see above).

EL   Executive Letter: Guidance of lesser importance issued by the Chief Executive of the NHS Executive (or deputy).

Welsh Guidance – social services

WOC   Welsh Office Circular: in general Welsh Office Guidance (ie, guidance prior to July 1999) was the same (or virtually the same) as the equivalent Department of Health guidance but labelled 'WOC' rather than an 'LAC'.

NAFWC   Social services guidance issued since July 1999 (when the Assembly came into being) is generally labelled 'NAFWC' (National Assembly for Wales Circular) followed by the number

---

53 *Shifting the Balance of Power: the next steps* (Department of Health, 2002) para 1.5.3 at www.doh.gov.uk/shiftingthebalance/nextsteps.pdf.

54 See note 52 above.

and year. Thus practice guidance concerning home care charging issued by the Assembly was issued as NAFWC 28/02 in
July 2002.

Welsh Guidance – health

WHC   Welsh Health Circular: health service guidance issued since
       July 1999 (when the Assembly came into being) has retained
       the same label (WHC). Thus guidance concerning the unified
       assessment of older people with community care needs was
       issued by the Assembly as WHC (2002) 32 (and since it also
       applied to Welsh social service authorities, it was also issued as
       NAFWC 09/02).

DGM   District General Manager Guidance. This is guidance of lesser
       importance issued by the Welsh Office, and generally equiva-
       lent to the Department of Health's 'EL' guidance.

1.44   Copies of all English guidance can be obtained free of charge from the
       Department of Health, PO Box 777, London SE1 6XH; Fax: 01623 724 524;
       e-mail: doh@prolog.uk.com. Such guidance is also available on the Inter-
       net at a site known as COIN (Circular on the Internet).[55] Since 2002 how-
       ever the Department of Health has moved away from issuing sequentially
       numbered circulars accessible at one web address; new guidance is
       now to be found in a variety of locations within the main Department
       of Health website. Accordingly information on residential charging is
       now located at www.dh.gov.uk/PolicyAndGuidance/OrganisationPolicy/
       FinanceandPlanning/ResidentialCare/fs/en; information on carers rights
       at www.carers.gov.uk/index.htm and so on. Where the location of the guid-
       ance is not already known, there is a search facility on the department's
       home site: additionally, each week it issues a 'Chief Executive Bulletin'
       which lists the most important guidance issued in the last seven days: this
       can be accessed at www.publications.doh.gov.uk/cebulletin/index.htm.
       Further information concerning recent developments can also be found on
       the department's press release site at www.dh.gov.uk/NewsHome/fs/en.

1.45   Copies of Welsh Assembly guidance can be obtained by writing to the
       relevant department (health or social services, etc) at the Welsh Assembly,
       Crown Buildings, Cathays Park, Cardiff CF10 3NQ – although this presup-
       poses awareness that such guidance has been issued. The Assembly's
       internet site, at www.wales.gov.uk/index.htm is difficult to navigate,
       appears to be updated on an occasional if not random basis and omits
       some important guidance for no discernible reason. Since policy guidance
       may have the force of law, it must be open to question whether the Assem-
       bly's site is itself vulnerable to a maladministration complaint[56] (if not legal

---

55 The details of local authority circulars can be obtained at www.dh.gov.uk/
    PublicationsandStatistics/LettersandCirculars/LocalAuthorityCirculars/fs/en.
    An effective mechanism for finding guidance is to use the 'A–Z' index at www.dh.
    gov.uk/Home/fs/en.

56 To the Welsh Administration Ombudsman under Government of Wales Act 1998
    s111 and Sch 9.

action)[57] – not least for its apparent failure to even comply with its own pub-lication scheme under the Freedom of Information Act 2000.[58]

Local Government Act 2000 Part I

1.46 As outlined above, the Local Government Act (LGA) 2000 provides local authorities with considerable flexibility in the way they approach their local leadership responsibilities. In particular LGA 2000 s2 empowers them to do anything which they consider will promote or improve the economic, social or environmental well-being of their area (whether for the benefit of all or part of it; or for all or any persons resident in it). In exercising these new powers councils are required to have regard to guidance issued by the secretary of state (LGA 2000 s3(5)). Such guidance was issued in March 2001[59] and at paragraph 6 stresses that the 'purpose in introducing the well-being power is to reverse that traditionally cautious approach, and to encourage innovation and closer joint working between local authorities and their partners to improve communities'.

1.47 The major restriction on the exercise of this power being, by section 3, that it cannot be used to do anything which is specifically prohibited, or limited by other statutory provisions.

1.48 Although general empowering provisions of this nature are not new,[60] LGA 2000 Part I provides considerably more freedom for councils than was previously the case – and the extent of this freedom to fund community care services has been the subject of analysis in a number of recent cases.[61]

1.49 *R (J) v Enfield LBC and Secretary of State for Health (intervener)*[62] con-cerned an applicant and her baby daughter who sought accommodation assistance from the local authority. The applicant, who was HIV positive, was unlawfully within the UK having overstayed her visa. At the time of the hearing it was considered that there was no power under Children Act 1989

---

57 As to the general duty to publish subordinate legislation (and now – arguably departmental guidance) see for instance *Blackpool Corporation v Locker* [1947] 1 KB 349 and the Australian High Court judgment in *Watson v Lee* (1979) 144 CLR 374.

58 See www.wales.gov.uk/keypubscheme/content/pub-scheme-e.htm#Publication_Scheme.

59 Issued by the Department of the Environment, Transport and the Regions (now the Office of the Deputy Prime Minister) in March 2001 as 'Power to promote or improve economic, social or environmental well-being' accessible at www.local-regions.odpm.gov.uk/wellbeing/pdf/wellbeing.pdf.

60 Local Government Act 1972 s111, for instance empowers authorities to 'do anything (whether or not involving the expenditure, borrowing or lending of money or the acquisition or disposal of any property or rights) which is calculated to facilitate, or is conducive or incidental to, the discharge of any of their functions'; – see for instance *R (A and B) v East Sussex CC (No 1)* [2002] EWHC 2771 (Admin); (2003) 6 CCLR 172 where the use of this power in relation to community care services was considered.

61 See also *R (Theophilus) v Lewisham LBC* [2002] EWHC 1371 (Admin), [2002] 3 All ER 851 which concerned further education funding.

62 [2002] EWHC 4321 (Admin); (2002) 5 CCLR 434.

s17 to provide accommodation.[63] Elias J concluded that in the absence of
any express statutory power to provide for the applicant and her daughter
then such a power existed under the LGA 2000 s2. He further held that if
the use of this power were 'the only way in which [the local authority] could
avoid a breach of the claimant's article 8 [of the European Convention on
Human Rights] rights, then . . . it would be obliged to exercise its discretion
in that way'.[64]

1.50   *R (Khan) v Oxfordshire CC*[65] concerned an applicant to whom Immigration and Asylum Act 1999 s115 applied,[66] such that she was not eligible
for any assistance unless she was able to obtain accommodation under
NAA 1948 s21 or LGA 2000 s2. The local authority had concluded that she
was excluded from assistance under the 1948 Act, by virtue of section
21(1A) which provides (in sum) that a person to whom IAA 1999 s115
applies may not be provided with residential accommodation if her need
for care and attention has arisen solely because of destitution (see para 7.27
where this provision is further considered). On the basis that the local
authority was correct, Moses J had to decide whether there remained a
power to provide assistance under the LGA 2000 s2. The problem being
that (by virtue of LGA 2000 s3) the power could not be used to provide anything which was otherwise prohibited, or limited by another statutory provision. Having considered Elias J's judgement in *R (J) v Enfield LBC and
Secretary of State for Health (intervener)*[67] Moses J concluded:[68]

> 33. I take the view that, unlike the absence of power under s17 of the
> Children Act 1989, the prohibition under s21(1A) is a prohibition within
> the meaning of section 3. Thus, it is not open to the local authority to
> provide finance under the Local Government Act 2000.

63 The Court of Appeal having held in *R (A) v Lambeth LBC* [2001] EWCA Civ 1624;
    (2001) 4 CCLR 486, that no such power existed: this finding was set aside by a
    differently constituted Court of Appeal in *R (W) v Lambeth LBC* [2002] EWCA Civ 613;
    (2002) 5 CCLR 203.
64 (2002) 5 CCLR 434 at [72]: a view affirmed by the Court of Appeal in *R (W) v Lambeth
    LBC* (2002) 5 CCLR 203 at [74]–[75], and in *R (A and B) v East Sussex CC (No 1)* [2002]
    EWHC 2771 (Admin) (but see *R(G) v Barnet LBC* [2003] UKHL 57 considered at para
    18.18 below, and see also *Anufrijeva v Southwark LBC* [2003] EWCA Civ 1406
    considered further at para 19.196 below).
65 [2002] EWHC 2211 (Admin); (2002) 5 CCLR 611.
66 Being a person subject to 'immigration control' who had leave to enter the UK subject
    to a condition that she did not have recourse to public funds. See para 7.27 where this
    provision is further considered.
67 (2002) 5 CCLR 434.
68 (2002) 5 CCLR 611 at [33]. This aspect of the judgment was upheld on appeal – see *R
    (Khan) v Oxfordshire CC* [2004] EWCA Civ 309; (2004) 7 CCLR June.

CHAPTER 2

Strategic planning

Introduction

2.1   This chapter is entitled 'strategic planning' – in part to distinguish its scope from the more specific care planning obligations owed to individual community care service users – which is considered at para 5.1 below. This chapter considers the wider public health and social care planning functions of social services authorities and NHS bodies, including the obligation of social services departments to prepare registers of disabled people.

2.2   Social services and NHS bodies have a number of statutory and non-statutory duties to prepare strategic plans. Increasingly in England, as the government seek to merge many health and social care functions, these strategic planning obligations are also converging.

Social services obligations

2.3   The duties upon social services authorities to plan, can be subdivided into a specific obligation to compile registers about the needs of disabled people in their area, and a more general duty to prepare strategic plans as to how best to deliver services to those 'in need' within their area.

Registration

2.4   National Assistance Act (NAA) 1948 s29(4)(g) and the directions made under that section[1] oblige social services authorities to maintain a register of disabled adults ordinarily resident in their area.[2] The purpose of such registers is to facilitate the obligation on social services authorities to inform 'persons to whom [section 29] relates of the services available for them [under section 29]'.[3]

2.5   The guidance accompanying the directions[4] explains that, for certain statutory purposes (ie, to establish a right to certain social security and tax benefits)[5] unconnected with NAA 1948 s29, there is a need to keep a register of the persons who come within the section's client group. The guidance points out that in addition the registers serve an important community care planning role – by helping to ascertain the demand and potential demand for domiciliary care services. Although the form of the registers is not prescribed, the guidance makes it clear that they need to contain

1   LAC (93)10 App 2 para 2(2). The material parts of which are to be found in appendix B, p605 below: for a discussion concerning this Direction, see para 8.18.

2   See chapter 6 for the definition of 'ordinary residence'.

3   LAC (93)10 App 2 para 2(1)(2) and NAA 1948 s29(4)(g).

4   LAC (93)10 App 2 para 2 onwards.

5   Various benefits for blind persons are dependent upon registration – most notably an extra income tax allowance; in addition such persons are exempt from the 'personal capability assessment' for incapacity benefit together with other miscellaneous benefits such as certain income support premiums and relief from non-dependent deductions for housing benefit and council tax benefit, certain car parking concessions, a small reduction in the TV licence and access to free NHS eye examinations.

sufficient information to produce the annual statistical returns required by the Department of Health.[6] The register aims at recording all persons who come within the NAA 1948 s29 client group – including 'mentally disordered persons'.

2.6 In many authorities the maintenance of a register of disabled people is seen as an administrative chore of little practical value. However, these registers have the potential to be used for strategic planning purposes and as important proactive tools for disseminating information about new services and resources and as databases to facilitate consultation exercises, mail-shots and so on.

2.7 For community care purposes however, the register is purely a planning tool; where a person comes within the NAA 1948 s29 client group and is assessed as requiring domiciliary services, then those services must be provided irrespective of whether he or she is registered. Indeed, the guidance makes clear that an individual has the right not to have his or her name included on the formal register if he or she so chooses.[7]

2.8 The NAA 1948 s29 client group comprises 'persons aged eighteen or over who are blind, deaf or dumb or who suffer from mental disorder of any description, and other persons aged eighteen or over who are substantially and permanently handicapped by illness, injury, or congenital deformity'. The meaning of these terms is considered in detail at para 8.21 below. The Department of Health guidance however requires social services authorities to divide their registers of 'substantially and permanently handicapped' persons into three categories,[8] namely:

1) *Very severe handicap*
   This category includes those persons who:
   a) need help going to or using the WC practically every night. In addition, most of those in this group need to be fed and dressed or, if they can feed and/or dress themselves, they need a lot of help during the day with washing and WC, or are incontinent; or
   b) need help with the WC during the night but not quite so much help with feeding, washing, dressing, or, while not needing night-time help with the WC, need a great deal of daytime help with feeding and/or washing and the WC; or
   c) are permanently bedridden or confined to a chair and need help to get in and out, or are senile or mentally impaired, or are not able to care for themselves as far as normal everyday functions are concerned, but who do not need as much help as categories (a) and (b) above.

2) *Severe or appreciable handicap*
   This category includes those persons who:
   a) either have difficulty doing everything, or find most things difficult and some impossible; or

---

6 See note 4 above.
7 LAC (93)10 App 4 para 3.
8 LAC (93) 10 App 4 para 9c and annex 1.

b) find most things difficult, or three or four items difficult and some impossible; or

c) can do a fair amount for themselves but have difficulty with some items, or have to have help with one or two minor items.

3) *Other persons*

This category is not defined, save only that it includes such persons as those suffering from a less severe heart or chest condition or from epilepsy.

2.9   An equivalent registration duty in relation to disabled children is found in the Children Act 1989 Sch 2 Part I para 2 – see para 18.8.

The social services duty to prepare strategic plans

2.10   Chronically Sick and Disabled Persons Act (CSDPA) 1970 s1(1) sought to increase the planning obligation on social services authorities by making them take a more proactive role. The section requires the authority to 'inform themselves' of the number of disabled people in its area (rather than passively waiting for people to register themselves as disabled). CSDPA 1970 s1(1) is, however, restricted in its ambit to disabled people. It provides as follows:

> It shall be the duty of every local authority having functions under section 29 of the National Assistance Act 1948 to inform themselves of the number of persons to whom that section applies within their area and of the need for the making by the authority of arrangements under that section for such persons.

2.11   DHSS Circular 12/70[9] explained the planning purpose underlying CSDPA 1970 s1(1) thus:

> . . . it requires the authorities concerned to secure that they are adequately informed of the numbers and needs of substantially and permanently handicapped persons in order that they can formulate satisfactory plans for developing their services . . . It is not a requirement of the section that authorities should attempt 100% identification and registration of the handicapped. This would be a difficult, expensive and time-consuming exercise, diverting excessive resources from effective work with those who are already known, involving a restrictive and artificial definition and likely to be counter-productive.

2.12   The need for a more effective planning obligation was highlighted by the White Paper Caring for People[10] which stated the government's intention that authorities would be required to draw up and publish plans for community care services, in consultation with health authorities and other interested agencies.[11] The intention was realised via National Health Service and Community Care Act (NHSCCA) 1990 s46 which gives to the

9   Para 5
10 HMSO, November 1989, Cm 849.
11 At para 5.3.

secretary of state powers to direct local authorities to prepare annual plans concerning the provision in their area of community care services. In 1991, detailed directions and guidance gave effect to this legislative intention:[12] namely that community care plans were to be the main vehicle for the strategic planning of adult care services by social services authorities.

2.13   In the last decade however many additional planning obligations have been imposed upon social services – including for instance Community Care Charters, the various National Service Frameworks (NSF); Local Action Plans and Local Strategic Partnerships; Local Health Partnership and Modernisation Board Plans; Health and Modernisation Plans (HIMPS); Joint Investment Plans (JIPs); Better Care, Higher Standards Charters; Local Community Strategy Initiatives; Carers strategies; and Best value plans. This proliferation of planning obligations combined with the government's increased emphasis on joint health and social services collaboration has effectively marginalised the importance of social services community care plans.[13] Accordingly the duty to prepare such plans was repealed on the 5 April 2002, in England as a consequence of the Care Plans (England) Directions 2003.[14] It now appears that the central functions that were fulfilled by community care plans will be addressed in Joint Investment Plans (discussed below) and the 'Better Care, Higher Standards' Charters (see para 3.9).[15]

Wales

2.14   The obligation in NHSCCA 1990 s46(1)[16] to prepare community care plans, continues in Wales although it has been updated to take account of the new statutory functions, including those under the Local Government Act

12 The Community Care Plans Direction 1991 and its accompanying guidance LAC(91)6. This was followed by Community Care Plans (Consultation) Directions 1993 and its guidance in LAC(93)4.

13 There is additional evidence to suggest that the increasing requirements of Whitehall for performance management data through the Performance Assessment Framework, which leads directly to the star-rating of social services departments, is to have a significant influence on the shape of individual strategic plans.

14 The Department of Health announced its intention to repeal the duty to prepare Community Care Plans (in England) in 2002. However, it was not carried through, leaving councils who had followed this advice in breach of their statutory duties. This was corrected by the 2003 Directions: accessible at www.dh.gov.uk/Home/fs/en [chose A–Z index: then 'community care plans'].

15 LAC(2001)6: HSC 2001/006, issued under LASSA 1970 s7(1). The 'Charters are for anyone 18 or over in England who has difficulties associated with old age, long term illness or disability and for carers who support people in these circumstances' (p1).

16 As detailed in WOC 55/91 secretary of state's directions – NHSCCA 1990 s46(1): Community Care Plans; WOC 20/93 Community Care Plans (Consultation) Directions 1993 and WOC 29/94 Social Care Plans (Independent Sector Non-Residential Care) Direction 1994. See also the Health, Social Care and Well-Being Strategies (Wales) Regulations 2003 SI No 154 which require the NHSCCA 1990 s46(1) plan to be integrated with the health, social care and well-being strategies that are required to be produced by local authorities and Local Health Boards under these regulations.

(LGA) 2000. The relevant guidance is now contained in circular NAFWC 36/00 and a policy document which accompanied it, Social Services Guidance on Planning (2000).[17] The guidance includes a requirement to produce five-year strategies monitored by annual reviews or business plans; a clear role for best value and performance management in setting targets and implementing service plans; and the need to produce and implement a strategy for informing the public of intentions included within plans.

2.15   The Welsh Assembly monitors all social services authority plans in Wales.[18] Ultimately, if a plan were out of line with national policies and priorities then the Assembly's powers under Local Authority Social Services Act (LASSA) 1970 s7A could be invoked.[19]

The NHS duty to prepare strategic plans

2.16   The White Paper, The New NHS Modern Dependable,[20] envisaged that the main planning tool for the NHS's community care functions would be through the development of Health Improvement Programmes. The White Paper explained that the programmes would span a three-year period and cover:

- the most important health needs of the local population and how these are to be met by the NHS and its partner organisations through broader action on public health;
- the main healthcare requirements of local people, and how local services should be developed to meet them either directly by the NHS, or where appropriate jointly with social services;
- the range, location and investment required in local health services to meet the needs of local people.

2.17   This proposal was realised with the enactment of Health Act 1999 s28(1) which obliges every health authority Local Health Board and Primary Care Trust, to prepare (in accordance with directions issued by the secretary of state) a plan which sets out a strategy for improving:

a) the health of the people for whom they are responsible; and
b) the provision of health care to such people.

2.18   Strategic health authorities are responsible for the monitoring and implementation of these plans by NHS trusts and primary pare trusts (PCTs) and have 'reserve powers'[21] to ensure that major decisions taken by such bodies are consistent with the programme. The key role of the local authority in the

---

17   Accessible on the website at
     www.wales.gov.uk/subisocialpolicy/content/pdf/guid_plan_e.pdf.
18   Social Services Guidance on Planning (2000) para 2.4 .
19   See para 1.24 above.
20   Cm 3807, para 4.7. The White Paper in Wales, *NHS Wales: putting patients first* (Jan 1998) Cm 3841 contained the same proposal – at para 4.9.
21   Under NHSA 1977 ss17A and 17B as amended by National Health Service Reform and Health Care Professions Act 2002 s3(3) and Sch 1(1) para 8.

development and implementation of the programme was initially under-scored by the creation of the new duty under Health Act 1999 s27 requiring co-operation between health bodies and local authorities and subsequently by Health and Social Care Act 2001 s11 which places a duty on NHS organ-isations to have arrangements for involving patients and the public in plan-ning development and provision of services.

2.19   Detailed guidance on these plans was issued as *Guidance for Developing Health Improvement Programmes*[22] and subsequently by a number of other circulars and guidance notes. In 2001 the Department of Health announced that Health Improvement Programmes would be renamed Health Im-provement and Modernisation Plans[23] and that these would constitute the main strategic plans for the NHS and its local partners – particularly when (as a consequence of the *Shifting the Balance of Power* initiative)[24] most health authority roles and responsibilities were devolved to PCTs. How-ever, with the abolition of health authorities and the emergence of strategic health authorities in 2002, the Department of Health announced in May 2003 that henceforth new Local Delivery Plans (LDPs)[25] – which 'focused on the health and social care priorities set out in the Planning and Priori-ties Framework (PPF)'[26] – would be the only plan that PCTs were obliged to prepare. In passing it stated that there would 'no longer therefore, be a formal requirement for PCTs to produce Health Improvement and Mod-ernisation Plans' (although of course the obligation to prepare a plan in accordance with the Health Act 1999 s28(1) remains). However the Depart-ment of Health advice note indicated that the new LDPs could:

> . . . build on or retain the structure of previous HIMP developments and might cover:
> • key health improvements issues drawn from national priority areas for locality (some may already feature in the LDP);
> • local priorities for PCT action agreed through partnership arrangements;
> • potential for alignment with health chapters in the Community Strategy;
> • presentation of the local picture, appropriate for and understandable to an Overview and Scrutiny Committee and public involvement forums.

Joint investment plans (JIPs)

2.20   The need for collaboration between the NHS and local authority welfare agencies has been the subject of discussion since the formation of the modern welfare state in 1948. With the inexorable trend towards structural

22 HSC 1998/167, LAC 98/23 (October 1998).
23 HIMPs Guidance Note issued 2 October 2001.
24 As at July 2003 the initiative comprised '*Shifting the Balance of Power: Securing Delivery*' (April 2001) and '*Shifting the Balance of Power: Next Steps*' (January 2002) – details of which are to be found at www.doh.gov.uk/shiftingthebalance/.
25 Guidance on these is to be found at www.dh.gov.uk/PolicyAndGuidance/ InformationTechnology/fs/en.
26 Planning and Priorities Framework (PPF) guidance (Oct 2002).

reconfigurations (if not mergers) between social services and NHS bodies (see para 10.10) the importance of joint planning has assumed greater importance.

2.21   Chapter 2 of the 1990 policy guidance gave general advice on what authorities were expected to achieve through planning, and throughout it placed considerable emphasis on the need for partnership and collaboration between authorities and the NHS:

> 2.3 Joint planning will be essential if the new planning agreements are to work. Many authorities believe there should be joint plans by LAs, [health authorities and primary care trusts] as this would most effectively ensure the 'seamless' service which they wish to achieve. The Department recommends that where ever possible joint plans are produced but recognises that in some areas problems exist (not least where authorities do not have coterminous boundaries) which mean that this objective would not be realistic at least in the short term. However, all authorities are expected to take a joint approach to planning and ensure their plans are complementary. Plans will be monitored to ensure this joint approach.

At para 2.11 the point is again emphasised:

> At an early stage [social services and health authorities/primary care trusts] should draw up joint resource inventories and analyses of need which enable them to reach agreement on key issues of 'who does what' for whom, when, at what cost and who pays.

2.22   The crucial importance of social services and local NHS bodies developing common procedures for recording information and 'mapping' the needs of their service users has been emphasised on many occasions, including in the highly influential Audit Commission Report, *The Coming of Age*[27] which stressed that: 'Health authorities, trusts and social services departments must map needs and the services available to meet them. They should share this information with each other as the basis for joint planning and commissioning.'

2.23   These messages were taken forward in 1997 guidance issued to both health and social services authorities as *Better Services for Vulnerable People* in 1997[28] which required them to prepare JIPs for older people including those with mental illness. Initially the requirement was little more than a joint mapping exercise, but it required 'a joint analysis' of such matters as local population needs; current resources; current investment and agreed service outcomes – with a view to agreeing gaps in service provision and 'present and future commissioning priorities'. Follow-up guidance has successively added detail to the requirements of JIPs and their scope (being extended to cover all adults with mental health needs and subsequently 'all other care groups'.[29]

---

27 (1997) Recommendation 1, page 77.

28 EL (97)62/CI (97)24.

29 See *Better Services for Vulnerable People – Maintaining the Momentum* letter issued by NHS and Social Care Regions in August 1998 CI(97) 24 which can be accessed at www.dh.gov.uk/PublicationsAndStatistics/LettersAndCirculars/fs/en.

2.24   JIPs have now (as noted above) subsumed the social services function to prepare 'community care plans' and are presently the main strategic planning tool for the provision of health and social care services for vulnerable people. Guidance concerning their development is posted on the Department of Health's 'Health and Social Care Change Agent Team's' web site.[30] The August 2002 guidance outlined the aims of the JIP as follows:

> 6. The aim of the JIP process is to enable the delivery of better services and therefore improved outcomes for service users. The emphasis must be on:
> *   promoting the independence of adults;
> *   using the plan to determine local targets and enabling the development of responsive services to meet the needs of the local population;
> *   improving the use of resources to meet joint objectives for health and social care; and
> *   transparency about current and planned investment.
>
> 7. In broad terms, the JIP process involves participating agencies setting out jointly to answer the following questions:
> *   what are the needs to be met?
> *   what is the prevalence of each need?
> *   what services are required to meet the needs?
> *   what is the provision actually made at this stage?
> *   what action is required to move services closer to what is required and so close the gaps that have been demonstrated?
> *   what are the agreed service outcomes?
> *   what outcomes are expected for the particular need being addressed at both a patient/user level and at a population level?

30 www.dh.gov.uk/PolicyAndGuidance/OrganisationPolicy/TertiaryCare/ ChangeAgentTeam/fs/en .

CHAPTER 3

Access to information, data protection and confidentiality

Introduction

3.1   In general the community care client group is a vulnerable client group. It includes many individuals with communication and mental capacity difficulties; many who are elderly or ill, unassertive and poorly informed. In order for the regime to be effective it is necessary therefore that the health and social care agencies are under a positive obligation to identify potential users of their services and then to provide active assistance in enabling them to access these services.

3.2   This chapter considers the various obligations on local authorities and health bodies to provide disabled people with relevant information. In addition it examines the specific data protection rights of disabled people and their carers/advocates and the extent of the obligation on social and healthcare agencies to preserve confidentiality.

The general duty to inform

3.3   This section reviews the obligations that local authorities and health bodies have to inform community care service users (and potential service users) of their rights. This is essentially a proactive obligation – to disseminate information regardless of an individual request. The subsequent section considers the obligations these bodies have to provide specific information when asked – the reactive obligation.

3.4   Although the duty on social services to provide general information, is primarily statutory (and in particular under Chronically Sick and Disabled Persons Act (CSDPA) 1970 s1) all public bodies have general public law obligations to provide information in certain situations. For instance, as discussed below (at para 19.166) there is a developing duty to provide reasons in certain situations. In addition the European Court of Human Rights has held that article 8 of the European Convention on Human Rights can oblige state authorities to proactively provide information – particularly when that information will enable individuals to make crucial decisions about the extent of a physical risk they may face.[1]

3.5   National Assistance Act (NAA) 1948 s29(1)(a)[2] empowers authorities to make arrangements 'for informing' disabled adults 'of the services available for them' under that section.

3.6   Section 1(2) of the Chronically Sick and Disabled Persons Act 1970 converts this discretionary power into an obligation and spells out in greater detail the nature of that duty. The provision only applies to disabled people and leaves considerable discretion as to the way in which the information is published. It remains, however, the most important statutory provision in relation to the duty to provide general information. It provides as follows:

---

1   See *Guerra v Italy* (1998) 26 EHRR 357; 14967/89; 26 February 1998; *McGinley and Egan v United Kingdom* (1998) 27 EHRR 1; and *LCB v United Kingdom* (1998) 27 EHRR 212.

2   As authorised by the secretary of state's directions – LAC(93)10 App 2 para 2(1), see para 8.38 below.

(2) Every such local authority –

(a) shall cause to be published from time to time at such times and in such manner as they consider appropriate general information as to the services provided under arrangements made by the authority under the said section 29 which are for the time being available in the area; and

(b) shall ensure that any such person as aforesaid who uses any of those services is informed of any other service provided by the authority (whether under any such arrangements or not) which in the opinion of the authority is relevant to his needs and of any service provided by any other authority or organisation which in the opinion of the authority is so relevant and of which particulars are in the authority's possession.

3.7   Paragraph 5 of DHSS Circular 12/70 explains the purpose of CSDPA 1970 s1(2) as ensuring that 'those who might benefit by help, and their families, should know what help is available to them and this is to be secured both by general publicity and by personal explanations'. While the duty to provide information to an individual service user is an essential part of the assessment process under National Health Service and Community Care Act (NHSCCA) 1990 s47, the general duty to publicise services is not specifically addressed by the 1990 Act. The 1990 Policy Guidance[3] only deals with this issue, at para 2.25, as an aspect of community care planning requiring that plans include details of what arrangements authorities intend to make to inform service users and their carers about services.

3.8   The 'Care Management and Assessment: A Practitioners' Guide'[4] states (at para 1.2) that 'a greatly increased emphasis on the sharing of information' is 'an essential feature' of community care planning and that this should include the publishing of information on the resources/services available and the assessment and review procedures. In this context it advises:

> 1.3 It is the responsibility of the practitioner to ensure that this published information reaches potential users and carers who are considering seeking assistance. The availability of such material should help practitioners in their task but will also mean that they will be more open to public challenge on the quality of service they provide.

3.9   Although the 1991 guidance remains in force, it has been updated such that the principal non-statutory obligation on social services and the NHS in England to publicise the availability of their services for adults now derives from the 'Better Care, Higher Standards' (BCHS) policy guidance issued in March 2001.[5] Relevant extracts from the guidance include:

> 2. Social services with their partners in housing and health should:
>   . . .
>   • Have a dissemination strategy for the charter which ensures all those in need of long term care can readily obtain a copy of the

---

3   *Community Care in the Next Decade and Beyond: policy guidance.* (HMSO, 1990).
4   Care Management and Assessment – A Practitioners' Guide (HMSO, 1991).
5   LAC(2001)6: HSC 2001/006, issued under LASSA 1970 s7(1). The 'Charters are for anyone 18 or over in England who has difficulties associated with old age, long term illness or disability and for carers who support people in these circumstances' (p1).

charter or summary which is accessible to people with sight, hearing, learning or other disabilities;

. . .

- Develop a jointly agreed strategy for the provision of information about long term care services across health, social services and housing for inclusion in charters for 2002/03;

. . .

10. It is strongly re-emphasised that charters must be accessible to people with sight, hearing, learning or other disabilities (this means authorities considering the availability of information in a range of formats including Braille, Moon, Maketon, audio tape and video tape) and for people whom English is not their first language.

. . .

The importance of developing an information strategy

19. A strategy for the provision of information should be developed including:

   A. Training of front-line staff in basic information about long term care services across health, social services, and housing and benefits as well as knowledge of where to refer for more detailed information. To support the charter authorities also need to continue to build the charter into their training programmes for all staff.

   B. Using the views expressed by users and carers to improve the accessibility of information. This would include making available accessible and user-friendly written information, including local BCHS charters. It should also include using and working with information/advice points such as libraries, Citizens' Advice Bureaux, local voluntary agencies and community groups; considering the use of electronic media, including terminals at publicly accessible points and times, and the use of the Internet.

   C. 'One-stop-shops' providing comprehensive information about long term care across health, social services, and housing and benefits. These may take different forms, including public enquiry offices open to personal callers, telephone help lines open through extended hours and outreach facilities to suit the environment and local population. In all cases, they require a high level of knowledge of local services for staff to answer enquiries with comprehensive, consistent and accurate information.

20. Care Direct will involve a 'one-stop-shop' service, covering the same services as Better Care, Higher Standards charters. Subject to the evaluation of the pilots, it will eventually offer a single national telephone help line number, linked to local help desks. Further, it will aim to go beyond the provision of information and will provide a service arranging appointments for assessment or access to services.

3.10   In addition to the 'Better Care, Higher Standards' policy guidance in England, there are an abundance of references to the duty to inform service users of their rights, in departmental guidance aimed at specific client groups. These include advice in the Single Assessment Process guidance[6]

6   Annex E – see para 14.3 below, where this guidance is considered further.

(Annex E), advice in the 'Valuing People' initiative[7] and the Fair Access to Care Services Guidance[8] which at para 29 advises that:

> ... councils should help individuals who may wish to approach them for support by publishing and disseminating information about access, eligibility and services, in a range of languages and formats. The information should also say what usually happens during assessment and care management processes, related timescales, and how individuals might access direct payments.

3.11   The practice guidance issued under the Carers and Disabled Children Act 2000[9] provides a useful overview of other government information dissemination initiatives, including reference to the strategy document: *A framework for improving quality in social care through better use of information and information technology*[10] and the government's internet strategy: *E-government: a strategic framework for public services in the information age.*[11]

Wales

3.12   There is no equivalent of 'Better Care, Higher Standards' in Wales. The principal guidance stems from the policy guidance: 'Health and social care for adults: creating a unified and fair system for assessing and managing care'. The guidance, at para 2.17 onwards and in Annex 10, requires agencies to 'work together to publish and disseminate a co-ordinated set of information about services and eligibility in a range of languages and accessible formats. The information should also say what usually happens during assessment and care management processes, related timescales, and how individuals might access direct payments'. In relation to the NHS; *Improving Health in Wales – A Plan for the NHS and its Partners,*[12] at chapter 3, made a commitment to publish improved information on accessing health and social care services[13] and required NHS trusts and local health groups to publish an annual prospectus providing information on available services.

---

7   See the White Paper 'Valuing People A New Strategy for Learning Disability for the 21st Century' (Department of Health) March 2001 Cm 5086 at para 4.30 and the policy guidance *Valuing People: A New Strategy for Learning Disability for the 21st Century: Implementation Guidance*: HSC 2001/016: LAC(2001)23, at Annex D and see also para 13.4 below where this initiative is considered in greater detail.

8   See para 4.48 below, where this guidance is considered further.

9   Paras 15–20 – see para 11.31 below, where this guidance is further considered.

10   Published in 2001, available at www.dh.gov.uk/PolicyAndGuidance/ InformationTechnology/InformationForSocialCare/fs/en.

11   Published in 2000 and available at www.e-envoy.gov.uk/EStrategy/ StrategicFramework/ fs/en.

12   Published in January 2001 and can be accessed at www.wales.gov.uk/subihealth/ content/keypubs/pdf/nhsplan-e.pdf.

13   Now published as the Health and Social Care Guide for Wales accessible at www. wales.nhs.uk/documents/4decH&SCareGuide.pdf.

Children

3.13   The obligations under the NAA 1948 and the CSDPA 1970 in relation to the provision of information relate only to persons aged 18 or over. The equivalent duty to inform in relation to services for disabled children and other children in need exists in Children Act 1989 Sch 2 Part I para 1. This duty is considered in volume 6 of the Children Act 1989 Guidance (Children with Disabilities), which makes the following observations:

> 3.6 ... [Social services departments] SSDs should build on their existing links with community groups, voluntary organisations and ethnic minority groups to involve them in planning services and as a sounding board when formulating policies. The publicity required must include information about services provided both by the SSD and, to the extent they consider it appropriate, about such provision by others (eg, voluntary organisations). Publicity should be clearly presented and accessible to all groups in the community, taking account of linguistic and cultural factors and the needs of people with communication difficulties. SSDs should take reasonable steps to ensure that all those who might benefit from such services receive the relevant information.

3.14   The Children Act 1989 guidance additionally deals with the need for professionals to communicate with disabled children in the assessment process and this aspect is considered at para 18.11 below.

3.15   A parallel duty to prepare plans in relation to services for disabled children and other children in need exists in Children Act 1989 Sch 2 Part I para 1.

The specific duty to inform

3.16   Access to non-confidential publicly held information is presently regulated by a variety of statutory and non-statutory provisions, including:

Local Government Act 1972

3.17   Prior to the coming into force of the Freedom of Information Act 2000 (below) the principal statute governing access to local authority information is Local Government Act 1972 (as amended) ss100A–100K which primarily concerns the public's right of access to meetings, and the papers considered at these meetings, including 'background papers' relating to reports considered at the meetings. Papers, agendas and minutes of meetings must generally be available three clear days prior to the date of the meeting.

Freedom of Information Act 2000

3.18   The Freedom of Information Act 2000 received Royal Assent on 30 November 2000. It is due to be implemented in stages and will be fully in force by January 2005.

3.19   The Act gives the general right of access to all types of 'recorded' information held by public authorities (and those providing services for them), sets out exemptions from that right and places a number of obligations on public authorities. A 'public authority' is widely defined in the Act and includes Parliament, government departments and local authorities, NHS bodies, GPs, etc.

3.20   The Act places two main responsibilities on public authorities, namely:

1) the adoption and maintenance of a 'Publication Scheme', and
2) the provision of information in response to requests from the public. This duty does not come into force in January 2005.

3.21   The duty to adopt a publication scheme has been phased in according to a fixed timetable with all authorities having to publish their schemes by June 2004. The scheme must detail the types of information the authority publishes, the form in which that information is published and details of any changes for accessing that information.

3.22   The scheme must be approved by the Information Commissioner[14] who is additionally responsible for enforcing and overseeing the Data Protection Act 1998.

Code of openness in central government

3.23   Under the Code of Practice on Access to Government Information (1994) most central government departments are under a general obligation to provide information to the public. The code is overseen by the Central Government Ombudsman.[15] The potential scope of the code is wide, although certain information is exempted – eg, information whose disclosure might harm national security or the administration of justice, personal information about a third party, commercial confidences, information which is requested in an unreasonably general way, or which would demand an unreasonable diversion of resources to supply it.

3.24   The procedure is for the request to be made initially in writing to the public authority (referring to the code) and then making a complaint via a sympathetic MP, if the information has not been provided, or is incomplete or has been unduly delayed (the code states that simple requests should be answered within 20 working days) or if the authority is imposing excessive charges for the disclosure.

The Code of Practice on Openness in the NHS

3.25   The Health Service Commissioner (often referred to as the NHS Ombudsman) was given responsibility for overseeing the Code of Practice on Openness in the NHS in England (1995).[16] The underlying principle of the code

14 Information Commissioner, Wycliffe House, Water Lane, Wilmslow, Cheshire, SK9 5AF; whose website is at www.informationcommissioner.gov.uk/index.htm.
15 Whose proper title is the Parliamentary Commissioner for Administration – whose website is at www.ombudsman.org.uk/index.html.
16 A similar but separate code was issued in respect of Wales.

is that information (not necessarily the documents from which the information derives) should be made available unless it can be shown to fall into one of the exempt categories (which largely parallel those for the above Code of Practice on Access to Government).

3.26   The code requires that: (i) each health body must publish the name of an individual in their employ responsible for the operation of the code; and (ii) how to request information through that individual should be publicised locally. Complaints about non-disclosure, or about delays in disclosure, or charges for information, should be made to that individual. The code provides that if complainants are dissatisfied with the response they receive they should write to the chief executive of the health body concerned. Time limits are set for each stage. Complainants still dissatisfied after receiving a reply from the chief executive are entitled then to complain to the Health Service Commissioner.

3.27   The Health Service Commissioner issued a special report on the workings of the scheme in 1996[17] in which he stated that, unlike his practice with other complaints, (where individuals must show some prima facie reason for their claim and to have suffered some hardship or injustice) in relation to complaints about non-disclosure he regarded the refusal as of itself a ground on which to claim injustice or hardship. To date, the Ombudsman has taken a robust approach to the enforcement of the code and required the health body to establish with precision the specific exemption relied upon, in order to justify any refusal to disclose information.

Access to personal information, data protection and confidentiality

3.28   The above statutory and non-statutory regimes relating to the provision of information all contain a general exemption in respect of the disclosure of personal information. The right of access to personal information and the associated right to have that information kept confidential are fundamental (and not infrequently complex) rights: they are not however absolute rights. Like all qualified rights they sometimes require a balance to be struck between competing interests and principles.

3.29   The striking of this balance has not been eased by the legal framework that has developed to regulate this important function. In essence there are presently three important legal domains that bear upon such decisions, namely:

- the Data Protection Act (DPA) 1998;
- the Human Rights Act (HRA) 1998; and
- the common law.

17 Health Service Commissioner (1996) First Report for Session 1996–97: Selected Investigations – Access to Official Information in the NHS; (1996) HC 6; London, TSO.

3.30 The relevant provisions of the DPA 1998, the HRA 1998 and the common law are reviewed below. However the interplay between them was considered in *R (S) v Plymouth CC*.[18] The case concerned 'C', a 27-year-old man with learning and behavioural difficulties and who had been assessed as lacking mental capacity to consent to the disclosure of his file to his mother (his nearest relative for the purposes of Mental Health Act 1983 s11). The local authority obtained a guardianship order in relation to C, since they believed that it was not in his best interests to live with his mother. The mother expressed concerns about the guardianship order, and in order to decide whether or not to object to its continuation, she asked to see the relevant papers in his social services and health care files. The local authority refused, initially asserting that it could not disclose the information because it was confidential. Subsequently it shifted its position, accepting that it had power to disclose, but that this could not occur without very good reasons (and it considered that no such reasons existed). The Court of Appeal disagreed with this approach. Reviewing the DPA 1998 it noted that all the information that the mother was seeking was 'sensitive personal data' within the meaning of DPA 1998 s2(e). This however did not mean that it could not be disclosed to third parties – since the Act permits disclosure in various situations, including:[19]

> . . . where it is necessary in order to protect the vital interests of the data subject or another person in a case where consent cannot be given by or on behalf of the data subject (Sch 3, para 3); or for the purpose of, or in connection with, any legal proceedings (including prospective legal proceedings) or for the purpose of obtaining legal advice, or where it is otherwise necessary for the purposes of establishing, exercising or defending legal rights (para 6); or where it is necessary for the administration of justice, or for the exercise of any functions conferred on any person by or under an enactment (para 7).

3.31 In the circumstances therefore the court considered that the Act provided little assistance and that the final decision on the disclosure of the confidential information[20] depended upon a careful analysis of the relevant common law and Human Rights Act 1998 principles – which required that 'a balance be struck between the public and private interests in maintaining the confidentiality of this information and the public and private interests in permitting, indeed requiring, its disclosure for certain purposes'.

3.32 Following a detailed analysis the 'court concluded as follows:

> 48. Hence both the common law and the Convention require that a balance be struck between the various interests involved. These are the confidentiality of the information sought; the proper administration of justice; the mother's right of access to legal advice to enable her to

18 (2002) 5 CCLR 251.

19 (2002) 5 CCLR 251 at [27].

20 The court was of the view that it was overly simplistic to consider that all the information in the file was confidential, commenting (at para 33) 'some of it may not be confidential at all: straightforward descriptions of everyday life are not normally thought confidential'.

decide whether or not to exercise a right which is likely to lead to legal proceedings against her if she does so; the rights of both C and his mother to respect for their family life and adequate involvement in decision-making processes about it; C's right to respect for his private life; and the protection of C's health and welfare. In some cases there might also be an interest in the protection of other people, but that has not been seriously suggested here.

49. C's interest in protecting the confidentiality of personal information about himself must not be under-estimated. It is all too easy for professionals and parents to regard children and incapacitated adults as having no independent interests of their own: as objects rather than subjects. But we are not concerned here with the publication of information to the whole wide world. There is a clear distinction between disclosure to the media with a view to publication to all and sundry and disclosure in confidence to those with a proper interest in having the information in question. We are concerned here only with the latter. The issue is only whether the circle should be widened from those professionals with whom this information has already been shared (possibly without much conscious thought being given to the balance of interests involved) to include the person who is probably closest to him in fact as well as in law and who has a statutory role in his future and to those professionally advising her. C also has an interest in having his own wishes and feelings respected. It would be different in this case if he had the capacity to give or withhold consent to the disclosure: any objection from him would have to be weighed in the balance against the other interests, although as *W v Edgell*[21] shows, it would not be decisive. C also has an interest in being protected from a risk of harm to his health or welfare which would stem from disclosure; but it is important not to confuse a possible risk of harm to his health or welfare from being discharged from guardianship with a possible risk of harm from disclosing the information sought. As *Re D*[22] shows, he also has an interest in decisions about his future being properly informed.

50. That balance would not lead in every case to the disclosure of all the information a relative might possibly want, still less to a fishing exercise amongst the local authority's files. But in most cases it would lead to the disclosure of the basic statutory guardianship documentation. In this case it must also lead to the particular disclosure sought. There is no suggestion that C has any objection to his mother and her advisers being properly informed about his health and welfare. There is no suggestion of any risk to his health and welfare arising from this. The mother and her advisers have sought access to the information which her own psychiatric and social work experts need in order properly to advise her. That limits both the context and the content of disclosure in a way which strikes a proper balance between the competing interests.

3.33   Public bodies should always analyse precisely why they are asserting 'confidentiality' and ask themselves whether this does indeed promote the best interests of the mentally incapacitated; is confidentiality being claimed

---

21 [1990] Ch 359; [1990] 2 WLR 471; [1990] 1 All ER 835, CA. See para 3.62 below.
22 *Re D (Minors)(Adoption Reports: Confidentiality)* [1996] AC 593; [1995] 3 WLR 483; [1995] 4 All ER 385, HL.

to protect themselves rather than the disabled person? At paragraph 5.8 of its guidance on protecting vulnerable adults, 'No Secrets' LAC(2000)7[23] the Department of Health emphasise this point, stating 'principles of confidentiality designed to safeguard and promote the interests of service users and patients should not be confused with those designed to protect the management interests of an organisation. These have a legitimate role but must never be allowed to conflict with the interests of service users and parents'.

Data Protection Act 1998

3.34　The Data Protection Act 1998 came into force on the 1 March 2000 and covers all social services and health records, repealing in large measure the previously applicable law under the Access to Files Act 1987, the Access to Health Records Act 1990 and the Data Protection Act 1984. Legal guidance on the Act has been issued by the Information Commissioner[24] in addition to which specific social services guidance has been issued by the Department of Health as LASSL(2000)2[25] – paragraph references below being to this circular (unless the context indicates otherwise). Any dispute concerning the refusal of access to information may be appealed to the Commissioner (or the courts); the Commissioner has, in addition, certain enforcement powers.

3.35　The 1998 Act applies to all 'accessible public records', no matter when they were compiled and includes electronic and manual data. An accessible public record is a record which contains any personal information held by the health body or social services department for the purposes of their health/social services functions, irrespective of when the information was recorded (DPA 1998 s68). The information held may include factual material as well as 'any expressions of opinion, and the intentions of the authority in relation to the individual' (para 5.4).

3.36　The Act applies eight basic principles to the disclosure of information. These essentially require data to be processed fairly, legally, accurately and that the information be retained no longer than necessary; they restrict the transfer of data as well as unnecessary reprocessing of data, and require organisations holding such information to take appropriate measures to restrict unauthorised access to it.

23　In Wales, as '*In Safe Hands*' (July 2000) para 9.5.

24　Formerly called the Data Protection Commissioner: the guidance 'Data Protection Act 1998 – Legal Guidance' is accessible on the internet at www.dataprotection.gov.uk and can be obtained from the Information Commissioner's Office, Wycliffe House, Water Lane, Wilmslow, Cheshire, SK9 5AF.

25　The volume of Guidance 'Data Protection Act 1998 – Guidance to Social Services' accompanying the circular. Guidance in Wales has been issued as '*Data Protection Act 1998 – Guidance to social services*' June 2000 and is virtually identical. Guidance to the NHS has been issued as HSC 2000/009 *Data Protection Act 1998: Protection and Use of Patient Information* March 2000 with follow up guidance in June 2003 as Guidance for Access to Health Records Requests under the Data Protection Act 1998 accessible at www.dh.gov.uk/PolicyAndGuidance/InformationTechnology/ PatientConfidentialityAndCaldicottGuardians/fs/en.

3.37   Where joint records are held, for example by social services and an NHS trust in a community mental health team, a request for access to that information can be made to either body (para 5.2): the guidance stating that:

> Authorities and their partners in joint record holding will therefore need to have procedures in place to ensure that the data subject is aware that he/she is not obliged to apply to all partners for access and to inform each other that access has been given.

3.38   The Act gives a right of access by individuals to any personal information held by the authority about them. Where the information concerns other individuals (for instance a local authority file on an entire family) one member is not in general entitled to see information about another member without that person's consent (paras 5.5–5.7). The Act permits the disclosure of information notwithstanding that it has been provided by a third party and that party has not consented to the disclosure, although in deciding whether to agree to disclosure regard is to be had to various factors, including the duty of confidence to the third party; the steps taken to obtain his or her consent (and whether he or she is capable of giving such consent) as well as the reasons for any refusal given by the third party (DPA 1998 s7(4); para 5.7 of guidance).

Access to information by or on behalf of children

3.39   The guidance (at para 5.8 onwards) makes clear that where a person aged under 18 seeks access to their records the authority must decide whether or not he or she has 'sufficient understanding to do so' which means 'does he or she understand the nature of the request'. If the requisite capacity exists then the request for access should be complied with. If however insufficient understanding exists, the request may be made by a person with parental responsibility who can make the request on the child's behalf. Disclosure to parents in such cases should only occur after the authority has satisfied itself:

(a) that the child lacks capacity to make a valid application, or has capacity and has authorised the parent to make the application; and

(b) (where the child does not have capacity) that the request made by the parent on the child's behalf is in that child's interest. (Para 5.9.)

3.40   This reflects the common law position, as put forward by the House of Lords in *Gillick v West Norfolk and Wisbech AHA*,[26] that the parents' right to make decisions on their child's behalf ends when the child achieves sufficient intelligence and understanding to make its own decision. The court cited with approval comments of Lord Denning[27] namely:

> ... the legal right of a parent to the custody of a child ends at the 18th birthday: and even up till then, it is a dwindling right which the courts will

26 [1986] AC 112; [1985] 3 WLR 830; [1985] 3 All ER 402.
27 In *Hewer v Bryant* [1970] QB 357 at 369.

hesitate to enforce against the wishes of the child, and the more so the older he is. It starts with a right of control and ends with little more than advice.

Requests made through another person (an agent)

3.41   Individuals with sufficient mental capacity are entitled to make their request for information via an agent. Paragraph 5.13 states that agents should provide evidence (normally in writing) of their authority and confirm their identity and relationship to the individual, and authorities (if satisfied that the agent is duly authorised) must treat the request as if it had been made by the individual concerned. Paragraph 5.14 accepts that some persons with profound physical impairments may not be able to give written consent to their agents and that in such cases the local authority should give the individual as much assistance as possible and ultimately could not always insist for permission in writing.

3.42   In a 1991 practice guidance the Department of Health advised that advocates should in general be given access to relevant information concerning the person for whom they advocate and are enabled to consult with appropriate individuals in order to establish the best interests of that person.[28] The local government ombudsman has also suggested that 'confidentiality' should not be used as a reason for not disclosing relevant information in such cases. In criticising a council for not sharing information with the parents of a 24-year-old man with serious learning difficulties, she commented:

> I accept that this would not be regular practice when the Council is looking after an adult: the privacy of the individual demands that the parents be kept at some distance. But [the user] had such a high level of dependency that the Council should have been willing to reconsider its approach to parental involvement in this case.[29]

Access to information on behalf of an adult lacking mental capacity

3.43   A general outline of the law concerning adults who lack mental capacity is contained at para 13.16 below.

3.44   The Act makes no special provisions about requests for access made on behalf of an adult who lacks sufficient understanding to make the request in his or her own name. The guidance however states (at para 5.11) that:

> . . . if a person lacks capacity to manage their affairs, a person acting under an order of the Court of Protection or acting within the terms of a registered Enduring Power of Attorney can request access on her or his behalf.

---

28 Care Management and Assessment Practitioners Guide HMSO 1991, para 3.28.
29 Local Government Ombudsman Complaint No 97/C/4618 against Cheshire (1999).

3.45   Although the wording in this respect is an improvement on the draft guidance,[30] the failure of the Act to deal with this issue and the inadequacy of the guidance on this point has been the subject of considerable criticism. However, these defects in the DPA 1998 are improved to a degree by the approach the courts have taken in relation to the powers available under the common law and consequent upon the implementation of the HRA 1998, as evidenced above in *R (S) v Plymouth CC*.[31]

Access procedures

3.46   Data Protection Act 1998 s7(2)(a) requires all requests for access to information to be in writing and DPA 1998 s7(8) requires the information to be disclosed 'promptly' and in any event within 40 days. All information must be disclosed, unless subject to any of the exceptions detailed below (most notably where the data includes information about another person).

3.47   The information should not be altered in any way (para 5.20) and should be the information which the authority held at the time of the request. Any amendment or deletion made between the time of request and supply should however be noted (if the changes would have occurred regardless of the request (para 5.21)). The Act contains procedures by which applicants can apply to have inaccurate information corrected.[32]

3.48   DPA 1998 s8(2) stipulates that the information should generally be provided in the form of a permanent copy although a copy need not be provided if is not possible, or would involve disproportionate effort or the applicant has agreed otherwise.

3.49   The 40-day time period for disclosure is subject to certain restrictions, namely:

1) *Sufficient description of information sought*
   The applicant must provide the authority with sufficient information to enable it to identify the person about whom the information is sought and where that information is likely to be held. Authorities are permitted to provide a standard request form for this purpose but are not permitted to insist on its use (para 5.16).

2) *Payment of the appropriate fee*
   Authorities are permitted to charge a fee for the provision of information, which must not however exceed the statutory maximum of £10, including the cost of supplying copies. The guidance requires authorities to advise applicants promptly of the need to pay a fee (if one is charged) and advises that procedures should exist for waiving the fee where the applicant's means or any other circumstances dictate such a course (para 5.17). Since the 40-day period only commences when the fee has been paid it may be appropriate to include payment in the initial

---

30 LASSL (99)16 at para 2.12. which stated such requests could 'only' be made by such persons.

31 (2002) 5 CCLR 251.

32 DPA 1998 s14 and see also para 5.31 onwards of the guidance.

letter of request (see appendix C at p624 below for a precedent letter of request).

The guidance advises (at para 2.18) that where authorities do not have the requested information, applicants should be informed as quickly as possible, and a decision then made as to whether the fee should be returned. In so deciding it should consider the applicant's circumstances, the effort involved in discovering that there was no data, and its own policy on charging.

3) *Repeated requests*

DPA 1998 s8(3) provides that access can be refused where the authority has previously complied with an identical or similar request from the applicant, unless a reasonable interval separates the requests.[33]

3.50   Not infrequently social services authorities suggest that the individual first view the data (eg, files) in the presence of a social worker, before providing such copies as are required. It is doubtful whether it is lawful for an authority to refuse to copy a file to an individual without his or her prior attendance to view it in the company of a social worker; since this imposes an extra non-statutory hurdle to access. Attendance at a social services office may be physically difficult for many service users and may be particularly daunting for the unassertive. If, however, the prior attendance requirement is put forward as good practice, to explain confusing or unclear aspects of the information and how it has been recorded, then providing this does not significantly delay the provision of copies and providing proper consideration is given to difficulties service users may have in attending, such a requirement may be sustainable.

Third party information

3.51   Data Protection Act 1998 s7(4) states that where an authority is unable to comply with a request for information without disclosing information relating to another individual (who can be identified from that information) then it is not obliged to comply with the request, unless, either:

(a) the other individual has consented to the disclosure, or
(b) it is reasonable in all the circumstances to comply with the request without the consent.

3.52   In deciding whether or not it is reasonable to make a disclosure without the third party's consent, DPA 1998 s7(6) requires the authority to have particular regard to the following factors:

(a) any duty of confidentiality owed to that other individual;
(b) any steps taken [by the authority] with a view to seeking the consent of the other individual;
(c) whether the other individual is capable of giving consent;
(d) any express refusal of consent by the other individual.

---

33 Para 5.19 of the guidance gives advice on what amounts to a 'reasonable interval'.

3.53   The guidance makes the following observations:

>   2.25 Section 7(6) is likely to be of particular relevance when a request is received for access to very old files and the possibility of tracing any third party is remote.

>   2.26 An authority should set itself a sensible timescale, within the 40 days allowed, in which to seek any third party consent. The 40 day period does not commence until the authority has received the written request, the appropriate fee, and if necessary, the further information required to satisfy itself as to the identity of the person making the request, and to locate the information sought.

>   2.27 If consent is not given by a third party within 40 days, an authority should give as much information as possible without identifying the third party (see DPA 1998 s7(5)). An authority should explain why some of the information requested has not been given. Where consent is or cannot be given and the authority considers it reasonable to comply with the request without consent then the authority may be required to justify its actions . . .

>   2.28 Where the authority is satisfied that the data subject will not be able to identify the other individual (the third party source) from the information, taking into account any other information which the authority reasonably believes is likely to be in or to come into the possession of the [applicant] then the authority must provide the information.

3.54   In addition to the above factors, the statutory exemptions detailed below also apply to decisions about disclosure, most importantly where it is considered that disclosure could result in serious harm to the other individual. Indeed, if the third party is a social worker, access cannot be refused unless the 'serious harm test' applies (para 2.37).

Statutory exemptions from disclosure

3.55   Data Protection Act 1998 Part IV provides that authorities do not have to disclose information in certain situations. The principle grounds of relevance for the purposes of community care being (in summary):

1)   *The prevention or detection of crime* (DPA 1998 s29).
      Where the authority considers that disclosure would be likely to prejudice criminal investigations, or crime prevention, it is exempt from the duty to disclose, although the guidance (para 3.37) advises that this only applies if there is a 'substantial chance' rather than a 'mere risk'.

2)   *Information about physical or mental health conditions* (DPA 1998 s30(1)).
      Social services are prohibited from disclosing any information without first consulting an appropriate health professional[34] normally this will be the person responsible for the data subject's current clinical care in connection with the matters to which the information relates – for example, be a GP or psychiatrist.

---

34 As defined in the relevant order, namely the Data Protection (Subject Access Modification)(Health) Order 2000 SI No 413.

The relevant exemption order in relation to health information specifically permits the refusal of disclosure to the extent to which it would be likely to cause serious harm to the physical or mental health or condition of the data subject or any other person.[35]

3) *Where disclosure is prevented by another enactment*
This category includes such examples as adoption records and reports, parental order records and reports under Human Fertilisation and Embryology Act 1990 s30.[36]

4) *Specific social services exemptions*
Information held for the purposes of social work is exempt from disclosure if it would be likely to prejudice the carrying out of social work, by causing serious harm to the physical or mental health (or condition) of the applicant or another person.[37]

3.56 If any of these exemptions are to be relied upon, the applicant must be notified as soon as practicable and in writing, even where the decision has also been given in person. Reasons should also be provided (para 5.39).

Appeals procedure

3.57 If disclosure is refused the applicant may apply either to the Information Commissioner or to the courts; the choice of remedy is up to the applicant.

Caldicott Guardians – information management and sharing

3.58 Considerable concern has been expressed about the way the NHS and other statutory bodies respect the confidential information they store. As a result of this concern in 1996 a review was commissioned by the Chief Medical Officer of England into the use of patient-identifiable information by the NHS in England and Wales and with the aim of ensuring that confidentiality was not being compromised. The review was chaired by Dame Fiona Caldicott, a distinguished academic.

3.59 Her subsequent report[38] made a number of recommendations, including the need to raise awareness of confidentiality and information security requirements among all staff within the NHS; the need to track all dataflows within the NHS; the need for protocols to protect the exchange of patient-identifiable information between NHS and non-NHS bodies and the appointment of a senior person, in every health organisation to act as a guardian, responsible for safeguarding the confidentiality of patient information. This latter person has come to be known as a 'Caldicott Guardian'

---

35 The Data Protection (Subject Access Modification) (Health) Order 2000 SI No 413 article 5.

36 These exemptions are listed in the Data Protection (Miscellaneous Subject Access Exemptions) Order 2000 SI No 419 (as amended by the Data Protection (Miscellaneous Subject Access Exemptions) (Amendment) Order 2000 SI No 1865.

37 Data Protection (Subject Access Modification) (Social Work) Order 2000 SI No 415.

38 The Caldicott Committee: Report on the review of patient-identifiable information – December 1997.

and the government has endeavoured to implement the recommendations of the report in a series of initiatives. Initially these were restricted to the NHS[39] although recently the process has been extended to cover all English social services departments.[40]

The common law and the Human Rights Act 1998

3.60   As has been noted above, the Data Protection Act 1998 is only one part of our domestic legal framework that seeks to both protect confidentiality and promote the right of access to personal information. The common law and the Human Rights Act (HRA) 1998 are also of great importance – particularly where questions arise concerning the exercise of discretion – for instance when a public authority is considering whether or not it would be appropriate to disclose confidential information to a third party (such as a carer or advocate for a person lacking sufficient mental capacity).

The common law

3.61   The common law has long recognised the concept of a person's right to confidentiality:[41] a right that it can be said to arise 'when confidential information comes to the knowledge of the person (the confidant) in circumstances where he has notice or is held to have agreed that the information is confidential with the effect that it would be just in all the circumstances that he should be precluded from disclosing the information to others'.[42] The common law of confidentiality is based upon a presumption (no more and no less) against disclosure to third parties.[43]

3.62   *W v Edgell*[44] concerned a doctor who disclosed a medical report commissioned from him by solicitors acting for a patient who was held in a secure hospital having killed a number of people. The patient applied to a tribunal with the eventual purpose of being discharged from detention. The doctor considered that the patient still posed a danger and although he stated this in his report, the solicitors decided not to disclose it. The doctor was so concerned about the potential risk that he gave a copy of the report to the hospital, which then copied it to the tribunal. The patient sued the doctor for breach his confidence.

3.63   In his judgment Bingham LJ, accepted that the doctor owed a duty of confidence:

39 Details of the implementation programme are given at www.dh.gov.uk/PolicyAndGuidance/InformationTechnology/ PatientConfidentialityAndCaldicottGuardians/fs/en and see HSC 1999/12 *Caldicott Guardians* (Jan 1999).

40 HSC 2002/003: LAC(2002)2 *Implementing the Caldicott Standard into Social Care* (Jan 2002)

41 *Prince Albert v Strange* (1849) 1 Mac & G 25.

42 *Attorney-General v Guardian Newspapers* [1988] 3 WLR 776; [1988] 3 All ER 545 *per* Lord Goff.

43 *R v Mid Glamorgan FHSA ex p Martin* [1995] 1 WLR 110.

44 [1990] Ch. 359; [1990] 2 WLR 471; [1990] 1 All ER 835.

He could not lawfully sell the contents of his report to a newspaper. Nor could he, without a breach of the law as well as professional etiquette, discuss the case in a learned article, or in his memoirs, or in gossiping with friends, unless he took the appropriate steps to conceal the identity of W.

3.64   However the Court of Appeal concluded that the 'public interest' justified Dr Edgell's limited disclosure – his limited breach of the obligation of confidentiality.

3.65   In *Woolgar v Chief Constable of Sussex Police and UKCC*[45] the Court of Appeal considered the extent of the 'public interest' defence and concluded that the disclosure of confidential information to a regulatory body (the UKCC) to assist them in their investigation of a matter which might affect the safety of patients, was sufficiently serious as to justify this action. The court came to a similar conclusion in *Maddock v Devon CC*[46] which concerned the disclosure of confidential information from the applicant's social services file to a university at which the applicant had obtained a place to study to become a social worker – the essence of the information being that she was potentially unsuited to become a social worker.

3.66   In *A Health Authority v X*,[47] where the court had to determine whether it was permissible to order the disclosure of personal health records held by a GP practice to a health authority (investigating various alleged irregularities in the way the practice had been run). The court held that since the proposed disclosure of the records did amount to an interference with that patient's rights under article 8 of the European Convention on Human Rights, it could only be justified where:

   (i) the authority reasonably required them for its regulatory or administrative functions, and

   (ii) there was a compelling public interest in their disclosure, and

   (iii) there was in place effective and adequate safeguards against abuse including safeguards of the particular patient's confidentiality and anonymity.

The Human Rights Act 1998

3.67   In *A Health Authority v X*,[48] the court considered the impact of the Human Rights Act (HRA) 1998 on the general domestic legal principles regulating the duty of confidentiality. HRA 1998 s6 requires public authorities to act in conformity with Convention rights, including article 8, which protects privacy. In a number of cases the European Court of Human Rights has confirmed that article 8 is both concerned with the duty on the state to

45   [2000] 1 WLR 25; [1999] 3 All ER 604 and see also *R v Chief Constable of North Wales ex p AB* (2000) 3 CCLR 25.

46   Lawtel 15 September 2003.

47   [2001] 2 FCR 634; [2001] 2 FLR 673 – upheld on appeal – [2001] EWCA Civ 2014; [2002] 2 All ER 780; [2002] 1 FLR 1045.

48   [2001] 2 FCR 634; [2001] 2 FLR 673 – upheld on appeal – [2001] EWCA Civ 2014; [2002] 2 All ER 780; [2002] 1 FLR 1045.

protect individuals from the unreasonable disclosure of publicly held confidential information[49] as well as the right of individuals to access such information.

3.68   In *Gaskin v United Kingdom*[50] the applicant sought access to his social services records. The request was refused in part on the ground that some of the information had originally been given in confidence and certain of the informants did not consent to their material being disclosed. The information was important to Mr Gaskin as he had spent almost all his life in care and he wanted it for identity purposes. His was a legitimate claim, as indeed was the refusal to divulge the information, which had been given to the local authority in confidence. The Court concluded that article 8 required a balancing of the conflicting interests in such a situation; and that this required an independent adjudication system to decide whether the papers should be disclosed. As no such system existed, it found a violation of article 8.

3.69   It has been suggested, that a useful checklist for determining whether a disclosure of confidential health care information is legally justified would include the following factors:[51]

1. Is the information in question of a confidential nature? For example anonoymised patient information is less likely to be given legal protection against disclosure.

2. Was the information imparted to the clinician on the understanding that it would not be disclosed, or only disclosed for limited reasons such as for diagnosis treatment and care? Most patients tell their doctors about themselves on the understanding that it will be communicated on a need-to-know basis to others involved in their care.

3. Has guidance issued by the relevant regulatory body (such as the General Medical Council) been complied with?

4. Is there a legal requirement that information be disclosed? There are some legislative provisions requiring disclosure of medical records to health service, government or other bodies.

5. Is the legislation proportionate to any legitimate objective being sought?

6. Is access reasonably required to permit the body to carry out its legal functions? If there is another way to access the information that is needed, or if anonymised information would suffice, then the courts would be unlikely to sanction unconsented disclosure of patient records.

7. Are there adequate safeguards against abuse? The body seeking access to the records must be able to show that they would protect any information coming into their hands against further unauthorised disclosure.

49 See for example *Z v Finland* (1997) 25 EHRR 371 and *MS v Sweden* (1997) 3 BHRC 248.

50 (1989) 12 EHRR 36. See also *MG v United Kingdom* (2002) 5 CCLR 525.

51 Association of Community Health Councils for England and Wales Briefing Paper April 2002: arguably this checklist is of relevance – with the necessary modifications – for other professionally held information.

CHAPTER 4

The duty to assess

continued

Diagram 1: Community care assessments – when is the duty triggered?

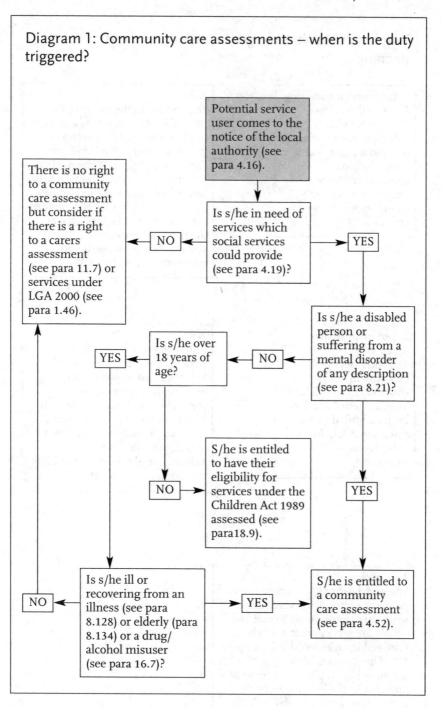

Diagram 2: The three stages in assessment and care planning

1 Information gathering
The social services department obtain sufficient information in order to make a decision about the most appropriate way of meeting the person's community care needs (see para 4.37).

Note
Depending on the extent of the person's care needs, this may be a brief process, or more complex, potentially requiring input from carers (see para 11.27), and others with relevant information such as health (see para 4.68) and housing (see para 4.68). It may also require consideration of factors such as the person's emotional, cultural and psychological needs and preferences (see para 4.38).

2 Service provision decision
The social services department decides which of the 'needs' and 'requirements' that have been identified in the assessment 'call for the provision of services' (see para 4.72).

Note
The social services department may not consider that it is 'necessary' to provide everything which is identified in the assessment as being of potential benefit to the person. In general it will only provide services which are essential or for which the assessed need meets its 'eligibility criteria' (see para 4.74).

3 Care plan
The social services department now prepares a 'care plan' which explains what 'care needs' must be met and details the services that are to be provided in order to do this (see para 5.2). The care plan also explains what health or housing services are to be provided by the housing or health authority (if any). The plan will take account of the user's preferences and also identify those 'unmet needs' which do not qualify for services (see para 5.38).

Introduction

4.1   The public provision of community care services is dependent in each case on a public authority making an administrative decision that the particular individual could not only benefit from the service, but also that the service should be provided. The decision-making procedure is known as the assessment process.

4.2   The assessment process commences with the potential service user coming to the notice of the social services authority and ends with a decision as to whether or not he or she is entitled to services. If services are required, then the next stage is the preparation of a care plan which describes and quantifies the services and specifies how (and by whom) they are to be delivered. This chapter is concerned with assessments and the chapter following with the care plans. The duty to assess carers is considered separately in chapter 11.

The theoretical framework

4.3   Assessment and care planning are central to the social work process. They are the bureaucratic response to the social services 'resource problem'. As Phyllida Parsloe commented over ten years ago:[1]

> The NHS and Community Care Act backs a whole field of horses, with the two front-runners being user choice and scarce resources. Local authorities are apparently expected to give equal weight to empowering users and keeping within their own budget.

4.4   The assessment process therefore seeks to reconcile the demand for services with the resources available. This is not a new problem, or one unique to community care. Over 20 years ago in his seminal analysis Michael Lipsky[2] charted the growth of street-level bureaucracies (legal aid lawyers, social workers, health care workers and so on). In his view their essential role is:

> . . . to make decisions about other people. Street-level bureaucrats have discretion because the nature of service provision calls for human judgment that cannot be programmed and for which machines cannot substitute . . . It is the nature of what we call human services that the unique aspects of people and their situations will be apprehended by public service workers and translated into courses of action responsive to each case within (more or less broad) limits imposed by their agencies.[3]

4.5   Lipsky argued that for this function to be exercised effectively, such employees had to be accountable both to their employers' preferences and to

---

1   Community Care, 'Making a bid for fair play', 5 August 1993.

2   Michael Lipsky, *Street-Level Bureaucracy* (Russell Sage Foundation, New York, 1980): the term 'street-level bureaucracies' encompassing 'schools, police and welfare departments, lower courts, legal services officers, and other agencies whose workers interact with and have wide discretion over the dispensation of benefits or the allocation of public sanctions' (p xi).

3   Michael Lipsky, *Street-Level Bureaucracy* at p162.

their clients' claims and that in order to maintain client confidence (given these twin roles) it was essential that the exercise of discretion was perceived as being independent: this in turn necessitated that street-level bureaucrats be seen to act as 'professionals'.[4] The organisational response to this quasi-independence has been to make:

> ... street-level bureaucrats more accountable by reducing their discretion and constraining their alternatives. [To] write manuals to cover contingencies. [To] audit performance of workers to provide retrospective sanctions in anticipation of which it is hoped future behaviour will be modified.[5]

4.6   Lipsky described how additionally street-level bureaucrats have been given mandated responsibilities that they are unable to fulfil – due primarily to their large case loads relative to their responsibilities. In his opinion, an organisational imperative of such systems is that they 'not appear to be rationing services or depriving social groups of their rights or entitlements'. They must:

> ... give evidence of strenuous efforts to avoid rationing services. They may be asked to 'trim the fat', but never to reduce the quality of their services or the quality of vital services. It is one of the best-kept secrets of government how agencies can forever find fat to trim and nonessential services to eliminate, while never affecting 'vital programs' and 'necessary services'.[6]

4.7   Many community care practitioners would identify with this analysis. Increasingly they are subject to micromanagement by unrealistically detailed central and local guidance (discussed below) and all pervasive performance audits. The development of 'managerialism'[7] within social services has unquestionably undermined the ability of social workers to carry out 'needs led' assessments. Increasingly they are budget or audit led exercises whose primary purpose is to conform to internal administrative imperatives, rather than the empowerment of service users and their carers.

4.8   At the heart of this dilemma is the issue of resources, and the extent to which the courts are prepared to defer to the problems of government (central and local) in ensuring that the state's finite resources are applied equitably. An analysis of the courts approach to this question, made more complex by the enactment of the Human Rights Act (HRA) 1998 is provided at para 4.116 below.

The duty to assess – the statutory framework

4.9   Arguably there has always been an implied duty on social services authorities to assess potential community care service users. Because of doubt

---

4   *Street-Level Bureaucracy* at p162.
5   *Street-Level Bureaucracy* at p162.
6   *Street-Level Bureaucracy* at p29.
7   See in particular, J Harris, *The Social Work Business* (Routledge, 2003).

about the extent of this obligation, in relation to the provision of services under Chronically Sick and Disabled Persons Act (CSDPA) 1970 s2, the Disabled Persons (Services, Consultation and Representation) Act (DP(SCR)A) 1986 s4 gave to disabled people (and their carers) the right to request an assessment. The circular accompanying the 1986 Act (LAC (87)6) explained the position thus:

> 3. However, section 2(1) does not make it explicit whether a local authority has a duty to determine the needs of a disabled person. It was suggested in the course of debates in Parliament on the Disabled Persons (Services, Consultation and Representation) Bill that as the duty to 'make arrangements' could be interpreted as applying only after the local authority are satisfied that such arrangements are necessary in order to meet particular needs, local authorities might refuse to come to a view as to what are those needs as a means of avoiding the obligation to make arrangements. It has never been the Government's view that subsection 2(1) should be interpreted in that way, and it is clear that this is shared by the vast majority of local authorities. However, it was agreed that the matter should be put beyond doubt.

> 4. Section 4 of the 1986 Act accordingly makes it clear that local authorities have a duty to decide whether the needs of a disabled person call for the provision of services under section 2 of the 1970 Act, if they are requested to do so by a disabled person (section 4(a)) or by anyone who provides care for him or her (section 4(c)) in the circumstances mentioned in section 8 of the 1986 Act.

4.10   Section 4 of the 1986 Act provides:

> When requested to do so by –
> (a) a disabled person,
> (b) . . .[8]
> (c) any person who provides care for him in the circumstances mentioned in section 8,[9]
> a local authority shall decide whether the needs of the disabled person call for the provision by the authority of any services in accordance with section 2(1) of the 1970 Act (provision of welfare services).

4.11   The right to request an assessment proved to be an unsatisfactory mechanism for disabled people to access services under the CSDPA 1970 as it required people to know of the existence of their right to services before they could access those services. As most people did not know of their rights under that Act, they were obviously unable to make the necessary request under DP(SCR)A 1986 s4. What was required, therefore, was a duty to assess regardless of any request from the potential service user: a duty that extended not only to services under CSDPA 1970 s2, but to all services under all the community care statutes.

4.12   The intention to create such a general duty to assess was announced in

---

8   This provision, which related to requests by 'authorised representatives' has not as yet been brought into force.

9   That is, someone 'who provides regular and substantial care for the disabled person – see para 11.7.

the 1989 white paper *Caring for People* (Cm 849) which at para 3.1.3 stated that social services authorities would be responsible for:

> . . . carrying out an appropriate assessment of an individual's need for social care (including residential and nursing home care), in collaboration as necessary with medical, nursing and other agencies, before deciding what services should be provided.

4.13   The effect of the changes has been to make social services departments the 'gate-keepers', controlling access to state-supported community care services. Such services can only be provided at public expense after an assessment of need has occurred[10] and a decision made by the social services authority that, having regard to the assessment of need, services should be provided.

The duty to assess: when does it arise?

4.14   National Health Service and Community Care Act (NHSCCA) 1990 s47(1) provides:

> (1) Subject to subsections (5) and (6) below, where it appears to a local authority that any person for whom they may provide or arrange for the provision of community care services may be in need of any such services, the authority –
> (a) shall carry out an assessment of his needs for those services; and
> (b) having regard to the results of that assessment, shall decide whether his needs call for the provision by them of any such services.

4.15   Section 47(1) obliges social services authorities to carry out an assessment of an individual's needs for community care services even where the individual has made no request for an assessment. All that is required in order to trigger the assessment obligation is that:

> (a) the individual's circumstances have come to the knowledge of the authority;
> (b) he or she may be in need of community care services.

Social services authority awareness of the individual

4.16   The first requirement for the triggering of the duty to assess is that the social services authority has the requisite knowledge of the user. It is the social services authority that must have the requisite knowledge, rather than the individual social services department. Thus, in the case of a unitary authority (which has responsibility for both housing and social services) the duty to assess will in general be triggered when, for instance, a 'vulnerable'[11] person presents him or herself as homeless (see para 17.13 below) or seeks help from an in-house welfare rights unit concerning potential disconnection of services due to payment arrears.

---

10   Except in emergencies – NHSCCA 1990 s47(5), see para 5.41.
11   Under Housing Act 1996 s189.

4.17   In *R (Patrick) v Newham LBC*,[12] the applicant, who had physical and mental health difficulties was living rough after the authority had determined that she was intentionally homeless. Lawyers acting on her behalf wrote to the authority, enclosing a doctor's letter confirming her significant psychiatric problems and requested urgent accommodation. In the subsequent judicial review proceedings it was argued (among other things) that this should have triggered an assessment under NHSCCA 1990 s47. Henriques J held:[13]

> I am wholly unable to accept any suggestion that the respondent has discharged its duty under section 47. The authority has not carried out any assessment of the applicant's needs for community care services. There is no record of any consideration of the applicant's individual circumstances at all . . .
>
> An assessment of needs is a formal task to be carried out in accordance with Central Government Guidance and involves collation of medical evidence, psychiatric evidence, etc, with a view thereafter to matching accommodation to needs. I am satisfied that the council have not complied with their duty under section 47. That duty plainly accrued [on the date when] the applicant's solicitors wrote to the respondent describing the applicant's circumstances and requesting urgent accommodation.

4.18   It follows that authorities should ensure that they have the necessary internal organisational networks so that the needs of vulnerable individuals are automatically referred to the relevant community care team irrespective of the point at which first local authority contact with that individual occurs.[14] A failure to make such arrangements may amount to maladministration.

Individuals who 'may be in need' of community care services

4.19   The local authority must not only have knowledge of the individual, it must also have knowledge[15] that he or she may be in need of services. In *R v Bristol CC ex p Penfold*,[16] the court held that this was 'a very low threshold test'. The Fair Access to Care Services (FACS) 2002 Policy Guidance, para 30,[17] stresses this point, namely that in deciding whether a person appears to be in need of community care services local authorities should 'set a low threshold, and avoid screening individuals out of the assessment process before sufficient information is known about them'.

---

12 (2000) 4 CCLR 48.

13 (2000) 4 CCLR 48 at 51–52.

14 See Fair Access to Care Services (FACS) 2002 policy guidance, para 68, which states (among other things) 'if individuals need other services, officers of the council should help them to find the right person to talk to in the relevant agency or organisation, and make contact on their behalf (see 'Better Care, Higher Standards').

15 Presumably this may include constructive knowledge.

16 (1998) 1 CCLR 315.

17 Para 2.23 of the Unified and Fair System for Assessing and Managing Care (UFSAMC) 2002 in Wales.

4.20   Not only is the duty to assess independent of any request from the potential service user, it also arises irrespective of:

a) there being any prospect of the potential service user actually qualifying for any services;[18]

b) the financial circumstances of the service user;[19] or

c) the service user being ordinarily resident[20] in the local authority's area.[21]

No need to 'request' an assessment

4.21   As has been noted above, NHSCCA 1990 s47(1) marked a major advance on the previous assessment obligation (under the (DP(SCR)A) 1986 s4) by dispensing with the need for a 'request' in order to activate the obligation. In *R v Gloucestershire CC ex p RADAR*,[22] it was held that the local authority could not discharge its obligation to potential service users (who had previously received services) simply by writing to them asking them to reply if they wanted to be considered for assessment. Carnwath J stated:

> The obligation to make an assessment for community care services does not depend on a request, but on the 'appearance of need' . . . Of course, the authority cannot carry out an effective reassessment without some degree of co-operation from the service user or his helpers. However, that is a very different thing from saying that they can simply rest on having sent a letter of the type to which I have referred.

4.22   In reaching this decision the court emphasised the essential frailty of many of the potential service users:

> In some areas of law that might be an adequate response, where those affected can be assumed to be capable of looking after their own interests, and where silence in response to an offer can be treated as acceptance or acquiescence. However, that approach cannot be and is not valid in the present context.[23]

4.23   Theoretically, therefore the duty is activated even when the potential service user objects to being assessed: strictly speaking, his or her consent is not required.[24] Of course in practice, an objection would generally be an

---

18 See *R v Bristol CC ex p Penfold* (1998) 1 CCLR 315 (discussed below) although in such cases the assessment may be rudimentary.

19 LAC (98)19 [WOC 27/98 in Wales] para 8 and FACS 2002 Policy Guidance para 70 and UFSAMC 2002 (Wales) para 2.33.

20 See chapter 6 where 'ordinary residence' is considered in greater detail.

21 See *R v Berkshire CC ex p P* (1996) 1 CCLR 141 (discussed below), although in general this will only be necessary for a local authority to carry out an assessment of someone who is not ordinarily resident in their area, if the person's residence is disputed or he or she has no settled residence.

22 (1998) 1CCLR 476; [1996] COD 253.

23 (1998) 1CCLR 476 at 482D.

24 Paragraph 11.2 of the practice guidance to the Carers (Recognition and Services) Act 1995 suggests that users can refuse an assessment; while this may be a statement of practice, as a matter of law it appears incorrect. All an individual can do, is not co-operate and if needs be, refuse any services which are offered.

end of the matter, provided the person has full mental capacity to make an informed decision on the question[25] – since, as Carnwath J observed without some degree of co-operation the effectiveness of any assessment will be significantly impaired.[26]

4.24   Clearly it will be a question of fact and degree, whether a local authority has, in any particular situation, sufficient knowledge of a potential service user, to trigger the duty to assess. In *R v Bexley LBC ex p B*[27] for instance, the court held that:

> Authorities are, however, under an obligation to make provision ...
> whenever they are satisfied that the relevant conditions have been met. A request by or on behalf of a disabled person is not one of those conditions. It seems to me that the court should look at the reality of the situation. In the present case, although no formal request was made by the applicant's mother for an assessment of the applicant's needs, that was the effect of what happened in the early months of 1994.

Entitlement to services is not relevant

4.25   The duty to assess is triggered when the authority is aware of an 'appearance of need' – and not the likelihood of entitlement to services. *R v Bristol CC ex p Penfold*[28] concerned a 52-year-old person who suffered from anxiety and depression. She was accepted as being homeless by the respondent council and was offered two properties, although she refused both as neither were in the part of the city where her relations (and support network) lived. Her solicitors then asked the authority to carry out a community care assessment of her needs, on the basis that she either be offered accommodation under National Assistance Act 1948 s21[29] or, if she moved elsewhere, that she would need support to replace her family.

4.26   The authority refused to carry out a community care assessment on the grounds (among others) that there was no prospect of meeting any needs that might have emerged in the course of the assessment (because their eligibility criteria were so tightly drawn, that only people at considerable risk were likely to be offered services). In relation to this argument, Scott Baker J held:

1) where there is an apparent need for community care services which a local authority is empowered to provide, then the authority must undertake an assessment under NHSCCA 1990 s47(1)(a) (and this duty is not a 'resource dependent' duty);

2) even if it were the case that a service user has no sensible prospect of being awarded services because of constraints upon resources, that

25 Presumably the mental capacity required would need to encompass an understanding of the potential consequences of that refusal – which may for instance be an exposure to significant direct and indirect risk of harm.

26 *R v Gloucestershire CC ex p RADAR* (1998) 1CCLR 476 at 482F.

27 (2000) 3 CCLR 15 at 22J

28 (1998) 1 CCLR 315.

29 See para 7.53 where this aspect of the case is considered.

does not absolve the local authority from conducting a section 47(1)(a) assessment;

3) the discharge by a housing authority of its obligations under the home-lessness legislation does not preclude the need for a community care assessment.

4.27   Of particular relevance, the judgment states as follows:[30]

It seems to me that Parliament has expressed section 47(1) in very clear terms. The opening words of the subsection, the first step in the three stage process, provide a very low threshold test. The reference is to community care services the authority *may* provide or arrange for. And the services are those of which the person *may* be in need. If that test is passed it is mandatory to carry out the assessment. The word *shall* emphasises that this is so. The discretionary element comes in at the third stage when the authority decides, in the light of the results of the assessment what, if any, services to provide.

Usually, but not inevitably, the section will be triggered by, or on behalf of, a person claiming to have a need. But the initiative could come from the local authority. In practice however only those who think they have a need will ask for a community care assessment. As a matter of logic it is difficult to see how the existence or otherwise of resources to meet a need can determine whether or not that need exists. The practical reality of success of the applicant's argument is that the potentially deserving cases will be prioritised in terms of:

(i)   assessed needs that are to be met;

(ii) assessed needs that must remain current but will be recorded in the local authority's records for planning purposes; and

(iii) aspirations that following an assessment turn out not to be a need.

I do not, therefore accept [the] submission that Parliament cannot have intended expenditure to a pointless end when it was clear that any established need could not be met. Even if there is no hope from the resource point of view of meeting any needs identified in the assessment, the assessment may serve a useful purpose in identifying for the local authority unmet needs which will help it to plan for the future. Without assessment this could not be done.

If the respondent's argument on construction is accepted, the consequence will be that not only can authorities set wholly disparate eligibility criteria for services they intend to provide but they may also utilise such criteria as a basis for whether they will undertake a community care assessment at all. This cannot be right. The mere fact of unavailability of resources to meet a need does not mean that there is no need to be met. Resource implications in my view play no part in the decision whether to carry out an assessment.

The duty to assess arises even when services are discretionary

4.28   The duty to assess is not dependent upon a collateral statutory duty 'to pro-vide' or upon the person being ordinarily resident in the local authority's

---

30   (1998) 1 CCLR 315 at 322.

area. In *R v Berkshire CC ex p P*,[31] the respondent local authority refused to assess the applicant, because it claimed that he was not 'ordinarily resident' within its area. Laws J held:[32]

> I reject the respondent's submission that section 47(1) imports a condition requiring the physical availability of services to a person before the duty of assessment arises in relation to that person. The word 'may' in the subordinate clause in question means, in the context of the subsection as a whole, that the duty to assess arises where the local authority possesses the legal power[33] to provide or arrange for the provision of community care services to the individual in question.

4.29 Accordingly the duty to assess is not conditional upon whether the service user is resident in the authority's area or indeed whether the local authority is prepared to exercise its discretion to make any such services available. The rationale behind this decision (in relation to the ordinary residence question) must be that without such a duty, persons whose residence was disputed by two or more authorities would effectively be in limbo until their residence was resolved.

Financial circumstances are not relevant

4.30 The financial circumstances of a person are irrelevant for the purposes of assessment. This point is made explicit by policy guidance LAC(98)19[34] which states:

> 8. Local authorities are under a legal duty under the NHSCCA 1990 to assess the care needs of anyone who, in the authority's view, may be in need of community care services. It is the Department's view that the law does not allow authorities to refuse to undertake an assessment of care needs for anyone on the grounds of the person's financial resources, eg, because they have capital in excess of the capital limit for residential accommodation. Even if someone may be able to pay the full cost of services, or make their own arrangements independently . . . they should be advised about what type of care they require, and informed about what services are available.[35]

4.31 This view is reinforced by the Fair Access to Care (FACS) guidance. The 2002 policy guidance at para 70[36] states:

> An individual's financial circumstances should have no bearing on whether a council carries out a community care assessment or not. Neither should the individual's finances affect the level or detail of the assessment

---

31 (1998) 1 CCLR 141.

32 (1998) 1 CCLR 141 at 147F.

33 Social services authorities have the power under NAA 1948 s29 to provide services for people who are not ordinarily resident in their area.

34 Para 8 WOC 27/98 in Wales.

35 The circular is expressed as being issued under Local Authority Social Services Act 1970 s7(1); see also para 12.12 below where it is further considered.

36 Para 2.33 UFSAMC 2002 in Wales makes the same point, but more briefly; see para 4.51 below.

process. Once an individual's care needs have been assessed and a decision made about the care to be provided, an assessment of their ability to pay charges should be carried out promptly, and written information about any charges payable, and how they have been calculated, should be communicated to the individual.

4.32   Importantly, this approach is amplified in the FACS 2003 practice guidance (at Q8.5):

> The carrying out and completion of a community care assessment should not be contingent on whether or not an individual can pay for care services, be they provided in a care home or the individual's own home.
>
> Following assessment, arranging residential care on behalf of service users is dealt with in paragraphs 71 and 72 of the FACS policy guidance. With respect to individuals receiving services at home, a council should arrange those services irrespective of the resources or capacity of the service user, if that is what the service user wants the council to do. Where an individual is to receive services under section 29 of the National Assistance Act 1948 and is ordinarily resident in a council area, that council has a duty to arrange services on his or her behalf.

4.33   Once a NHSCCA 1990 s47 assessment has been undertaken, a duty to provide care home accommodation may subsist even where the subsequent financial assessment reveals that the person has capital in excess of the upper capital limit. In this respect LAC(98)19 advises (at para 10):

> It is the Department's view that having capital in excess of the upper limit . . . does not in itself constitute adequate access to alternative care and attention. Local authorities will wish to consider the position of those who have capital in excess of the upper limit . . . and must satisfy themselves that the individual is able to make their own arrangements, or has others who are willing and able to make arrangements for them, for appropriate care. Where there is a suitable advocate or representative (in most cases a close relative) it is the Department's view that local authorities should provide guidance and advice on the availability and appropriate level of services to meet the individual's needs. Where there is no identifiable advocate or representative to act on the individual's behalf it must be the responsibility of the local authority to make the arrangements and to contract for the person's care.

The nature of an assessment

4.34   Despite the central importance of the assessment process in community care law, there is no effective legislative description of what the process actually consists of. The assessment process was defined with some precision by Disabled Persons (Service, Consultation and Representation) Act (DP(SCR)A) 1986 s3, but this section has not been brought into force and previous secretary of states have indicated that it will be long delayed (if indeed ever brought into force) because of its 'resource and administrative implications'. However, given that such procedures have received Royal

Assent, it may be difficult for the executive to issue directions that are radically different to the scheme prescribed by the 1986 Act.[37]

4.35   The NHSCCA 1990 empowers the secretary of state to give directions as to the form assessments should take.[38] In the debates on the Community Care (Delayed Discharge, etc) Act 2003 the government undertook to issue directions[39] under NHSCCA 1990 s47(4) to require local authorities to 'take all reasonable steps to reach agreement' with the service user on a care plan. Pursuant to this undertaking, in December 2003 the Department of Health consulted on draft directions under section 47(4). If promulgated in their draft form they are likely to have a minimal impact on practice, in that they would merely require social services, when undertaking an assessment under section 47(1), to:

- consult the person being assessed and, where they think it appropriate, any carer for that person.
- take all reasonable steps to reach agreement with the person and, where they think it appropriate, any carer for that person, on the community care services which they are considering providing to him.
- provide information to the person and, where they think it appropriate, any carer for that person, about the amount of the payment (if any) which the person will be liable to make in respect of the community care services which they are considering providing to him.

4.36   In the absence of directions NHSCCA 1990 s47(4) provides that assessments are to be carried out in such manner and take such form as the local authority considers appropriate. It follows that the adequacy of an assessment in any given case will depend upon its compliance with the relevant principles of public law, including:

1) that the aim of the process adopted by the social services department must be to determine the section 47(1)(b) question, ie, which of the applicant's needs 'call for' the provision of services. This therefore requires the local authority to:
   a) gather sufficient data about the applicant in order to make an informed decision about what his or her needs are; and
   b) have some general standard or formula by which it can make consistent decisions as to what needs do and do not 'call for' services;

2) that the process must be conducted fairly – ie, ensuring the individual understands what is occurring and has a full opportunity to contribute and respond to any third party evidence; that the process be non-discriminatory and completed within a reasonable period of time, etc;

---

37 See for instance *R v Secretary of State for Home Department ex p Fire Brigades Union* [1995] 2 All ER 244, where 'the secretary of state could not validly . . . resolve to give up his statutory duty to consider from time to time whether or not to bring the statutory scheme into force' (per Lord Browne-Wilkinson at 256B) and so could not introduce a conflicting non-statutory criminal injuries compensation scheme.

38 Section 47(4); see also Carers (Recognition and Services) Act 1995 s1(4), where a similar provision applies, and likewise no directions have been issued.

39 Baroness Andrews, House of Lords, *Hansard*, 27 March Col 976–979.

3) that all relevant matters are taken into account – ie, central and local government guidance, the views of important persons (other professionals, carers and friends, etc) who have relevant information to the section 47(1)(b) judgment.

The assessment and 'presenting needs'

4.37   The first stage of the NHSCCA 1990 s47(1) assessment process obliges authorities to identify those needs which could potentially be satisfied by the provision of a community care service. In the terminology of the Department of Health these are now known as 'presenting needs'.[40] The assessor is required to collect sufficient data concerning these 'presenting needs' (under section 47(1)(a)) in order to determine the section 47(1)(b) question, namely: 'which of the applicant's presenting needs call for the provision of community care services?'.

4.38   The scope and depth of the assessment of 'presenting needs' will depend upon the nature and complexity of the person's situation; thus, if the principal purpose of the assessment is to assess whether he or she should receive a disabled person's parking badge, the assessment will be materially different to one assessing the needs of a frail elderly person awaiting discharge from hospital.

4.39   *R v Haringey LBC ex p Norton*[41] concerned the adequacy of the local authority's assessment, undertaken in response to a complaint about a decision to reduce the applicant's community care services. In the assessment the council only considered its obligation to provide 'personal care needs' rather than other needs such as social, recreational and leisure needs. The court held this to be unlawful; the assessment had to investigate all potential needs.

4.40   In *R v Avon CC ex p M*[42] the applicant had Down's syndrome, a symptom of which was that he had formed an entrenched view that he wanted to go to a particular residential home even though an alternative, cheaper home objectively catered for all his other needs. The authority, in deciding what accommodation he needed, had regard to a psychologist's report which stated that M's entrenched position was attributable to his Down's syndrome. The authority refused to fund the more expensive home on the ground that it would set a precedent by accepting psychological need as being part of an individual's needs which could force it to pay more than it would usually expect to pay in such cases. Rejecting this argument, Mr Justice Henry held:[43]

---

40   Para 13 FACS 2002 Policy Guidance, 'presenting needs' mean 'the issues and problems that are identified when individuals contact, or are referred to, councils seeking social care support': the Welsh Assembly document, UFSAMC 2002(Wales) does not use this term or any other specific term of art.

41   (1998) 1 CCLR 168, QBD.

42   (1999) 2 CCLR 185; [1994] 2 FLR 1006.

43   (1999) 2 CCLR 185 at 195–196.

The [local authority's report] . . . proceeds on the basis that the psychological need can simply be 'excluded': . . . M's needs are thus arbitrarily restricted to the remainder of his needs, which are then described as 'usual'. Meeting his psychological needs is then treated as mere 'preference', a preference involving payments greater than usual.

The law is clear. The council have to provide for the applicant's needs. Those needs may properly include psychological needs.

4.41　Early practice guidance on the assessment process[44] described the concept of 'presenting needs' (without using the term) as follows:

> 11.　Need is a complex concept which has been analysed in a variety of different ways. In this guidance, the term is used as a shorthand for the requirements of individuals to enable them to achieve, maintain or restore an acceptable level of social independence or quality of life, as defined by the particular care agency or authority.
>
> . . .
>
> 16.　. . . Need is a multi-faceted concept which, for the purposes of this guidance, is sub-divided into six broad categories, each of which should be covered in a comprehensive assessment of need:
> - Personal/social care
> - health care
> - accommodation
> - finance
> - education/employment/leisure
> - transport/access

4.42　While there cannot be an exhaustive description of all potential 'presenting needs', their general range has been categorised in the Single Assessment Process policy guidance (2002),[45] a copy of which is reproduced as Table 1 overleaf.

Assessments prepared by other social services authorities

4.43　Relevant information will include (for instance) assessments and associated evidence obtained by other authorities, the opinions of experts and other professionals and other people with knowledge of the person being assessed. In this respect the FACS 2002 policy guidance states:[46]

> When a service user permanently moves from one council area to another, the 'receiving' council should, pending an assessment, take account of the services that were previously received and the effect of any substantial changes on the service user when reaching an interim decision about what services to provide. The 'receiving' council should have regard to these factors, as well as the outcomes that were previously pursued, when carrying out the assessment and reaching longer-term decisions about

---

44　*Care Management and Assessment, A Practitioners' Guide* (Department of Health Social Services Inspectorate, HMSO, 1991).

45　At Annex F – see Table 1 at p72 below. A similar list appears at para 4.24 of the Unified and Fair System for Assessing and Managing Care (UFSAMC) 2002 (Wales).

46　Para 56; para 5.43 UFSAMC 2002 in Wales.

Table 1: Single assessment process (SAP) Annex F

The domains and sub-domains of the single assessment process

User's perspective
- Needs and issues in the users' own words
- Users' expectations, strengths, abilities and motivation

Clinical background
- History of medical conditions and diagnoses
- History of falls
- Medication use and ability to self-medicate

Disease prevention
- History of blood pressure monitoring
- Nutrition, diet and fluids
- Vaccination history
- Drinking and smoking history
- Exercise pattern
- History of cervical and breast screening

Personal care and physical well-being
- Personal hygiene, including washing, bathing, grooming, toilet use
- Dressing
- Pain
- Oral health
- Foot-care
- Tissue viability
- Mobility
- Continence and other aspects of elimination
- Sleeping patterns

Senses
- Sight
- Hearing
- Communication

Mental health
- Cognition and dementia, including orientation and memory
- Mental health including depression, reactions to loss, and emotional difficulties

Relationships
- Social contacts, relationships, and involvement in leisure, hobbies, work, and learning
- Carer support and strength of caring arrangements, including the carer's perspective

Safety
- Abuse and neglect
- Other aspects of personal safety
- Public safety

Immediate environment and resources
- Care of the home and managing daily tasks such as food preparation, cleaning and shopping
- Housing – location, access, amenities and heating
- Level and management of finances
- Access to local facilities and services

what services will be provided. Where 'receiving' councils intend to pursue significantly different outcomes, or provide significantly different services, they should produce clear and written explanations for service users.

Policy and practice guidance

4.44   A plethora of guidance exists concerning the assessment process: some of it of general application and some of it specific to certain user groups.

4.45   Although the original policy guidance accompanying the community care reforms contained only six paragraphs concerning the assessment process[47] this was buttressed by detailed practice guidance *Care Management and Assessment: A Practitioners' Guide*[48] (referred to in this chapter as the '1991 practice guidance').

4.46   However, the lack of firm policy guidance, combined with severe financial pressures on local authorities, led to a fragmented system which was, in the opinion of an influential 1998 Audit Commission report, unfair and extremely confusing for service users. The report commenting:

> The effect of all this is to produce a maze of different criteria which are complex and difficult for people to understand. People who qualify for care in one authority may not qualify in another. The price of freedom of local decision-making is considerable variation in access to services between areas. Authorities may be able to reduce the worst effects of the inequities that result by comparing approaches and, here again, guidance may be useful.[49]

4.47   Such criticisms were accepted in the 1998 White Paper 'Modernising Social Services'[50] which pledged the government to introduce a series of National Service Frameworks (NSFs)[51] that would set national standards and define service models for specific services or care groups (para 2.34). Additionally the Government undertook to 'introduce greater consistency in the system for deciding who qualifies' for community care services – by developing guidance on 'Fair Access to Care' (para 2.36).

4.48   The product of this commitment is a series of NSFs and other guidance concerning the assessment of various care groups and generic policy and practice guidance on the assessment process, known as the Fair Access to Care Services (FACS) initiative The relationship between these guidance documents is depicted in Diagram 3 on page 74.

4.49   As has been noted at para 1.37, in *R (B and H) v Hackney LBC* (2003)[52] Keith J held that policy guidance issued under LASSA 1970 s7(1) was not

---

47   *Community Care in the Next Decade and Beyond: Policy Guidance* (1990) paras 3.15–3.20.

48   Department of Health Social Services Inspectorate, HMSO, 1991.

49   Balancing the Care Equation: Progress with Community Care (HMSO, 1996) para 32.

50   Cm 4169, Department of Health, TSO.

51   At the time of writing (April 2004) there are currently two NSFs of direct relevance to social services (Older People and Mental Health) which can be accessed at www.dh.gov.uk/Home/fs/en [chose A–Z index: then 'National Service Frameworks'].

52   [2003] EWHC 1654 (Admin).

Diagram 3: Department of Health Guidance concerning the assessment process

General Assessment Guidance Adults with community care needs
- Fair Access to Care Services – Policy Guidance (2002) [*FACS (2002) Policy Guidance*] (see para 4.48
- Fair Access to Care Services – Practice Guidance (2003) [*FACS (2003) Practice Guidance*] (see para 4.50)
- Community Care in the Next Decade and Beyond: policy guidance (1990) [*the 1990 Policy Guidance*] (see pvii)
- Care Management and Assessment: Practitioners' Guide (1991) (see para 4.50)

Carers
FACS guidance is not of direct relevance as carer's assessments are not governed by s47 NHSCCA 1990. Guidance on carer's assessments is in *The Carers and Disabled Children Act 2000: a practitioners' guide to carers assessments* (2001) (see para 11.31)

Disabled children
FACS guidance is not of direct relevance. Specific guidance exists as *The Framework for the Assessment of Children in Need and their Families* (2000) Policy and Practice Guidance (see paras 18.12 and 18.14)

Specific user group assessment guidance

Older people
- NSF of Older People (see para 14.2)
- Single assessment process (2002) (see para 14.3)

Mental Health Service users
- NSF for Mental Health (1999) (see para 15.2)
- Effective Care Co-ordination in Mental Health Services – Modernising the Care Programme Approach (1999) (see para 15.5)

People with learning disabilities
- Valuing people: White Paper (2001) (see para 13.4)
- Valuing people: implementation policy guidance LAC(2001)23 (see para 13.6)

For the Welsh Assembly equivalent guidance, see footnotes 55–60 at pp75–76 below.

'strong guidance' in relation to the assessment process under NHSCCA 1990 s47. In his view, since section 47(4) states that in the absence of directions local authorities are entitled to conduct assessments as they deem appropriate – then it logically follows that it is only a direction that can materially restrict this latitude. If this view is correct, then it conflicts with other High Court decisions and the Court of Appeal in the *Gloucestershire* judgment (it was the subject of detailed argument in the *Hackney* proceedings). It would also downgrade the force of the key FACS and Single Assessment Process guidance (see below) – although only so far as this guidance relates to the actual assessment process under NHSCCA 1990 s47 (ie, information gathering and the service provision decision): the guidance would remain strong 'policy guidance' in so far as it relates to care planning and service provision.

General guidance on assessment

4.50 Everyone entitled to a community care assessment has the right to be assessed according to the FACS guidance.[53] This guidance does not replace the earlier guidance (for instance the 1991 practice guidance) but 'builds on' it.[54] In the FACS 2003 Practice Guidance (which is in a questions and answers format) at Q8.1. it is stated that:

> In general, councils should in the first instance refer to the FACS guidance, and to the recent guidance on assessment and care planning for specific groups. They can usefully refer to the 1991 practice guidance for fuller information, where appropriate.

Specific user group assessment guidance

4.51 The 'user group specific' guidance can be broken down into the various categories listed below. The guidance relating to the assessment of older people is considered below, whereas the guidance specifically relating to people with mental health problems, learning disabilities, disabled children and carers are more specifically considered in the chapters that deal with these client groups (as indicated):

Older people
- The NSF for Older People (March 2001).[55]
- The Single Assessment Process (SAP) Policy Guidance (2002).[56]

This guidance is considered at para 14.2 below.

---

53 The FACS guidance comprises policy guidance (which was published on 28 May 2002, under cover of a local authority circular, LAC(2002)13) and practice guidance. It is intended that the practice guidance be regularly updated – the most recent, at the time of writing (April 2004) was issued on 6 March 2003. The guidance can be found at www.dh.gov.uk/PolicyAndGuidance/HealthAndSocialCareTopics/SocialCare/FairAccessToCare/fs/en.

54 Para 31 FACS 2002 Policy Guidance.

55 The Strategy for Older People in Wales (2003).

56 The Unified and Fair System for Assessing and Managing Care (UFSAMC) 2002 (Wales).

Mental health service users
- The NSF for Mental Health (Sept 1999).[57]
- Effective Care Co-ordination in Mental Health Services – Modernising the Care Programme Approach (1999).[58]

This guidance is considered at paras 15.2 and 15.5 below.

People with learning disabilities
- Valuing people: a new strategy for learning disability for the 21st century (2001).
- Valuing people: implementation policy guidance LAC(2001)23.

This guidance is considered at paras 13.4 and 13.6 below.

Disabled children
The right of disabled children to be assessed primarily stems from the Children Act 1989, although they also have certain rights under the community care regime (see para 18.1 below). However FACS is not of direct application: the specific guidance of relevance being:
- The Framework for the Assessment of Children in Need and their Families (2000) Policy Guidance.[59]
- Assessing Children in Need and the Families (2000) Practice Guidance.

This guidance is considered at paras 18.2 and 18.4 below.

Carers
Carers' assessments are not governed by NHSCCA 1990 s47 and accordingly the FACS guidance is not of direct relevance. Guidance on carers assessments is provided in 'The Carers and Disabled Children Act 2000: a practitioners guide to carers' assessments' (2001)[60] which is considered at para 11.31 below.

Disabled parents
Although not formal guidance, 'A Jigsaw of Services' (2000) constitutes important guidance concerning the rights of disabled parents in the assessment process, and is considered at para 18.2 below.

The assessment process

The scope of the assessment

4.52   The scope and depth of an assessment will be determined in large measure by the complexity of the person's needs. The assessment may consist of little more than a single conversation with a social worker or may involve complex analysis of data, protracted interviews and multi-disciplinary meetings spanning many months.

---

57 Adult Mental Health Services: A National Service Framework for Wales (April 2002).
58 Adult Mental Health Services in Wales: Equity, Empowerment, Effectiveness, Efficiency. A Strategy Document (2001).
59 In Wales, the 'Framework for the Assessment of Children in Need and their Families' (2001) Policy Guidance.
60 With the same name and date in Wales.

4.53   The SAP 2002 policy guidance (specifically directed at assessments of older people) lists four types of assessment[61] (considered in greater detail at para 14.3):

- contact assessment;
- overview assessment;
- specialist assessments; and
- comprehensive assessment.

4.54   In reality, however, these merely describe arbitrary points on a line between the very simple and the highly complex. The FACS 2002 policy guidance cautions against an overly prescriptive approach to these categories of assessment, stating (at para 34):

> . . . councils should not operate eligibility criteria to determine the complexity of the assessment offered; rather the depth and breadth of the assessment should be proportionate to individuals' presenting needs and circumstances. Based on their judgment, professionals may wish to carry out initial assessments, or assessments to take stock of wider needs, or specialist assessments of particular needs, or comprehensive assessment across all potential needs. In many cases, combinations of these assessment types may be used.

4.55   Accordingly authorities still retain a wide discretion in determining the scope of any particular assessment, and in this respect the 1991 practice guidance advice (at para 3.3) remains apposite:

> . . . the scope of an assessment should be related to its purpose. Simple needs will require less investigation than more complex ones. In the interests of both efficiency and consumer satisfaction, the assessment process should be as simple, speedy and informal as possible.[62]

4.56   The courts have been unenthusiastic about guidance that dictates an overly prescriptive approach to the assessment process. The 1991 practice guidance for instance put forward six models of assessment, from simple to comprehensive and then stated that all disabled people had the right to a comprehensive assessment (regardless of how complex their needs might be). This advice was considered by Carnwath J in *R v Gloucestershire CC ex p RADAR*[63] where (referring to the 1991 practice guidance) he held:

> I have some sympathy with those trying to write these sort of guides since the complexity of the legislative chain, combined with the length of the titles of most of the Acts, makes short and accurate exposition particularly difficult. However, if what is intended is to define the legal obligation in respect of the disabled, then it can only be intended as a reference to the decision referred to in Disabled Persons (Services, Consultation and Representation) Act 1986 s4, that is, as to the range of services required under section 2 of the 1970 Act. I take that to be the intended meaning of the word 'comprehensive'. If it is intended to mean anything else, it is misleading.

61 Annex E p12.

62 FACS 2002 policy guidance at para 35 advises that they be 'be as simple and timely as possible'.

63 (1998) 1 CCLR 476 at 484.

Screening assessments

4.57   Certain basic matters must be considered in even the most rudimentary interview for it to amount to an assessment. In *R v Bristol CC ex p Penfold*[64] the respondent sought to argue that a mere consideration by the council of an applicant's request for an assessment, was itself an assessment. Rejecting this, Scott Baker J held that an assessment 'cannot be said to have been carried out unless the authority concerned has fully explored the need in relation to the services it has the power to supply. In some cases the exercise will be very simple; in others more complex'.[65]

4.58   As noted above, FACS 2002 policy guidance para 30[66] cautions against individuals being screened out of the assessment process before sufficient information is known about them. This is amplified in the FACS 2003 practice guidance at para 8.2, where it is stated:

> There is considerable evidence that screening systems operated by councils can turn people away without their needs being identified. Some councils go further by declaring that they do not help particular groups of individuals, such as those with higher functioning autism/Asperger syndrome, and make no attempt to assess needs as they should do. This is unacceptable. Often these screening systems are not connected to assessment and care management systems, which cannot be helpful. Councils should always bear in mind that almost all adults approach social services for support only when they feel they need to.

The setting of an assessment

4.59   The 1991 practice guidance (at paras 3.12–3.15) emphasises the importance of the assessment being conducted in an appropriate location, as this may have a material effect on its outcome. It points out that office interviews, while administratively convenient and less costly than domiciliary assessments, may give false results if the interviewee is not at ease; and that the applicant is more likely to relax in the home setting. The following important points are also made:

> 3.13 Where the assessment is concerned with the maintenance of a person at home, the assessment should take place in that setting. If users are considering admission to residential or nursing home care, involving irreversible loss of their home, they should always be given the opportunity of experiencing that setting before making their final decision.

> 3.14 There may be advantages to some part of the assessment being undertaken in settings external to the home, for example, day or residential care settings, so that staff have longer contact with the individual. In such circumstances, assessors will be working in close collaboration with service providers.

---

64 (1998) 1 CCLR 315.
65 (1998) 1 CCLR 315 at 321C.
66 Para 2.23 UFSAMC 2002 in Wales. See also para 3.20 of the 1990 policy guidance.

3.15 In considering such options, care should be taken to avoid exposing individuals to unnecessary disruption. In addition, it is necessary to avoid assuming that behaviour will be replicated in other settings. Such considerations may, occasionally, affect assessment arrangements for hospital discharges.

User involvement

4.60 The draft Community Care (Assessment) Directions (see para 4.35 above) requirement to consult the user is amplified in the FACS 2002 policy guidance which advises that assessments should be 'rounded and person-centred' and that (at para 35):

> Councils should recognise that individuals are the experts on their own situation and encourage a partnership approach to assessment. They should help them prepare for the assessment process and find the best way for each individual to state their views. The use of interpreters, translators, advocates or supporters can be critical in this regard.

4.61 The 1991 policy guidance also stressed the importance of involving users in the assessment process so that the resulting services fully take into account their preferences (and so far as possible those of their carers).[67] It highlighted the need for the assessor to establish a relationship of trust and to clarify what the assessment will entail. The FACS 2002 policy guidance at para 36 states that assessments should be carried out in such a way, and be sufficiently transparent, for individuals to:

- Gain a better understanding of their situation.
- Identify the options that are available for managing their own lives.
- Identify the outcomes required from any help that is provided.
- Understand the basis on which decisions are reached.

4.62 In *R v North Yorkshire CC ex p Hargreaves*,[68] the social services authority came to a service provision decision without taking into account the preferences of the disabled person – largely because (in Dyson J's opinion) her carer was very protective and probably considered by the social services authority as obstructing its ability to communicate with the disabled person. Nevertheless this did not discharge the authority's obligation to discover what her preferences were, and accordingly the decision was quashed.

Potential service users with communication or mental capacity difficulties

4.63 Individual involvement in the assessment process becomes a more difficult question where the potential service user is unable to participate fully due to lack of ability to communicate or mental capacity. The issue becomes controversial where the potential service user chooses not to participate in (or actively objects to) the assessment.

67 At paras 3.16 and 3.25.
68 (1997) 1 CCLR 104.

4.64   Much of the general and specific user group assessment guidance stresses the importance of endeavouring to communicate with service users, no matter how severe their impairments, and of the particular importance of advocacy services in this respect.[69] The FACS 2002 policy guidance (at para 35), for example, advises that:

> Councils should recognise that individuals are the experts on their own situation and encourage a partnership approach to assessment. They should help them prepare for the assessment process and find the best way for each individual to state their views. The use of interpreters, translators, advocates or supporters can be critical in this regard.

4.65   The 1990 policy guidance states that 'where a user is unable to participate actively [in the assessment] it is even more important that he or she should be helped to understand what is involved and the intended outcome'.[70] The 1991 practice guidance elaborates on this advice, stating that where it is clear that a user or carer would benefit from independent advocacy, he or she should be given information about any schemes funded by the authority or run locally. It goes on to state that it is consistent with the aims of basing service provision on the needs and wishes of users that those who are unable to express their views, for example, those with severe learning disabilities or dementia, or those who have been previously disadvantaged, for example, those from minority ethnic groups, should, as a matter of priority, be supported in securing independent representation.[71]

4.66   In *R (A and B) v East Sussex CC (No 2)*,[72] a case concerning the appropriate way to lift and move two young women (A and B) with profound physical and learning difficulties, Munby J stressed the importance of ascertaining their views on the process:

> 132. I have said that the assessment must take account of the disabled person's wishes, feelings and preferences. How are these to be ascertained?
>
> 133. In a case where the disabled person is, by reason of their disability, prevented, whether completely or in part, from communicating their wishes and feelings it will be necessary for the assessors to facilitate the ascertainment of the person's wishes and feelings, so far as they may be deduced, by whatever means, including seeking and receiving advice – advice, not instructions – from appropriate interested persons such as X and Y involved in the care of the disabled person.
>
> 134. Good practice, Miss Foster suggests, would indicate, and I am inclined to agree that:
> (i)   A rough 'dictionary' should be drawn up, stating what the closest carers (in a case such as this, parents and family, here X and Y) understand by the various non-verbal communications, based on their intimate long-term experience of the person. Thus with familiarisation

---

69 See paras 13.11 and 14.10 for further considerations of the role of advocacy services.
70 At para 3.16.
71 See paras 3.25–3.27.
72 [2003] EWHC 167 (Admin); (2003) 6 CCLR 194.

and 'interpretation' the carers can accustom themselves to the variety of feelings and modes of expression and learn to recognise what is being communicated.

(ii) Where the relatives are present with the carers and an occasion of 'interpretation' arises, great weight must be accorded to the relatives' 'translation'.

(iii) As I commented in *Re S*:[73]

'the devoted parent who ... has spent years caring for a disabled child is likely to be much better able than any social worker, however skilled, or any judge, however compassionate, to 'read' his child, to understand his personality and to interpret the wishes and feelings which he lacks the ability to express.'

(iv) That said, in the final analysis the task of deciding whether, in truth, there is a refusal or fear or other negative reaction to being lifted must ... fall on the carer, for the duty to act within the framework given by the employer falls upon the employee. Were the patient not incapacitated, there could be no suggestion that the relative's views are other than a factor to be considered. Because of the lack of capacity and the extraordinary circumstances in a case such as this, the views of the relatives are of very great importance, but they are not determinative.

4.67   The 1991 practice guidance accepts that an individual's involvement in the assessment process may be involuntary (at para 3.17) and that any individual can withdraw at any stage from active involvement. The effect of such 'wilful lack of co-operation' may be that the social services authority finds it impossible to ascertain the preferences of the user and/or carer.[74] The 1991 practice guidance makes a number of further and important observations:

3.17 Individuals who enter voluntarily into the assessment process should also be made aware of their entitlement to withdraw at any stage. Where the assessment is on an involuntary basis, for example as a prelude to possible compulsory admission to psychiatric hospital, it is even more important that the individuals are helped to understand, as far as they are able, the nature of the process in which they are engaged. It is less clear cut where practitioners are dealing with someone, with failing capacities, for example, relapse of a psychotic illness, where intervention has been on a voluntary basis but, at a certain threshold of risk or vulnerability, it is likely to tip over into compulsory admission. That threshold should be clearly defined in policy terms and agreed with other relevant agencies, for example, police and health authorities. All practitioners should be clear on the distinction between using assessment as an instrument of social support as opposed to social control. The former offers choices to the user while the latter imposes solutions. The one should not be allowed to shade into the other without all parties appreciating the full implications of that change.

---

73 [2003] 1 FLR 292 at para [49] – see para 13.57 below.
74 Per Dyson J in *R v North Yorkshire CC ex p Hargreaves* (1997) 1 CCLR 104 at 111J.

The section 47(3) referral duty in relation to health and housing needs

4.68　Where the assessment discloses a possible housing or medical need, NHSCCA 1990 s47(3) obliges the authority to notify the relevant housing or health authority.[75] Section 47(3) provides:

> If at any time during the assessment of the needs of any person under subsection (1)(a) above, it appears to a local authority –
>
> (a) that there may be a need for the provision to that person by such Primary Care Trust or Health Authority[76] as may be determined in accordance with regulations of any services under the National Health Service Act 1977, or
>
> (b) that there may be a need for the provision to him of any services which fall within the functions of a local housing authority (within the meaning of the Housing Act 1985) which is not the local authority carrying out the assessment,
>
> (c) the local authority shall notify that Primary Care Trust, Health Authority or local housing authority and invite them to assist, to such extent as is reasonable in the circumstances, in the making of the assessment; and, in making their decision as to the provision of the services needed for the person in question, the local authority shall take into account any services which are likely to be made available for him by that Primary Care Trust, Health Authority or local housing authority.

4.69　In relation to this obligation, the 1990 policy guidance advised as follows:

> 3.47 It is expected that, as a matter of good practice, GPs will wish to make a full contribution to assessment. It is part of the GP's terms of service to give advice to enable patients to avail themselves of services provided by a local authority.
>
> 3.48 Where advice is needed by the local authority in the course of assessment, this should be obtained from the GP orally (eg, by telephone) as far as possible. A record should be kept of the advice given. In addition to the information that only the patient's own GP can provide, local

---

75　The consequent obligations on the health and housing authorities are considered below at paras 10.32, 17.9 and 17.19 respectively. Although there is no duty on the notified authority to respond following notification, the service user will benefit where parallel duties are triggered.

76　Although the section has been amended (as a result of the demise of health authorities in England and Wales) to insert 'Primary Care Trusts' (National Health Service Reform and Health Care Professions Act 2002 Sch 2(2) para 56), no equivalent amendment has occurred in Wales – to insert the term 'Local Health Boards'. It appears however that this is not strictly necessary, as a result of a combination of Welsh Statutory Instrument: the Health Authorities (Transfer of Functions, Staff, Property, Rights and Liabilities and Abolition) (Wales) Order 2003 SI No 813 (W 98) – which transfers all functions of health authorities in Wales to the Assembly – and the Local Health Boards (Functions) (Wales) Regulations 2003 No 150 (W 20) which provides (subject to exceptions) that functions that were exercised by Health Authorities and were transferred to the Assembly by SI No 2003/813 are to be exercised by Local Health Boards.

authorities may, on occasion, also require a clinical examination or an interpretation of the medical report provided by the GP. Local authorities should, therefore, be aware that GPs have a personal duty to, and a relationship with, their patients, and may not be best placed to act in addition as an assessor on the authority's behalf. In such circumstances local authorities may wish other practitioners to act in, this capacity.

4.70 The specific obligations on health bodies and housing authorities, when so notified, are considered at paras 10.32 and 17.9 below. However a social services failure to make such a referral may, in appropriate cases, undermine the legality of the assessment process.

4.71 In general however, the courts have considered such cases from the public law perspective as a failure to take into account a material consideration (see para 19.149). Thus in *R v Birmingham CC ex p Killigrew*,[77] the point relied upon was a failure to follow the above quoted 1990 Policy Guidance. The applicant was profoundly disabled and a re-assessment of her needs failed to seek up-to-date medical evidence. Given the severity of her condition, Hooper J considered this to be a fundamental breach of the assessment obligation and accordingly quashed the resulting care plan.[78]

The service provision decision: what needs must be satisfied by the provision of services?

4.72 Once the authority has complied with its obligations under NHSCCA 1990 s47(1)(a) – ie, it has gathered together all the data it considers necessary (reports, interviews, etc) – section 47(1)(b) requires it to make a decision: to decide which of the individual's 'presenting needs' 'call for' the provision of community care services. 'Community care services' are defined by NHSCCA 1990 s46, as services which a local authority may provide or arrange to be provided under:

(a) Part III of the National Assistance Act 1948;
(b) Health Services and Public Health Act 1968 s45;
(c) National Health Service Act 1977 s21 and Sch 8; and
(d) Mental Health Act 1983 s117.

4.73 NHSCCA 1990 s47(1)(b) obliges the authority to 'have regard to' the results of the section 47(1)(a) assessment, rather than obliging it to provide services to meet all the presenting needs. It is this decision that is generally referred to as the 'service provision decision'. It is of considerable importance, since it determines which community care services an individual is legally entitled to receive. It is the point, at which the individual's needs are reconciled with the local resources that are available to meet such needs.

---

77 (2000) 3 CCLR 109.
78 See also para 4.141 below.

As Swinton-Thomas LJ observed in the Court of Appeal decision in *R v Gloucestershire CC ex p Barry*:[79]

> Section 47(1)(a) provides for the provision of community care services generally, the need for such services, the carrying out of an assessment and then, section 47(1)(b) gives the local authority a discretion as to whether to provide those services. The discretion in making the decision under section 47(1)(b) arises by reason of the words 'having regard to the results of that assessment'. In making that decision they will be entitled to take into account resources.

Eligibility criteria and 'eligible needs'.

4.74   Social services officers need some external scale, formula or criteria in order to make consistent and sensible service provision decisions. It is not merely consistency that demands such criteria: it is also economics. Local authorities have finite resources and they need to ensure that these are applied equitably – to those whose needs (however this concept is defined) are greatest.

4.75   Early guidance on eligibility criteria was provided in 1994, in what was termed the 'Laming Letter'.[80] It was this guidance that was considered in a number of early community care cases.[81] The guidance suggested that:

> 14. Authorities can be helped in this process by defining eligibility criteria, ie, a system of banding which assigns individuals to particular categories, depending on the extent of the difficulties they encounter in carrying out everyday tasks and relating the level of response to the degree of such difficulties. Any 'banding' should not, however, be rigidly applied, as account needs to be taken of individual circumstances. Such eligibility criteria should be phrased in terms of the factors identified in the assessment process.

4.76   The guidance was considered in the *Gloucestershire* proceedings;[82] Lord Clyde stating as follows:[83]

> In deciding whether there is a necessity to meet the needs of the individual some criteria have to be provided. Such criteria are required both to determine whether there is a necessity at all or only, for example, a

---

79 [1996] 4 All ER 421; (1997) 1 CCLR 19, CA; although reversed by the House of Lords ([1997] AC 584; (1997) 1 CCLR 40; [1997] 2 All ER 1; [1997] 2 WLR 459) these observations concerning the effect of NHSCCA 1990 s47(1) were not contradicted by the Lords.

80 CI (92) 34; although the guidance was expressed as being cancelled on 1 April 1994, Sedley J accepted that 'in the sense that it gives plainly sensible advice' its content is still relevant although not mandatory – see *R v Islington LBC ex p Rixon* (1996) 1 CCLR 119 at 127B.

81 (1997) 1 CCLR 40; [1997] 2 All ER 1; [1997] 2 WLR 459.

82 *R v Gloucestershire CC ex p Barry* (1997) 1 CCLR 40 at 54; [1997] 2 All ER 1; [1997] 2 WLR 459.

83 In relation to an assessment of a person's need for services under Chronically Sick and Disabled Persons Act 1970 s2.

desirability, and also to assess the degree of necessity. Counsel for the respondent suggested that a criterion could be found in the values of a civilised society. But I am not persuaded that that is sufficiently precise to be of any real assistance. It is possible to draw up categories of disabilities, reflecting the variations in the gravity of such disabilities which could be experienced. Such a classification might enable comparisons to be made between persons with differing kinds and degrees of disability. But in determining the question whether in a given case the making of particular arrangements is necessary in order to meet the needs of a given individual it seems to me that a mere list of disabling conditions graded in order of severity will still leave unanswered the question at what level of disability is the stage of necessity reached. The determination of eligibility for the purposes of the statutory provision requires guidance not only on the assessment of the severity of the condition or the seriousness of the need but also on the level at which there is to be satisfaction of the necessity to make arrangements. In the framing of the criteria to be applied it seems to me that the severity of a condition may have to be to be matched against the availability of resources.

4.77 Although there are many theoretical models by which such criteria may be constructed, the Department of Health and Welsh Assembly have now issued detailed (and prescriptive) policy guidance with a view to stand-ardising individual local authority eligibility criteria for community care services. These are the 'Fair Access to Care Services' (FACS) 2002 Policy Guidance, in England and the 'Unified and Fair System for Assessing and Managing Care' (UFSAMC) 2002 in Wales. The eligibility criteria sections of these two documents differ in only minor respects and both base their criteria on the issue of 'independence'. As the FACS 2002 policy guidance states (at para 15):[84]

> Councils should use the following eligibility framework to specify their eligibility criteria. In other words, they should use the framework to describe those circumstances that make individuals, with the disabilities, impairments and difficulties described in paragraph 14, eligible for help. The eligibility framework is based on the impact of needs on factors that are key to maintaining an individual's independence over time. The framework makes no reference to age, gender, ethnic group, religion, disabilities, impairments or similar difficulties, personal relationships, location, living and caring arrangements, and similar factors. In themselves, these factors do not threaten independence; however, they may need to be taken into account as needs are assessed and services considered.

4.78 The framework detailed in the FACS 2002 policy guidance (at para16) is reproduced as Table 2 overleaf.

4.79 Every social services authority must use the framework overleaf and must use the exact wording. However they are permitted to 'add additional risk factors as extra bullet points within a band'.[85]

---

84 UFSAMC 2002 (in Wales) paras 5.16–5.17.
85 Q3.1 of the FACS 2003 practice guidance.

Table 2: FACS policy guidance para 16

Critical[86] **– when**

- life is, or will be, threatened; and/or
- significant health problems have developed or will develop; and/or
- there is, or will be, little or no choice and control over vital aspects of the immediate environment; and/or
- serious abuse or neglect has occurred or will occur; and/or
- there is, or will be, an inability to carry out vital personal care or domestic routines; and/or
- vital[87] involvement in work, education or learning cannot or will not be sustained; and/or
- vital social support systems and relationships cannot or will not be sustained; and/or
- vital family and other social roles and responsibilities cannot or will not be undertaken.

Substantial – when

- there is, or will be, only partial choice and control over the immediate environment; and/or
- abuse or neglect has occurred or will occur; and/or
- there is, or will be, an inability to carry out the majority of personal care or domestic routines; and/or
- involvement in many aspects of work, education or learning cannot or will not be sustained; and/or
- the majority of social support systems and relationships cannot or will not be sustained; and/or
- the majority of family and other social roles and responsibilities cannot or will not be undertaken.

Moderate – when

- there is, or will be, an inability to carry out several personal care or domestic routines; and/or
- involvement in several aspects of work, education or learning cannot or will not be sustained; and/or
- several social support systems and relationships cannot or will not be sustained; and/or
- several family and other social roles and responsibilities cannot or will not be undertaken.

Low – when

- there is, or will be, an inability to carry out one or two personal care or domestic routines; and/or
- involvement in one or two aspects of work, education or learning cannot or will not be sustained; and/or
- one or two social support systems and relationships cannot or will not be sustained; and/or
- one or two family and other social roles and responsibilities cannot or will not be undertaken.

86 Critical means that life is threatened or individuals are at great risk of serious illness or harm (Q3.6 of the FACS 2003 practice guidance).

87 Vital means that without help, individuals are at great risk of *either* losing their independence, possibly necessitating admission to institutional care *or* making very little, damaging or inappropriate contributions to family and wider community life with serious consequences for the individual and others . . . [however] 'what may be "vital" to one individual may not be "vital" to another' (Q3.6 of the FACS 2003 practice guidance).

4.80   Although all social services authority eligibility criteria must adopt the above framework, this does not mean that they must all come to the same service provision decisions. The guidance allows individual local authorities to decide how high on the scale an individual must be, before he or she qualifies for services. Effectively, therefore, the guidance sanctions a continuation of the existing local variations in eligibility for services: the so called 'postcode lottery'.

4.81   Arguments concerning the need for local authorities to have flexibility over their eligibility criteria are not wholly convincing. The justification for such variations is based on the proposition that criteria must accommodate local financial and demographic variables: for instance that an area might be relatively poor, or have a relatively high population of elderly people or relatively high morbidity, etc. However, these are the very factors that the government seeks to iron out, by its sophisticated Local Government Finance Formula Grant.

4.82   In order to determine the annual grant for each local authority, the government calculates a Formula Spending Share (FSS)[88] which is based on formulae that include detailed information on the population profile, social structure and other characteristics of each authority. The FSS therefore allocates the central government grant according to authorities' relative circumstances. In theory therefore it puts each authority – so far as the funding of social welfare services are concerned – in the same financial situation.

4.83   Notwithstanding this criticism, the guidance, advises as follows:[89]

> For any given planning period . . . a council should estimate the numbers of adults currently receiving services, and who potentially may be referred to it. The council should attempt to categorise these individuals' needs into the four bands of the eligibility framework. The council should then estimate the kinds of services that typically would be required to meet the needs arising in each band, including immediate needs and developing needs. It should cost this service provision with respect to prices typically faced when commissioning and purchasing services. (A council should also reflect on the longer-term costs of not meeting low level needs that would considerably worsen for the lack of timely help.) The council should then add up the costs of meeting needs falling into each eligibility band. Starting with the critical band, if the estimated costs of providing services to individuals with needs in this band equals the resources locally available to adult social care, then the council's eligibility framework would simply comprise the critical band. If a council's resources could cover the cost of services for individuals whose needs fall within the critical or substantial bands, then the council's eligibility criteria should comprise the critical and substantial bands; and so on.

4.84   In the English guidance, therefore it is explicit (whereas in the Welsh it is

---

88 In April 2003 Formula Spending Shares replaced the previous formula grant system, known as Standard Spending Assessments. This change took place in order to ensure that the formula was as responsive as possible to local variations in need: see the local government White Paper *Strong Local Leadership – Quality Public Services* (Dec 2001).

89 Q3.9 of the FACS 2003 practice guidance.

merely implicit) that if a council considers that it only has resources to fund service users whose eligible needs fall into the critical category, then that would be acceptable. Both English and Welsh guidance, however, contain caveats: the UFSAMC 2002 policy guidance, at para 5.21 comments 'any set of criteria must also allow for exceptional cases . . . [and] . . . must remain in line with the implications of case law'. The FACS 2003 practice guidance contains the somewhat curious statement (in response to Q3.9) that in deciding where to strike the eligibility line a council should be 'observant of its statutory duties under community care legislation'. The legality of this approach is considered at para 4.116 below.

4.85   The guidance[90] emphasises that (with the exception of life threatening circumstances in the critical band) there is no hierarchy of needs and related risks within an eligibility band. It also explains what should happen where a council considers that it has sufficient resources to meet all the eligible needs in (for instance) both the critical and substantial bands, and can extend into the moderate band without being able to meet all needs that would fall into the moderate band. The guidance[91] advises that in such cases local authorities have a discretion on how to proceed, and suggests two possible alternatives; the first being:

> . . . to separate the moderate band into two sub-bands termed, 'moderate – greater' and 'moderate – lesser'. In doing the separation the council should regard each of the current four elements of the band as having equal weight, and split each element up into risks of greater or lesser importance. The costs of meeting the greater risks should be equal to the resources that are left over once needs falling into the critical and substantial bands are met. The council's eligibility criteria comprise the critical and substantial bands and the 'moderate – greater' sub-band.

The second being to:

> . . . take a less formal approach. Instead of reclassifying the moderate band, they could ask their professionals to make judgments as to whether risks, arising from an individuals' needs, lean more to substantial than 'mainstream' moderate. In doing so the council should again regard each of the current four elements of the moderate band as having equal weight. Councils would need to monitor professionals' judgments to ensure both consistency and that they stay within budget.

4.86   The process prescribed in the English and Welsh guidance accordingly follows the following sequence:

1) the local authority ascertain the extent of the individual's 'presenting needs';
2) these presenting needs are subjected to a risk analysis (risk of harm to the user and others and risks to independence);
3) these risks are then compared to the above framework categories 'critical, substantial, medium or low';

90 Q3.3 of the FACS 2003 practice guidance.
91 Q3.10 of the FACS 2003 practice guidance.

4) if the individual's 'presenting needs' fall into one or more of the categories of risk that the local authority has decided that it will provide services to meet, then the local authority must meet those needs: such needs being termed 'eligible needs'.[92]

4.87 To assist in the second stage of the above analysis, the FACS 2002 policy guidance, states at para 40:

> As presenting needs are fully described and explored, the individual and professional should consider and evaluate the risks to independence that result from the needs both in the immediate and longer-term. This evaluation should take full account of how needs and risks might change over time and the likely outcome if help were not to be provided. The evaluation of risks should focus on the following aspects that are central to an individual's independence:
> • Autonomy and freedom to make choices.
> • Health and safety including freedom from harm, abuse and neglect, and taking wider issues of housing and community safety into account.
> • The ability to manage personal and other daily routines.
> • Involvement in family and wider community life, including leisure, hobbies, unpaid and paid work, learning, and volunteering.

4.88 Thus in each case the assessor should ask 'what are the risks to a persons (autonomy or health and safety, etc) if no services are provided'; or put another way, what would be the consequences for the individual, if services are not provided? The answer is then categorised in terms of critical, substantial, medium or low.

4.89 The key paragraphs[93] in the FACS 2002 policy guidance, which explain how the various elements of the assessment process culminate in a service provision decision, are as follows:

> 42. Eligibility for an individual is determined following assessment. As part of the assessment, information about an individual's presenting needs and related circumstances is established, and should be recorded. This information is then evaluated against the risks to his/her autonomy, health and safety, ability to manage daily routines, and involvement in family and wider community life. Councils may wish to facilitate the risk evaluation by asking their professionals to identify risks using the framework in paragraph 16 above. These identified risks to independence will then be compared to the council's eligibility criteria. Through identifying the risks that fall within the eligibility criteria, professionals should identify eligible needs.

> 43. Once eligible needs are identified, councils should meet them. However, services may also be provided to meet some presenting needs as a consequence of, or to facilitate, eligible needs being met.

---

92 FACS 2002 Policy Guidance, para 13; UFSAMC 2002 policy guidance, para 5.14.
93 Q3.12 of the FACS 2003 practice guidance describes para 42 of the policy guidance as the paragraph 'which spells out the logic of how to go from the assessment to a determination of eligibility'.

Revising eligibility criteria

4.90   The formulation of eligibility criteria is a core policy function of social services authorities. The FACS 2002 policy guidance directs that once determined, the criteria 'should be published in local 'Better Care, Higher Standards' charters, and made readily available and accessible to service users, the public more generally, and other relevant local bodies'.[94] The clear implication of this requirement is that eligibility criteria should be set for a reasonable period – presumably for the duration of the relevant Better Care, Higher Standards charter. Obviously if an unforeseen financial crisis arises (for instance of the type that resulted in the *Gloucestershire* proceedings) then emergency changes to the criteria may have to be instigated,[95] but absent such situations, criteria should not be the subject of frequent amendments. If this were otherwise, and criteria were changed frequently (to reflect the annual cycle of local authority economic woes)[96] then service users would have no idea from day to day, where their entitlements lay – effectively comparing their need against a moving target. Such a situation would be giving pre-eminence to short term financial issues – if not making them determinative.

Resources and the limits of eligibility criteria

4.91   In *R v Gloucestershire CC ex p Barry*[97] the House of Lords considered the legality of eligibility criteria. The case arose because the authority had its resources for community care drastically cut by an unexpected change in the size of the grant made by the Department of Health. The authority wrote to those people (about 1,500) on its lowest priority level advising them it had decided that their home care service would be reduced or withdrawn. Some of the people who were affected, who were receiving their services under Chronically Sick and Disabled Persons Act (CSDPA) 1970 s2, sought a judicial review of the decision. Their basic argument was straightforward; their condition had not changed and so their need for services remained. How could the state of an authority's finances make their individual need no longer a 'need'? The solution adopted by the House of Lords (a majority 3:2 judgment) was that authorities could (within limits) change their eligibility criteria and if they then become more austere, they could reassess existing service users against these new criteria. If on such a reassessment it was found that the service user was no longer eligible for assistance, then the service can be withdrawn. Accordingly it had been lawful for Gloucestershire to take into account its resources when framing its eligibility criteria, but unlawful for it to withdraw services without a prior reassessment.

94   FACS 2002 policy guidance, para 20, and UFSAMC 2002 policy guidance, para 2.17.
95   See FACS 2002 policy guidance, para 19 and UFSAMC 2002 policy guidance, para 5.22.
96   As the 2003 practice guidance concedes (Q11.3), local authority budgeting 'is not a science'.
97   (1997) 1 CCLR 40; [1997] 2 All ER 1; [1997] 2 WLR 459.

4.92   The majority decision, in relation to the resource argument, has been criticised[98] and the Lords themselves have sought to restrict the impact of the judgment. Subsequently, in *Re T (A Minor)*,[99] a differently constituted House of Lords held that 'resource arguments' in the *ex p Barry* decision were in large measure restricted to cases concerning CSDPA 1970 s2, the statutory construction of which the Lords held to be a 'strange one'.[100] Indeed the court found certain aspects of the majority's reasoning in *ex p Barry* to be 'with respect . . . very doubtful . . .'.[101] A similar line was taken by the Court of Appeal in *R v Sefton MBC ex p Help the Aged*[102] where the Master of the Rolls felt 'compelled' to follow the reasoning of the majority in the *ex p Barry* decision, but only to a limited degree. The Court of Appeal effectively distinguished the *ex p Barry* decision, as one peculiar to the situation under CSDPA 1970 s2. This line was also adopted by Scott Baker J in *R v Bristol CC ex p Penfold*[103] when he rejected the respondent's argument that its resource problems justified its refusal to carry out a community care assessment. It was also adopted by Dyson J in *R v Birmingham CC ex p Taj Mohammed*[104] where he held that housing authorities were not entitled to take resources into account when deciding whether or not to approve a disabled facilities grant.

4.93   The courts have further restricted the ability of local authorities to make blanket 'shortage of resources' assertions, by requiring that in appropriate cases contentions of this nature be supported by strong evidence.[105]

4.94   The effect of the *Gloucestershire* and subsequent judgments is that social services authorities are entitled to take their available resources into account, when framing their general eligibility criteria. This principle is, however, subject to four significant constraints. These can be summarised as:

1) the reassessment obligation;
2) resources shape eligibility criteria not assessments;
3) resources cannot be the sole criterion;
4) the Human Rights Act (HRA) 1998 obligation.

The reassessment obligation

4.95   As noted, local authorities are entitled (within limits) to change their eligibility criteria (for instance when they have a budgetary problem – as occurred in the *Gloucestershire* case). However when criteria are revised and made more severe, existing service users must be the subject of a full

---

98 See for instance, B Rayment, '*Ex p Barry in the House of Lords*' and L Clements, '*The collapsing duty*' both in 'Judicial Review' (1997) vol 2, issue 3.

99 Sub nom *R v East Sussex CC ex p Tandy* (1998) 1 CCLR 352; [1998] 2 WLR 884; [1998] 2 All ER 769.

100 (1998) 1 CCLR 352 at 359I.

101 (1998) 1 CCLR 352 at 360G.

102 (1997) 1 CCLR 57 at 67H.

103 (1998) 1 CCLR 315.

104 (1998) 1 CCLR 441.

105 See para 5.26 below.

community care reassessment before any decision can be taken on the withdrawal of services. The logic for this requirement is two-fold: first, that the service users' circumstances may have altered since their previous assessment and so they may be eligible under the new, more austere criteria; and second, even if their needs do not satisfy the revised criteria, the criteria are not 'determinative' (see para 4.114 below) and so there may be special reasons why the services should continue notwithstanding.

4.96   McCowan LJ highlighted this requirement in the first instance hearing of the *Gloucestershire* case[106] when he held:

> It would certainly have been open to the Gloucestershire County Council to reassess the individual applicants as individuals, judging their current needs and taking into account all relevant factors including the resources now available and the competing needs of other disabled persons. What they were not entitled to do, but what in my judgment they in fact did, was not to reassess at all but simply to cut the services they were providing because their resources in turn had been cut. This amounted to treating the cut in resources as the sole factor to be taken into account, and that was, in my judgment, unlawful.

Resources shape eligibility criteria not assessments

4.97   The 1992 'Laming Letter'[107] stated as follows:

> 13. An authority may take into account the resources available when deciding how to respond to an individual's assessment. However, once the authority has indicated that a service should be provided to meet an individual's needs and the authority is under a legal obligation to provide it or arrange for its provision, then the service must be provided. It will not be possible for an authority to use budgeting difficulties as a basis for refusing to provide the service.

4.98   The legality of the Laming Letter advice on resources was in issue (and upheld) in the *Gloucestershire* case. McCowan LJ in the first instance hearing expressed the legal position thus:[108]

> . . . once they have decided that it is necessary to make the arrangements, they are under an absolute duty to make them. It is a duty owed to a specific individual and not a target duty. No term is to be implied that the local authority are obliged to comply with the duty only if they have the revenue to do so. In fact, once under that duty resources do not come into it.

106 *R v Gloucestershire CC ex p Mahfood* (1997) 1 CCLR 7; 94 LGR 593, DC.

107 CI (92) 34; although the guidance was expressed as being cancelled on 1 April 1994, Sedley J accepted that 'in the sense that it gives plainly sensible advice' its content is still relevant although not mandatory – see *R v Islington LBC ex p Rixon* (1997) 1 CCLR 119 at 127B.

108 *R v Gloucestershire CC ex p Mahfood* (1997) 1 CCLR 7; 94 LGR 593, DC; and see also *R v Kirklees MBC ex p Daykin* (1998) 1 CCLR 512 at 525D, where Collins J expressed the proposition in the following terms: 'once needs have been established, then they must be met and cost cannot be an excuse for failing to meet them. The manner in which they are met does not have to be the most expensive. The Council is perfectly entitled to look to see what cheapest way for them to meet the needs which are specified'.

4.99   In the House of Lords, Lord Clyde reiterated this point in the following
        terms:[109]

> The right given to the person by section 2(1) of the Act of 1970 was a right
> to have the arrangements made which the local authority was satisfied
> were necessary to meet his needs. The duty only arises if or when the
> local authority is so satisfied. But when it does arise then it is clear that
> a shortage of resources will not excuse a failure in the performance of
> the duty.

4.100   Lord Clyde's approach was followed by Lord Woolf MR in *R v Sefton MBC
        ex p Help the Aged*[110] in relation to the duties under National Assistance
        Act (NAA) 1948 s21 and is expressed by the FACS 2002 policy guidance (at
        para 52)[111] as follows:

> Councils are also reminded that they may take their resources into
> account when drawing up their eligibility criteria against which they assess
> individuals' needs, and when deciding which services will be provided to
> meet those needs. However, this does not mean that councils can take
> decisions on the basis of resources alone. Once a council has decided it is
> necessary to provide services to meet the eligible needs of an individual, it
> is under a duty to provide those services.

4.101   The principle underlying this formulation is of fundamental importance.
        All local authorities have limited resources and all are required to fulfil a
        variety of statutory obligations. If a council could assert resource shortages
        as a reason for not complying with a statutory duty, then this would
        effectively result in these duties being 'collapsed into powers' (as Richard
        Gordon QC, argued in the *Gloucestershire* case). The resolution of this prob-
        lem is achieved in the *Gloucestershire* judgment by the court holding that
        the duty to provide community care services only arises once a service
        provision decision under NHSCCA 1990 s47(1)(b) has occurred. However
        once a local authority has decided that a person has 'eligible needs'
        then these must be met irrespective of resource arguments. In *Re T (A
        Minor)*,[112] Lord Browne-Wilkinson dealt with this issue as follows:

> There remains the suggestion that, given the control which central
> Government now exercises over local authority spending, the court cannot,
> or at least should not, require performance of a statutory duty by a local
> authority which it is unable to afford . . . My Lords, I believe your Lordships
> should resist this approach to statutory duties.
>   . . . The argument is not one of insufficient resources to discharge the
> duty but of a preference for using the money for other purposes. To permit
> a local authority to avoid performing a statutory duty on the grounds that it
> prefers to spend the money in other ways is to downgrade a statutory duty
> to a discretionary power. A similar argument was put forward in the *Barry*
> case but dismissed by Lord Nicholls (at 470F–G) apparently on the ground
> that the complainant could control the failure of a local authority to carry

---

109 (1997) 1 CCLR 40 at 54F; [1997] 2 WLR 459 at 474G.
110 (1997) 1 CCLR 57 at 67I.
111 UFSAMC 2002 policy guidance para 5.32.
112 (1998) 1 CCLR 352 at 360; [1998] 2 WLR 884; [1998] 2 All ER 769.

out its statutory duty by showing that it was acting in a way which was *Wednesbury* unreasonable in failing to allocate the necessary resources. But with respect this is a very doubtful form of protection. Once the reasonableness of the actions of a local authority depends upon its decision how to apply scarce financial resources, the local authority's decision becomes extremely difficult to review. The court cannot second-guess the local authority in the way in which it spends its limited resources: see also *R v Cambridge District Health Authority ex p B* [1995] 1 WLR 898, especially at p906D–F. Parliament has chosen to impose a statutory duty, as opposed to a power, requiring the local authority to do certain things. In my judgment the courts should be slow to downgrade such duties into what are, in effect, mere discretions over which the court would have very little real control. If Parliament wishes to reduce public expenditure on meeting the needs of sick children then it is up to Parliament so to provide. It is not for the courts to adjust the order of priorities as between statutory duties and statutory discretions.

Failure to meet an assessed need

4.102   It follows that once a local authority has assessed an individual as having 'eligible needs' then any failure to provide services to meet those needs, will be open to legal challenge. In *R v Wigan MBC ex p Tammadge*,[113] for example, the applicant lived with her four children, three of whom had severe learning disabilities. Over a considerable period of time she sought a larger property in order to be able to better provide for their needs. In due course a complaints panel concluded that the family needed a larger property and asked the director of social services to investigate the possibility of one being found. Following the hearing a social worker visited the applicant on 22 October and made it clear that the social services department accepted the panel's recommendations. Subsequently on 15 November a multi-disciplinary meeting was convened where it was again agreed that a larger property was needed. The matter was then referred to a meeting of senior officers and councillors. This meeting decided however that 'it was not appropriate to commit the authority to the purchase or adaptation of a larger property'. In quashing that decision, Forbes J held that by the 22 September at the latest Wigan's 'own professionally qualified staff and advisors' had concluded that that her need for larger accommodation had been established.

4.103   Once the duty had arisen in this way, it was not lawful of Wigan to refuse to perform that duty because of shortage of or limits upon its financial resources.

Waiting lists and delayed service provision decision

4.104   Rather than refusing to provide a service to meet an eligible need, councils may merely delay their decision: for instance by simple prevarication or by adopting unnecessary processes (eg, continually referring the case back for further information or reports, etc) or by the use of a lengthy waiting list.

113 (1998) 1 CCLR 581.

4.105　　In *R v South Lanarkshire Council ex p MacGregor*,[114] the applicant was one of 199 people in the Council's area who (due to the local authority's limited resources) were on a waiting list for a place in a nursing home, of whom 106 were in hospitals. The court (the Outer House of the Court of Session) held that the policy was unlawful, and that:

> ... once a local authority determines that an individual's needs call for a particular provision the local authority is obliged to make that provision. In particular having decided that an individual requires the provision of a permanent place in a nursing home ... a local authority could not ... refuse to make such a provision simply because it did not have the necessary resources.

4.106　The local government ombudsman has made similar findings. For instance, the Ombudsman upheld in a 2001 complaint against Cambridgeshire that a resource led policy that delayed the provision of residential care (once the person had been assessed as needing it) was maladministration[115] and in a complaint against Essex[116] stated:

> The Council believes it does not have to provide a care service or funding for care immediately it has decided that it is necessary to provide the service to meet a person's assessed needs. It considers that it is acting correctly by having a waiting list on which the time a person may have to wait for resources to become available is indeterminate and depends to a significant extent on the needs and priority of other people on the waiting list and those who may come on to the list. That cannot, in my view, be correct.

Physical resource shortages

4.107　The courts have reacted differently where the shortage concerns physical or human resources as opposed to financial. In such cases the courts have generally been more sympathetic to the local authority position – provided it is taking reasonable steps to resolve the problem. Thus in *R v Lambeth LBC ex p A1 and A2*,[117] the Court of Appeal held that provided the authority was making a 'sincere and determined' effort to resolve the physical resource problem, then it would not intervene.

4.108　　However where an authority makes no such effort, the situation will be otherwise. In *R v Islington LBC ex p Rixon*,[118] for instance Sedley J considered that a local authority could not assess someone as needing a service (for instance a Day Centre placement) and then fail to provide it, merely because none was available. This reason, alone would be insufficient:

> There are two points at which, in my judgment, the respondent local authority has fallen below the requirements of the law. The first concerns the relationship of need to availability ... the local authority has, it

114　(2000) 4 CCLR 188.
115　Complaint against Cambridgeshire 99/B/04621, 29 January 2001.
116　Complaint against Essex 00/B/00599, 3 September 2001.
117　(1998) 1 CCLR 336 and see also *R v Islington BC ex p McMillan* (1997) 1 CCLR 7 at 17.
118　(1998) 1 CCLR 119 at 130F.

appears, simply taken the existing unavailability of further facilities as an insuperable obstacle to any further attempt to make provision . . .

4.109   It also follows that where the first choice service is not available, then in addition to demonstrating that it is taking purposeful steps to resolve the service supply problem, the local authority will be required to make alternative interim arrangements; as the FACS 2002 policy guidance[119] states:

> Councils should provide services promptly once they have agreed to do so, but where waiting is unavoidable they should ensure alternative services are in place to meet eligible needs.

Allocation and funding panels

4.110   Many local authorities use 'panels' of various types (sometimes termed 'allocation panels', 'funding panels' or 'purchasing panels') as a means of rationing services. In effect they constitute a non-statutory 'post-service provision decision' hurdle that applicants must traverse. The *R v Wigan MBC ex p Tammadge*,[120] (para 4.102 above) case is an example: objectively the authority had made a decision that the applicant's presenting needs called for the provision of services. However, the individual officers were unable to progress this, since the local authority's procedures stated that only a panel meeting was able to make a formal decision on resource allocation. This is not untypical of the procedures adopted by many local authorities. In response to judicial and ombudsmen doubts concerning the legality of these panels, some authorities have endeavoured to project these panels as 'quality control' mechanisms – namely to ensure that their social workers have completed the assessment correctly.[121] Not infrequently the panel will refer a funding application back for further analysis or paperwork to be completed. The effect of this is to create delay, which arguably is the whole point of the exercise: the protection of resources by (among other things) deferring service provision. Occasionally however – as in *R v South Lanarkshire Council ex p MacGregor*,[122] (above at para 4.105) – the panel is more blatant: in that case it openly restricted access to residential care solely on the basis of the authority's budget.

4.111   The local government ombudsman has considered a number of complaints concerning such panels. A 2001 complaint against Essex[123] concerned its 'purchasing panel'. A council social worker had assessed the complainant's mother as in need of residential care and prepared a care

---

119   Para 53; and UFSAMC 2002 policy guidance, para 5.35.

120   (1998) 1 CCLR 581.

121   Many of those authorities that suggest their panels are quality control mechanisms have difficulty in sustaining this argument, when their council's minutes are reviewed. Not unusually it can be shown that the panel was created as a response to a budgetary problem – rather than as a response to a concern about the quality their of social workers' assessments. Indeed if this were the problem one would assume that a logical response would be to improve their training.

122   (2001) 4 CCLR 188.

123   Complaint No 00/B/00599, 3 September 2001.

plan naming an appropriate care home. This came before the 'purchasing panel' which accepted the plan, but decided that the need was not of sufficient priority to justify immediate funding and so her name was placed on a waiting list. The local government ombudsman considered that this amounted to maladministration; that there was 'no justification for the council's use of a waiting list for funding care which was otherwise available and which only comes into operation *after* the council has decided that it will provide a service to meet particular needs'.

4.112   A 2003 complaint against East Sussex[124] concerned a young man with learning disabilities due to leave college. His parents wanted him to move to an independent residential provider for his post college needs (as many of his co-pupils were moving to this provider). The local authority assessed his needs and concluded (1) that this provider would meet his needs and (2) there was no suitable alternative local provision available. The provider however indicated that the council should make a speedy decision as other students were also seeking the place identified. The council's internal policies however required that the placement be approved by a series of funding panels which met throughout the year. The funding panel initially refused funding and placed the request on a 'service pending list'. As a consequence the placement ceased to be available and although the council made temporary arrangements, the young man's placement in the independent facility was delayed by two years. In finding maladministration (and recommending over £30,000 compensation) the ombudsman held:

> ... clearly the council's social services budget is under heavy pressure ... however, the Council knew of [the disabled person's] needs, has accepted its duty to fund the provision and was happy that the provision offered by [the independent provider] was suitable. Therefore it was unacceptable for it not to have made specific budgetary provision that would enable it to respond more quickly once a placement was offered.

4.113   There is, however, nothing objectionable about a panel, whose role is to determine the reasonableness of a care package (for instance one with the expertise to review complex care packages). Thus in *R (Rodriguez-Bannister) v Somerset NHS Trust*,[125] the court found not unreasonable the role of a panel whose primary task was to determine the kind of accommodation that was required, 'whether residential, supported living or other' and not to make recommendations about the necessary levels of support in any particular setting. Where there is conflict about the true purpose of a panel, it can be instructive to examine the minutes of the relevant local authority committee: not infrequently it will reveal that the panel was created as a response to a budgetary crisis rather than concerns about the quality control arrangements for care packages.

124 Complaint No 00/B/18600, 29 January 2003.
125 [2003] EWHC 2184 (Admin).

Resources cannot be the sole criterion

4.114   Although councils are entitled to take into account the extent of their available resources when they frame their eligibility criteria, they cannot make resource availability the sole criterion: resource availability alone cannot be 'determinative'.

4.115   In the *Gloucestershire* decision Hirst LJ (in the Court of Appeal) held that resources were 'no more than one factor in an overall assessment, where no doubt the objective needs of the individual disabled person will always be the paramount consideration'.[126] In the first instance decision McCowan LJ – when quashing the decision of the county council (to withdraw services without reassessment) – stated that this 'amounted to treating the cut in resources as the sole factor to be taken into account, and that was, in my judgment, unlawful'.[127]

The Human Rights Act 1998 obligation[128]

4.116   There is a point at which resource availability ceases to be a legitimate reason for refusing to provide services: or put another way, there is a level of austerity beyond which eligibility criteria cannot venture. This aspect of the argument was articulated by McCowan LJ in the first instance *Gloucestershire* judgment,[129] when he observed:

> I should stress, however, that there will, in my judgment, be situations where a reasonable authority could only conclude that some arrangements were necessary to meet the needs of a particular disabled person and in which they could not reasonably conclude that a lack of resources provided an answer. Certain persons would be at severe physical risk if they were unable to have some practical assistance in their homes. In those situations, I cannot conceive that an authority would be held to have acted reasonably if they used shortage of resources as a reason for not being satisfied that some arrangement should be made to meet those persons' needs.

4.117   The *Gloucestershire* proceedings took place prior to the enactment of the Human Rights Act (HRA) 1998; using the language of the European Convention on Human Rights (the 'Convention') McCowan LJ was, in effect, stating that limited resources could not be used as a reason for allowing a violation of article 3 to take place. There can be little doubt that domestic law recognises a core set of 'positive' justiciable, non-resource dependent rights – the uncertainty relates to their scope. As Lord Hoffman has commented:[130]

126 (1997) 1 CCLR 19 at 31G.
127 *R v Gloucestershire CC ex p Mahfood* (1997) 1 CCLR 7 at 16I; 94 LGR 593, DC.
128 For a brief review of the relevant provisions of the European Convention on Human Rights see para 19.172.
129 *R v Gloucestershire CC ex p Mahfood* (1997) 1 CCLR 7; 94 LGR 593, DC.
130 L Hoffman, (2001) *The 'Separation of Powers'*; Annual Commercial Bar Lecture; unpublished transcript. London: COMBAR.

Human rights probably include not only freedom from certain forms of state interference but also a positive obligation upon the state to provide every citizen with certain basic necessities which he requires in order to be able to function as a human being.

4.118 Arguably, therefore, there is a point at which simple decisions about the provision of community care services, cross over from the realm of socio-economic rights and into the domain of those civil and political rights protected by the Convention. Although this may be an overly simplistic reading of these two categories of rights, it nevertheless serves as a useful device for considering the 'austerity' limits of eligibility criteria.

4.119 In relation to social care services, it is perhaps self evident that services could not be denied (on resource grounds) if the consequence were that the disabled person's life was at risk, or that significant health problems would develop or that there was a risk of serious abuse or neglect occurring. In effect, therefore, the core set of social care rights are at least those detailed in the 'critical' category of the prescribed eligibility framework (see para 4.79 above): these being risks associated with articles 2 and 3 of the Convention.

4.120 The same could be argued in relation to article 5. *R v Manchester CC ex p Stennett*,[131] for instance, concerned the right of detained patients to 'free' aftercare services under Mental Health Act 1983 s117. The court accepted that in many cases patients were only discharged from their detention in psychiatric wards if they 'agreed' to move into a specialist care home. It was argued, therefore that to require payment for this service would, in effect be requiring a patient to pay for his or her freedom. Lord Steyn found such a proposition compelling, stating:

> It can hardly be said that the mentally ill patient freely chooses such accommodation. Charging them in these circumstances may be surprising ... If the argument of the authorities is accepted that there is a power to charge these patients such a view of the law would not be testimony to our society attaching a high value to the need to care after the exceptionally vulnerable.

4.121 The European Court of Human Rights' wariness of allowing resource arguments to excuse states from their core 'administration of justice obligations' under articles 5 and 6[132] has been adopted by our domestic courts;[133] Lord Bingham for instance commenting:[134]

> It is plain that contracting states cannot blame unacceptable delays on a general want of prosecutors or judges or courthouses or on chronic underfunding of the legal system.

4.122 It follows that a resource argument alone will seldom dispose of a claim to

---

131 [2002] UKHL 34; (2002) 5 CCLR 500; [2002] 3 WLR 584; [2002] 4 All ER 124.
132 See for instance *Zimmermann and Steiner v Switzerland* (1983) 6 EHRR 17; and *Koendjbiharie v Netherlands* (1990) 13 EHRR 820.
133 See for instance *R (KB and others) v Mental Health Review Tribunal and the Secretary of State for Health* [2002] EWHC 639 (Admin); (2002) 5 CCLR 458; [2002] ACD 85.
134 *Dyer v Watson* [2002] SLT 229 the Privy Council at 242.

respect for a Convention right. In relation to the absolute Convention articles, financial resource arguments will rarely if ever be relevant. In relation to the positive obligations under these articles (for instance a duty to provide health care or social care) the state can play the resource card, but it cannot assume it will trump all others – particularly where the consequences of inaction for the applicant are dire.

4.123   In relation to the qualified rights, it is likely the extent of available resources will be a relevant factor in determining whether a negative obligation has been respected, although courts will require evidence that the impugned act is 'proportionate' and that the resource difficulties are 'made out by evidence, and cannot assumed to be present'.[135] The level of scrutiny will inevitably be less for those positive obligations under the qualified articles, but again, where the consequences of a failure to act are likely to be severe, then any assertion of poverty by the state will again call for heightened scrutiny by the court.

Timescale for assessments

4.124   There is no general statutory timescale for the completion of community care assessments – although such timescales have been prescribed in policy guidance for assessments under the Children Act 1989 (see para 18.12) and in directions under the Community Care (Delayed Discharge, etc) Act 2003 (see para 10.172). It is intended however that by December 2004, all assessments of older people under the Single Assessment Process should begin within 48 hours and be completed within a month.[136]

4.125   As a matter of statutory interpretation, where a provision is silent on the time for compliance, the law implies that it be done within a reasonable time, and that what is a 'reasonable time' is a question of fact, depending on the nature of the obligation and the purpose for which the computation is to be made.[137]

4.126   The FACS guidance[138] requires that local 'Better Care, Higher Standards' charters (see para 3.9) contain information about the authority's timescales for assessments and that individuals will be told how long they have to wait for assessment, and how long the assessment process will take. When considering complaints about delayed assessments the local government ombudsman has regard to the timescales set out in the relevant local authorities charter[139] – and this would appear to be an appropriate starting point for any such review.

135 *R v Southwark LBC ex p Khana and Karim* (2001) 4 CCLR 267 at 282I, per Mance LJ.
136 FACS 2003 practice guidance at para 8.7.
137 See for instance *Re North ex p Hasluck* [1895] 2 QB 264; *Charnock v Liverpool Corporation* [1968] 3 All ER 473.
138 FACS 2002 policy guidance at para 29 and FACS 2003 practice guidance at para 8.7.
139 See for instance complaint 01/C/15434 against South Tyneside Metropolitan Borough Council, 20 January 2003, where the Charter stipulated 21 days for the completion of community care assessments.

4.127   A further and significant factor concerning the speed with which assessments are undertaken stems from the pressure on English local authorities to meet a variety of Department of Health imposed 'Social Services Performance Assessment Framework Indicators'. For instance 'Indicator D43' measures delay by requiring authorities to record: 'For new adult and older clients, the percentage where the time from first contact to first service is more than six weeks'.[140]

4.128   Authorities frequently adopt a grading scheme for assessments – with a view to prioritising the most urgent. The arrangements for these schemes being detailed in the authority's 'Better Care, Higher Standards' charter. While the idea of a scheme setting priorities for assessment is to a degree anomalous (given that in general the object of assessment is to identify the extent and urgency of need) the local government ombudsman has accepted that such a system 'does not seem unreasonable'.[141] LAC(93)2 (although primarily aimed at the particular needs of persons who misuse alcohol and/or drugs) makes a number of observations of more general application to assessments[142] and supports the idea of some assessments being carried out faster than others, stating that authorities 'should have criteria for determining the level of assessment that is appropriate to the severity or complexity of the need' (at para 14). It further advocates that the need for authorities to develop 'fast-track assessment' procedures (at paras 16–20). The circular is considered in detail in chapter 16.

4.129   The local government ombudsman has investigated a considerable number of complaints concerning delayed assessments relating to home adaptations (see para 8.87). By way of example, in a 1996 report[143] a delay of six months in assessing a disabled person's needs was held to be maladministration and another 1996 report found seven months for an assessment and a further four months' delay by the authority in processing the disabled facilities grant approval to be maladministration.[144] In this complaint the local ombudsman reiterated her view that if the authority has a shortage of occupational therapists, then it should not use them for assessment purposes if this will result in unreasonable delay, stating: 'If such expertise is not available, councils need to find an alternative way of meeting their statutory responsibilities'. While the local ombudsman has approved in principle the idea of prioritising certain assessments, she has

140 Note 28, at p15 above, provides details of how the Performance Assessment Framework Indicators can be accessed at www.doh.gov.uk/paf/ and for a critique of the pressure these targets creates within social services authorities, see J Harris, *The Social Work Business*, Routledge, 2003.

141 Paragraph 33 of complaint 00/B/00599 against Essex County Council, 3 September 2001.

142 See, for instance, para 27 concerning the applicability of its observations to the needs of homeless people, quoted at para 16.9 below.

143 Complaints against South Bedfordshire District Council and Bedfordshire County Council Nos 93/B/3111 and 94/B/3146.

144 Complaints against Middlesbrough District Council and Cleveland County Council Nos 94/C/0964 and 94/C/0965.

criticised the way such a scheme is administered. In a 1995 complaint[145] she stated:

> The council's system of priorities is over-simple. Within the category of 'complex' cases there is no provision for relatively simple solutions to tide people over until a full assessment can be made. Also, there will be cases which cannot be described as 'emergencies' but need to be dealt with more urgently within the 'complex' category than others. The council's over-simple system of priorities resulted in a failure to meet [the complainants' disabled daughter's] needs promptly and I consider that to be an injustice resulting in maladministration.

4.130   Where there is unreasonable delay in assessing (or an intimation that there will be), the potential service user should consider making a complaint about the delay. The effect of this, if it is coupled with a request that the complaint enter at stage two of the complaints process,[146] is that the 28-day timescale is triggered and, hopefully, this should ensure a rapid acceleration in the assessment process. The complainant should emphasise (if it be the case) that the duty to assess commenced when his or her potential needs first came to the notice of the authority rather than at the time of any later request he or she may have made to be assessed.

Delegation of duty to assess

4.131   The duty to assess under National Health Service and Community Care Act (NHSCCA) 1990 s47 is a social services function (for the purposes of Local Authority Social Services Act (LASSA) 1970 Sch 1, see para 1.14). There is no general power for social services authorities to delegate this function to other bodies.[147] The only situation in which it can be legally delegated, is where the social services authority has entered into a formal partnership arrangement with an NHS body (either a primary care trust (PCT) or an NHS trust pursuant to the Health Act 2001 s31 and the regulations made there under[148] (see para 10.196).

4.132   In the absence of such partnership arrangements, there is no express power for the authority to delegate the function to another agency. In practice authorities often request third parties to carry out key tasks in the assessment, for instance, an occupational therapist employed by a PCT in assessing the need for home adaptations. In such cases, an authority may be, to all intents and purposes, bound by that third party's view on need – especially if it has expertise which the social services authority lacks. Another common situation where key assessment functions are in effect

---

145   Complaint against Rochdale Metropolitan Borough Council No 93/C/3660.
146   See para 19.19.
147   *R v Kirklees MBC ex p Daykin* (1998) 1 CCLR 512 at 525D.
148   NHS Bodies and Local Authorities Partnership Arrangements Regulations 2000 SI No 617 and National Health Service Bodies and Local Authorities Partnership Arrangements (Wales) Regulations 2000 SI No 2993 (W 193): see generally the SAP 2002 policy guidance p16 and UFSAMC 2002 policy guidance, p10, note 2.

delegated, concerns the assessment of detained drug and alcohol misusers wishing to attend community rehabilitation facilities: frequently key aspects of such assessments are carried out by expert probation officers on behalf of social services (see para 16.9 where this is further considered).

Assessment under NHSCCA 1990 s47(2)

4.133 NHSCCA 1990 s47(2) states:

> If at any time during the assessment of the needs of any person under subsection (1)(a) above it appears to a local authority that he is a disabled person, the authority –
> (a) shall proceed to make such a decision as to the services he requires as is mentioned in section 4 of the Disabled Persons (Services, Consultation and Representation) Act 1986 without his requesting them to do so under that section; and
> (b) shall inform him that they will be doing so and of his rights under that Act.

4.134 As noted above (see para 4.56) Carnwath J in *R v Gloucestershire CC ex p RADAR*,[149] found that the Department of Health had misunderstood the effect of NHSCCA 1990 s47(2) when issuing its 1991 practice guidance. The guidance mistakenly advised that the subsection entitled all disabled people to a 'comprehensive assessment' regardless of the complexity of their needs.

4.135 In the House of Lords *ex p Barry* decision Lord Clyde took the view that section 47(2) was a modest provision aimed at flagging up the duty to provide services under LASSA 1970 s2:

> So far as the twofold provision in section 47(1) and (2) is concerned the obligation on the local authority introduced by section 47(1) was to carry out an assessment on its own initiative and the separate provision made in subsection (2) cannot have been intended merely to achieve that purpose. It seems to me that there is sufficient reason for the making of a distinctive provision in subsection (2) in the desire to recognise the distinctive procedural situation relative to the disabled. But it does not follow that any distinction exists in the considerations which may or may not be taken into account in making an assessment in the case of the disabled as compared with any other case.[150]

The written record of the assessment

4.136 There is no statutory requirement that assessments be recorded in writing, although in practice all social services authorities have pro forma assessment documentation – which although frequently completed in manuscript is generally then keyed into the authorities IT system. The FACS

149 (1998) 1 CCLR 476 at 484.
150 (1997) 1 CCLR 40 at 56C.

2002 policy guidance is silent on the right of service user's to a copy of their assessment documentation, although it states that service users should receive a copy of their care plan.[151] The 1991 practice guidance however states (at para 3.54) that a 'copy of the assessment of needs should normally be shared with the potential service user, any representative of that user and all other people who have agreed to provide a service. Except where no intervention is deemed necessary, this record will normally be combined with a written care plan'.[152]

4.137   Where a service user has difficulty obtaining a copy of their assessment and/or care plan, a formal request can be made under the Data Protection Act 1998 (see para 3.38), although in practice it will generally be more effective to make the failure the subject of a formal complaint.[153]

Disputed service provision decisions

4.138   The 1990 community care reforms made social services the 'gate keepers' of the community care regime: ultimately it is the local authority that decides what a person's 'eligible needs' are and what they are not. Judges are not expert in the practice of social work and so must defer to their professional expertise – even when the decisions they reach appear harsh.

4.139   As has been noted above, (see para 4.6) social workers are subjected to intense internal administrative scrutiny – primarily to ensure that their decisions do not place undue pressure on local authority budgets – notwithstanding the rhetoric that 'counsels against trimming the assessment of need to fit available provision'.[154] On one level this is entirely reasonable, and on another it can lead to assessments being 'service' or 'budget' driven – in effect social workers being so constrained by organisational pressures that they do not assess individuals as needing services which are not available or which might exceed the available budget.

4.140   Given that judicial review is a blunt legal instrument and that courts are seldom prepared to consider a service provision decision '*Wednesbury*' unreasonable[155] (see para 19.139 below) the question arises, as to how errant authorities can be called to account – particularly if their complaints panels are insufficiently robust or well informed to address such problems.

4.141   The evidence suggests that the courts and ombudsmen adopt a variety of public law mechanisms to find fault with the decision-making process when they encounter an improbably austere service provision decision. In general, the harsher the apparent service provision decision, the greater

---

151 Para 49 and UFSAMC 2002 policy guidance, para 2.49.

152 See also para 7.78 which concerns the obligation to ensure the care plan is copied to the care home.

153 Local authorities are audited on the percentage of people receiving copies of their care plans – see Performance indicator D39 (see note 28, at p15 above).

154 *R v Islington LBC ex p Rixon* (1998) 1 CCLR 119 at 129B, per Sedley J.

155 *Associated Provincial Picture Houses v Wednesbury Corporation* [1948] 1 KB 223, CA. Although not invariably – see for instance *R v Sutton LBC ex p Tucker* (1998) 1 CCLR 251 at 275J.

the courts/ombudsmen's insistence on 'due process' – particularly on compliance with policy and practice guidance. For example, *R v Birmingham CC ex p Killigrew*,[156] concerned an applicant with severe disabilities and whose condition (multiple sclerosis) was deteriorating. Her husband and main carer was also a disabled person. At the end of 1997 she was assessed as requiring 12 hours continuous care each day seven days a week. The council undertook a manual handling assessment in 1998 and decided that Mrs Killigrew required two care assistants to move her, rather than the one that had previously done this. A community care reassessment then occurred, as a result of which the council proposed to reduce the day care from 12 to 3.5 hours. Hooper J held that no such reduction could occur without compliance with the 1990 policy guidance which in his view required: (1) detailed reasons as to why 12 hours were no longer required; and (2) up to date medical evidence – which the local authority had failed to obtain (1990 policy guidance paras 3.47–3.48).

4.142   Although the decision in *R v Ealing LBC ex p C*[157] involved an assessment under the Children Act 1989 (see chapter 18) the principles in issue are identical. The case concerned a profoundly disabled 9-year-old boy who lived with his mother and 15-year-old brother in a two-bedroomed council flat. An assessment in 1998 stated that 'the family would benefit from provision for aids and adaptations. Transfer to a larger property'. The council however asserted that the property was suitable provided that sufficient adaptations/aids were made available.

4.143   The High Court (Scott Baker J) considered the decision harsh as it meant that the mother was sharing a bed with the child who was incontinent and whose sleep was very disturbed; nevertheless applying the classic *Wednesbury* formulation he did not feel that the decision was one which 'no reasonable authority' could have reached. The Court of Appeal overruled this, stating that the appropriate test was 'did the local authority ask itself the right question, and take reasonable steps to acquaint itself with the relevant information to enable it to answer it correctly?' In essence the Court of Appeal found 'due process' reasons to quash what it considered an excessively harsh decision.

4.144   The local government ombudsman has adopted a similar approach to what appear to be 'resource led' reassessments. In a 2001 complaint[158] he held that although the final decision on what was the appropriate care plan, lay with social services, any proposed reductions should be communicated to other professionals that were involved (ie, physiotherapists, voluntary organisations that provided volunteers, occupational therapists, district nurses, etc) and their views on its suitability obtained, before deciding on its adoption.

---

156 (2000) 3 CCLR 109: see also, for example, *R v Lambeth LBC ex p K* (2000) 3 CCLR149 where the court quashed a budget-driven harsh service provision decision on the basis that the council had not followed the 1990 policy guidance and had confused 'needs' and 'services'.

157 (2000) 3 CCLR 122.

158 Complaint against Southwark No 99/A/00988, 12 March 2001.

The provision of services and the care plan

Introduction

5.1   Once an authority has made a decision under National Health Service and
        Community Care Act (NHSCCA) 1990 s47(1)(b) that a person's presenting
        needs are such that community care services are called for, then the
        authority must make arrangements for those services to be provided.[1] This
        process is generally referred to as 'care planning'. Good practice requires
        that the authority specify in a written care plan what services the individual
        is entitled to receive and all other salient information connected with the
        delivery of those services.

Care plans

5.2   In *R v Islington LBC ex p Rixon*,[2] Sedley J accepted the respondent's sub-
        mission that 'nowhere in the legislation is a care plan, by that or any other
        name required' and that 'a care plan is nothing more than a clerical record
        of what has been decided and what is planned'. In his view, however, this
        state of affairs:

>   . . . far from marginalising the care plan, places it at the centre of any
>   scrutiny of the local authority's due discharge of its functions. As
>   paragraph 3.24 of the [1990] policy guidance indicates, a care plan is the
>   means by which the local authority assembles the relevant information
>   and applies it to the statutory ends, and hence affords good evidence to any
>   inquirer of the due discharge of its statutory duties. It cannot, however, be
>   quashed as if it were a self-implementing document.

5.3   On this basis, Sedley J scrutinised the care plan, in order to ascertain the
        adequacy of the assessment process, observing:

>   The care plan . . . does not comply either with the [1990] policy guidance or
>   the [1991] practice guidance issued by central government. There has been
>   a failure to comply with the guidance contained in paragraph 3.24 of the
>   [1990] policy document to the effect that following assessment of need,
>   the objectives of social services intervention as well as the services to
>   be provided or arranged should be agreed in the form of a care plan . . .
>   The care plan also fails at a number of points to comply with the
>   [1991] practice guidance on, for example, the contents of a care plan,
>   the specification of its objectives, the achievement of agreement on
>   implementation on all those involved, leeway for contingencies and the
>   identification and feeding back of assessed but still unmet need.
>   In such a situation I am unable to [agree] that the failures to follow the
>   policy guidance and practice guidance are beyond the purview of the court.

5.4   In *R v Sutton LBC ex p Tucker*,[3] Hidden J held that a document put forward
        by the respondent as a care plan, was not, since (among other things):

---

1   In cases of emergency the services can be provided before the assessment: NHSCCA
    1990 s47(5).
2   (1998) 1 CCLR 119 at 128.
3   (1998) 1 CCLR 251.

There are no stated overall objectives in terms of long-term obligations, carers' obligations or service providers, there are no criteria for the measurement of objectives because the objectives themselves are not recorded in any care plan. There are no costings, no long-term options, no residential care options considered, there are no recorded points of difference, there is no reference to unmet need and there is no reference to a next date of review.

5.5 The importance that the courts attach to policy and practice guidance in this area is illustrated by the relief ordered in the *Tucker* case, which included:

> ... [firstly] an order of mandamus to provide within 21 days a care plan which complies, as far as possible, with the [1991] practitioner's guide and with paragraph 3.25 of the [1990] policy guidance. Secondly, a declaration that the respondent has acted unlawfully and in breach of paragraphs 3.24 and 3.41[4] of the policy guidance in failing to make a service provision decision under section 47(1)(b) of the National Health Service and Community Care Act 1990, as to the long-term placement of the applicant. Thirdly, a declaration that the respondent has acted unlawfully and contrary to paragraph 3.25 of the policy guidance in failing to produce a lawful care plan.

5.6 Given the importance attached to the 1990 policy guidance by Sedley J and Hidden J in the *Rixon* and *Tucker* cases, it is appropriate to quote this portion of the 1990 policy guidance in full:

> **CARE PLANS**
> 3.24 Once needs have been assessed, the services to be provided or arranged and the objectives of any intervention should be agreed in the form of a care plan. The objective of ensuring that service provision should, as far as possible, preserve or restore normal living implies the following order of preference in constructing care packages which may include health provision, both primary and specialist, housing provision and social services provision:
> * support for the user in his or her own home including day and domiciliary care, respite care, the provision of disability equipment and adaptations to accommodation as necessary;
> * a move to more suitable accommodation, which might be sheltered or very sheltered housing, together with the provision of social services support;
> * a move to another private household, ie, to live with relatives or friends or as part of an adult fostering scheme;
> * residential care;
> * nursing home care;
> * long-stay care in hospital.
>
> 3.25 The aim should be to secure the most cost-effective package of services that meets the user's care needs, taking account of the user's and carers' own preferences. Where supporting the user in a home of their own would provide a better quality of life, this is to be preferred to

4 Which provides (among other things) that 'it is most undesirable that anyone should be admitted to, or remain in, hospital when their care could be more appropriately provided elsewhere'.

admission to residential or nursing home care. However, local authorities also have a responsibility to meet needs within the resources available and this will sometimes involve difficult decisions where it will be necessary to strike a balance between meeting the needs identified within available resources and meeting the care preferences of the individual. Where agreement between all the parties is not possible, the points of difference should be recorded. Failure to satisfy particular needs can result in even greater burdens on particular services, for example where a person becomes homeless as a result of leaving inappropriate accommodation which has been provided following discharge from hospital.

3.26 Decisions on service provision should include clear agreement about what is going to be done, by whom and by when, with clearly identified points of access to each of the relevant agencies for the service user, carers and for the care manager. No agency's resources should be committed without its prior agreement. However, where the agencies have agreed as a result of the assessment and care planning process to provide a service, they will be expected to deliver it. With the service user's permission, the assessment information should be passed on to those responsible for care delivery. This applies particularly to any risks that may be associated with the care of the user.

5.7   Paragraph 4.37 of the 1991 practice guidance provides greater detail as to the required contents of the care plan:[5]

Care plans should be set out in concise written form, linked with the assessment of need. The document should be accessible to the user, for example, in Braille, or translated into the user's own language. A copy should be given to the user but it should also, subject to constraints of confidentiality, be shared with other contributors to the plan. The compilation and distribution of such records has implications for the necessary levels of administrative support.

A care plan should contain:
- the overall objectives;
- the specific objectives:
  – users;
  – carers;
  – service providers;
- the criteria for measuring the achievement of these objectives;
- the services to be provided by which personnel/agency;
- the cost to the user and the contributing agencies;
- the other options considered;
- any point of difference between the user, carer, care planning practitioner or other agency;
- any unmet needs with reasons – to be separately notified to the service planning system;
- the named person(s) responsible for implementing , monitoring and reviewing the care plan;
- the first date of the first planned review.

5   Care Management and Assessment – A Practitioners' Guide, para 4.37, (HMSO 1991).

5.8   By comparison the Fair Access to Care Services (FACS) 2002 policy guidance (at para 47) restricts itself to advising on the six key requirements of a care plan, namely:

> The written record of the care plan should include as a minimum:
> - A note of the eligible needs and associated risks.
> - The preferred outcomes of service provision.
> - Contingency plans to manage emergency changes.
> - Details of services to be provided, and any charges the individual is assessed to pay, or if direct payments have been agreed.
> - Contributions which carers and others are willing and able to make.
> - A review date.

Care plans and the single assessment process guidance

5.9   Although the single assessment process (SAP) guidance[6] sets out a more prescriptive care planning regime for older people, it provides a useful checklist for the categories of information that such plans should generally contain:

> Care planning should lead to an appropriate single care plan. Care plans should include:
> - A summary of identified/eligible needs indicating the intensity, instability, predictability, and complexity of needs, the associated risks to independence, and the potential for rehabilitation.
> - A note on whether or not the service user has agreed the care plan, and a reason where this was not possible.
> - A note on whether or not the user has consented for care plan information to be shared among relevant agencies, and a reason where this was not possible.
> - The objectives of providing help and anticipated outcomes for users.
> - A summary of how services will impact on identified/eligible need and associated risks.
> - The part the user will play in addressing needs, including the strengths and abilities he or she will bring to this.
> - Details on managing risk as appropriate. Where it has been agreed that users will accept a certain degree of risk, this must be written in the care plan.
> - Details of what carers are willing to do, and related needs and support.
> - A description of the level and frequency of the help that is to be provided, stating which agency is responsible for what service.
> - Details of any contributions to care costs that users are asked to make.
> - A nursing plan (integrated not attached) where appropriate.

6   HSC 2002/001 and LAC(2002)1 'Guidance on the Single Assessment Process for Older People', January 2002, Annex E p24–25 (accessible at www.dh.gov.uk/ PolicyAndGuidance/HealthAndSocialCareTopics/SocialCare/ SingleAssessmentProcess/fs/en); in Wales broadly similar wording is adopted – the Unified and Fair System for Assessing and Managing Care (in Wales) (UFSAMC) 2002 policy guidance para 2.44.

- The level of Registered Nurse Care Contribution for admissions to care homes which provide nursing care.
- The name of the person co-ordinating the care plan and their contact number.
- A contact number or office in case of emergencies, and a contingency plan if things go wrong.
- Monitoring arrangements and a date for review.

Care plans should be recorded for all older people who receive services. The detail of the care plan should be in proportion to the assessed/eligible needs and service provision. For people who receive one-off support or treatment of a very basic nature, a simple statement of service delivery and purpose is all that is needed. Service users should be given their own copy of the care plan or statement of service delivery, in the most appropriate format.

It is at the care planning stage that consideration should be given as to whether direct payments are appropriate or not.

Some health professionals may currently use the term 'service plan' instead of 'care plan'. It would be helpful for agencies and professionals to agree to use the definitions of this guidance.

Confusing 'needs' and 'services'

5.10   The 1991 practice guidance mirrors the statutory requirements of NHSCCA 1990 s47(1) by emphasising the importance of treating the assessment of need as a separate exercise from consideration of service response, stating (at para 3.1):

It is easy to slip out of thinking 'what does this person need?' into 'what have we got that he/she could have?' The focus on need is most clearly achieved where practitioners responsible for assessment do not also carry responsibility for the delivery or management of services arising from that assessment (at para 22 of the guide's summary).[7]

5.11   Commonly there will be several possible services that may address an eligible need. For example, an assessment might reveal that a person, who lives alone needs to be helped with many activities, such as dressing, bathing, feeding and that there is a general need for someone to keep a watchful eye on him to ensure there are no falls or other neglectful acts. These are all likely to be 'eligible needs' since a failure to address them could have critical or at least serious consequences. The services that could meet these needs are many: home help, day centre, meals on wheels, a residential home, and so on. The care plan determines which services most appropriately meet the eligible needs. Thus, in care planning terminology, no one has a 'need' for a place in a day centre: what they might have is a

---

7   In *R v Islington LBC ex p Rixon* (1998) 1CCLR 119 at 129B Sedley J put it thus: 'The practice guidance . . . counsels against trimming the assessment of need to fit the available provision'.

Diagram 4: Common service provision problems

Is the need particularly compelling in the sense that significant harm to the disabled person or a carer would result if services are not provided (see para 4.79)?

→ YES → The service should be provided; a failure to provide would be *Wednesbury* unreasonable and/or a breach of Human Rights Act 1998 (see paras 4.140 and 4.119).

↓ NO →

Is the service already being provided (or only recently terminated)? → YES →

Service cannot be withdrawn unless there has been a reassessment and either:
1) the service is now no longer needed, or
2) the council has new criteria and the user no longer meets these criteria, and in either case (see para 4.95)
3) rational reasons are given for why the service is no longer needed (see paras 4.141 and 4.144).

Once a need has been identified it must be met; the resource difficulties of a council are not a relevant factor (see para 4.105).

↓ NO

Is the failure to provide the service due to the council's financial problems (or resulting from an 'allocation panel refusal') (see paras 4.104 and 4.110)?

YES ← / → NO

The council must identify and fund an alternative service (or make direct payments): the duty to provide arises out of an assessed need, not the availability of an existing service (see para 5.32).

← YES ← Is the failure to provide the service due to a 'service failure': eg, a service provider has stopped providing the service?

↓ NO

YES ← Is the failure due to a dispute with another agency as to responsibility (ie, the NHS or education department)? ← NO

Formal complaint should be made against each agency (see paras 19.63 and 19.67). In general, social services should arrange provision and then resolve liability directly with the other agency (see para 10.37).

→ NO → If appropriate, request a full reassessment and the provision of adequate reasons for the failure to provide services (see para 5.29).

need to be kept occupied or in a safe environment during the day. One of the services that could meet this need is a place in a day centre – but obviously it is not the only one (for instance the service user might prefer to have a sitting service or to have direct payments instead).

5.12   In *R v Kirklees MBC ex p Daykin*,[8] Collins J observed that it was 'not always easy to differentiate between what is a need and what is merely the means by which such need can be met'. The case concerned a disabled person who had been assessed as being unable to manage the stairs to his council flat. Collins J considered the 'need' in this case was to be able to get into and out of his dwelling. In his opinion 'the means by which this need could be met included, among other things, the provision of a stair-lift or re-housing'.

Choosing between alternative care packages

5.13   The assessment process may identify needs which are capable of being met by two or more alternative care packages. If the choice concerns a care home placement, then the choice of accommodation provisions may apply (see para 7.84). Where the authority can meet the assessed need by two or more different care packages, it is not unreasonable for the authority to consider the relative cost of each option. As the above quoted 1991 policy guidance (at para 3.25) states that the local authority should seek to 'secure the most cost-effective package of services that meets the user's care needs, taking account of the user's and carers' own preferences'.

5.14   Although the question has not as yet been litigated, it is by no means obvious how one can compare the relative cost of two alternative services: a problem expressed by the Audit Commission thus:

> The financial incentive for authorities to use residential care remains strong. In nearly all situations it is substantially cheaper for local authorities to place people in residential care, even where there is no difference between the gross cost of residential care and care at home.[9]

5.15   In constructing a care plan, the issue of resources (the 'cheaper option') only arises if there is objectively real and present choice of care packages available. *R v Avon CC ex p M*,[10] for example, concerned a disputed care plan. The parties agreed that the best interests of the applicant were served by his going to a residential care home. However because of M's learning disabilities he had formed a fixed psychological attachment to a particular home which was more expensive than the alternative proposed by the local authority. A complaints panel heard the uncontroverted evidence

---

8 (1998) 1 CCLR 512. See also, for example, *R v Lambeth LBC ex p K* (2000) 3 CCLR 141 where the court quashed a service provision decision on the basis that the council had not followed the 1990 policy guidance and the care plan had confused 'needs' and 'services'.

9 Balancing the Care Equation (HMSO, 1996) at para 40.

10 (1999) 2 CCLR 185; [1994] 2 FLR 1006.

concerning his psychological needs and unanimously recommended the placement in the more expensive home. The local authority refused. Henry J, in finding for the applicant, stated as follows:

> Here, there was a clear finding by a body set up for detailed fact finding that M's needs included his psychological needs and, unless that finding could be disposed of, the authority was liable to meet those needs. Without that finding being overthrown, there were not two options before the social services committee, as the paper suggests, there was only one: to meet M's needs, including his psychological needs.

5.16   *R v Sutton LBC ex p Tucker*,[11] like the *ex p M* case, concerned the care needs of a person with learning disabilities – in this case a Rubella impaired applicant. She had been in short-term NHS accommodation for over two years awaiting a decision from the authority concerning her long-term placement. All agreed that this would need to be in a small residential unit shared with one or two other residents with similar impairments. The local authority favoured a home in Birmingham run by the specialist charity SENSE, but the applicant's family, clinicians and indeed the SENSE staff considered that this would not be viable since she needed to be close to her family in Richmond. No such facility existed in Richmond and the local authority balked at the cost of commissioning a purpose created unit solely for the applicant; the net result being that nothing concrete happened and she remained inappropriately placed in short-term NHS accommodation.

5.17   In the judicial review proceedings, the local authority sought to explain their inaction, by reference to the family's unreasonable refusal of a care option – namely the placement in Birmingham. Hidden J disagreed. This was not a situation where there was a choice of care plans; indeed this was a case where there was no care plan at all. In his view, the local authority preference for the Birmingham placement was untenable. The only option therefore was a local placement. Since there was no 'choice of care plan' the issue of resources was not relevant and the local authority had to prepare a plan to this effect. He ordered that this be done within 21 days (ie, within 21 days the local authority was to produce a care plan which spelt out how within a reasonable period of time it would provide a local placement for the applicant).

5.18   Where, however, a real choice of potential care packages does exist, the key issue is how the balance is to be struck between 'cost effectiveness' and 'user preferences'. What happens, for instance, if an assessment discloses that a disabled person has substantial eligible needs and the local authority determine that the cost of a package of care in a residential home would be cheaper than a package of domiciliary care? Since this is a fairly frequent situation, is it reasonable for the local authority to have cost ceilings: for instance, that home care packages cannot exceed 20 hours home help per week?

11 (1998) 1 CCLR 251.

5.19   In *R v Lancashire CC ex p Ingham*,[12] Hidden J held:

> In taking the decision the respondent was deciding that under section 47(1)(b) of the 1990 Act the provision of residential care within section 21 to section 27 of the 1948 Act, rather than 24-hour care in the home, was called for and that under section 2 of the 1970 Act it was not necessary to meet the applicant's needs by [practical assistance in the form of 24-hour care service being provided], as her needs were best met by the provision of residential care under the 1948 Act.
>
> In so far as the council had regard to the fact that the residential placement was a more cost-effective means of meeting needs than 24-hour care in the home, it was entitled to do so. It was always aware that identified needs must be met, but that cost-effective use of resources might be relevant to the type of service provision.[13]

5.20   The judgment was upheld by the Court of Appeal,[14] where Swinton Thomas LJ held:

> It is true that resources played a part in the decision that was made as to placement, but I am not persuaded that the Lancashire County Council behaved in any way improperly or unlawfully in carrying out the duties laid on them by section 2 of the 1970 Act.

5.21   In *R v Southwark LBC ex p Khana and Karim*,[15] the applicants, an elderly couple, sought judicial review of the council's decision to meet their care needs by provision of a placement in a residential care home. The applicants wanted, for personal and cultural reasons, to live in the community independently in a home of their own with the support of their relatives and the statutory services. Mance LJ giving judgment of the Court of Appeal made the following points:

> In some circumstances, instanced by *R v Avon CC ex p M*[16] . . . a person may have a need . . . as distinct from a preference, to reside in a particular place. Here, it seems to me that Mrs Khana . . . is in reality seeking to insist, as against Southwark, on the – no doubt strongly held – preferences or beliefs of Mrs Khana and her family as to what community services should be provided to Mrs Khana and in what way. Under the relevant legislation and guidance, Southwark must take into account Mrs Khana's and Mr Karim's beliefs and preferences, but the assessment of any needs regarding, inter alia, accommodation and how to provide for them rests ultimately with Southwark.[17]
>
> . . . section 47 of the 1990 Act contemplate[s] an assessment by the local authority of a person's accommodation needs, which takes very full account of their wishes, including the very fundamental aim of preserving the independence of elderly people in the community and in their own homes for as long and as fully as possible. A certain degree of risk-taking is

12   5 July 1995 (unreported), QBD.
13   From the uncorrected draft transcript of the judgment.
14   *R v Lancashire CC ex p RADAR and another* [1996] 4 All ER 421.
15   (2001) 4 CCLR 267, CA.
16   See para 5.15 above.
17   (2001) 4 CCLR 267 at 281H.

often acceptable, rather than compromise independence and break family or home links. But, where a local authority concludes, as Southwark did here, that 'the only way in which Mrs Khana's needs can properly be met is for her to go into a full-time residential home', and makes a corresponding offer, and where this assessment and the reasonableness of the offer made cannot be challenged as such, then the local authority has in my judgment satisfied its duties under the legislation.[18]

If this had been a case where Mrs Khana's assessed needs could be met in different ways, then . . . Southwark would have been entitled to take into account its resources in deciding which way to adopt . . . [However] . . . any problem of resources would require to be made out by evidence, and cannot be assumed to be present. There is no material enabling comparison between the cost of a two bedroom ground floor flat provided by the authority with or without further community care services – and the costs of living in a residential home.[19]

5.22 It follows that where there is a choice between care packages, then:

- 'very full account' should be taken of the users' wishes;
- a 'very fundamental aim' of the care plan should be to preserve the independence of elderly people in the community and in their own homes for as long and as fully as possible (for which a 'certain degree of risk-taking is often acceptable');
- that the relative cost of alternative care packages is a legitimate consideration. However if the authority wish to put this forward as a relevant factor, then it 'would require to be made out by evidence, and cannot be assumed to be present'.

5.23 In general, therefore, authorities are unlikely to be able to insist upon a care package that institutionalises a disabled person, merely because it is the cheaper option; they will have to demonstrate (as Southwark did in the instant case) that the residential package is the most suitable to meet the user's eligible needs. Avoidable or unnecessary institutionalisation will be vulnerable to a challenge involving article 8 of the European Convention on Human Rights (see para 19.198 below).

5.24 The FACS 2003 practice guidance (Q6.4) advises that costs ceilings are not unlawful from a general/strategic planning perspective, but cannot be imposed in an arbitrary way, stating:

If an individual is eligible for support, the council should provide services that are cost-effective and appropriate. Cost-ceilings may be used as a guide, but they should not be used rigidly. Councils should always base their decisions on their assessment of a particular individual's needs, and if spending above a cost-ceiling can make a significant difference to an individual, then the council should consider doing so. They should also consider that more may be needed to be spent on certain service users because the costs of providing services to them are higher than for other groups. An example of this is the higher costs often associated with providing culturally sensitive services in people's own homes or day care

18 (2001) 4 CCLR 267 at 281K.
19 (2001) 4 CCLR 267 at 282I.

and residential establishments. Cost-ceilings used in this sensible way can ensure fairness to both individuals whose needs might call for extra help or for whom the costs of services are higher and other service users.

5.25   In her 1998 report concerning a complaint against Liverpool City Council[20] the local government ombudsman considered a council imposed financial ceiling (of £110pw) on the level of domiciliary care provided, which reflected the average cost to the council for an older person in residential care. She found that in setting the limit the council had fettered its discretion since there was no evidence that it had ever exceeded the limit and that such a fees policy was unfair and unreasonably discriminated against elderly people (as opposed to other service users).

5.26   In this context the point made by Mance LJ in *ex p Khana and Karim* concerning the need for local authorities to adduce cogent evidence of resource shortages is a general principle of importance (see para 5.21 above). Public bodies cannot assume that the courts will accept general unsupported assertions of resource difficulties. A similar approach was taken in *Sabah Mohamoud v Greenwich LBC*,[21] where the council had argued that it could not re-house an overcrowded household because overcrowding was not uncommon in its area and many people lived in unfit houses. The court held that such 'general assertions' about other accommodation was not satisfactory; what had to be shown was there were others who were experiencing the same degree of overcrowding – particularly as the applicant's overcrowding appeared to be gross and possibly in a class of its own.

Rejection of a care package

5.27   Disabled people are entitled to refuse services, either explicitly or by their behaviour. In *R v Kensington and Chelsea RLBC ex p Kujtim*,[22] for instance, Potter LJ for the Court of Appeal held that the duty to provide accommodation (under National Assistance Act (NAA) 1948 s21, see paras 7.1 and 7.44 above) can be treated as discharged if the applicant 'either unreasonably refuses to accept the accommodation provided or if, following its provision, by his conduct he manifests a persistent and unequivocal refusal to observe the reasonable requirements of the local authority in relation to the occupation of such accommodation'. The same would presumably hold true of a disabled person who behaved offensively to a home care assistant or refused to comply with the reasonable requirements of a day centre, etc, although in deciding whether to withdraw the service the applicant's mental health and its treatability may be relevant factors.[23]

20 Complaint 96/C/4315 against Liverpool CC, 20 August 1998; (1999) 2 CCLR 128.
    A sum of £10,000 compensation was recommended by the ombudsman.
21 January 2003 *Legal Action* 23.
22 (1999) 2 CCLR 340 at 354I.
23 See *Croydon LBC v Moody* (1999) 2 CCLR 92 and para 17.6 below.

5.28   In *R v Southwark LBC ex p Khana and Karim*,[24] it was alleged that Mrs Khana (the disabled party subject to the community care assessment) refused to accept the offer of a residential care home placement proposed by the local authority – and insisted upon the provision of a community based care package. In finding that the local authority had acted appropriately, Mance LJ commented:

> . . . although I do not consider that the case requires analysis in these terms, I would, if necessary, also treat Mrs Khana's refusal of the offer of residential home accommodation – the only course that would meet her assessed needs – as unreasonable in the sense intended by Potter LJ, when he was considering in *ex p Kujtim* what would discharge a local authority from any further duty for so long as such refusal was maintained.

Reviews and reassessments

5.29   The FACS 2002 policy guidance[25] requires all care plans to be regularly reviewed and to have a review date. Service users should be made aware of the arrangements for review and, where appropriate, advised that services may be withdrawn or changed as a result of the review. Service users can of course request reviews, themselves. Reviews should:[26]

- Establish how far the services provided have achieved the outcomes set out in the care plan.
- Reassess the needs and circumstances of individual service users.
- Help determine an individuals' continued eligibility for support.
- Confirm or amend the current care plan, or lead to closure.
- Comment on the effectiveness of direct payments, where appropriate.

5.30   Reviews should (except in exceptional circumstances) consist of a face to face meeting between the user and a 'council professional responsible for the review'[27] and should generally involve all relevant parties: for instance carers; the service user's advocate; the purchasers and the providers of the care services. The outcome of reviews should be recorded in writing and care plans updated accordingly.[28]

5.31   Councils should only withdraw services after a review if satisfied that the person's needs will not significantly worsen or increase in the foreseeable future for the lack of help (and this includes involvement in employment, training and education and parenting responsibilities). In making

---

24 (2001) 4 CCLR 267, CA.

25 FACS 2002 policy guidance paras 47–67 and the UFSAMC 2002 policy guidance paras 2.44–2.51. This advice largely reiterates advice given in the 1990 policy guidance (para 3.51–3.53) and CI (92) 34, para 31.

26 FACS 2002 policy guidance paras 47–67 and the UFSAMC 2002 policy guidance paras 2.44–2.51.

27 That is an officer of the authority that commissions and purchases the care services – but not in general an officer actually responsible for the provision of the services (FACS 2002 policy guidance para 61).

28 FACS 2002 policy guidance para 61.

such decisions, councils should not make assumptions about the capacity of family members or close friends to offer support. Service users must have such decisions fully explained to them – and interpreters, translators, advocates and supporters will be required in this process where appropriate. All decisions must be in writing and individuals must be advised of their right to use the complaints procedures.[29]

Breakdowns in care plan arrangements and reviews

5.32   Since formal reviews of a care plan amount to a reassessment, they too must be 'needs led' even if the reason for the reassessment is a service provision problem. This point is well illustrated by a 2002 local government ombudsman's complaint[30] concerning the care plan of a young adult with multiple and profound mental and physical disabilities. In 1994 her needs were assessed and provision made for her to have one weekend per month respite care in a residential unit, paid by the local authority, but provided by a charitable organisation. In 2000 the family were notified that owing to funding problems the unit was closed at weekends. Although the council had no record of their assessment, it argued that the need was for three days respite care a week, not necessarily at weekends. The family made a formal complaint arguing that weekend respite was essential as it gave them a substantial break (as during the week their daughter was at a residential special school).

5.33   The complaints panel noted that the 1994 assessment was 'not as sophisticated as current assessments' but concluded that since it did not specify an entitlement to weekend respite there was no obligation to provide this. The ombudsman found it 'astonishing that the council acknowledges managing . . . regular periods of respite care for six years with neither a proper assessment nor a care plan'. However having regard to the records of the service provider (and the history of weekend service provision) she was satisfied that weekend respite had been agreed. She then stated:

> The council says that because it was not responsible for the closure of [the respite facility] it cannot be held responsible for the withdrawal of [the complainants] provision. I do not accept this. It is the council, not [the charitable provider] which has statutory responsibility for providing for [the complainants] needs. If [the respite facility] could not, for whatever reason, meet those needs, the council had a duty to find, in the locality, somewhere else where [the complainant] would feel equally settled and in which her parents would have confidence.

5.34   The ombudsman reached the same conclusion in a complaint concerning adult care respite arrangements that broke down because of problems with the centre providing the care (which included an allegation of abuse during a respite period). The ombudsman noted:[31]

---

29 FACS 2002 policy guidance para 61.
30 Complaint 01/C/03521 against North Yorkshire, 19 August 2002. [The names used are not the real names.]
31 Complaint 02/B/16654 against Bedfordshire County Council, 16 October 2003.

I understand why the council found it difficult to identify alternative opportunities for respite care. And I appreciate the fact that the solution proposed [by the parents] requires resources that the department did not necessarily have. But there is case law to say that a want of resources in a particular budget does not excuse the council from carrying out its statutory duty.

5.35 A further ombudsman's report[32] on the question of service delivery difficulties concerned a severely disabled person and his main carer, both aged over 90. He was assessed as needing help getting up and going to bed; the weekend and evening cover being provided by an agency. Because of recruitment problems the agency gave notice to the council that it proposed to withdraw its service and the council was unable to find another agency willing to provide this service unless the council would pay travel costs to the staff, above the flat rate fee for the service and the council refused as this was against its policy. In finding a fettering of discretion and maladministration the ombudsman commented:

It cannot be easy to arrange for home care in the rural parts of the county's area, and even the best contractual agreements must fail from time to time. But it seems to me that when a service failure occurs, the council might well have to seize any realistic opportunity to make the service good. Here it had such an opportunity. Another home care contractor offered to provide the . . . service but only if the council would pay its staff travel costs over and above the flat rate fee for providing home care. Doubtless there are many tussles between the council and its providers over such arrangements and I can understand why the council might have considered this a precedent and the thin end of the wedge, but what was that to Mr and Mrs Derwent? It seems to me that Mr Derwent's home care was entirely sacrificed to maintain the purity of the council's contractual arrangements . . . This was a classic case of the council fettering its discretion, and was maladministration.

5.36 In a 2003 report, the ombudsman reviewed a complaint concerning the failure of a social services authority to respond to a breakdown in care arrangements. The complainant's adult daughter (who had severe physical and visual disabilities and learning disabilities) decided that she wished to return home from a specialist residential care placement in which she had been living for some time. Her father made interim arrangements and requested an urgent reassessment by the council with a view to producing a new care plan – potentially funded by direct payments and the Independent Living Fund. The council delayed such that the complainant had little or no choice but to make the support arrangements himself.

5.37 The ombudsman concluded that the council should have produced a final care plan within three months and the failure to do this amounted to maladministration. The ombudsman accepted that the complainant had spent £70,000 in supporting his daughter during the two year period of council inaction – and in his view the council itself had probably saved about £100,000 by not making any services available. Accordingly an award of £80,000 was recommended.

32 Complaint 99/B/00799 against Essex 29 March 2001.

Unmet need

5.38   The 1991 practice guidance advised that unmet need be recorded in a care plan and at the time some controversy arose as to whether the concept of 'unmet need' was lawful. However there can be no legal problem with the term if defined (as in the Welsh guidance)[33] as 'presented needs that are not evaluated as eligible needs or where eligible needs are met but an alternative more appropriate/desirable service should ideally be available'. Effectively therefore, unmet needs are those needs which the individual (or others) consider of relevance (ie, 'presenting needs') but which on assessment are not deemed sufficiently important to be 'eligible needs'.

5.39   The FACS 2003 practice guidance[34] adopts the same approach to the concept of unmet need, stating that the difference between presenting needs and eligible needs should be monitored, and the results used to inform service delivery, planning and commissioning. It is however coy about requiring councils to specifically record unmet need in writing (unlike the Welsh guidance[35] and the 1991 practice guidance[36]) – merely requiring that the information on the user's presenting needs be recorded and placed on his or her file. This is particularly unhelpful. In effect it means that in order to assess what 'presenting' needs are not being met, the individual (or someone on his or her behalf) will have to gain access to their file and find the relevant statement. This will then have to be compared against the care plan and a list prepared of those needs that the local authority has decided can be 'unmet'. Given that the Welsh policy guidance and the 1991 practice guidance specifically advise that unmet need should be recorded; that this is not specifically contradicted by the FACS guidance (which is merely oblique on the question); that recording unmet need will be relatively straight forward (if done during the assessment process) and given the bureaucratic run around that service users may have to pursue if it is not recorded – the balance of administrative fairness strongly favours it being recorded on the care plan.

5.40   The recording of unmet need is also an essential component of a local authority's strategic planning obligations. In *R v Bristol CC ex p Penfold*,[37] Scott Baker J held that the duty to assess was not predicated upon the likelihood of a service being provided, stating:

> I do not, therefore accept [the] submission that Parliament cannot have intended expenditure to a pointless end when it was clear that any established need could not be met. Even if there is no hope from the resource point of view of meeting any needs identified in the assessment, the assessment may serve a useful purpose in identifying for the local authority unmet needs which will help it to plan for the future. Without assessment this could not be done.

33   The UFSAMC 2002 policy guidance Annex 9, p101.

34   At Q.11.1–Q11.3: see also UFSAMC 2002 policy guidance paras 2.45; 6.22; 8.8; footnote 4 on p16; Annex 9 p101.

35   UFSAMC 2002 policy guidance paras 2.45; 6.22; 8.8; footnote 4 on p16; Annex 9 p101.

36   At para 4.32.

37   (1998) 1 CCLR 315 at 322.

Provision of services without an assessment

5.41 Where an individual's need is so pressing that there is not time even to carry out a 'fast-track' assessment, then a service can be provided without an assessment. NHSCCA 1990 s47(5) provides:

> Nothing in this section shall prevent a local authority from temporarily providing or arranging for the provision of community care services for any person without carrying out a prior assessment of his needs in accordance with the preceding provisions of this section if, in the opinion of the authority, the condition of that person is such that he requires those services as a matter of urgency.

5.42 While authorities are not obliged by NHSCCA 1990 s47(5) to make such provision, it would be an unlawful fettering of discretion for authorities to reach a policy decision prohibiting the provision of any community care service without a prior assessment. The 1993 guidance suggested that the power under NHSCCA 1990 s47(5) should be used sparingly[38] and the FACS 2002 policy guidance advises:[39]

> Councils should provide an immediate response to those individuals who approach them, or are referred, for social care support in emergencies and crises. After this initial response, they should inform the individual that a fuller assessment will follow, and services may be withdrawn or changed as a result of this assessment.

Disputed care plans

5.43 The appropriate procedure for disputing the content of a care plan will generally be through the local authority complaints procedures (see para 19.4 below). This may additionally include a complaint concerning the adequacy of the assessment – and particularly the needs that have been identified as 'eligible needs' (see para 4.74 above). In *R (Lloyd) v Barking and Dagenham LBC*,[40] the Court of Appeal held that it was not an appropriate organ to prescribe the degree of detail that should go into a care plan.

---

38 See for instance LAC(93)2 para 17 but compare paras 21–22.
39 At para 69; and the UFSAMC 2002 policy guidance para 5.36.
40 (2001) 4 CCLR 196 at 205G, CA.

CHAPTER 6

Ordinary residence

Introduction

6.1   The provision of community care services is primarily a local authority responsibility. Accordingly it is important that the relevant legislation spell out which particular authority is responsible – and generally this is done by reference to the service user's ordinary residence.[1] Not all of the statutes regulating the provision of community care services, however, contain specific 'ordinary residence' restrictions: broadly speaking the situation can be summarised as in Table 3 below.

Table 3: Ordinary residence

Statute	Ordinary residence			
	of direct relevance	*of indirect relevance*	*of no relevance*	*For further detail see paragraph*
NAA 1948	✓			7.51
HSPHA 1968			✓	14.17
CSDPA 1970	✓			8.64
NHSA 1977			✓	8.127
HASSASSAA 1983			✓	14.30
MHA 1983	✓			15.23
CA 1989	✓			6.15
NHSCCA 1990			✓	4.28
CC(DP)A 1996		✓		9.5
CDCA 2000		✓		11.36
HSCA 2001		✓		9.5
CC(DD)A 2003	✓			10.181

Ordinary residence and the National Assistance Act 1948

6.2   The National Assistance Act (NAA) 1948 places primary responsibility for the provision of its services (under sections 21 and 29) on the authority in which the relevant person is 'ordinarily resident'. In relation to the accommodation obligation under section 21, section 24 provides as follows:

---

1   Similar but distinct from the device of local connection used under Housing Act 1996 Part VII; in this respect, see LAC(93)7 paras 16–17.

Authority liable for provision of accommodation

24(1) The local authority empowered under this Part of this Act to provide residential accommodation for any person shall subject to the following provisions of this Part of this Act be the authority in whose area the person is ordinarily resident.

...

(3) Where a person in the area of a local authority –
   (a) is a person with no settled residence, or
   (b) not being ordinarily resident in the area of the local authority, is in urgent need of residential accommodation under this Part of this Act,
   the authority shall have the like power to provide residential accommodation for him as if he were ordinarily resident in their area.

(4) Subject to and in accordance with the arrangements under section twenty-one of this Act, a local authority shall have power, as respects a person ordinarily resident in the area of another local authority, with the consent of that other authority to provide residential accommodation for him in any case where the authority would have a duty to provide such accommodation if he were ordinarily resident in their area.

(5) Where a person is provided with residential accommodation under this Part of this Act, he shall be deemed for the purposes of this Act to continue to be ordinarily resident in the area in which he was ordinarily resident immediately before the residential accommodation was provided for him.

(6) For the purposes of the provision of residential accommodation under this Part of this Act, a patient in a hospital vested in the Secretary of State, a Primary Care Trust or an NHS trust shall be deemed to be ordinarily resident in the area, if any, in which he was ordinarily resident immediately before he was admitted as a patient to the hospital, whether or not he in fact continues to be ordinarily resident in that area.

(7) In subsection (6) above 'NHS trust' means a National Health Service trust established under Part I of the National Health Service and Community Care Act 1990 or under the National Health Service (Scotland) Act 1978 and 'Primary Care Trust' means a Primary Care Trust established under section 16A of the National Health Service Act 1977.

6.3   Under NAA 1948 s24(4) (as confirmed by the secretary of state's directions – see para 7.50) authorities have the power (but not a duty) to provide services for persons who are ordinarily resident elsewhere. In relation to the accommodation obligation, NAA 1948 s24(3) also apportions responsibility in situations of urgency and for people who lack 'ordinary residence' (ie, because they have 'no settled residence').

6.4   Although the Act fails to provide any statutory definition for the term 'ordinary residence', the department of health has issued interpretative guidance in circular LAC(93)7,[2] which includes reference to a number of

2   WOC 41/93 in Wales.

reported decisions in which its meaning has been considered. The Department of Health is committed to a revision of LAC(93)7 during 2004[3] – as it anticipates a growth in disputes concerning ordinary residence (consequent upon the Community Care (Delayed Discharge, etc) Act 2003 (see para 10.170 below). In Wales, guidance on ordinary residence and the process for disputes resolution has been issued in 2003 as WOC 41/93.[4]

6.5   The key to the term is in the word 'residence'; it will generally be the place where a person's normal residential address is to be found. The circular states that the phrase involves questions of fact and degree, and factors such as time, intention[5] and continuity.

6.6   The leading case on ordinary residence is the House of Lords' decision in *Shah v Barnet LBC*.[6] In Lord Scarman's judgment a person's long-term future intentions or expectations are not relevant; the test is not what is a person's real home[7] but whether a person can show a regular, habitual mode of life in a particular place, the continuity of which has persisted despite temporary absences.[8] A person's attitude is only relevant in two respects; the residence must be voluntarily adopted, and there must be a settled purpose in living in the particular residence. 'Ordinary residence' is to be given its 'ordinary and natural meaning', namely 'a man's abode in a particular place or country which he had adopted voluntarily and for settled purposes as part of the regular order of his life for the time being, whether of short or long duration'.[9]

6.7   *R v Waltham Forest LBC ex p Vale*[10] concerned a 28-year-old applicant with profound learning disabilities such that she was totally dependent on her parents. In these circumstances the court held that 'concepts of voluntarily adopted residence and settled purpose did not arise'. Importing principles from child care law,[11] it determined that her ordinary residence was that of her parents, not because it was her real home, but because it was her 'base'. The court further held that a person's ordinary residence could result after a stay in one place of only short duration; and that there was no reason why one month should be regarded as being too short.

6.8   The *Waltham Forest* decision was tested in *R v Redbridge LBC ex p East Sussex CC*,[12] which concerned two adult male autistic twins with profound

---

3   LAC HSC 2003/009 (2003) 21 para 68.
4   26 June 1993 'Ordinary Residence – Personal Social Services' accessible at www.wales.gov.uk/subisocialpolicy/content/circulars/per-soc-serv-e.htm.
5   In view of the comments of Lord Scarman in *Shah v Barnet LBC* [1983] 1 All ER 226, intention must be given a restrictive interpretation.
6   [1983] 1 All ER 226: although the case concerned the interpretation of 'ordinary residence' for the purposes of the Education Act 1962, it is accepted that the term has the same meaning in both statutes.
7   [1983] 1 All ER 226 at 239.
8   [1983] 1 All ER 226 at 236.
9   [1983] 1 All ER 226 at 235.
10   (1985) *Times* 25 February, QBD.
11   See for instance, *In re P (GE) (an infant)* [1965] Ch 568.
12   (1993) *Times* 3 January; [1993] COD 256, QBD.

learning disabilities who were boarded at a school in East Sussex, but whose parents lived in Redbridge. Applying the principles enunciated in the *Waltham Forest* decision, the court held that the twins were at law ordinarily resident in Redbridge. Subsequently, however, the parents went to live in Nigeria. It was held that when this occurred the twins ceased to have any settled residence and accordingly became the responsibility of East Sussex. LAC(93)7 advises, however, that except in cases involving persons with severe learning difficulties, 'an adult with learning disabilities should be regarded as capable of forming his own intention of where he wishes to live'.[13]

6.9   Where a person is provided with residential accommodation by a social services authority, he or she is deemed to continue to be ordinarily resident in the area in which he or she was ordinarily resident immediately before the residential accommodation was provided.[14] This will be the case, even if the person is in effect a 'self-funder' (see para 7.15), but has relied upon the local authority to make the placement and contract with the care home.

6.10   Likewise where a person is in NHS care he or she is deemed to be ordinarily resident in the area in which he or she was ordinarily resident immediately before admission as a patient to the NHS facility.[15] Where a person was not ordinarily resident in any area prior to admission, then the responsible social services authority will be the one in whose area he or she is at that time.[16] The guidance suggests that these principles should also be followed when assessing responsibility for people leaving prisons, resettlement units and other similar establishments.[17]

No settled residence

6.11   When a person presents him or herself to a social services authority and claims to be of no settled residence or of no fixed abode, the authority is advised that it should normally accept responsibility.[18] If this were not the case, authorities could argue that they owed no duty to such persons, as the secretary of state's direction in LAC(93)10 Appendix 1 (with one exception)[19] limits their duty to those ordinarily resident in the area, or in urgent need. It is submitted therefore that if a person has no settled residence, his or her ordinary residence is the place where he or she is actually living (or perhaps – in extreme cases – the place where the previous night

13 LAC(93)7 para 12: and see also *R v Kent CC and Salisbury and Pierre* (2000) 3 CCLR 38 (at para 6.24 below).

14 NAA 1948 s24(5). The situation will generally be otherwise where the person has independently admitted him or herself to the home and without financial assistance from the local authority – see LAC(93)7 paras 10 and 15.

15 NAA 1948 s24(6).

16 NAA 1948 s24(3).

17 LAC(93)7 para 14.

18 LAC(93)7 para 16.

19 LAC(93)10 Appendix 1, para 2(3).

was spent).[20] Guidance accompanying the Community Care (Delayed Discharge, etc) Act 2003 suggests that the ordinary residence of people of no fixed abode who are admitted to hospital will be determined by the postcode of the place they were at immediately prior to admission.[21]

6.12   Guidance on the special needs of homeless people has been given in LAC(93)2, including the following.

RESIDENTIAL CARE FOR HOMELESS PEOPLE WITH OTHER NEEDS

26. There may be other vulnerable people who are homeless and who are in need of residential care. Many of the above considerations apply to them as much as to alcohol and drug misusers. Like any other section of the population, homeless people may be in need of care because of frailty, physical disability, mental disorder of any description or a combination of any of these. They may have complex needs which also include alcohol and drug misuse. Their needs may be hard to classify by standard client groups.

27. As with alcohol and drug misusers, [local authorities] LAs should have flexible systems of assessment and care management that allow such people access to the services they need in a way that meets their special circumstances. Their homelessness may in itself mean that an urgent response is called for. LAs will be aware that there are a wide variety of agencies which specialise in providing care for homeless people. As with specialist alcohol and drug providers, these agencies may be in a position to assist in assessment procedures. Some of these homes receive additional support from the Home Office specifically to reserve places for vulnerable offenders and ex-offenders whose care needs require residential support. As above, LAs will need to collaborate with the Probation Service to make best use of these resources.

Urgent need

6.13   The secretary of state's direction places a duty on authorities to make arrangements not only for persons ordinarily resident in their area, but also for 'other persons who are in urgent need thereof'.[22] Urgent need is not defined; in this context however it is only relevant when the person is ordinarily resident in another authority's area. It would appear therefore that the duty to persons in urgent need will almost invariably be a short-term duty, only subsisting during the currency of the urgency, and even then, only until such time as the other authority assumes responsibility.

20 In *R v Eastleigh BC ex p Betts* [1983] 2 AC 613 (which concerned a different phrase 'normally resident') Lord Brightman suggested that 'in appropriate circumstances a single day's residence may be enough to enable a person to say that he was normally resident in the area in which he had arrived only yesterday'. Patrick Eccles QC argues that this finding is capable of being read across into the interpretation of 'ordinary residence: see 'Ordinary Residence and Community Care: An Overview' P Eccles QC (1999) 2 CCLR 100 at 104.

21 HSC 2003/009 :LAC(2003)21 para 33.

22 LAC(2003)21 at para 2(1)(b), and see also NHSCCA 1990 s47(5) concerning the provision of community care services in cases of urgency.

Ordinary residence and the Chronically Sick and Disabled Persons Act 1970

6.14 The definition of ordinary residence in Chronically Sick and Disabled Persons Act (CSDPA) 1970 s2 is identical to that under the NAA 1948, and accordingly the same considerations apply. However the process for resolving disputes concerning ordinary residence is materially different to that under the NAA 1948, and this is considered at para 6.24 below.

Ordinary residence and the Children Act 1989

6.15 As a matter of principle, children are presumed to have the ordinary residence of their parents.[23] The Children Act (CA) 1989, however, adopts a different test for determining responsibility for children in need. The duty under CA 1989 s17 (to safeguard and promote the welfare of children in need)[24] and the duty under CA 1989 s20 (to accommodate) are owed by social services authorities to children 'within their area'. However financial responsibility for certain accommodation services provided under the Act[25] rests with the local authority in whose area the child is 'ordinarily resident'. Thus a child may be ordinarily resident in local authority A but 'within the area' of local authority B. Accordingly provision is made in CA 1989 s20(2) for local authority A to take over the responsibilities of local authority B.

Within the area

6.16 A series of cases have concerned the question of which authority is responsible for carrying out an assessment of children in need – and thus the true construction of the phrase 'within their area'. In *R (Stewart) v Wandsworth LBC, Hammersmith and Fulham LBC and Lambeth LBC,*[26] the claimant applied to Hammersmith LBC for housing (under the homelessness provisions). Hammersmith accommodated her in a hostel in Lambeth and then determined that she was intentionally homeless and obtained a possession order against her. The claimant then requested that Hammersmith assess her children's needs under CA 1989 s17. Hammersmith refused on the basis that this was Lambeth's responsibility. Lambeth LBC refused, as did Wandsworth LBC (the children's school being within their area). The court decided that 'within their area' was simply a question of physical presence (even though that might mean that more than one authority could be under the duty to assess). Accordingly it held that Lambeth and Wandsworth were responsible but Hammersmith was not.

---

23 See for instance, *In re P (GE) (an infant)* [1965] Ch 568.
24 See para 18.3.
25 See CA 1989 ss20(2); 21(3); 29(7) and 29(9).
26 [2001] EWHC Admin 709; (2001) 4 CCLR 466; [2002] 1 FLR 469.

6.17   The decision was followed in a similar fact case, *R (M) v Barking and Dagenham LBC and Westminster CC*,[27] where the court agreed that the relevant test was physical presence. It noted that no formal guidance existed to deal with such jurisdictional problems and encouraged inter-authority co-operation in such cases:

> . . . to avoid any impression that local authorities are able to pass responsibility for a child on to another authority . . . To put it shortly, the needs should be met first and the redistribution of resources should, if necessary take place afterwards. It is also important, quite plainly, that the parents of children should not be able to cause inconvenience or extra expense by simply moving on to another local authority . . .

Ordinary residence: the Children Act 1989/National Assistance Act 1948 interface

6.18   In *R v Lambeth LBC ex p Caddell*[28] the applicant had been placed by the respondent London borough with paid carers who lived in Kent. When he became 18 years of age, the borough determined that he had ceased to be their responsibility since he was no longer a child, and accordingly the ordinary residence rules under the NAA 1948 applied. Kent County Council contended however, that Lambeth was still the responsible authority since CA 1989 s24 allowed for social services authorities to continue to provide advice and assistance to young persons who had been in care once they achieved their majority. Connell J rejected this line of argument, holding that the duty under CA 1989 s24 was owed by the authority in whose area the young person resided, ie, Kent.

6.19   Children Act 1989 s24 (which specifically concerns the needs of looked after children who are leaving care) has since been amended by the Children (Leaving Care) Act 2000. In effect the financial obligations imposed by the 2000 Act (particularly in the substituted sections 24A and 24B of the 1989 Act) are now the responsibility of the local authority which looked after the young person immediately before he or she left care. This responsibility continues until the age of 21 (or beyond in the case of certain education and training costs).

6.20   It follows that when services are being provided under Mental Health Act 1983 s117 or CSDPA 1970 s2 (or indeed under the Children Act 1989), the procedures laid down by NAA 1948 s32(3) will not be available to determine ordinary residence disputes.

---

27 [2002] EWHC 2663 (Admin); (2003) 6 CCLR 87.
28 [1998] 1 FLR 253.

Ordinary residence and Mental Health Act 1983 s117

6.21   The duty to provide services under Mental Health Act (MHA) 1983 s117 is
a joint health and social services responsibility. MHA 1983 s117(3) stipulates that the responsible health bodies are 'the Primary Care Trust[29] or
Health Authority' and that these together with the relevant social services
authority are those 'for the area in which the person concerned is resident
or to which he is sent on discharge by the hospital in which he was
detained'.

6.22   It might appear, therefore, that MHA 1983 s117(3) gives a choice of
responsible authorities – either the health/social services authorities in
whose area he or she was resident at the time of admission to hospital[30] or
those to which he or she is sent on discharge. In *R v Mental Health Review
Tribunal ex p Hall*,[31] Scott Baker J considered this question. He noted:

> The word 'or' in subsection (3) clearly envisages an alternative so that
> there is always some authority that will be responsible when a patient is
> discharged; if not that of his residence that of the place to which he is sent.
> One or the other authority is responsible but not both; otherwise there
> would be a recipe for disaster with the prospect of endless disagreements
> and failures to make arrangements. Section 117 does not provide for multi
> social services department or health authority responsibility. The words
> 'or to whom he is sent on discharge from tribunal' are included simply
> to cater for the situation where a patient does not have a current place of
> residence. The subsection does not mean that a placing authority where
> the patient resides suddenly ceases to be 'the local social services authority'
> if on discharge the applicant is sent to a different authority.

Disputed 'ordinary residence'

Disputed 'ordinary residence' and the National Assistance Act 1948

6.23   Where two or more social services authorities are in dispute over a person's
ordinary residence, NAA 1948 s32(3) provides that the question is to be
determined by the secretary of state. This procedure is however only

---

29   Inserted by the NHS Reform and Health Care Professionals Act 2002, Sch 2(2) para
47. Specific reference to local health boards in Wales appears not to be strictly
necessary, as a result of a combination of Welsh Statutory Instrument 2003 No 813 (W
98) The Health Authorities (Transfer of Functions, Staff, Property, Rights and
Liabilities and Abolition) (Wales) Order 2003 – which transfers all functions of health
authorities in Wales to the Assembly – and Welsh Statutory Instrument 2003 No 150
(W 20) The Local Health Boards (Functions) (Wales) Regulations 2003 which provides
(subject to exceptions) that functions that were exercised by Health Authorities and
were transferred to the Assembly by SI 2003/813 are to be exercised by Local Health
Boards.

30   A person does not cease to be resident in the area of an authority by reason only of
his/her admission to hospital – *Fox v Stirk* [1970] 2QB 463.

31   (1999) 2 CCLR 361 at 371I–J. Although the case went to the Court of Appeal ((1999) 2
CCLR 383) the question of the responsible department was not argued in that Court.

available for disputes which concern potential services under the NAA 1948. LAC(93)7[32] Part II sets out the procedure to be followed by authorities in such cases, namely:

(a) Before the secretary of state is approached, one of the authorities must provisionally accept responsibility and be providing services.
(b) An agreed written statement of facts, signed by all authorities involved, must be sent, together with the application for determination. The statement should include:
  – full information about the person whose ordinary residence is in dispute
  – details relating to the prior residence of the person
  – details of the statutory provisions under which services have been provided.
  Copies of all relevant correspondence between the authorities should be annexed to the agreed statement.
(c) In addition each authority may also send separate written representations concerning the agreed statement (ie, a legal submission).

Disputed 'ordinary residence' and the Chronically Sick and Disabled Persons Act 1970

6.24   In *R v Kent CC and Salisbury and Pierre*,[33] a dispute arose as to the potential service user's ordinary residence and the council argued that the court could not determine this question since NAA 1948 s32(3) provided for this to be decided by the Minister. The dispute arose, however, in the context of services under the CSDPA 1970 and not the NAA 1948. Latham J held:[34]

> The difficulty with this submission is that . . . it is raised not under the National Assistance Act 1948, but under the 1970 Act. There is no equivalent provision in this latter Act. The reference to section 29 of the 1948 Act is not, in my judgment, sufficient to justify the conclusion that the provisions of section 32(3) of that Act apply to the determination of any issue under section 2 of the 1970 Act. The phrase 'are satisfied in the case of any person to whom that section applies' does not involve consideration of ordinary residence. It is a reference to the nature of the disabilities which trigger consideration of the question whether a person is one to whom, the duty under section 2 of the 1970 Act is owed. That is why it was necessary to include the phrase 'who is ordinarily resident in their area' in that section. That being so, it seems to me that the present claim requires me to determine whether or not [the service user] is ordinarily resident in Kent.

6.25   The judge then determined the question of ordinary residence on the basis of the existing legal authorities. The service user had learning difficulties,

32   The Department of Health propose to amend the LAC(93)7 in 2004 (see note 3 above).
33   (2000) 3 CCLR 38.
34   (2000) 3 CCLR 38 at 43J.

but these were not so severe as those considered in *R v Waltham Forest LBC ex p Vale*,[35] and accordingly it was held that:

> In the present case, the papers show that [the service user] has expressed a clear and consistent desire to stay with [her paid carers who lived in Kent]. I think that is sufficient to justify the conclusion that she is in her present abode voluntarily, and with a settled intention to remain there for the time being. Her disabilities do not appear to be such as to prevent her from having the requisite understanding for both mental elements. That is sufficient to justify the conclusion that she is ordinarily resident in Kent. If I am wrong, she is nonetheless to be treated, in my view, as if [her paid carers] were her parents, and she were a child. This would produce the same result.

Disputed 'ordinary residence' and the Children Act 1989

6.26 Although, as noted above, no formal dispute resolution process exists where authorities are unable to agree on whether or not a child is 'within their area', CA 1989 s30(2) provides a formal process for disputes concerning ordinary residence. This is essentially the same secretary of state process as with the NAA 1948 s32(3) (above).

Disputed 'ordinary residence' and Mental Health Act 1983 s117

6.27 Where doubt arises as to a person's area of residence, non-statutory guidance exists on determining the responsible health body and social services authority[36] (as the statutory procedure for determining ordinary residence under NAA 1948 s32(3) does not apply to disputes under MHA 1983 s117, see para 6.20). The social services guidance deals with issues of good practice and provides a procedure for resolving disputes between authorities over responsibility.

Disputed 'ordinary residence' and the Community Care (Delayed Discharge, etc) Act 2003

6.28 The process for resolution of such disputes is considered at para 10.181 below.

---

35 (1985) *Times* 25 February, QBD.
36 See the joint Association of Metropolitan/County Councils' guidance 'AMA/Social Services Circular 9/1988' and guidance letter 4.10.89 (which merely confirms that the effective date for 9/1988 is 11/2/88).

Care home accommodation

continued

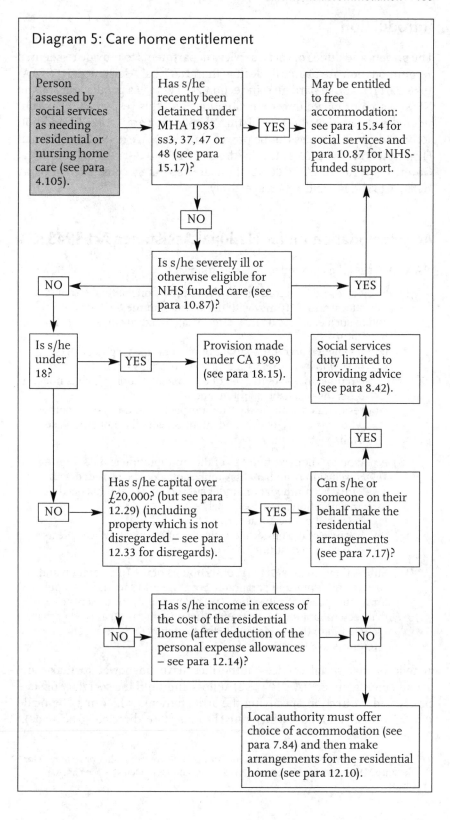

Diagram 5: Care home entitlement

Person assessed by social services as needing residential or nursing home care (see para 4.105).

Has s/he recently been detained under MHA 1983 ss3, 37, 47 or 48 (see para 15.17)?

YES → May be entitled to free accommodation: see para 15.34 for social services and para 10.87 for NHS-funded support.

NO ↓

Is s/he severely ill or otherwise eligible for NHS funded care (see para 10.87)?

NO ← / → YES

Is s/he under 18? → YES → Provision made under CA 1989 (see para 18.15).

Social services duty limited to providing advice (see para 8.42).

YES

NO →

Has s/he capital over £20,000? (but see para 12.29) (including property which is not disregarded – see para 12.33 for disregards). → YES → Can s/he or someone on their behalf make the residential arrangements (see para 7.17)?

NO →

Has s/he income in excess of the cost of the residential home (after deduction of the personal expense allowances – see para 12.14)? → NO

NO

Local authority must offer choice of accommodation (see para 7.84) and then make arrangements for the residential home (see para 12.10).

Introduction

7.1   The powers and duties of social services departments to provide residential accommodation are primarily dealt with in National Assistance Act (NAA) 1948 Part III, and in particular in section 21. There is a parallel duty on the NHS to accommodate in certain situations and this responsibility is considered separately at the end of this chapter at para 7.142. In addition accommodation services can be provided under NAA 1948 s29(4), Mental Health Act (MHA) 1983 s117, Children Act 1989 (CA) 1989 s17 and Local Government Act (LGA) 2000 s2; these are separately considered at paras 7.143, 7.145, 7.147 and 1.49 respectively.

Accommodation under National Assistance Act 1948 s21

7.2   NAA 1948 s21(1) as amended reads as follows:

(1)   Subject to and in accordance with the provisions of this Part of this Act, a local authority may with the approval of the Secretary of State, and to such extent as he may direct shall, make arrangements for providing –
(a)   residential accommodation for persons aged eighteen or over who by reason of age, illness, disability or any other circumstances are in need of care and attention which is not otherwise available to them; and
(aa) residential accommodation for expectant and nursing mothers who are in need of care and attention which is not otherwise available to them.

(1A) A person to whom section 115 of the Immigration and Asylum Act 1999 (exclusion from benefits) applies may not be provided with residential accommodation under subsection (1)(a) if his need for care and attention has arisen solely –
(a)   because he is destitute; or
(b)   because of the physical effects, or anticipated physical effects, of his being destitute.

(1B) Subsections (3) and (5) to (8) of section 95 of the Immigration and Asylum Act 1999, and paragraph 2 of Schedule 8 to that Act, apply for the purposes of subsection (1A) as they apply for the purposes of that section, but for the references in subsections (5) and (7) of that section and in that paragraph to the Secretary of State substitute references to a local authority.

7.3   It follows that social services authorities have no power to make any arrangements under NAA 1948 s21 unless and until the secretary of state has issued a direction specifying the arrangements which may be made (are 'approved') and those which must be made (are 'directed' to be made).[1]

---

1   Authority to provide accommodation may however derive from other provisions – for instance MHA 1983 s117 – see para 7.143 below and LGA 2000 s2 – see para 1.49 above.

7.4   The secretary of state's most recent direction in England is found at Appendix 1 to LAC(93)10[2] and came into force on 1 April 1993 (see appendix B for the full text of the direction).

7.5   NAA 19948 s21 specifies two hurdles which a person must (with one exception) surmount before being considered by a social services authority for residential accommodation under this section: the exception relates to expectant and nursing mothers, for whom the age requirement does not apply (see below). The two requirements are:

a) the person must be 18 or over, and
b) the person must be in need of care and attention which is not otherwise available.

Care and attention

7.6   Accommodation under NAA 1948 s21 is only available to persons who (among other things) are in need of 'care and attention'; a phrase which is not defined in the legislation. The courts have adopted a reasonably generous approach to its interpretation – based on the supposition that this is the intention of the secretary of state[3] – thus in *R v Hammersmith LBC ex p M*,[4] the Court of Appeal observed that '[t]hose who needed assistance because they lacked care and attention have always remained the subject of s21(1)(a) . . .'

7.7   The *Hammersmith* case (as with so many under NAA 1948 s21) concerned asylum-seekers. As a consequence of the Asylum and Immigration Act (AIA) 1996 they were not entitled to either public housing assistance or to social security benefits and became destitute: being variously described as 'traumatised', 'penniless', 'having no means to buy food or shelter', 'no friends or contacts' and 'had not eaten for some time'. The applicants sought accommodation under NAA 1948 s21 claiming that they were in need of care and attention, which was not otherwise available.

7.8   The respondent local authorities denied responsibility claiming that for the purposes of NAA 1948 s21, a need of accommodation alone was insufficient – there had also to be a need for care and attention. The Court of Appeal summarised a key part of the local authority argument as follows:[5]

> . . . [counsel for the local authority] submitted that the effect of the legislation was to provide three separate solutions for three different problems. The problems; lack of resources which had originally been dealt with under Part II of the 1948 Act;[6] lack of care and attention which alone continued to be dealt with by Part III of the 1948 Act and finally lack of

---

2   WOC 35/93 in Wales; since the texts are virtually identical the English direction is referred henceforth.
3   *R v Westminster CC ex p M, P, A and X* (1997) 1 CCLR 85 at 92D, CA.
4   This being a consolidated appeal, comprising *R v Hammersmith LBC ex p M; R v Lambeth LBC ex p P and X and R v Westminster CC ex p A* (1997) 1 CCLR 85.
5   (1997) 1 CCLR 85 at 92K–93C.
6   This provided for 'National Assistance': a means tested benefit – see para 1.8.

accommodation which initially had been dealt with by section 21(1)(b) of the 1948 Act.[7]

Basing their submissions upon this division, the appellants argue that the purpose of section 21(1)(a) was not to provide money for those in need of money or to provide accommodation for those who need 'accommodation per se' but to provide accommodation for those who required care and attention. Such persons could be rich and own their own homes but still could need the local authority's assistance under section 21(1)(a). The accommodation was not in itself an end but a means whereby the required care and attention can be provided.

From this base the appellants urge that it is only necessary to take one further and final step. They contend that asylum-seekers' needs are for food and accommodation and not for care and attention and consequently asylum-seekers cannot avail themselves of section 21(1)(a).

7.9   Although the court accepted that there were 'three paths of legislative pro-vision' this did not mean that their 'paths could not overlap making an applicant prima facie eligible for more than one form of assistance'. It held that:

> ... personal characteristics can be caused by external conditions. For example one of the problems of the asylum-seeker is that they have to sleep rough and go without food. This can bring about illness and disability which can result in their needing 'care and attention which is not otherwise available to them'.[8]

and

> ... it is for the authority to decide whether they qualify ... [but they] ... can anticipate the deterioration which would otherwise take place in the asylum-seekers condition by providing assistance under the section.[9]

7.10   In *R (Mani) v Lambeth LBC and Secretary of State for the Home Department*,[10] the Court of Appeal also rejected a subtly different argument; namely that the need for care and attention had to be an 'accommodation related need'.

7.11   'Care and attention' for the purposes of NAA 1948 s21, does not there-fore suggest care services of an intrusive nature – for instance attention with bodily functions, or care of an intimate or of a specifically personal character. It can be precautionary – and primarily related to external factors (sleeping rough and going without food). The courts however insist that the construction that they have given to NAA 1948 s21 does not undermine the importance of there being a need for care and attention in addition to the provision of accommodation: a need that can only be addressed if residential accommodation is provided. As Hale LJ held in *R (Wahid) v Tower Hamlets LBC*:[11]

---

7   This provided for the temporary accommodation of homeless people – and was repealed by the Housing (Homeless Persons) Act 1977 – see para 1.9.
8   (1997) 1 CCLR 85 at 94B.
9   (1997) 1 CCLR 85 at 95C–D.
10 [2003] EWCA Civ 836; (2003) 6 CCLR 376.
11 [2002] EWCA Civ 287; (2002) 5 CCLR 239 at 248G–J. The judgment was cited with approval by Lord Hoffman in *Westminster CC v National Asylum Support Service* [2002] UKHL 38; (2002) 5 CCLR 511 at 518H.

[The duty under section 21(1)] is premised on an unmet need for 'care and attention' (a 'condition precedent', as this Court put it in the *Westminster* case, at 93E).[12] These words must be given their full weight. Their natural and ordinary meaning in this context is 'looking after': this can obviously include feeding the starving, as with the destitute asylum-seekers in the *Westminster* case. Ordinary housing is not in itself 'care and attention'. It is simply the means whereby the necessary care and attention can be made available if otherwise it will not (I do not understand this Court to have rejected that part of the local authority's argument in the *Westminster* case, at 93B–D). The destitute asylum-seekers in the *Westminster* case had a claim because their destitution would reduce then to a situation in which they required such care and attention and it could not be made available to them in any other way because of the restrictions placed upon their ability to seek other forms of support by the Asylum and Immigration Act 1996.

7.12   In spite of the courts insistence on the importance of a need existing for 'care and attention' it is difficult to see what the phrase adds in any given situation. Without materially changing the outcome of the various cases, NAA 1948 s21(1) could have been worded to direct that accommodation can only be provided if (1) the person is in imminent risk of significant harm and (2) absent the provision of residential accommodation there is no other way of avoiding this harm. Section 21 is not however so framed: although the second factor exists ('not otherwise available') the first does not – it speaks instead of a 'need for care and attention'. Nevertheless (and notwithstanding judicial protestations to the contrary) the present interpretation of NAA 1948 s21 conforms more closely to the former 'risk assessment' wording than to the latter 'care assessment' wording – and although linked, these are different concepts. This point is illustrated by Hale LJ's observation (above) that 'care and attention' means 'looking after' or merely 'feeding the starving'. The problem with this approach is that feeding the hungry also amounts to 'looking after' or 'care and attention'. It is therefore questionable whether the requirement materially affects the legal determination of need in any particular case.

7.13   If in practice the key test is the establishment of a risk of harmful consequences, then this element is already addressed in the assessment process under National Health Service and Community Care Act (NHSCCA) s47(1); namely that the need for accommodation must be sufficiently pressing to 'call for' the provision of accommodation: Pill LJ in *Wahid* accepted that the section 47(1) process envelopes (if not makes redundant) the NAA 1948 s21 requirement for 'care and attention', observing:

The material available in the section 47(1) assessment was relevant to an assessment under the 1948 Act. There was no need for the judge to make a specific reference to the fact that two statutory provisions were engaged in the exercise.[13]

12 This being a consolidated appeal, comprising *R v Hammersmith LBC ex p M; R v Lambeth LBC ex p P and X and R v Westminster CC ex p A* (1997) 1 CCLR 85, CA.
13 (2002) 5 CCLR 239 at 245I.

'Not otherwise available to them'

7.14   The social services' obligation to provide residential accommodation only arises when the care and attention that a person needs, is 'not otherwise available'. Other options may of course include a package of domiciliary care services to enable the person to remain in his or her own home, and/or the provision of accommodation under the Housing Act 1996[14] or assistance from the NHS under its continuing care responsibilities.[15] It was the fact that such help (ie, public housing and social security assistance) was not 'otherwise available' to asylum-seekers, that proved crucial in establishing their entitlement to support under NAA 1948 s21.

7.15   The interpretation of this phrase has been considered by the House of Lords in *Steane v Chief Adjudication Officer*,[16] which concerned the payment of attendance allowance to persons placed in independent residential accommodation by social services authorities but whose residential home fees were not being funded by the authority.[17] The effect of this decision was to confirm that accommodation is not being provided under NAA 1948 s21 if the resident is a 'self-funder', ie, is paying for the accommodation without any support from the local authority *and* making direct payment to the home owner. In effect, therefore, the duty on the social services authority to provide residential accommodation is one of last resort.[18]

7.16   The proposition, that local authorities did not owe a duty to provide residential accommodation for 'self-funders'[19] was tested in *R v Sefton MBC ex p Help the Aged*.[20] Here the authority decided that it would not accept responsibility for any person already in residential care or nursing home accommodation until such time as his or her capital fell below £1,500 (notwithstanding that the charging rules at that time required capital below £10,000 to be disregarded). The Court of Appeal held such a policy to be unlawful, and that 'care and attention is not to be regarded as "otherwise available" if the person concerned is unable to pay for it according to' the charging rules (see para 12.9).

7.17   The matter has been put beyond question, initially through the Community Care (Residential Accommodation) Act 1998 s1 (and now the Health and Social Care Act 2001 s53), which inserted a new subsection (2A)

---

14   See chapter 17.

15   See para 10.64.

16   (1998)1 CCLR 538, HL and see also *Chief Adjudication Officer v Quinn and Gibbon* (1998) 1 CCLR 529, HL.

17   Social Security (Attendance Allowance) Amendment (No 3) Regulations 1983 SI No 1741 reg 4(1)(c) provided that attendance allowance was not payable for any period during which a person is living in accommodation provided in circumstances in which the cost of the accommodation may be borne wholly or partly out of public funds: now with minor amendment to be found in the Social Security (Attendance Allowance) Regulations 1991 SI No 2740.

18   As stated in *Adjudication Officers Guidance* para 11 (DSS 1994) concerning the payment of attendance allowance and disability living allowance.

19   That is, persons already in such accommodation who were paying there own fees.

20   (1997) 1 CCLR 57.

into NAA 1948 s21, stipulating that for the purposes of deciding whether care and attention are otherwise available to a person, a local authority shall disregard so much of the person's capital as does not exceed the capital limit for the purposes of NAA 1948 s22.[21] The Guidance which accompanies the Act[22] makes it clear that even if a person's capital exceeds the statutory limit, there will nevertheless be situations where they cannot decide that care and attention is not required (for instance because of lack of mental capacity).[23]

Client group

7.18   NAA 1948 s21 lists the criteria which may cause a person to be considered in need of the necessary care and attention, namely:

– age
– illness
– disability
– an expectant or nursing mother
– any other circumstances.

7.19   The list should be contrasted with that under NAA 1948 s29 (which deals with domiciliary services – see para 8.23). The NAA 1948 s29 list does not include age as a qualifying criterion and is generally more restrictive in its requirements (for instance, an illness must substantially and permanently handicap the person before he or she qualifies).

Age

7.20   Age is usually taken as a reference to the frail elderly: people who as a result of the aging process alone, have become frail. Age is, of course, frequently accompanied by disabling conditions or illness, which are alternative qualifying conditions for the purpose of NAA 1948 s21. The NHS has responsibilities for very frail elderly people (particularly for respite and rehabilitation services) and this obligation is considered in greater detail at para 10.87 below.

Illness

7.21   Illness is not defined by the NAA 1948, although by National Health Service Act (NHSA) 1977 s128 it is defined as including mental disorder within the meaning of the Mental Health Act 1983 and any injury or disability requiring medical or dental treatment or nursing. The care and attention may be required, not merely because the person is ill; it may arise in order to prevent that person becoming ill, or by way of after-care.[24] The residential accommodation duties parallel the obligations under NHSA 1977

21 See para 12.29.
22 LAC(98)19; WOC 27/98 in Wales (both being 'policy guidance').
23 LAC(98)19 para 9; and see para 13.16 below where this issue is considered further.
24 LAC(93)10 Appendix 1 para 2(5).

Sch 8 para 2, which enable social services authorities to provide domiciliary services for people who are or have been ill (or for the prevention of illness – see para 8.124). The criterion of 'illness' was inserted into NAA 1948 s21 by NHSCCA 1990 s42(1)(a). Prior to this amendment a parallel social services accommodation obligation existed under NHSA 1977 Sch 8 para 2.[25] This power to accommodate was generally used to provide accommodation for people who were able to live more independently than those accommodated under NAA 1948 s21, but who nevertheless required some degree of care and support. These were mostly (but not always) people under pension age.[26]

Disability

7.22   Unlike in NAA 1948 s29, disability is not qualified in NAA 1948 s21. It follows that the condition need not necessarily be substantial or permanent.

Expectant or nursing mothers

7.23   The secretary of state's direction specifically states that residential accommodation can be provided for expectant and nursing mothers of any age, ie, irrespective of whether or not they are over the age of 18.[27]

Any other circumstance

7.24   The secretary of state's direction[28] does not limit the potential client group entitled to services under NAA 1948 s21 (as the direction also refers to persons whose need arises as a result of any other circumstance). The direction nevertheless specifically refers to two categories of condition:

Mental disorder   Residential accommodation can be provided for persons who are or have been suffering from mental disorder, as well as for the purpose of the prevention of mental disorder – see below.[29]

Alcohol or drug dependency   In this case however the residential accommodation is for those actually dependent (rather than for prevention).[30] The provision of accommodation for persons who are alcohol or drug-dependent is considered in greater detail in chapter 16.

---

25   Duties under this head repealed by NHSCCA 1990 Sch 10.
26   See charging for residential accommodation guidance (CRAG) para 2.003 – discussed at para 12.73 below.
27   LAC(93)10 Appendix 1 para 3.
28   LAC(93)10 Appendix 1
29   LAC(93)10 Appendix 1 at para 2(3).

Asylum-seekers and other persons who are 'destitute'

7.25 As noted above at para 7.7 the Asylum and Immigration Act 1996 removed from entitlement to public housing and social security assistance, people seeking political asylum. This prohibition had applied to people in the UK in breach of immigration control (eg, people who had overstayed their visa or people whose asylum application had been refused) since 1987.[31] As also noted above, as a consequence of the 1996 amendment a number of asylum-seekers became destitute and sought assistance under NAA 1948 s21 on the basis that they came within the 'any other circumstance' category. Their claims succeeded in *R v Hammersmith LBC ex p M*,[32] where the Court of Appeal nevertheless stressed that NAA 1948 s21 was not a 'safety net' provision on which anyone who is short of money and/or short of accommodation can rely'.[33]

7.26 The *Hammersmith* judgment caused not inconsiderable financial problems for a number of local authorities. A 1998 government white paper described the position thus:[34]

> The Court of Appeal judgment . . . meant that, without warning or preparation, local authority social services departments were presented with a burden which is quite inappropriate, which has become increasingly intolerable and which is unsustainable in the long term, especially in London, where the pressure on accommodation and disruption to other services has been particularly acute.

7.27 The government accordingly amended the community care legislation (including NAA 1948 s21) with the aim of ensuring that 'social services departments should not carry the burden of looking after healthy and able-bodied asylum-seekers'.[35] In future such 'able-bodied' asylum-seekers were to be provided for by a new organisation known as the National Asylum Support Service (NASS). The amendment was effected by the Immigration and Asylum Act (IAA) 1999 s116, which inserted into NAA 1948 s21 a new subsection (1A) namely:

> A person [subject to immigration control, including asylum-seekers] may not be provided with residential accommodation under subsection (1)(a) if his need for care and attention has arisen solely –
> (a) because he is destitute; or
> (b) because of the physical effects, or anticipated physical effects, of his being destitute.

30 LAC(93)10 Appendix 1 at para 2(6).

31 Lord Hoffman in *Westminster CC v National Asylum Support Service* [2002] UKHL 38; (2002) 5 CCLR 511 at 517–518 briefly recounts the legislative history curtailing social welfare entitlements of asylum-seekers and others in breach of immigration control.

32 This being a consolidated appeal, comprising *R v Hammersmith LBC ex p M; R v Lambeth LBC ex p P and X and R v Westminster CC ex p A* (1997)1 CCLR 85.

33 (1997)1 CCLR 85 at p 94K.

34 'Fairer, Faster and Firmer – A Modern Approach to Immigration and Asylum' Home Office 1998 (Cm 4018) para 8.14 – cited by Lord Hoffman in *Westminster CC v National Asylum Support Service* (2002) 5 CCLR 511 at 519C.

35 Cm 4018 at para 8.23.

7.28   NASS was provided with power to make provision for the support of all
destitute asylum-seekers and their dependants[36] – but (and importantly) in
deciding whether a person was eligible for support from NASS, Asylum
Support Regulations 2000[37] reg 6(4) required that account be taken of any
other support which is available to the person.

7.29   However, it became apparent that the amendment did not achieve its
objective of relieving social services authorities from the bulk of their obligations to asylum-seekers. As Lord Hoffman noted in *Westminster CC v
National Asylum Support Service*:[38]

> 29. What may have escaped notice in the aftermath of *ex p M*[39] was that
> the 1996 Act had brought into the scope of section 21 of the 1948 Act *two*
> distinct classes of asylum-seekers who would not have been entitled to
> Part III accommodation if the 1996 Act had not excluded them from the
> normal social security system. The first class were the able-bodied asylum-
> seekers who qualified solely because, being destitute, they were already
> or were likely to become in need of care and attention. This was the class
> highlighted in *ex p M*. I shall call them 'the able-bodied destitute', who
> came within section 21 solely because they were destitute. The second
> class were asylum-seekers who had some infirmity which required the
> local social services to provide them with care and attention, but who
> would not ordinarily have needed to be provided with accommodation
> under section 21 because it was available in other ways, for example,
> under the homelessness legislation. They would not have come within
> the section 21 duty because they would not have satisfied the third
> condition which I have quoted from the judgment of Hale LJ in *Wahid's*
> case[40] . . .

7.30   The problem highlighted by Lord Hoffman was that use of the word 'solely'
in the new NAA 1948 s21(1A) had the effect of only excluding the 'able-
bodied' destitute. The second class (which he referred to as the 'infirm
destitute') were able to claim assistance from social services authorities
under NAA 1948 s21, not 'solely' because of their destitution, but additionally because of their infirmity. And since they had access to such assistance
they were excluded from the NASS scheme by virtue of the above mentioned stipulation in the Asylum Support Regulations 2000. He accordingly held:[41]

> The present case has been argued throughout on the footing that [the
> applicant] has a need for care and attention which has not arisen solely
> because she is destitute but also (and largely) because she is ill. It is also
> common ground that she has no access to any accommodation in which

36   IAA 1999 s95.

37   SI No 704.

38   (2002) 5 CCLR 511 at 519E.

39   This being a consolidated appeal, comprising *R v Hammersmith LBC ex p M; R v
Lambeth LBC ex p P and X and R v Westminster CC ex p A* (1997) 1 CCLR 85.

40   Namely that 'the care and attention which is needed must not be available otherwise
than by the provision of accommodation under section 21': *R (Wahid) v Tower
Hamlets LBC* [2002] EWCA Civ 287; (2002) 5 CCLR 239 at [30].

41   [2002] UKHL 38; (2002) 5 CCLR 511 at [49].

she can receive care and attention other than by virtue of section 21 or under Part VI of the 1999 Act. The first question for your Lordships is whether in those circumstances she comes prima facie within section 21(1)(a) and, if so, the second is whether she is excluded by section 21(1A). In my opinion, the answers to these questions are yes and no respectively. The third question is whether the existence of a duty under section 21 excludes [the applicant] from consideration for asylum support. Again, in agreement with the Court of Appeal, I think that the answer is yes.

Nationality, Immigration and Asylum Act 2002

7.31   The Nationality, Immigration and Asylum Act (NIAA) 2002 (which entered into force in January 2003) is a response, in part , to the failure of the IAA 1999 to deter sufficient numbers of unlawful immigrants and asylum-seekers from entering the UK. In addition it sought to deal with what the government termed 'entitlement shopping' – namely 'individuals who move to the UK for the sole or main purpose of accessing residential accommodation and other services in preference to similar services in the EEA[42] country of origin'.[43]

7.32   NIAA 2002 s54 and Sch 3 prohibit local authorities from providing community care services, services under CA 1989 s17 (except for unaccompanied minors) and services under LGA 2000 s2 for:

- individuals with refugee status in other EEA countries,
- citizens of other EEA countries,
- failed asylum-seekers who have not co-operated with removal directions, and
- individuals who are unlawfully in the UK.

7.33   The NIAA 2002 does not therefore change the law concerning social services responsibilities to asylum-seekers (whose claims have not been determined) although it materially changes the obligations of NASS to asylum-seekers who failed to make their asylum claim 'as soon as reasonably practicable' after their arrival in the UK.[44]

7.34   The prohibition in NIAA 2002 s54 against social services providing care services does not apply where a failure to provide assistance would constitute a breach of the person's rights under the European Convention on Human Rights (ECHR) or a European Union (EU) Treaty. The Department of Health considers that the EU exception will mean that:

> EEA nationals who work or have worked in the UK, their families, self-employed and former self-employed EEA nationals, and students should be provided with social care services by councils if they are eligible for such

42   European Economic Area – this consists of the EU countries together with Iceland, Liechtenstein and Norway.

43   Department of Health 'Note of Clarification' para 4 concerning NIAA 2002 s54 which can be accessed at: www.doh.gov.uk/jointunit/delayeddischarge/ asylums54clarification11mar.

44   NIAA 2002 s55: See *R (Q and others) v Secretary of State for the Home Department* [2003] EWCA Civ 364; [2003] 2 All ER 905; [2003] 3 WLR 365.

care in order to protect their freedom of movement. They are entitled on the same basis as UK nationals.[45]

7.35   The scope of the ECHR exception was considered by the Court of Appeal in *R (Q and others) v Secretary of State for the Home Department*.[46] Although the case concerned a refusal by the Secretary of State to provide accommodation, the court's findings concerning the requirements of ECHR art 3 would apply with equal force to local authorities. The court held (among other things):[47]

...

(iv)   The burden of satisfying the Secretary of State that such support is necessary is on the applicant. Under article 3 the applicant must satisfy the Secretary of State that such support is necessary to avoid his or her being subjected to 'inhuman or degrading treatment'. The threshold is a high one.

(v)   The regime imposed on asylum-seekers who are denied support by reason of section 55(1) constitutes 'treatment' within article 3 because, although treatment implies something more than passivity on the part of the State, there is here more than passivity. Asylum-seekers cannot lawfully be removed but, while they remain, which they must do if they are to press their claims, they cannot lawfully work unless the Secretary of State gives them special permission to do so.

(vi)   The threshold is a high one but the ECHR said in paragraph 52 of its judgment in *Pretty*:[48]
    '52. As regards the types of "treatment" which fall within the scope of article 3 of the Convention, the Court's case law refers to 'ill-treatment' that attains a minimum level of severity and involves actual bodily injury or intense physical or mental suffering. Where treatment humiliates or debases an individual showing lack of respect for, or diminishing, his or her human dignity or arouses feelings of fear, anguish or inferiority capable of breaking an individual's moral and physical resistance, it may be characterised as degrading and also fall within the prohibition of article 3. The suffering which flows from naturally occurring illness, physical or mental, may be treatment, where it is, or risks being, exacerbated by treatment, whether flowing from conditions of detention, expulsion or other measures, for which the authorities can be held responsible.'

(vii)   Where the condition of an applicant verges on that described in *Pretty*, section 55(5) permits and section 6 of the Human Rights Act 1998 obliges the Secretary of State to arrange for the provision of support.

7.36   In *R (S, D and T) v Secretary of State for the Home Department*,[49] the Court of Appeal applied this test in a case concerning claimants to whom NIAA 2002 s54 and Sch 3 applied. It distinguished between two claimants,

---

45   Department of Health 'Note of Clarification' para 13 concerning s54 NIAA 2002.
46   [2003] EWCA Civ 364; [2003] 2 All ER 905; [2003] 3 WLR 365.
47   [2003] EWCA Civ 364 at [119].
48   *Pretty v UK* (2002) 35 EHRR 1.
49   [2003] EWCA Civ 1285; (2004) 7 CCLR 53.

finding that assistance was required in order to avoid a breach ECHR art 3 in one case and not the in relation to the other.

7.37   The first claimant, 'S' was sleeping rough on the streets and a doctor's report found symptoms of psychological disturbance and considerable malnutrition. He had to beg for money in order to eat, but received very little. He begged for shelter, but without success. His physical condition deteriorated, and a further medical report from the hospital where he had gone because of abdominal pains confirmed his loss of weight. He became unable to eat more than a few mouthfuls of food when it was available. In respect of this cliamant the Court of Appeal agreed with the first instance judge (Maurice Kay J)[50] that to 'fail to provide him with support at that stage debased him and diminished his human dignity in the manner described in *Pretty*'. The Court added that 'this does not mean that other cases have to reach the same or a similar degree of severity in order to engage article 3'.

7.38   The second claimant 'T' who was described as living a vagrant's life at Heathrow; he found it difficult to rest or sleep because of the noise and the light and because he would be moved on by the police. Any ablutions were confined to public lavatories and he was unable to wash his hair or his clothes or to bathe or shower. He developed a problem with his left eye and also a cough. He carried his belongings around with him in holdalls and became increasingly worried demoralised and humiliated. The Court of Appeal considered that his case had neither reached (nor was verging on) the inhuman or the degrading. 'He had shelter, sanitary facilities and some money for food. He was not entirely well physically, but not so unwell as to need immediate treatment'.

7.39   In *R (Zardasht) v Secretary of State for the Home Department*,[51] Newman J gave further guidance on when a person's condition fell below the human rights threshold: that in the majority of cases of asylum-seekers they would have no home, income, few or no possessions, little or no money, be strangers to the UK, have little or no English, be lonely, disconcerted, anxious about their welfare and vulnerable. Merely because some or all of those factors existed would not normally be sufficient to justify support. However in *R (Limbuela) v Secretary of State for the Home Department*,[52] and *R (Adam) v Secretary of State for the Home Department*,[53] a less onerous approach was taken.

Asylum and Immigration (Treatment of Claimants) Bill

7.40   The Asylum and Immigration (Treatment of Claimants) Bill 2004, if enacted, will provide for the withdrawal of support from failed asylum-seekers who refuse to leave the UK and who have children.

---

50 [2003] EWHC 1941 (Admin); (2004) 7 CCLR 32.
51 23 January 2004 (unreported).
52 (2004) *Times* 9 February.
53 17 February 2004 (unreported).

Powers and duties

7.41   The differences between statutory powers and duties are considered at para 1.3. Certain of the accommodation obligations placed on authorities by NAA 1948 s21 are discretionary (ie, powers), whereas the majority are mandatory (ie, duties); these two categories are dealt with separately below.

Duty

7.42   As a result of the secretary of state's direction contained in Appendix 1 to circular LAC(93)10[54] the social services authorities are under a duty to provide residential accommodation for all of the categories of persons described in NAA s21(1)(a), namely persons aged 18 or over who by reason of age, illness, disability or any other circumstance are in need of care and attention not otherwise available to them (but subject to the asylum and immigration exceptions discussed above).

7.43   The duty does not therefore extend to expectant or nursing mothers per se (although presumably they may nevertheless come within the ambit of 'any other circumstance'). The secretary of state's direction restricts the general duty to such persons who are either:

(a) ordinarily resident in the social services authority's area, or
(b) in urgent need of residential accommodation.

These terms are considered in greater detail in chapter 6.

Discharge of the duty to accommodate

7.44   In *R v Kensington and Chelsea RLBC ex p Kujtim*,[55] the Court of Appeal held that the duty can be treated as discharged if the applicant 'either unreasonably refuses to accept the accommodation provided or if, following its provision, by his conduct he manifests a persistent and unequivocal refusal to observe the reasonable requirements of the local authority in relation to the occupation of such accommodation'.

7.45   In *R (Patrick) v Newham LBC*[56] the applicant, who had mental health difficulties, was evicted on the grounds of neighbour nuisance. She sought assistance from the respondent authority who decided that she was intentionally homeless and in due course evicted her from the temporary accommodation it had provided. Shortly afterwards she started sleeping rough. Lawyers wrote on her behalf, enclosing a doctor's letter confirming her significant psychiatric problems and requested urgent accommodation. Three weeks later the authority replied stating that they had offered the applicant accommodation in a charitable hostel for people with mental health problems, but that she had refused this offer. The respondent authority sought to rely on the judgement in *Kujtim* – namely that she had

---

54   The full text of the Directions is at appendix B.
55   (1999) 2 CCLR 340 at 354I and see para 7.55 below.
56   (2001) 4 CCLR 48.

had unreasonably refused the accommodation offered. In rejecting this argument, Henriques J held:

> I do not myself consider that an apparent refusal of accommodation by a psychiatrically ill applicant puts an end to the respondent's continuing duty to provide Part III accommodation when she may well have been labouring under a complete misapprehension as to the nature of the accommodation.[57]

and

> If the respondent sought to put an end to its section 21 duties to provide accommodation, they ought in my judgment at the very least to have ensured that the applicant was legally represented when the offer was made to her to ensure not only that she understood what the offer was, both in terms of location and services offered, but also that she understood the legal consequences or potential legal consequences of refusing the offer.[58]

7.46 For the purposes of the Community Care (Delayed Discharge, etc) Act 2003 the responsibility of the local authority ceases (for reimbursement purposes) where appropriate services have been offered to the patient, and despite the authority's 'active encouragement' the patient has unreasonably refused to move to take up these services (see para 10.180 below).

Mental disorder

7.47 In relation to persons who are or who have been suffering from mental disorder (or for the purpose of the prevention of mental disorder) the duty to provide residential accommodation is specifically stated as including those with no settled residence who are in the authority's area.[59]

Alcoholic or drug-dependent

7.48 The secretary of state's direction specifically refers to persons who are alcoholic or drug-dependent as being persons for whom a social services authority is empowered to provide residential accommodation.[60] It would appear to follow that there is therefore a duty to provide residential accommodation for such persons when they are ordinarily resident in the authority's area and have been assessed as needing care and attention not otherwise available to them. NAA 1948 s21 sets out the full extent of the potential client group. The secretary of state cannot add new categories to the list; he or she can merely select who from this group is to qualify. As the direction states that social services authorities have a potential to accommodate all of the categories of persons specified in NAA 1948 s21(1)(a), it must therefore follow that this includes persons who are alcoholic or drug dependent.

---

57 (2001) 4 CCLR 48 at 53D.
58 (2001) 4 CCLR 48 at 53H.
59 LAC(93)10 Appendix 1 at para 2(3).
60 LAC(93)10 Appendix 1 at para 2(6).

Power

7.49   Social services authorities have the power (but not the duty) to provide residential accommodation for persons described in NAA 1948 s21(1)(a) and (aa) who are ordinarily resident in the area of another local authority, provided that the other authority agrees.[61]

7.50   The secretary of state's direction empowers (but does not direct) social services authorities to provide residential accommodation for expectant and nursing mothers.[62] There is not therefore a duty to accommodate such persons, although if the woman is over 17, some other circumstance would appear to include being an expectant or nursing mother; in which case she may then come within the ambit of NAA 1948 s21(1)(a) rather than NAA 1948 s21(1)(aa).

Ordinary residence

7.51   The nature of the obligation under NAA 1948 s21 is conditioned by the ordinary residence of the applicant (see chapter 6 where the meaning of ordinary residence is considered in detail). The position can however summarised as follows in the Table below.

Table 4: Residential accommodation – NAA 1948 s21

	Ordinarily resident	No settled residence	Not ordinarily resident
P O W E R	Expectant or nursing mothers (although they may also come within the ambit of 'any other circumstance' if over 18 – see column below)		Persons aged 18 or over who by reason of age, illness, disability or any other circumstance AND the other authority agrees
D U T Y	Persons aged 18 or over who by reason of age, illness, disability or any other circumstance (which includes a mental disorder of any description and alcohol or drug dependent persons).	Persons aged 18 or over who by reason of age, illness, disability or any other circumstance AND are living in the authority's area when the need arises	Persons aged 18 or over who by reason of age, illness, disability or any other circumstance AND who are in urgent need

61 LAC(93)10 Appendix 1 para 2(1)(a) and see NAA 1948 s24(4).
62 LAC(93)10 Appendix 1 para 3.

The nature of residential accommodation

7.52   The duty under NAA 1948 s21, is to make arrangements for providing
'residential accommodation'. While typically this will be in a care home,
the duty is not limited to the provision of such accommodation. As Hale LJ
observed in *R (Wahid) v Tower Hamlets LBC*:[63]

> It can no longer be assumed that a need for care and attention can only
> be properly met in an institutional setting. There are people who are
> undoubtedly in need of care and attention for whom local authority social
> services authorities wish to provide residential accommodation in ordinary
> housing.

Ordinary housing

7.53   In *R v Newham LBC ex p Medical Foundation for the Care of Victims of Torture
and others*[64] the respondent argued that under NAA 1948 s21 it was unlawful to provide residential accommodation in the form of simple bed
and breakfast accommodation, or indeed ordinary private sector flats or
houses. In rejecting this assertion, Moses J held that the word 'residential'
meant no more than 'accommodation where a person lives'. In his judgment, an authority might be obliged to provide accommodation under
NAA 1948 s21 notwithstanding that it had decided that the person did not
need board or any other services. A similar local authority submission was
rejected by Scott Baker J in *R v Bristol CC ex p Penfold*,[65] where he held that
NAA 1948 s21 can:

> In appropriate circumstances extend to the provision of 'normal'
> accommodation. 'Normal' housing can be provided . . . when it is
> the answer to a need which would otherwise have to be met by other
> community care services.

7.54   In *ex p Penfold*, the court further held that discharge by a housing authority
of its obligations under the homelessness legislation does not preclude the
need for a community care assessment. It follows therefore that a person
may be entitled to housing under the community care legislation notwithstanding that he or she has been refused such accommodation under the
homelessness legislation. In general however (as was the case in *ex p Penfold*), the mere fact that a person is entitled to a community care assessment
is no guarantee that their 'assessed need' will be sufficiently substantial to
warrant such a service.

7.55   A series of subsequent cases (notably *R v Wigan MBC ex p Tammadge*,[66]
R v Kensington and Chelsea RLBC ex p Kujtim,[67] and the 'asylum-seeker

---

63   (2002) 5 CCLR 239 at 248D.
64   (1998) 1 CCLR 227.
65   (1998) 1 CCLR 315; see also *R v Wigan MBC ex p Tammadge* (1998) 1 CCLR 581 at
       584A, where the respondent did not dispute that NAA 1948 s21 permitted the
       provision of 'normal' or 'bare accommodation, ie, without any board or services.
66   (1998) 1 CCLR 581.
67   (1999) 2 CCLR 340.

cases – referred to above) confirmed the view of the High Court that ordinary housing was capable of being provided under NAA 1948 s21. This acceptance may have been seen by some as a way of circumventing the traditional route of obtaining publicly provided housing accommodation – most notably under the Housing Act 1996. Thus an increasing number of applicants argued that they were entitled to more appropriate accommodation, because this need had been referred to in their community care assessments. Thus, by way of example in *R v Richmond LBC ex p H*,[68] the applicant was assessed as ready to return from supported (mental health) lodgings to ordinary housing in the community. His doctor wrote: 'He is requesting to get accommodation in a street house in a residential area which I believe is entirely justified considering his metal health needs'. The council failed to offer a suitable property. Newman J held that the description of the accommodation put forward was not mere preference but part of the individual applicant's needs. He accordingly made a mandatory order that the council (ie, social services) provide the 'accommodation in accordance with his lawfully assessed needs, including his psychological needs, within three months'.

7.56   A similar outcome was reached in *R (Batantu) v Islington LBC*,[69] where the social services department had assessed the applicant (who lived in a 12th floor property) as needing (1) a ground floor property with enough space to house him and his family; and (2) safe, secure and easily accessible accommodation. It then referred him to the housing department. Henriques J held that the duty to accommodate lay with social services, not the housing department; that since nine months had elapsed since the assessment and the case was an emergency, the court made a mandatory order to provide the accommodation.

7.57   Judicial disquiet about this trend was however expressed in *R (Wahid) v Tower Hamlets LBC*.[70] The case concerned a claimant who suffered from schizophrenia and lived in a two-bedroomed house with his wife and eight children. His community care assessment stated that 'mental stability can only be maintained by his transfer to a more congenial and relaxed environment'. Mr Wahid sought a judicial review to compel the provision of appropriate accommodation. In finding that there was no duty to provide this alternative accommodation under NAA 1948 s21 (and when giving leave) Stanley Burnton J was quoted as saying that this area of law cried out for 'comprehensive analysis and clarification by the Court of Appeal'.[71] This analysis and clarification was provided by the Court of Appeal judgment which upheld Stanley Burnton J's first instance decision.[72]

7.58   Hale LJ confirmed that ordinary housing could be provided under NAA 1948 s21 without the provision of any ancillary services, even though when

---

68   20 July 2000 (unreported), Admin Ct. Referred to in *R (Batantu) v Islington LBC* (2000) 4 CCLR 445 and as *R v Richmond LBC ex p T* January 2001 *Legal Action* 28.

69   (2001) 4 CCLR 445.

70   (2002) 5 CCLR 239.

71   October 2001 *Legal Action* 17.

72   *R (Wahid) v Tower Hamlets LBC* [2002] EWCA Civ 287; (2002) 5 CCLR 239.

originally enacted 'the kind of accommodation originally envisaged was in a residential home or hostel'. She gave as an example:

> ... small groups of people with learning disabilities who are able to live in ordinary houses with intensive social services support; or single people with severe mental illnesses who will not receive the regular medication and community psychiatric nursing they need unless they have somewhere to live.[73]

7.59 However the court held that the mere fact that ordinary housing could be provided under NAA 1948 s21 and the applicant was in need of this did not mean that a duty arose under NAA 1948 s21. In the opinion of Hale LJ:

> Such care and attention as the claimant did need as a result of his illness was being met by his wife and other members of the family together with the community mental health team. He was free of hallucinations and happier than he had been for a long time. The family does have a housing problem, alleviation of which would have a beneficial effect upon the claimant's mental health. But the housing problem is the family's rather than the claimant's alone. The claimant's problem is his fragile mental health. While together they might sometimes give rise to a need for care and attention, [the social services authority] was entitled to conclude that this was not so in this case.[74]

7.60 In the court's opinion (and that of the first instance judge) the case could be distinguished from *Batantu* (above) since in that case it had been accepted that the family's unsatisfactory housing situation was likely to have been one of the factors, which maintained the applicant's psychiatric illness;[75] that the local authority had actually assessed the need for accommodation and the situation was urgent – whereas in *Wahid* the local authority had not assessed accommodation as being an eligible need and in the court's opinion the need was not urgent.[76]

7.61 Hale LJ concluded by highlighting a significant additional hurdle that applicants seeking ordinary housing will have to surmount; namely NAA 1948 s21(8). It meant, she noted, that:

> Nothing in section 21 allows, let alone requires, a local social services authority to make any provision authorised or required to be made, whether by them or by any other authority, by or under any enactment other than Part Ill of the 1948 Act. The asylum-seekers succeeded because there was no other power, let alone duty, to provide them with the care needed to sustain life and health. There is power to meet ordinary housing needs, either through the procedures for allocating social housing under Part VI of the Housing Act 1996, or through the provisions for assisting and accommodating the homeless under Part VII of that Act.

7.62 On one reading, NAA 1948 s21(8) could be interpreted as prohibiting the provision of ordinary housing (under NAA 1948 s21(1)) to anyone not

---

73 (2002) 5 CCLR 239 at 248C.
74 (2002) 5 CCLR 239 at 249B.
75 (2002) 5 CCLR 239 at 246K per Pill LJ.
76 *R (Wahid) v Tower Hamlets LBC* [20001] EWHC Admin 641; (2001) 4 CCLR 455 at 465D.

specifically excluded from accessing housing under the Housing Act 1996. It is clear that this was not the Court of Appeal's interpretation (for otherwise it would pose an insuperable barrier rather than mere 'hurdle'). In *R v North and East Devon Health Authority ex p Coughlan*,[77] the Court of Appeal considered NAA 1948 s21(8) from the perspective of the provision of local authority funded nursing care (see para 10.75 below) and concluded that the section 'should not be regarded as preventing a local authority from providing any health services' – albeit that the court considered that NAA 1948 s21(8) made a material distinction between NHS services and other services (eg, housing). However the approach adopted by the Court of Appeal in *Coughlan* is a useful guide: arguably therefore where a housing department has resolved that a person does not qualify for housing (eg, because of intentional homelessness) or does not qualify for urgent rehousing (as in *Batantu*) then whatever general powers there may have been under the Housing Act 1996, will be deemed to have been determined, such that the authority will no longer be 'authorised or required to provide the accommodation by or under any other enactment'.

7.63   The interface between local authorities' community care and housing obligations is further considered at chapter 17 below.

Accommodation in care homes

7.64   As noted above, the duty under NAA 1948 s21 is generally discharged by social services authorities making arrangements for the provision of accommodation in care homes. This accommodation may be provided by:

a) the social services authority itself;[78]
b) another social services authority;[79]
c) a voluntary organisation;[80] or
d) a private for reward provider.[81]

7.65   A key aim of the community care reforms was the promotion of a flourishing independent sector (providing services such as residential accommodation) alongside good quality public services.[82] To encourage social services authorities to contract with the private sector, they were initially required to spend 85 per cent of their special transitional grant (STG)[83] on the purchase of non-local authority services.

77 [2000] 2 WLR 622; [2000] 3 All ER 850; (1999) 2 CCLR 285, CA.
78 NAA 1948 s21(3).
79 NAA 1948 s21(3).
80 NAA 1948 s26(1).
81 NAA 1948 s26(1).
82 White Paper *Caring for People* (1989) para 1.11.
83 The Treasury grant which was paid to compensate local authorities for the transfer to them of the previous Department of Social Security responsibility for funding residential and nursing care. The STG was paid for the first six years after April 1993; from 1 April 1999 the compensation monies have been added to the general block funding.

7.66 In *R v Wandsworth LBC ex p Beckwith*,[84] a proposal by the respondent council to close all its residential care homes for elderly people was challenged by an elderly resident on the ground that the council was under a legal duty under NAA 1948 ss21 and 26 to maintain some accommodation for the elderly under its own management. The House of Lords rejected the argument. Provided there is sufficient residential accommodation in the local authority's area, there is no requirement that any be actually provided by the authority; it can consist entirely of arrangements made with voluntary organisations or other persons. Although LAC(93)10 para 4 states that authorities are required to maintain some public provision, this was, in the Lords' judgment 'simply wrong'.

Duties to care home proprietors

7.67 The courts have proved resistant to care home proprietors' claims concerning the inadequate fees they receive from local authorities[85] – suggesting that these are not so much public law issues as 'fiercely contested private law' actions.[86] Thus in *R v Cumbria CC ex p Cumbria Professional Care Ltd*,[87] it was held that the council's preference for its own in-house care services and its failure to enter into block contracts with private sector respite care providers was not unlawful; did not breach its obligations under the or the Public Service Contract Regulations 1993[88] or EEC Directive 92/50 article 1 or its general duty to promote a 'mixed economy' of care. In *R (Birmingham Care Consortium) v Birmingham CC*[89] a challenge that home care fees were insufficiently high to enable residents to exercise a reasonable choice of accommodation under the National Assistance Act 1948 (Choice of Accommodation) Directions 1992 was likewise dismissed – so too in *R v Coventry CC ex p Coventry Heads of Independent Care Establishments and others*[90] was a classic public law claim[91] by care home proprietors challenging the fees paid by the local authorities.

The regulation of care homes

7.68 The following is a summary of the care home regulatory framework, focusing on the issues of relevance to the provision of community care services.

---

84 [1996] 1 All ER 129; [1996] 1 WLR 60, HL.

85 In *Douce v Staffordshire CC* [2003] EWCA Civ 506; (2002) 5 CCLR 347 the court was prepared to consider 'arguable' that the authority's (then) regulatory functions under the Registered Homes Act 1984 could give rise to a duty of care to care home proprietors – but on the facts the claim (in tort) was rejected.

86 In *R v Cumbria CC ex p Cumbria Professional Care Ltd* (2000) 3 CCLR 79, per Turner J at 97K.

87 (2000) 3 CCLR 79.

88 SI No 3228.

89 [2002] EWHC 2188 (Admin); (2002) 5 CCLR 600.

90 (1998) 1 CCLR 379.

91 Alleging, among other things, a failure to consult, a failure to consider relevant factors and that the local authority was acting 'beyond its powers.

For detailed analysis and guidance on the registration regime reference should be made to a specialist text on the subject[92] and the websites of the Commission for Social Care Inspection (CSCI) in England and the Care Standards Inspectorate for Wales (CSIW).[93]

Commission for Social Care Inspection

7.69   The regulation of care homes in England and Wales is now governed by the Care Standards Act (CSA) 2000. The CSA 2000 repealed the Registered Homes Act (RHA) 1984 which had previously been the principal statute regulating residential care homes and nursing homes (as they were then termed) and a plethora of regulations and 'National Minimum Standards'.[94]

7.70   On 1 April 2002 responsibility for the registration and inspection of services provided by care homes (as residential care and nursing homes are now termed) became the responsibility of the National Care Standards Commission (NCSC) in England and the Care Standards Inspectorate for Wales (CSIW) in Wales. Previously registration and inspection had been a local authority responsibility (for independent residential care homes) and a health authority responsibility (for nursing homes). In addition the NCSC/CSIW assumed responsibility for (among other things) the inspection and registration of local authority care homes and domiciliary care agencies. In April 2004 the CSCI took over the responsibilities of the NCSC in England as a result of the enactment of the Health and Social Care (Community Health and Standards) Act 2003 s102.[95] The CSCI/CSIW have extensive enforcement powers and operate a complaints procedure through which service users and family members can lodge complaints about registered services.

7.71   It is a criminal offence for any person to carry on, or manage, a care home without being registered.[96] CSA 2000 s3 defines a care home as follows:

> 3(1) For the purposes of this Act, an establishment is a care home if it provides accommodation, together with nursing or personal care, for any of the following persons.

---

92 See for instance P Ridout, *Care Standards: A Practical Guide* (Jordans, 2003).

93 The CSCI website is at www.csci.org.uk/ and the CSIW website at www.wales.gov.uk/subisocialpolicycarestandards/index.htm. The Welsh site was (at the time of writing: April 2004) in the 'early stages of development'.

94 The principal regulations in England are the Care Homes Regulations 2001 SI No 3965 and in Wales the Care Homes (Wales) Regulations 2002 WSI 2002 No 324 (W 37). The regulations and standards in England can be accessed at www.carestandards.org.uk/nation+min.+standards/default.htm and in Wales at www.wales.gov.uk/subisocialpolicycarestandards/content/regulationsfinal-e.htm.

95 See also para 19.62 below.

96 CSA 2000 s1.

(2) They are –
    (a) persons who are or have been ill;[97]
    (b) persons who have or have had a mental disorder;[98]
    (c) persons who are disabled[99] or infirm;
    (d) persons who are or have been dependent on alcohol or drugs.
(3) But an establishment is not a care home if it is –
    (a) a hospital;
    (b) an independent clinic; or
    (c) a children's home,
or if it is of a description excepted by regulations.

Personal care

7.72   Establishments that cater for such persons as are listed in CSA 2000 s3(2), by the provision of accommodation 'together with nursing or personal care' must be registered with the CSCI/CSIW. Under the RHA 1984 s1, 'board' was required, in addition to 'personal care' however under the CSA 2000 this is no longer the case. Personal care is not defined, although CSA 2000 s121(3) states that the expression 'does not include any prescribed activity' and CSA 2000 s121(9) says that the care that is provided must include 'assistance with bodily functions (eg, toileting, eating) where such assistance is required'.

7.73   The CSA 2000 does not define 'personal care'[100] and it remains to be determined whether in that Act it bears the same meaning as that given to the same phrase in the RHA 1984, although it would appear that Parliament intended it to be so construed.[101] In *Harrison v Cornwall CC*,[102] the Court of Appeal considered that the concept of 'personal care' was wider than the mere provision of assistance with bodily functions and embraced 'care in many forms; emotional or psychiatric as well as physical'.[103] The

---

97 Under CSA 2000 s121(1) 'illness' includes injury.

98 Under CSA 2000 s121(1) 'mental disorder' means mental illness, arrested or incomplete development of mind, psychopathic disorder, and any other disorder or disability of mind.

99 CSA 2000 s121(2) provides that, for the purposes of the CSA 2000, a person is disabled if (i) his sight, hearing or speech is substantially impaired; (ii) he has a mental disorder; or (iii) he is physically substantially disabled by any illness, any impairment present since birth, or otherwise.

100 CSA 2000 s121(3) states that the expression 'does not include any prescribed activity and section 121(9), that an establishment is not a care home for the purposes of this Act unless the care which it provides includes assistance with bodily functions where such assistance is required.

101 See for instance the statement of the Minister of State, Department of Health (Mr John Hutton) House of Commons Standing Committee G Tuesday 4 July 2000 (Hansard) 'I remind the Committee that the proposed requirements are the same as those in the Registered Homes Act 1984, which were clarified by the *Harrison v Cornwall County Council* judgment with which the Committee is familiar . . . we intend that the homes that are currently required to register under the 1984 Act should be required to register under the Bill.

102 (1991) 11 BMLR 21; 90 LGR 81.

103 The RHA 1984, however (at section 20) defined 'personal care' as meaning care which includes assistance with bodily functions 'where such assistance is required' and the words in parenthesis do not appear in the CSA 2000.

Department of Health[104] and Welsh Assembly[105] guidance on the CSA 2000 however define personal care as care requiring:

- assistance with bodily functions such as feeding, bathing, and toileting;
- care which falls just short of assistance with bodily functions, but still involving physical and intimate touching, including activities such as helping a person get out of a bath and helping them to get dressed.

7.74　The guidance has been the subject of criticism[106] and it has been suggested that its definition of personal care is considerably narrower than that under the RHA 1984. In other contexts the phrase 'bodily functions' has been held not to include 'general counselling and support'[107] but physical contact is not necessary essential.[108] It may include the reading to or guiding a person with a severe visual impairment,[109] or the provision of any similar assistance in relation to the 'operation of the senses' for instance the provision of an interpreter to a severely deaf person.[110]

7.75　The mere fact that accommodation and care services are provided by separate legal entities (as may happen in 'supported housing' for instance – see para 17.55) does not in itself mean that the unit is not a care home. The Act speaks of an 'establishment' providing the accommodation 'together with' care services.

7.76　In *Alternative Futures Ltd v National Care Standards Commission*,[111] the Care Standards Tribunal held that whether an establishment was a 'care home' for the purposes of the CSA 2000 was, in borderline cases, a difficult question for which no single factor could be considered determinative. Thus the fact that the care and accommodation are provided by separate companies was not conclusive (especially if these services remained closely co-ordinated) nor was the level of personal care provided,[112] nor was the provision of tenancies to the residents. In the tribunal's view, if there was one issue more important than others, it was the issue of choice. Where it is was alleged that accommodation and care services are delivered separately, it is important that service users are genuinely able to choose who it is that provides them with their personal care. Likewise where a

---

104　*Supported Housing and Care Homes Guidance on Regulation*, August 2002.

105　*Clarification of the Registration Requirements for Supported Housing and Extra Care Schemes under the Care Standards Act 2000 Guidance* August 2002.

106　See for instance the criticisms voiced in *Alternative Futures Ltd v National Care Standards Commission* [2002] 101–111 NC at paras 59 and 78. The judgment is accessible at www.carestandardstribunal/cstdecisions0101_0111.htm.

107　*R v North Cornwall DC ex p Singer* (1993) *Times* 12 January 1994.

108　*Mallinson v Secretary of State for Social Security* [1994] 2 All ER 295; [1994] 1 WLR 630.

109　[1994] 2 All ER 296.

110　*Secretary of State for Social Security v Fairey (aka Halliday)* [1997] 1 WLR 799; [1997] 3 All ER 844.

111　Accessible at www.carestandardstribunal/cstdecisions0101_0111.htm – the case is subject to a pending appeal.

112　As the tribunal noted: 'the level of personal care is not on its own the determining factor. We agree . . . that section 121(9) must not be read to mean that where bodily assistance is provided or required then registration as a care home is required'.

home is seeking to de-register on the basis that it has become an independent living scheme, the organisation has to demonstrate that it has genuinely altered its operation to promote service user choice and in particular that service users are able to exercise an informed choice to move to the new arrangement.

Care homes providing nursing

7.77   Under the RHA 1984 quite separate regimes existed for the registration and inspection of residential care homes and nursing homes – albeit that it was possible to have 'dual registration'. Under the CSA 2000 (and the regulations thereto) the CSCI/CSIW has power when issuing a certificate of registration to impose conditions, including the categories of person the home can accommodate – for instance authorising the accommodation of people requiring nursing care.[113] The current terminology therefore for what formerly was called a nursing home is a 'care home with nursing'.

Registration criteria

7.78   As with the RHA 1984, where different persons are responsible for the carrying on and the management of a care home they must both be registered.[114] The CSA 2000 sets out a broad range of regulation making powers covering, among other matters, the management, staff, premises and conduct of social care and independent healthcare establishments and agencies. The regulations[115] list and describe in some detail the requirements that must be satisfied in order for an establishment to be registered and to retain its registration. These include:

- that the registered provider and manager be 'fit' to carry on the running of the home (together with an explanation as to what this entails – regs 7–10);
- that the care home is conducted to promote and make proper provision for the health and welfare of service users (including where appropriate their treatment, education and supervision – regs 12–13);
- that accommodation should not be provided until (in so far as it is practicable) the service user has been assessed by a suitably trained person; and the registered person has obtained a copy of the assessment; and there has been appropriate consultation regarding the assessment with the service user or his or her representative; and the home has confirmed in writing to the service user that having regard to the assessment it is suitable for the purpose of meeting his or her needs in respect of his health and welfare; and that the assessment of the service user's needs is kept under review; and revised as and when necessary (reg 14);

---

113 National Care Standards Commission (Registration) Regulations 2001 SI No 3969, reg 9(f).

114 Care Homes Regulations 2001 reg 2 describes the person carrying on the home (ie, the person in ultimate control) as the 'registered provider': this of course can now include a local authority.

115 Principally the Care Homes Regulations 2001 SI No 3965.

- that after consultation with the service user or his or her representative (in so far as it is practicable) a written plan be prepared as to how the service user's health and welfare needs are to be met and this plan be available to the service user[116] and kept under review (reg 15);
- that facilities and services are provided in accordance with the care home's written statement (under reg 4). These include such matters as telephone facilities; furniture, laundry, kitchen equipment, wholesome and nutritious food, the maintenance of satisfactory standards of hygiene, secure deposit arrangement for money and valuables, arrangements for social, recreational, religious and community activities (reg 16).

7.79   Additionally the regulations address such issues as the proper keeping of records, the adequacy of staffing arrangements, staff training and procedures for their concerns to be registered; complaints procedures for service users (see para 19.65 below).

7.80   All care homes are liable to a minimum of two inspections a year by the NCSC/CSIW; such inspections may be unannounced.[117]

National minimum standards

7.81   CSA 2000 s23 gives power to the secretary of state/Welsh Assembly to publish 'national minimum standards' which the National Care Standards Commission must take into account when making its decisions. These standards form the basis for judgments made by the Commission regarding registration and the imposition of conditions for registration, variation of any conditions and enforcement of compliance with the Care Standards Act 2000 and associated regulations, including proceedings for cancellation of registration or prosecution.

7.82   Both the Department of Health and the Welsh Assembly have now published a series of national minimum standards, which in effect flesh out the basic requirement of the regulations. Although not legally binding they must be taken into account by the CSCI/CSIW when making decisions about whether or not the regulations have been complied with (eg, whether to approve a registration or to cancel a registration). The standards are revised from time to time. As at April 2004, national minimum standards had been approved in England in respect of the following categories:[118]

---

116 A failure by a local authority to provide a care home with a copy of the service user's care plan will constitute maladministration: see complaint 99/B/3078 against Kent, March 2001, para 97.

117 National Care Standards Commission (Fees and Frequency of Inspections) Regulations 2001 SI No 3980, reg 6.

118 The national minimum standards in England can be accessed at www.csci.org.uk/information_for_service_providers/national_minimum_standards/default.htm, and in Wales at www.wales.gov.uk/subisocialpolicycarestandards/content/regulationsfinal-e.htm.

- Care homes for older people
- Adult placements
- Care homes for adults 18–65
- Domiciliary care
- Nurses agencies
- Children's homes
- Adoption
- Residential family centres
- Fostering services
- Boarding schools
- Residential special schools
- Accommodation of students under 18 by Further Education Colleges.

Domiciliary care agencies

7.83 The CSA 2000 brings domiciliary care agencies (including those run by local authorities) within the CSCI/CSIW regulatory framework.[119] These provisions came into effect in England on 1 April 2003 and in Wales on 1 March 2004. See para 8.13 where the registration obligations for such agencies is considered further.

Choice of accommodation

7.84 The National Assistance Act 1948 (Choice of Accommodation) Directions 1992 constitute one of the few examples of genuine choice that individuals have in relation to their community care services. In general service user's wishes and preferences must be taken into account – but not necessarily satisfied. However, when they are engaged, the Choice of Accommodation Directions give service users a legal right to choose the setting of their care.

7.85 The 1992 directions have been the subject of amendment in England[120] as a result of the deferred payments scheme[121] (see para 12.34) and draft revised guidance on the amended directions was issued in October 2003,[122] referred to in the following section as the '2003 draft guidance'.

---

119 By CSA 2000 s11 it is a criminal offence for a person to carry on or manage a domiciliary care agency without being registered in respect of it.

120 Accessible at www.dh.gov.uk/PublicationsAndStatistics/Legislation/ DirectionsFromSecretaryState/fs/en. At the time of writing (April 2004) no amendment has as yet been made in Wales to the Directions and circular WOC12/93 accordingly remains current albeit draft guidance exists at www.wales.gov.uk/ subisocialpolicy/content/consultations/choice-e.htm.

121 Direction 4 of the 1992 Directions was repealed by the National Assistance Act 1948 (Choice of Accommodation) (Amendment) (England) Directions 2001. The revised text of relevance to '*Preferred accommodation outside local authority's usual limit*' – is now found in the National Assistance (Residential Accommodation) (Additional Payments and Assessment of Resources) (Amendment) (England) Regulations 2001 SI No 3441. The guidance accompanying the 1992 Directions was revised as a result of LAC(2001)29. The revised Directions, the 2001 regulations and the revised guidance is contained at appendix B below.

122 Consultation for which closed on 15 December 2003.

7.86   Once a social services authority has assessed a person as eligible for accommodation under NAA 1948 s21, then it is obliged to make arrangements for accommodating in a care home that person at a place of his or her choice (if any choice of preferred accommodation has been indicated) provided that the conditions specified in direction 3 of the National Assistance 1948 (Choice of Accommodation) Directions 1992 (as amended) are satisfied. The directions are set out in appendix B below. The conditions which need to be satisfied are:

- the preferred accommodation appears to the authority to be suitable[123] in relation to his or her needs as assessed by it;
- the cost of making the arrangements at the preferred accommodation would not require the authority to pay more than it would usually expect to pay having regard to the assessed needs;
- the preferred accommodation is available; and
- the persons in charge of the preferred accommodation will provide it subject to the authority's usual terms and conditions, having regard to the nature of the accommodation, for providing accommodation for such a person under National Assistance Act 1948 Part III.

7.87   The preferred accommodation must be in either England, Wales or Scotland.[124] Health and Social Care Act 2001 s56 provides regulatory powers to the secretary of state to make provision for cross border placements by local authorities in Scotland, Northern Ireland, the Channel Islands and the Isle of Man, however at the time of writing (April 2004) the only regulations made concern the Isles of Scilly. It is possible that the restriction of funded accommodation to Great Britain could be vulnerable to an EU law challenge as constituting an unreasonable restriction on the free movement of services.[125]

7.88   A local authority will be guilty of maladministration if it fails to explain clearly to clients and their carers what their rights are under the directions, or if it puts the onus on them to find accommodation at an acceptable cost to the authority.[126]

---

123 Accommodation will not necessarily be unsuitable simply because it fails to conform with the authority's preferred model of provision – see 2003 draft guidance para 3.5.2.

124 National Assistance Act 1948 (Choice of Accommodation) Directions 1992 direction 2, extended to Scotland by National Assistance Act 1948 (Choice of Accommodation) (Amendment) Directions 1993. Pending approval of the '2003 draft guidance', guidance on the 1992 Directions is contained in LAC(92)27 (WOC 12/93 in Wales and WOC 47/93 in relation to the 1993 Scottish amendment).

125 See, for instance, article 49 (ex article 59) of the Treaty establishing the European Community which prohibits restrictions on the freedom to provide services within the Community. A reported case challenging the discriminatory impact of the restriction in Great Britain on access to care home accommodation ((1996) *Independent* 4 March) was – it appears – withdrawn it appears as a result of the death of the applicant.

126 Complaint 97/A/3218 against Merton LBC, 25 October 1999.

More expensive accommodation

7.89   Where a person's preferred accommodation is more expensive than the accommodation proposed by the authority, then he or she may nevertheless require the authority to support him or her in that accommodation, provided either:

a) a third party agrees to top-up the difference – and that third party can reasonably be expected to pay the sum for the duration of the proposed placement[127] (in this category the directions exclude residents from topping up their own fees[128] and also residents' spouses); or[129]

b) the resident is subject to the 12-weeks property disregard – during which the resident can top-up his or her own fees (see para 12.33a); or

c) the resident has entered into a deferred payment scheme with the local authority under the Health and Social Care Act 2001 s53 – in which case the resident can top-up his or her own fees (see para 12.34).

7.90   The amount of top-up is calculated as the difference between –

a) the cost which the authority would usually expect to pay for the accommodation having regard to the person's assessed need, and

b) the full standard rate for the accommodation.[130]

7.91   The 2003 draft guidance emphasises that it is the usual cost that must be used for comparative purposes.[131] In the guidance accompanying the original 1992 directions it was stated that 'there may be circumstances where an authority might judge the need to move to another part of the country to be an integral part of the individual's assessed needs'[132] and in such cases the authority would have to pay the 'usual' cost applicable for that area. Although this advice is absent from the 2003 draft guidance – authorities must remain under such an obligation in such cases.

7.92   The type of care may also affect the usual cost, for instance the cost an authority might usually expect to pay for respite care might be different from its usual cost for permanent care.[133] Local authorities are not, however, obliged to accommodate service users in the least expensive available accommodation commensurate with that person's assessed needs.[134]

---

127 2003 draft guidance para 4.5.4.

128 This exclusion was confirmed in *R v East Sussex CC ex p Ward* (2000) 3 CCLR 132.

129 Since 1 October 2001 a resident's spouse cannot enter into a topping up agreement (National Assistance (Residential Accommodation) (Additional Payments and Assessment of Resources) (Amendment) (England) Regulations 2001 SI No 3441, regulation 4) however liable relatives who were making maintenance contributions to the care costs of their spouses (under NAA 1948 s42 – see para 12.79) prior to 1 October 2001 may continue to do so. There is, however, nothing in principle to stop a resident transferring capital to a third party to enable that person to make the top-up payments (provided the transfer does not amount to a deprivation designed to reduce the residents liability for residential fees (see para 12.44 below).

130 LAC(2001)29 Annex 1 para 10; as specified in NAA 1948 s22(2) or pursuant to NAA 1948 s26(2) and (4).

131 2003 draft guidance para 3.5.4.

132 LAC(92)27 para 7.6.

133 2003 draft guidance para 3.5.8.

134 LAC (2001) 29 Annex 1 para 4.

7.93   The local ombudsman has stressed that since councils have a discretion to exceed the normal amount that they are willing to contribute to the costs of residential care, they must have regard to the particular circumstances of each case.[135]

7.94   The right to exercise choice over accommodation extends not only to prospective residents, but also to existing residents who wish to move to different or more expensive accommodation.[136]

7.95   While the Choice of Accommodation Directions enable an individual to opt for more expensive accommodation (and to enter into a topping-up agreement) this only applies if the usual cost figure used by the authority would genuinely secure the person a placement in a less expensive home which met his or her assessed needs (including in certain situations psychological needs).[137] The directions do not mean that authorities may set an arbitrary ceiling on the amount they are willing to contribute towards residential care and require third parties routinely to make up the difference. If challenged, an authority should be able to demonstrate that its usual cost is sufficient to allow it to provide people with the level of service they could reasonably expect if the possibility of third party contributions did not exist.[138] The 2003 draft guidance explains (at para 3.5.5.):

> Individual residents should not be asked to pay more towards their accommodation because of market inadequacies or commissioning failures. For example, where an individual has not expressed a preference for more expensive accommodation, but there are not sufficient places at a given time at the council's usual cost, the council should make a placement in more expensive accommodation and meet the cost difference itself. Only when an individual has expressed a preference for more expensive accommodation than a council would usually expect to pay, can a third party or the resident be asked for a top-up (see paragraph 4.1). From time to time, due to unforeseen circumstance, there may be insufficient care home places available to councils (at the usual cost) to meet the current assessed care needs of supported residents. In these circumstances, neither the resident nor a third party should be asked to contribute more than the resident would normally be expected to contribute. That is, in these circumstances, councils should make up the difference between the resident's assessed contribution and the actual care home fees.

7.96   There is a duty on social services authorities to explain to residents and prospective residents (and their carers) their rights under the direction.[139] In addition, authorities are advised to have a written agreement with the resident, third party and the person providing the accommodation when they seek to exercise their right to use more expensive accommodation. It is suggested that the agreement specifies:[140]

135   Complaint 97/A/3218 against Merton LBC 25 October 1999.
136   2003 draft guidance para 5.1.
137   *R v Avon CC ex p M* [1994] 2 FCR 259, QBD.
138   LAC(2001)29 Annex 1 para 3.
139   2003 draft guidance para 8.1.
140   LAC(2001)29 Annex 1 para 13.

- failure to keep up top-up payments will normally result in the resident having to move to other accommodation. (Where resident's top-ups are being made against the value of property subject to a deferred payments agreement, a council will have assured itself from the outset that top-up payments are viable and recoverable when the home is sold);
- an increase in the resident's income will not necessarily lessen the need for a top-up contribution, since the resident's own income will be subject to charging by the council in the normal way;[141]
- a rise in the accommodation's fees will not automatically be shared equally between council, resident (if making a top-up), and third party; and
- if the accommodation fails to honour its contractual conditions, the council must reserve the right to terminate the contract.

Where the preferred care home is full

7.97   Not infrequently the care home of choice will be full, and the question arises as to what arrangements should then be made for the service user. The situation is generally of most concern to the statutory agencies, if the patient is in hospital awaiting discharge to such a home. The 2003 draft guidance para 3.5.9 states as follows:

> Waiting for the preferred care home should not mean that the person's care needs are not met in the interim or that they wait in a setting unsuitable for their assessed needs, and this includes an acute hospital bed, until the most suitable or preferred accommodation becomes available. In view of the Community Care (Delayed Discharges, etc) Act 2003, councils should have contingency arrangements in place, that address the likelihood that an individual's preferred accommodation will not always be readily available. These arrangements should meet the needs of the individual and sustain or improve their level of independence. For some, the appropriate interim arrangement could be an enhanced care package at home.

7.98   The 2003 Department of Health hospital discharge guidance '*Discharge from hospital: pathway, process and practice*' (see para 10.157) states at para 7.6:

> If admission to a care home is agreed as the best option, any patient who is being placed with public support is able to choose a home under the *Direction on choice*. The directions are currently undergoing a review to update them in the light of forthcoming legislation and further information will be available.
> Because residential placements can be delayed considerably while people wait for a place in their home of choice to become available, transition or interim placement should be considered when the first choice of home is not available. If the interim placement meets a person's needs, it is acceptable for a person to move from an acute setting to a transitional placement until a permanent/alternative choice becomes available.
> In circumstances where waiting for a care home placement is causing

141 See chapter 12.

an unacceptable delay in care transfer, the following processes should be put in place:

- Patients and carers should be informed about the possibility of an interim placement as soon as possible. It is important that people understand that it is inappropriate for them to remain on an acute ward indefinitely while they are waiting for admission to a care home.
- The interim or transitional placement must be able to meet the assessed care needs of the patient and they must receive active help to move on to the home of their choice when a place is available.
- There must be support (such as an independent advisory service) to patients and their carers in making important decisions. Self-funders should also be offered support in making such choices.
- Practitioners should be signed up to the use of transitional placements with appropriate protocols.
- Trusts should have in place agreed policies and procedures to address situations in which patients and their families refuse to move from an acute bed to another setting.

The guidance stresses that when a person's acute episode of ill-health has been treated, it is not appropriate for them to remain on an acute hospital ward. This is providing they are clinically fit and have been assessed as safe to transfer. Remaining in an acute ward has disadvantages for the patient and capacity of the whole system.

The *Direction on choice* states that where an individual expresses a preference for a particular type of accommodation within the UK, the placing local authority has to accommodate this request, provided that:

- the accommodation is suitable in relation to the individual's assessed needs;
- to do so would [not] cost the local authority more than it would usually expect to pay for someone with the individual's assessed needs;
- the accommodation is available;
- the person in charge of the accommodation is willing to provide accommodation subject to the local authority's usual terms and conditions for such accommodation.

7.99   For a consideration of local authority liability for reimbursement payments under the Community Care (Delayed Discharge, etc) Act 2003 – where a patient is refusing to leave hospital because the preferred care home is not available, see para 10.180 below.

NHS funded nursing home placements

7.100   Patients in NHS-funded nursing homes do not have a statutory right of choice; the government expects, however, that before any placement there will be 'considerable consultation with the patient and his or her family and [hospitals should] take account of the patient's wishes'.[142]

---

142 Statement of the Minister for Health, John Bowis, to Health Committee, recorded at para 79 of *First Report into Long-Term Care* (HMSO 1995).

Other aspects

National Assistance Act 1948 s47: local authority's removal powers

7.101   Environmental health departments have power under NAA 1948 s47 to apply to a magistrates' court for an order removing chronically sick, disabled or elderly persons to more suitable accommodation.[143]

7.102   The application for removal requires that the vulnerable person or 'some person in charge of him' be given seven days' notice of the intended application, unless the case is urgent, in which case an ex parte application is permitted to a single justice.[144]

7.103   The requirements for a removal order to be made are:

1. that the respondent is either suffering from grave, chronic disease or being aged, infirm or physically incapacitated is living in unsanitary conditions. Thus the 'unsanitary conditions' requirement does not apply to persons suffering from grave or chronic disease.
2. is 'unable to devote to himself and is not receiving from other persons proper care and attention' and;
3. the community physician has provided an appropriate certificate.[145]

7.104   Where the court is satisfied it can order the removal of the person concerned to a suitable hospital or other place[146] for a period of up to three months and the order can be renewed indefinitely. Inappropriate use of the provision has the clear potential to violate the European Convention on Human Rights (ECHR) (see para 19.172 below): its scope extends beyond the categories of persons specified in ECHR art 5(1)(e) and of particular concern is the possibility of removal for a lengthy period as a result of a hearing at which the person may not be present based on the authority of limited medical evidence.

National Assistance Act 1948 s48: duty to protect property

7.105   Where a person is provided with accommodation under NAA 1948 s21 or removed from their home by the local authority using its powers under NAA 1948 s47, section 48 obliges the authority to take steps to protect that persons property, if there is a danger of loss/damage to it and no other suitable arrangements have been made to protect it. Authorities are empowered to enter premises in order to take steps to protect property and to

143 NAA 1948 s47 (as amended) enables a person to be detained for up to three weeks on the authority of only the most limited of medical evidence without having any prior notice of the application or right to be heard. The certifying doctors need have no particular knowledge of the detained person.

144 National Assistance (Amendment) Act 1951.

145 Essentially that he or she is satisfied that it is either in the interests of the person concerned; or for the prevention of injury to the health of, or serious nuisance to other persons; and that it is necessary to remove the person concerned from the premises in which he is residing. In addition, if the application is made ex parte, that it is in the interests of the person concerned that he or she be removed without delay.

recover from the resident any reasonable expenses incurred in taking such action.

Closure of residential and nursing homes

7.106 The closure of residential homes for the elderly has proved to be one of the more controversial effects of the community care changes. The period 1990–1995 saw a 25 per cent reduction in the number of local authority homes in England (amounting to almost 40,000 fewer residents). The decline in the NHS provision of long-term geriatric beds has been no less dramatic, with the loss of 30 per cent of such beds between 1983 and 1993.[147]

7.107 In relation to the closure of long-stay NHS accommodation, there is now an obligation on health bodies to consult with the appropriate social services authority (see paras 10.23 and 10.35 below) and (in Wales) the community health council.[148] The Housing Ombudsman has determined that registered social landlords (RSL) are also subject to a similar duty to consult when contemplating the closure of a supported living scheme as well as ensuring that suitable alternative accommodation is secured for licensees/tenants.[149]

7.108 The numerous challenges that have been mounted to local authority and NHS decisions to close care homes have raised many different public law arguments which can be broadly categorised under the following five general headings. The courts have however, indicated that they consider home closure decisions to be an area where litigation should be avoided if at all possible. In *Cowl and others v Plymouth CC*,[150] the Court of Appeal spoke of the heavy obligation on lawyers in such disputes to resort to litigation only if it is really unavoidable and in *R v Barking and Dagenham LBC ex p Lloyd*,[151] the Court of Appeal held that it was not an appropriate organ to prescribe the amount of consultation to be carried out with a patient's advisers.

Promises for life

7.109 Not infrequently existing residents assert that they were given a promise – or at least formal or informal assurances that on moving to the particular home, they would be able to remain there for the rest of their lives. Moving into a care home is a very major step for many people, and often taken at a

---

146 Which hospital or other place (usually a residential or nursing home) has also been given seven days' notice of the intended application.

147 T Harding, et al, *Options for Long Term Care* (HMSO, 1996), p8.

148 Community Health Council Regulations 1996 SI No 640 and see also EL(90)185. See also *R v North and East Devon Health Authority ex p Pow* (1997) 1 CCLR 280 and *R v North and East Devon Health Authority ex p Coughlan* (1999) 2 CCLR 285 considered at paras 10.23 and 10.24 below.

149 See the case digest at www.ihos.org.uk: 'Closure of sheltered accommodation'.

150 [2001] EWCA Civ 1935; (2002) 5 CCLR 42 at 49B. Views reiterated by Maurice Kay J in *R (Dudley and Whitbread and others) v East Sussex CC* [2003] EWHC 1093 Admin.

151 (2000) 4 CCLR 196 at 205G.

time when they are frail and uncertain about the wisdom of giving up their independence. Such explicit or implicit assurances can be pivotal in the making of these crucial decisions.

7.110 *R v North and East Devon Health Authority ex p Coughlan*,[152] concerned such a promise. The Court of Appeal took as its starting point that the health authority could break its promise 'if, and only if, an overriding public interest required it' (at para 52). Having considered the reasons advanced by the health authority (essentially budgetary) the court undertook an extensive review of the public law principles underlying the concept of legitimate expectation (see para 19.59) and considered that such expectations can fall into three broad categories:

1. where the public authority need only bear in mind its assurance when reaching a decision;
2. where the assurance was such as to require the authority to follow a particular procedural course in its decision-making process (for instance consulting the relevant parties);
3. where the assurance was so specific that it gave rise to substantive rights – in which case the court must determine 'whether to frustrate the expectation is so unfair that to take a new and different course will amount to an abuse of power'.

7.111 The court considered that the *Coughlan* case fell into the third category. After weighing up the competing questions it held:

> 89. We have no hesitation in concluding that the decision to move Miss Coughlan against her will and in breach of the Health Authority's own promise was in the circumstances unfair. It was unfair because it frustrated her legitimate expectation of having a home for life in Mardon House. There was no overriding public interest which justified it. In drawing the balance of conflicting interests the court will not only accept the policy change without demur but will pay the closest attention to the assessment made by the public body itself. Here, however, as we have already indicated, the Health Authority failed to weigh the conflicting interests correctly . . .

7.112 The courts will in general only accept that a promise for life has been made, when 'convincing' evidence is advanced by the applicant of a 'clear and unequivocal assurance'.[153] The assurance should however be viewed from the perspective of the resident – the test being 'what would the ordinary resident think that the [statement in question] was trying to convey'.[154]

Failure to properly consult

7.113 *R v Devon CC ex p Baker* and *Durham CC ex p Curtis and others*,[155] concerned the proposed closure of residential homes in Devon and in Durham. The

---

152 (1999) 2 CCLR 285; [2000] 2 WLR 622; [2000] 51 BMLR 1; [2000] 3 All ER 850.
153 *R (Phillips and Rowe) v Walsall MBC* (2001) 5 CCLR 383 at 387D; and see also *R (Lloyd) v Barking and Dagenham LBC* (2000) 4 CCLR 27.
154 *R (Bodimeade) v Camden LBC* (2001) 4 CCLR 246 at 255H.
155 [1995] 1 All ER 73, CA.

Court of Appeal held that (in respect of the procedure followed by Durham County Council) the decision to close a particular home was unlawful; the council had failed to consult the residents properly. The court approved the proposition that consultation contained four elements,[156] namely:

> First, that consultation must be at a time when proposals are still at a formative stage. Second, that the proposer must give sufficient reasons for any proposal to permit of intelligent consideration and response. Third, that adequate time must be given for consideration and response and, finally, fourth, that the product of consultation must be conscientiously taken into account in finalising any statutory proposals.

7.114   The consultation process must include a statement setting out the relevant context for the proposals under consideration – for instance that some residents may have been promised a home for life. Although a failure to refer to such key topics may not vitiate the consultation process it may render the decision-making process vulnerable to challenge on the basis of having omitted a relevant consideration.[157]

7.115   The court also approved the proposition that if a resident is to be transferred from one home to another (for whatever reason), he or she must be consulted over his or her removal from the existing home as well as over the home to which he or she is to be transferred.[158]

7.116   Provided the key stages of the consultation process are followed and the product of the consultation 'conscientiously taken into account'[159] then the court will 'not strain to find technical defects which will make the obligations imposed on local authorities unworkable'.[160] The courts will also be slow to add additional obligations, for instance that a proposal could only be adopted (after consultation) if it enjoyed 'consensus or the agreement or consensus of the consultees'.[161] Whether or not there is a duty to 're-consult' if new issues emerge during the consultation process will depend upon the facts of a given case'[162] but in general there is 'no duty to consult further on [an] amended proposal which had itself emerged from the consultation process'.[163]

156   These elements first being propounded in *R v Brent LBC ex p Gunning* (1986) 84 LGR 168 and adopted by the Court of Appeal in *ex p Coughlan* (1999) 2 CCLR 285, CA at para [108]; [2000] 2 WLR 622; [2000] 51 BMLR 1; [2000] 3 All ER 850.

157   *Merton, Sutton and Wandsworth Health Authority ex p Perry and others* (2000) 3 CCLR 378 at para 112.

158   [1995] 1 All ER 73, CA at 86.

159   *R v North and East Devon Health Authority ex p Coughlan* (1999) 2 CCLR 285, CA at para 108.

160   *R (Smith) v East Kent NHS Hospital Trust and Medway Health Authority* (2003) 6 CCLR 251 at 276C.

161   (2003) 6 CCLR 251 at 267C.

162   (2003) 6 CCLR 251 at 271F.

163   *R v Islington LBC ex p East* [1996] ELR 74 at 88 cited with approval by Silber J in *R (Smith) v East Kent NHS Hospital Trust and Medway Health Authority* (2003) 6 CCLR 251 at 266H.

Failure to properly assess existing residents

7.117 In *Coughlan* it was argued that prior to consulting on the closure of her nursing facility there should have been a multi-disciplinary assessment of her individual needs and a risk assessment of the effects of moving her to new accommodation.[164] The argument being that if her needs were incapable of being met elsewhere then closure of the facility would not have been possible.

7.118 The health authority denied that such an obligation existed arguing that under the relevant guidance (HSG 1998/048 – see para 7.129) it was only after a closure decision that the detailed transfer procedures (set out in the 1998 guidance) applied and it was:

> . . . impracticable and unrealistic in the vast majority of cases to carry out the assessments and to identify alternative placements prior to a closure decision, let alone prior to consultation on a proposed closure. Funds for the development of alternative facilities might only become available after the closure decision is taken; only then would the range of alternative available placements become clear; large closure programmes might take years to implement, in which case assessments and alternative facilities considered at the time of consultation or closure would change over time; and in practice the necessary co-operation of individual patients for effective assessments and alternative placements might be more difficult to obtain before rather than after a final decision has been taken on closure.[165]

7.119 On the facts of this particular case (and in view of its other findings against the health authority) the court considered that it was unnecessary to rule separately in the legality of the health authorities actions in this regard.

7.120 However *Merton, Sutton and Wandsworth Health Authority ex p Perry and others*[166] concerned a decision to close a long-stay hospital and provide alternative community-based replacement services for over a hundred long-stay residents who had profound learning disabilities, and physical impairments such as lack of mobility, incontinence and eating problems. Some of the residents who challenged the closure decision had been at the facility for almost 30 years. They argued (among other things) that they had not had a full assessment of their needs prior to the consultation on closure, and the health authority responded by citing the Court of Appeal's judgment in *Coughlan* that a failure to undertake such an assessment did not necessarily render the process unlawful. Jackson J found in favour of the residents stating:[167]

> It should be remembered that Miss Coughlan was not a person with learning disabilities. The government guidance which is applicable in the

---

164 *Coughlan* reference and at para 94 'as required both by the Guidance in both HSG(95)8 (paras 17–20) and HSC 1998/048 and also by the general obligation to take all relevant factors into account in making the closure decision'.

165 HSG(95)8 at para 98.

166 (2000) 3 CCLR 378.

167 (2000) 3 CCLR 378 at paras 91–93.

present case, but which was not applicable in Coughlan, is HSG(92)42.
This circular states on page 2 as follows:

> 'The large majority of people with learning disabilities not living with
> their families can be cared for in residential accommodation arranged
> through the relevant social services authority. There are, however,
> likely to be a small number of people with severe or profound learning
> disabilities and physical, sensory or psychiatric conditions who need
> long term residential care in a health setting. Where this seems to be
> the case a multi-professional assessment and consultation with parents
> or carers are necessary to determine whether the services they need can
> only be provided by the NHS or whether other alternatives would be
> more appropriate and cost effective.'

The residents of Orchard Hill, whose problems are far greater than
those of the average person with learning disability, require a detailed
assessment of the kind set out in HSG(92)42 before any decision can be
taken about moving them out of NHS care.

7.121   In the absence of special factors, such as existed in the *Merton, Sutton and
Wandsworth* proceedings, it would appear that as a general principle specialist assessments (eg, specifically addressing the psychological and risk
impacts of a relocation) are 'not necessary or appropriate when making a
decision on closure'.[168]

Failure to consider relevant matters

7.122   In *R (Dudley and Whitbread and others) v East Sussex CC*,[169] the claimant
argued that the authority had reached its closure decision without considering relevant guidance, including (1) a report prepared at the request of
Plymouth City Council[170] following *Cowl and others v Plymouth CC*[171] and
(2) Department of Health guidance concerning 'The transfer of frail older
NHS patients to other long-stay settings' HSG 1998/048 (see para 7.129
below). In relation to the former the court held that notwithstanding the
eminence of the report's author, Plymouth did not have the authority to
promulgate guidelines for the world at large and so the material was not
something to which East Sussex had to have regard. In relation to HSG
1998/048, since it was specifically NHS guidance and not addressed to
social services (although it had been copied to them) it was again not something to which the authority had to have regard.

---

168 *R (Phillips and Rowe) v Walsall MBC* (2001) 5 CCLR 383 at 387J.
169 [2003] EWHC 1093 Admin, 16 April 2003.
170 *Report and Findings of the Extraordinary Complaints Panel – Closure of Granby Way
Residential Care Home for Older People, Plymouth – November* (2003) 6 CCLR 393 and
see also *Scrutiny Inquiry into Care Homes, Gloucestershire County Council* June 2003,
Chair – D Latham; www.gloucestershire.gov.uk/index.cfm?articled=4397. See also
J Williams and A Netten (2003) *Guidelines for the Closure of Care Homes for Older
People: Prevalence and Content of Local Government Protocols* A (PSSRU discussion
paper 1861/2) accessible at http://www.pssru.ac.uk/pdf/dp1861_2.pdf.
171 [2002] 1 WLR 803; (2002) 5 CCLR 42, CA.

The Human Rights Act 1998

7.123　Many home closure cases have invoked the provisions of the Human Rights Act (HRA) 1998. In part this stems from research evidence that indicates that relocating institutionalised elderly people to a new residence may have a dramatic effect on their mental health and life expectancy,[172] some studies suggesting that the increase in mortality rates might be as high as 35 per cent.[173] The arguments therefore concern allegations that a closure may result in premature death or cause severe distress and so violating the positive obligations of the public authority under ECHR arts 2 and 3 (see paras 17.176 and 19.178). Such arguments need to be considered carefully: in *ex p Coughlan*,[174] for instance, the Court of Appeal, whilst primarily considering the impact of the closure on ECHR art 8, noted:[175]

> Miss Coughlan views the possible loss of her accommodation in Mardon House as life-threatening. While this may be putting the reality too high, we can readily see why it seems so to her; and we accept, on what is effectively uncontested evidence, that an enforced move of this kind will be emotionally devastating and seriously anti-therapeutic.

Article 2

7.124　In *R (Dudley and Whitbread and others) v East Sussex CC*[176] a closure decision was challenged on (among others) human rights grounds. Maurice Kay J accepted that ECHR art 2 (the right to life) had been given 'an extended meaning' observing:

> As was said by the Strasbourg Court in *Osman v United Kingdom* [1998] 29 EHRR 245 at paragraph 115:
>
>> Article 2 of the Convention may also imply in certain well-defined circumstances a positive obligation on the authorities to take preventative operational measures to protect an individual whose life is at risk.
>
> Although the risk in that case was of criminal acts, the principle is not so limited. However, the evidence does not point to a breach of article 2 in this case. No particularised medical evidence has been filed showing that the life of any particular resident is seriously at risk. What the claimant needs to establish is that 'the authorities did not do all that could reasonably be expected of them to avoid a real and immediate risk to life of which they have or ought to have knowledge' – see *Osman*. The claimants have not established that in this case.

172　See, for instance, *International Journal of Geriatric Psychiatry* (1993) vol 8, p521; also see (1994) *Times* July, 'Elderly patients die within weeks of transfer'.

173　'Relocation of the aged and disabled: A mortality study' *Journal of American Geriatric Society*, vol 11, 185.

174　(1999) 2 CCLR 285, CA.

175　(1999) 2 CCLR 285 at para 92.

176　[2003] EWHC 1093 Admin 16 April 2003 at paras 27–33.

Article 3

7.125   Again in *R (Dudley and Whitbread and others) v East Sussex CC*[177] Maurice Kay J assessed the submissions concerning a violation of ECHR art 3 in the following terms:

> The issue here is whether the closure decision crosses the threshold of the minimum level of severity required which depends on the circumstances of the particular case . . . the threshold is simply not reached in this case – see for example *R v North West Lancashire Health Authority ex parte A* [2000] 1 WLR 977 at pages 1000 to 1001, per Buxton LJ:
>
> > Article 3 of the ECHR addresses positive conduct by public officials of a high degree of seriousness and opprobrium. It has never been applied to merely policy decisions on the allocation of resources, such as the present case is concerned with. That is clear not only from the terms of article 3 itself, and the lack of any suggestion in any of the authorities that it could apply in a case even remotely like the present, but also from the explanation of the breach of article 3 that has been given by the Convention organs. Thus in *Tyrer v United Kingdom* [1978] 2 EHHR 1, a case concerned with corporal punishment, the Strasbourg Court held, at paragraphs 30 and 35 of its judgment that:
> >
> > > . . . in order for a punishment to be 'degrading' and in breach of article 3, the humiliation or debasement involved must attain a particular level . . . the court finds that the applicant was subjected to a punishment in which the element of humiliation attained the level inherent in the notion of 'degrading punishment.
> >
> > More generally, the Strasbourg Commission has on a number of occasions stressed the degree of seriousness of the conduct that article 3 addresses. For instance, the Commission said in *East African Asians v United Kingdom* [1973] 3 EHRR 76, 81, paragraph 195:
> >
> > > The Commission finally recalls its own statement in the first *Greek* case (1969) 12 YB Eur Conv HR 1 that treatment of an individual may be said to be degrading in the sense of article 3 'if it grossly humiliates him before others or drives him to act against his will or conscience' . . . the word 'grossly' indicates that article 3 is only concerned with 'degrading treatment' which reaches a certain level of severity.
> >
> > These strong statements clearly demonstrate, if demonstration were needed, that to attempt to bring the present case under article 3 not only strains language and common sense, but also, and even more seriously, trivialises that Article in relation to the very important values that it in truth protects.
>
> In my judgment, the same considerations apply to the present case.

Article 8

7.126   The Court of Appeal in *ex p Coughlan*[178] considered the finding of the first instance judge that Miss Coughlan's rights under ECHR art 8 had been violated, in the following terms:[179]

---

177 [2003] EWHC 1093 Admin 16 April 2003 at paras 27–33.
178 (1999) 2 CCLR 285, CA.
179 (1999) 2 CCLR 285 at paras 92–93.

Miss Coughlan views the possible loss of her accommodation in Mardon House as life-threatening. While this may be putting the reality too high, we can readily see why it seems so to her; and we accept, on what is effectively uncontested evidence, that an enforced move of this kind will be emotionally devastating and seriously anti-therapeutic.

The judge was entitled to treat this as a case where the Health Authority's conduct was in breach of article 8 and was not justified by the provisions of article 8(2). Mardon House is, in the circumstances described, Miss Coughlan's home. It has been that since 1993. It was promised to be just that for the rest of her life. It is not suggested that it is not her home or that she has a home elsewhere or that she has done anything to justify depriving her of her home at Mardon House.

7.127   In *R (Madden) v Bury MBC*,[180] the local authority accepted at the hearing that the closure decision engaged ECHR art 8, and accordingly Richards J held that:

> . . . its implications had to be considered, it seems to me important that such consideration requires a clear recognition of the interests at stake under article 8 and of the matters relied on by way of justification of an interference with those interests, with an appropriate balancing exercise to ensure that the principle of proportionality is observed. This can be done on a relatively generalised basis looking at the interests of residents as a whole and does not, in the absence of special circumstances, require an individualised balancing exercise by reference to an assessment of the needs of each individual resident. The detailed individual assessment can follow. It may well be that in a situation of this kind, the balancing exercise does not need to be elaborate, and that its outcome is reasonably predictable, especially given the existence of what are plainly substantial public interest considerations in favour of closure.
>
> The fact remains that the point needs to be addressed. There is no evidence in this case that is was addressed . . . Thus there was a failure to consider article 8; a failure to reach a proper assessment that the admitted interference with the rights of residents under article 8 was justified. In my judgment that amounts to a further and independent reason for upholding the decision to be unlawful.

7.128   In *R (Dudley and Whitbread and others) v East Sussex CC*,[181] however, Maurice Kay J was satisfied (on the facts of this case) that any interference with ECHR art 8(1) could be justified under article 8(2)[182] stating:

> I am prepared to assume, without deciding, that article 8 is engaged. That may be a generous assumption in a case which does not have the *Coughlan* element of a particular home for life, and when the Council will be finding alternative accommodation for the residents. The issue then becomes justification under article 8(2). In my judgment, the council has clearly established justification. It is relevant that the East Sussex area contains a higher proportion of residents aged 65-plus than any other local authority.

180 [2002] EWHC 1882 (Admin); (2002) 5 CCLR 622 at 636–637.
181 [2003] EWHC 1093 Admin at paras 27–33.
182 See also Lloyd *R (Lloyd) v Barking and Dagenham LBC* (2001) 4 CCLR 27, another disputed home closure case where the Court of Appeal upheld the first instance judge's finding that arguments under ECHR art 8 added 'nothing the case'.

It has also been 'zero'-rated by the Audit Commission which restricts the level of finance available. That is not a matter for congratulation, but it highlights the circumstances in which the council was carrying out its review of residential care homes. These are plainly relevant considerations as the council seeks the most effective ways of fulfilling its various statutory responsibilities within existing financial constraints. It is hardly surprising that it was anxious not to lose the prospect of a £1 million grant from central government. The court is slow to interfere with decisions which 'involve a balance of competing claims on the public purse in the allocation of economic resources', see Neill LJ in *R v Criminal Injuries Compensation Board ex p P* [1995] 1 WLR 845 at 857. This has been reaffirmed in home closure cases since the coming into force of the Human Rights Act. In *R (Phillips and Rowe) v Walsall MBC* [2001] ECHR Admin 789, Lightman J said, paragraph 11:

> I may add that if (contrary to my view) a move such as is presently contemplated could possibly constitute an interference with a fundamental right under article 8, it would surely be justified as required for the economic wellbeing of the council and of those in need of its services. Resources of public authorities are notoriously limited and it must be a matter for elected authorities such as the council to have leeway in how they are husbanded and applied.

HSC 1998/048

7.129   In response to a particular incident at an NHS facility, guidance on the 'transfer of frail elderly patients to other long stay settings' (HSC 1998/048) was issued on 2 April 1998. Although primarily aimed at NHS bodies, the circular was copied to all directors of social services in England.

7.130   The guidance provides checklists of steps to be taken during the closure process and emphasises the importance of consultation at all stages. A key part of any strategy should be a 'project plan' 'which is flexible enough to adapt to changing circumstances is central to the planning process'. Authorities should set up a steering group to see the whole project through, with a project manager, a patient transfer co-ordinator, a key worker who works at the hospital and knows the patient and their needs and will liaise with the patient and their relatives or carers as well as with staff in the receiving care setting. Contingency plans must be prepared for all aspects of the project and the vital importance of information sharing (both between all professionals and with patients and carers) is stressed.

7.131   The guidance advises against winter and weekend transfers and that whenever possible groups of friends should be moved together. There should be a named staff member authorised to postpone or cancel the transfer of any individual should this become necessary – even if this means that the patient has to be moved within the hospital.

Health and safety issues

7.132   A detailed consideration of general health and safety issues in care homes is beyond the scope of this text and reference should be made to guidance issued by the Health and Safety Executive in its booklet HS(G)104, *Health and Safety in Residential Care Homes.*[183] The guidance details the main heads of legal responsibility to employees and residents under the Health and Safety at Work Act 1974 as well as in tort and contract. The guidance gives practical advice on the handling and reporting of incidents, occupational health, training, the working environment, kitchen, laundry and outdoor safety, as well as covering other issues such as violence to staff.

Manual handling

7.133   Of increasing and particular concern, however, is the question of the avoidance of procedures that involve manual handling. This question arises not only in residential care settings, but also in general domiciliary and community care situations. HS(G)104 emphasises the importance of proper manual handling arrangements, thus:

> 89.   Almost four of every ten accidents reported in the health care sector arise from manual handling. In residential care homes there will be a range of manual handling tasks from the simple lifting of provisions to complicated lifts involving residents. Sprains and strains of backs and limbs are often sustained from manual handling. Injuries may also occur as a result of cumulative damage often sustained over a considerable period, which can result in physical impairment, or even permanent disability.

7.134   Because of the general prevalence of such injuries throughout all types of work environment, European Directive 90/269/EEC required all member states to take specific legislative action to reduce such injuries at work. In consequence, the Manual Handling Operations Regulations 1992[184] were issued and more recently the Management of Health and Safety at Work Regulations 1999.[185] Detailed guidance on the 1992 regulations has been issued by the Health and Safety Executive under reference L23. Regulation 4 of the 1992 regulations (as amended) provides that:

> 4(1) Each employer shall –
>   (a) so far as is reasonably practicable, avoid the need for his employees to undertake any manual handling operations at work which involve a risk of their being injured;
>   (b) where it is not reasonably practicable to avoid the need for his employees to undertake any manual handling operations at work which involve a risk of their being injured –
>   (i)   make suitable and sufficient assessment of all manual handling operations to be undertaken by them, having regard to the factors which are specified in column 1 of Schedule 1 to these Regulations and considering the questions which are specified in the corresponding entry in column 2 of that Schedule,

183   Obtainable from HSE Books, PO Box 1999, Sudbury, Suffolk, CO10 6FS. Tel: 01787 881165.
184   SI No 2793.
185   SI No 3242.

(ii) take appropriate steps to reduce the risk of injury to those employees arising out of their undertaking any such manual handling operations to the lowest level reasonably practicable,

(iii) take appropriate steps to provide any of those employees who are undertaking any such manual handling operations with general indications and, where it is reasonably practicable to do so, precise information on–

(aa) the weight of each load, and

(bb) the heaviest side of any load whose centre of gravity is not positioned centrally.

(2) Any assessment such as is referred to in paragraph (1)(b)(i) of this regulation shall be reviewed by the employer who made it if –

(a) there is reason to suspect that it is no longer valid; or

(b) there has been a significant change in the manual handling operations to which it relates;

and where as a result of any such review changes to the assessment are required, the relevant employer shall make them.

(3) In determining for the purposes of this regulation whether manual handling operations at work involve a risk of injury and in determining the appropriate steps to reduce that risk regard shall be had in particular to –

(a) the physical suitability of the employee to carry out the operations;

(b) the clothing, footwear or other personal effects he is wearing;

(c) his knowledge and training;

(d) the results of any relevant risk assessment carried out pursuant to regulation 3 of the Management of Health and Safety at Work Regulations 1999;

(e) whether the employee is within a group of employees identified by that assessment as being especially at risk; and

(f) the results of any health surveillance provided pursuant to regulation 6 of the Management of Health and Safety Regulations 1999.

7.135   As the guidance L23 states, regulation 4 establishes a clear hierarchy of measures which an employer is required to adopt, namely:

a) avoid hazardous manual operations so far as is reasonably practicable;

b) assess any hazardous manual handling operations that cannot be avoided;

c) reduce the risk of injury so far as is reasonably practicable.

7.136   The very detailed guidance given by the Health and Safety Executive is of great practical importance, analysing the appropriate use of hoists and other possible lifting mechanisms when moving patients. What the regulations do not do, however, is prohibit the lifting of patients. Frequently it appears that social services authorities and health authorities are adopting an extremely restrictive interpretation of the regulations which has the end result that a patient does not receive a service (such as a bath) because it involves some element of manual handling.

7.137   In *R (A and B) v East Sussex CC (No 2)*,[186] Munby J was asked to give

186 [2003] EWHC 167 (Admin); (2003) 6 CCLR 194.

general guidance concerning how local authorities should seek to resolve the relative interests of disabled people – to be lifted safely and with dignity – and their paid carers, to avoid risks of injury from manual handling. By the time of the hearing the local authority had accepted that its previous inflexible 'no manual handling' policy was unlawful and had revised it. Nevertheless a dispute remained as to the application of the new policy to the needs of the applicants – two young women with profound physical and learning disabilities. The judge reviewed:

- the relevant legislation (as detailed above); and
- the relevant guidance/advice publications, and considered that in the context of the handling of incapacitated people in their own homes, that the most relevant was 'Handling home care: Achieving safe, efficient and positive outcomes for care workers and clients' (2001) Health and Safety Executive (HSG 225); and
- the relevant domestic case law, in particular *King v Sussex Ambulance NHS Trust*,[187] which concerned an injury sustained by an ambulance man in carrying an elderly person down the stairs of a cottage. In Munby J's view the case established a principle:

  > . . . that an employee whose job is to lift people (the ambulance man) may have to accept a greater degree of risk than one who is employed to move inanimate objects (the furniture remover) and that what is reasonable (and . . . practicable) has to be evaluated having regard to the social utility of the operation and a pubic authority's duties to the public and to the particular member of the public who has called for the authority's help. At the same time one has to recognise, of course, that none of this can justify exposing an employee to . . . 'unacceptable risk'.

  From this analysis the judge concluded that there maybe situations where 'some manual handling is on any view an inherent – an inescapable – feature of the very task for which those who care . . . – are employed';

- the relevant human rights instruments and Strasbourg case law, including the European Convention on Human Rights, the Charter of Fundamental Rights of the European Union, *Price v United Kingdom*[188] which case he considered established that profoundly disabled people were entitled to an 'enhanced degree of protection' under the Convention, and *Botta v Italy*[189] which he considered endorsed the principle recognised in article 26 of the Charter, namely 'the rights of persons with disabilities to benefit from measures designed to ensure their independence, social and occupational integration and participation in the life of the community'.[190]

187 [2002] EWC Civ 953; (2002) 68 BMLR 177.
188 [2001] 34 EHRR 1285.
189 26 EHRR 241.
190 (2003) 6 CCLR 194 at 220D.

7.138   Munby J did not make a definitive decision as to what degree of manual handling was required in the particular case. He however gave general guidance, as to how the balance of interest should be struck. In his view this was not a 'situation in which the disabled person's rights 'trump' those of the carer, though equally . . . the carers rights do not 'trump' those of the disabled person'. There is no doubt but that such cases raise extremely challenging issues, and in difficult cases the resolution may require the installation of specialist (and expensive) equipment beyond that which has generally been sanctioned by local authorities and health bodies.

7.139   The judge gave guidance on how the assessment should be conducted and how the disabled person's wishes, feelings and preferences should be ascertained. At the end of this process, a decision had to be made:

> Once the balance has been struck, if it comes down in favour of manual handling, then the employer must take appropriate assessments and take all appropriate steps to minimise the risks that exist.

7.140   In those cases where authorities are using the regulations as a reason for refusing to provide a service, they are often willing to admit that in consequence the task is carried out by a carer instead. Although such a person is not an employee for the purposes of the regulations and other health and safety at work legislation, he or she is someone to whom the authority prima facie owes a duty of care (respect for, and the support of, carers being at the heart of the community care reforms). If an authority fully conversant with the good practice and knowledge engendered by the regulations stands by and allows a carer to carry out tasks it believes to be unduly hazardous for its own employees, then it may well be liable in negligence for any injuries that result (unless, perhaps, it has taken steps to inform and/or train the carer in safe lifting techniques, etc).

7.141   Such health risks are foreseeable: well publicised research has shown that over 50 per cent of carers have suffered a physical injury such as a strained back since they began to care. In addition the research reveals that, caring also subjects carers to other health related problems, with over half receiving treatment for stress-related illness since becoming carers.[191]

Residential accommodation services and the NHS overlap

7.142   Both social services authorities and the NHS have obligations to care for people who are disabled, ill or who have learning difficulties. In the context of care home accommodation, however, the overlap takes three forms:

---

191 M Henwood, *Ignored and Invisible? Carers Experience of the NHS* (Carers National Association, 1998): cited in 'Caring about Carers: A National Strategy for Carers'; LASSL (99)2; and see also para 10.159 below.

1) the duty on the NHS to deliver specific services to persons in accommodation secured by the social services authority (eg, district nursing services). This responsibility is considered at para 10.129 below.

2) the duty on the NHS to make 'free nursing care' contributions (Health and Social Care Act 2001 s49). This responsibility is considered at paras 10.59 and 10.144 below.

3) the duty on the NHS in certain cases to pay the full care home fees (where the resident is deemed to have 'continuing health care needs). This responsibility is considered at para 10.64 below.

Accommodation under Mental Health Act 1983 s117

7.143   The duty to provide accommodation (and other community care services) under Mental Health Act (MHA) 1983 s117 is a quite separate community care service to the duty under NAA 1948 s21.[192] The duty only arises in respect of persons who have been detained under MHA 1983 s3,[193] or admitted to a hospital under MHA 1983 s37[194] or transferred to a hospital under a transfer direction made under MHA 1983 ss47 or 48[195] and then cease to be detained and leave hospital.

7.144   The duty to provide accommodation under MHA 1983 s117 only arises after the patient has been assessed as requiring this service. Accommodation provided under MHA 1983 s117 differs from the service under NAA 1948 s21 in that authorities are not permitted to charge for this service. MHA 1983 s117 services are considered at paras 12.2 and 15.34.

Accommodation under National Assistance Act 1948 s29(4)(c)

7.145   NAA 1948 s29(4) empowers social services authorities (subject to direction by the secretary of state) to provide hostel accommodation for disabled people engaged in workshops provided by the authority under that section. The secretary of state's direction empowers (but does not oblige) authorities to provide such facilities.[196]

7.146   The provision of workshop activities is considered at para 8.48. The effect of NAA 1948 s29(4A) is to make the hostel accommodation subject to the same charging provisions as apply to residential accommodation services under NAA 1948 s21 (see para 12.4 below).

---

192   National Health Service and Community Care Act 1990 s46(3).
193   Admission to hospital for treatment of a mental disorder.
194   A hospital order made in criminal proceedings.
195   Transfer to hospital of a prisoner suffering from a mental disorder.
196   LAC(93)10 Appendix 2 para 2(4).

Accommodation under Children Act 1989 s17

7.147   Children Act 1989 s17 requires social services authorities to safeguard and promote the welfare of children in need in their area; this includes the provision of an almost unlimited range of services, of which accommodation (in a care home or ordinary rented dwelling) may be one. The duties owed to children in need (including disabled children) are considered in chapter 8 below.

Domiciliary and community-based services

continued

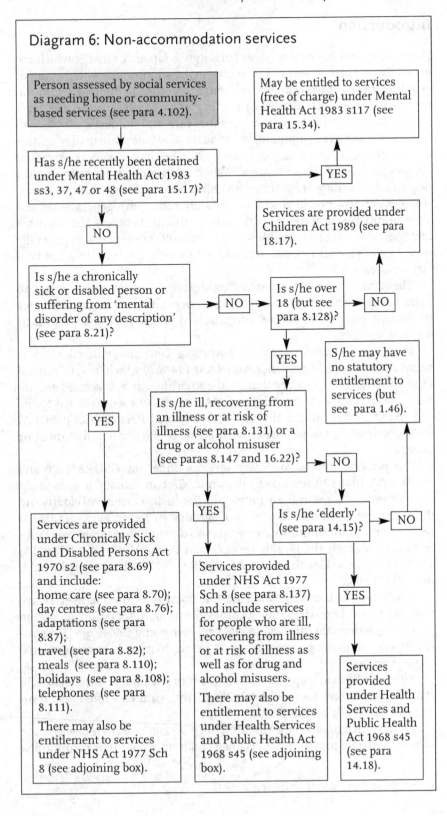

Diagram 6: Non-accommodation services

Person assessed by social services as needing home or community-based services (see para 4.102).

May be entitled to services (free of charge) under Mental Health Act 1983 s117 (see para 15.34).

Has s/he recently been detained under Mental Health Act 1983 ss3, 37, 47 or 48 (see para 15.17)?

YES

NO

Services are provided under Children Act 1989 (see para 18.17).

Is s/he a chronically sick or disabled person or suffering from 'mental disorder of any description' (see para 8.21)?

NO → Is s/he over 18 (but see para 8.128)? → NO

YES

YES

Is s/he ill, recovering from an illness or at risk of illness (see para 8.131) or a drug or alcohol misuser (see paras 8.147 and 16.22)?

S/he may have no statutory entitlement to services (but see para 1.46).

NO

YES

Is s/he 'elderly' (see para 14.15)? → NO

Services are provided under Chronically Sick and Disabled Persons Act 1970 s2 (see para 8.69) and include:
home care (see para 8.70);
day centres (see para 8.76);
adaptations (see para 8.87);
travel (see para 8.82);
meals (see para 8.110);
holidays (see para 8.108);
telephones (see para 8.111).

There may also be entitlement to services under NHS Act 1977 Sch 8 (see adjoining box).

Services provided under NHS Act 1977 Sch 8 (see para 8.137) and include services for people who are ill, recovering from illness or at risk of illness as well as for drug and alcohol misusers.

There may also be entitlement to services under Health Services and Public Health Act 1968 s45 (see adjoining box).

YES

Services provided under Health Services and Public Health Act 1968 s45 (see para 14.18).

Introduction

8.1   Domiciliary and day care services constitute a range of services which are generally provided or secured by social services authorities with the aim of enabling those people who receive them to continue to live in the community (rather than in residential care or nursing homes). The services available include help in the home (personal care and domestic assistance); transport; disability equipment; home adaptations; day care (in day centres or workshops); leisure facilities; and other services aimed at providing support for individuals and carers.[1] Where such services are delivered to a person's home they are referred to collectively as 'domiciliary' services, whereas services provided in a community setting are generally termed 'community-based services', although in this text, unless the contrary intention is made clear, the phrase 'community care services' is generally used to embrace all non-accommodation services (ie, including domiciliary services).

8.2   The haphazard development of community care law over the last 50 years has resulted in community care services for separate client groups (ie, 'elderly people', 'ill people' and 'disabled people') being dealt with by separate statutes.

8.3   The present statutory regime governing community-based services stems from National Assistance Act (NAA) 1948 s29 which lists, in general terms, the range of services that local authorities are empowered to provide. The statutory shortcomings of NAA 1948 s29 eventually led to the enactment of the Chronically Sick and Disabled Persons Act (CSDPA) 1970 which spells out in greater detail some of the services that must be provided.

8.4   The persons entitled to receive services under the CSDPA 1970 and under NAA 1948 s29 are broadly the same. Certain vulnerable groups are not, however, covered by these provisions (for instance, the frail elderly and those recovering from an illness). Such groups are nevertheless entitled to receive various community care services as a result of separate legislative provisions (namely the Health Services and Public Health Act (HSPHA) 1968, the National Health Service Act (NHSA) 1977 and the Mental Health Act (MHA) 1983.

8.5   In addition, as noted above at para 1.46, local authorities have extensive powers to provide services under Local Government Act (LGA) 2000 s2 to promote (among other things) 'social well being' and under the 'Supporting People' programme (see para 17.55 below) to provide housing-related support services.

8.6   Although limited steps have been taken to harmonise these disparate statutory provisions, they still retain distinctive features – often incongruous and frequently overlapping.

8.7   With the enactment of the Children Act (CA) 1989, an attempt was made to make separate provision for disabled children; accordingly community-

---

1   See White Paper: *Caring for People* para 3.61.

based services for children are now primarily governed by CA 1989 Part III and CSDPA 1970 s2. The CA 1989 amended NAA 1948 ss21 and 29 so that in general, services under these sections are not available to children. Accordingly the community care statutes are often considered to be restricted to providing services for adults. There are, however, exceptions to this rule (most significantly, services under NHSA 1977 Sch 8 para 3 are available for adult or child alike).

8.8   NHSCCA 1990 Part III made a further attempt to introduce some logical structure into the various community care statutes; section 46(3) defining (for the purposes of the Act) 'community care services' as being services under:

- National Assistance Act 1948 Part III
- Health Services and Public Health Act 1968 s45
- National Health Service Act 1977 s21 and Sch 8
- Mental Health Act 1983 s117.

8.9   Confusingly, however, NHSCCA 1990 s46 does not refer to services provided under CSDPA 1970 s2. The Court of Appeal has however determined that services under section 2 are 'community care services' notwithstanding this omission. The particular difficulties caused by the wording of CSDPA 1970 s2 in this respect are considered in detail at para 8.112.

8.10   It is little wonder that such confusion exists, given the various statutory provisions have been enacted during a period of unparalleled development in public and administrative law. The contradictions and inconsistencies however, run like fault lines through the community care legislation, which has been well described as a set of sometimes incomprehensible and frequently incompatible principles. Nowhere is this statement truer than in relation to domiciliary and community-based services; these services have developed erratically since the war, first by way of cautious general provisions (eg, NAA 1948 s29), and subsequently by way of more idealistic and specific rights (such as those provided by CSDPA 1970 s2). Fundamental contradictions have emerged between these statutes, as a result of both poor and hurried drafting and the absence of any coherent theory underlying the provision of community care. Put plainly, this is an area of law in need of radical codification.

NAA 1948 s29 (see para 8.17 below) } **Major provisions**
CSDPA 1970 s2 (see para 8.62 below)

HSPHA 1968 s45 (see para 14.18 below)
NHSA 1977 Sch 8 (see para 8.124 below) } **Minor provisions**
MHA 1983 s117 (see para 15.16 below)

8.11   Each of the various community care statutes entitles similar (but not identical) client groups to similar (but not identical) services. An analysis of these statutory provisions could therefore either focus on client groups or the services they deliver. Given the substantial overlap between the client groups covered by each statute and the overwhelming legal and practical importance of NAA 1948 s29 and CSDPA 1970 s2, this chapter will focus on the legal entitlements that derive from these two so-called 'major provisions'. These two provisions apply to people who are disabled, or chronically sick or who have a mental disorder (including a learning disability) of any description. The final section of this chapter will consider NHSA 1977 s21 and Sch 8A. Although the social care obligations created by NHSA 1977 s21 and Sch 8 are in practice of primary legal relevance to drug and alcohol misusers, these provisions encompass many other potential services users (including disabled people and expectant and nursing mothers) and accordingly more conveniently fall to be considered in this general chapter.

8.12   The remaining minor community care statutory provisions (namely HSPHA 1968 s45 – which applies only to frail elderly people and MHA 1983 s117 which applies only to certain formerly detained psychiatric patients) are considered separately in the chapters addressing these specific client groups (namely chapter 14 for older people and chapter 15 for mental health service users).

Registration of domiciliary care agencies

8.13   As noted above at para 7.83 the Care Standards Act (CSA) 2000 brought domiciliary care agencies (including those run by local authorities) within the Commission for Social Care Inspection/Care Standards Inspectorate for Wales (CSCI/CSIW) regulatory framework.[2] These provisions came into effect in England on 1 April 2003 and in Wales with effect from 1 March 2004 (Domiciliary Care Agencies (Wales) Regulations 2004).[3a]

8.14   Section 4 of the 2000 Act defines a 'domiciliary care agency' as:

> An undertaking[3] which consists of or includes arranging the provision of personal care in their own homes for persons who by reason of illness, infirmity or disability are unable to provide it for themselves without assistance.

8.15   The registration and inspection regimes for such undertakings are in broad measure the same as for care homes and detailed in the Domiciliary Care Agencies Regulations 2000.[4] A national minimum standards statement has been published by the CSCI for domiciliary care agencies (see para 7.82 above).

8.16   The requirement to register as a domiciliary agency is limited to undertakings that provide care to persons who are 'unable to provide [the personal care] for themselves'. Although, therefore, the provision of 'personal care' (see para 7.72 above) is a necessary requirement for registration, this is qualified by the requirement that it only becomes registerable when the service users are unable to provide it for themselves – accordingly, it has

---

2   By CSA 2000 s11 it is a criminal offence for a person to carry on or manage a domiciliary care agency without being registered in respect of it.

3   Widely defined in CSA 2000 s121(2).

3a SI No 219 (W 23).

4   SI No 3214.

a narrower meaning than that for the registration of care homes. As the Minister noted during the debate on the Bill:

> I hope that it is clear from the words 'unable to provide it for themselves without assistance' that personal care in this context has a narrower meaning than in the context of a care home. It will clearly include assistance with bodily functions and physical care, which falls short of assistance such as helping a person to get dressed. However, it could not extend to encouragement and emotional support, as that is not a form of personal care that a person could be said to be unable to provide for themselves. Within the normal meaning of the words, a person cannot be said to be either able or unable to provide themselves with emotional support.[5]

Services under National Assistance Act 1948 s29

Welfare arrangements under section 29

8.17   The cross-heading to NAA 1948 s29 reveals the profound change in terminology (if not social attitude) that has occurred in the last 50 years – describing the content of the section as: 'Welfare arrangements for blind, deaf, dumb and crippled persons, etc'. The amended text of NAA 1948 s29(1) now reads as follows:

> 29(1)   A local authority may, with the approval of the Secretary of State, and to such extent as he may direct in relation to persons ordinarily resident in the area of the local authority shall make arrangements for promoting the welfare of persons to whom this section applies, that is to say persons aged eighteen or over who are blind, deaf or dumb or who suffer from mental disorder of any description, and other persons aged eighteen or over who are substantially and permanently handicapped by illness, injury, or congenital deformity or such other disabilities as may be prescribed by the Minister.

8.18   As with NAA 1948 s21 (see para 7.3), it follows that social services authorities have no power to make any arrangements for the promotion of anyone's welfare under this section[6] unless and until the secretary of state has issued a direction specifying the arrangements which may be made (are 'approved') and those which must be made (are 'directed' to be made). The secretary of state's most recent direction in respect of NAA 1948 s29 is found at appendix 2 to LAC(93)10[7] and came into force on 1 April 1993 (the full text of the direction is in appendix B below).

8.19   It is generally considered that the statutory duties created by NAA 1948 s29 are 'target' duties rather than duties owed to a specific individual[8] (see

---

5   Hansard: The Minister of State, Department of Health (Mr John Hutton), House of Commons Standing Committee G, Tuesday 4 July 2000 (pm).

6   Authority to provide services may however derive from other provisions – for instance NHSA 1977 Sch 8 – see para 8.124 below and LGA 2000 s2 – see para 1.46 above).

7   WOC 35/93 in Wales.

8   *R v Islington LBC ex p Rixon* (1997) 1 CCLR 119 at 131H.

para 1.5). Although this means that the local authority obligations under section 29 are limited, in practice this problem (from the service user's perspective) has been remedied by CSDPA 1970 s2 which was enacted with the purpose of creating individual rights to certain specified domiciliary services for the NAA 1948 s29 client group (see para 8.69).

18 or over and ordinarily resident

8.20   Section 29 services are only available if they promote the welfare[9] of persons who are 18 or over. The duty to provide NAA 1948 s29 services[10] applies only to persons, who are ordinarily resident in the local authority's area, whereas a power exists to provide services for other persons.[11] There are no exceptions to these two basic requirements (eg, no exception for cases of urgency). Ordinary residence has the same meaning as NAA 1948 s21 (see para 6.2) with a minor exception under NAA 1948 s29(7) in relation to certain service users who are (or have been) employed in a workshop or an equivalent occupational activity promoted by the social services authority. In *R v Berkshire CC ex p P*,[12] Laws J described the arrangement of the section as follows:

> In my judgment section 29(1) confers two distinct functions on local authorities; one permissive, the other mandatory. Within it the duty to make arrangements is confined to cases where the secretary of state has given a direction relating to persons ordinarily resident in the authority's area. The power to make arrangements is not so confined; it arises where the secretary of state has given his approval to arrangements being made, and his approval may be given without regard to the place of residence of any potential beneficiary.

Disabled people – statutory definition

8.21   The definition provided in NAA 1948 s29, of the persons who may potentially qualify for its services, is generally accepted as the principal definition of a 'disabled person' for the purposes of the community care legislation. It applies to:

> . . . persons . . . who are blind, deaf or dumb or who suffer from mental disorder of any description, and other persons aged eighteen or over who are substantially and permanently handicapped by illness, injury, or congenital deformity . . .

8.22   People who fall within this definition are entitled to services, not only under NAA 1948 s29 but also under CSDPA 1970 s2. It is this definition (with amendment as to age alone) that was also adopted in Children Act

---

9   The wording of NAA 1948 s29(1) is such that the service need not be provided *to* the disabled person, ie, a service provided to a carer may be an 'arrangement which promotes the welfare of the disabled person'.

10   LAC(93)10 appendix 2, para 2(1); albeit that it is only a target duty, see para 1.5.

11   *R v Berkshire CC ex p P* (1997) 1CCLR 141.

12   (1997) 1CCLR 141 at 148G.

1989 s17(1) (see para 18.5). NAA 1948 s29 does not, however, permit the provision of services to people whose need arises by virtue of age alone – ie, because their age has made them frail. The social care needs of this group are addressed by HSPHA 1968 s45 which is considered at para 14.18 below.

8.23   In order to be eligible for any of the services available under NAA 1948 s29, a person must be:

- blind, or
- deaf, or
- dumb, or
- suffering from mental disorder of any description, or
- substantially and permanently handicapped by 'illness, injury, congenital deformity or such other disabilities as may be prescribed by the Minister'.

8.24   The list should be contrasted with that under NAA 1948 s21 (see para 7.18) which deals with local authorities' duties to provide residential accommodation. The NAA 1948 s21 list is less restrictive, including such groups as frail elderly people, expectant mothers and disabled persons (without having to establish that their 'handicap' is either permanent or substantial).

8.25   As already noted, NAA 1948 s29 places a duty on social services authorities to maintain registers of people in their area who may be entitled to its services (at para 2.4 above). The test, however, of whether a person qualifies for services under NAA 1948 s29 is independent of whether or not he or she is on a particular authority's register – ie, registration is not a prerequisite to obtaining assistance.[13]

Blind

8.26   Although NAA 1848 s29 makes no reference to partially sighted persons, previous guidance[14] confirms that the phrase 'other persons who are substantially and permanently handicapped' covers persons who are partially sighted.

8.27   Social services authorities have well established procedures for determining whether a visually impaired person is blind or partially sighted and thus whether the terms of NAA 1948 s29(1) – and registration – apply. The procedure is initiated by a consultant ophthalmologist completing the relevant form (a substantial form known as BD8). The form is completed in collaboration with the patient, who is provided with a copy of the first part only (relating to the consultant's certification of sight loss). The patient has a right to seek a review of the assessment.[15] The circular guidance advises that the effective date of registration should be the same as that of certification.[16] The guidance further recommends that social services authorities have separate sections in their register for each of the groups of persons to

13 LAC(93)10 appendix 4, para 3.
14 LAC 13/74 para 11(i).
15 For further information see LASSL(90)1.
16 LAC(93)10 appendix 4, para 6.

whom NAA 1948 s29 applies (ie, that blind and partially sighted persons be separately recorded).[17]

8.28   Concern has been expressed by the Local Government Ombudsman about delays in the assessment of people who have suffered sight loss – and of inadequate referral arrangements between the NHS and social services.[18] The Department of Health has however sought to improve the co-ordination of services for such persons, with the development of a web site containing information on service arrangements[19] and the distribution of a joint Chief Inspector Social Services Inspectorate/NHS Executive letter entitled 'Identifying and Assessing People With Sensory Impairment' in October 2000[20]. In addition the Association of Directors of Social Services have sought to establish a national standard for services in this field, namely 'National Visual Impairment Standards. Progress in Sight'.[21] Among other things this states that 'the waiting time for an assessment should be closely monitored to ensure that it is not more than four weeks from the date of referral'.[22]

Deaf

8.29   Although NAA 1948 s29 makes no specific reference to people with impaired hearing, previous guidance[23] confirms that the phrase 'other persons who are substantially and permanently handicapped' covers persons who are hard of hearing.

8.30   There are no formal examination procedures for determining whether a person is deaf for the purposes of NAA 1948 s29.[24] Social services authorities are advised that all persons who suffer from a disabling loss of hearing should be regarded as being deaf for the purposes of section 29.[25] The guidance suggests, however, that this single class should be subdivided into three categories:[26]

Deaf without speech: Those who have no useful hearing and those whose normal method of communication is by signs, finger spelling or writing.

Deaf with speech: Those who (even with a hearing aid) have little or no

---

17 LAC(93)10 appendix 4, para 9.
18 Complaint No 02/C/03831 against Stockport MBC 28 August 2003.
19 Accessible at www.dh.gov.uk/PolicyAndGuidance/HealthAndSocialCareTopics/ Optical/fs/en.
20 www.dh.gov.uk/PolicyAndGuidance/HealthAndSocialCareTopics/Optical/fs/en.
21 Association of Directors of Social Services: October 2002 accessible at http://www.adss.org.uk/eyes/progress.pdf.
22 'National Visual Impairment Standards. Progress in Sight' at para 11.2 – the four-week period being the limit recommended by the Social Services Inspectorate in its report 'A sharper focus: Inspection of services for adults who are visually impaired or blind' (DoH) 1998.
23 LAC 13/74 para 11(i); see also LAC(93)10 appendix 4, para 7.
24 LAC(93)10 appendix 4, para 7.
25 LAC(93)10 appendix 4 at annex 2, para 2.
26 LAC(93)10 appendix 4 at annex 2, para 2.

useful hearing but whose normal method of communication is by speech and lip-reading.

Hard of hearing: Those who (with or without a hearing aid) have some useful hearing and whose normal method of communication is by speech, listening and lip-reading.

8.31 The guidance in LAC(93)10 appendix 4, annex 2 makes a number of general statements concerning the importance the government attaches to services for deaf people; these statements are directed principally at the training and duties of specialist social workers in this field rather than being specific statements about the type of services to be provided.

Deafblind

8.32 The Department of Health has issued policy guidance concerning the arrangements that individual local authorities must make to cater for the needs of people who are deafblind: LAC(2001)8 'Social Care for Deafblind Children and Adults'[27]. Among other things it requires authorities to:

- ensure that assessments are carried out by specifically trained persons and in particular to assess need for one-to-one human contact, assistive technology and rehabilitation;
- ensure services provided to deafblind people are appropriate;
- ensure that one member of senior management includes, within his or her responsibilities, overall responsibility for deafblind services.

Dumb

8.33 The guidance gives no advice regarding the criteria for determining whether or not a person with limited speech comes within the scope of NAA 1948 s29 (other than by reference to persons who are 'deaf without speech' – see above). By implication, however, persons who have little or no useful speech must come within the scope of the phrase 'substantially and permanently handicapped'.[28]

Suffering from a mental disorder of any description

8.34 Persons suffering from a mental disorder of any description (ie, within the ambit of Mental Health Act (MHA) 1983 s1) are included in the NAA 1948 s29 client group.[29] However, as is detailed below, NAA 1948 s29 services cannot be provided to a person if the same service has been 'authorised or required' to be provided under the NHSA 1977.[30] The relevant part of the NHSA 1977 (and the secretary of state's direction issued under it) has been so drafted that NAA 1948 s29 services are generally of little relevance to persons suffering from a mental disorder. The importance, however, of including such persons within section 29 is that they are thereby included

---

27 Accessible at www.dh.gov.uk/PolicyAndGuidance/HealthAndSocialCareTopics/ SensoryImpairment/fs/en?CONTENT_ID=4015702&chk=O5RFTt.

28 See LAC 13/74 para 11(i) and LAC(93)10 appendix 4, annex 2 para 2.

29 LAC(93)10 appendix 4, para 14.

30 NAA 1948 s29(6) see para 8.58.

and eligible for services under CSDPA 1970 s2. Persons who suffer from a mental disorder are entitled to community care services under NHSA 1977 Sch 8 and/or under MHA 1983 s117 (see paras 8.131 and 15.34 respectively) in addition to CSDPA 1970 s2.[31]

8.35   Whereas all the other potential service users under NAA 1948 s29 (and/or CSDPA 1970 s2) are persons whose 'handicap' is permanent and substantial, this is not however a requirement for persons suffering from a mental disorder.

Substantially and permanently handicapped

8.36   Circular guidance[32] states:

> It has not proved possible to give precise guidance on the interpretation of the phrase 'substantially and permanently handicapped'. However, as hitherto, authorities are asked to give a wide interpretation to the term 'substantial', which the Department fully recognises must always take full account of individual circumstances. With regard to the term 'permanent', authorities will also wish to interpret this sufficiently flexibly to ensure that they do not feel inhibited from giving help under section 29 in cases where they are uncertain of the likely duration of the condition.

'Illness, injury, or congenital deformity or such other disabilities as may be prescribed by the Minister'

8.37   To qualify for services under NAA 1948 s29 a person who is substantially and permanently handicapped must be so by virtue of an illness, an injury, or congenital deformity; no further disabilities have been prescribed by the minister. Further, persons who are disabled as a result of an illness or congenital deformity will not be entitled to receive NAA 1948 s29 services where those services are available under the NHSA 1977.[33] It is undecided whether substantial and permanent handicap resulting from drug or alcohol misuse can be defined as arising out of illness or injury to qualify the person for NAA 1948 s29 services; in practice domiciliary services to such persons will generally be delivered under the NHSA 1977 (and are considered at para 8.131).

Services

8.38   NAA 1948 s29 leaves to the secretary of state the power to determine the type of domiciliary services which can be provided; the only limitations being:

a) that the purpose of the services must be the promotion of the welfare of the NAA 1948 s29 client group;[34]

---

31 LAC(93)10 appendix 4, para 13 incorrectly states that such services are generally provided under HSPHA 1968 s12 – this section has been repealed and reference should have been made to NHSA 1977 Sch 8 (although since CSDPA 1970 s2 applies to persons suffering from a mental disorder of any description, arguably this section is of greater importance).

32 LAC(93)10 appendix 4, para 8.

33 NAA 1948 s29(6).

34 But see note 27 at p325.

b) by virtue of NAA 1948 s29(6)(a) that the direct payment of money to service users is not permitted under section 29 (except if a payment for their work or produce). However the impact of this restriction has been neutered by the direct payments legislation); and

c) by virtue of NAA 1948 s29(6)(b) that no accommodation or services can be provided under section 29 if the accommodation or services have been 'authorised or required' to be provided under the NHSA 1977.[35]

8.39 Although NAA 1948 s29(4) contains an illustrative list of the type of services that may be made available, the Act leaves to the secretary of state the power to decide what services must and what services may be provided. The services referred to by section 29(4) are:

(a) for informing persons to whom arrangements under that subsection relate of the services available for them thereunder;

(b) for giving persons instruction in their own homes or elsewhere in methods of overcoming the effects of their disabilities;

(c) for providing workshops where such persons may be engaged (whether under a contract of service or otherwise) in suitable work, and hostels where persons engaged in the workshops, and others to whom arrangements under subsection (1) of this section relate and for whom work or training is being provided in pursuance of the Disabled Persons (Employment) Act 1944, or the Employment and Training Act 1973 may live;

(d) for providing persons to whom arrangements under subsection (1) of this section relate with suitable work (whether under a contract of service or otherwise) in their own homes or elsewhere;

(e) for helping such persons in disposing of the produce of their work;

(f) for providing such persons with recreational facilities in their own homes or elsewhere;

(g) for compiling and maintaining classified registers of the persons to whom arrangements under subsection (1) of this section relate.

8.40 The secretary of state's most recent directions in respect of NAA 1948 s29 services were issued as appendix 2 to LAC(93)10[36] in March 1993. The directions distinguish between services[37] which a social services department *may* provide (ie, has a power to provide – generally known as an 'approval') and those which it *must* provide (ie, is under a duty to provide).

Services which social services departments have a duty to provide

8.41 As noted above, the duty on social services departments to provide services under NAA 1948 s29 are restricted to persons who are ordinarily resident in the authority's area. The services being:

---

35 The provision of accommodation is however specifically excluded from NHSA 1977 Sch 8.

36 The full text of which is at appendix B below. The Directions were issued in Wales as WOC 35/93.

37 The local authority may provide the services alone, or in conjunction with another authority or by employing an independent or private providers: see NAA 1948 s30 and LAC(93)10 appendix 2, paras 3 and 4.

Social work service, advice and support

8.42   Social services authorities are required to *'provide a social work service and such advice and support as may be needed for people in their own homes or elsewhere'.*[38] This duty is complemented by Local Authority Social Services Act 1970 s6(6) which obliges local authorities to provide 'adequate staff for assisting' the director of social services in the exercise of his or her functions.[39] 'Advice and support' would cover such services as welfare rights advice and counselling. Previous circular guidance[40] advised that the provision of advice and support would frequently necessitate offering advice and other help to the families of the disabled person; and that authorities should bear in mind the part which voluntary workers can play in delivering this service. Welfare rights advice is increasingly seen as a core local authority activity. Thus guidance requires this advice when charges are being assessed for residential and non-residential care services (see paras 12.11 and 12.102 respectively) and in relation to hospital discharge arrangements (see para 10.163).

Social rehabilitation or adjustment to disability

8.43   Social services authorities are required to *'provide, whether at centres or elsewhere, facilities for social rehabilitation and adjustment to disability including assistance in overcoming limitations of mobility or communication'.*[41] These services will generally be provided for a short or medium-term period covering the disabled person's rehabilitation or adjustment to his or her disability. The reference to 'social' rehabilitation makes the point that medical rehabilitation is either a service to be provided under the NHSA 1977 Sch 8 (and thus excluded from provision under NAA 1948 s29)[42] or is one which should be provided by the NHS. The bundle of services referred to in this category covers, in many cases, services for which there is an overlapping responsibility between the NHS and the social services authority – and particularly 'intermediate care' (see para 10.113).

8.44   The direction, in respect of these services, subsumes (and extends) the services referred to in NAA 1948 s29(4)(b), which merely refers to arrangements for 'giving persons instruction in their own homes or elsewhere in methods of overcoming the effects of their disabilities'.

Registers of disabled people

8.45   Social services authorities are required to make arrangements *'for informing persons to whom [section 29] relates of the services available for them [under section 29]'.*[43] The extent and nature of this duty is considered at para 2.4 above.

---

38 LAC(93)10 appendix 2, para 2(1)(a).
39 See para 1.16 above.
40 DHSS Circular 13/74, para 11(ii) – cancelled by LAC(93)10.
41 LAC(93)10 appendix 2, para 2(1)(b).
42 NAA 1948 s29(6)(b).
43 LAC(93)10 appendix 2, para 2(1)(2) and NAA 1948 s29(4)(g).

Day centres and other facilities

8.46 Social services authorities are required to *'provide, whether at centres or else-where, facilities for occupational, social, cultural and recreational activities and, where appropriate, the making of payments to persons for work undertaken by them'.*[44] These services include the day centre in its various forms, work-shops, recreational and educational activities and so on. In relation to people with learning disabilities (in particular) the government is seeking to reduce reliance on these services (see *Valuing People* para 7.21, considered at para 13.4 below).

8.47 The direction, in respect of these services, overlaps with the workshop services referred to in NAA 1948 s29(4)(c) and subsumes (and extends) the services referred to in section 29(4)(f) which merely refers to arrangements for 'providing such persons with recreational facilities in their own homes or elsewhere'. In most cases services of this nature will in fact be provided to the eligible NAA 1948 s29 service user through CSDPA 1970 s2(1)(c).

Workshop and workshop hostel services

8.48 The provision of facilities for occupational activities often takes the form of a local authority workshop which provides employment (paid or otherwise) for particular user groups – frequently people with learning disabilities. In addition to the power to pay users employed in the workshops,[45] social services authorities are specifically empowered to help such persons dispose of the products of their work. The use of workshops continues the tradition of the segregated workhouse of the pre-welfare state. In the early post-war years many such workshops were former poor-law workhouses which continued to be devoted to menial mechanical tasks – and hence a few are still to be found located on the old industrial estates.

8.49 The social services authorities' duty to provide workshops is coupled with the power to provide hostel accommodation (including board and other services, amenities and requisites)[46] for those engaged in the work-shop or other occupational activity under NAA 1948 s29(4). Section 29(4A) applies the same charging rules for the provision of such accommodation as applies to residential accommodation provided under NAA 1948 s21 (see para 12.4).

Services which social services departments have power to provide

8.50 The directions[47] give social services authorities the discretion to provide the following services (regardless of the potential service user's ordinary residence).

---

44 LAC(93)10 appendix 2, para 2(1)(c).
45 LAC(93)10 appendix 2, para 2(1)(c) contains an express power for local authorities to pay disabled persons who undertake work in workshops.
46 NAA 1948 s29(4)(c) and LAC(93)10 appendix 2, para 2(4).
47 LAC(93)10 appendix 2, para 2(3) and (4).

Holiday homes

8.51   The discretion to provide holiday homes under NAA 1948 s29 should be contrasted with the duty under CSDPA 1970 s2(1)(f) to facilitate the taking of a holiday (see para 8.108).

Free or subsidised travel

8.52   '*Provide free or subsidised travel for all or any persons who do not otherwise qualify for travel concessions, but only in respect of travel arrangements for which concessions are available*'. Travel concessions are dealt with under the Transport Act 1985 s93(7)[48] which sets out the minimum eligibility requirements and are more fully considered below at para 8.82. Under the 1985 Act the persons concerned must be:

(a) men over 65 and women over 60; or
(b) persons under 16; or
(c) persons 16–18 undergoing full-time education; or
(d) blind persons; or
(e) persons suffering from any disability or injury which, in the opinion of the authority, seriously impairs their ability to walk.

Assistance in finding accommodation

8.53   '*Assist a person in finding accommodation which will enable him or her to take advantage of any arrangements made under section 29(1) of the Act*'. Social services authorities have been given the power to provide this service (and those detailed in paras 8.54 and 8.55 below) to meet the needs of disabled people, similar to the powers approved for elderly persons under DHSS Circular 19/71 para 4 (see paras 14.20–14.28).

Subsidy of warden costs

8.54   '*Contribute to the cost of employing a warden on welfare functions in warden assisted housing schemes*'. See the note to para 8.53 above.

Warden services

8.55   '*Provide warden services for occupiers of private housing*'. See the note to para 8.53 above.

Information on disability services

8.56   The power under section 29 to provide information services for disabled people[49] has been subsumed into the wider duty set out in CSDPA 1970 s1 (see paras 3.5 and 3.6).

---

48 See also The Greater London Authority Act 1999 s151; the Travel Concessions (Eligibility) Act 2002 and the Transport for London (Consequential Provisions) Order 2003 SI No 1615.

49 NAA 1948 s29(4)(a) and LAC(93)10 appendix 2, para 2(4).

Direct payments to service users under NAA 1948 s29

8.57 Although NAA 1948 s29(6)(a) prohibits authorities from making cash payments (under section 29) to service users to enable them to procure their own care,[50] its impact has been largely neutralised by the provisions of the Community Care (Direct Payments) Act 1996 and Health and Social Care Act 2001 s57 which provisions are considered at para 9.5 below.

Overlap with services under NHSA 1977 Sch 8

8.58 NAA 1948 s29(6)(b) excludes services being provided under section 29 where such services 'are required to be provided' under the NHSA 1977.

8.59 The use of the word 'required' suggests that it is only where there is an obligation to provide the service under the 1977 Act that the service provision must be under this statute (if at all) rather than under NAA 1948 s29. A consideration of the similar exclusionary provision which exists in relation to accommodation services under NAA 1948 s21[51] supports this interpretation. The section 21 provision was considered by the Court of Appeal in *R v North East Devon Health Authority ex p Coughlan.*[52] Amending the relevant judgment to accommodate the slightly different wording of NAA 1948 s29(6)(b)[53] the Court's interpretation would appear to be as follows:

> The subsection should not be regarded as preventing a local authority from providing any health services. The subsection's prohibitive effect is limited to those health services which, in fact, [are] . . . required to be provided under the [NHSA 1977]. Such health services would not therefore include services which the secretary of state legitimately decided under section 3(1) of the [NHSA 1977] it was not necessary for the NHS to provide . . . The true effect is to emphasise that [the National Assistance Act 1948] provision . . . is secondary to [the NHSA 1977] provision.

8.60 Physiotherapy[54] and chiropody are examples of services which social services departments are probably prohibited from providing, by virtue of NAA 1948 s29(6)(b), since these are specifically referred to as being health services under LAC(95)5.[55] Technically these are services which local authorities might otherwise have been obliged to consider providing, in that they clearly come within the definition of services which help 'overcome limitations of mobility or communication'.[56] It must however be noted that the mere fact that services under NAA 1948 s29 might be excluded, does not of itself exclude social services responsibility, since such authorities also have functions under the NHSA 1977 (by virtue of s21 and Sch 8): see para 8.124 below.

50 This provision is mirrored in NHSA 1977 Sch 8 para 2(2) (see para 8.142).

51 NAA 1948 s21(8); although this subsection prohibits social services from providing any services which are '*authorised or* required' to be provided under the NHSA 1977.

52 (1999) 2 CCLR 285 at [29].

53 That is by excluding reference to the phrase '*authorised or*'.

54 Although it has been determined that physiotherapy may be provided as part of a child's special educational needs – *Bromley LBC v Special Educational Needs Tribunal and others* (1999) 2 CCLR 239.

55 See para 10.131 below.

8.61   In *R v Gloucestershire CC ex p Mahfood*,[57] the council sought to argue that there was a further consequence which flowed from NAA 1948 s29(6)(b). The argument hinged on whether or not services provided by virtue of CSDPA 1970 s2 are NAA 1948 s29 services or free-standing CSDPA 1970 s2 services.[58] This general question is considered in greater detail at para 8.112. In the context of NAA 1948 s29(6)(b) McCowan LJ disposed of the respondent counsel's submissions as follows:

> His argument was that it is a pre-condition of the duty under section 2 of the 1970 Act that the local authority has power to provide the service under section 29 of the 1948 Act. If there is no power under section 29 there can be no duty under section 2. But section 29(6) of the 1948 Act positively provides that there is no power to exercise certain functions, in particular those which involve services which have to be provided under the National Health Service Act 1977. There is a duty to provide home helps for the aged and handicapped, but it is a duty under the 1977 Act. Therefore, the power to provide the service is excluded and home help services could not lawfully have been provided to Mr Mahfood and Mr Barry under section 2 of the 1970 Act.
>
> The submission is an unattractive one because it would follow that if the local authority was satisfied by reason of the fact that general arrangements had not been made for the home help, it would have no power and thus no duty to make these arrangements. The short answer to the point, however, is that section 29(6) of the 1948 Act merely states 'nothing in the foregoing provisions of this section shall authorise or require'. What is authorising the local authority to make arrangements under section 2 is section 2. Thus the provisions which authorise the local authority to meet the needs of a disabled person if those needs are not being otherwise met are section 2 itself.[59]

Services under Chronically Sick and Disabled Persons Act 1970 s2

8.62   The Chronically Sick and Disabled Persons Act (CSDPA) 1970, sponsored by Alf Morris MP, is the first of a distinguished line of private members' Bills in this field[60] and represents an early marker in the continuing struggle by disabled people for full civil rights. Writing 25 years after its enactment, Alf Morris commented:

> It seems incredible and outrageous now, but from 1945–1964, there was not one debate in the Commons on disability. Westminster and Whitehall

---

56   LAC(93)10 appendix 2, para 2(1)(b).

57   (1997) 1 CCLR 7.

58   The respondent did not pursue this argument in the Court of Appeal or the House of Lords.

59   (1997) 1 CCLR 7 at 16K.

60   The Disabled Persons (Services, Consultation and Representation) Act 1986 was promoted by Tom Clarke MP and the Carers (Recognition and Services) Act 1995 was promoted by Malcolm Wicks MP.

always had more pressing things to do than respond to the claims of people with disabilities. No-one even knew how many disabled people there were in Britain. They were treated not so much as second-class citizens, more as non-people: seen or heard only by families or, if they were in institutions, by those who controlled their lives.[61]

8.63 The speed with which the Act was drafted resulted in ambiguities which have frustrated its interpretation; most significantly the extent to which CSDPA 1970 s2 is distinct from NAA 1948 s29; this question is considered in greater detail below. The underlying purpose of CSDPA 1970 s2 was undoubtedly to convert the vaguely worded, generally discretionary services under NAA 1948 s29 into a set of specific services to which individual disabled people had an enforceable right. CSDPA 1970 s2(1) reads as follows:

Where a local authority having functions under section 29 of the National Assistance Act 1948 are satisfied in the case of any person to whom that section applies who is ordinarily resident in their area that it is necessary in order to meet the needs of that person for that authority to make arrangements for all or any of the following matters, namely –
(a) the provision of practical assistance for that person in his home;
(b) the provision for that person of, or assistance to that person in obtaining, wireless, television, library or similar recreational facilities;
(c) the provision for that person of lectures, games, outings or other recreational facilities outside his home or assistance to that person in taking advantage of educational facilities available to him;
(d) the provision for that person of facilities for, or assistance in, travelling to and from his home for the purpose of participating in any services provided under any arrangements made by the authority under the said section 29 or, with the approval of the authority, in any services provided otherwise than as aforesaid which are similar to services which could be provided under such arrangements;
(e) the provision of assistance for that person in arranging for the carrying out of any works of adaptation in his home or the provision of any additional facilities designed to secure his greater safety, comfort or convenience;
(f) facilitating the taking of holidays by that person, whether at holiday homes or otherwise and whether provided under arrangements made by the authority or otherwise;
(g) the provision of meals for that person whether in his home or elsewhere;
(h) the provision for that person of, or assistance to that person in obtaining, a telephone and any special equipment necessary to enable him to use a telephone,
then, [subject to the provisions of section 7(1) of the Local Authority Social Services Act 1970 (which requires local authorities in the exercise of certain functions, including functions under the said section 29, to act under the general guidance of the Secretary of State)], it shall be the duty of that authority to make those arrangements in exercise of their functions under the said section 29.

61 DW Issues: June 1995.

'Ordinarily resident'

8.64   CSDPA 1970 s2 services are only available to persons who are ordinarily resident in the local authority's area. Ordinary residence has the same meaning as that in NAA 1948 s21, although the statutory procedure for resolving disputes about 'ordinary residence' (under NAA 1948 s32(3)) is not available where the disagreement concerns services under CSDPA 1970 s2[62] – see para 6.24 above.

Client group

8.65   CSDPA 1970 s2 services are available to both disabled children and disabled adults (unlike services under NAA 1948 s29, which are only available to disabled adults). Section 2 requires social services authorities to make arrangements 'for that person' – whereas NAA 1948 s29 speaks of the need to make arrangements to 'promote the welfare' of a class of people. It follows therefore that services under CSDPA 1970 s2 must only be provided to the disabled person, whereas it is arguable that NAA 1948 s29 services can be provided to third parties so long as they thereby 'promote the welfare' of the person in question.[63]

Disabled adults

8.66   Section 2 services are available to the same group of persons as specified in NAA 1948 s29, namely persons aged 18 or over who are blind, deaf, dumb or who suffer from mental disorder of any description, and other persons aged 18 or over who are substantially and permanently handicapped by illness, injury, or congenital deformity (see para 8.21 where these terms are considered).

Disabled children

8.67   By virtue of CSDPA 1970 s28A, section 2 services are additionally available to disabled children within the meaning of Children Act (CA) 1989 s17(11), namely a child who is 'blind, deaf, dumb or suffers from mental disorder of any kind or is substantially and permanently handicapped by illness, injury or congenital deformity'. It will be seen that the CA 1989 follows the wording used in NAA 1948 s29, and accordingly the comments made in respect of the adult client group apply equally to disabled children.

8.68   Whilst the CA 1989 itself makes provision for a wide range of services for disabled children (considered at para 18.17 below), in general, if the service is capable of being provided under both Acts, then it will (as a matter of law) be provided under the CSDPA 1970.[64]

---

62 *R v Kent CC and Salisbury and Pierre* (2000) 3 CCLR 38.
63 See note 9 above.
64 *R v Bexley LBC ex p B* (2000) 3 CCLR 15, see para 18.16 below where this question is considered in greater detail.

Services under CSDPA 1970 s2

8.69 As already noted (see para 4.102), once a social services authority has carried out an assessment of the needs of a disabled person and decided that the provision of services under CSDPA 1970 s2 is necessary in order to meet that person's needs, then the authority is under an absolute duty to provide that service.[65] The services detailed in section 2 are described below.

Practical assistance in the home

8.70 The potential services covered by CSDPA 1970 s2(1)(a) include those primarily concerned with the maintenance of the home (eg, house cleaning, ironing, decorating, etc) and those concerned with the personal care of the disabled person (eg, help with getting out of and into bed, dressing, cooking, laundry, a sitting service, etc). While a rigid policy of not providing the former services under CSDPA 1970 s2 would constitute a fettering of a statutory duty, it is the case that personal care will generally be of higher priority in any system of eligibility criteria (because of the greater likelihood of consequent harm if this service is not provided).

8.71 Some authorities have policies that only permit 'cleaning only' services, where there is medical evidence to support its necessity (ie, acute eczema or asthma): however an unkempt home might also cause clinical depression in an elderly person – and this too could constitute medical evidence for the provision of cleaning services. Non-personal care services under CSDPA 1970 s2(1)(a) could also be justified where the provision of a house cleaning service would free a carer to provide an equivalent amount of intensive personal care.

8.72 The Local Government Ombudsman has held it to be maladministration for a council to have criteria which stipulate that no domestic assistance can be provided – unless accompanied by a need for personal care[66] and guidance to the Carers and Disabled Children Act 2000 emphasises this point:[67]

> . . . local authorities that have decided not to provide or commission certain services as community care services – such as shopping only, cleaning only, or other low-level services – should review their positions. Such services, if targeted purposively, can be of genuine assistance in sustaining the caring relationship, and be cost effective.

8.73 There is appreciable overlap between the duty under CSDPA 1970 s2(1)(a) and that under NHSA 1977 Sch 8 para 3, which places a duty on social services authorities to provide home help for households where such help is required owing to the presence of a person who is suffering from illness, lying in, an expectant mother, aged, or 'handicapped' as a result of having

---

65 *R v Gloucestershire CC ex p Mahfood* (1997) 1 CCLR 7.
66 Complaint No 01/C/17519 against Salford CC, 11 December 2003.
67 'Practitioners Guide to Carers' Assessments under the Carers and Disabled Children Act 2000' para 80 (Department of Health, March 2001).

suffered from illness or by congenital deformity (see para 8.148). The main differences between these two provisions are:

a) The NHSA 1977 service is available to a wider client group (ie, the 'handicap' need not be permanent or substantial; expectant mothers, the temporarily ill and the elderly are covered), but it does not cover persons 'handicapped' as a result of injury.

b) The service under the NHSA 1977 is generally regarded as a target duty, whereas the duty under CSDPAS 1970 s2 can create an individual right to the service (see para 1.5).

c) The NHSA 1977 service is provided to 'households' (ie, a direct beneficiary may be the carer), whereas the CSDPA 1970 s2 service can only be provided to the disabled person (ie, a carer could only be an indirect beneficiary).

d) The NHSA 1977 uses the phrase 'home help' whereas CSDPA 1970 s2(1)(a) refers to 'practical assistance' in the home – although it is difficult to see whether anything of significance can be discerned from this difference.

8.74   In *R v Islington LBC ex p McMillan*,[68] the applicant complained that, among other things, although he had been assessed as needing regular home care assistance, this had on occasions not materialised (because of staff being on leave or ill). The court held that this did not amount to a breach of duty since the applicant had been notified in the care plan that the service might suffer from such interruptions and, given his comparative need, that this was not unreasonable.[69]

The provision of a wireless, television, library, etc

8.75   The service described by CSDPA 1970 s2(1)(b) consists of the social services authority actually providing (or helping with the acquisition of) equipment to satisfy a recreational need. The items referred to (ie, wireless, television, library or similar recreational facilities) are illustrative not exhaustive and presumably equipment such as a personal computer, hi-fi system could also be provided under section 2(1)(b).

The provision of recreational/educational facilities

8.76   CSDPA 1970 s2(1)(c) requires social services authorities to provide two separate types of service, namely:

Recreational facilities

8.77   This service is complementary to the home-based service detailed in CSDPA 1970 s2(1)(a) above, and must be provided outside the person's home. Included within this provision are traditional day centres and 'drop-

68   (1997) 1 CCLR 7 at 17
69   See para 4.107 above where this decision is also considered in greater detail.

in' clubs as well as such recreational activities as outings and so on. In *R v Haringey LBC ex p Norton*,[70] the respondent council, when carrying out its assessment, only considered its obligation to provide 'personal care needs' rather than other needs such as social, recreational and leisure needs (such as those available under section 2(1)(c)). The court held this to be unlawful, the assessment had to investigate all potential needs (see para 4.39 above).

8.78   Where a person is assessed as needing a place in a day centre, and his or her name is put on a waiting list because no such places are currently available, then in effect the authority will be failing to meet assessed need. If the waiting list is reasonably short, then this may be acceptable. If, however, it is a chronic problem, the authority will be liable to challenge, unless it is taking expeditious steps to increase the number of available places. This aspect was considered by Sedley J in *R v Islington LBC ex p Rixon*[71] where he held:

> The duty owed to the applicant personally by virtue of section 2(1) of the Chronically Sick and Disabled Persons Act 1970 includes the provision of recreational facilities outside the home to an extent which Islington accepts is greater than the care plan provides for. But the local authority has, it appears, simply taken existing unavailability of further facilities as an insuperable obstacle to any further attempt to make provision. The lack of a day care centre has been treated, however reluctantly, as a complete answer to the question of provision for Jonathan's needs. As McCowan LJ explained in the *Gloucestershire* case, the section 2(1) exercise is needs-led and not resource-led. To say this is not to ignore the existing resources either in terms of regular voluntary care in the home or in budgetary terms. These, however, are balancing and not blocking factors.

For further consideration of waiting lists – see para 4.104 above.

Educational facilities

8.79   The educational service required in this case may be either home-based or otherwise. The wording suggests that the service provided by the authority consists of enabling the disabled person to have access to an (already existing) educational facility – rather than the provision of the educational facility itself. Potentially the scope of the educational obligation created by CSDPA 1970 s2(1)(c) is wide. In particular the subsection appears to enable the provision of:

a)   services for which there is an overlapping NHS responsibility (eg, communication assistance via speech synthesisers, speech therapy, hearing and writing aids, etc); and

b)   services to support disabled (adult) students. LAC(93)12[72] gives specific guidance on the these responsibilities, and in particular stresses that CSDPA 1970 s2(1)(c) covers funding the personal care requirements of such students to enable them to pursue their studies (even if those

---

70   (1998) 1 CCLR 168.
71   (1998) 1 CCLR 119 at 126D.
72   See paras 9–11.

studies are undertaken outside the local authority's area). The relevant part of the circular stating as follows:

> 9. Social services departments have been reminded of their duty under section 2(1)(c) of the Chronically Sick and Disabled Persons Act 1970 to make arrangements for assisting a disabled person who is ordinarily resident in their area in taking advantage of educational facilities available to him or her, (even where provision is made outside that local authority's area), if they are satisfied that it is necessary in order to meet that person's needs. Such assistance might, in appropriate cases include the funding by the local authority of the personal care required to enable the student in question to pursue his or her studies. It is, of course, for the authority to decide, in each case, what the individual's needs are, and how they are to be met.

> 10. Disabled students attending higher education courses may be eligible to receive up to three Disabled Students Allowances from the local education authority, as part of their mandatory award. These allowances are for a non-medical helper, major items of special equipment, or minor items such as tapes or braille paper. They are aimed at helping students with costs related to their course, and are not intended to meet other costs arising from their disability which would have to be met irrespective of whether or not they were in a course. For those attending further education courses, similar support may be provided at the discretion of the [local education authority] LEA.

> 11. There may be occasions where the social services department is asked to consider the provision of additional care support for an individual who will receive a Disabled Students Allowance or discretionary support from the LEA. It will, therefore, be appropriate in some circumstances for the support for an individual's personal care needs to be provided jointly by the SSD and the LEA.

8.80   The *ex p Rixon* judgment (above) also considered the interplay between the duties owed under CSDPA 1970 s2(1)(c) and the general duty under Education Act 1944 s41[73] which obliges education authorities to secure adequate further education facilities for (among others) adults who have learning difficulties. Sedley J observed that for persons with the gravest learning difficulties the duty under Education Act 1944 s41 might be met by the provision of facilities under CSDPA 1970 s2. He suggested however, that if this was the case, then the appropriate remedy for an alleged breach of the section 41 duty was (in the first instance) through the secretary of state procedures under Education Act 1944 ss68 or 99.

8.81   *R v Further Education Funding Council and Bradford MBC ex p Parkinson*,[74] concerned a 20-year-old applicant with severe mental and physical impairments. He was unable to take advantage of a place at a further education college without first being able to communicate to the required

---

73 As substituted by Further and Higher Education Act 1992 s11. See also, DFE Circular 1/93 'The Further and Higher Education Act 1992 Guidance [WOC 15/93 in Wales] and 'Duties and Powers: The Law Governing the Provision of Further Education to Students with Learning Difficulties and/or Disabilities (HMSO) 1996.

74 (1996) *Times* 31 October.

standard. He sought to compel the respondents to provide the necessary facilities either under Education Act 1944 s41 or Higher Education Act 1992 Sch 2. In dismissing the application, Jowitt J observed that although 'purely education facilities' could not be provided under the community care legislation, the applicant might be eligible for services under CSDPA 1970 s2(1)(c) 'as providing assistance to take advantage of education facilities which are available to him'.

Travel and other assistance

8.82 CSDPA 1970 s2(1)(d) concerns the provision of travel assistance or facilities to enable a disabled person to travel from his or her home in order to participate in any community-based services provided under CSDPA 1970 s2 and NAA 1948 s29 – or indeed any other services of a similar nature (for example, services provided under HSPHA 1968 s45 or NHSA 1977 Sch 8). While social services authorities are empowered (but not obliged) to charge for such transport services (see para 12.85), in assessing a person's ability to pay, his or her mobility component of disability living allowance (if received) must be ignored.[75]

8.83 In general, where transport is required in order that a disabled child attend a school specified in a special educational needs statement, it will be for the education department to provide this.[76]

Blue Badge Scheme

8.84 CSDPA 1970 s21 (as subsequently amended) requires motor vehicle badges to be made available for the benefit of disabled people and for regulations to be issued concerning the operation of this scheme, now known as the Blue Badge Scheme[77] (formerly the Orange Badge Scheme). Persons who meet at least one of the following criteria have a statutory right to a badge:

- receive the higher rate of the mobility component of the Disability Living Allowance (DLA);
- are registered blind;
- use a vehicle supplied by a government department;
- receive a grant from a government department for their vehicle;
- receive a War Pensioners' Mobility Supplement; or
- have a severe disability in both upper limbs, regularly drive a motor vehicle but cannot turn the steering wheel of a motor vehicle by hand, even if that wheel is fitted with a turning knob.

---

75 Social Security Contributions and Benefits Act 1992 s73(14).

76 This may even be the case where the statement provides that 'the mother to be responsible for transport to and from the school at her own expense', see *R v Havering LBC ex p K* (1997) *Times* 18 November.

77 The Disabled Persons (Badges For Motor Vehicles) (England) Regulations 2000 SI No 682, as amended by the Disabled Persons (Badges for Motor Vehicles) (England) (Amendment) Regulations 2000 SI No 1507 and see also the Disabled Persons (Badges For Motor Vehicles) (Wales) Regulations 2000 WSI No 1786.

8.85   An additional ground exists (at the discretion of the local authority) under which a disabled person may be issued with a badge if they have a permanent and substantial disability that means they are unable to walk or have very considerable difficulty in walking.

8.86   Travel assistance is also available under NAA 1948 s29 (see para 8.52).

Home adaptations and disabled facilities

8.87   CSDPA 1970 s2(1)(e) reads as follows:

> The provision of assistance for that person in arranging for the carrying out of any works of adaptation in his home or the provision of any additional facilities designed to secure his greater safety, comfort or convenience.

8.88   Section 2(1)(e) is therefore in two parts; one relating to adaptations (ie, significant works, possibly of a structural nature) and the other to the provision of additional facilities (ie, works involving the provision of fixtures and fittings and equipment).

8.89   In relation to 'additional facilities' the duty on the authority is to provide these ('the provision of'), whereas in relation to adaptations the duty is stated as being the 'provision of assistance . . . in arranging for the carrying out of'. Whether the difference in wording is legally significant is not clear. The subsection does not oblige social services authorities to carry out (or otherwise provide) the adaptations, merely to provide assistance for that person in arranging for the carrying out of the works. Arguably this might be no more than assistance in finding a suitable architect or builder or assistance with a grant application form. The circular guidance in relation to disabled facilities grants (see below) suggests, however, that the duty is more substantial, namely a duty to ensure that appropriate works are carried out including, for instance, the provision of financial assistance.

Adaptations

8.90   The social services obligation under CSDPA 1970 s2(1)(e) to assist in arranging works of adaptation is a specific duty and arises once an assessment has concluded that it is necessary for this service to be provided (see para 4.102 above). In legislative terms it is quite separate from the responsibility born by the housing authority[78] under Housing Grants, Construction and Regeneration Act (HGCRA) 1996 to provide (subject to a means test)[79] disabled facilities grants for such works. The procedures for securing such grants are considered at para 17.21 below. Unfortunately, however, the manner in which authorities discharge these two responsibilities often results in considerable confusion and delay and has resulted in numerous complaints to the Local Government Ombudsman.

---

78   Notwithstanding that the two authorities will frequently be one and the same.

79   The means test for disabled facilities grants depends upon the financial resources of the disabled person and their partner. If the disabled person is under 18 his or her parents means are assessed.

8.91 CSDPA 1970 s2(1)(e) places a specific duty on the social services authority to help a disabled person arrange for adaptations to his or her home to be carried out. Frequently the social services department (in providing this assistance) requires the disabled person to make an application to the housing authority for a disabled facilities grant. At this stage delay may arise due to the housing authority's failure;[80] this does not however discharge the social services department from its separate (and separately enforceable) duty under section 2(1)(e).

8.92 When such delay occurs, the appropriate response from a social services department to assist the disabled person in resolving the problem – by actively intervening in the process if needs be. Likewise, the refusal of a grant application by the housing authority does not of itself absolve the social services authority from its separate responsibility under CSDPA 1970 s2(1)(e). This point is emphasised in circular LAC(90)7,[81] which refers to the social services department as the 'lead body', and (as noted below) that its duty to act remains regardless of the housing authority's actions.[82]

8.93 Typically home adaptations concern such matters as stair lifts, ground-floor extensions, doorway widening, ramps and wheelchair accessible showers. Unlike under HGCRA 1996 Part I (considered at paras 17.31 and 17.32 below), the 1970 Act imposes no requirement that work be either 'appropriate' or 'reasonable and practicable'. All the 1970 statute requires is that the social services authority be satisfied that the works are necessary in order to meet the needs of the disabled person (by securing his or her greater safety, comfort or convenience).

8.94 Department of Health guidance, LAC(90)7, illustrates this difference of approach (at paras 15–17 and also at para 58):

> 15. The existing responsibilities of [social services authorities] under s2 of the CSDP Act are unchanged. In cases of their duty to make arrangements for home adaptations, under s2(1)(e), the responsibility will, in many instances, be effectively discharged on their behalf by the housing authority, by the giving of a disabled facilities grant. However the [social services authority's] duty to act remains, and they may be called upon to meet this duty in two ways. The first is where the needs as assessed by the [social services] authority exceed the scope for provision by the housing authority under s114(3) of the 1989 [Local Government and Housing] Act[83] and where the authority decline to use their discretionary powers under s114(4). If the [social services] authority deem the need to be established, then it will be their responsibility in these circumstances to make arrangements for this need to be met under s2 of the CSDP Act.

---

80 See para 4.129 for a general analysis of the Ombudsman's comments on such delay.

81 At para 14. LAC(90)7 was issued jointly as Department of the Environment Circular 10/90. Whilst DoE Circular 10/90 has been withdrawn (and superseded by new guidance, Circular 17/96) LAC(90)7 remains in force (see DoE 4/98 and LASSL (99)21).

82 LAC(90)7 para 15.

83 Now Housing Grants, Construction and Regeneration Act 1996 Part I, see para 17.21 below.

16. Such a responsibility might arise when for instance the [social services] authority considers there is need related to the individual's social needs that demands a greater level of provision than is required for the disability alone, and where the housing authority chooses not to exercise its discretionary powers. This may occur, for example, where the size of a bedroom for a disabled child is required to be greater than is necessary for sleeping, because it needs to fulfil the role of bed/sitting room to provide more independent social space.

17. The second instance where the [social services] authority may find they have a continuing duty to provide assistance concerns cases where a disabled person asks the [social services] authority for financial assistance, under section 2(1)(e) of the CSDP Act, with that part of the costs of an adaptation which he is expected to finance himself in the light of the test of resources for the disabled facilities grant. On occasion, this could be as much as the total costs of the adaptation. In such cases, the [social services] authority still has a duty to assist. However, in order to maintain consistency with the new arrangements for disabled facilities grants, the [social services] authority may wish to use their existing powers to charge for their services (under section 17 of the [Health and Social Services and Social Security Adjudications] Act 1983) to recover the full cost of any assistance given, provided that they consider that the client is able to afford to repay this. In examining the question of financial assistance, [social services] authorities are recommended to bear in mind that the amount of grant approved will have been calculated on the basis of a test of resources (described in more detail in paragraphs 64 and 65 and Appendix II below). [Social services] authorities should not try to make their own separate assessment of what a grant applicant is expected to pay; but they might consider whether, in their opinion, the meeting of those costs would cause hardship.[84] The method of charging or of recovery of costs is for the [social services] authority to decide; but alternatives which might be considered include loans, with or without interest, possibly secured in either case by a charge on the property[85] or the placing of a charge on the property for a set period.

8.95   The Department of the Environment guidance, Circular 17/96, deals with the interface between the two statutory obligations in the following terms:

Role of the social services authority to assist with adaptations

5. Social services authorities' responsibilities under s2 Chronically Sick and Disabled Persons Act 1970 to make arrangements for home adaptations are not affected by the grants legislation. Where an application for [disabled facilities grant] DFG has been made, those authorities may be called upon to meet this duty in two ways:

---

84 Charging for domiciliary services is considered in detail at para 12.85. The reference to 'hardship' in the circular is unhelpful: Health and Social Services and Social Security Adjudications Act 1983 s17 merely requires that the disabled person satisfy the authority that his or her means are insufficient for it to be reasonably practicable for him or her to pay for the service – in this respect see in particular para 12.68 below.
85 Such a charge could presumably only be secured on the property with the owner's consent as Health and Social Services and Social Security Adjudications Act 1983 s17 does not empower authorities to create such charges – (unlike s22).

(a) where the assessed needs of a disabled person exceeds the scope for provision by the housing authority under section 23 of the 1996 Act; and

(b) where an applicant for DFG has difficulty in meeting is assessed contribution determined by the means test and seeks financial assistance from the authority.

6. In such cases, where the social services authority determine that the need has been established, it remains their duty to assist even where the local housing authority either refuse or are unable to approve the application. Social services authorities may also consider using their powers under section 17 of the Health and Social Services and Social Security Adjudications Act 1983 to charge for their services where appropriate.

Delay

8.96 The carrying out of such adaptations has been frequently characterised by delay. In assessing whether the delay is unlawful or constitutes maladministration, it is necessary to consider separately the statutory obligations under CSDPA 1970 s2 and HGCRA 1996 Part I. In relation to the duty under CSDPA 1970 s2, the general principles relevant to the assessment and provision of services timetable (under NHSCCA 1990 s47) apply and are considered at para 17.52 above. The assessment will generally require specialist involvement and this may result in delay. The Local Government Ombudsman has produced a number of reports on this issue.[86] In a 1991[87] report the ombudsman dealt with a situation where the complainant had (among other things) waited nine months for an occupational therapist's (OT) assessment. In finding maladministration, she commented:

> The Council say that they suffered from a shortage of OTs during 1989; while I recognise that this is a national problem, nevertheless the Council still retain their responsibility to assess their client's needs. If sufficient OTs are not available, they may need to find another way of assessing those needs.

8.97 Her finding in this case does not of course mean that delays of less than nine months are acceptable. Her finding means that any council, knowing that the use of OTs for an assessment will cause a substantial delay, is guilty of maladministration when it opts to use OTs nevertheless (ie, it is maladministration the moment such a procedure is adopted).

8.98 Unlike the CSDPA 1970, HGCRA 1996 s36 allows for the delayed payment of a disabled facilities grant – up to a maximum of 12 months following the date of the application. However guidance to the Act stresses that 'this power should be used only in exceptional circumstances and not where the applicant would suffer undue hardship'.[88] The 12-month delay, however only runs from the submission of a completed grant application to the housing authority; and prior to its completion an OT assessment and

---

86 See paras 4.129 above and 19.101 below where the ombudsman's role is considered.
87 Complaint No 90/C/0336, 3 October 1991.
88 Department of the Environment as Circular 17/96 para 7.5.4 (see para 17.27 below where this is considered further).

building tenders may have to be obtained. This itself can cause very substantial delays, such that the relevant minister has stated that 'waiting times for any adaptation of more than 250 working days, from the point of initial inquiry to completion, are unacceptable'.[89]

Equipment and additional facilities

8.99   CSDPA 1970 s2(1)(e) also covers the provision of 'additional facilities' designed to secure the disabled person's greater safety, comfort or convenience. This includes all manner of fittings and gadgets such as handrails, alarm systems, hoists, moveable baths, adapted switches and handles, and so on.

8.100   The importance of the provision of appropriate equipment in promoting the independence and quality of disabled peoples' lives has been emphasised in much guidance. The National Service Framework for Older People,[90] for instance, at para 2.48 advises that:

- services should take a preventive approach, recognising that effective equipment provision (including for people with moderate disabilities) is likely to:
  - help older people to maintain their independence and live at home;
  - slow down deterioration in function and consequent loss of confidence and self-esteem;
  - prevent accidents;
  - prevent pressure sore damage;
  - support and better protect the health of carers;
- services should be timely and resolve the frequently long delays which inhibit older people's discharge from hospital, or their safety and confidence in coping at home.[91]

8.101   In 2000 and 2002 the Audit Commission published highly critical reports on the state of public provision of equipment for disabled people.[92] The 2002 report found that equipment services were in a parlous state; that users reported 'long delays for equipment of dubious quality'. Its recommendation of a substantial overhaul of the service, led to a government initiative to establish integrated 'community equipment services' where both NHS and social services equipment could be accessed at a single point.[93] Each integrated community equipment service is required to meet the following criteria:[94]

89 House of Commons Hansard 27 January 2003: Column 696 The Parliamentary Under-Secretary of State, Office of the Deputy Prime Minister (Mr Tony McNulty). – and see para 17.52 below

90 See para 14.2 below.

91 This final point is given considerable emphasis in the NHS hospital discharge guidance: 'Discharge from hospital: pathway, process and practice' Department of Health February 2003, appendix 5.3.1 pp71–72 (see also para 10.157 below).

92 *Fully Equipped: The Provision of Equipment to Older or Disabled People by the NHS and Social Services in England and Wales* 29 March 2000 and *Fully Equipped 2002 – Assisting Independence* 27 June 2002 accessible at www.audit-commission.gov.uk/.

93 See 'Guide to Integrating Community Equipment Services', 27 March 2001 accessible at www.dh.gov.uk/PublicationsAndStatistics/Publications/PublicationsLibrary/fs/en.

94 Community Equipment Services HSC 2001/008: LAC(2001) 13 para 8.

- Revenue funding from pooled health and social services contributions using Health Act 1999 flexibilities.
- A single operational manager for the service.
- A board to advise the manager, whose members include representatives of stakeholder organisations.
- Unified stock.

8.102 The guidance accompanying this initiative[95] defined community equipment as follows:

> Community equipment is equipment for home nursing usually provided by the NHS, such as pressure relief mattresses and commodes, and equipment for daily living such as shower chairs and raised toilet seats, usually provided by local authorities. It also includes, but is not limited to:
> - Minor adaptations, such as grab rails, lever taps and improved domestic lighting.
> - Ancillary equipment for people with sensory impairments, such as liquid level indicators, hearing loops, assistive listening devices and flashing doorbells.
> - Communication aids for people with speech impairments.
> - Wheelchairs for short-term loan, but not those for permanent wheelchair users, as these are prescribed and funded by different NHS services.[96]
> - Telecare equipment such as fall alarms, gas escape alarms and health state monitoring for people who are vulnerable.

8.103 The above guidance makes plain that the provision of some forms of equipment may be construed as joint social services/NHS responsibility. Similarly, some forms of equipment can be viewed as a joint social services/housing authority responsibility. Circular LAC(90)7 seeks to clarify this position (at para 19):

> ... equipment which can be installed and removed with little or no structural modification to the dwelling should usually be considered the responsibility of the [social services] authority. However, items such as stair lifts and through-floor lifts, which are designed to facilitate access into or around the dwelling would, in the view of the Secretaries of State, be eligible for disabled facilities grant. With items such as electric hoists, it is suggested that any structural modification of the property – such as strengthened joists or modified lintels – could be grant aidable under the disabled facilities grant, but that the hoisting equipment itself should be the responsibility of the [social services] authority.

Charging for equipment

8.104 The general rules concerning social services' ability to charge for community care services is considered in detail at para 12.85. However specific issues arise in relation to charging for equipment and additional facilities, particularly when there is a question on whether the item is in fact a social services or an NHS or a housing responsibility. In relation to NHS provided equipment, there is no power to charge – since such NHS services

---

95 Community Equipment Services HSC 2001/008: LAC(2001) 13 para 7.
96 See para 10.136 below concerning the provision of permanent wheelchairs.

are free at the point of delivery (unless made available under prescription – see para 10.51 below).

8.105   In relation to items that are provided as part of adaptations funded by a disabled facilities grant, the Department of the Environment guidance, Circular 17/96 advises:

Funding considerations

7. It is for housing authorities and social services authorities between them to decide how particular adaptations should be funded either through CSDP Act or through a DFG.

8. However, since DFGs were introduced in 1990 under the Local Government and Housing Act 1989, it has been common practice that equipment which can be installed and removed fairly easily with little or no structural modification of the dwelling is normally the responsibility of the social services authority.

9. For larger items such as *stairlifts* and *through-floor lifts* which normally require such structural works to the property, help is normally provided by housing authorities through DFG. However, some routine installations, may not involve structural work. To ensure that such adaptations are progressed quickly, the respective authorities should jointly agree a standard line on the installation of lifts which will apply unless there are exceptional circumstances. Authorities will wish to include arrangements for routine servicing, maintenance, removal and possible re-use.

8.106   This guidance is complimented by that in circular LAC (90)7 (para 19) which states:

[Social services] authorities can, under s17 of the HASSASSA Act,[97] charge for the provision of equipment.[98] If the [social services] authority choose to make only a revenue charge (for example to cover maintenance), or not to charge at all, they would retain ownership of the equipment, and be able if they so wished to re-use it in another property if no longer required by the original recipient. [Social services] authorities are encouraged to make maximum use of their opportunities to recover and re-use equipment such as stairlifts, and to foster local arrangements for direct provision of such equipment where this can be done effectively and economically.

8.107   In relation to items of equipment provided by English social services authorities, their power to charge under has now been curtailed by Community Care (Delayed Discharges, etc) Act 2003 s15,[99] which provides the secretary of state with power to make regulations requiring certain community care services to be provided free of charge. This power has been exercised in relation to (among other things)[100] 'community equipment services' – which are defined as the provision of an aid, or minor adapta-

---

97 See para 12.86 below.

98 This must now be read as subject to the limitations imposed by the Community Care (Delayed Discharges, etc) Act 2003 – see para 8.107 below.

99 Community Care (Delayed Discharges, etc) Act 2003 s16 gives to the Welsh Assembly similar powers – but as of December 2003 these had not been exercised.

100 See para 10.113 in relation to intermediate care services which are also to be provided free.

tion to property, for the purposes of assisting with nursing at home or aiding daily living, and an adaptation is minor if the cost of making the adaptation is £1,000 or less.[101] Guidance on this provision states that:[102]

> Any item of community equipment which a person (or their carer) is assessed as needing as a community care service, and for which the individual (or their carer) is eligible, is required to be provided free of charge. All minor adaptations costing £1,000 or less (which includes the cost of buying and fitting the adaptation) are required to be provided free of charge. Councils retain the discretion to make a charge in relation to minor adaptations that exceed £1,000 to provide.

Holidays

'Facilitating the taking of holidays by that person, whether at holiday homes or otherwise and whether provided under arrangements made by the authority or otherwise'

8.108   The power of social services authorities to provide holiday homes under NAA 1948 s29 (see para 8.51) is complemented by the duty under CSDPA 1970 s2(1)(f) to facilitate the taking of holidays by disabled persons. In *R v Ealing LBC ex p Leaman*,[103] the council refused to consider a request made by the applicant for financial assistance in taking a privately arranged holiday – on the ground that it would only grant such assistance which it itself had arranged or sponsored. In quashing the council's decision Mann J held that:

> The effect of the general policy adumbrated by the council is, in my judgement, to excise the words 'or otherwise' where they second occur in section 2(1)(f). Accordingly, the London Borough were wrong in declining to consider any application which the applicant might have made for assistance with his private holiday. Whether, having regard to a proper consideration of a person's needs, those needs required the making of a grant to a private holiday is an entirely different question. It is a question wholly within the province of the local authority. However, it was quite wrong for them to deprive themselves of the opportunity of asking that question.[104]

8.109   In appropriate cases, the local authority will have to fund the full cost of such a holiday, and not merely the additional costs attributable to the user's impairment. This may include the full cost of a holiday as well as the costs of a carer's attendance if that is the only way to 'facilitate the taking of the holiday': *R v North Yorkshire CC ex p Hargreaves (No 2)*.[105]

---

101 The regulations apply, not only to equipment provided under CSDPA 1970 s2, but also to equipment provided under NAA 1948 s29, HSPHA 1968 s45 (1), NHSA 1977 Sch 8 and CDCA 2000 s2.

102 Changes to Local Authorities Charging Regime for Community Equipment and Intermediate Care Services LAC(2003) 14: June 2003, para 3.2.

103 (1984) *Times* 10 February, QBD.

104 From pp4–5 of the transcript of the judgement.

105 (1998) 1 CCLR 331.

Meals

'The provision of meals for that person whether in his home or elsewhere'

8.110   CSDPA 1970 s2(1)(g) covers the provision of meals at day centres (or indeed anywhere) as well as meals in the disabled person's home such as meals-on-wheels. The equivalent service for the elderly is governed by Health Services and Public Health Act (HSPHA) 1968 s45 (see para 14.21).

Telephone and ancillary equipment

'The provision for that person of, or assistance to that person in obtaining, a telephone and any special equipment necessary to enable him to use a telephone'

8.111   CSDPA 1970 s2(1)(h) may cover the installation of a telephone line as well as the provision of an appropriate handset, loud telephone bell (or a flashing visual or vibrating signal), amplifiers, inductive couplers for personal hearing aids and visual transmission machines such as minicoms, faxes and possibly modems for computer e-mail transmission, etc.

Chronically Sick and Disabled Persons Act 1970 s2 and National Assistance Act 1948 s29

8.112   The rapid drafting[106] of CSDPA 1970 s2 has led to considerable confusion as to its status. The section commences with the clause: 'Where a local authority having functions under section 29 of the National Assistance Act 1948 are satisfied . . . ' and concludes 'it shall be the duty of that authority to make those arrangements in exercise of their functions under the said section 29'. It is not surprising therefore that CSDPA 1970 s2 has been considered as an extension to NAA 1948 s29 – to the extent that services identified under CSDPA 1970 s2 are in fact NAA 1948 s29 services: ie, delivered as 'arrangements in exercise of . . . s29'.

8.113   In the courts' view it is for this reason that CSDPA 1970 s2 services are not specifically listed as 'community care services' in National Health Service and Community Care Act (NHSCCA) 1990 s46 – since the reference in section 46 to services under NAA 1948 Part III include CSDPA 1970 s2 services.[107] However, and conversely, when statutory provisions make specific reference to CSDPA 1970 s2 in addition to NAA 1948 s29, the courts have generally explained this in terms of *ex abundarte cautela*[108] (from an abundance of caution).

---

106 For a description of the speed with which the Bill was drafted see *Be it Enacted* (RADAR, 1995). Unfortunately there is nothing in the Hansard reports on the passage of the Bill through Parliament to elucidate the confusing references to NAA 1948 s29.

107 Hansard (House of Commons) Standing Committee E, 15 February 1990 cols 1055 onwards.

108 *R v Powys CC ex p Hambidge* (1998) 1 CCLR 182 at 189D per Popplewell J.

8.114   It follows, that the assessment duty under NHSCCA 1990 s47(1), will require consideration of whether services under CSDPA 1970 s2 are 'called' for (see para 4.72 above) notwithstanding the absence of specific reference to this provision. This requirement was explained by Collins J in *R v Kirklees MBC ex p Daykin*[109] in the following terms:

> ... section 47 and section 2 go hand in hand. Parliament may in other Acts have specifically mentioned section 2 but that was for the purposes of those Acts and no doubt for the avoidance of any doubt. It seems to me quite clear that in the context of section 2 and section 47 the definition of 'community care services' is apt to include the services provided under section 2.

8.115   This interpretation of the status of CSDPA 1970 s2 adult care services must now be considered as settled law. It is probably the 'best fix' that can be achieved in terms of reconciling these two radically different statutes – both in terms of their origins and their philosophical outlook – and in terms of their relations with the other community care statutes.

8.116   However, having accepted that CSDPA 1970 s2 services are essentially a specifically enforceable species of services provided under the generic umbrella of NAA 1948 s29, certain collateral interpretative difficulties arise. For example NHSCCA 1990 s47(2) appears to create a different assessment procedure for CSDPA 1970 s2 services to those under the NHSCCA 1990 s46 community care statutes. As noted above (see para 4.134) the explanation advanced for this difference of treatment by the Department of Health (namely that section 47(2) assessments are required to be 'comprehensive') was rejected by Carnwath J in *R v Gloucestershire CC ex p RADAR*.[110]

8.117   A similar incongruity was exposed in *R v Gloucestershire CC ex p Mahfood*.[111] Here the respondent argued that if CSDPA 1970 s2 services were provided under NAA 1948 s29 it followed that a home help service could not be provided under CSDPA 1970 s2 notwithstanding that section 2(1)(a) is concerned with precisely such a service. The argument turned upon NAA 1948 s29(6), which prohibits services being provided under section 29 if they can be provided under the NHSA 1977. The 1977 Act makes provision for a home help service.[112] The argument, as already noted at para 8.61 was described as unattractive by McCowan LJ.[113]

8.118   In *R v Powys CC ex p Hambidge*[114] the point in issue was the ability of local authorities to charge for services provided under CSDPA 1970 s2 notwithstanding that the provision that authorises charges to be levied for non-accommodation services (the Health and Social Services and Social Security Adjudication Act 1983 s17 – see para 12.85 below) made no

---

109 (1998) 1 CCLR 512 at 525A.
110 (1998) 1 CCLR 476.
111 (1997) 1 CCLR 7; (1996) 160 LG Rev 321.
112 This aspect is also considered at para 8.58.
113 (1997) 1 CCLR 7 at 17C.
114 (1998) 1 CCLR 458.

reference to services under CSDPA 1970 s2. The Court of Appeal accepted the view of the Department of Health that section 2 services 'are arranged by local authorities in exercise of their functions under section 29 of the 1948 Act'[115] – and since HASSASSAA 1983 s17 refers to NAA 1948 s29 services, that was sufficient authority for charges to be levied.

Chronically Sick and Disabled Persons Act 1970 s2 and the Children Act 1989

8.119   An additional difficulty stems from the differences between the CSDPA 1970 s2 and NAA 1948 s29 client groups. Chronically Sick and Disabled Persons Act 1970 s28A[116] provides that:

> This Act applies with respect to disabled children in relation to whom the local authority have functions under Part III of the Children Act 1989 as it applies in relation to persons to whom section 29 of the National Assistance Act 1948 applies.

8.120   Accordingly the CSDPA 1970 s2 client group includes all disabled people, whereas NAA 1948 s29 applies only to disabled people over 18 years of age. It follows that children's services provided under CSDPA 1970 s2 cannot be provided 'in exercise of ... functions under ... s29'.

8.121   In *R v Bexley LBC ex p B*[117] (see para 18.16 below) the respondent council sought to argue (among other things) that home care services provided to a disabled child were provided under the Children Act (CA) 1989 rather than under CSDPA 1970 s2. Latham J rejected the argument; holding that such services were provided under section 2 itself.[118]

8.122   Although the *Bexley* decision is authority for the fact that community-based services provided to disabled children are generally provided under CSDPA 1970 s2, it is necessary to establish whether they are also delivered under the generic CA 1989 Part III umbrella. If they are, then it may be lawful for local authorities to charge for such services (in pursuance of their powers under CA 1989 (see para 18.47 below). Given the pragmatic approach taken by the courts to the difficulties in interpreting CSDPA 1970 s2 it is likely that they will seek to resolve this question merely by substituting the references in section 2, to NAA 1948 s29 with references to CA 1989 Part III such that the material parts of the section would then read:

> Where a local authority having functions under Children Act 1989 Part III are satisfied in the case of a disabled child ... it shall be the duty of that authority to make those arrangements in exercise of their functions under the said Part III.

8.123   Statutory recognition of the distinctiveness of CSDPA 1970 s2 services and services under the CA 1989 is found in the Carers (Recognition and

---

115 Note 2 to the Social Services Inspectorate advice note on non-accommodation charges, January 1994 – see para 12.92 below.
116 Inserted by CA 1989 s108(5), Sch 13 para 27.
117 (1995) 3 CCLR 15.
118 (1995) 3 CCLR 15 at 23C.

Services) Act 1989 s1(2)(a). This provision only applies when 'a local authority assess the needs of a disabled child for the purposes of the CA 1989 Part III or s2 of the CSDPA 1970'.

Services under National Health Service Act 1977 Sch 8

8.124 Most disabled people receive their domiciliary/community-based services from social services authorities under CSDPA 1970 s2. These services, however, are only available to people who are 'substantially and permanently handicapped'[119] or who 'suffer from a mental disorder of any description'. Section 2 services are not therefore available to person's whose impairment is not 'permanent' notwithstanding that it may be substantial. Domiciliary and community-based services for such persons are generally provided by social services pursuant to duties under NHSA 1977 s21 and Sch 8. Frequently the persons covered by these provisions are referred to as 'ill people'; ie, people who have a substantial impairment as a result of an accident or severe illness, but whose prognosis is that they will make a full recovery (and will not therefore be 'permanently handicapped'). The Act, however, also covers services for a wider client group including elderly people, expectant mothers, drug and alcohol misusers as well as disabled people.

8.125 In discussing the provision of care services for ill people, one enters the minefield that marks the medical/social divide; a subject considered further in chapter 10. The NHSA 1977 attempts to demarcate the duties of the NHS and the social services authorities. Sections 1–5 spell out the general nature of the NHS obligation in relation to disease prevention, the care and after-care of ill people. Section 21 then outlines the services which are the responsibility of the social services authorities – these being amplified in Sch 8. Sections 22–28 contain empowering provisions designed to foster co-operation between health and social care service providers (see para 10.32 below).

8.126 The texts of NHSA 1977 s21(1) and Sch 8 paras 1–3 as amended are set out below:

21(1) Subject to paragraphs (d) and (e) of section 3(1)[120] above, the services described in Schedule 8 to this Act in relation to –
(a) care of mothers,
(b) prevention, care and after-care,
(c) home help and laundry facilities,
are functions exercisable by local social services authorities, and that Schedule has effect accordingly.

---

119 See para 8.21 above.

120 It is NHSA 1977 s3(1) which enables the secretary of state to direct that certain facilities for the care, the prevention of illness and the after-care of the 'ill' and nursing or expectant mothers are the responsibility of the health service rather than social services authorities – see for example LAC(95)5 and chapter 10 below.

Schedule 8: Local Social Services Authorities
Care of mothers and young children

1(1) A local Social Services Authority may, with the Secretary of State's approval, and to such extent as he may direct shall, make arrangements for the care of expectant and nursing mothers (other than for the provision of residential accommodation for them).

Prevention, care and after-care

2(1) A local Social Services Authority may, with the Secretary of State's approval, and to such extent as he may direct shall, make arrangements for the purpose of the prevention of illness and for the care of persons suffering from illness and for the after-care of persons who have been suffering and in particular for–

(a) . . .

(b) the provision for persons whose care is undertaken with a view to preventing them from becoming ill, persons suffering from illness and persons who have been so suffering, of centres or other facilities for training them or keeping them suitably occupied and the equipment and maintenance of such centres;

(c) the provision, for the benefit of such persons as are mentioned in paragraph (b) above, of ancillary or supplemental services; and

(d) for the exercise of the functions of the Authority in respect of persons suffering from mental disorder who are received into the guardianship under Part II or III of the Mental Health Act 1983 (whether the guardianship of the local Social Services Authority or of other persons).

Such an Authority shall neither have the power nor be subject to a duty to make under this paragraph arrangements to provide facilities for any of the purposes mentioned in section 15(1) of the Disabled Persons (Employment) Act 1944.

(2) No arrangements under this paragraph shall provide for the payment of money to persons for whose benefit they are made except–

(a) in so far as they may provide for the remuneration of such persons engaged in suitable work in accordance with the arrangements, of such amounts as the local social services authority think fit in respect of their occasional personal expenses where it appears to that Authority that no such payment would otherwise be made.

(b) . . .

(2A) No arrangements under this paragraph may be given effect to in relation to a person to whom section 115 of the Immigration and Asylum Act 1999 (exclusion from benefits) applies solely –

(a) because he is destitute; or

(b) because of the physical effects, or anticipated physical effects, of his being destitute.

(2B) Subsections (3) and (5) to (8) of section 95 of the Immigration and Asylum Act 1999, and paragraph 2 of Schedule 8 to that Act, apply for the purposes of subsection (2A) as they apply for the purposes of that section, but for the references in subsections (5) and (7) of that section and in that paragraph to the Secretary of State substitute references to a local social services authority.'

(3) The Secretary of State may make regulations as to the conduct of premises in which, in pursuance of arrangements made under this

paragraph, are provided for persons whose care is undertaken with a view to preventing them from becoming sufferers from mental disorder within the meaning of that Act of 1983 or who are, or have been, so suffering, facilities for training them or keeping them suitably occupied.

(4A) This paragraph does not apply in relation to persons under the age of 18.

(4AA) No authority is authorised or may be required under this paragraph to provide residential accommodation for any person.

Home help and laundry facilities

3(1) It is the duty of every local Social Services Authority to provide on such a scale as is adequate for the needs of their area, or to arrange for the provision on such a scale as is so adequate, of home help for households where such help is required owing to the presence of a person who is suffering from illness, lying-in, an expectant mother, aged, handicapped as a result of having suffered from illness or by congenital deformity, and every such Authority has power to provide or arrange for the provisions of laundry facilities for households for which home help is being, or can be, provided under this sub-paragraph.

Client group

8.127 The Act requires social services authorities to provide a variety of services for a diverse client group, certain services being restricted to particular client groups. There is no requirement that the persons be ordinarily resident within the social services authority's area.

8.128 The potential client group is wide, in that services can be provided for any adult in order to prevent illness – to which everyone is, of course, vulnerable. The provision of home help under NHSA 1977 Sch 8 para 3 has no age restriction on the person whose need triggers the service (ie, it applies to children as well as adults). It should also be noted that the provision of home help is specified as being for the benefit of the 'household', rather than merely for the qualifying individual within the home.

8.129 NHSA 1997 Sch 8 paras 1 and 2 are subject to directions issued by the secretary of state (presently LAC(93)10 appendix 3[121] – see para 8.139 below).

Mothers

8.130 The client group is restricted to 'expectant and nursing mothers (of any age)'.[122] The services available are without restriction, save only that the provision of accommodation is not permitted. The accommodation needs of such mothers are covered by NAA 1948 s21(1)(aa) (see para 7.23).

The ill

8.131 NHSA 1977 s128(1) defines illness as including mental disorder within the meaning of the MHA 1983 and any injury or disability requiring medical or

---

121 WOC 35/93 in Wales.
122 LAC(93)10 appendix 3.

dental treatment or nursing. Persons who are alcoholic or drug-dependent are specifically included.[123] Services can also be provided for the purpose of preventing illness and for the after-care of persons who have been so suffering; the client group is therefore limited only by the size of the adult population.

8.132   The client group is generally restricted to persons aged 18 or over.[124] The exception to this general rule, being that home help and laundry services (under para 3) are available to ill adults or children alike).

Mothers lying-in

8.133   At first sight it might appear incongruous that separate reference be made to mothers 'lying-in' (literally, 'the being in childbed'), when nursing mothers are already included as a category. The reason for this is related to the different services available. Where the need exists, there is a duty to provide home help for mothers lying-in, whereas the other services available to expectant and nursing mothers are discretionary. The mother may be of any age (ie, over or under 18).

The aged

8.134   No definition is provided for 'aged'.[125] The overlap with the corresponding provision under Health Services and Public Health Act (HSPHA) 1968 s45 (see para 14.12) is presumably explained on the basis that (where need for home help is assessed) section 45 services are discretionary whereas the NHS provision is obligatory.

The handicapped

8.135   The 'handicapped' person may be of any age (ie, over or under 18) and there is no requirement that the 'handicap' be either substantial or permanent (unlike the requirement in NAA 1948 s29; see para 8.36 above); it must, however, result from either illness or congenital deformity. Excluded, therefore, are those whose impairment results from injury (NAA 1948 s29 covers this category if the consequent impairment is both permanent and substantial). The apparent lacuna is however largely academic – the definition of illness in NHSA 1977 (as detailed above) includes an injury which requires medical or dental treatment or nursing – and the Act covers the provision of services for the after-care of such persons.

Excluded groups

8.136   The effect of Immigration and Asylum Act 1999 s117, by amending NHSA 1977 Sch 8, is to exclude from services people who are asylum-seekers

---

123 LAC(93)10 appendix 3, para 3(g); see para 16.22 where services for alcohol and drug misuers are considered in greater detail.

124 NHSA 1977 Sch 8 para 4A.

125 See NAA 1948 s21, where no definition is given of 'age' and likewise HSPHA 1968 s45, which uses the phrase 'old people' – dealt with at paras 7.20 and 14.21 respectively.

and are in need of community care services solely on account of being 'destitute'.[126]

Services

8.137 Before the implementation of the National Health Service and Community Care Act (NHSCCA) 1990, the services that could be provided under NHSA 1977 Sch 8 included the provision of accommodation. The NHSCCA 1990 by amendment[127] removed this power, and all social services authority community care accommodation obligations for adults (with the exception of their joint MHA 1983 s117 obligations, see para 7.143) are now dealt with under NAA 1948.[128]

8.138 NHSA 1977 Sch 8 paras 1–3 deal with three separate services:

Paragraph 1 Services for expectant and nursing mothers.
Paragraph 2 Services for the prevention of illness, and the care and after-care of sufferers.
Paragraph 3 Home help and laundry services.

8.139 Paragraphs 1 and 2 follow the traditional community care drafting convention; they do not authorise the provision of any services but leave to the secretary of state the power to specify in directions what services may and what services must be provided. The most recent directions in this respect were issued on 17 March 1993 as LAC (93)10 appendix 3.[129] Paragraph 3 is, however, a free-standing statutory provision which is not the subject of any direction.

8.140 These three categories of services are dealt with separately below.

Services for expectant and nursing mothers

8.141 The directions merely state[130] that 'the Secretary of State approves the making of arrangements . . . for the care of expectant and nursing mothers (of any age) other than the provision of accommodation for them'.[131] For mothers under the age of 18 there is of course an overlapping responsibility under CA 1989 Part III (if the mother or child are considered to be 'in need' – see para 18.3). No circular or other guidance has been issued concerning the nature or extent of these services – they remain at the discretion of the social services authority. There is no reason why the service provided by the social services authority should not include the giving of assistance in kind or, in exceptional circumstances, in cash.[132] The only

---

126 NHSA 1977 Sch 8 para 2A inserted by Immigration and Asylum Act 1999 s117.
127 NHSCCA 1990 Sch 9 para 18(4). See also para 12.73.
128 NAA 1948 s21 as amended by NHSCCA 1990 s42 (see LAC(93)10 para 6) – and the provision of certain hostel accommodation under NAA 1948 s29 – see para 7.145.
129 WOC 35/93 in Wales.
130 LAC(93)10 appendix 3, para 2.
131 Accommodation services being covered by NAA 1948 s21(1)(aa).
132 The general prohibition on making payment to service users under the community care legislation does not apply in this case; compare NAA 1948 s29(6)(a) and NHSA 1977 Sch 8 para 2(2) and also compare CA 1989 s17(6).

restrictions (which follow from the actual wording of the direction) are that the service must be a 'care' service and that the service must be for the care of the mother (ie, not for the infant or any one else in the household).

Services for the prevention of illness, etc

8.142　Detailed directions have been issued in relation to the range of services that can be provided for the prevention of illness and the care and after-care of those who have been ill (see appendix B for the full text). While the directions oblige social services authorities to provide services for the prevention of mental disorder (or for the care of persons who have been suffering from mental disorder) they leave the provision of services for the alleviation of 'non-mental disorder' to the discretion of the social services authority. These two services are therefore dealt with separately below. The services are, in both cases, only available to adults and (subject to the specific exceptions detailed below) may not include the payment of money to the service user (but see para 9.1 below).

The duty to provide services to alleviate mental disorder

8.143　The secretary of state's directions oblige social services authorities to make domiciliary care arrangements (detailed in (a) and (b) below) for the purpose of preventing mental disorder, as well as for persons who are or who have been suffering from mental disorder[133] (see appendix B for full text). The directed services are the provision of:

a) Centres (including training centres and day centres) or other facilities (including domiciliary facilities), whether in premises managed by the local authority or otherwise, for training or occupation of such persons; including the payment of persons engaged in suitable work at the 'centres or other facilities'.[134]

b) Social work and related services to help in the identification, diagnosis, assessment and social treatment of mental disorder and to provide social work support and other domiciliary and care services to people living in their own homes and elsewhere.

8.144　The directions would appear to be so widely drafted as to cover most of the commonly encountered domiciliary care services, ie, day centres, drop-in centres, educational, occupational and recreational facilities, transport, meals,[135] home helps and so on. Accommodation services are, however, specifically excluded by NHSA 1977 Sch 8 para 2(4AA).

8.145　The directions additionally require local authorities to appoint sufficient social workers in their area to act as approved social workers for

133　LAC(93)10 appendix 3, para 3(2).

134　LAC(93)10 appendix 3, para 3(3)(b) – but subject to NHSA 1977 Sch 8 para 2(2)(a), which provides that the amount of such remuneration shall be limited to payment of such persons' occasional personal expenses if their work would not normally be remunerated.

135　Meals and meals-on-wheels for housebound people are specifically included by virtue of NHSA 1977 Sch 8 para 3(3)(a).

the purposes of Mental Health Act (MHA) 1983 and to make arrangements to enable them to exercise their guardianship functions under that Act.

8.146 As has been noted above at para 8.58, NAA 1948 s29(6)(b) excludes services being provided under section 29 where such services are 'required to be provided' under the NHSA 1977. The inclusion of the phrase 'mental disorder of any description' within NAA 1948 s29 and in the secretary of state's direction relating to services under NHSA 1977 Sch 8, would tend to suggest that NAA 1948 s29 is of limited relevance to persons suffering from a mental disorder. It is, however, unlikely that this exclusion applies to services under CSDPA 1970 s2 (for the reasons stated by McCowan LJ noted at para 8.61 above). The tortuous relationship between the almost irreconcilable provisions in these Acts is so unsatisfactory, that only primary legislation can lead to a rational resolution.

The power to provide services to alleviate 'illness'

8.147 The secretary of state's direction empowers (but does not oblige) social services authorities to make the domiciliary care arrangements detailed below. In each case the service can only be provided for the purpose of either preventing illness, or for the care or after-care of a person suffering or recovering from an illness. The directed services are the provision of:

a) Centres or other facilities for training such persons or for keeping them suitably occupied (and the equipment and maintenance of such centres), together with any other ancillary or supplemental services for such persons.[136] The services provided by a social services authority may include the payment of 'persons engaged in suitable work at the centres or other facilities'.[137] The equivalent services for disabled people (under CSDPA 1970 s2) are considered at para 8.76 and for elderly people (under HSPHA 1968 s45) at para 14.21.

b) Meals at the centres referred to in (a) above, or at other facilities (including domiciliary facilities) and meals-on-wheels for housebound people, provided they are not available under HSPHA 1968 s45(1)[138] or from a district council under HASSASSA Act 1983 Sch 9 Part II para 1.[139] The equivalent services for disabled people (under the CSDPA 1970) are considered at para 8.110 and for elderly people (under HSPHA 1968) at para 14.21.

c) Social services (including advice and support) for the purposes of preventing the impairment of physical or mental health of adults in families where such impairment is likely, and for the purposes of preventing the break-up of such families, or for assisting in their rehabilitation; the equivalent services for disabled people (under NAA 1948 s29) are considered at para 8.42.

136 LAC(93)10 appendix 3, paras 3(1)(a) and (b).
137 See note 132 above.
138 See para 14.2.
139 The paragraph empowers a district council to make arrangements (or to employ a suitable voluntary organisation to make these arrangements) for providing meals and recreation for old people in their homes or elsewhere, see para 14.30 below.

d) Night-sitter services. Such a service is a specific form of 'practical assist-ance within the home' (as covered by CSDPA 1970 s2(1)(a)) and 'home help' (as covered by NHSA 1977 Sch 8 para 3 – see below). The inclusion of specific reference to this service is therefore probably unnecessary.

e) Recuperative holidays. CSDPA 1970 s2(1)(f) covers holidays for dis-abled people (see para 8.108) and NAA 1948 s29 enables authorities to provide holiday homes (see para 8.51).

f) Facilities for social and recreational activities; this is an equivalent power to the duty under CSDPA 1970 s2(1)(c) (see para 8.76) and under HSPHA 1968 s45 (see para 14.21).

g) Services specifically for persons who are alcoholic or drug-dependent. Such services are considered separately at para 16.22.

Home help and laundry services

Home help

8.148　The Act requires social services authorities to provide[140] a home help ser-vice for households where such help is required owing to the presence of a person who is suffering from illness, lying-in, or is an expectant mother, aged, or handicapped as a result of having suffered from illness or by con-genital deformity.[141] The potential extent of the service, as well as the over-lap (and differences) between this provision and that under CSDPA 1970 s2(1)(a) has been noted above at paras 8.70 and 8.117. The NHSA 1977 home help service, unlike the 1970 Act service, can be provided for the of 'the household' rather being restricted to the disabled service user's needs.

Laundry service

8.149　Social services authorities are empowered (but not obliged) to provide[142] a laundry service for households where they assess it as being required owing to the presence of a person who is suffering from illness, or lying-in, an expectant mother, aged, or handicapped as a result of having suffered from illness or by congenital deformity. Laundry services can therefore be provided in any situation where the Act enables the provision of home help: they are not, however, dependent on the household actually receiving that home help service.

8.150　　The NHS has overlapping responsibilities for laundry services, particu-larly as a consequence of incontinence (see para 10.142) or the involvement of the district nursing services or as part of a continuing care package (see para 10.87).

140　The services may either be provided by the authority or arranged by the authority but provided by another authority, a voluntary organisation or private person – see LAC(93)10 appendix 3, para 4.

141　NHSA 1977 Sch 8 para 3.

142　See note 140 above.

CHAPTER 9

Direct payments and the Independent Living Fund

Introduction

9.1   Direct payments are a different way by which local authorities can discharge their community care responsibilities. Having assessed a need, social services satisfy that need, not by the provision of care services but by the payment of cash to the service user or someone on his or her behalf. Historically such an arrangement was not possible: although the principal social care statutes provided social services with flexibility as to how they discharged their obligations, they almost invariably prohibited the payment of cash directly to the service user.[1]

9.2   The inability of service users to make their own care arrangements was frequently seen as disabling and disempowering.[2] In addition, research suggested that the making of direct payments could result in much improved user satisfaction, and indeed cost savings to local authorities.[3] Kestenbaum, for instance, drew attention to the high value placed by service users on choice and control and that in general this could not be provided by local authorities:

> It is not simply a matter of resource levels, though these are significant. As important are the qualities that any large-scale service providing organisation would find hard to deliver: choice of care assistant, flexibility, consistency, control of times and tasks, etc.[4]

9.3   As a consequence of this pressure for reform a number of direct payment options have been developed over the last 15 years. These initially consisted of 'indirect' or 'third-party schemes' whereby the local authority paid the cash to an intermediary who then brokered the care arrangements that the service user required. In 1988 there was development of the first 'Independent Living Scheme' which specifically allowed for direct payments to a restricted group of disabled people. In 1996 the provisions of the Community Care (Direct Payments) (CC(DP)A) Act 1996 brought the possibility of direct payments to almost all disabled people. The 1996 Act was augmented by the Carers and Disabled Children Act (CDCA) 2000 which extended direct payments to certain carers and parents of disabled children, and then superseded (in England) by the provisions of Health and Social Care Act (HSCA) 2001 ss57–58. At the time of writing,[5] the relevant parts of the 2001 Act have not been brought into effect in Wales – where accordingly the 1996 Act remains relevant (see para 9.34).

---

1   See, for instance, National Assistance Act (NAA) 1948 s29(6)(a) and National Health Service Act (NHSA) 1977 Sch 8 para 2. Although Children Act (CA) 1989 s17(6) (prior to its amendment by the CDCA 2000) permitted the payment of cash, this was only in 'in exceptional circumstances'.

2   See, eg, J Morris, *Independent Lives: Community Care and Disabled People* Basingstoke (Macmillan, 1993).

3   See, for instance, A Kestenbaum, 'Independent Living: a Review' (Joseph Rowntree Foundation, 1996).

4   'Independent Living: a Review' at p77.

5   April 2004.

9.4   This chapter reviews the law concerning direct payments, as follows:

- Direct payments and the HSCA 2001 (ie, England) – see immediately below;
- Direct payments and the CC(DP)A 1996 (ie, Wales) – see para 9.34 below;
- Indirect payments/third-party schemes – see para 9.36 below;
- The Independent Living Funds – see para 9.42 below.

Direct payments and the Health and Social Care Act 2001

9.5   The power to provide direct payments under the Community Care (Direct Payments) Act 1996 has now been superseded in England by the provisions of HSCA 2001 ss57–58. The Act repealed the relevant parts of the 1996 Act[6] (in England) and provided the secretary of state with the power to make regulations compelling local authorities to make direct payments in specified situations. Regulations have been issued (the '2003 regulations') which provide:[7]

- that payments can only be made to persons who appear to be capable of managing a direct payment alone or with 'such assistance as may be available to him' (regs 2 and 3);
- an obligation to make direct payments where (reg 4):
  - the person is entitled to services under the community care legislation or the Carers and Disabled Children Act (CDCA) 2000 or (in the case of a parent of a child in need) the Children Act 1989;
  - that person agrees to the making of the direct payment;
  - the person is not a proscribed person (effectively someone who is subject to certain court or tribunal orders)(reg 2(2));
  - the local authority is satisfied that the person's needs for the relevant service can be met by securing the provision of it by means of a direct payment (or in the case of a child in need – that his or her welfare will be safeguarded and promoted by securing it by the provision of it by means of the direct payment) (reg 2(3));
- for the possibility of gross payments (reg 5);
- for payments to be made to relatives or persons living in the same household if the local authority 'is satisfied that securing the service from such a person is necessary for promoting the persons need for the service/the welfare of the child in need' (reg 6).

---

6   HSCA 2001 s67 and Sch 6.

7   The Community Care, Services for Carers and Children's Services (Direct Payments) (England) Regulations 2003 SI No 762.

8   Direct Payment Guidance. Community Care, Services for Carers and Children's Services (Direct Payments) Guidance England 2003 (Sept 200) accessible at www.dh.gov.uk/PolicyAndGuidance/OrganisationPolicy/FinanceAndPlanning/ DirectPayments/fs/en.

9.6   In addition to the regulations, detailed practice guidance has been issued
       by the Department of Health[8] (referred to below as the '2003 guidance').
       The government is eager to increase the number of service users taking up
       direct payments[9] and to ensure that internal authority budgeting arrange-
       ments are not used to stifle schemes – as the 2003 guidance at para 23
       states:

> Problems with internal budget management procedures may not be used
> as a reason to refuse or delay the offering or start of a direct payment to a
> person to whom there is a duty to make a direct payment.

9.7   The key entitlement principles under HSCA 2001 can be summarised as
       follows:

   1) Direct payments must relate to the users assessment (be it a commu-
      nity care assessment, an assessment under the CDCA 2000 or under
      the CA 1989).
   2) The service user must consent to the arrangement.
   3) The service user must be able to 'manage' the payment – alone or with
      assistance.
   4) The exclusion of certain service users.
   5) The exclusion of certain service providers.
   6) The exclusion of certain services.
   7) The amount of the payment.
   8) The obligations upon the recipient of direct payments.

A prior assessment

9.8   Direct payments can only be made after an assessment has taken place
       under the relevant legislation (ie, under National Health Service and Com-
       munity Care Act (NHSCCA) 1990 s47, the CDCA 2000 or the CA 1989).
       The recipient of the direct payment must ensure that it is spent on services
       to meet the assessed need. The 2003 regulations provides that where a
       social services authority believe that the payment has not been used to
       secure the provision of the service to which it relates it may require repay-
       ment (reg 9 – see para 9.32 below).

Consent

9.9   The 2003 guidance at para 45 states:

> The council should . . . make clear that a person does not have to agree to
> a direct payment and that it would arrange services in the normal way if
> someone decides not to accept direct payments. They should also discuss
> with people who are to receive direct payments what they should do if they
> no longer wish to receive direct payments.

---

9   See 2003 guidance para 10 and Section III: PSS Performance Assessment Framework
     for 2003/2004 at www.dh.gov.uk/assetRoot/04/07/03/99/04070399.pdf.

The ability to manage the payment – alone or with assistance

9.10 A direct payment is only permitted if (among other things) it:

> . . . appears to the responsible authority [that the person is] . . . capable of managing a direct payment by himself or with such assistance as may be available to him (reg 3).

9.11 Three significant considerations arise out of this requirement:

a) The test is subjective to the extent that it is the local authority's opinion that is determinative. Accordingly the courts will be slow to interfere with their assessment in any particular situation, provided it is based upon evidence and rational.

b) The test is 'capability' not 'capacity'. Accordingly a person may be deemed incapable by a local authority, not because he or she lacks sufficient mental capacity, but because he or she is not considered sufficiently responsible to ensure that the payments are properly managed. This might arise because of a variety of factors, for instance because of mental health problems, a chaotic lifestyle, drug or other dependency.

c) If there is doubt as to whether the service user is capable of managing the payment, consideration must be given to what assistance may be available to enable the payment to be properly managed.

9.12 The 2003 guidance primarily focuses upon the issue of capacity, namely whether a service user has sufficient mental capacity to manage a payment – alone or with assistance – advising (at paras 48–49):

> Councils should not make blanket assumptions that whole groups of people will or will not be capable of managing direct payments. A council is not under a duty to make a direct payment if it does not appear to it that the person is capable of managing the payment, or to do so with assistance. However, very many people will be able to do so, in particular, if they have access to help and support.
>
> If a council is concerned that a person who wishes to receive a direct payment may not be able to manage the payment, the council should ensure that it takes into account all relevant factors before making a decision not to make a direct payment. These decisions may need to involve professional staff who are trained to assess capacity and to help people make decisions, and who should consider:
> • the person's understanding of direct payments, including the actions required on their part;
> • whether the person understands the implications of taking or not taking on direct payments;
> • what help is available to the person;
> • the nature of the services the person is assessed as needing;
> • what arrangements the person would make to obtain services.

9.13 At para 58 the 2003 guidance advises, in relation to enduring powers of attorney:

> A person with legal capacity can make an enduring power of attorney (EPA). He or she makes the EPA in the expectation that if they lose

capacity the person appointed as attorney will lawfully be able to continue to deal with his or her property and affairs once the power is registered. If a person receives direct payments, then the attorney under the EPA could continue to receive payments on his or her behalf.

The provision of assistance in the managing of the direct payment

9.14　It is not only people with limited mental capacity that are likely to benefit from assistance in the managing of the direct payment, and in this respect the 2003 guidance (at paras 24–26) advises:

> When discussing direct payments with people, local councils will wish, wherever possible, to offer the option for them to be put in touch with a support group or local centre for independent living, or a peer support group of people who already manage direct payments.
>
> Experience has shown that developing support services is a key element of successful implementation of direct payment schemes . . . The experience of existing recipients of direct payments is that they find it easier to seek advice from someone who is independent of the council.

9.15　The guidance contains considerable advice on how service users' should be enabled to cope with some of the more complex aspects of managing payments – particularly if this requires that they employ care assistants – including:

> *Health and safety* (para 96)
> Councils . . . should avoid laying down health and safety policies for individual direct payment recipients. Individuals should accept that they have a responsibility for their own health and safety, including the assessment and management of risk. They should be encouraged to develop strategies on lifting and handling and other tasks both in the home and outside it where lifting equipment, for example, may not be available.
>
> *Employee responsibilities* (paras 100–101)
> Individuals should be made aware of their legal responsibilities in terms of providing a statement of employment particulars, meeting the national minimum wage, taxes and statutory benefits such as sick pay and annual leave. If support services are provided, local councils may wish to include a payroll service which will take responsibility for administering wages, tax and National Insurance for the direct payment recipient. A written contract will help ensure that all those involved have the same understanding about the terms of employment.
>
> The aim should be to inform the potential recipient accurately, responsibly, constructively and supportively. It should not be done in such a way as to put off the recipient, for example, by over-stressing the extent and complexity of these responsibilities, but neither should the council fail to make recipients aware of what is involved.

9.16　The employment obligations of direct payment recipients may be of particular complexity if the employed person is to care for a disabled child, and the guidance in this respect is considered separately at para 18.25 below.

Excluded service users

9.17 Regulation 2(2) of the 2003 regulations lists those service users who are prohibited from receiving direct payments. The list comprises persons who are subject to specific court or tribunal controls, the imposition of which being deemed evidence of their unsuitability to manage direct payments. The following list comprises only those persons subject to English statutory orders, although regulation 2(2) also lists persons subject to orders imposed by Scottish courts/tribunals:[10]

(a) required to submit to treatment for his mental condition or for his drug or alcohol dependency by virtue of a requirement of a community rehabilitation order within the meaning of Powers of Criminal Courts (Sentencing) Act (PCC(S)A) 2000 s41 or a community punishment and rehabilitation order within the meaning of section 51 of that Act;

(b) subject to a drug treatment and testing order within the meaning of PCC(S)A 2000 s52;

(c) released on licence under the Criminal Justice Act 1991 s37 subject to a mental health or drug or alcohol dependency treatment condition;

(d) placed under guardianship in pursuance of:
   (i) Mental Health Act (MHA) 1983 s7; or
   (ii) MHA 1983 s37;

(e) absent from hospital under MHA 1983 s s17 leave;

(f) subject to after-care under supervision under MHA 1983 s25A.

(g) subject to a condition imposed under MHA 1983 ss42(2) or 73(4) (including one varied under MHA 1983 ss73(5) or 75(3));

(h) subject to a supervision and treatment order under the Criminal Procedure (Insanity and Unfitness to Plead) Act 1991 Sch 2, Pt 1.

Excluded service providers

9.18 Regulation 6 of the 2003 regulations restricts the ability of the recipients of direct payments to use the monies to purchase care services from their close relatives or partners. These restrictions are less onerous than those that previously applied under the CC(DP)A 1996. Regulation 6 provides

---

10 The Scottish orders referred to in 2003 regulations reg 2(2) comprise persons: (i) who are patients subject to after-care under a community care order under the Mental Health (Scotland) Act 1984 s35A; (j) who are patients absent from hospital on leave under Mental Health (Scotland) Act 1984 s27; (k) subject to a guardianship order under Adults with Incapacity (Scotland) Act 2000 s57 by reason of, or by reasons which include, incapacity through mental disorder; (l) who are restricted patients within the meaning of the Mental Health (Scotland) Act 1984 s63(1) who have been given a conditional discharge under ss64 or 68 of that Act; (m) subject to an order under the Criminal Procedure (Scotland) Act 1995 ss57(2)(a), (b), (c) or (d), 58 or 59; (n) required to submit to treatment for their mental condition or drug or alcohol dependency by virtue of a requirement of a probation order within the meaning of the Criminal Procedure (Scotland) Act 1995 ss228 to 230 or subject to a drug treatment and testing order within the meaning of section 234B of that Act; (o) released on licence under the Prisons (Scotland) Act 1989 ss22 or 26 of the or under the Prisoners and Criminal Proceedings (Scotland) Act 1993 s1 and subject to a mental health or for his drug or alcohol dependency treatment condition.

that direct payments cannot (subject to the proviso listed below) be used to purchase services from:

    (a) the direct payment recipient's spouse or common law partner
    (b) anyone living in the same household as the direct payment recipient who is also his or her:
        (i)   parent or parent-in-law (or their spouse or common law partner);
        (ii) son or daughter (or their spouse or common law partner);[11]
        (iii) son-in-law or daughter-in-law (or their spouse or common law partner);[12]
        (iv) stepson or stepdaughter (or their spouse or common law partner);
        (v) brother or sister (or their spouse or common law partner);
        (vi) aunt or uncle(or their spouse or common law partner); or
        (vii) grandparent (or their spouse or common law partner).

9.19   Regulation 6(1) of the 2000 regulations provides that a direct payment recipient can purchase services from one of the above excluded service providers if the social services authority 'is satisfied that securing the service from such a person is necessary to meet satisfactorily the prescribed person's need for that service'. There is however no statutory restriction on the direct payment recipient paying any other relation to provide care.

9.20   Where the payment is made to the parent of a disabled child then payments can be made to 'live-in' close relatives provided the social services authority 'is satisfied that securing the service from such a person is necessary for promoting the welfare of the child in need' (reg 6(1)(b)). This issue is considered separately at para 18.25 below.

9.21   The 2003 guidance (at paras 94–95) advises as follows:

> Unless a council is satisfied that it is necessary to meet satisfactorily a person's needs, a council may not allow people to use direct payments to secure services from a spouse (husband or wife), from a partner (the other member of an unmarried couple with whom they live), or from a close relative (or their spouse or partner) who live in the same household as the direct payment recipient.
>
>   This restriction is not intended to prevent people using their direct payments to employ a live-in personal assistant, provided that that person is not someone who would be usually excluded by the Regulations. The restriction applies where the relationship between the two people is primarily personal rather than contractual, for example, if the people concerned would be living together in any event.

9.22   The Department of Health have moved to encourage the use of direct payments to pay close relatives – the Minister issuing a press release stating:[13]

---

11 This exclusion does not apply in the case of a person mentioned in CA 1989 s17A(2)(c), namely 'a disabled child aged 16 or 17, and a local authority ('the responsible authority') have decided for the purposes of section 17 that the child's needs (or, if he is such a disabled child, his needs) call for the provision by them of a service in exercise of functions conferred on them under that section' – reg 6(3) of the 2003 regulations.

12 Ibid.

13 Department of Health Press Release 26 January 2004 at www.dh.gov.uk/PublicationsAndStatistics/PressReleases/PressReleasesLibrary/fs/en.

. . . some councils say they are confused over the rules governing how individuals can use their direct payments to pay close relatives. We're reminding councils that there is no legal restriction on individuals using their direct payment to pay close relatives who don't live with them . . . [and that] . . . in exceptional circumstances, people can also use their direct payment to pay a relative who lives with them, if they and their local council decide this is the only satisfactory way of meeting their care needs.

Excluded services

9.23   Direct payments cannot be used to purchase prolonged periods of residential care (reg 7). The guidance (at paras 74–75) clarifies the scope of this prohibition in the following terms:

> Direct payments may not pay for adults to live for the long-term in a care home. They may be made to enable people to purchase for themselves short stays in care homes, but this cannot be for more than a four-week period in any twelve-months. Where two successive periods of such care are less than four weeks apart, they are added together to make a cumulative total which may not exceed four weeks. If the two periods are more than four weeks apart they are not added together. It is unlikely that direct payments will be appropriate for emergency (unplanned) residential care.
>
> People can receive additional weeks in a care home once they have reached the four-week maximum. They cannot purchase the stay using their direct payments, but if the council considers that a longer stay is needed, it can still arrange and fund stays for the person itself in the normal way. There is no restriction on the length of time for which the council may arrange such accommodation for someone.

9.24   Although the 2003 guidance and regulations are silent on the issue of local authority provided services, it appears that practice guidance issued in 2000, holds true, namely that:

> . . . direct payments cannot be used to purchase local authority provided services, as local authorities are not permitted to sell their services in this way. However, an individual could receive both direct payments, and services provided by the local authority in the normal way, within his or her care package.[14]

9.25   With the exception of 'in-house' local authority services and prolonged periods of residential care, there is no limit on the services to which direct payments can be applied (provided they are within the scope of the community care legislation, the CDCA 2002 or CA 1989 Part III). It follows that direct payments can, for instance, be used to purchase equipment, as the guidance (paras 78–79) explains:

> Councils may make direct payments to enable people to purchase for themselves equipment that would otherwise have been provided by the social services department. Direct payments may also be made to enable

14   LAC(2000)1 practice guidance para 32.

people to pay for adaptations which would otherwise have been provided or arranged by the social services department.

Direct payments cannot be used to purchase services or equipment for which the council is not responsible, for example, services that the NHS provides. Direct payments are not a substitute for disabled facilities grants.

The amount of the payment

9.26   Direct payments must be calculated on the basis of the 'reasonable cost of securing the cost of the service concerned' albeit that the legislation permits them to be paid gross or net of any charge the local authority deems it is reasonably practicable for the service user to pay.[15] In some cases the calculation of the appropriate amount of a direct payment may be complex. Advice on how this should be done is given in the 2003 guidance and in specialist guidelines produced by CIPFA for local authorities.[16] The guidance comments at paras 82–83:

> It is up to the council to decide on the amount of a direct payment. However, the direct payments legislation provides that it must be equivalent to the council's estimate of the reasonable cost of securing the provision of the service concerned, subject to any sum paid by the recipient. This means that the direct payment should be sufficient to enable the recipient lawfully to secure a service of a standard that the council considers is reasonable to fulfil the needs for the service to which the payment relates. There is no limit on the maximum or minimum amount of a direct payment either in the amount of care it is intended to purchase or on the value of the direct payment.
>
> In estimating the reasonable cost of securing the provision of the service concerned, local councils should include associated costs that are necessarily incurred in securing provision, without which the service could not be provided, or could not lawfully be provided. The particular costs involved will vary depending upon the way in which the service is secured, but such costs might include recruitment costs, national insurance, statutory holiday pay, sick pay, maternity pay, employers' liability insurance, public liability insurance and VAT.

The obligations upon the recipient of direct payments

9.27   In some cases direct payments will place a considerable administrative burden on the service user; requiring detailed records and accounts to be kept (as the local authority will need to audit these) as well as obligations in relation to employment contracts, grievance procedures, the payment of PAYE and national insurance, VAT and so on. Local authorities are advised to provide appropriate support services (including advocacy support – 2003 guidance para 36).

---

15 HSCA 2001 s57(4) and (5) and reg 5 of the 2003 regulations.
16 'Community Care (Direct Payments) Act 1996; accounting and financial management guidelines'. Chartered Institute of Public Finance and Accountancy (1998).

9.28   In relation to support services (at paras 24–26) the 2003 guidance states:

> When discussing direct payments with people, local councils will wish, wherever possible, to offer the option for them to be put in touch with a support group or local centre for independent living, or a peer support group of people who already manage direct payments.
>
> Experience has shown that developing support services is a key element of successful implementation of direct payment schemes. Councils are encouraged to consider ways in which they can offer support in connection with direct payments. Councils might decide that they can provide a support service directly, in partnership with a local voluntary organisation, or by some other means. Support provided through voluntary/recipient-run organisations has been shown to be particularly effective and valued by recipients.
>
> The experience of existing recipients of direct payments is that they find it easier to seek advice from someone who is independent of the council . . .

9.29   In relation to the monitoring and auditing of the payments the guidance advises (paras 146–148):

> The frequency of monitoring will be dictated by the length of time the person has managed a direct payment (either alone or with help) and their particular circumstances. Once a council is satisfied a person is managing the direct payments satisfactorily, reviews should be at the same intervals as for other people receiving services. For example, people with fluctuating conditions might need monitoring every few months, rather than once or twice a year . . .
>
> Each council should set up financial monitoring arrangements for audit purposes. This will fulfil its responsibility to ensure that public funds are spent to produce the intended outcomes. CIPFA issues up-to-date guidance for local councils on this point and local councils should ensure this advice is being used. Before people decide to accept direct payments, local councils should discuss with them the information they will be expected to provide and the way in which monitoring will be carried out.
>
> Councils should pay particular attention to ensuring that audit arrangements are as simple and easy to understand as possible. Complicated paperwork can be a significant disincentive for people considering direct payments. It is worth taking time to discuss with individuals what is required so as to avoid being needlessly intrusive.

9.30   Direct payment users are legally responsible for the services they purchase with the monies they receive from social services. It follows that in respect of any problem they encounter with the service they purchase, they cannot make a complaint to social services, although they can seek the authority's assistance – in this respect the 2003 guidance advises at para 154:

> Councils should make people aware that they should plan for the unexpected and discuss with each person what arrangements he or she will make for emergencies, to ensure that the person receives the care he or she needs when the usual arrangements break down (eg, through sickness of one of the person's personal assistants). The council will need to be prepared to respond in these circumstances just as it would with any other person using a service. It may decide to step in and arrange the

services where this is necessary to meet its responsibilities. The council could also explore other ways of providing assistance to enable the person to continue to manage his or her own care by using direct payments, particularly if the difficulty is temporary or unforeseen.

9.31   It has been suggested that the decision of the Scottish Employment Appeal Tribunal in *South Lanarkshire Council v Smith and others*[17] means that local authorities remain liable in employment disputes between a recipient of direct payments and the person he or she chooses to employ as his or her carer. Although the judgment is at times difficult to follow (because it fails to explain material background detail) the case did not concern direct payments under the 1996 legislation. It appears to be of only limited relevance to direct payment arrangements; indeed Lord Johnstone in his judgment noted that 'we would not for a moment seek to suggest that disabled persons cannot be an employer, particularly over someone caring for them'.

Repayment and discontinuance

9.32   Authorities have power to seek repayment of direct payments if they are satisfied that it has not been used to secure the provision of the service to which it relates. The 2003 guidance at para 161 advises that:

> Councils should bear in mind that repayment should be aimed at recovering money which has been diverted from the purpose for which it was intended, or where services have been obtained from someone who is ineligible to provide them, or which has simply not been spent at all. It should not be used to penalise honest mistakes, nor should repayment be sought where the individual has been the victim of fraud.

9.33   The 2003 Regulations additionally provide that a council shall cease making direct payments if the person no longer appears to the council to be capable of managing the direct payment or of managing it with help (reg 10).

Direct payments – Wales

9.34   The Welsh Assembly have (as at April 2004) yet to bring into force HSCA 2001 ss57–58 and accordingly direct payments in Wales are primarily governed by the Community Care (Direct Payments) Act 1996. It is anticipated that the 2001 Act's regime will come into force in Wales in stages between August 2004 and December 2005.[18]

9.35   The major difference between the scheme in Wales (which is the subject of detailed guidance issued by the Assembly) and the scheme under

---

17 Transcript 19 January 2000.

18 Details of the current guidance are at www.wales.gov.uk/subisocialpolicy/content/direct/contents_e.htm and the details of the proposed scheme are at www.wales.gov.uk/subisocialpolicy/content/ consultations/direct-payments/reg-appraisal-e.pdf and www.wales.nhs.uk/ documents/13390.pdf. Full details of the working of the 1996 legislation are detailed in the second edition of this text.

the 2001 Act, is that the former is discretionary and the latter (subject to exceptions) mandatory. In most other respects the two schemes are very similar.

Third party/indirect payments

9.36   Prior to the implementation of the 1996 Act social services departments were (with very minor exceptions)[19] subject to a specific prohibition against making payments of cash to disabled people, in lieu of services.[20] They were however permitted by NAA 1948 s30 (see below) to pay third parties (such as independent home care service providers) that had undertaken to deliver the assessed services. A number of authorities accordingly developed 'third party' schemes whereby they made payments to an intermediary (typically a trust fund or brokerage scheme) which then worked closely with the disabled person in the purchasing of his or her care. Such schemes gave the disabled person effective control over the purchasing of care services and also provided assistance with the administrative obligations inherent in any employment situation (recruitment and appointment of carers, employment contracts, grievance procedures, PAYE, etc).

9.37   Although cash payments can now be made directly to disabled people in certain situations by virtue of the 1996 and 2001 Acts, there remain a number of instances whereby third party schemes are still of value: most notably where the service user lacks the necessary mental capacity to manage their payments – even with assistance.

9.38   During the passage through Parliament of (what became) the CC(DP)A 1996, the Minister was asked to confirm that the new possibilities created by the Act would not affect the status of these pre-existing third-party schemes. He confirmed that such 'schemes that are in place now should not be affected. We are not seeking to undermine such schemes'.[21]

9.39   Despite the Minister's reassurance, questions remained about whether such arrangements were lawful, ultimately resulting in the issue being determined by the court. In *R (A and B) v East Sussex CC (No 1)*[22] Munby J considered the legality of an arrangement whereby a local authority made a payment to a specially created independent trust (known as a 'user independent trust') whose sole purpose was then to arrange the care of two young women with profound physical and learning disabilities. The trust in this case was a company limited by guarantee with relatively sophisticated control arrangements designed to ensure that the best arrangements possible were made for the disabled persons.

---

19   See for instance para 8.141 above.
20   Most particularly by virtue of NAA 1948 s29(6)(a), see para 8.57 above, and NHSA 1977 Sch 8 para 2(2)(a) – see para 8.142.
21   Minister for Health, John Bowis, at col 380 House of Commons Hansard 6 June 1996.
22   [2002] EWHC 2771; (2003) 6 CCLR 177.

9.40   The claimants argued – among other things – that NAA 1948 s30 permitted such payments. Section 30 provides that:

> A local authority may, in accordance with arrangements made under
> section 29 of this Act, employ as their agent for the purposes of
> that section any voluntary organisation or any person carrying on,
> professionally or by way of trade or business, activities which consist of or
> include the provision of services for any of the persons to whom section 29
> above applies, being an organisation or person appearing to the authority
> to be capable of providing the service to which the arrangements apply.

9.41   NAA 1948 s64 defines a 'voluntary organisation' as 'a body the activities of which are carried on otherwise than for profit, but does not include any public or local authority'. Since the judge concluded that the independent trust in question came within this definition it followed that such a third party scheme was perfectly compatible with the legal requirements of NAA 1948 s29. Had this not been the case, he expressed himself satisfied that the scheme would have been lawful in any event by virtue of both the Local Government Act 1972 s111 and Local Government Act 2000 s2.

The Independent Living Fund

9.42   The Independent Living Fund (ILF) was established by the Department of Health and Social Security in 1988 as an independent trust[23] to provide a weekly payment to severely disabled people who suffered significant financial loss as a result of the abolition of supplementary benefits 'additional requirements' payments in that year.[24] The fund is financed by the government, but administered by seven independent trustees.

Independent Living (Extension) Fund

9.43   The original trust was wound up in 1993 as part of the community care reforms with the fund monies being transferred to local authorities through the special transitional grant. However the payments that were being made to disabled people at the time it was wound up, have been preserved and are paid from what is known as the Independent Living (Extension) Fund.

9.44   There is provision for payments made from the Independent Living (Extension) Fund to be increased to recipients if they experience a 'significant change in their circumstances'. The current maximum award is £715 per week. Payments are suspended (as with the 1993 Fund below) during any period when the disabled person is accommodated in a hospital, residential or nursing home, although they can be reinstated on discharge.

---

23 The trust deeds for the various funds are held by the solicitor to the Department of Social Security; the original trust deed being dated 8 June 1988 and the Independent Living (Extension) Fund dated 25 February 1993.

24 R Means and R Smith, *Community Care Policy and Practice* (Macmillan, 1994).

Independent Living (1993) Fund

9.45 After the original fund was wound up in 1993, a new fund, known as the Independent Living (1993) Fund, was created for new applicants: the entitlement terms of the 1993 Fund are, however, more stringent and the benefits less generous. The ILF entitlement terms are periodically reviewed and guidance notes on the workings of the ILF schemes are available from the ILF website.[25]

9.46 In order to qualify for a grant from the 1993 fund, an applicant must:

- be at least 16 and under 66 years of age;
- live alone or with people who cannot fully meet his or her care needs; and
- be assessed by the local authority as being at risk of entering residential care, or capable of leaving it to live in the community; and
- receive at least £200 worth of services per week from the local authority (net of any charge) and be assessed as needing additional care;
- receive the highest rate care component of the Disability Living Allowance (DLA) and be able to live in the community for at least the next six months;
- be on Income Support; or income-based job seekers allowance or have an income which is insufficient to cover the cost of the care needed (ie, at or around Income Support levels after care costs paid); and
- have less than £18,500 capital (a tariff income of £1 per week is assumed for every £250 of capital between £11,500. and £18,500).

9.47 The maximum sum that the 1993 Fund can pay is £420 per week. In addition, the combined contribution from the local authority and the ILF must be no greater than £715 per week although the total cost of the care package may be more than this. As the guidance notes explain, any monies contributed by the applicant (by way of DLA, Severe Disability Premium, available income or money from savings), or by some other contributor (such as a friend or relative) do not count towards this maximum. Likewise, Health Authority funding is not included within the limit.[26]

9.48 The ILF award is made on the basis that the care package will remain within the £715 per week limit for the first six months. If the applicant's circumstances change within that period the Fund may be prepared to increase its funding – provided that it is satisfied that the change in circumstances was not foreseeable. However, if after the six month period the local authority wishes to increase its contribution taking the joint input to above £715 per week, the award from the Fund will not normally be withdrawn.

9.49 If the local authority contribution is variable, meaning that the combined weekly cost would occasionally exceed £715, the Fund may still be prepared to contribute – for instance where the variation in local authority

---

25 Accessible at www.ilf.org.uk/guidancenotes.htm.
26 It appears also that supporting people's payments are not counted in this sum – see para 17.55 below.

contribution is part of a regular and established pattern and the overall cost averaged over 52 weeks is £715 a week or less.

9.50   Although applications can be made directly to the Fund (see below) in general the social services department should first carry out a full community care assessment and agree to support the application to the Fund. If an applicant appears to meet all the criteria, the Fund will arrange for an assessment visit to be made. The visit will be carried out jointly, by one of the Fund's visiting social workers together with a local authority social worker.

9.51   Applicants are required to contribute towards the overall cost of the care package, including all of their Severe Disability Premium and half of their Disability Living Allowance. Earnings are however disregarded and if the applicant is not in receipt of income support, then specific charging rules apply – details of which are available from the ILF. The contact address for which is: Independent Living Funds, PO Box 7525, Nottingham, NG2 4ZT. Tel: 0845 601 8815. Their web address is: www.ilf.org.uk.

CHAPTER 10

NHS responsibilities for community care services

continued

Introduction

10.1 At no time since the formation of the NHS has there been a clear separation between its responsibilities for health services and those of the local authorities for care services.

10.2 Until 1990, successive governments sought, by simultaneous amendment[1] of the community care and NHS legislation, to transfer most health functions from local authorities to the NHS. During this period, however, perceptions of what a 'health function' was changed. In consequence the NHS tended to concentrate upon the provision of acute health care and sought to shed its responsibilities for the long-term health care needs of people with mental health problems. During the 1980s responsibility for people who would formerly have been resident in a long-stay mental hospital or geriatric ward was in large measure transferred to the social security budget, leading to a substantial increase in the number of private residential and nursing homes. Accordingly the legislative changes of the last 20 years have been dominated by the tripartite tension between these three agencies. The National Health Service and Community Care Act (NHSCCA) 1990 radically altered the respective responsibilities of the DHSS (as the Department for Work and Pensions was then called) and local authorities, but left virtually unchanged the interface between the NHS and local authorities. In contrast, however, the present reforms of the NHS seek to redraw the relationship between the NHS and local authorities: indeed in relation to primary care services these may result in an effective merger of the two bodies' primary care and social services responsibilities.

Health care and the NHS – a historical overview

10.3 At the beginning of the twentieth Century the majority of institutional health and social care was provided through the poor law boards. Gradually as the century progressed local authorities assumed greater responsibilities for both functions. The 1929[2] poor law reforms led to the creation of local authority health committees, which took control of the better poor law hospitals (then known as public health hospitals). The remaining poor law institutions, workhouses and basic poor law hospitals were also transferred from the poor law boards becoming the responsibility of the county and county borough councils.

10.4 The creation of the National Health Service in 1948 did not initially wrest responsibility for health services from local authorities. Although today it is convenient to see the National Health Service Act (NHSA) 1946

---

1 The National Health Service Act 1946 and the National Assistance Act 1948 came into force on the same day, as did the Health Services and Public Health Act 1968 and the Local Authority Social Services Act 1970; as did the Local Government Act 1972 and the NHS Reorganisation Act 1973.

2 Local Government Act 1929.

and the National Assistance Act (NAA) 1948 as demarcating the responsibilities of what we now call social services departments and the NHS, this separation of responsibilities has in fact developed largely as a consequence of subsequent legislation. The 1946 Act stipulated that many services we would today label as 'health services', such as ambulances (s27), midwifery (s23), health visitors (s24), were to be the responsibility of local authority health committees (called 'local health authorities').[3] Indeed NAA 1948 s21(7)(b), as originally enacted, authorised the provision by local authorities of 'health services,[4] not being specialist services or services of a kind normally provided only on admission to hospital'.

10.5   While minor changes to the health/social care responsibilities of NHS/local authorities occurred over the next 25 years,[5] major reform did not take place until 1974, when the Local Government Act 1972 and the National Health Service Reorganisation Act 1973 came into force. The 1973 Act sought to transfer all nursing functions (whether in hospital, at home or elsewhere) to the NHS. It abolished local health authorities (ie, local authority health committees) and in their place created free standing Regional, Area and District health authorities.

10.6   In 1977, the NHSA 1946 was repealed and replaced by a consolidating Act, the NHSA 1977. Although the 1977 Act has itself been much amended, it remains the primary statute governing the NHS.

10.7   In 1990[6] major reform of the NHS was effected by the creation of general practitioner (GP) fundholding practices and by the removal of health authority responsibility for providing hospital, community health and ambulance services. The responsibility for the management and running of these services was placed in hands of an entirely new institution, the NHS trust. Health authorities henceforth became purchasers of health care.[7] Secondary and tertiary health care (ie, general and specialist hospitals) being provided by acute trusts while primary care (ie, community health and GP services) was to be provided by fundholding and non-fundholding GPs and community NHS trusts.

10.8   In 1996 District and Regional Health Authorities were abolished[8] by the Health Authorities Act 1995 and replaced by a single tier health authority system, which, in England, received funding from the Executive branch of the Department of Health known as the NHS Executive. In Wales responsibility for funding health authorities devolved, in 1999, to the Welsh Assembly.

---

3   NHSA 1946 Sch 4 Pt II.
4   Including nursing services by virtue of NHSA 1946 s25.
5   Most notably the Health Services and Public Health Act 1968 which transferred to local health authorities responsibility for health visitors and nursing other than in a person's home; and the Local Authority Social Services Act 1970 which in its first schedule sought to delineate the responsibilities of local authority social services departments.
6   Through the NHSCCA 1990.
7   This separation of purchaser/provider being known as the 'internal market'.
8   Largely because the 1990 legislation had stripped away many of their responsibilities.

10.9 In 1997 the government in England published its plans for reform of the NHS, as *The New NHS: Modern, Dependable*[9] and the Assembly in Wales published its proposals as *NHS Wales: putting patients first.*[10] Both papers proposed (among other things) the abolition of GP fundholding and improved procedures to enable local authorities and health bodies to share funds and work in partnership. These changes were effected by the Health Act 1999 with the local commissioning of health care services in England passing to Primary Care Trusts (PCTs)[11] and subsequently in Wales to Local Health Boards (LHBs).[12]

10.10 The Health and Social Care Act (HSCA) 2001 Part III heralded the next phase of the reform programme (in England) with the creation of 'care trusts' – bodies that have the potential to combine both the commissioning and delivery of adult health and social care services. Care trusts are created once a PCT and local authority have established partnership working arrangements (see para 10.196) and undertaken consultations on the effective 'merger' of the two bodies.[13] As at December 2003, eight such care trusts had been established in England.[14] Care trusts are separate entities and presumably legally responsible for the discharge of their health and social care functions (which should be compared with the situation concerning partnership working arrangements – see para 10.197 below).

10.11 Further reform of the structure of the NHS was signalled in 2001 with the publication in England of *Shifting the Balance of Power within the NHS – Securing Delivery*[15] and in Wales of *Improving Health in Wales.*[16] The former document proposed the abolition of the 95 English health authorities and the latter the abolition of the five Health Authorities in Wales.[17] These changes were implemented through the National Health Service Reform and Health Care Professions Act 2002.[18] In England most of the former health authority functions have been transferred to PCTs, with health service resources being allocated directly to PCTs by the Department of Health. Twenty eight Strategic Health Authorities (SHAs) have been created to act as a key link between the Department and the local health bodies. SHAs have strategic planning functions and are responsible for ensuring that national priorities are integrated into local health service

9 Cm 3807, December 1997.

10 Stationery Office, January 1998.

11 Health Act 1999 s2.

12 The National Health Service Reform and Health Care Professions Act 2002 s6 and the Local Health Boards (Establishment) (Wales) Order 2003 SI No 148 (W18) and see the Local Health Boards (Constitution, Membership and Procedures) (Wales) Regulations 2003 SI No 149 (W 19).

13 The Care Trusts (Applications and Consultation) Regulations 2001 SI No 3788.

14 See www.dh.gov.uk/PolicyAndGuidance/OrganisationPolicy/TertiaryCare/CareTrusts/fs/en.

15 See www.dh.gov.uk/assetRoot/04/07/65/22/04076522.pdf.

16 Available at http://www.wales.nhs.uk/publications/NHSStrategydoc.pdf.

17 Government of Wales Act 1988 s27.

18 See also the National Health Service (Functions of Strategic Health Authorities and Primary Care Trusts and Administration Arrangements) (England) Regulations 2002 SI No 2375.

plans and that local health bodies develop high quality and responsive services. In Wales LHBs fulfil similar functions to PCTs in England with the Assembly assuming the core health authority functions.[19]

The National Health Service Act 1977

10.12   The National Health Service Act (NHSA) 1977 is the principal statute governing the health service. The structure of the Act reflects the fact that the NHS in reality contains two quite different systems. Part I is primarily concerned with the provision of health care in hospitals and 'community health services'; for example, the services provided by district nurses, midwives or health visitors in clinics or individuals' homes, and the provision of medical services to pupils in state schools. The responsibility for securing the provision of these services rests with the secretary of state in England and the Assembly in Wales to whom the NHSA 1977 gives power to delegate the discharge of their functions.[20] In large measure these functions have in England been delegated to PCTs and SHAs[21] and in Wales, to a lesser degree, to the LHBs.[22]

10.13   The second aspect of the NHS, sometimes described by governments as 'the NHS in the high street', is dealt with under Part II of the 1977 Act. This governs the arrangements made for the provision of services by GPs, dentists, opticians and chemists.

10.14   The separateness of these two systems has been slightly blurred by the National Health Service (Primary Care) Act 1997 which enables (in essence) doctor and dentist services to be provided under Part I of the Act, through a salaried service.[23]

Hospital and community health services (Part I)

10.15   NHSA 1977 s1 places the general NHS duty upon the secretary of state in England and the Assembly in Wales.[24] The extent and nature of the duty under section 1, is dealt with in detail below (see para 10.20), however the Act provides:

> 1 (1) It is the Secretary of State's duty to continue the promotion in England and Wales of a comprehensive health service designed to secure improvement –

19 For a detailed explanation of the structure of the NHS in Wales see *Guidance on the Establishment of Local Health Boards in Wales* (2003) accessible at www.wales.gov.uk/ healthplanonline/workinggroups/scp/content/lhb-guid-handbook-e.pdf.

20 NHSA 1977 ss16, 16B, 16D, 17, 17A(4),18, 51(2) and 126.

21 The National Health Service (Functions of Strategic Health Authorities and Primary Care Trusts and Administration Arrangements) (England) Regulations 2002 SI No 2375.

22 The Local Health Boards (Functions)(Wales) Regulations 2003 SI No 150 (W 20).

23 See HSC 1999/116 – NHS primary care walk-in centres.

24 Government of Wales Act 1998 and the National Assembly for Wales (Transfer of Functions) Order 1999 SI No 672.

(a) in the physical and mental health of the people of those countries, and

(b) in the prevention, diagnosis and treatment of illness,

and for that purpose to provide or secure the effective provision of services in accordance with this Act.

(2) The services so provided shall be free of charge except in so far as the making and recovery of charges is expressly provided for by or under any enactment, whenever passed.

10.16   NHSA 1997 s2 confers wide ranging powers for the secretary of state to provide such services as are appropriate, namely:

2   Without prejudice to the Secretary of State's powers apart from this section, he has power –

(a) to provide such services as he considers appropriate for the purpose of discharging any duty imposed upon him by this Act; and

(b) to do any other thing whatsoever which is calculated to facilitate, or is conducive or incidental to, the discharge of such a duty.

10.17   NHSA 1977 s3 sets out those general services which it is the secretary of state's duty to provide – to such extent as he or she considers necessary – to meet all reasonable requirements. Most of the services that may be described as hospital and community health services are included under this section.[25]

10.18   Section 3(1) provides:

3 (1) It is the Secretary of State's duty to provide throughout England and Wales, to such extent as he considers necessary to meet all reasonable requirements –

(a) hospital accommodation;

(b) other accommodation for the purpose of any service provided under this Act;

(c) medical, dental, nursing and ambulance services;

(d) such other facilities for the care of expectant mothers and young children as he considers are appropriate as part of the health service;

(e) such facilities for the prevention of illness, the care of persons suffering from illness and the after care of persons who have suffered from illness as he considers are appropriate as part of the health service;

(f) such other services as are required for the diagnosis and treatment of illness.

10.19   As noted above, the responsibility for actual provision of services under NHSA 1977 Part I was, as a result of the NHSCCA 1990, transferred to NHS trusts. Trusts are semi-autonomous bodies set up to assume responsibility for the ownership and management of hospitals or other establishments or facilities previously managed or provided by a health authority.[26]

25 By virtue of s3(1A) there is power to secure these services from outside England and Wales.

26 A trust's functions are conferred by its establishment order made under NHSCCA 1990 s5(1) and Sch 2.

NHS trusts do not receive funding in the way that PCTs do, but rather through obtaining contracts for their services from PCTs.[27]

Section 1: the duty to promote a 'comprehensive' health service

10.20 In contrast to the detailed legislative duties laid upon social services authorities, the NHS's statutory duties are general and indeterminate. Accordingly the courts have been reluctant to disturb NHS administrative decisions where these general public law duties are involved. In *R v Cambridge Health Authority ex p B*[28] the decision in question concerned 'the life of a young patient'. At first instance Laws J criticised the authority's justification for its decision not to fund any further chemotherapy treatment for the child as consisting 'only of grave and well-rounded generalities', stating that:

> . . . where the question is whether the life of a 10-year-old child might be saved, however slim a chance, the responsible authority . . . must do more than toll the bell of tight resources . . . they must explain the priorities that have led them to decline to fund the treatment.

10.21 The Court of Appeal felt unable to sustain this line, holding instead:

> Difficult and agonising judgements have to be made as to how a limited budget is best allocated to the maximum advantage of the maximum number of patients. That is not a judgement which the court can make . . . It is not something that a health authority . . . can be fairly criticised for not advancing before the court . . .
>
> It would be totally unrealistic to require the authority to come to court with its accounts and seek to demonstrate that if this treatment were provided for B then there would be a patient, C, who would have to go without treatment. No major authority could run its financial affairs in a way which would permit such a demonstration.

10.22 The *ex p B* decision should not be seen as an abrogation by the court of its duty to scrutinise 'anxiously' questions which engage fundamental human rights. In that case the court heard evidence of the lengths to which the health authority had gone to weigh up the likelihood of the treatment being successful, the adverse effects of the treatment and had consulted with the family. The Court accepted that it was a bona fides decision taken on an individual basis and supported by respected professional opinion. In such cases, where the key consideration is expertise that the court does not possess, even with the enactment of the Human Rights Act 1998, the court will inevitably hesitate to substitute its opinions. The situation will however be otherwise where the issue concerns questions of law or logic.

27 Under NHSCCA 1990 s4, these 'NHS contracts' are not legally enforceable but are subject to arbitration by the secretary of state/Welsh Assembly. For details of the contracting and commissioning responsibilities of PCTs, see generally 'The NHS Contractors' Companion' accessible at www.dh.gov.uk/assetRoot/04/06/54/62/04065462.pdf.

28 [1995] 2 All ER 129, CA.

10.23   Health bodies must, therefore, comply with the law, respect fundamental human rights and ensure that their decisions are reached in accordance with established public law principles. They must not, for instance, ignore circular guidance,[29] operate a perverse policy which (in practice) fetters their discretion to fund treatment[30] or fail to consult before reaching certain decisions. Thus in *R v North West Lancashire Health Authority ex p A*[31] the court ruled as unlawful a health authority policy that allowed for the funding of gender reassignment surgery only upon the patient satisfying unattainable conditions. The policy was simply irrational. Likewise in *R v North East Devon Health Authority ex p Pow*[32] the health authority, faced with severe cash shortages, decided to close certain hospitals without consulting the Community Health Council (which consultation was then required where substantial changes to services were contemplated). In quashing the health authority's decision Moses J held:

> It would seriously undermine the purpose of regulation 18 [Community Health Council Regulations 1996] . . . if a Health Authority could allow time to pass to the point where matters were so urgent that there was no time left for consultation.
>
> I was told . . . that if I grant relief it will not be possible to use the closure of the hospitals as a means of making savings at all . . . Even though, the task [of making budget savings] . . . is far harder, in my view the importance of the duty to consult is such that I do not think the greater burden of the task facing the Health Authority, caused by its own error in law, justifies the refusal of relief.

10.24   The core provisions of NHSA 1977 ss1 and 3 were subjected to considerable scrutiny by the Court of Appeal in *R v North and East Devon Health Authority ex p Coughlan*.[33] There the Court noted that:

> Section 1(1) does not place a duty on the Secretary of State to provide a comprehensive health service. His duty is 'to continue to promote' such a service. In addition the services which he is required to provide have to be provided 'in accordance with this Act'.[34]

and

> . . . the Secretary of State's section 3 duty is subject to two different qualifications. First of all there is the initial qualification that his obligation is limited to providing the services identified to the extent that he considers that they are *necessary* to meet *all reasonable requirements* . . .[35]

and

---

29 *R v North Derbyshire Health Authority ex p Fisher* (1998) 1 CCLR 150 (see below).
30 *R v North West Lancashire Health Authority ex p A* [2000] 1 WLR 977; (1999) 2 CCLR 419.
31 [2000] 1 WLR 977; (1999) 2 CCLR 419.
32 (1998) 1 CCLR 280.
33 (1999) 2 CCLR 285; [2000] 2 WLR 622; [2000] 51 BMLR 1; [2000] 3 All ER 850.
34 (1999) 2 CCLR 285 at [22].
35 (1999) 2 CCLR 285 at [23].

24. The first qualification placed on the duty contained in section 3 makes it clear that there is scope for the Secretary of State to exercise a degree of judgment as to the circumstances in which he will provide the services, including nursing services referred to in the section. He does not automatically have to meet *all* nursing requirements. In certain circumstances he can exercise his judgment and legitimately decline to provide nursing services. He need not provide nursing services if he does not consider they are reasonably required or necessary to meet a reasonable requirement.

25. When exercising his judgment he has to bear in mind the comprehensive service which he is under a duty to promote as set out in section 1. However, as long as he pays due regard to that duty, the fact that the service will not be comprehensive does not mean that he is necessarily contravening either section 1 or section 3. The truth is that, while he has the duty to continue to promote a comprehensive free health service and he must never, in making a decision under section 3, disregard that duty, a comprehensive health service may never, for human, financial and other resource reasons, be achievable. Recent history has demonstrated that the pace of developments as to what is possible by way of medical treatment, coupled with the ever increasing expectations of the public, mean that the resources of the NHS are and are likely to continue, at least in the foreseeable future, to be insufficient to meet demand.

26. In exercising his judgment the Secretary of State is entitled to take into account the resources available to him and the demands on those resources. In *R v Secretary of State for Social Services and other ex p Hincks* [1980] 1 BMLR 93 the Court of Appeal held that section 3(1) of the Health Act does not impose an absolute duty to provide the specified services. The Secretary of State is entitled to have regard to the resources made available to him under current government economic policy.

European community law

10.25 A further and detailed analysis of NHSA 1977 s1 took place in *R (Watts) v Bedford Primary Care Trust*[36] where Munby J reviewed the domestic and Strasbourg jurisprudence concerning the public law obligations to provide health care services. He concluded that notwithstanding the enactment of the Human Rights Act 1998, NHSA 1977 s1 remained a 'target' duty (see para 1.5). The case concerned an elderly claimant who had been put on a waiting list for urgent hip replacement surgery (her wait was expected to be about 12 months). She accordingly applied to have the surgery in Belgium (where the operation could be undertaken within two weeks) and sought agreement from the NHS to refund her Belgian medical expenses. When this was refused she took proceedings alleging that this constituted an unreasonable restriction on the free movement of goods and services within the European Union (EU). In doing so she relied upon a decision of the European Court of Justice (ECJ) in *Geraets-Smits v Stichting Ziekenfonds VGZ, Peerbooms v Stichting CZ Groep Zorgverzekeringen*[37] in which the

36 [2003] EWHC2401 (Admin); (2003) 6 CCLR 566: the case has subsequently been referred on appeal, to the European Court of Justice.
37 Case C-157/99; [2002] QB 409.

court had held that article 49 of the European Community Treaty could entitle such patients to reimbursement of such medical costs. It held, however, that states could legitimately restrict their funding of health care purchased by patients in other EU countries. However such a restriction would not be legitimate if the patient was seeking routine[38] treatment and that treatment was not available in the relevant state within an adequate time. On the question of what constituted undue delay Munby J observed that:[39]

> . . . any national authority properly directing itself in accordance with the principles laid down by the ECJ would have been bound to conclude . . . that the anticipated delay of approximately one year was on any view 'undue', and thus such as to trigger the claimant's right under article 49 to reimbursement of the cost of obtaining more timely treatment in another member state.

NHS Guidance Directions

10.26   The main types of health circular which concern community care are detailed at para 1.43 above. Increasingly however, guidance is no longer issued as sequentially numbered circulars, but in subject specific domains – generally only accessible on the internet (see para 1.44 above).

10.27   While NHSA 1977 s17 empowers the secretary of state to issue directions to NHS bodies (and NHSA 1977 s17A empowers SHAs to direct PCTs) in much the same way as he or she can to social services departments under Local Authority Social Services Act (LASSA) 1970 s7A, there is no specific provision in the 1977 Act concerning the issuing of guidance.[40] Under NHSA 1977 s2(b) however, the secretary of state has power to do 'anything whatsoever which is calculated to facilitate or is conducive or incidental to, the discharge of' the duty to promote a comprehensive health service. Such a power clearly authorises the issuing of guidance. In all other respects however the Act is silent on the effect of such guidance. It would appear however that such guidance must, in certain situations, be equivalent to the policy guidance issued to social services, ie, by obliging the health body 'to follow the path charted by the secretary of state's guidance, with liberty to deviate from it where the . . . authority judges on admissible grounds that there is good reason to do so, but without freedom to take a substantially different course'.[41] By way of example, the guidance given to health authorities (and other health bodies) concerning the preparation of Health Improvement Programmes as (Health Service Circular) HSC 1998/176 was also issued as LAC(98)23 to social services authorities. Since the circular was primarily aimed at health authorities, it is not unreasonable

---

38 Treatment that was considered 'normal within the professional circles concerned' – para 60 of the *Geraets-Smits* judgment.

39 (2003) 6 CCLR 566 at [164].

40 Although by virtue of the HSCA 2001 s45(10) care trusts (see para 10.10) are subject to such LASSA 1970 s7 guidance

41 *R v Islington LBC ex p Rixon* (1998) 1 CCLR 119 at 123; (1996) *Times* 17 April.

to assume that its legal force was no less in relation to them than it was to social services authorities, especially as the circular states that it is 'policy guidance'[42] in so far as it applies to social services.

10.28   In *R v North Derbyshire Health Authority ex p Fisher*[43] Dyson J had to decide whether an Executive Letter [EL(95)97 – which concerns the prescribing of Beta-Interferon drugs to people with Multiple Sclerosis] was a 'direction' under the NHSA 1977,[44] and if not, how much weight a health authority was required to afford it. He held that directions could be contained in such a circular, but that the wording of the circular was not sufficiently mandatory to be a 'direction'. Accordingly it was to be construed as 'strong guidance'. This meant that the health authority, although not obliged to follow the circular, could only depart from it by giving clear reasons for so doing and that those reasons would be susceptible to a *Wednesbury* challenge (see para 19.139). In finding against the health authority the judge held that it had failed to properly understand the circular and therefore its actions were defective (as if it had had no regard to the circular at all). Since *ex p Fisher* some degree of formality in relation to NHS directions has been introduced by virtue of NHSA 1977 s18.

10.29   Although NHS guidance may have considerable force (as in *ex p Fisher*) it cannot be used as a device to amend primary or subordinate legislation. Thus in *R v Secretary of State for Health ex p Pfizer Ltd*[45] Collins J held that HSC 1998/158, which suggested that GPs should not prescribe Viagra, was unlawful in that it sought (among other things) to restrict the GPs duty to provide patients with all necessary and appropriate personal medical services pursuant to NHS (General Medical Services) Regulations 1992 Sch 2 para 12(1) (these regulations are considered below at para 10.45).[46]

The medical/social divide

10.30   The conflict between health and social care is not a new one. What is a social need and what is a medical need is an intractable problem. It is only of practical importance to community care service users because a service provided by the NHS is generally free at the point of need, whereas a service provided by the social services department is generally subject to a means-tested charge. Help with bathing is therefore free if provided in a person's home by the district nurse (or NHS auxiliary), whereas if provided by a social services care assistant it may be subject to a charge. The argument is repeated in a hundred different ways with such items as walking sticks, hoists, commodes and speech therapy.

42   See para 1.30 above for an explanation as to the effect of 'policy guidance'.
43   (1998) 1 CCLR 150.
44   At that time the relevant section being NHSA 1977 s13.
45   (1999) 2 CCLR 270; (1999) *Times* 17 June.
46   Accordingly the Regulations were subsequently amended by NHS (General Medical Services) Amendment (No 2) Regulations 1999 SI No 1627; See HSC 1999/115.

10.31   Exhortations to organisations, professionals and other service providers to work together more closely and effectively litter the policy landscape, yet the reality is all too often a jumble of services fractionalised by professional culture and organisational boundaries and by tiers of governance.[47] The period since 1998 has however been marked by a series of legislative interventions designed to improve joint working in this sector – most notably by strengthening the duty to co-operate (see the Health Act (HA) 1999), the creation of care trusts (through the Health and Social Care Act (HSCA) 2001) and the duty to co-ordinate hospital discharge procedures (through the Community Care (Delayed Discharges, etc) Act (CC(DD)A) 2003.

The duty to co-operate

10.32 There are a number of statutory duties on local authorities and 'health bodies' (ie, health authorities, NHS trusts and primary care trusts) to work together constructively. These fall into two broad categories, namely:

1) the obligation to co-operate at the strategic level, ie, in the preparation of plans for the improvement of the health of the general population and in relation to the closure of hospitals or other facilities; and

2) the obligation on a general day-to-day level requiring co-operation in the delivery of services to individuals who are disabled, elderly or ill.

Local delivery plans

10.33 The strategic planning obligations of local authorities include the duty to prepare joint investment plans in collaboration with PCTs (see para 2.20). A reciprocal duty rests with PCTs in the preparation of their local strategic plans – presently referred to as 'local delivery plans'. The present planning obligation on PCTs stems from HA 1999 s28(1) which required the preparation, by health authorities, of plans for the improvement of the health of the general population.[48] Initially these were known as Health Improvement Programmes[49] and subsequently renamed Health Improvement and Modernisation Plans). The White Paper *The New NHS: Modern,*

---

47 Webb, *Policy and Politics* (1991) vol 19.4, p29; quoted in Means and Smith *Community Care* (Macmillan, 1994). There has been considerable criticism of successive governments' concentration upon creating administrative joint planning structures, on creating coterminosity, and other organisational devices to promote joint working. The research evidence suggesting however that 'where mutual trust has existed between senior officers from health and local authorities, the relationship has appeared to be far more important than joint planning machinery. R Davidson and S Hunter *Community Care in Practice*, (1994); see also L Clements and P Smith 'A Snapshot' *Survey of Social Services' Responses to the Continuing Care Needs of Older People in Wales*, (1999).

48 The emphasis here is collaboration by the local authority as a whole, recognising that the causes of ill-health are related to social, economic, environmental, housing, education and transport factors and their alleviation are not merely the responsibility of social services and the NHS: 'Our Healthier Nation' Department of Health, Cm 3852, February 1998.

49 Health Act 1999 s28(1) and see circular guidance HSC 1998/167.

Dependable[50] explained the need for strategic programmes of this nature covering:

- the most important health needs of the local population and how these are to be met by the NHS and its partner organisations through broader action on public health;
- the main healthcare requirements of local people, and how local services should be developed to meet them either directly by the NHS, or where appropriate jointly with social services;[51]
- the range, location and investment required in local health services to meet the needs of local people.

10.34 With the metamorphosis of local health authorities into regional SHAs the Department of Health has signalled that PCTs are no longer under a formal requirement to produce Health Improvement and Modernisation Plans. PCTs must however produce Local Delivery Plans which ensure that the government's priorities in the NHS (eg, waiting list and other performance targets) are translated into concrete local action. These priorities are identified in guidance issued to SHAs (most recently on 2 October 2002) as Planning and Priorities Framework (PPF) guidance. SHAs have powers[52] to ensure that major investment decisions taken by PCTs are consistent with the PPF guidance.

Specific duties to collaborate

NHSA 1977 s22

10.35 Health Act 1999 s27 amended NHSA 1977 s22 by substituting a more extensive duty to co-operate. The amendment was required, not least because of the proliferation of health bodies (PCTs, NHS trusts, LHBs, etc). Accordingly NHSA 1977 s22 provides that in exercising their respective functions, NHS bodies and local authorities are required to co-operate with one another 'in order to secure and advance the health and welfare of the people of England and Wales'.

10.36 The notes of guidance to the HA 1999 explained that the purpose of the amendment was to extend the duty of partnership in order to:

> . . . secure and advance the health and welfare of the people of England and Wales, to cover Primary Care Trusts and NHS trusts as well as Health Authorities and Special Health Authorities. This recognises the need to work in partnership in commissioning and delivering care, as well as at the strategic planning level. Welfare is used in its wide general sense and is designed to cover functions relating to social services, education, housing and the environment.

---

50 Cm 3807, December 1997.

51 Cm 3807(1997, Stationery Office). At para 4.8 it emphasised that this duty of co-operation would be underscored by a duty to 'promote the economic, social and environmental well being of their areas' – subsequently enacted (as a power only) as Local Government Act 2000 s2.

52 Health Act 1999 s17B.

10.37   Where a community care service user suffers as a result of an inter-agency dispute, it is generally appropriate for complaints to be made against each authority primarily on the basis that they have failed to 'work together' in violation of their specific statutory obligations.[53] The Local Government Ombudsman has repeatedly criticised authorities for failing to provide services while they squabbled over their respective obligations. A 1996 complaint, for example, concerned the failure of a health authority and social services department to co-operate. Although the Ombudsman considered that the health authority's involvement had been 'reluctant, if not unhelpful' she nevertheless found the social services authority guilty of maladministration. In her opinion, having accepted that a need existed, social services should have 'grasped the nettle' and secured the provision, before entering into protracted negotiations with the NHS on liability for the care costs.[54]

10.38   HSCA 2001 s11 takes the duty further by requiring community collaboration and involvement in the health care planning and development process. Section 11 requires health bodies to make arrangements 'with a view to securing, as respects health services for which it is responsible, that persons to whom those services are being or may be provided are, directly or through representatives, involved in and consulted' in the planning of the provision of those services.

NHSCCA 1990 s47(3)

10.39   A specific duty to co-operate exists under NHSCCA 1990 s47(3) which provides:

> If at any time during the assessment of the needs of any person under subsection (1)(a) above, it appears to a local authority –
>
> (a) that there may be a need for the provision to that person by such Primary Care Trust or Health Authority[55] as may be determined in accordance with regulations of any services under the National Health Service Act 1977, or
>
> (b) that there may be a need for the provision to him of any services which fall within the functions of a local housing authority (within the meaning of the Housing Act 1985) which is not the local authority carrying out the assessment,

---

53 See para 19.63 where the issues are further considered.

54 Complaint 96/C/3868 against Calderdale MBC.

55 Although the section has been amended (as a result of the demise of health authorities in England and Wales) to insert 'Primary Care Trusts' (National Health Service Reform and Health Care Professions Act 2002 Sch 2 (2) Para 56), no equivalent amendment has occurred in Wales to insert the term 'Local Health Boards'. It appears however that this is not strictly necessary, as a result of a combination of Welsh Statutory Instrument 2003 No 813 (W 98) the Health Authorities (Transfer of Functions, Staff, Property, Rights and Liabilities and Abolition) (Wales) Order 2003 – which transfers all functions of health authorities in Wales to the Assembly – and Welsh Statutory Instrument 2003 No 150 (W 20) the Local Health Boards (Functions) (Wales) Regulations 2003 which provides (subject to exceptions) that functions that were exercised by Health Authorities and were transferred to the Assembly by SI No 2003/813 are to be exercised by LHBs.

the local authority shall notify that Primary Care Trust, Health Authority or local housing authority and invite them to assist, to such extent as is reasonable in the circumstances, in the making of the assessment; and, in making their decision as to the provision of the services needed for the person in question, the local authority shall take into account any services which are likely to be made available for him by that Primary Care Trust, Health Authority or local housing authority.

10.40   It follows that where during the assessment process a 'health care' need is disclosed, the assessing authority is obliged to notify the PCT/LHB and at the same time to specify what assistance it is that the authority is requested to provide in order to facilitate the assessment. The health authority is not however under any statutory duty to respond or co-operate.[56] A failure to respond – or failure to respond within a reasonable time or in a reasonable manner – would inevitably be vulnerable to challenge as maladministration. The same applies to a housing authority where a housing need is disclosed (see para 17.9).

10.41   During the passage of the HA 1999 through Parliament, an attempt was made to insert an amendment which would have required a positive response from health authorities to any request for assistance by a local authority (of a similar nature to that required under Children Act (CA) 1989 s27). On the amendment being withdrawn, the government gave an assurance that guidance would be issued requiring health and local authorities to publish details as to how they will work together to ensure that all the assessment needs of individuals are met.[57]

MHA 1983 s117(2)

10.42   In respect of formerly detained patients, specific co-operation is required by Mental Health Act 1983 s117(2), which stipulates that it shall be the duty of the PCT/LHB and the local social services department to provide, in co-operation with the relevant voluntary agents, after-care services for any such person until satisfied that the person concerned is no longer in need of such services.

10.43   In *R v Mental Health Review Tribunal and others ex p Hall*[58] the Divisional Court held that the duty to provide after-care services under MHA 1983 s117(2) was jointly shared by the health and social services authority in which the patient was resident at the time he was detained: see para 15.16 where MHA 1983 s117 services are considered further.

---

56 Unlike the equivalent duty under Children Act 1989 s27. Circular guidance places a positive obligation on the NHS in certain situations, eg, the Single Assessment Process (SAP) Policy Guidance (2002) and the Unified and Fair System for Assessing and Managing Care (UFSAMC) 2002 (Wales).

57 Lord Hunt of Kings Heath, House of Lords Hansard 18 Mar 1999, column 851. With the exception of the SAP guidance (note 56 above) it appears that this assurance has not been honoured.

58 [1999] 3 All ER 132; (1999) 2 CCLR 361. Although the case was appealed, this issue was not re-argued before the Court of Appeal.

Community Care (Delayed Discharges, etc) Act 2003

10.44 The NHS/social services obligations under this Act are considered at para 10.170 below. In large measure, however, the obligations are one way – on the social services to facilitate a discharge.

NHS primary health care responsibilities

General practitioner services

10.45 NHSA 1977 s29 places a duty of each PCT/LHB to arrange with medical practitioners to provide personal medical services for all persons in their area who wish to take advantage of the arrangements. These services are described as 'general medical services'. As with hospital services, it is not the PCT/LHB itself which provides the service, instead, it enters into separate statutory arrangements with independent practitioners for the provision of those services. GPs are therefore not employees of the PCT/LHB, but are independent professionals who undertake to provide general medical services in accordance with regulations which govern that activity; currently the National Health Service (General Medical Services) Regulations 1992[59] (as amended).[60] The Regulations are of particular relevance in three specific respects.

GPs' obligation to provide general medical services

10.46 Schedule 2 paragraph 12 of the 1992 Regulations require GPs to render to their patients all necessary and appropriate medical services including:

(a) giving advice, where appropriate, to a patient in connection with the patient's general health, and in particular about the significance of diet, exercise, the use of tobacco, the consumption of alcohol and the misuse of drugs or solvents;

(b) offering to patients, consultations and, where appropriate, physical examinations for the purpose of identifying, or reducing the risk of disease or injury;

(c) offering to patients, where appropriate, vaccination or immunisation against measles, mumps, rubella, pertussis, poliomyelitis and tetanus;

(d) arranging for the referral of patients, as appropriate, for the provision of any other services under the [NHSA 1977]; and

(e) giving advice, as appropriate, to enable patients to avail themselves of services by a local social services authority.

10.47 Considerable concern has been expressed about the general performance of GPs in fulfilling their community care obligations, primarily the

---

59 SI No 635.

60 The regulations are subject to annual amendment – the most recent being by the National Health Service (General Medical Services) (Amendment) (Wales) Regulations 2002 SI No 916 (W 104) and the National Health Service (General Medical Services) Amendment Regulations 2002 SI No 554.

responsibility of ensuring that people in need of community care services are provided with the necessary assistance to obtain them.[61]

10.48   The obligation created by paragraphs (d) and (e) above includes more than merely advising patients of the availability of the community care services for which the local authority is responsible. This obligation nevertheless presupposes that GPs properly inform themselves of the social services' community care responsibilities. Where the patient may be entitled to other services under the NHSA 1977, the obligation on the GP is not merely to advise; it is to refer, to enable the patient to receive the service. It follows that a GP is required to refer patients to social services authorities where they may be entitled to receive the wide range of community care services available under NHSA 1977 Sch 8 (see para 8.124).

10.49   In those cases where the patient lacks mental capacity or it is otherwise unlikely that he or she will respond to such advice or referral, there will frequently be an equivalent duty owed to the patient's carer. This will most obviously be the case where the carer is also a patient of the GP (as he or she will also be entitled to many of the same services). LAC(96)7 describes this responsibility in the following terms:

> 30. Primary care staff, including GPs and community nurses through their contact with users and carers, are in a good position to notice signs of stress, difficulty or rapidly deteriorating health particularly in carers. The provisions of the [Carers (Recognition and Services) Act 1995] will help primary care staff to meet the medical and nursing needs of their patients who are carers. When making a referral for a user's assessment they should be able to inform the carer that they may also have a right to request an assessment and will be well-placed to encourage patients whom they consider will benefit most to take up the opportunity. Social services departments should make sure that primary care staff have relevant information about social services criteria and know who to contact to make referral.

10.50   National Health Service (General Medical Services) Regulations 1992 Sch 2 para 16 stipulates that (in relation to patients over 75) GPs must offer each of them a domiciliary visit every 12 months with a view to assessing whether the patient requires personal medical services; the assessment must take into account a variety of factors which might affect the patient's health, including his or her mobility and social environment.

GPs' obligation to prescribe drugs and appliances

10.51   The obligation on GPs to render general medical services for their patients brings with it a need to prescribe. This requirement is addressed by Sch 2 para 43 of the 1992 Regulations which provides:

> 43 (1) Subject to paragraph 44, a doctor shall order any drugs or appliances which are needed for the treatment of any patient to whom he is providing treatment under these terms of service by issuing to that patient a prescription form, and such a form shall not be used in any other circumstances.

---

61 See for instance EL(96)8 para 11.

10.52 The prescribing powers of GPs are restricted in relation to the provision of controlled drugs[62] and other substances (which are listed in Sch 10 of the 1992 Regulations) notably proprietary medicines which are generally brought over the counter at chemists.[63] Where the government wishes to restrict the power of GPs to prescribe any drug 'needed for a patients treatment' it must do so through the medium of regulatory amendment and not guidance.[64]

10.53 Regulation 43 of the 1992 Regulations additionally enables GPs to prescribe 'appliances'; ie, medical aids, dressings, pads, etc, as well as basic equipment to help overcome the effects of disability. In relation to disability equipment there is frequently an overlap of responsibility with the local social services department's community care duties. It is therefore common practice for health and social services to arrange joint equipment stores which can be accessed by both social services and the relevant NHS trust (see para 8.101).

10.54 The appliances which a GP can prescribe are detailed in two lists known as the 'Drug Tariff' and the 'Appliance List'.[65] The lists enable GPs to provide a range of general items (considered below). If more specialist equipment is needed however, this may be obtained through a hospital consultant (see below).

10.55 The appliance list includes such items as:

- Stoma and some incontinence care equipment. See also para 10.131 below where health authority responsibility for incontinence supplies is considered.
- Equipment for people with diabetes.
- Elastic hosiery, dressings, bandages, trusses, etc.
- Respiratory equipment (including oxygen cylinders and oxygen concentrators).
- Chiropody appliances. GPs can refer patients to NHS chiropodists and consultants for more specialist equipment. PCTs must also ensure that adequate chiropody services are available to residents placed by social services in nursing home accommodation (see para 10.131 below).
- Wheelchairs for permanent use (see para 10.136 below).

GPs' obligation to provide medical certificates

10.56 GPs have an important role in providing certificates for the purpose of contributory benefits and non-contributory social security benefits.

---

62 That is drugs listed in Misuse of Drugs Regulations 1985 SI No 2066 Sch 2; National Health Service (General Medical Services) Regulations 1992 Sch 2 para 43(3) as amended.
63 1992 Regulations Sch 2 para 44.
64 *R v Secretary of State for Health ex p Pfizer Ltd* (1999) 2 CCLR 270; see para 10.29 above.
65 The 'Drug Tariff' is a statement published under National Health Service (Pharmaceutical Services) Regulations 1992 SI No 662 reg 18. The 'Appliance List' contains the details of appliances which have been approved by the secretary of state for the purposes of NHSA 1977 s41.

Accordingly the 1992 Regulations Sch 2 para 37(1) provides that GPs are required to issue free of charge to their patients (or their personal representatives) any medical certificate which is reasonably required for certain specified purposes; these being set out in Schedule 9 of the 1992 Regulations (as amended).

Hospital consultant services

10.57   NHS trusts are the major providers of secondary health services in hospitals and similar institutions. Doctors and consultants working for such trusts[66] are directly employed by the trusts under an employment contract; a quite different arrangement to the 'independent' provider status of GPs.

10.58   Such a doctor/consultant may prescribe any drug, appliance or piece of equipment which he or she considers necessary for a patient's treatment. In general their employment contract with the NHS trust will restrict this prescribing power, or at least make the provision of expensive items subject to validation by the trusts' managers. In certain situations however, it may be unlawful for a health authority to restrict the availability of specialist drugs. In *R v North Derbyshire Health Authority ex p Fisher*[67] for instance, the court held that the respondent authority had failed, without good reason, to follow government guidance[68] on the prescription of Beta-Interferon drugs to people with Multiple Sclerosis, and accordingly its actions were unlawful.

Free nursing care in care homes

10.59   In 1999 the Royal Commission on long-term care published its report *With respect to old age*[69] recommending that personal care and nursing services should be provided free of charge to all persons assessed as being in need of these services (regardless of whether they were living in the community, a care home or a hospital). The government in England felt unable to accept the full recommendations and opted instead to fund only the registered nursing care costs of residents in nursing homes.[70] In England, primary care trusts (PCTs) were charged with responsibility for deciding the extent of this obligation, and the Department of Health issued guidance to explain how this should be achieved. The Department issued guidance defining three different bands of nursing need (in contrast, in Wales, the Assembly, opted for a much simpler approach – that every nursing home resident would receive the same contribution from the health authority, namely £105 per week).

---

66 That is consultants or junior doctors (which description includes senior registrars, registrars, senior house officers and house officers).

67 (1998) 1 CCLR 150.

68 Executive Letter EL(95)97 – see para 10.28 above.

69 *With respect to old age: The Royal Commission on Long-Term Care* Cm 4192 (The Stationery Office).

70 Announced in *The NHS Plan* at paragraph 15.181 (Department of Health, July 2000.) and enacted as Health and Social Care Act 2001 s49.

10.60   The policy proposal was brought into effect in England and Wales by HSCA 2001 s49 which provides:

> (1) Nothing in the enactments relating to the provision of community care services shall authorise or require a local authority, in or in connection with the provision of any such services, to –
> (a) provide for any person, or
> (b) arrange for any person to be provided with,
> nursing care by a registered nurse.
> (2) In this section 'nursing care by a registered nurse' means any services provided by a registered nurse and involving –
> (a) the provision of care, or
> (b) the planning, supervision or delegation of the provision of care,
> other than any services which, having regard to their nature and the circumstances in which they are provided, do not need to be provided by a registered nurse.

10.61   Directions concerning the impact of HSCA 2001 s49 in England were issued in 2001[71] and in 2003[72] (in this section referred to as the 2001 and the 2003 directions). In England all nursing home residents (regardless of whether self-funding or supported by social services) are provided with an assessment by their local PCT, which determines the extent of their nursing care needs (known as the 'registered nursing care contribution – 'RNCC'). These needs are banded[73] into 'high', 'medium' and 'low' and a contribution made by the PCT in relation to each (as at April 2003, these amounted to either £40, £75.50 or £125 per week). In Wales all residents in nursing homes receive a flat rate payment of £105 per week – detailed in a 2001 direction.[74]

10.62   Prior to April 2004 only self funding residents in Wales received an 'RNCC' payment. This created a problem when residents funded by an English local authority moved to a home in Wales. A protocol was agreed to deal with this situation[75] and guidance issued by the Assembly.[76] In such cases the receiving Welsh local authority accepted initial responsibility for the registered nursing contribution (before seeking reimbursement from – among others – the Local Health Board). The relationship between HSCA 2001 s49 payments and the continuing health care responsibilities of the NHS are considered further below at para 10.144.

---

71 HSC(2001)17; LAC (2001)26.

72 HSC 2003/006; LAC(2003)7.

73 These are detailed in '*NHS Funded Nursing Care Practice Guide and Workbook*' Department of Health, August 2001 see www.dh.gov.uk/assetRoot/04/07/67/20/04076720.pdf.

74 Guidance on Free Nursing Care in Nursing Homes NAWC 34/01.

75 Protocol on cross-border issues for NHS-funded nursing care in care homes providing nursing care in England and Wales during the period from 1 April 2003 to 31 March 2004.

76 NAFWC 12/2003 and WHC (2003)33.

Responsible commissioner

10.63   In England the PCT responsible for the funding of the HSCA 2001 s49 payments to nursing home residents is based upon the location of the care home (ie, whether it lies within the geographic boundary of the PCT). The guidance[77] however advises that:

> In some cases, for instance where care homes are close to the boundary of a neighbouring PCT, it may be sensible for responsibility for the management of the contract with the care home to be transferred to a neighbouring PCT if the majority of residents are registered in that PCT.[78]

The NHS's continuing care responsibilities

Historical overview

10.64   The debate over continuing health care responsibilities is not new. Means, Morbey and Smith[79] chart the organisational tensions that have existed over the health/social care divide since the formation of the NHS. They conclude that these have been characterised by a failure of the NHS to invest in community health services or to transfer significant resources to social services (p85). They describe how the conflict has generally been expressed in debates over what is health care and what is social care.

10.65   One example they cite is the Boucher Report of 1957 – which addressed local authority concerns that their residential homes cared for many people who ought to be cared for in hospital. The Report led to circular guidance outlining the respective responsibilities of the welfare and hospital authorities; welfare authorities were to provide:

- care of the otherwise active resident in a welfare home during minor illness, which may well involve a short period in bed;
- care of the infirm (including the senile) who may need help in dressing, toilet, and so on, and may need to live on the ground floor because they cannot manage stairs, and may spend part of the day in bed (or longer periods in bad weather);
- care of those older persons in a welfare home who have to take to bed and are not expected to live more than a few weeks (or exceptionally months). Who would, if in their own homes, stay there because they cannot benefit from treatment or nursing care beyond help that can be given at home, and whose removal to hospital away from familiar surroundings and attendance would be felt to be inhumane.[80]

Hospital authorities, however, were to take responsibility for:

77 See HSC 2003/006; LAC(2003)7 paras 66–68 and HSC2001/17; LAC(2001)26 guidance 'Establishing a Responsible Commissioner' accessible at www.dh.gov.uk/assetRoot/04/06/97/97/04069797.pdf.

78 HSC 2003/006; LAC(2003)7 para 67.

79 Means, Morbey and Smith, *From Community Care to Market Care?* (Policy Press, 2002).

80 Ministry of Health (1957) Local authority *services for the chronic sick and infirm* Circular 11/50 London: MoH, as cited by Means, Morbey and Smith at page 78.

- care of the chronic bedfast who may need little or no medical treatment, but who do require prolonged nursing care over months or years;
- convalescent care of older sick people who have completed active treatment, but who are not yet ready for discharge to their own homes or to welfare homes;
- care of the senile confused or disturbed patients who are, owing to their mental condition, unfit to live a normal community life in a welfare home.[81]

10.66   Although the demarcation of the health/social care boundary described in the Boucher Report is a long way from the situation today, legally there has been no material change in the scope of the NHS's continuing health care responsibilities since that time. There has been no amendment to the primary statutory obligation (albeit that the duty is now to be found in the consolidated NHSA 1977). There has been no Ministerial statement, no direction by the secretary of state or any other kind of announcement to the effect that the entitlement to continuing health care has been curtailed.

10.67   The material changes have been in terms of policy and funding arrangements – most significantly in the last 25 years, the availability of supplementary benefit payments (later income support) to cover the cost of private nursing home accommodation. This situation led to the closure of many NHS continuing care wards,[82] with the patients being transferred to privately run nursing homes funded by the social security budget.

10.68   On 1 April 1993 the higher-rate income support payments for nursing and residential care homes were withdrawn and the social services authorities became the 'gate-keepers' for such community placements. This led to a general, but incorrect, assumption that the NHS no longer had the same responsibility for funding long-term care. The fact that social services authorities were (for the first time) empowered to make payments towards the cost of independent nursing home placements also encouraged the view that the NHS was no longer an agency responsible for making similar payments. In fact, the responsibility for the care of persons in need of nursing home accommodation is an overlapping one between the two services.

10.69   The effect of this shift in the provision of continuing care was the subject of comment by the Audit Commission, which noted a significant rise in local authority funding for nursing home placements (over and above what would have been predicted), describing this trend as 'worrying' and suggesting that it was due to 'a combination of rising demand from within the community and increasing pressure from hospitals'.[83]

---

81   Ministry of Health (1957) *Geriatric services and the care of the chronic sick* HM(57) 86 London: MoH, as cited by Means, Morbey and Smith at page 78.

82   Between 1983 and 1993 there was a 30 per cent (17,000) reduction in number of long-term geriatric and psychogeriatric NHS beds – Harding et al 'Options for Long Term Care (HMSO, 1996) p8 and between 1988 and 2001 a loss of 50,600 such beds, see House of Commons Select Committee (2002) Delayed Discharges: Third Report, Vol 1 HC 617-I, 35 at www.publications.parliament.uk/pa/cm200102/cmselect/cmhealth/617/617.pdf.

83   Audit Commission report *Taking Stock* (December 1994), commenting on the pattern of hospital discharges (at para 32).

The Health Service Commissioner's 1994 Report

10.70   Throughout this period many individuals, their carers and relatives paid substantial sums to private nursing homes in situations where previously the care would have been provided without charge by the NHS. This aspect came prominently to the fore with the publication by the Health Service Commissioner of a highly critical report into a premature hospital discharge by the Leeds Health Authority. The complaint concerned a patient who was discharged from a neuro-surgical ward in the Leeds General Infirmary, forcing his wife to pay for his continuing care in a private nursing home.[84] The Commissioner in his report stated (at para 22):

> No one disputes that by August 1991 his condition had reached the stage where active treatment was no longer required but that he was still in need of substantial nursing care, which could not be provided at home and which would continue to be needed for the rest of his life. Where was he to go? Leeds Health Authority's policy, as explained by their chief executive, was (and still is) to make no provision for continuing care at NHS expense either in hospital or in private nursing homes. In particular I note that the contract for neurosurgical services makes no reference to continuing institutional care. This patient was a highly dependent patient in hospital under a contract made with the Infirmary by Leeds Health Authority; and yet, when he no longer needed care in an acute ward but manifestly still needed what the National Health Service is there to provide, they regarded themselves as having no scope for continuing to discharge their responsibilities to him because their policy was to make no provision for continuing care. The policy had the effect of excluding an option whereby he might have the cost of his continuing care met by the NHS. In my opinion the failure to make available long-term care within the NHS for this patient was unreasonable and constitutes a failure in the service provided by the Health Authority. I uphold this complaint. I recommend that Leeds Health authority make an ex gratia payment to the complainant to cover those costs which she has already had to incur and to provide for her husband's appropriate nursing care at the expense of the NHS in the future. I recommend that the Authority review their provision of services for the likes of this man in view of the apparent gap in service available for this particular group of patients.

10.71   The Health Ombudsman was so concerned about the situation disclosed by the Leeds complaint that he took the exceptional step of having his report separately published.[85] In response, the government undertook to issue guidance, indicating:

> If in the light of the guidance, some health authorities are found to have reduced their capacity to secure continuing care too far – as clearly happened in the case dealt with by the Health Service Commissioner – then they will have to take action to close the gap.[86]

84   Health Service Commissioner Second Report for Session 1993–94; Case No E62/93–94 (HMSO).

85   Normally only an abbreviated selection of his reports is published twice yearly.

86   Virginia Bottomley, Secretary of State for Health, 4 November 1994.

10.72 The Health Service Ombudsman commented in similar terms in relation to other complaints concerning continuing care. In 1996 he published a short digest of investigations his office had made into complaints concerning long-term care.[87] A number of these have concerned health authorities who made no provision for continuing care arrangements[88] or whose arrangements were inadequate. Complaint E985/94–95,[89] for example, concerned an elderly patient who suffered a stroke and became unable to swallow and was fed by means of a gastric tube. After her condition had stabilised in hospital her husband felt compelled to acquiesce in her discharge although she remained ill and incapacitated, and indeed died shortly after her admission to the nursing home. Although the husband had had contact with a consultant, the ward staff, the hospital social worker and the GP, no one had properly explained the various options available[90] including the possibility that she would meet the criteria for NHS-funded continuing care in a nursing home. As a result of the Ombudsman's intervention the health authority accepted responsibility for the nursing home fees.

The 1995 continuing care guidance

10.73 In February 1995, as a consequence of the Health Ombudsman's 'Leeds report',[91] continuing care guidance was published as a first step towards defining with greater precision the boundaries between the responsibilities of the NHS and social services authorities for continuing care.[92] The guidance required every health authority to prepare and publish local 'continuing health care statements' which spelt out which patients would be entitled to free continuing health care funded by the NHS. As part of this process the government also announced procedures that enabled patients to challenge their discharge from in-patient hospital care.[93]

10.74 Although in 1996 the Department of Health issued follow up guidance to improve the quality of continuing health care statements[94] the evidence suggests that the 1995 guidance (which was repealed by the 2001 guidance – see below) was misapplied by health authorities and that the Department

---

87 Fifth Report for session 1995–96, *Investigations of Complaints about Long-Term NHS Care*, HMSO.

88 See for instance No E264/94-95 which concerned a 55-year-old stroke patient (in the selected investigations April–September 1995); W478/89-90 which involved the failure to provide NHS after-care to a woman who had suffered severe brain injuries (in the selected volume for October 1990–March 1991)

89 Against North Worcestershire Health Authority, selected volume for April–September 1996.

90 See para 10.162 below for details of the duty to provide information on hospital discharge.

91 At para 3 it stated that the guidance 'addresses a number of concerns raised in the report made last year by the Health Service Ombudsman'.

92 LAC(95)5; HSG(95)8 'NHS Responsibilities for Meeting Continuing Health Care Needs: WOC 16/95 and WHC(95)7 in Wales.

93 LAC(95)17; HSG(95)39.

94 See for instance EL(96)8 and EL(96)89 – discussed below.

of Health was inactive in policing individual health authority continuing care statements.[95]

The Coughlan judgment

10.75   In 1999 the Court of Appeal delivered its judgment in *R v North and East Devon Health Authority ex p Coughlan*.[96] It reinforced the finding of the Health Service Commissioner in the Leeds Health Authority complaint; that entitlement to NHS continuing care support arose, not merely when a patient's health care needs were complex, but also when they were substantial – the so called 'quality/quantity' criteria (see below).

10.76   The medical condition of Pamela Coughlan was described by the court as follows (para 3):

> She is tetraplegic; doubly incontinent, requiring regular catheterisation; partially paralysed in the respiratory tract, with consequent difficulty in breathing; and subject not only to the attendant problems of immobility but to recurrent headaches caused by an associated neurological condition.

10.77   The Court of Appeal held that social services could only lawfully fund low-level nursing care – low in terms of its quality and quantity. The court expressed this as follows (at para 30):

> (d) ... There can be no precise legal line drawn between those nursing services which are and those which are not capable of being treated as included in such a package of care services.
>
> (e) The distinction between those services which can and cannot be so provided is one of degree which in a borderline case will depend on a careful appraisal of the facts of the individual case. However, as a very general indication as to where the line is to be drawn, it can be said that if the nursing services are:
>
> - merely incidental or ancillary to the provision of the accommodation which a local authority is under a duty to provide to the category of persons to whom section 21 refers and
> - of a nature which it can be expected that an authority whose primary responsibility is to provide social services can be expected to provide, then they can be provided under section 21.
>
> It will be appreciated that the first part of the test is focusing on the overall quantity of the services and the second part on the quality of the services provided.

10.78   Additionally the court emphasised that the setting of a person's care, was not determinative of eligibility for continuing health care funding. In its view 'where the primary need is a health need, then the responsibility is that of the NHS, even when the individual has been placed in a home by a

---

95   Indeed the evidence suggests the contrary – as the NHS Ombudsman noted in her Second Report for Session 2002–2003: *NHS funding for long term care*; Stationery Office. HC 399 (at para 21) 'My enquiries so far have revealed one letter (in case E814/00–01) sent out from a regional office of the Department of Health to health authorities following the 1999 guidance, which could justifiably have been read as a mandate to do the bare minimum'.

96   *R v North and East Devon Health Authority ex p Coughlan* [2000] 2 WLR 622; [2000] 3 All ER 850; (1999) 2 CCLR 285, CA (see also para 10.24 above).

local authority' (para 31) and 'the fact that a case does not qualify for in-patient treatment in a hospital does not mean that the person concerned should not be a NHS responsibility' (para 41).

10.79   The continuing care policies of North and East Devon Health Authority were, it appears, not unusual. A 1999 Royal College of Nursing Report *Rationing by Stealth* suggested that the continuing care policies of over 90 per cent of health authorities were equally deficient.

The 1999 continuing care guidance

10.80   The *Coughlan* judgment was pronounced on the 16 July 1999 and the following month the Department of Health issued follow up guidance; HSC 1999/180; LAC(1999)30. This guidance stated that it was 'interim guidance' and did little more than ask health and local authorities to 'satisfy themselves that their continuing care policies were in line with the judgement'. Unfortunately it gave a clear indication that further guidance would be issued 'later this year' (at para 2) and this expectation of this further guidance led to many health authorities taking no decisive action in the wake of the *Coughlan* judgment.[97]

The 2001 continuing care guidance

10.81   The Department of Health took two years to issue further guidance (HSC 2001/015; LAC (2001)18). Although this guidance has been the subject of robust criticism by the Health Service Commissioner[98] (see below) it remains the relevant guidance[99] and is considered in detail at para 10.87 below.

The 2003 Health Service Commissioner's Special Report

10.82   In February 2003 the Health Service Commissioner published a special report concerning continuing health care.[100] The need for such a report stemmed from the large number of complaints that the Commissioner had received on this issue (as had been the case with her predecessor in 1994). She was trenchant in her criticism of the Department of Health's failure to provide clear guidance in conformity with the Court of Appeal's judgment in *Coughlan*; commenting (at para 31):

> I do not underestimate the difficulty of setting fair, comprehensive and easily comprehensible criteria . . . But that is all the more reason for the Department to take a strong lead in the matter: developing a very clear, well-defined national framework. One might have hoped that the

---

97 In this respect, see the comments of the Health Service Commissioner in her Second Report for Session 2002–2003 *NHS funding for long term care*; Stationery Office. HC 399.

98 Health Service Commissioner's Second Report for Session 2002–2003 *NHS funding for long term care*; Stationery Office. HC 399 para 38.

99 At the time of writing – December 2003.

100 Second Report for Session 2002–2003 *NHS funding for long term care*; Stationery Office. HC 399.

comments made in the *Coughlan* case would have prompted the Department to tackle this issue . . . [however] authorities were left to take their own legal advice about their obligations to provide continuing NHS health care . . . The long awaited further guidance in June 2001 . . . gives no clearer definition than previously of when continuing NHS health care should be provided: if anything it is weaker, since it simply lists factors authorities should 'bear in mind' and details to which they should 'pay attention' without saying how they should be taken into account . . . I fear I would find it even harder now to judge whether criteria were out of line with current guidance. Such an opaque system cannot be fair.

10.83   Her report considered a number of complaints, including one against Wigan and Bolton Health Authority and Bolton Hospitals NHS Trust.[101] The complaint concerned a patient who had suffered several strokes, as a result of which she had no speech or comprehension and was unable to swallow, requiring feeding by PEG tube (a tube which allows feeding directly into the stomach). She was subsequently discharged to a nursing home. In response to the health authority's refusal to accept continuing care responsibility for the patient, the Commissioner commented:

> I cannot see that any authority could reasonably conclude that her need for nursing care was merely incidental or ancillary to the provision of accommodation or of a nature one could expect social services to provide (paragraph 15). It seems clear to me that she, like Miss Coughlan, needed services of a wholly different kind.

10.84   The importance of this determination, is that the Commissioner expressed the view (incontrovertible though it must be) that the patient could not by any stretch of the imagination, be considered to be a 'borderline' case. Effectively that the health authority's decision was *Wednesbury* unreasonable (see para 19.139 below).

The 2003 periodical Report of the Health Service Commissioner

10.85   The Health Service Commissioner's fifth (periodic) report – for the session 2002–03[102] carried summaries of three further investigations – all of which were indicative of inflexible and overly restrictive policies being operated by health authorities.

Directions

10.86   As a consequence of the Health Service Commissioner's 2003 special report the Department of Health issued directions; 'The Continuing Care (National Health Service Responsibilities) Directions 2004'.[103] These provide, among other things, that each Strategic Health Authority shall:

- establish a single set of eligibility criteria for the provision of continuing care by PCTs in its area;

---

101   HC 399 at p24, para 1; Complaint No E420/00-01.
102   24 June 2003, HC 787.
103   Available at www.dh.gov.uk/assetRoot/04/07/46/91/04074691.pdf.

- take such steps as it considers reasonable to obtain the agreement to the proposed criteria of each local authority in its area;
- create a review procedure for patients (where the dispute cannot be resolved informally) who wish to challenge PCT continuing care decisions. In such cases he or she may apply in writing to the SHA on receipt of which it 'may' refer the matter to a panel (the membership of which is spelt out in the draft directions).

NHS responsibilities for meeting continuing health care needs

10.87 The following section details the NHS's responsibilities by reference to the English guidance. In Wales draft (revised) guidance was issued in 2004.[103a]

Patients covered by the guidance

10.88 The 2001 guidance applies only to adults and is primarily concerned with the needs of older people, older people with mental health needs, people with dementia and younger adults requiring continuing NHS health care as a result of illness or accidents (and who may have resulting physical disability). The guidance stresses that it does not detract in any way from the requirements set out in previous guidance for other categories of patient – particularly for children; adolescents and adults with a mental illness or with learning disabilities (para 8). The duties of the NHS for the continuing care of adults with a mental illness are considered at paras 15.5 and 15.24; those for persons with learning disabilities at para 10.89, and in relation to children's services at para 18.37.

Learning disability services and continuing care

10.89 Circular guidance HSG(92)43 and LAC(92)17 has referred to the historically anomalous position of people with learning difficulties; essentially that although their needs are primarily social, historically the NHS has provided for people with learning difficulties and therefore the NHS has received the funding for the continuing care needs of such people. Thus the guidance states that:

> . . . it is well recognised that many people (ie, people with learning difficulties) traditionally cared for in long-stay hospitals are predominantly in need of social care, and should be cared for in the community. In order to support in the community ex-long-stay patients and people who might in earlier times have been cared for in long-stay hospitals, health finance may be spent on social services rather than on health services.

10.90 Until the large scale closure of the large NHS hospitals specifically catering for people with learning disabilities, one fifth of people with severe or

103a www.wales.gov.uk/subihealth/content/consultations/continuing-care-draft-con-guidance-e.pdf.

profound learning disabilities received their care services from the NHS.[104] The guidance advocates, therefore, not only that the NHS transfer monies to social services for the present support of such persons (and their successors)[105] but also that it should develop new and innovative services to meet the social (as opposed to health) needs of such persons.

Continuing care – the key concepts

10.91   Crucial to an understanding of the continuing health care responsibilities of PCTs/LHBs is an appreciation of the status of the relevant circular guidance. Important as the guidance is, it is secondary to any judicial determinations (notably in this case, the *Coughlan* judgment). Given the inadequate nature of the 2001 guidance and the reliance placed upon earlier guidance by both the Court of Appeal and the Health Service Commissioner – the earlier guidance is, where relevant, considered below. Although much of the earlier guidance has been formally 'cancelled' by the 2001 guidance (at Annex A) this does not mean that it ceased to be relevant to an understanding of legal responsibilities in this domain.

10.92   An additional and instructive concept to bear in mind when approaching any practical determination as to whether an individual is entitled to continuing health care funding is to compare his or her needs against those of Pamela Coughlan (para 10.76 above) and the patients considered in the various Health Service Commissioner's reports – notably the Leeds Health Authority patient (para 10.70 above) and the Wigan and Bolton Health Authority patient (para 10.83 above). The Health Service Commissioner and the government have found such comparisons useful (see paras 10.71, 10.83 above and 10.101 below). A summary of the key cases is provided in Table 5 on pages 278–280.

Key issues identified by the 2001 guidance

10.93   Paragraph 16 of the 2001 guidance gives examples of the range of health services which all PCTs/LHBs must arrange and fund to meet the needs of their population 'either at home, in a nursing home or a residential home' – these include:

- primary health care;
- assessment involving doctors and registered nurses;
- rehabilitation and recovery (where this forms part of an overall package of NHS care as distinct from intermediate care);
- respite health care;
- community health services;
- specialist health care support;
- healthcare equipment;

---

104 LAC(92)15.
105 HSG(92)43; LAC(92)17.

- palliative care;
- specialist transport services.

10.94 Annex C to the 2001 guidance then lists a number of key issues that must be considered in the framing of continuing health care eligibility criteria, stating:

1. The eligibility criteria or application of rigorous time limits for the availability of services by a health authority should not require a local council to provide services beyond those they can provide under [NAA 1948 s21] . . .
2. The nature or complexity or intensity or unpredictability of the individual's health care needs (and any combination of these needs) requires regular supervision by a member of the NHS multidisciplinary team, such as the consultant, palliative care, therapy or other NHS member of the team.
3. The individual's needs require the routine use of specialist health care equipment under supervision of NHS staff.
4. The individual has a rapidly deteriorating or unstable medical, physical or mental health condition and requires regular supervision by a member of the NHS multidisciplinary team, such as the consultant, palliative care, therapy or other NHS member of the team.
5. The individual is in the final stages of a terminal illness and is likely to die in the near future.
6. A need for care or supervision from a registered nurse and/or a GP is not, by itself, sufficient reason to receive continuing NHS health care.
7. The location of care should not be the sole or main determinant of eligibility. Continuing NHS health care may be provided in an NHS hospital, a nursing home, hospice or the individual's own home.

10.95 The key principles and concepts that emerge from the *Coughlan* judgment and the above guidance, can be summarised as:

- The concept of 'intensity'
- Multiple criteria
- Specialist interventions
- Continuing health care in community settings

The concept of intensity

10.96 The 2001 guidance (like the earlier 1995 guidance) lists four key factors of crucial relevance, namely the nature or complexity or intensity or unpredictability of the individual's health care needs. Of these, however, an appreciation of the concept of 'intensity' is arguably central to an understanding of the NHS's continuing care responsibilities. It was a misunderstanding of this factor that led to the maladministration determination by the Health Service Commissioner in the Leeds Health Authority complaint (see para 10.70 above) and to the judgment of the Court of Appeal in ruling unlawful the North and East Devon Health Authority's continuing care criteria. In the Leeds case, the authority had failed to appreciate that a need for 'substantial nursing' (ie, the 'intensity' of the general nursing need) without any specialist medical interventions was in itself sufficient to

Table 5: Summary of patients involved in continuing care disputes

R v North and East Devon Health Authority ex p Coughlan

Miss Coughlan was grievously injured in a road traffic accident in 1971. She is tetraplegic; doubly incontinent, requiring regular catheterisation; partially paralysed in the respiratory tract, with consequent difficulty in breathing; and subject not only to the attendant problems of immobility but to recurrent headaches caused by an associated neurological condition (para 3 of judgment).

The court concluded at para 3:

The secretary of state accepts that, where the primary need is a health need, then the responsibility is that of the NHS, even when the individual has been placed in a home by a local authority . . . Here the needs of Miss Coughlan . . . were primarily health needs for which the Health Authority is as a matter of law responsible.

Leeds Ombudsman Report Case No E62/93–94 January 1994

A man suffered a brain haemorrhage and was admitted to a neuro-surgical ward . . . He received surgery but did not fully recover. After 20 months in hospital he was in a stable condition but still required full time nursing care. His condition had reached the stage where active treatment was no longer required but that he was still in need of substantial nursing care, which could not be provided at home and which would continue to be needed for the rest of his life (para 22 of report).

The importance of this assessment was emphasised in NHS guidance EL(96)8 which (at para 16) criticised continuing care statements which placed an *'over-reliance on the needs of a patient for specialist medical supervision in determining eligibility for continuing in-patient care' and specifically referred to the fact that this was not considered by the ombudsman in the Leeds case as an acceptable basis for withdrawing NHS support.*

Wigan and Bolton Health Authority and Bolton Hospitals NHS Trust Case No E420/00–01[106]

Mrs N had suffered several strokes, as a result of which she had no speech or comprehension and was unable to swallow, requiring feeding by PEG tube (a tube which allows feeding directly into the stomach). Mrs N was being treated as an in-patient in the Trust's stroke unit and was discharged to a nursing home (p24, para 1).

Health Services Commissioner concluded (at p32, para 30)

I cannot see that any authority could reasonably conclude that her need for nursing care was merely incidental or ancillary to the provision of accommodation or of a nature one could expect Social Services to provide (para 15). It seems clear to me that she, like Miss Coughlan, needed services of a wholly different kind.

---

106 From the NHS Ombudsman's Second Report for Session 2002–2003 *NHS funding for long term care*; Stationery Office. HC 399.

Dorset Health Authority and Dorset Health Care NHS Trust
Case No E208/99–00[107]

Mr X suffered from Alzheimer's disease and admitted to a nursing home (p11, para 1) and allegedly receiving services very similar to Miss Coughlan's (p20, para 23).

Health Services Commissioner concluded (at p21, para 26)

I ... recommend that the ... Authority should, with colleague organisations, determine whether there were any patients (including Mr X senior) who were wrongly refused funding for continuing care, and make the necessary arrangements for reimbursing the costs they incurred unnecessarily ... Mr X senior suffered a degenerative condition, so he was more likely to be eligible for funding as time went by.

Berkshire Health Authority Case No E814/00–01[108]

Mrs Z, a 90-year-old admitted to a hospital suffering with vascular dementia (p35, para 1) and in need of 'all help with daily living, except feeding' and resistant to help and needing supervision if she was to take the medication she needed (p38, para 12).

Health Services Commissioner concluded (at p46, para 39)

It is certainly very possible (but not entirely certain) that, if appropriate criteria had been applied, Mrs Z would have qualified for fully funded care.

Birmingham Health Authority Case No E1626/01–02[109]

Mrs R, a 90-year-old admitted to hospital following a severe stroke, which had left her immobile, incontinent, and confused (and unlikely that her condition would change) (p49, para 1).

Health Services Commissioner concluded (at p54, para 23)

Had Mrs R been assessed against criteria which were in line with the then guidance and the Coughlan *judgment, she might (though it is not possible to be certain) have been deemed eligible for NHS funding for her nursing home care.*

Complaint against the former Shropshire Health Authority
Case No E5/02–03[110]

Mrs F has Alzheimer's disease and in June 2000 was assessed by a consultant psychiatrist as needing specialist elderly mentally ill (EMI) care. A nursing assessment in November 2000 noted that she required full assistance with all her personal tasks including washing, dressing, feeding and toiletting. She was also doubly incontinent, was dependent upon others for her safety, and could only mobilise with assistance.

The Ombudsman was advised by her independent clinical assessor that Mrs F required significant nursing care and it was debatable whether that could properly be regarded as merely incidental or ancillary to the accommodation which Mrs F also needed. The Ombudsman upheld the complaint.

continued

107 HC 399

108 HC 399.

109 HC 399.

110 From the 2003 periodical Report of the Health Service Commissioner 5th Report – for the session 2002–03; 4 June 2003 HC 787.

**Complaint against the former Shropshire Health Authority
Case No E2119/01[111]**

Mr C suffered a severe stroke and the clinical assessment found that he was
unable to manage any aspect of personal care independently. The notes
recorded that he had an in-dwelling urinary catheter, occasional faecal
incontinence (largely avoided by regular toiletting by hoist transfer to
commode/toilet); that he required to be fed soft pureed diet with thickened
oral fluids, that he had a PEG gastrostomy tube in place – used to
administer additional fluids overnight if necessary . . . that an hoist used for
all transfers; that all pressure areas remain intact . . . with repositioning two
hourly; that communication was by eye contact and head movement; that
he could not speak.

The Ombudsman's specialist assessor concluded that from the
information provided Mr C's needs were primarily health needs.

**Complaint against Cambridgeshire Health Authority and Primary Care
Trust (the 'Pointon' case)[112]**

Mr P is severely disabled with dementia and unable to look after himself.
His wife cared for him at home. She took a break one week in five but had
to pay more than £400 for the substitute care assistant. The NHS would not
pay because Mrs P was not a qualified nurse (and could not therefore be
offering nursing care). It was held that the fact that Mr P was receiving
(what was in effect) nursing care from his wife, did not mean he could not
qualify for continuing health care; that the health bodies had failed to take
into account his severe psychological problems and the special skills it
takes to nurse someone with dementia; that the assessment tools used by
the NHS were skewed in favour of physical and acute care; the fact that Mr
P needed care at home – rather than in a nursing care home was not
material to the question of continuing health care responsibility.

entitle a patient to NHS continuing health care funding. Likewise in
Coughlan the Court of Appeal commented (at para 41 onwards):

> Where the issue is whether the services should be treated as the
> responsibility of the NHS, not because of their nature or quality, but
> because of their quantity or the continuity with which they are provided,
> the distinction between general and specialist services is of less assistance.
> The distinction certainly does not provide an exhaustive test. The
> distinction does not necessarily cater for the situation where the demands
> for nursing attention are continuous and intense. In that situation the
> patient may not require in-patient care in a hospital under the new policy,
> but the nursing care which is necessary may still exceed that which can be
> properly provided as a part of social services care provision.

10.97   The authority had predicated its funding support on the patient needing
specialist health care – care of a nature which it was unreasonable to expect
from a social services department. It had however failed to appreciate that
a substantial need for low level nursing (as in the Leeds case) would also

111 HC 787.
112 Accessible at www.ombudsman.org.uk/hsc/document/pointon.htm.

trigger NHS responsibility (the so called 'quantity' test – see para 10.77 above).

10.98   The Health Service Commissioner has (as noted at para 10.82 above) been critical of the quality of the 2001 guidance. The statement in the guidance (at Annex C, para 6) that 'a need for care or supervision from a registered nurse and/or a GP is not, by itself, sufficient reason to receive continuing NHS health care' can also be criticised as likely to mislead. Although this statement is correct, it could (and arguably should) have been expressed in the opposite way namely: 'a need for care or supervision from a registered nurse and/or a GP is not an essential prerequisite to qualifying for continuing NHS health care'. The failure of the 2001 guidance to emphasise this point raises further questions about its objectivity. Accordingly in the *Pointon* complaint[113] the patient was not receiving any NHS input (his wife was caring for him at home) but nevertheless held to be entitled to continuing health care funding.

Multiple criteria

10.99   The four key factors listed above are alternatives – they are not cumulative. Accordingly a need for substantial general nursing alone – is sufficient to qualify a patient for continuing health care funding. Guidance issued by the Department of Health in 1996 (EL(96)8)) was critical of a number of continuing care statements which, rather than being sensitive to the complexity *or* intensity *or* unpredictability of a person's needs, placed too much emphasis on the need for people to meet multiple criteria for NHS-funded care. Follow up guidance (EL(96)89)[114] noted with concern that of the 25 Health Authority Continuing Care Statements considered, 10 required individuals to meet at least two or more criteria. It criticised, by way of example, a statement which required adults to fulfil all these criteria:

- unable to initiate purposeful movements even with aids;
- poor physical condition which requires constant observation or active intervention supported by technical means and a clinical specialist;
- need feeding by technical means;
- requires on going supervision at least weekly by a specialist health professional, either NHS Consultant or Specialist Nurse.

10.100 The 2001 guidance is, itself, seriously defective in this respect. It lists the four factors (the nature or complexity or intensity or unpredictability – see para 10.94 above) and then states that they must additionally require 'regular supervision by a member of the NHS multidisciplinary team, such as the consultant, palliative care, therapy or other NHS member of the team'. This would seem to be in direct opposition to the *Coughlan* decision, where it was held that satisfying the quantity test alone would disqualify a patient from social service support. As noted above in Table 5 the requirement

---

113 Complaint against Cambridgeshire Health Authority and Primary Care Trust, see Table 5 above for summary of the facts.

114 Annex 1 at para 4.14.

for such regular supervision was not considered necessary in the *Pointon*
complaint.[115]

Specialist interventions

10.101 Considerable concern has been expressed over the repeated use in continuing health care statements of undefined terms such as 'specialist'.
EL(96)8 at para 16, for instance, criticised statements which placed an
'over-reliance on the needs of a patient for specialist medical supervision in
determining eligibility for continuing in-patient care' and specifically
referred to the fact that this was not considered by the ombudsman in the
Leeds case as an acceptable basis for withdrawing NHS support.

10.102   In the *Coughlan* judgment the Court noted that a differentiation of
responsibility based upon the need for 'specialist nursing' was not statutory in origin, but introduced into the guidance by the Department of
Health. It considered that in many cases the concept of 'specialist' was
devoid of meaning and agreed with the Royal College of Nursing that such
a demarcation was unhelpful: it was 'elusive' and 'idiosyncratic' (at paras
13 and 41). In the *Pointon* complaint[116] it appears to have been accepted that
a need for nurses with special skills that enabled them to deal with the
patient's severe psychological problems associated with his dementia was
qualitatively the type of nursing care to be the responsibility of the NHS. It
could be argued that this will also be the case where the patient requires
nurses with psychiatric nursing skills (eg, a Community Psychiatric Nurse
(CPN)).

Continuing health care in community settings

10.103 In *Coughlan* the Court held that 'the fact that the resident at a nursing
home does not require in-patient treatment in a hospital does not mean
that his or her care should not be the responsibility of the NHS' (at para 42)
and where the primary need is a health need, then the responsibility is that
of the NHS, even when the individual has been placed in a home by a local
authority (at para 31).

10.104   This finding accorded with the 1992 guidance[117] which stated that where
a patient's need is primarily for health care, any placement (in a nursing
home or elsewhere) must be fully funded by the health authority. The 2001
guidance made this point explicit, stating that (see para 10.94 above):

> The location of care should not be the sole or main determinant of
> eligibility. Continuing NHS health care may be provided in an NHS
> hospital, a nursing home, hospice or the individual's own home.

---

115 Complaint against Cambridgeshire Health Authority and Primary Care Trust, see
   Table 5 above.

116 Complaint against Cambridgeshire Health Authority and Primary Care Trust, see
   Table 5 above.

117 LAC(92)24 Annex A para 7.

10.105 In a 2003 complaint the Health Service Commissioner[118] criticised an authority whose continuing health care statement had the effect of requiring 'on-site medical provision' (ie, hospital based) in order to qualify for full NHS funding (see Table 5 above).

Specific continuing health care issues

Likely to die in the near future

10.106 Paragraph 18 of the 2001 guidance makes it clear that the NHS is responsible for the continuing health care funding of patients who require palliative care and whose prognosis is that they are likely to die in the near future. It states that such patients:

> ... should be able to choose to remain in NHS funded accommodation (including in a nursing home), or to return home with the appropriate support. Patients may also require episodes of palliative care to deal with complex situations (including respite palliative care). The number of episodes required will be unpredictable and applications of time limits for this care are not appropriate.

10.107 Although the 1995 guidance contained a similar provision, it was expressed as applying to patients 'likely to die in the *very* near future' (emphasis added). In relation to such persons, EL(96)8 stated that 'very short time limits (for instance of the order of a couple of weeks) are not appropriate and any time limits should be applied flexibly in the light of individual circumstances'. In general health authorities appear to have interpreted the phrase 'likely to die in the near future' as a period of between 6 and 12 weeks. It would seem to follow that the deletion of the word 'very' from the 2001 guidance should have led to a relaxation in these timescales.

10.108 In a research report annexed to EL(96)89[119] it was noted that some health authorities were placing inappropriate limitations on this obligation, for instance suggesting that such a package would only be provided in unusual circumstances. It would also be inappropriate to suggest that such patients' could only be provided with a package of health and social care at home if it was less expensive than the package if provided in a hospital or nursing home.

Rehabilitation and recovery

10.109 Much of the continuing care guidance has advocated NHS after-care services which help promote independent living. If with the assistance of rehabilitation or respite services, a patient can live independently in the

---

118 Berkshire Health Authority Case No E814/00-01; Second Report for Session 2002–2003 *NHS funding for long term care*; Stationery Office, HC 399.
119 Continuing Health Care: Analysis of a sample of final documents, M Henwood (1996).

community, then resources should be devoted towards this end.[120] Thus the 1995 guidance suggested that 'the existence of good rehabilitation services and well developed community health services and social care support may lessen, although not eliminate, the need for continuing inpatient care.[121] The importance of developing rehabilitation and recovery services was described as a 'crucial priority' in EL(96)89.[122]

10.110   The 1995 guidance required health authorities to take full account of the need for services:[123]

> . . . to promote the effective recovery and rehabilitation of patients after acute treatment so as to maximise the chances of the successful implementation of long-term care plans. This is particularly important for older people who may need a longer period to reach their full potential for recovery and to regain confidence. Local policies should guard against the risk of premature discharge in terms of poorer experiences for patients and increased levels of readmissions.

10.111   Follow-up guidance in February 1996 on the local eligibility criteria (EL(96)8) expressed concern over certain rehabilitation and recovery criteria, stating (at para 16) that they would be unduly:

> . . . restrictive if they limit NHS responsibility for rehabilitation to post-acute care and do not take account of responsibilities to contribute to longer-term rehabilitative care which is needed as part of a care package for someone in their own home or in a residential care home or nursing home. Some eligibility criteria include time limits for rehabilitation or recovery. While perhaps helpful in ensuring that services are well focused, such limits will be restrictive if applied rigidly. They will usefully act as a trigger for reassessment.

10.112   The reference to 'longer-term' rehabilitative care is of importance and is echoed by the 1995 guidance in relation to respite services (see para 10.120 below). Health authorities are required to provide rehabilitation services for persons with chronic conditions, as well as acute needs. In general this obligation is not fulfilled; while the NHS provides rehabilitation following an acute episode, such as a stroke, hip operation or accident, such services are not commonly available to people with chronic conditions such as Parkinson's disease. 'Active rehabilitation' for such patients can improve their ability to cope with daily living skills and so prolong their ability to live in the community and relieve some of the pressure on their carers.

Intermediate care

10.113   In 2000 a major initiative was launched by the government to improve rehabilitation services as well as services that avoided the unnecessary

---

120   The Audit Commission noted however that '[r]ehabilitation is currently advocated by many as the "missing factor" in the care of elderly people. What is clear is that many health authorities lack basic knowledge about the rehabilitation services for older people in their area' *Coming of Age*, Audit Commission 1997.

121   Annex A, p14.

122   At para 6; and this emphasis was underscored by its inclusion in the NHS Priorities and Planning guidance of 1996/97 and 1997/98.

123   EL(96)89.

hospital admission of vulnerable people. Henceforth the NHS and social services were to provide such persons with 'intermediate care' – guidance upon which was provided in circular LAC(2000)1; HSC 2000/01. The intermediate care initiative is aimed at freeing up acute hospital beds and promoting the independence of older people. This includes, for instance community teams (of social workers, occupational therapists, physiotherapists, community nurses, etc) that provide intensive short-term support services to prevent unnecessary admissions and facilitate earlier discharge, either back home or via 'step-down' community hospital/nursing home facilities.

10.114   Although the provision of intermediate care services will often satisfy a patient's needs for rehabilitation and recuperation – this will not always be the case. Given the time limited nature of the service, it will frequently be only a first stage of a programme – for which the NHS may have full responsibility.[124]

Intermediate care – definition

10.115 LAC(2000)1; HSC 2000/01 (at para 7) defines intermediate care as services that meet all the following criteria:

(a) are targeted at people who would otherwise face unnecessarily prolonged hospital stays or inappropriate admission to acute in-patient care, long-term residential care, or continuing NHS in-patient care;

(b) are provided on the basis of a comprehensive assessment, resulting in a structured individual care plan that involves active therapy, treatment or opportunity for recovery;

(c) have a planned outcome of maximising independence and typically enabling patient/users to resume living at home;

(d) are time-limited, normally no longer than six weeks and frequently as little as 1–2 weeks or less; and

(e) involve cross-professional working, with a single assessment framework, single professional records and shared protocols.

10.116 The guidance states that such services should 'generally be provided in community-based settings or in the patient/user's own home, but may be provided in discrete step-down facilities on acute hospital sites' (para 11) and time limited, para 8 explaining that:

Based on current practice, an intermediate care episode should typically last no more than six weeks. Many episodes will be much shorter than this, for example 1–2 weeks following acute treatment for pneumonia, or 2–3 weeks following treatment for hip fracture. Exceptionally, for example following a stroke, patients may require intermediate care for slightly longer than six weeks. Nevertheless, all individual care plans for people receiving intermediate care should include a review date within the six-week period. Exceptional extensions beyond six weeks should be subject to a full re-assessment and should be authorised by a senior clinician. Individual care plans should specifically address what care, therapy or support may be needed on discharge from intermediate care.

124 See in this respect 'Discharge from hospital: pathway, process and practice' at para 6.1; Department of Health (2003) accessible at www.publications.doh.gov.uk/ hospitaldischarge/index.htm.

Service models

10.117   For planning purposes, intermediate care can be categorised into various service models, which are identified in para 14 of the 2000 guidance as:

- *rapid response*: a service designed to prevent avoidable acute admissions by providing rapid assessment/diagnosis for patients referred from GPs, A and E, NHS Direct or social services and (if necessary) rapid access on a 24-hour basis to short-term nursing/therapy support and personal care in the patient's own home, together with appropriate contributions from community equipment services and/or housing-based support services . . .

- *'hospital at home'*: intensive support in the patient's own home, including investigations and treatment which are above the level that would normally be provided in primary care but do not necessarily require the resources of an acute hospital . . .

- *residential rehabilitation*: a short-term programme of therapy and enablement in a residential setting (such as a community hospital, rehabilitation centre, nursing home, or residential care home) for people who are medically stable but need a short period of rehabilitation to enable them to regain sufficient physical functioning and confidence to return safely to their own home. This may range from around 1–2 weeks (eg, for pneumonia) to 4–6 weeks (eg, following major surgery) or slightly longer (eg, for frail older people recovering from major trauma). It will typically involve input from nurses, care managers and a range of allied health professions (eg, physiotherapists, occupational therapists, speech/language therapists, psychologists, dieticians), supported by auxiliary care staff, to maximise patients'/clients' residual functions and equip them with skills for independent living. Residential rehabilitation may be 'step-down', ie, following a stay in an acute hospital; or it may be 'step-up', ie, following a referral by (say) a GP, social services or rapid response team and following full assessment (including medical assessment) in cases which would otherwise necessitate acute admission or admission to longer-term residential care;

- *supported discharge*: a short-term period of nursing and/or therapeutic support in a patient's home, typically with a contributory package of home care support and sometimes supported by community equipment and/or housing-based support services, to enable earlier transfer of care from an acute hospital and to allow a patient to complete their rehabilitation and recovery at home . . .

- *day rehabilitation*: a short-term programme of therapeutic support, provided at a day hospital or day centre. This may be used in conjunction with other forms of intermediate care . . .

Charging

10.118   Although the 2000 guidance advised that intermediate care should be free at the point of use (para 19) a number of authorities nevertheless levied charges. Community Care (Delayed Discharge, etc) Act (CC(DD)A) 2003 ss15 and 16 accordingly provides the secretary of state and Welsh Assembly (respectively) with power to make regulations which require such services to be provided free of charge.

10.119 Regulations under CC(DD)A 2003 s15 have been issued in England[125] and stipulate that intermediate care and community equipment services (see para 8.101 above) are to be provided free of charge. The regulations define intermediate care in the following terms:

> . . . a service which consists of a structured programme of care provided for a limited period of time to assist a person to maintain or regain the ability to live in his home, and is required to be provided free of charge to any person to whom it is provided for any period up to and including six weeks.

Respite

10.120 The 2001 guidance provides little in the way of detail as to the nature of the respite care that the NHS should provide. Paragraph 18 refers to it in the context of 'palliative care' and at para 25 it is stated:

> Local councils will usually have the lead responsibility for arranging and funding respite care. However, the NHS also has important responsibilities for respite health care, including people who, during a period of respite care, require or could benefit from rehabilitation (which may include a package of intermediate care).

10.121 The 1995 guidance however required health authorities to 'arrange and fund an adequate level of such care' and gave three examples of the type of patient who ought to be able to access NHS funded respite services, namely:

- people who have complex or intense health care needs and will require specialist medical or nursing supervision or assessment during a period of respite care;
- people who during a period of respite care require or could benefit from active rehabilitation; and
- people who are receiving a package of palliative care in their own homes but where they or their carer need a period of respite care.

10.122 As noted above, in relation to rehabilitation services, the reference to 'active rehabilitation' is of importance in that it is directed towards the needs of people whose condition is chronic rather than acute. By providing such persons with regular periods of respite care where they also receive such services as intensive physiotherapy, speech and occupational therapy, the NHS can prolong their ability to live independently in the community and reduce the pressure on their carers.

10.123   Follow up guidance in 1996[126] advised that eligibility criteria will in general be too restrictive if they confined themselves to the above three examples, suggesting that they should cover other contingencies, such as 'where carers have been providing a level of health care which is not reasonably available in a residential setting'.

---

125 The Community Care (Delayed Discharges, etc) Act (Qualifying Services)(England) Regulations 2003 SI No 1196.

126 EL(96)8 at para 16.

Palliative health care

10.124   The 2001 guidance makes a number of references to palliative care (eg, at paras 16, 18, 23, 29 and in Annex C). Earlier guidance (EL(93)14 and EL(94)14) had urged authorities to work closely with the voluntary sector (ie, hospices), and provide palliative care services.[127] Palliative care must be distinguished from the care of 'terminally-ill people', who are defined by the Department of Health (at EL(93)14 Annex F) as people with an active and progressive disease for which curative treatment is not possible or not appropriate and whose death can reasonably be expected within 12 months.

10.125   The 1995 guidance expressly required health authorities to provide:

- palliative health care, on an inpatient basis, fully funded by the NHS in hospital, hospice or in a limited number of cases in nursing homes capable of providing this level of care;
- specialist palliative health care to old people already in nursing homes;
- palliative health care support to people in their own homes or in residential care.

10.126   In relation to the community care overlap between social services and health authorities, EL(93)14 gives the following guidance (at Annex C paras 10–14):

> 10. Under the wider community care reforms, from April 1993, local authorities will be responsible for assessing people's needs for care, including residential care and nursing home places. Where people have health as well as social needs, appropriate NHS staff will be involved in these assessments.
>
> 11. Where assessment reveals that a person is terminally ill and requires specialist in-patient palliative care, it will be for the health authority to arrange that, whether in a voluntary hospice, an NHS facility or an independent sector nursing home capable of providing such care. This applies equally to respite palliative care.
>
> 12. Where it is decided on the basis of assessment that a person's needs make a placement in a residential care or nursing home appropriate, the local authority will generally be responsible for arranging such a placement (although precise responsibilities will have been agreed between local authorities and health authorities).[128] Although not in need of specialist in-patient palliative care at the time of their initial assessment

---

127 The World Health Organisation defines palliative health care as: 'The total active care of patients whose disease is not responsive to curative treatment. Control of pain, and other symptoms of psychological, social and spiritual problems is paramount. The goal of palliative care is achievement of the best quality of life for the patients and their families'.

128 The wording used here is tendentious. Whether a person has a health or a social need is in every case a question of fact and agreement; whether the majority of such persons end up as the responsibility of the NHS or social services cannot be relevant in an individual's case; the Executive Letter guidance is here echoing the wording used in the draft guidance which preceded LAC(95)5; the 1994 draft stated: 'The expectation will be that the significant majority of people who require continuing care in a nursing home setting are likely to have their needs met through social

and placement, some people placed in this way may eventually become terminally ill[129] or enter the terminal phase of a long-term condition. Some of these patients may come in time to require specialist palliative care. Health authorities will be responsible for providing such specialist care. Depending on the individual's needs, specialist palliative care could be provided by means of a placement for temporary or permanent specialist in-patient care elsewhere (for which new placement the health authority would bear the cost) or by additional specialist health care to the person in the home where they live (in which case the health authority would fund only the additional care).

13. There has been some confusion about whether nursing homes which currently attract the 'Terminal Illness' level of Income Support should, therefore, automatically look to health authorities for funding. This is not necessarily the case. Responsibility for funding depends on the care needs as described above.

14. HSG(92)50, issued to health authorities and Trusts in December 1992, sets out health authorities' responsibilities for the health care of people placed in residential care and nursing homes under local authority contracts. Broadly, health authorities would be expected to provide specialist palliative care to people in residential care homes as if they were living at home, and in nursing homes to provide any necessary additional specialist palliative health care in addition to general nursing (which will continue to be included in the local authority's contract with the home). Arrangements for this need to be agreed locally between health and local authorities. Local discussion and agreement are the key to seamless and responsive care.

10.127 EL(96)8 (at para 16) reminded authorities that eligibility criteria which applied time limits for palliative care would be inappropriate; such care should be provided by the NHS purely on the basis of clinical need.

10.128 Reference has been made above (at para 10.106) to the additional responsibilities of the NHS for patients 'likely to die in the near future'.

NHS specialist or intensive services for people in care homes

10.129 It is a basic tenet of the NHS that all medical and nursing services are provided free at the point of need. Whilst this principle is curtailed in so far as it applies to the needs of residents in nursing homes not funded by the NHS, the limitation only applies to the general (non-registered nursing[130] needs) of such residents.

10.130 The respective responsibilities of the two authorities are the subject of further guidance in LAC(92)24, which emphasises at para 2:

2. Local authority contracts for independent sector residential care should not include provision of any service which it is the responsibility of the

services'. This draft was the subject of substantial criticism (see for instance *Community Care* magazine 29 September 1994 at p24) and in consequence heavily rewritten with this passage omitted.

129 That is, have (among other things) a life expectancy of less than 12 months.

130 See paras 10.59 above and 10.144 below.

NHS to provide. It will continue to be the responsibility of the NHS to provide where necessary community health services to residents of LA and independent residential care homes on the same basis as to people in their own homes. These services include the provision of district nursing and other specialist nursing services (eg, incontinence advice) as well as the provision, where necessary, of incontinence and nursing aids, physiotherapy, speech and language therapy and chiropody. Where such services are provided they must be free of charge to people in independent sector homes as well as to residents of local authority Part III homes.

10.131 The 1995 guidance clarified this distinction in the following terms:

Some people who will be appropriately placed by social services in nursing homes, as their permanent home, may still require some regular access to specialist medical, nursing or other community health services. This will also apply to people who have arranged and are funding their own care. This may include occasional continuing specialist medical advice or treatment, specialist palliative care, specialist nursing care such as incontinence advice, stoma care or diabetic advice or community health services such as physiotherapy, speech therapy and language therapy and chiropody. It should also include specialist medical or nursing equipment (for instance specialist feeding equipment) not available on prescription and normally only available through hospitals . . .

Assessment procedures and arrangements for purchasing care should take account of such needs and details should be identified in individual care plans. In such cases the NHS can either provide such services directly or contract with the home to provide the additional services required. Such additional services should be free at the point of delivery.

10.132 LAC(92)24 also defines specialist nursing as 'primarily continence advice and stoma care, but also other specialist nursing such as diabetic liaison and other community health services (primarily physiotherapy, speech and language therapy and chiropody)'. It then makes clear that such services should be provided by the NHS to patients in local authority-funded nursing home accommodation.

10.133 The 2001 guidance (at paras 23 and 29) states that PCTs are responsible for arranging the following services for residents of care homes (without charge):

- access to GP and other primary care services (including community nursing);
- physiotherapy, occupational therapy, speech and language therapy, dietetics and podiatry;
- continence pads and equipment and nursing aids (see below);
- the provision of district nursing (in residential care homes) and other nursing services, eg, continence advice and stoma care;
- specialist medical and nursing equipment (in nursing homes, eg, specialist feeding equipment) normally only available through hospitals;
- palliative care;
- and access to hospital care, which should also be arranged whenever it is required.

Specialist medical equipment

10.134 The joint responsibilities of social services and the NHS for the community equipment services is considered at para 8.101 above. However, the issue of NHS responsibility for the provision of 'specialist medical and nursing' equipment can cause problems. In general however, a care home providing nursing only has to provide the general equipment which is a prerequisite for its registration. Thus if a patient is in need of equipment which is not part of the basic registration requirement it may be argued that this is therefore 'specialist' in the sense that it ought to be funded by the health authority.[131] The NHS Ombudsman has, for instance, investigated a complaint[132] concerning an elderly nursing home resident who had to be fed by means of a gastric tube. Although the liquid feed was supplied on prescription she was required to pay for the tubes through which the feed was delivered (at £25 per week). The health authority accepted that this was incorrect and refunded the cost of the tubes.

10.135   The 2001 guidance (para 23) states that specialist medical and nursing equipment (eg, specialist feeding equipment) normally only available through hospitals should be provided as a continuing health care service. Guidance has now been issued concerning the provision of such equipment through joint community equipment stores[133] (see para 8.101). Circular HSC 2001/17; LAC (2001)26 additionally makes the following comments concerning specialist equipment:

> 8. For the majority of care home residents, much of the equipment necessary for their care will be available in the care home. Equipment is also available on prescription from a GP or a prescribing nurse. Details are contained in the Drug Tariff. This covers a range of appliances, including stoma and incontinence appliances, as well as the domiciliary oxygen therapy service.
>
> 9. Care home residents should have access to the full range of specialist NHS support that is available in other care settings and to people receiving care at home. In addition to equipment that is provided or secured by the care home in accordance with the minimum standards, the NHS should also consider whether there is a need to provide residents with access to dietary advice, as well as to the full range of available community equipment services, including pressure redistributing equipment, aids to mobility, and communication aids, etc, that are available in other settings. Specialist equipment needs for individual use should be specified in the assessment and subsequent care plan, together with the arrangements for

---

131 Para 5.3.1 of the pathways guidance (see para 10.157) states that 'care homes providing nursing care are expected to have, as part of the facilities they provide, some standard items of equipment for anyone needing them and for the safety of staff. These should include hoists, wheelchairs for occasional use, bath and shower seats and fixed items such as grab rails. All other items of equipment to meet the needs of an individual should be, or should have been, provided to them on the same basis as if they were living in a private house, applying the same eligibility criteria'.

132 Case No E985/94, p61. Selected Investigations April – September 1996.

133 HSC 2001/008; LAC(2001)13 *Community Equipment Services* available at www.doh. gov.uk/pdfs/hsc2001008.pdf.

getting the equipment in place, and any aftercare that may be necessary. Residents should have access to other NHS services, such as the wheelchair service, and staff working for the NHS should be responsible for assessing them.

Wheelchairs

10.136   As noted above (para 10.55) wheelchairs may be obtained from NHS trusts for temporary use on discharge from hospital. Wheelchairs for longer term use are provided as part of the 'general medical service' obligation under NHSA 1977 s29 (see para 10.45): wheelchairs being included in the 'appliance list' under the National Health Service (General Medical Services) Regulations 1992[134] Sch 2 para 43.

10.137   The assessment of need for (and provision of) wheelchairs is in practice undertaken by local NHS Wheelchair Services. The assessment is undertaken by a specialist, usually an occupational therapist, physiotherapist or consultant who will then identify the most suitable wheelchair. If the disabled person has difficulty using a manual wheelchair the trust can supply an electric model, including one for outdoor use if appropriate (see below).[135] The NHS in England additionally operates a 'wheelchair voucher scheme' that gives users the option of purchasing from an independent supplier or from the wheelchair service. In either case the user can top up the voucher cost (which covers only the cost of a 'standard' wheelchair to meet the users' needs) to enable a more expensive model to be acquired. However if the chair is purchased from an independent supplier it is owned by the user who is responsible for its maintenance and repair, whereas if the 'wheelchair services' option is chosen, the trust retains ownership but is also responsible for its maintenance.[136]

10.138   Considerable concern has been expressed about the poor state of NHS wheelchair services over many years, not least due to 'inequitable variations in prescribing, management structures, staffing, criteria, funding, costs and levels of services' and the lack of any national minimum standards.[137] As a consequence draft 'National Standards for Wheelchair Services' guidelines have been prepared which are likely to be finalised and adopted in early 2004.[138] These stipulate that 'users should not be discriminated against with regard to age' in the provision of services. Concern has been expressed that discrimination does occur in relation to care home residents, for some of whom access to wheelchair services has proved to be difficult, due to the erroneous suggestion that the care homes 'equipment' obligations should suffice for such residents.

---

134 SI No 635.

135 HSG(96)34.

136 HSG(96)53.

137 See the 'National standards for wheelchair services: Final Consultation Draft Document' accessible at http://www.wheelchairmanagers.nhs.uk/ servicestandards.doc and also the comments of the Minister for Health in her press release 27 November 2002.

138 Accessible at http://www.wheelchairmanagers.nhs.uk/servicestandards.doc.

10.139   The draft guidelines contain response times for various actions, for instance 15 working days[139] from receipt of a referral to an assessment; variable times for the provision of equipment – depending upon whether it is locally held (15 days), ordered from a manufacturer (30 days), or made to measure (65 days maximum). Likewise urgent repairs should be carried out within 24 hours and non-emergency repairs within 3 days.

10.140   Since 1996 funding has been available for the provision of electrically powered indoor/outdoor wheelchairs (EPIOCs), although targeted on 'more severely disabled users (including children) who could benefit from them to enjoy enhanced levels of independent mobility inside and outside their home'. The suggested (1996) criteria for such wheelchairs being that the severely disabled person is:[140]

- unable to propel a manual chair outdoors;
- able to benefit from the chair through increased mobility leading to improved quality of life;
- able to handle the chair safely.

10.141   Research has however suggested that these criteria exclude significant numbers of potential beneficiaries and the availability of EPIOCs[141] is currently being reviewed.

Incontinence supplies

10.142   Paragraph 23 of the 2001 guidance reiterates that 'PCTs are responsible for arranging . . . the provision of nursing advice, eg, continence advice and stoma care' and para 29 reiterates their responsibility to provide 'continence pads and equipment and nursing aids'.[142] Since April 2004 all continence supplies should be provided free of charge by PCTs.

10.143   Circular HSC 2001/17; LAC(2001)26 makes the following comments concerning continence services:

- From 1 October 2001 continence products should be made available by the NHS to residents of nursing homes who are also receiving NHS funded nursing care. An overview assessment for continence needs (see Annex E of the single assessment process guidance) should be carried out as part of the initial NHS assessment and registered nursing care contribution (RNCC) determination of current residents of nursing homes. A subsequent assessment (referred to as the 'initial assessment' at 3.9 of GPCS) should be carried out by a continence adviser or other suitably qualified nurse professional where this is indicated. GPCS should also inform the continence aspects of any comprehensive assessment of needs for people newly entering a nursing home.

139 The days referred to in this paragraph are to working days.

140 NHS Executive, HSG(96)34. Powered indoor/outdoor wheelchairs for severely disabled people, May 1996.

141 Department of Health funded research undertaken by the York Health Economics Consortium 'The Evaluation of the Powered Wheelchair and Voucher Scheme Initiatives March 2000.

142 See also 'Good Practice in Continence Services', Department of Health, April 2000 which provides guidance on the organisation and range of continence services.

- Systems should be established to ensure nursing homes receive the continence supplies required by residents.[143] It is up to PCTs or Community Trusts to make the necessary local arrangements, and it is for the NHS locally to determine how distribution is arranged. It is also for PCTs/Community Trusts to arrange a suitable payment mechanism with nursing homes for funding these products for self-funders (either using the system for paying for free nursing care or systems for paying for continuing NHS healthcare, existing payment systems that councils have with homes or amending current NHS systems to include provision to nursing homes). The provision of continence products should always follow an assessment of the patient's needs . . .

- £6 million is being made available to support the introduction of free continence products from 1 October 2001, distributed through Health Authority baseline allocations according to the number of self funders in the Health Authority's area. . . . From 1 April 2003 the responsibility of those residents whose nursing fees are currently paid for by councils will transfer to the NHS. The NHS will be expected to fund the cost of continence products for those patients from this date. Until 1 April 2003, councils will remain solely responsible for the provision of continence products for these residents. Continence advisers, nurses and PCTs should use the period until 1 April 2003 to establish processes for assessment of continence needs for patients currently funded by councils, and prepare themselves for providing continence services for all those in nursing homes in assessed need of services from 1 April 2003.

NHS continuing care responsibilities and HSCA 2001 s49 payments

10.144 As noted above (at para 10.60) Health and Social Care Act (HSCA) 2001 s49 made PCTs and LHBs responsible for the registered nursing care costs of residents in care homes. It could argued that with the introduction of HSCA 2001 s49, continuing health care responsibilities came to an end, since the section provided a clear demarcation between the respective responsibilities of the NHS and social services. This is not the case. The obligation under HSCA 2001 s49 is entirely separate. As the explanatory note accompanying section 49 states, its purpose is to remove:

> . . . local authorities' functions to purchase nursing care by a registered nurse under community care legislation. This is intended to strengthen the incentives for the NHS to ensure effective rehabilitation after acute illness or injury. It is estimated that around 35,000 people who are currently paying for their nursing care will receive free nursing care through the NHS.

10.145 The payments made by the PCTs/LHBs are in any event recycled social services monies[144] – in that the funds to pay for these contributions have been deducted from social services Formula Spending Share (see para 4.82) and transferred to PCTs/LHBs.

10.146   The English guidance on Free Nursing Care in Nursing Homes HSC

---

143 Nursing homes should not therefore charge fees for continence products required by residents.

144 For details of how the PCT contributions are actually paid – see the 2003 directions paras 49–56.

2001/17; LAC(2001)26, at appendix 6, is explicit about the distinction between payments made as a consequence of the HSCA 2001 s49 'free nursing care' obligation and continuing care:

> *Relationship with Continuing Care*
> Nothing in this guidance changes the duties of HAs to arrange and fully fund services for people whose primary needs are for healthcare rather than for accommodation and personal care.
>
> HSC 2001/15; LAC(2001)18 asked HAs to review their criteria for fully funded continuing NHS healthcare. People whose primary needs are for health care rather than accommodation continue to be eligible for fully funded continuing NHS health care. Criteria for fully funded continuing NHS health care define a level of overall care needs (including, but not limited to care from a registered nurse) which mean that the person has a primary need for healthcare and needs care beyond that which social services is able to provide under section 21 of the National Assistance Act 1948. Criteria are based on the scale, range, nature, continuity and intensity of the individual's health care needs and may involve consultant, palliative care, therapy or other NHS input. Where an individual's primary need is health care then the whole package of care must be paid for by the NHS.
>
> The first decision in any assessment process should always be whether or not an individual's needs meets the local criteria for fully funded continuing NHS health care and therefore their primary need is for health care. The RNCC should only be used for deciding the registered nurse's input (and hence the NHS's funding contribution) to a package of continuing health and social care which is incidental or ancillary to accommodation that could be arranged by social services under section 21 of the National Assistance Act 1948. The majority of nursing home residents are likely to fall into this category.
>
> The RNCC tool should be used to determine the registered nurse's *contribution* as part of a care package. 'Complex' and 'unpredictable' in the context of the RNCC refer to an individual's care needs which require care from a registered nurse, such as fluctuating care needs which require for frequent intervention and monitoring from a registered nurse. They should not be confused with similar terminology used to assess an individual's overall healthcare needs when assessing against continuing health care criteria.

10.147 Notwithstanding this guidance, the very existence of the RNCC bands create a conceptual problem in relation to the scope of the NHS's continuing health care responsibilities. This stems from an appreciation of status of these 'bands' – namely that they are the creation of the Department of Health, not Parliament, and the three bands[145] (high, medium and low) are arbitrary to the extent that the Department of Health had an almost entirely free hand in determining the eligibility criteria for each band of support.

10.148 It is arguable that the Department set the high level of support (ie, the 'high' band) above the level defined by the Court of Appeal as the point at which a person could expect full continuing care funding. By so doing, the

145 These are detailed in '*NHS Funded Nursing Care Practice Guide and Workbook*' Department of Health, August 2001 see www.dh.gov.uk/assetRoot/04/07/67/20/ 04076720.pdf.

Department caused very considerable confusion amongst PCTs. If the 'high band' only triggered a PCT contribution liability of £120 per week how could someone with a lesser health care need be entitled to full continuing care? Para 3.8 of the guidance[146] describes the 'high band' as follows:

> 3.8 People with high needs for registered nursing care will have complex needs that require frequent mechanical, technical and/or therapeutic interventions. They will need frequent intervention and re-assessment by a registered nurse throughout a 24-hour period, and their physical/mental health state will be unstable and/or unpredictable.

10.149   The patient the subject of the Leeds NHS Ombudsman complaint does not meet these criteria, nor does Pamela Coughlan. Indeed the high band accurately describes the condition of the Wigan and Bolton nursing home resident whom the Health Service Commissioner considered to be un- questionably entitled to continuing health care funding.

10.150   It is likely that some patients assessed as falling within the 'medium band' will also be entitled to continuing care. Para 3.9 describes the medium band in the following terms:

> 3.9 People whose needs for registered nursing care are judged to be in the medium banding may have multiple care needs. They will require the intervention of a registered nurse on at least a daily basis, and may need access to a nurse at any time. However, their condition (including physical, behavioural and psychosocial needs) is stable and predictable, and likely to remain so if treatment and care regimes continue.

10.151   Both Pamela Coughlan and the patient the subject of the Leeds NHS Ombudsman complaint would have had difficulty qualifying for this band (see Table 5 above).

10.152   It could be argued that the RNCC banding system does not in fact con- flict with the continuing health care responsibilities of the NHS – on the basis that the RNCC is a measure of the 'quality' of nursing required (ie, by a registered nurse) and not of the 'quantity' (ie, the second limb of Court of Appeal's test of eligibility). Such an argument would only be tenable if the Court had decided that Pamela Coughlan qualified on the 'quantity' grounds, and this is not the case. Neither does it explain why the Health Service Commissioner considered that the Wigan and Bolton patient to be unquestionably entitled to continuing care funding when she would appear only to qualify for the higher band RNCC. It must be the case, how- ever, that where there is a conflict between a determination based on the RNCC guidance and the Court of Appeal's assessment in *Coughlan* the Court of Appeal's judgment takes precedence.

NHS discharge procedures

10.153   The law that regulates the hospital discharge responsibilities of the NHS and social services is an amalgam of statute and tort. The patient is owed a

146 The '*NHS Funded Nursing Care Practice Guide & Workbook*' Department of Health, August 2001 see www.doh.gov.uk/jointunit/freenursingcare.

duty of care (in the tort of negligence) by both the social services authority and the relevant NHS body. The NHS has a statutory responsibility to provide care under the National Health Service Act (NHSA) 1977 – albeit a weak duty (see para 1.5) and social services have responsibilities under the community care legislation to assess and provide services. Patients have in general[147] no right to remain in an NHS facility and can be discharged against their wishes – provided that the NHS and social services authorities consider that it is safe (ie, have satisfied themselves that it would not be negligent – by exposing the patient to an unnecessary or involuntary risk of harm). In this respect the two bodies are subject to considerable Department of Health and Welsh Assembly guidance.

10.154   The relationship between the NHS and social services in the discharge process is also shaped by central government guidance, and (in England)[148] by statute – the Community Care (Delayed Discharge, etc) Act (CC(DD)A) 2003. The regulations and guidance accompanying the Act[149] also contain significant material relating to the rights of the patient and their carers in the discharge process.

10.155   The relevant event in this process is the discharge of the patient from NHS care – not his or her transfer to another NHS facility. Patients do not have the right to choose the place at which they receive NHS care.[150] The decision that they are safe to be transferred to another NHS facility is primarily that of the responsible consultant and the NHS team on the receiving ward. When discussing hospital discharge therefore, the issue is not of internal transfer but discharge from an NHS funded setting. A consultant's decision that a patient is safe to be transferred is however a fundamental requirement – a key triggering event – in the discharge planning process.[151]

10.156   When such a decision has been made, and the patient has (or may have)

---

147 Unless they are entitled to continuing health care support, detained under the MHA 1983 or have been in NHS accommodation for a prolonged period – such that it might be deemed their 'home' for the purposes of ECHR art 8 (see paras 7.126 and 19.187).

148 There is no present intention to bring the reimbursement provisions of the 2003 Act into force in Wales.

149 The Delayed Discharges (England) Regulations 2003 SI No 2277 (the '2003 Regulations') and guidance as HSC 2003/009; LAC(2003)21 on the 24 September 2003. In addition a host of other materials (directions, protocols, draft forms, question and answer statements, etc, have been issued – most of which are accessible at the Department of Health site www.dh.gov.uk/PolicyAndGuidance/OrganisationPolicy/TertiaryCare/DelayedDischarge/fs/en.

150 See para 7.100 above.

151 The NHS/social services cannot (without invoking their powers under the Mental Health Act 1983) prevent patients from discharging themselves – provided they have sufficient mental capacity to make the decision (see para 13.16). Para 5.4.3 of the pathways guidance (see para 10.157) explains that 'self-discharge or discharge against medical advice may fall into one of the following categories. The patient (1) understands the risks they are taking in discharging themselves; (2) is not competent to understand the risks associated with discharge due to his or her medical condition; (3) is not competent to understand the risks associated with discharge due to mental health problems. The discharge policy must set out the procedure to be followed by the ward-based care co-ordinator in such circumstances.

a need for community care services, then a safe discharge cannot occur until the NHS and social services are satisfied that the patient is not only (1) ready for discharge, but also (2) safe to be discharged. In essence this is therefore a twin key process. Once the consultant activates the system, the discharge conveyor belt only starts to move when two keys have been turned; the first is primarily the responsibility of the NHS and the second, primarily the responsibility of social services. Once the two keys have been turned and the belt in motion, then (if the process is regulated by the CC(DD)A 2003) social services are generally unable to stop the system without paying compensation to the NHS.

Key guidance

10.157   Three central documents give key guidance on the process that should be followed to ensure a discharge is safe. These being *Discharge from hospital: pathway, process and practice*;[152] the safe discharge protocol *Definitions – Medical Stability and 'Safe to Transfer'*[153] and the *CCDDA 2003 Guidance for Implementation*[154] (referred to in the following section as the 'pathways guidance', the 'discharge protocol' and the 'delayed discharge guidance' respectively). In terms of good practice, the pathways guidance should be viewed as the core guidance shaping the basic structure, processes and the collaborations that are essential to a sympathetic and effective hospital discharge system. The provisions of the CC(DD)A 2003 are designed to synchronise with the good practice guidance; thus the service of a notice under the Act should not be seen as an event that dominates or in any way undermines the operation of the system.

Patient and carer involvement

10.158   The pathways guidance states that 'the engagement and active participation of individuals and their carers as equal partners is central to the delivery of care and in the planning of a successful discharge' (para 1.4) and stresses the importance of them being 'kept fully informed by regular reviews and updates of the care plan'.[155] This awareness is not restricted to older people: para 4.1 notes that young people may also be carers and 'should be offered a carer's assessment if they are under 16 years of age, when the adult receives a community care assessment'.

10.159   The pathways guidance acknowledges that carers have often considered

---

152 Department of Health, accessible at: www.publications.doh.gov.uk/
hospitaldischarge/index.htm. Only limited discharge guidance exists in Wales. The draft continuing care guidance (para 10.87) above simply refers to the UFSAMC guidance (see note 56 at p75 above).

153 Department of Health, accessible at www.dh.gov.uk/PolicyAndGuidance/
OrganisationPolicy/TertiaryCare/DelayedDischarge/fs/en.

154 The Community Care (Delayed Discharges, etc) Act 2003, *Guidance for Implementation*, September 2003. HSC 2003/009; LAC(2003)21.

155 Pathways guidance para 1.2. And para 4.5.1 provides a detailed 'carer's checklist' of relevant factors to be considered.

themselves marginalised by discharge arrangements, particularly with patients being sent home too early (para 4.1) leaving their carers to cope with unacceptable caring situations.[156] Working with carers is a responsibility of discharge co-ordinators – and it should not be seen merely as a social services function. If a patient refuses permission to allow their carer to be involved in decisions about their future care, carers should be informed of this and their right to an assessment reinforced. Carers should be given time to consider their options 'in making what are often life changing decisions' and they should be 'informed about the support networks and services that may be available to them' (para 4.3).

10.160   At para 4.3 the pathway's guidance makes the following points:

> The need of the carer should be under constant review to take account of their personal health and social care needs as well as the caring role they are undertaking. The assessment and review process should consider the need for a short-term break from caring.
>
> Patients may also have responsibilities such as being the parent of young children or as a carer of someone who has a disability and who is unable to live independently. It is important to identify whether an adult has dependent children and to ensure that arrangements are in place for their care during the period of admission. If the child is the carer of an adult with a chronic illness or disability, the child's own needs for support must be addressed. It is vital that every effort is made to ensure that the family has sufficient services to ensure that children are not left with unacceptable caring responsibilities that affect their welfare, education or development. In addition, patients can also be carers, and it is important to ensure that if they are caring for someone that they have the right services upon discharge, to ensure that they can look after their own needs, as well as the person they are caring for.

Mental capacity

10.161   In relation to patients with limited mental capacity the pathways guidance (at para 5.3) states that 'where patients cannot represent themselves, the next of kin, and/or an advocate, should be involved'; that 'advocates might enable views that differ from the carers' views to be heard' and that it is necessary therefore for staff to have access to interpreting and advocacy services (see para 13.11).

Information/communication

10.162   In a number of investigations the NHS Ombudsman has been critical of trusts who have failed to provide adequate information to patients and their carers, such that a right to challenge discharge from NHS funded care was lost. He has stressed that where the obligation to inform is a joint one with the social services, this does not excuse a failure by the trust to provide

---

156   Carers England (2002). *Hospital discharge practice briefing.* London: Carers UK which reported that 43% of carers considered they were not given adequate support when the person returned home. See also J Mather et al, *Carers 2000,*Office of National Statistics, 2000.

the information (ie, it cannot assume that social services will discharge its duty).[157] He has also criticised as inadequate the provision of general brochures to patients and situations where staff provided patients with only limited advice on their possible options.[158]

10.163   The pathway's guidance stresses the importance of patients and their carers being 'provided with information, both verbal and written, and in a range of media formats (to take into account any sensory or spoken language needs) on what to expect and their contribution to the process'. This should include details of arrangements, contact details and any relevant information regarding their future treatment and care (para 3.4) and para 4.2 advises that:

> Any form of communication must take account of the individual's ability to understand and absorb information. The same information will need to be available in plain language and in a variety of appropriate forms. This should include, for example, appropriate minority and ethnic languages and presentations in large print, Braille and British Sign Language. Other formats might also be appropriate including audiotapes and visual formats such as interactive CD-Rom. For some patients it will be necessary to involve an advocate or interpreter to provide further assistance. Every effort must be made to ensure consistency and continuity of information from different personnel.[159]

Ward-based care co-ordinator

10.164   Central to the operation of an effective and sympathetic discharge process is the presence of a 'ward care co-ordinator'. This 'important' and 'highly skilled role' requires an 'experienced practitioner who has a good understanding of discharge planning' and although usually undertaken by nurses 'it may be appropriate in a transitional or rehabilitation service for a therapist or social worker to be the care co-ordinator' (pathways guidance at para 5.4.1). The guidance additionally observes (at para 5.4):

> On admission to the ward a named individual from the ward staff should be identified to co-ordinate all stages of the patient journey to proactively support and facilitate the work of the multidisciplinary team in delivering the best outcomes for the patient and guide them through the system to receive what they need, when they need it [160] This role, henceforth referred to as the ward-based care co-ordinator, should focus on the needs of patients who have been identified as requiring additional support in discharge planning . . . If the patient is transferred to another ward it is the responsibility of the ward-based care co-ordinator to provide a formal transfer of responsibility.

---

157 Fifth Report for Session 1995–96, *Investigations of Complaints about Long-Term NHS Care*, HMSO. Complaint E685/94-95.

158 Complaint E672/94–95.

159 Department of Health (2000). *Patient and public involvement in the new NHS.*

160 House of Commons Health Committee Delayed Discharges (2001–02), Vol 1. The Stationery Office.

Safe discharge

10.165 The pathways guidance stresses that 'planning for hospital discharge is part of an ongoing process that should start prior to admission (for planned admissions) and as soon as possible for all other admissions. It explains the nature of the shared responsibility of the NHS and social services in the discharge decision in the following terms (para 5.4.3):

> A decision that a patient is medically fit for discharge can only be made by the patient's consultant (or by someone to whom the consultant has delegated his or her authority) or by another doctor who is responsible for the care of the patient. Patients, who have both health and social care needs, must only be discharged when they are clinically fit. This is a decision made by the multidisciplinary team when considering all the factors, which will include the relative safety of remaining in hospital or being elsewhere and the patient's and carer's view of these risks. It is also important to include the carer as part of the team as they will have expertise regarding the patient's home environment.

10.166 The 1994 *Hospital Discharge Workbook*[161] expressed this responsibility in a rather more direct way, namely:

> The decision that a patient is medically fit for discharge can only be made by a consultant (or by someone to whom the consultant has delegated his authority), or by another doctor who is responsible for the care of an individual patient (such as a general practitioner responsible for GP beds). However, the decision to discharge a patient should be the result of a jointly agreed, multidisciplinary process in which social services are responsible for assessing the needs of people for social care.

10.167 The discharge protocol lists three key criteria for the making of the discharge decision and emphasises that they 'are not separate or sequential stages; all three should be addressed at the same time whenever possible'.

1. a clinical decision has been made that the patient is ready for transfer,
2. a multidisciplinary team decision has been made that the patient is ready for transfer, and
3. the patient is safe to discharge/transfer.

10.168 The discharge protocol comments that:

> In some cases we are told the process consists almost entirely of the consultant deciding a patient is medically fit for discharge, followed by referral to social services. Hence the multidisciplinary input to the decision making process is minimal and – in extreme cases – non-existent. In addition this does not fulfil the, now legal, requirement to begin planning for discharge as soon as possible during the hospital stay.

---

161 Department of Health (1994) p1, para 1 of the pathway guidance explains that it 'builds on the very successful *Hospital Discharge Workbook* first published by the Department of Health in 1994'.

10.169 It goes on to analyse the critical questions in relation to each of the three steps:

> 1. *The clinical decision (ready to transfer/discharge)*
> *   Does the patient need to remain in an acute bed to receive intensive medical input from a consultant team?
> *   Does the patient need intensive or specialist nursing, therapy or other clinical support only available in an acute setting, such as the administration of specialist drugs or intensive monitoring through the use of specialist equipment?
> *   Has the patient's condition been monitored within an agreed period?
> *   Is the patient's health likely to deteriorate significantly if moved elsewhere?
> *   Has the patient recovered from the acute episode sufficiently to be able to return home or move to another setting?
> *   Could the patient be managed at home by primary care or in a nurse or therapy led unit?
>
> 2. *The multidisciplinary team decision (ready to transfer/discharge)*
> *   Will the patient benefit from further acute treatment and/or rehabilitation?
> *   Can rehabilitation or recuperation be provided in an alternative setting, including the patient's own home and has the team come to a decision about where the patient should be managed?
> *   What are the risks of remaining in the acute bed?
> *   Has the patient (and have any carers) been involved in the assessment?[162]
>
> 3. *The objective decision (safe to transfer/discharge)*
> *   Does the multidisciplinary team have a clear picture of the patient's living circumstances prior to this episode and know enough to be able to make a decision that the person is safe to discharge/transfer?
> *   Can the assessment be continued/completed in another setting, including the person's own home?
> *   What does the patient want and expect?
> *   Has the carer been consulted and what are their views?
> *   Has a similar level of need for this patient previously been met by primary and community care services?
> *   Does everyone, including the patient and carer, understand the risk of transferring the patient?

Delayed discharge payments

10.170 The charging arrangements (known as 'reimbursement') apply to local authorities who delay the discharge of adults who are (1) safe to be discharged and (2) have been receiving acute medical care and (3) are in need of community care services. A lack of capacity in a community care service (for instance the absence of any available care home places) does not exempt social services from their liability to make a payment.

---

162 Although the protocol uses the word 'assessment' this does not appear to refer to a 'community care assessment' but merely whether the patient and carer have been involved in the multidisciplinary decision that he or she is safe to transfer.

Acute medical care

10.171 The reimbursement rules only apply to patients receiving 'acute medical care' – defined as 'intensive NHS-funded medical treatment provided by or under the supervision of a consultant which is for a limited time after which the patient no longer benefits from that treatment'. Maternity care, mental health care,[163] palliative care, intermediate care and care provided for recuperation or rehabilitation are excluded from the definition of acute care. Community Care (Delayed Discharge, etc) Act (CC(DD)A) 2003 s14 enables the Minister, by Order, to extend the scope of the reimbursement provisions to cover NHS patients in care homes. The explanatory notes to CC(DD)A 2003 s14 state that the intention is to include in time 'patients receiving intermediate care in a care home setting . . . as well as those receiving intermediate care in a hospital'.

The timings of the CC(DD)A 2003 notices

10.172 The NHS is required to give social services two notifications:

1) The first, known as an Assessment Notification (under section 2) gives notice of the patient's possible need for services on discharge. Following this notification, social services have a minimum of three days to carry out an assessment and arrange care.

2) The second, a Discharge Notification (under section 5) gives notice of the day on which it is proposed that the patient will be discharged.

10.173 Reimbursement liability commences on the day after the minimum period (the third day after an Assessment Notification) or the day after the proposed discharge date, whichever is the later. A notification after 2pm is counted from the next day.

10.174   The technicalities of the notifications are slightly involved.[164] Initially (that is, during the first year of the scheme) notifications sent on Sundays and Bank Holidays will be deemed to have been sent on the following days as will notifications sent after 2pm on a Friday or after 5pm on any other day.[165]

The CC(DD)A 2003 assessment obligations

The NHS

10.175 Before the NHS can issue the first notification (under section 2) it must:

- undertake an assessment as to whether the patient is eligible for continuing care support;[166]

---

163 As detailed in Delayed Discharges (Mental Health Care) (England) Order 2003 SI No 2276 art 2.

164 Detailed explanations are given in guidance at www.doh.gov.uk/reimbursement/pdf/notificationissuing.pdf.

165 The 2003 Regulations regs 10 and 11.

166 The Delayed Discharge (Continuing Care) Directions 2003 dir 2.

- consult with the patient about involving social services (and the notification to social services must clarify the outcome of this consultation and provide certain minimum information – detailed in the regulations);
- identify the patient's responsible social services authority.[167]

Social services

Community care assessment obligation

10.176 On receiving the 'assessment' notification social services are required to undertake an assessment of the patient's needs for community care services – and this 'is to be treated as done' under National Health Service and Community Care Act (NHSCCA) 1990 s47.[168] In this respect the discharge guidance states:[169]

> Assessment for discharge covers the services needed to allow the patient to move from the acute bed – a further assessment may then be needed to put in place a longer term package of care or the next step, eg, from intermediate care to home.

Social services – carers assessment obligation

10.177 The 'assessment' notification also triggers social services' obligations under the Carers and Disabled Children Act 2000[170] and in this respect the discharge guidance states:[171]

> Just as assessment for discharge need not be a full community care assessment, a carer's assessment related to a patient discharge may be only part of a full assessment which continues after the patient is discharged. Where the carer will be undertaking lifting, or other tasks that need training to ensure that the carer or patient is not put at risk, staff should ensure that appropriate training is provided.

The CC(DD)A 2003 reimbursement liability

10.178 To be liable for reimbursement, it must be social services provision and only social services provision which is not available.[172] The discharge guidance goes into considerable detail as to how responsibility can arise in various situations – for instance when jointly commissioned care services are delayed; where the patient receives direct payments and so on.

10.179   If social services do not have services in place by 11am of the day after the proposed discharge date, such that the discharge cannot take place, then they are liable for a charge[173] – provided this is the sole reason for the delay. The charge, which may be increased by regulation,[174] is currently £100 per day for the majority of social services authority areas, but £120 for

---

167 HSC 2003/009; LAC (2003) 21 para 65.
168 CC(DD)A 2003 s4(9).
169 HSC 2003/009; LAC (2003) 21 para 36.
170 CC(DD)A 2003 s4(3).
171 HSC 2003/009; LAC (2003) 21 para 47.
172 CC(DD)A 2003 s6; HSC 2003/009; LAC (2003) 21 para 55.
173 CC(DD)A 2003 s6 and the 2003 Regulations regs 10 and 11.
174 Currently detailed in the 2003 Regulations reg 7.

authorities in the Home Counties, London and the South East.[175] Liability ends when the patient is discharged[176] or the patient needs to remain in hospital for other treatment or dies.[177]

Choice of accommodation and delayed discharge

10.180 Patients leaving hospital or a place in a care home supported by a local authority have rights under the Choice of Accommodation Directions (see para 7.84). Not inconsiderable numbers of patients considered to be inappropriately occupying NHS beds are doing so because they have been assessed as requiring a care home place and the home of their choice has no current vacancies. In this respect the pathways guidance states (para 2.2):

> Although *patient choice* is considered extremely important, patients who have been assessed as not requiring NHS continuing in-patient care, do not have the right to occupy, indefinitely, an NHS bed (with the exception of a very small number of cases where a patient is being placed under Part II of the Mental Health Act 1983). They do, however, have the right to refuse to be discharged from NHS care into a care home.

10.181 The discharge guidance deals with this problem as follows:

> 97. ... [local protocols] should make it clear that an acute bed is not an appropriate place to wait and the alternatives that will be offered. Where social services are responsible for providing services and a person's preferred home of choice is not immediately available, they should offer an interim package of care. All interim arrangements should be based solely on the patients assessed needs and sustain or improve their level of independence. If no alternative is provided which can meet the patient's needs, social services are liable for reimbursement.

> 98. Social services should take all reasonable steps to gain a patient's agreement to a care package, that is to provide a care package which the patient can be reassured will meet the needs identified and agreed in the care plan ...

> 99. If the patient continues to unreasonably refuse the care package offered by social services they cannot stay in a hospital bed indefinitely and will need to make their own arrangements so that they can be discharged safely. If at a later date further contact is made with social services regarding the patient, the council should re-open the care planning process, if it is satisfied that the patient's needs remain such to justify the provision of services and there is no longer reason to think that the patient will persist in refusing such services unreasonably. Councils may wish to take their own legal advice in such circumstances.

> 100. Where appropriate alternative services, which take account of the patient's views, have been offered, and active encouragement given to the patient to transfer, but they unreasonably refuse to move to the alternative, social services will not be held responsible ...

---

175 Known as 'Higher Rate' authorities and listed in the Schedule to the 2003 Regulations.

176 CC(DD)A 2003 s6(4)(b).

177 The 2003 Regulations reg 9.

10.182 A questions and answers statement (on the CC(DD)A 2003) issued by the Department of Health addresses the question of patient choice, by adding the additional comment:[178]

> NHS staff will have to make a judgement about whether the patient will be safe to discharge without any help from social services. If they do not think it will be safe, they will need to explain further to the patient their concerns and this might be helped by contacting social services to discuss options with the patient. If the patient still refuses any help from social services the NHS will need to consider providing NHS services to help the patient go home safely.

Delayed discharge and ordinary residence

10.183 Difficult questions are likely to arise, concerning 'ordinary residence' – since responsibility for the assessment process (and ultimately the reimbursement liability) depends upon the NHS body serving notice upon the correct local authority. The responsible authority is the one in which the patient is ordinarily resident (considered generally in chapter 6 above). The basic duties are detailed in the 2003 Regulations (reg 18). Paragraph 65 of the discharge guidance advises that although the NHS trust is not required to undertake lengthy investigations to establish with certainty which council is responsible – if it serves the wrong council it will have to withdraw the notice and 'risks causing a delay in the patient's discharge, as the time allowed for the assessment and care planning process starts again for the new council'. At para 67 it advises:

> . . . if a council receives an assessment notification in respect of a patient who it believes is ordinarily resident elsewhere, it should inform the issuing NHS body, which should withdraw the notice if it agrees with the council's opinion. If the NHS body does not agree and the matter cannot be resolved locally and informally, the council receiving the assessment notification must proceed with assessment and care planning as if it were the responsible authority.

10.184 However if after services have been provided or reimbursement has been paid, the council which has been dealing with the case is entitled to reclaim the costs incurred in providing services or any reimbursement payments, if made, from the correct council (discharge guidance para 69).

10.185 Disputes about ordinary residence will be determined by the Department of Health unless the dispute involves a Welsh council and an English council – in which case it is the country in which the patient is located which will indicate who has responsibility for determining ordinary residence (ie, either the Department of Health or the Welsh Assembly).

Reviews/challenges to discharge decisions

10.186 Strategic Health Authorities (SHAs) are required to set up disputes panels to arbitrate between social services and the PCTs over disputes as to

---

178 Community Care (Delayed Discharges, etc) Act 2003 – Frequently Asked Questions on Reimbursement (Q29) at www.dh.gov.uk/assetRoot/04/07/19/26/04071926.pdf.

reimbursement. These panels are not for use by patients challenging their discharge (for whom a separate process exists – see below). The panels comprise an independent chair person and two wing members, one from a local authority and the other an NHS representative – both of whom must be from a different local authority/NHS body to the ones involved in the dispute (2003 regulations, reg 15).

Patient's right to seek a review of a discharge decision

10.187 The 2001 Continuing Care guidance (at Annex E) re-issued with little change the 1995 guidance concerning the establishment of panels to adjudicate where a patient/carer challenges an NHS decision that the patient is not eligible for continuing care funded by the NHS (or is being discharged contrary to the good practice guidance). The key change concerned the extension of the procedure to 'other decisions regarding the NHS arranged and funded element of services for people in receipt of continuing health and social care and, once implemented, free nursing care' (para 33). Previously the procedure was only available for patients about to be discharged from continuing NHS health care.

10.188   The review process is a SHA function and directions have now been issued which regulate the composition and functions of the continuing care review panels.[179] Direction 4(3) provides that:

> 3 (1) Where a patient, or a person acting on a patient's behalf –
>   (a) is dissatisfied about –
>   (i) the procedure followed by a Primary Care Trust or an NHS trust in reaching a decision about the patient's need for continuing care, or
>   (ii) the application by a Primary Care Trust or an NHS trust of the criteria referred to in direction 2(2)(a) in relation to such a decision; and
>   (b) has been unable to resolve the matter informally,
> he may apply in writing to the Strategic Health Authority for a review of the decision.

10.189 The directions specify in detail the process followed in such cases and stipulate that the SHA must provide the applicant with its decisions (and reasons) in writing within two weeks of it receiving a request for a review (except in exceptional circumstances).

10.190   The 2001 guidance confirms that the review procedure applies to all patients who have been receiving NHS in-patient care, whether in hospital, or arranged and funded by the NHS in a hospice, nursing home, or elsewhere, and to all client groups covered in local eligibility criteria. It describes the scope of the review procedure as being twofold:

> (a) to check that proper procedures have been followed in reaching the decisions about the need for NHS health care, and

---

179 The Continuing Care (National Health Service Responsibilities) Directions 2004 accessible at www.dh.gov.uk/assetRoot/04/07/46/90/04074690.PDF.

(b) to ensure that the health authority's eligibility criteria for NHS continuing in-patient care are properly and consistently applied. The procedure is not, however, a formal appeals mechanism or a complaints procedure, and does not therefore affect patients' rights under NHS or social services complaints procedures.

10.191 The procedure cannot be used to challenge the content (as opposed to the application) of the [SHAs] eligibility criteria; the type and location of any offer of NHS-funded continuing in-patient care; the content of any alternative care package offered; or such matters as the patient's treatment or any other aspect of his or her stay in hospital.

10.192 Each PCT is required to appoint a 'designated officer' who is responsible for the efficient operation of the review procedure. This will encompass checking (in liaison with the provider) that all appropriate steps have been taken to resolve the case informally as well as the collection of information for the panel, including interviewing patients, family members and any relevant carer(s).

10.193 If the PCT resolution process fails, then the dispute is then referred to the SHA's standing review panel (as detailed above).

Budget sharing arrangements between the NHS and social services

10.194 Historically the ability of the NHS and social services authorities to pool budgets, or transfer resources from one to another had been severely curtailed. In consequence it has been argued that innovation has been stifled and 'cost shunting' between authorities encouraged.[180]

10.195 This situation was relaxed as a consequence of Health Act (HA) 1999 ss29–31, which amended National Health Service Act (NHSA) 1977 s28 enabling health bodies and social services to enter into a wide range of 'partnership arrangements'. NHSA 1977 s28A (as amended) enables SHAs and PCTs to make payments to local authorities in respect of any local authority function that is 'health-related'. NHSA 1977 s28BB provides a reciprocal power for local authorities to make payments to SHAs or PCTs in relation to 'prescribed functions'. Regulations made under this section have[181] defined 'prescribed functions' widely[182] excluding only such matters as 'surgery, radiotherapy, termination of pregnancies, endoscopy, [certain] laser treatments and other invasive treatments'.

---

180 Partnership in Action (September 1998) Department of Health discussion paper.

181 The National Health Service (Payments by Local Authorities to NHS Bodies) (Prescribed Functions) Regulations 2000 SI No 618 and the the National Health Service (Payments by Local Authorities to Health Authorities) (Prescribed Functions) (Wales) Regulations 2001 SI No 1543 (W 108)

182 Including services under NHSA 1977 ss2, 3(1), 5(1), (1A), (1B) and Sch 1 as well as functions under the MHA 1983 ss25A to 25 H and 117.

Partnerships arrangements under HA 1999 s31

10.196 HA 1999 s31 allows the NHS and local authorities to pool their resources, delegate functions and transfer resources from one party to another and enable a single provider to provide both health and local authority services. In effect it permits:

- **The pooled fund arrangements:** where authorities pool resources so that they will effectively 'lose their health and local authority identity', allowing staff from either agency to develop packages of care suited to particular individuals irrespective of whether health or local authority money is used.

- **Delegation of functions – lead commissioning:** where PCTs and local authorities delegate functions to one another (including the secondment or transfer of staff). In the case of health and social care this enables one of the partner bodies to commission all mental health or learning disability services locally.

- **Delegation of functions – integrated provision:** this consists of the provision of health and local authority services from a single managed provider. The arrangement can be used in conjunction with lead commissioning and pooled fund arrangements.

10.197 As with the budget sharing regulations above, most NHS functions can be the subject of partnership arrangements (with the same exceptions – see para 10.195 above).[183] Likewise a wide range of social services functions can be the subject of partnership arrangements – including in England (but not Wales) charging for care home accommodation under the NAA 1948 and for non-accommodation community care services.[184] HA 1999 s31(5) provides that any partnership arrangements made under section 31 will not affect the liability of the NHS body or the local authority for the exercise of their functions. Liability remains, therefore with the body primarily responsible for the discharge of the function (ie, the body with this responsibility prior to the partnership arrangement).

10.198 Guidance on these arrangements has been issued as HSC 2000/010; LAC (2000)9 in England.

Other partnership arrangements

10.199 The government's discussion paper 'Partnership in Action' noted that not all the perceived constraints to joint working were legislative and that in 'many areas, health and social services authorities have not taken advantage

---

183 NHS Bodies and Local Authorities Partnership Arrangements Regulations 2000 SI No 617 and the National Health Service Bodies and Local Authorities Partnership Arrangements (Wales) Regulations 2000 SI No 2993 (W 193)

184 The NHS Bodies and Local Authorities Partnership Arrangements (Amendment)(England) Regulations 2003 SI No 629.

of opportunities allowed within the existing framework'.[185] A detailed list of these legal mechanisms was provided in a 1998 Report 'Pathways to Partnership': Legal Aspects of Joint Working in Mental Health',[186] and included:

- *Housing and Social Services*
  Housing Act 1996 s213(1): the duty on a housing authority to respond to any request for assistance from a social services authority.

- *The duty to co-operate*
  NHSA 1977 s22: the duty on health and local authorities to co-operate in order to advance the health and welfare of the people of England and Wales.

- *Sharing of staff*
  NHSA 1977 s26: so far as is reasonably necessary and practicable health authority staff should be made available to enable local authorities to help them discharge their social services, education and public health functions.
  NHSA 1977 s27: this provides a reverse obligation to s26, so far as it is reasonably necessary and practicable in order to enable health authorities to discharge their functions under the NHSA 1977 and the NHSCCA 1990.

- *Staff transfers*
  Local Government Act 1972 s113: enables local authority staff to be seconded to the NHS and vice versa.

- *Supply of goods and services*
  Local Authorities (Goods and Services) Act 1970: this Act enables local authorities to enter into agreements with health authorities for the supply of goods and services.

Dowry payments

10.200 Prior to its amendment by the HA 1999, NHSA 1977 s28A only permitted payments by health authorities to local authorities, housing associations and certain other bodies and voluntary organisations in respect of personal social services, education for disabled people and housing. Detailed guidance[187] and directions[188] were issued in relation to these payments. These provisions permitted various scheme, including an arrangement known as 'dowry' payments.

10.201   Dowry payments were used to facilitate the transfer of patients from long-stay hospitals into the community. They involved a lump-sum payment or annual payment to a local authority taking over the patient's care;

---

185 Partnership in Action (September 1998) Department of Health discussion paper, paragraph 4.5.
186 Camilla Parker with Richard Gordon for the Sainsbury Centre for Mental Health.
187 LAC(92)17, HSG (92) 43 and HSG(95)45.
188 Directions under NHSA 1977 s28A being contained as Annex C to HSG(92)43.

the amount of the lump-sum or annual payment and the length of time for which annual payments were to be made being negotiated by the respective authorities. In this respect HSG(95)45 advised (at Annex para 4.1):

> . . . in respect of people being discharged from long stay institutions, the NHS is responsible for negotiating arrangements with local authorities, including any appropriate transfer of resources which assist the local authority meeting the community care needs of such people *and of their successors* who may otherwise have entered the institution.

10.202 The relevance of such arrangements (or more precisely the lack of these) was spelt out in LAC(92)17 (para 10 Annex A) which stated that:

> Where residential care arrangements in the community for a person who was formerly a patient in a long-stay hospital appear to be breaking down . . . then the LA . . . should take the lead in seeing that the appropriate arrangements are secured . . . Where no agreement has been made between the HA responsible for the hospital care before discharge and the LA about respective responsibilities, the HA should assist the LA . . . and if the resecuring or reprovisioning of care leads the LA to incur additional expenditure, the HA will be expected to use its powers under s28A to assist the LA to fund the care.

CHAPTER 11

Carers

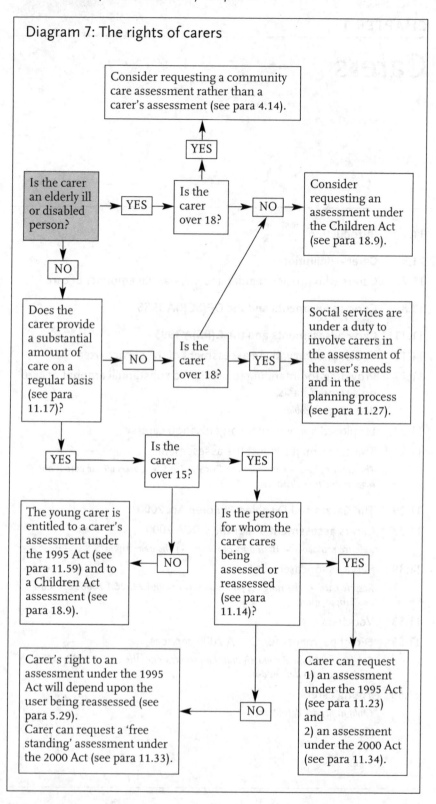

Diagram 7: The rights of carers

Consider requesting a community care assessment rather than a carer's assessment (see para 4.14).

YES

Is the carer an elderly ill or disabled person? → YES → Is the carer over 18? → NO → Consider requesting an assessment under the Children Act (see para 18.9).

NO

Does the carer provide a substantial amount of care on a regular basis (see para 11.17)? → NO → Is the carer over 18? → YES → Social services are under a duty to involve carers in the assessment of the user's needs and in the planning process (see para 11.27).

YES

Is the carer over 15? → YES

The young carer is entitled to a carer's assessment under the 1995 Act (see para 11.59) and to a Children Act assessment (see para 18.9). ← NO

Is the person for whom the carer cares being assessed or reassessed (see para 11.14)? → YES

Carer's right to an assessment under the 1995 Act will depend upon the user being reassessed (see para 5.29).
Carer can request a 'free standing' assessment under the 2000 Act (see para 11.33). ← NO

Carer can request 1) an assessment under the 1995 Act (see para 11.23) and 2) an assessment under the 2000 Act (see para 11.34).

Introduction

11.1 There are 6 million 'carers' in Britain (one in eight people, one in six house-holds) of which, 855,000 provide care for more than 50 hours a week. Half of all carers are in full or part-time work whereas only a quarter are retired. Carers are most commonly aged between 45 and 64; 58 per cent are women; 9 out of 10 care for a relative and half of all carers look after some-one aged over 75.[1] The task of providing care has subjected over half of all carers to a health-related problem (see para 7.141 above).

11.2 A key objective of the community care reforms was to ensure that 'service providers make practical support for carers a high priority'.[2] The white paper[3] emphasised the crucial role played by carers in the provision of community care:

> The reality is that most care is provided by family, friends and neighbours. The majority of carers take on these responsibilities willingly, but the Government recognises that many need help to be able to manage what can become a heavy burden. Their lives can be made much easier if the right support is there at the right time, and a key responsibility of statutory service providers should be to do all they can to assist and support carers. Helping carers to maintain their valuable contribution to the spectrum of care is both right and a sound investment. Help may take the form of providing advice and support as well as practical services such as day, domiciliary and respite care.[4]

11.3 Since 1986 three statutes have given greater recognition and rights to carers: (1) the Disabled Persons (Services, Consultation and Representation) Act 1986 (2) the Carers (Recognition and Services) Act 1995 and (3) the Carers and Disabled Children Act 2000. These Acts are referred to below as the DP(SCR)A 1986, the C(RS)A 1995 and the CDCA 2000 respectively. The common principle underlying these three provisions is an acknowledgement that the ability of carers to provide care is often dictated by the type of services received by the disabled person. If there is no shared care (respite care), no night-sitting service, no home-help, etc, then it is more likely that the carer will have difficulty managing, with the risk that he or she might withdraw from the caring role. For this reason the legislation requires social services authorities (when requested) to carry out a separate assessment of:

a) the carer's ability to provide and to continue to provide care (under the 1995 Act); and

b) the carer's need for services (under the 2000 Act).

---

1 Caring about Carers: A National Strategy for Carers; LASSL(99)2.
2 *Caring for People* (HMSO, 1989) Cm 849, quotation from para 1.11.
3 *Caring for People.*
4 *Caring for People*, para 2.3.

Carer – definition

11.4   There is no single definition of a 'carer' although its use in this text excludes persons who are under a contract of employment to provide the care. National Health Service and Community Care Act (NHSCCA) 1990 s46(3) defines a private carer (for the purposes of strategic planning – see para 2.12 above) as:

> . . . a person who is not employed to provide the care in question by any body in the exercise of its function under any enactment.

11.5   Such a definition includes non-resident carers and makes no stipulation as to the age of the carer or the quantity or quality of care provided. In general any reference to a 'carer' (unless the context shows otherwise) must therefore be to such a heterogeneous group; indeed the Policy Guidance makes clear that the term may encompass 'families, friends and neighbours'.[5] The common denominator for such carers is that they all provide some 'service', even though this might be, for instance, in the form of advocacy or emotional support, rather than a personal care service of the kind delivered by the social services authority. Even if a person does not come within an authority's definition of 'carer', he or she may be a 'significant other' whose views should properly be taken into account in the assessment and decision-making process.[6]

11.6   'Carer' has a more restricted meaning when used in the context of certain aspects of the assessment process and this is dealt with in greater detail below.

Carers who provide regular and substantial amounts of care

11.7   The meaning of the words 'regular and substantial' is considered at para 11.17 below. Carers who provide regular and substantial amounts of care have rights under both DP(SCR)A 1986 s8 and C(RS)A 1995 s1 to be involved in the assessment process. Although there is considerable overlap between the two statutory provisions, they differ in a number of respects. The principal differences are displayed in Table 6 opposite.

Carer assessments and the DP(SCR)A 1986

11.8   DP(SCR)A 1986 s8(1)[7] provides that where:

> (a) a disabled person is living at home and receiving a substantial amount of care on a regular basis from another person (who is not a person

---

5   Policy Guidance para 3.28: the same phrase as used in *Caring for People*, see note 1 above.

6   *Empowerment, Assessment, Care Management and the Skilled Worker* (see note 25 below).

7   This subsection of the Act came into force on 1 April 1987; subsections (2) and (3) are still not in force.

Table 6: Principal differences between the 1986 and 1995 Acts

DP(SCR)A 1986 s8	C(RS)A 1995 s1
Duty of assessor to consider the ability of the carer arises irrespective of a request.	Duty of assessor to consider the ability of the carer arises only if a request has been made by the carer.
Social services merely required to 'have regard' to the ability of the carer to provide care.	Social services required to carry out an actual 'assessment' of the ability of the carer to provide care.
The definition of 'carer' includes voluntary organisation volunteers and (possibly) voluntary organisation employees who provide the care.	Voluntary organisation employees and volunteers who provide the care are excluded from the definition of 'carer'.
Only applies where the carer is already providing a substantial amount of care on a regular basis.	Applies where a person 'intends' to provide the care (ie, to those not as yet providing such care).
Does not cover carers who care for a person receiving care services under the Mental Health Act 1983 or Health Services and Public Health Act 1968 (ie, the frail elderly).	Covers carers who care for persons receiving care services under Mental Health Act 1983 and the Health Services and Public Health Act 1968 (ie, the frail elderly).

---

employed to provide such care by any body in the exercise of its functions under any enactment), and

(b) it falls to a local authority to decide whether the disabled person's needs call for the provision by them of any services for him under any of the welfare enactments,

the local authority shall, in deciding that question, have regard to the ability of that person to continue to provide such care on a regular basis.

11.9 Although the 1986 Act gives less substantial rights to carers than the 1995 and 2000 Acts it nevertheless remains of importance in certain situations. Most obviously the obligation it imposes (to have regard to the ability of such carers) exists in all cases and does not have to be triggered by a request from the carer. Guidance on the 1986 Act is given in Circular LAC(87)6.

11.10 A number of the terms used in DP(SCR)A 1986 s8 are also to be found in the 1995 and 2000 Acts (such as 'regular' and 'substantial' and 'ability of carer') and these are considered below.

Carer assessments and the C(RS)A 1995

11.11   The 1995 Act originated as a private member's Bill[8] aimed at securing for carers recognition of their central importance as providers of community care services. This recognition is provided by requiring the social services authority (if so requested) to carry out a separate assessment of the carer at the same time as it assesses the person for whom the care is provided. The right of a carer to an 'assessment' under the 1995 Act is to be contrasted with the situation under the 1986 Act which merely requires the social services authority to 'have regard to' the carer's ability. The 1995 Act is however misnamed, in that there is only one service it provides for carers, namely an assessment.[9]

11.12   Section 1(1) of the Act is aimed at carers (of whatever age) who care for adults and C(RS)A 1995 s1(2) at carers (of whatever age)[10] who care for disabled children. Policy and practice guidance concerning the 1995 Act has been issued as circular LAC(96)7[11] (referred to in the rest of this section as the 1996 policy and the 1996 practice guidance).

11.13   Carers, in order to be eligible for an assessment under the 1995 Act, must cross four hurdles:

a)   the person for whom they care must be 'being' assessed;

b)   they must be providing (or intending to provide) a substantial amount of care on a regular basis;

c)   they must not be under a contract to provide the care or doing so as a voluntary organisation volunteer; and

d)   they must request the carer's assessment.

In conjunction with an assessment of the service user

11.14   Carers do not have a right to a 'free-standing' assessment (unless of course they are entitled to a community care assessment in their own right, by virtue of being an elderly, ill or disabled person). Carers only qualify for a carer's assessment when the person for whom they care 'is being' assessed. The carer's assessment must therefore coincide with the service user's assessment. The 1996 policy guidance (at para 8) confirms that this will also arise:

> . . . where a re-assessment of the service user is taking place, either as part of a review or because of a change in circumstances of either the user or carer arising for example, from a deterioration in the health of the user or a change in the carer's ability to continue to provide care.

---

8   Sponsored by Malcolm Wicks MP.

9   Local Authority Social Services Act 1970 Sch 1 was amended to include the assessment under C(RS)A 1995 s1 as a social services authority function.

10   It would include young carers, for example, if caring for disabled siblings, etc.

11   Virtually identical policy guidance was issued in Wales as WOC 16/96 and WHC(96)21.

11.15 Some concern was expressed about this provision; it being suggested that if a disabled person refuses a community care assessment, then this denies the carer the right to an assessment under the 1995 Act. This view is questionable for two reasons:

1) there is doubt whether a disabled person can (as a matter of law) refuse an assessment (as opposed to refusing to take part in the process) – see para 4.63 above;

2) although a carer might, in such cases, lack a statutory right to an assessment, there is nothing to prevent the local authority assessing the carer in any event.

11.16 In practice, however any such theoretical problems have been circumvented by the CDCA 2000 providing a free-standing right to a carers assessment (see para 11.33 below).

Providing (or intending to provide) a substantial amount of care on a regular basis

11.17 Although the 1996 guidance was singularly unhelpful in clarifying how this phrase should be interpreted[12] the question has now been addressed by the guidance accompanying the 2000 Act. The CDCA 2000 uses the same phrase and its practice guidance[13] states as follows:

> 67. It is not only the time spent each week caring that has an impact on carers. For some, such as those caring for adults with learning disabilities, the caring role can have the additional impact of being a life long commitment. For others, such as those caring for adults with severe mental health problems, caring can be a sporadic or cyclical responsibility. The carer may not be physically or practically caring at all at certain times, but still be anxious and stressed waiting for, or actively seeking to prevent, the next crisis. In addition, caring responsibilities may conflict with other family responsibilities, such as parenting or holding down a job. Any assessment of the carer's need for support has to look at the impact of the whole caring situation.

> 68. The term 'substantial and regular' is not defined in this guidance. In any given situation, the test that a practitioner should apply will relate to the impact of the caring role on the individual carer. In particular the practitioner will need to address the following questions.

> - Is the caring role sustainable?
> - How great is the risk of the caring role becoming unsustainable?

12 See LAC(96)7 para 11 simply advised that it is 'for local authorities to form their own judgement about what amounts to "regular" and "substantial"'.

13 Department of Health: Carers and Disabled Children Act 2000: Carers and people with parental responsibility for disabled children: practice guidance at paras 67–68 and at para 4.11–12 of the Welsh practice guidance – see para 11.31 below.

The English practice guidance to the 2000 Act suggests that in determining what is 'sustainable' the following four factors should be considered,[14] namely:

Autonomy: ie, the extent to which the carer has choice over the tasks they will perform and over the time to which they give to their caring role.

Health and Safety: ie, the risks to the carers own health of maintaining the caring role at its current level.

Managing daily routines: ie, the extent to which carers are able to look after their own domestic needs and other daily routines.

Involvement: ie, the extent to which carers have freedom to maintain relationships, employment, interests and other commitments.

11.18   The English practice guidance then requires the local authority to categorise these factors of risk into four bands, 'critical, substantial, medium and low'. A critical risk includes (para 70) – the development of major health problems; an extensive loss of autonomy; an inability to look after one's own domestic needs and other daily routines; a risk to employment or other responsibilities; a risk to significant social support systems or relationships.

'Intending to provide'

11.19   A carer may be entitled to a carer's assessment even if he or she is presently providing no care – provided the authority is satisfied that he or she is intending to provide a substantial amount of care on a regular basis for the user. This provision covers all such 'intending' carers, and is explained by LAC(96)7 (at para 16) thus:

> By including carers both providing or intending to provide care, the Act covers those carers who are about to take on substantial and regular caring tasks for someone who has just become, or is becoming, disabled through accident or physical or mental ill health. Local and health authorities will need to ensure that hospital discharge procedures take account of the provisions of the Act and that carers are involved once planning discharge starts.

11.20   The provision (although not restricted to such cases) is of particular relevance to potential users who are about to be discharged from hospital. The importance of good collaborative working practices between social services and the NHS is emphasised in the 1996 practice guidance which suggested at para 29 that local authorities should 'review with NHS commissioning agencies and NHS providers how they might best be involved in the carer's assessment', and then stating:

---

14   The following two paragraphs do not appear in the Welsh Guidance. Instead the Welsh guidance stated that the issue would be the subject of guidance in the Fair Access to Care. Although this did not occur (see para 4.77 above where the Welsh FAC guidance is considered) the Welsh FAC guidance in common with that issued in England did adopt the same four factors as sustainability criteria (see para 4.87).

30. Primary care staff, including GPs and community nurses through their contact with users and carers, are in a good position to notice signs of stress, difficulty or rapidly deteriorating health particularly in carers. The provisions of the Act will help primary care staff to meet the medical and nursing needs of their patients who are carers. When making a referral for a user's assessment they should be able to inform the carer that they may also have a right to request an assessment and will be well-placed to encourage patients whom they consider will benefit most to take up the opportunity. Social services departments should make sure that primary care staff have relevant information about social services criteria and know who to contact to make a referral. GPs nurses and other members of multi-disciplinary teams may be able to assist in an assessment of a carer's ability to provide and continue to provide care.

11.21 The English guidance on the hospital discharge process, *Discharge from hospital: pathway, process and practice*, contains substantial advice concerning the involvement of carers, and is considered at para 10.158 above.

Employed and voluntary organisation carers

11.22 The Act excludes from consideration (at C(RS)A 1995 s1(3)) persons who provide care by virtue of a contract of employment or as a volunteer for a voluntary organisation. This will not exclude carers who are in receipt of carers allowance[15] or similar social security benefits, but foster carers of disabled children or care assistants working in their capacity as part of a home care service (whether private or public) will be excluded. Anyone who is paid by the user (eg, using their own money, direct payments from the authority or independent living funds) will also be excluded.

The carer must request the assessment

11.23 The English and Welsh policy guidance under the 1995 and the English policy guidance under the 2000 Act require social workers 'to inform any carer who appears to be eligible under [each] Act of their right to request an assessment' (LAC(96)7 at para 20).[16] The English policy guidance under the 2000 Act additionally requires (at para 9) that 'to ensure that the carer has been made aware of this right the assessor should give the carer a copy of the Department of Health's leaflet *How to get help in looking after someone – A carers guide to a carers assessment*. While this obligation is omitted from the Welsh policy guidance, the 'Welsh Guide to Assessments'[17] requires potential carers 'to be notified of their right to an assessment and to be handed a leaflet *A carers guide to a carers assessment*.

---

15 A taxable, non-contributory benefit for people aged 16 or over caring for more than 35 hours a week for someone who is getting Attendance Allowance or the middle/higher rate care component of Disability Living Allowance.

16 WOC 16/96 and WHC (96)21 in Wales. See also *R (AB and SB) v Nottingham CC* (2001) 4 CCLR 295 at 307G where it was held that no duty to assess under the C(RS)A 1995 arose until a formal request had been made.

17 At paras 4.12 and 4.13 – see para 11.32 below.

11.24   Young carers are in particular unlikely to know of their right to seek a carer's assessment, or to request one when told of their right. Accordingly the 1996 practice guidance states (at para 15.5) that even where no assessment is requested, 'the care manager should still consider whether there is a need to assist or relieve the child either through the provision of community care services for the user or through the provision of services to promote the welfare of the child'.

The carer's assessment under the C(RS)A 1995

11.25   A carer's assessment differs markedly from a user's assessment. Under NHSCCA 1990 s47(1) the object of a user's assessment is to identify that person's need for community care services. The object of a C(RS)A 1995 carer's assessment is to identify his or her 'ability to provide and to continue to provide care' (section 1(1) and (2)). The process by which such an assessment provides benefits to the carer can best be illustrated by the following example:

C(RS)A 1995 assessment example

A carer in her sixties, still in full time work, provides all the morning and evening care for her disabled husband, whose care needs are substantial. While she is at work, a care package involving a call by the district nurse, meals-on-wheels and a short visit by the home care service occurs. On the annual review of the care plan, the user assessment discloses that his condition has deteriorated slightly, but that the present care package meets his needs adequately. During her carer's assessment she discloses that her GP has recently told her that she has suffered a slight stroke and in the GP's opinion if she continues with the stressful routine of caring and working, then there is a risk of a significantly more serious stroke (in which case there will be two service users in the household). Having regard to the user's assessment, his need for services remains; having regard to the carer's assessment, her ability to continue to provide care is in jeopardy, such that some extra local authority services may be required to ensure that she can otherwise continue to provide care. Essentially her assessment informs and amends the user's care package.

The extra services are community care services delivered to the disabled husband.

11.26   C(RS)A 1995 s1(4) enables the secretary of state to issue directions as to the manner in which a carer's assessment is to be carried out.[18] To date no such direction has been issued. The 1996 policy guidance gives limited and general advice on the form such assessments should take (at paras 21–25), whereas slightly more detail is provided in the practice guidance,[19] including:

> 9.1 The assessment is not a test for the carer. It should not be prescriptive but recognise the carer's knowledge and expertise. The assessment should

---

18 Mirroring NHSCCA 1990 s47(4)C.

19 For adult carers at paras 9–11 and for young carers at para 16.

listen to what they are saying and offer an opportunity for private[20] discussion in which carers can candidly express their views . . .

9.3 Carers often give most of the assistance needed by the person for whom they care, and may only want a fairly small amount of help to enable them to continue caring. A Personal Social Services Research Unit (PSSRU) study[21] found that some of the most cost effective care packages were where carers continued to perform caring tasks but were given sufficient support and respite to enhance their well being and maintain their own health. Equally it is important that care managers do not make assumptions about carers' willingness to undertake the range of caring tasks, particularly those related to intimate personal care. This is highlighted in a discussion of spouse carers[22] which emphasises the difficulties faced by some husbands or wives when their ability to cope with changed behaviour or personality and/or tasks involving physical intimacy is taken for granted . . .

9.8 In assessing the carer's ability to care or continue to care, care managers should not assume a willingness by the carer to continue caring, or continue to provide the same level of support. They will wish to bear in mind the distinction between caring *about* someone and caring *for* them. Many carers continue to care deeply *about* a person even though their ability to care for them may change.

Carers whose care is not regular and/or substantial

11.27 The statutory rights in the DP(SCR)A 1986 and C(RS)A 1995 only apply to carers who (among other things) provide a substantial amount of care on a regular basis. The 1990 policy guidance[23] sets out the way social services authorities should deal with all carers, ie, regardless of whether the care they provide is either regular or substantial. Paragraph 3.25 emphasises that assessments and care plans must take account of 'user's and the carer's own preferences', and (at para 3.16) that they 'must feel that the process is aimed at meeting their wishes'.[24] It continues:

Role of carers in the assessment
3.27 Service users and carers should be informed of the result of the assessment and of any services to be provided. In the case of carers, due regard should be had to confidentiality, particularly where the carer is not a close relative. Where care needs are relatively straightforward the most appropriate way of conveying decisions can best be determined taking individual circumstances into account. A written statement will normally be needed if a continuing service is to be provided. Written statements should always be supplied on request.

20 Authorities will need to ensure that the carer is aware that his or her comments may be placed on the user's file and accordingly advised of the right to withhold consent to them being copied to the user.
21 D Challis, et al, *Care Management and Health Care of Older People* (Canterbury, 1995).
22 K Atkin, 'Similarities and Differences Between Informal Carers', in *Carers: Research and Practice* (HMSO, 1992).
23 *Community Care in the Next Decade and Beyond* (HMSO, 1990).
24 And any failure to take into account user and carer preferences will normally render invalid any assessment, *R v North Yorkshire CC ex p Hargreaves* (1997) 1 CCLR 104.

3.28 Most support for vulnerable people is provided by families, friends and neighbours. The assessment will need to take account of the support that is available from such carers. They should feel that the overall provision of care is a shared responsibility between them and the statutory authorities and that the relationship between them is one of mutual support. The preferences of carers should be taken into account and their willingness to continue caring should not be assumed. Both service users and carers should therefore be consulted – separately, if either of them wishes – since their views may not coincide. The care plan should be the result of a constructive dialogue between service user, carer, social services staff and those of any other agency involved.

Carers' own needs
3.29   Carers who feel they need community care services in their own right can ask for a separate assessment. This could arise if the care plan of the person for whom they care does not, in their view, adequately address the carer's own needs.

11.28   This advice is reiterated in the 1993 Department of Health guidance – that the views and interests of carers who do not come within this category (ie, who do not provide substantial or regular care) should be taken into account when an assessment is undertaken.[25]

The Carers and Disabled Children Act 2000

11.29   In 1999 the Department of Health published *Caring about Carers: A national strategy for carers* in which it acknowledged that the then legislation prevented carers receiving help in their own right. It undertook 'when Parliamentary time allowed' to rectify this situation, and to ensure that:

> Individual carers . . . have greater flexibility and choice . . . [via] . . . direct payments or credit scheme arrangements to enable them – with the consent of the person needing care – to arrange for services to be given to them in a way that was useful and at a time and a form that was appropriate.[26]

11.30   These undertakings were discharged with the enactment of the Carers and Disabled Children Act (CDCA) 2000. The 2000 Act, as its name suggests, is directed at two particular client groups, namely carers and disabled children. In relation to the 'carers' part of the Act, the following chart identifies the material differences/similarities between it and the 1995 Act: the

---

25 *Empowerment, Assessment, Care Management and the Skilled Worker* (HMSO, 1993) uses the term 'significant others' as a separate category from 'carer'; although neither term is defined, the report accepts the importance of involving 'members of the user's networks to negotiate and sustain arrangements which integrate resources from the statutory and independent sectors with the help given through family and/or neighbourhood networks'.

26 *Caring about Carers: A national strategy for carers*. London, Department of Health, 1999. LASSL(99)2, chapter 6 para 12–14.

Table 7: A comparison of 'carer's' provisions of the 1995 and 2000 Acts

The 1995 Act	The 2000 Act
Carer's right depends upon the service user 'being assessed'	Carer has free standing right to an assessment
Rights available to: Carer – any age Service user – any age	Rights available to: Carer – 16 or over Service user – 18 or over
Carer must be providing or intending to provide substantial and regular care	
Carer must request assessment	
Assessment considers the carer's ability to provide and continue to provide care	Assessment considers the carer's need for services

---

principal difference is that the 2000 Act makes allowance for services to be provided directly to the carer.[27]

11.31 In March 2001 guidance concerning the implementation of the Act was issued in England (accessible at: www.carers.gov.uk/carersdisabledchildact2000.htm) as follows:

- Carers and Disabled Children Act 2000: Carers and people with parental responsibility for disabled children: Policy Guidance (referred to below as the 2001 policy guidance)
- Carers and Disabled Children Act 2000: Carers and people with parental responsibility for disabled children: Practice Guidance (referred to below as the 2001 practice guidance).
- Practitioner's Guide to Carers' Assessments under the Carers and Disabled Children Act 2000 (referred to below as the 2001 assessment guidance).
- Carers and Disabled Children Act 2000: Direct payments for young people: Policy Guidance and Practice Guidance.
- Carers and Disabled Children Act 2000: Practice Guidance on the provisions of the Act as they affect Disabled 16 and 17 year old young people.

---

27 Prior to the CDCA 2000 a common misconception existed – namely that that local authorities were not empowered to provide services directly to carers. Such services could have (and still could be) provided (for instance) under Local Government Act 1972 s111 and under NHSA 1977 Sch 8 para 2(1) (see LAC(96)7 para 5(a) where the Department of Health assert this opinion) additionally the CA 1989 s17(3) makes specific provision for services to the parents of disabled children. It has also been suggested that NHS Act 1977 Sch 8 para 3, NAA 1948 s29 are also capable of being construed so as to enable services to be provided to carers (see the second edition of this text, para 7.35).

11.32   In September 2001 equivalent guidance was issued in Wales, namely:[28]

- 'Guidance 2000 Act'.
- Practitioners Guide to Carers' Assessment.

Carer's assessment under the CDCA 2000

11.33   CDCA 2000 s1 entitles carers aged 16 or over who provide or intend to provide a substantial amount of care on a regular basis for another person aged 18 or over, to an assessment even where the person cared for has refused an assessment by the local authority social services department or has refused the delivery of community care services following assessment.

11.34   The assessment under the 2000 Act is focussed on the question of carers' services and accordingly is materially different from that under the C(RS)A 1995. As with the 1995 Act, employed and volunteer carers provided by voluntary organisations are not covered by the CDCA 2000 (see para 11.22 above). As noted in para 11.23 above, social workers, must not only advise potential carers of their rights – they must also hand them a specific leaflet setting out the benefits of being assessed. Although technically it may be necessary for a carer to make two requests, one for an assessment under the C(RS)A 1995 and one for an assessment under the CDCA 2000, good practice would no doubt dictate that a request for an assessment under one Act would be deemed a request to be assessed under both.

Referral protocols

11.35   The 2001 policy guidance (paras 11–13)[28a] attempts to deal with the problem of how a local authority can determine whether the carer is providing regular and substantial care if the disabled person refuses to co-operate or agree to an assessment, advising that 'referral protocols' be developed. Paragraph 21 of the practice guidance explains that:

> Such a form would record that in the opinion of a professional, GP, voluntary sector worker, carers' group representative, etc, that the carer being referred was a substantial and regular carer within the terms of the Act and local eligibility criteria.

Paragraph 21 additionally contains a simple pro forma example.

Boundary problems

11.36   The 2001 practice guidance (at paras 24–27)[29] gives guidance on boundary problems; where the carer lives some distance away from the user. It advises that in general it will be the disabled person's home authority (not the carer's) which will be responsible for the assessment and the provision of any services under the 2000 Act.

---

28 Accessible at www.wales.gov.uk/subicarersnew/content/infoforprofs.htm.

28a The Welsh guidance only makes brief reference to this issue, at para 3.3.3.

29 Para 4.3 of the Welsh guidance.

The assessment

11.37 The 2001 practice guidance stresses that assessments should focus on 'simple pragmatic responses to carers' presenting needs' and that they are not a 'process for its own sake' (para 47). Many local authorities provide carers who have asked to be assessed, with 'pro forma' documents to complete. In relation to these the 2001 practice guidance states (para 61) 'self-assessment forms can help [social services] prepare for assessment [but] best practice suggests that they cannot replace face-to-face assessment'. On this question the 2001 assessment guidance at para 29[30] advises that assessments should 'not be a bureaucratic process based on ticking boxes' they should 'focus on outcomes the carer would want to see help them in their caring roles and maintain their health and well-being'.

11.38 In order that the carer has an opportunity to opt for a confidential meeting with the assessor, he or she is advised to make arrangements for the assessment 'over the phone, and away from the home or while the cared for person is out' (2001 practice guidance, para 59) and to advise the carer of the right to have a friend or advocate present (para 60).[31]

Services for carers

11.39 CDCA 2000 s2 enables local authorities to provide services to carers following a carer's assessment under section 1. Services to carers are not defined in the Act. The local authority may provide any services they see fit to provide and which in their view help the carer care for the person cared for (CDCA 2000 s2(2)). These services may take the form of physical help, for example assistance around the house, or other forms of support such as the provision of equipment, training or counselling for the carer. Section 2(3) seeks to address the problem of a disabled person refusing to accept services which might be of benefit to their carer (and this provision is dealt with separately below under the subheading 'fictional carers services').

Respite care

11.40 Respite care (frequently referred to as 'shared care') is not a service referred to as such by any statute. It is a generic term for temporary care; care which temporarily relieves a carer from his or her caring role. Respite care is a service highly valued by carers although it is not as a matter of law, a 'carer's service' within the meaning of the 2000 Act: this being explained by the Department of Health in a 'question and answer' statement issued shortly after the 2000 Act received Royal Assent:

> *Q7. Are short-term breaks (respite care) a service for carers or cared for people?* People who care may be assessed as needing a break from their caring role. This need will be clearly recorded on their own assessment documentation.

---

30 These references are also contained in section 3.6 of the Welsh Guidance.
31 These references are also contained in section 3.11 of the Welsh Guidance.

The person they care for will then be assessed for the additional support that they will need to allow their usual carer to take a break. This need will be recorded on their assessment documentation. The additional service remains a community care service delivered to the cared for person, not a carer service under this Act.

11.41   Respite care can take place in the service user's home – while the carer goes elsewhere. In such situations, the care is practical assistance in the home, or home help (ie, a service under Chronically Sick and Disabled Persons Act (CSDPA) 1970 s2(1)(a) (see para 8.70) or National Health Service Act (NHSA) 1977 Sch 8 para 3 (see para 8.148) or Health Services and Public Health Act (HSPHA) 1968 s45 (see para 14.26). If the respite care consists of the service user leaving his or her home for a short period (and staying temporarily in a care home) then it will generally be a service under National Assistance Act (NAA) 1948 s21 (see para 7.6).

The range of potential services under CDCA 2000 s2

11.42   In relation to the range of services available under the 2000 Act, the practice guidance (para 80)[32] states as follows:

> The Act provides new opportunities for authorities to be flexible and innovative in the way services are provided to people within caring relationships. As a guiding principle, authorities should be prepared to provide the most appropriate and cost-effective support to meet assessed needs. Much of the support that carers need may already be provided through the delivery of community care services. Focusing on the outcomes the carer and user want will help to ensure best value solutions. Anecdotally, carers sometimes say that they have approached councils to be told that they can have help with personal care (which they do not want) but not cleaning (which they do). In this context, local authorities that have decided not to provide or commission certain services as community care services – such as shopping only, cleaning only, or other low-level services – should review their positions'. Such services, if targeted purposively, can be of genuine assistance in sustaining the caring relationship, and be cost effective.

11.43   The 2001 practice guidance (para 38)[33] stresses the importance of local authorities 'focusing on outcomes' when they construct their eligibility criteria for services. Criteria based solely upon 'risk' could award services regardless of whether they were likely to make a real difference. By focusing on outcomes, criteria should ensure 'best value solutions' (para 80) and enable more suitable services to be delivered 'ie, laundry, gardening, taxi fares, etc' (para 38). The range of services and equipment capable of being provided to the carer under CDCA 2000 s2 is very wide and may include (for instance) the provision of: help with housework; relaxation therapy/ counselling; mobile phones; trips/holidays/special events; driving lessons; travel assistance; training and so on.

---

32   The Welsh guidance contains no equivalent statement.

33   In Wales this appears only in the 'Practitioners Guide to Carers' Assessments, para 3.2.

11.44 Local authorities in England and Wales receive an annual grant, known as the Carers Special Grant to 'stimulate diversity and flexibility of services provision that enable carers to take a break from caring, and to help provide carers' services'.[34] The grant in England is subject to greater control than in Wales, but in general the grant is to be spent primarily on providing services that enable the carer to take a break (ie, respite care services) but additionally the grant may be used to fund carer specific services under the 2000 Act.[35]

11.45 CDCA 2000 s8 empowers local authorities to charge for services provided under the Act, although few at present do so.

11.46 In certain situations it may be unclear whether a service provided by a local authority is done so under the CDCA 2000 to the carer or under the community care legislation to the disabled person. Most obviously this would arise where a home help service had been provided pursuant to Carers Act and community care assessment in respect of a carer and a disabled person living in the same household. The question arises as to whether this is a service to the carer under the 2000 Act or a service to the disabled person under the community care legislation. This is a real issue, since the recipient is liable to be charged for the service and only he or she is able to complain if it is defective. CDCA 2000 s4 requires authorities in such cases to ensure that the relevant care plans stipulate for whom such a service is provided. Section 4(5) states that in making this decision the authority should disregard the financial means of the carer or of the person cared (otherwise – presumably – it might be tempted to determine that the service was delivered to the party from whom it could extract the highest charge).

Carers and employment

11.47 The 2001 practice guidance contains an important section (para 35–37)[36] which stresses the need to for 'carers of adults' to be supported so that they can stay in work or be helped to return to work. It also notes that:

> ... people with parental responsibility for disabled children will also benefit from joining or re-joining the workforce ... many parents of disabled children would like to return to work and, if they were able to do so, would benefit socially and emotionally, as well as financially.[37]

11.48 In order to take this obligation forward, local authorities are advised (para 37) to investigate various matters, including how they treat their own staff

34 *Caring about Carers: A national strategy for carers.* Department of Health, 1999. The grant for England for the period 2004/05 amounted to £125 million

35 For details of the grant conditions see www.carers.gov.uk/2004_05carers_grant_guidance.PDF and in Wales www.wales.gov.uk/subicarersnew/content/infoforprofs.htm.

36 This section does not appear in the Welsh guidance.

37 The draft guidance – circulated for consultation – contained a proviso – to the effect that this would only be the case 'provided it promoted and safeguarded the interests of the child'. After strong objection from a number of carers' and disabled children's support organisations this phrase was dropped from the final version of the guidance.

who are carers – and how the experiences of these staff members can be harnessed to improve employment practices.

Fictional carer's services (under CDCA 2000 s2)

11.49 As noted above, the 2000 Act seeks to address the problem of disabled persons refusing to accept services which might be of benefit to their carer. Section 2(3) provides that a service, although provided to the carer –

    (a) may take the form of a service delivered to the person cared for if it is one which, if provided to him instead of to the carer, could fall within community care services and they both agree it is to be so delivered; but

    (b) if a service is delivered to the person cared for it may not, except in prescribed circumstances, include anything of an intimate nature.

11.50 Accordingly certain care services, that would otherwise be construed as community care services, may be deemed to be services under the CDCA 2000. Such services can only be delivered to the carer, if:

- they could be a community care service;
- both the disabled person and the carer agree to them being provided to the carer; and
- the services are not of an intimate nature (except in prescribed circumstances).

11.51 In respect of these services the 2001 policy guidance (para 25)[38] states:

> Cared for people may not be forced to accept services they do not wish to receive. However, in some circumstances they may accept a level of contact with social services that helps the person who cares for them. A cared for person who has refused an assessment may agree to the delivery of a non-intimate sitting service provided as a carer's service to give their usual carer a short break.

11.52 Regulation 2(1) of the Carers (Services) and Direct Payments (Amendment) (England) Regulations 2001[39] concerns the meaning of 'intimate care'. It stipulates that a service is deemed to be of an 'intimate' nature if it involves physical contact such as lifting, washing, grooming, feeding, dressing, bathing or toileting the person cared for'. Such service cannot be provided to the cared for person under CDCA 2000 s2(3) (ie, where the cared for person is refusing the service him or herself and so it is 'fictionally' being provided to the carer) except in 'prescribed circumstances'. Regulation 2(2)[40] explains that 'prescribed circumstances' arise where (essentially):

    (a) the person cared agrees to the intimate care; or

    (b) in an emergency (which is likely to cause the cared for person serious personal harm) either –

        (i) the cared for person is unable to consent; or

---

38 This section does not appear in the Welsh guidance.

39 SI No 441 and in Wales, the Carers (Services) and Direct Payments (Amendment) (Wales) Regulations 2001 SI No 2186 (W 150).

40 See also 2001 policy guidance para 28 (para 2.3 of the Welsh Guidance).

(ii) he or she does not consent but the intimate care is necessary to alleviate the imminent risk of serious personal harm.

Vouchers

11.53 Section 3 of the 2000 Act empowers local authorities to provide vouchers which can be used to obtain respite/short-term break services. It is the government's view that voucher schemes 'offer flexibility in the timing of carers' breaks and choice in the way services are delivered to persons cared for while their usual carer is taking a break'.[41]

11.54 Regulations[42] made under CDCA 2000 s3 have come into effect in England; the essential details of these being:

1) All voucher schemes must now be in accordance with these regulations.

2) Vouchers may be expressed in terms of money; or a period of time but a 'time voucher' must specify the service for which the voucher may be redeemed; and may specify the supplier of services authorised by the local authority to supply that service.

3) Community care time vouchers may be issued:
   - to a person cared for, or
   - a carer, provided the person cared for either consents to this or is unable to consent through lack of capacity.[43]

4) Children Act 1989 vouchers, may be issued to a parent-carer.

5) Money vouchers may only be issued in the case of a community care voucher to a person cared for, or in the case of Children Act 1989 vouchers to a parent-carer.

6) Vouchers must not be issued to persons who are proscribed under the Direct Payment regulations (see para 9.17 above).

7) All vouchers must be redeemed within the financial year during which they are is issued; a voucher is redeemed on the day on which the service that is secured against the value of the voucher is delivered.

8) A voucher may only be redeemable for services supplied by – (a) the local authority that issued the voucher (the 'issuing authority'); or (b) a relevant supplier of services.

9) Where the voucher holder indicates he or she wants to use a supplier with whom the local authority does not have a contract the authority must enter into a contract with this supplier provided the preferred supplier agrees and complies with the authorities usual terms and conditions.

---

41 2001 policy guidance at para 42.

42 The Carers and Disabled Children (Vouchers) (England) Regulations 2003 SI No 1216.

43 It appears to follow that where a 'cared for person' lacks mental capacity, the carer can use the voucher to purchase respite care which includes 'intimate personal care' – even though this would not be permissible under the 'fictitious carer services' arrangements under section 2 (see para 11.52 above).

10) If the service user ceases to be ordinarily resident in the issuing authority's area without the full value of any vouchers held in relation to him being redeemed, any vouchers which remain unredeemed on the day on which that person ceases to be so ordinarily resident must be returned to the issuing authority.

11) Where a voucher holder wishes the supplier to provide additional or more expensive services, this may occur if a third party agrees to pay to the supplier the difference between the cost which will be met by the voucher and the actual cost of the service supplied ('third party' means someone other than the service user, the parent-carer, or the issuing authority).

12) A voucher must not be used to secure residential accommodation –
    a) for a period in excess of 28 consecutive days; and
    b) in any period of 12 months for periods which exceed 120 days in total.

Direct payments for CDCA 2000 services

11.55   CDCA 2000 s5 provided for any carer's services under CDCA 2000 s2 to be delivered by way of direct payments. This was achieved by amending the Community Care (Direct Payments) Act 1996 s1 to include services under the CDCA 2000 s2. In England, however, such direct payments are now governed by Health and Social Care Act (HSCA) 2001 s57[44] (see para 9.5 above). Where therefore a social services authority has decided that a service should be delivered to a carer under the 2000 Act, then it is obliged (in England)[45] to offer the carer cash payments as an alternative to arranging social care services to meet their assessed support needs. This option exists for all carers aged 16 or over who care for a person aged 18 or over. In relation to young carers aged 16–18 the 2001 policy guidance at para 38 advises:

> . . . it is unlikely that there will be many situations where such an arrangement would be the best option for a young carer aged 16 or 17 receiving services under the provisions of the Act. The facility is available to allow for flexibility in the small number of circumstances where a 16 or 17 year old is choosing to undertake a substantial caring role for a period and that decision is supported by the local council. It could in some circumstances be more helpful to the young carer to receive a direct payment, for example, to allow them to arrange for carer services to be delivered in such a way as to minimise any disruption to their education that would result from their decision to care.[46]

Services for disabled children and their carers under the CDCA 2000

11.56   The 2000 Act entitles the parents of disabled children to an assessment of their needs and for them (and disabled children aged 16 or over) to receive

---

44   CDCA 2000 s5 being repealed in England by HSCA 2001 Sch 6 (3) Para 1.
45   But only empowered in Wales – see para 9.35 above)
46   See also para 11.59 below.

services by way of direct payments and vouchers. These provisions are considered separately at para 18.25 below.

Time off work to care for dependants

11.57 Employment Relations Act 1999 s8 and Sch 4, Part II inserted a new section 57A into the Employment Rights Act 1996, subsection (1) of which provides:

> An employee is entitled to be permitted by his employer to take a reasonable amount of time off during the employee's working hours in order to take action which is necessary –
> (a) to provide assistance on an occasion when a dependant falls ill, gives birth or is injured or assaulted,
> (b) to make arrangements for the provision of care for a dependant who is ill or injured,
> (c) in consequence of the death of a dependant,
> (d) because of the unexpected disruption or termination of arrangements for the care of a dependant, or
> (e) to deal with an incident which involves a child of the employee and which occurs unexpectedly in a period during which an educational establishment which the child attends is responsible for him.

11.58 'Dependant' is defined widely in relation to persons who live in the same household (Employment Rights Act 1996 s57A (3)) and there is a general obligation upon carers who take such time off work, to tell the employer the reason for the absence as soon as practicable and how long the absence is likely to last (section 57A (2)). It will be noted that the event which requires the carer to take time off need not be 'unexpected' in relation to the situations detailed in subsections (a)–(c) above. Any time off work claimed as a result of this statutory provision is to be taken as unpaid leave.

Young carers

11.59 The Carers (Recognition and Services) Act (C(RS)A) 1995 applies to all carers irrespective of their age, whereas the rights provided by the CDCA 2000, only apply to carers aged 16 or over (caring for a person aged 18 or over). Carers who are under the age of 18 are generally referred to as 'young carers'.

11.60 There is no legislation which specifically refers to young carers. Guidance concerning young carers has, however, been issued by the Social Services Inspectorate (SSI) in 1995.[47] The guidance adopts a definition of a 'young carer' as 'a child or young person who is carrying out significant caring tasks and assuming a level of responsibility for another person, which would usually be taken by an adult'. Such duties as are owed to young carers by a social services authority are primarily contained in the Children Act 1989 and in the guidance issued by the Department of Health.[48]

47 Guidance letter 28 April 1995; CI(95)12.
48 Two volumes of guidance have been issued under the Children Act 1989 of relevance to young carers – Volume 2: *Family Support* and Volume 6: *Children with Disabilities* (both HMSO 1991).

Child in need – definition

11.61   Children Act (CA) 1989 s17(10) provides that a child is 'in need' if:

(a) he is unlikely to achieve or maintain, or to have the opportunity of achieving or maintaining, a reasonable standard of health or development without the provision for him of services by a local authority . . .; or

(b) his health or development is likely to be significantly impaired, or further impaired, without the provision for him of such services; or

(c) he is disabled.

11.62   In relation to young carers, since they are not usually 'disabled children', it is necessary to establish that the child comes within category (a) or (b). The policy guidance under the 1995 Act (at para 14) referred to, and adopted, advice given in the 1995 SSI guidance[49] which stated that:

> . . . many young people carry out a level of caring responsibilities which prevents them from enjoying normal social opportunities and from achieving full school attendance. Many young carers with significant caring responsibilities should therefore be seen as children in need.[50]

11.63   The key issue therefore is whether the young carer's caring responsibilities are 'significant'. In this respect the 1996 practice guidance stresses (at para 15.2) that young carers should not be expected to carry out 'inappropriate' levels of caring (that is, inappropriate to their age, sex, culture, etc).

11.64   A local authority can of course provide services for a sibling carer even if that child is not considered to be a 'child in need'. CA 1989 s17(3) specifically provides that social services may provide services to (among others) such a child 'if it is provided with a view to safeguarding and promoting the welfare' of the disabled child.

11.65   The 2000 policy guidance that regulates the process for assessments under the CA 1989 (*The Framework for the Assessment of Children in Need and their Families*), makes the following observations concerning the assessment of young carers:[51]

> **Assessing the Needs of Young Carers**
>
> 3.61 A group of children whose needs are increasingly more clearly recognised are young carers for example those who assume important caring responsibilities for parents and siblings. Some children care for parents who are disabled, physically or mentally ill, others for parents dependent on alcohol or involved in drug misuse. For further information and guidance refer to the *Carers (Recognition and Services) Act 1995: Policy Guidance and Practice Guide* (Department of Health, 1996a) and *Young Carers: Making a Start* (Department of Health, 1998).
>
> 3.62 An assessment of family circumstances is essential. Young carers

---

49 Guidance letter CI(95)12, Annex A para 1.1.

50 See also para 2.4 of Volume 2 Guidance which emphasises that 'the definition of 'need' in the Act is deliberately wide to reinforce the emphasis on preventive support and services to families'.

51 Department of Health, *Framework for the Assessment of Children in Need and their Families* (policy guidance), The Stationery Office, 2000.

should not be expected to carry inappropriate levels of caring which have an adverse impact on their development and life chances. It should not be assumed that children should take on similar levels of caring responsibilities as adults. Services should be provided to parents to enhance their ability to fulfil their parenting responsibilities. There may be differences of view between children and parents about appropriate levels of care. Such differences may be out in the open or concealed. The resolution of such tensions will require good quality joint work between adult and children's social services as well as co-operation from schools and health care workers. This work should include direct work with the young carer to understand his or her perspective and opinions. The young person who is a primary carer of his or her parent or sibling may have a good understanding of the family's functioning and needs which should be incorporated into the assessment.

3.63 Young carers can receive help from both local and health authorities. Where a child is providing a substantial amount of care on a regular basis for a parent, the child will be entitled to an assessment of their ability to care under section 1(1) of the *Carers (Recognition and Services) Act 1995* and the local authority must take that assessment into account in deciding what community care services to provide for the parent. Many young carers are not aware that they can ask for such an assessment. In addition, consideration must be given as to whether a young carer is a child in need under the Children Act 1989. The central issue is whether a child's welfare or development might suffer if support is not provided to the child or family. As part of the *National Strategy for Carers* (1999), local authorities should take steps to identify children with additional family burdens. Services should be provided to promote the health and development of young carers while not undermining the parent.

11.66 Children Act 1989 s17(1) places a general duty on social services authorities to safeguard and promote the welfare of children within their area who are 'in need', and empowers authorities to provide almost unlimited services towards this goal. Accordingly although the carers legislation provides assessment (and limited service provision) rights for young carers, it will generally be appropriate that their primary assessment be under the CA 1989 process.

11.67 The CA 1989 assessment procedures and service provision arrangements for young carers are the same as for any other child in need (and are considered at para 18.9 below). A fear often expressed by young carers and their disabled parents is that of child protection proceedings being initiated by social services were they to appreciate the extent of the child's caring responsibilities.[52] However CA 1989 s17(1)(b) emphasises that a principal purpose for the provision of services is to promote the upbringing of such children by their families.

---

52 See, for instance, *Community Care* No 1020 p14, 'Lost Childhood'; 'There is a conspiracy of silence around young carers. This silence is often the result of fear, fear of separation from their families either by the institutionalisation of the care recipient or by the instigation of care proceedings'. Volume 2 Guidance para 2.15 states: 'The Act gives a positive emphasis to identifying and providing for the children's needs rather than focusing on parental shortcomings in a negative manner'.

11.68   The English 2001 policy guidance[53] for the CDCA 2000 states that:

para 20 – 'in most circumstances the local council should ensure that the person cared for is receiving sufficient services so that a young person aged 16 or 17 is not undertaking a regular and substantial load of caring responsibilities'.

---

53   Para 2.5.1 of the Welsh guidance.

Charges for community care services

continued

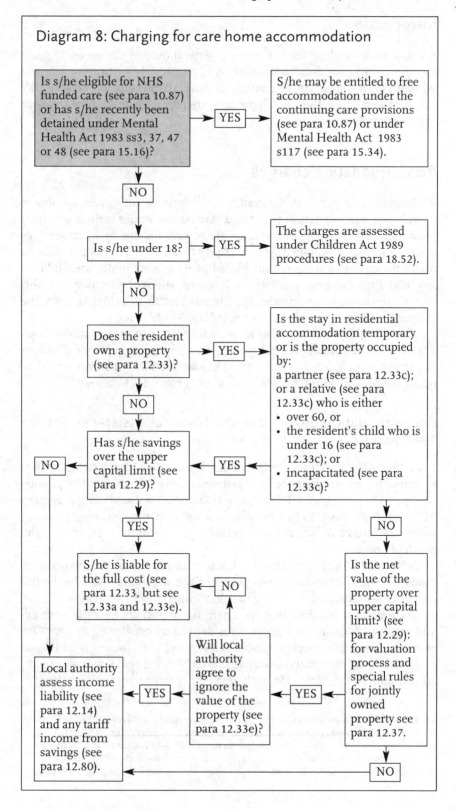

Diagram 8: Charging for care home accommodation

Introduction

12.1   Social services authorities are under a general duty to charge individuals for whom they provide accommodation in registered care homes. There is no equivalent obligation to charge for non-accommodation community care services. Since the two charging systems are distinct they are dealt with separately below.

Accommodation charges

12.2   As Diagram 8 on page 339 illustrates, social services authorities are able to provide accommodation in registered care homes under various statutory provisions. The majority of residents are accommodated by social services under National Assistance Act (NAA) 1948 Part III although residents under the age of 18 are generally placed using powers under the Children Act (CA) 1989. In certain situations, however, where the resident was formerly a detained patient under the Mental Health Act (MHA) 1983, the accommodation is provided under MHA 1983 s117.

12.3   The charging rules relating to accommodation provided under NAA 1948 Part III are considered below. The charging rules under the Children Act 1989 are considered at paras 18.52 below, and those relating to accommodation provided under MHA 1983 s117 at paras 15.34 below.

Accommodation provided under National Assistance Act 1948 Part III

12.4   NAA 1948 s22(1) places a general obligation on social services authorities to charge for accommodation in registered care homes which they provide under NAA 1948 Part III (except temporary accommodation).[1] Section 22(1) refers to NAA 1948 s26, which deals with the charging situation where the authority has provided residential accommodation in an independent home.

12.5   NAA 1848 s22(2) stipulates that the maximum charge for such accommodation shall be fixed by the local authority but that this must be the full cost to the authority of providing that accommodation.

12.6   Section 22(3) requires that the charging provisions be means-tested, and section 22(4) directs that every resident must be allowed to retain (or receive) a minimum weekly personal allowance. The amount is laid down each year by the National Assistance (Sums For Personal Expenses) Regulations and is the same for each resident whether in a social services

---

1   Local authorities are not obliged to charge for temporary periods of accommodation of less that eight weeks, NAA 1948 s22(5A), see para 12.33 below. As a result of Community Care (Delayed Discharge, etc) Act (CC(DD)A) 2003 ss15 and 16 and the Community Care (Delayed Discharges, etc) Act (Qualifying Services)(England) Regulations 2003 SI No 1196 intermediate care services are to be provided free of charge.

authority-run home or an independent sector home (see para 12.16 for details of the allowance).

12.7   Most importantly, however, NAA 1948 s22(5) stipulates that the way the means-tested charging system operates is to be specified in separate regulations made by the secretary of state. The principal regulations in this respect are the National Assistance (Assessment of Resources) Regulations 1992,[2] although they are the subject of regular amendments. Detailed guidance has been issued by the Department of Health on the interpretation of the Assessment of Resources Regulations (subsequently referred to in this section as 'the Regulations'). The guidance, known as CRAG (Charging for Residential Accommodation Guide) is issued separately by the Department of Health and the Welsh Assembly.[3]

12.8   References in the following section to paragraph numbers are to paragraphs in the English CRAG unless otherwise stated. The details given below are those applying as at April 2004. The CRAG guidance specifically states that it is 'policy guidance' for the purposes of Local Authority Social Services Act 1970 s7(1). It is therefore guidance which local authorities must follow in all but the most exceptional of circumstances.[4]

The assessment of charges

12.9   Where a resident is unable to pay the standard rate care home charges or the actual cost incurred by the local authority (either for a local authority or independent home)[5] the authority is obliged to assess that person's ability to pay by reference to the Regulations and to CRAG. If, having carried out such an assessment, the authority is satisfied that the resident is unable to pay the standard rate (or in the case of an independent home, make a full refund of the fees) the authority must decide on the basis of the assessment what the person's contribution should be. If the resident refuses to co-operate with the financial assessment, then the authority will charge the full standard rate.

12.10   Residents can pay their assessed charge direct to the local authority. However, under NAA 1948 s26(3A) where residents have been placed by local authorities in independent sector homes (and where the resident, the authority and the organisation or person managing the home all agree)

---

2   SI No 2977.

3   Up-to-date versions of CRAG in England can be accessed at www.dh.gov.uk/
     PolicyAndGuidance/OrganisationPolicy/FinanceAndPlanning/ResidentialCare/
     fs/en. In Wales CRAG is also available on the internet at www.wales.gov.uk/
     index.htm or by post from Parc Cathays/Cathays Park, Caerdydd/Cardiff, CF10 3NQ;
     e-mail: assemblylibrarycathayspark@wales.gsi.gov.uk.

4   See para 1.29 above for consideration of 'policy guidance'.

5   The standard rate for local authority homes is the 'full cost' to the authority of
     providing the accommodation (NAA 1948 s22(2)); the standard rate for
     accommodation in homes not managed by the local authority is the full cost to the
     authority of providing or purchasing the accommodation under contract with the
     independent-sector home (NAA 1948 s26(2)).

then the resident may pay the assessed charge direct to the home with the authority paying the remainder. The advantage of such an arrangement is not only administrative convenience; it may also enable the resident to have a direct contractual relationship with the home owner (rather than having to rely on the authority's contract). Where such a three way arrangement exists the authority remains liable to the home owner for any arrears, should the resident fail to pay the home as agreed (paras 1.023–1.024).

Preliminary financial advice

12.11　CRAG obliges authorities to ensure that residents are given a clear explanation (usually in writing) of how their assessed contribution has been calculated and why this figure may fluctuate, particularly where a new resident's charge may vary in the first few weeks of admission because, for instance, of the effect of benefit pay-days of income support/pension credit or the withdrawal of attendance allowance (para 1.015).

12.12　Guidance issued under the Community Care (Residential Accommodation) Act 1998[6] – LAC(98)19 – required local authorities to have in place procedures to ensure that when the net capital of a resident (who is self-funding) reduces below the upper capital limit (see para 12.29) that they undertake an assessment and if necessary step in and take over funding arrangements to ensure that the resident is not forced to use capital below the upper capital limit (other than the notional income from that capital). It follows that a failure to provide appropriate advice in such cases could amount to maladministration and may render the authority liable to reimburse the 'spent down' monies.

12.13　Similar advice is provided in LAC(2000)11 and LAC(2001)25 which states (at para 25):

> . . . once a council is aware of the resident's circumstances, any undue delay in undertaking an assessment and providing accommodation if necessary would mean that the council has not met its statutory obligations. Consequently, the council could be liable to reimburse the resident for any payment he has made for the accommodation which should have been met by the council pursuant to its duties.

The treatment of income

12.14　Part II of the Regulations contains the procedure by which a resident's income (earned and unearned) is assessed for charging purposes; the provisions adopt many of the same rules used in the assessment of income for income support[7] and are the subject of detailed guidance in CRAG sections 8 and 9. A major difference between the two assessment regimes is that the income taken into account for CRAG purposes is that of the resident's alone. Under the NAA 1948 the authority has no power to assess a couple

---

6　Repealed and re-enacted by HSCA 2001 s53 and Sch 6.
7　Under the Income Support (General) Regulations 1987.

(whether or not married) according to their joint resources. Each person entering residential care should be assessed according to their individual means (para 4.001).

12.15　If, however, at the conclusion of the assessment process the local authority provide support for a resident in circumstances where it believes that the resources of his or her spouse are such that he or she ought to make a contribution, then the authority can invoke the 'liable relative' rules under NAA 1948 s42. The liable relative rules only apply to spouses (ie, married partners) and are considered in greater detail at para 12.79 below.

Personal expenses allowance

12.16　The basis of the charging provisions is that residents are required to pay all of their assessed income (above the personal allowance) towards the charge for the residential accommodation: 'The personal allowance is intended to enable residents to have money to spend as they wish, for example on stationery, personal toiletries, treats and small presents for friends and relatives' (para 5.001). The minimum amount of the personal expenses allowance is stipulated each year in the National Assistance (Sums For Personal Requirements) Regulations,[8] although by virtue of NAA 1948 s22(4) there is power to allow a different amount from that prescribed for personal expenses in special circumstances (see below).

12.17　The allowance of the period April 2004 – March 2005 is £18.10 in England and £18.40 in Wales.

Discretion

12.18　Under NAA 1948 s22(4) authorities have the power in special circumstances to allow a different amount from that prescribed for personal expenses. CRAG gives various examples[9] where it may be appropriate for an authority to allow a resident to retain a higher amount, including:

- where a person in residential accommodation has a dependent child, the authority should consider the needs of the child in setting the personal allowance;

- where a person temporarily in residential accommodation receives income support/pension credit including an amount for a partner who remains at home;

- where the resident is the main recipient of an unmarried couple's overall income, the authority can use its discretion to increase the resident's personal expenses allowance in special circumstances to enable the resident to pass some of that income to the partner remaining at home (see also para 12.26 below);

8　National Assistance (Sums for Personal Requirements) (England) Regulations 2003 SI No 628, for Wales SI No 892 (W 112).

9　At para 5.005.

- someone who does not qualify as a 'less dependent' resident solely because their care home accommodation provides board and so cannot be assessed under the rules relating to 'less dependent' residents (see para 12.71 below). In such cases the local authority can increase the personal expenses allowance if it considers that this could enable the resident to lead a more independent life, for example if he or she is working;

- where the resident is responsible for a property that has been disregarded, for example because the stay is temporary (see para 12.33b below) or the property is otherwise being disregarded the local authority should consider increasing the allowance to meet any resultant costs. In such cases the authority should disregard any reasonable housing related expenditure (see para 3.012).

12.19   The above examples are illustrative, not exhaustive. Accordingly in any case where a resident is experiencing hardship, an application can be made for an increase in the allowance. This may be because the lack of income means that he or she is unable to live as independent life as possible (for instance being unable to take part in community activities or attend family gatherings, etc) or for any other reason. Such a claim would be made by way of a request for a review (see para 12.84 below). Presumably in any such complaint it would be relevant for the local authority to have regard to their 'anti-poverty' strategy: on the basis that this must apply too all people within its area, including care home residents.

Income disregards

12.20   In general all income is taken into account in full. The situation can however be briefly summarised as follows:

12.21   *Income taken into account in full:* Most income is taken into account in full. This includes, for instance, net earnings,[10] most social security benefits, annuity income, pensions, trust income, etc (paras 8.005–8.020).

12.22   *Income partly disregarded:* Some income is partly ignored, for instance £10 of certain war pensions, up to half of pensions (see below) and modest amounts of the income from lodgers/sub-letting are ignored (paras 8.031–8.032).

12.23   *Pension credit:* The pension credit scheme provides a minimum income guarantee for people aged over 60. In addition, people over 64 can benefit from 'savings credit' which is designed to reward those who have made provision for their old age through second-tier pensions or similar savings. The scheme therefore allows them to keep a portion of their additional income – over and above the traditional cut off figure for income support (there is no upper maximum capital threshold for savings credit purposes). People who get a savings credit are entitled to keep some or all of it when they go into a care home. The relevant figures for April 2004–05 are:

10   Subject to a £5 or £20 disregard; see paras 9.018– 9.020.

- a savings disregard of up to £4.65 per week for individual supported residents with pre-Pension Credit assessed income between £79.60 and £105.45. The actual level of the disregard equals the savings credit actually received or £4.65 whichever is less. A flat rate disregard of £4.65 per week applies to all individual supported residents with pre-Pension Credit assessed income in excess of £105.45.

- a savings disregard of up to £6.75 for couples in residential care (and to couples where one partner is in temporary residential care and the other at home) with pre-Pension-Credit assessed income between £127.25 and £160.95. The actual level of the disregard equals the savings credit actually received or £6.75 whichever is less. A flat rate disregard of £6.75 applies to such couples with pre-Pension Credit assessed income in excess of £160.95.

12.24   The specified 'disregard' sums are retained by the residents as increased Personal Expense Allowances.

12.25   *Income fully disregarded:* Some income is fully disregarded, ie, Disability Living Allowance (DLA), Mobility Component (and Mobility supplement) DLA, Attendance Allowance for temporary residents (these cease in any event after four weeks for permanent residents), Christmas Bonus payments, income from the Independent Living Funds and social fund payments and any payments made to people who have been infected with hepatitis C as a result of NHS treatment with blood products.[11]

12.26   *Occupational pensions:* Where the resident has an occupational pension and has a spouse who is not living in the same residential home, 50 per cent of the occupational pension should be disregarded, providing the resident is actually paying such a sum over to the spouse. The disregard applies to *occupational* and private pensions between married partners and only where the spouse actually pays over at least 50 per cent of the pension. In all other cases the use of the 'discretion' detailed above should be considered (para 8.024A–C).

The treatment of capital

12.27   Part III of the Regulations deals with the capital entitlement rules. These differ from those that apply for income support and pension credit purposes (not least in respect of the maximum permissible sums and the disregards). Reference should be made to a specialist text for an analysis of the interplay between these differing regimes.[12]

12.28   Capital is widely defined for care home charging purposes, and includes all land and buildings (unless disregarded – see below). It also includes savings, shares, bonds and the like. It does not however include the surrender value of an insurance policy or annuity; or the value of any

---

11   Announced in the 'consultation' paper preceding the April 2004 uprating: and to be included in CRAG guidance for April 2004.
12   See 'Paying for care handbook', Child Poverty Action Group.

payment made from the social fund, independent living fund, payments 'in kind' from a charity, or student loans. Full details of the disregards are contained in Schedule 4 of the Regulations and at chapter 6 of CRAG.

Capital limits

12.29 The capital limits are generally increased each year; the limits for the period April 2004–March 2005 are as follows (with the Welsh figures in brackets)

Lower limit   £12,250   (£13,500)
Upper limit   £20,000   (£20,500)

12.30 Capital under the lower limit is disregarded for the purpose of the means test. For as long as the resident's assessed capital exceeds the upper limit then he or she is not entitled to receive financial assistance from the local authority in respect of the payment of residential home fees. Capital between the upper and lower limits is taken into account by attributing a 'tariff income' of £1.00 per week for each £250 (or part of £250) above the lower limit. Thus if a resident in England has £12,630 capital, £12,500 is disregarded and a tariff income of £2.00 per week is taken into account as income.

Couples

12.31 As with income, the authority is only permitted to take into account the capital of the resident. CRAG is explicit on this point, stating:

> The LA has no power to assess a couple according to their joint resources. Each person entering residential care should be assessed according to their individual means, although liability of a married person to maintain their spouse [see para 12.79 below] should be considered in each case (para 4.001).

12.32 Where a resident is one of a couple, the resident is liable to pay the standard rate or full contracted fee if he or she has more than the upper capital limit, or in respect of jointly held capital his or her share exceeds the upper capital limit (reg 20 and para 6.003). If the capital is in a joint account,[13] then there will be a presumption that it is owned in equal shares, thus if the account is held by the resident and his or her partner it will be presumed that half of it is owned by the resident (para 6.010).

The treatment of residential property

12.33 In general the capital value of a property or former home is taken into account in full (less 10 per cent for disposal costs – para 6.011); there are however a number of circumstances in which it may be disregarded. These are:

a) the value of a resident's home is disregarded for the first 12 weeks of a permanent admission to residential care. CRAG clarifies this provision as follows (at para 7.003B):

13 Different rules apply in relation to jointly owned interests in land – see para 12.37 below.

Where a person leaves residential care (where they have been living on permanent basis), before the end of the 12 weeks and then re-enters on a permanent basis within 52 weeks they will be entitled to the remaining balance of the 12 week disregard. If a resident leaves permanent care and then re-enters more than 52 weeks later, they will qualify for the disregard again.

b) The value of a dwelling normally occupied by a resident as his or her home should be ignored if his or her stay in a residential care or nursing home is temporary and:

- he or she intends to return to that dwelling, and the dwelling is still available to him or her; or
- he or she is taking reasonable steps to dispose of the property in order to acquire another more suitable property for the resident to return to.

If the resident's stay is initially thought to be permanent but turns out to be only temporary, the dwelling should be treated as if the stay had been temporary from the outset (para 7.002; Regulations Sch 4 para 1). Regulation 2(1) allows an authority to regard a person's stay as temporary if it is likely to last for any period not exceeding 52 weeks, or, in exceptional circumstances, is unlikely to exceed that period substantially.

c) Where the resident no longer occupies a dwelling as his or her home, its value should be disregarded where it is occupied in whole or in part by:

- the resident's partner or former partner[14] (except where the resident is estranged or divorced from the former partner – unless a lone parent); or
- a relative[15] of the resident or member of his or her family (ie, another person for whom the resident is treated as responsible) who:
  - (i) is aged 60 or over, or
  - (ii) is aged under 16 and is a child whom the resident is liable to maintain, or
  - (iii) is incapacitated.[16]

d) Where the resident has acquired property which he or she intends eventually to occupy as his or her home, the value should be disregarded for up to 26 weeks from the date the resident first takes steps to take up

14 This need not therefore be a 'spouse'. CRAG does not provide any clarification as to how 'partner' should be interpreted. It is possible that it may now be deemed to include a same sex partner – see *Mendoza v Ghaidan* [2002] EWCA Civ 1533; [2002] 4 All ER 1162; [2003] 2 WLR 478.

15 'Relative' is specified as including: parents, parents-in-law, sons, sons-in-law, daughters, daughters-in-law, step-parents, step-sons, step-daughters, brothers, sisters, grandparents, grandchildren, uncles, aunts, nephews, nieces and the spouse or unmarried partner of any except the last five (para 7.004).

16 The meaning of 'incapacitated' is not defined by the Regulations, but CRAG suggests that it includes a person receiving (or whose incapacity is sufficient to that required to qualify for) one of the following: 'incapacity benefit, severe disablement allowance, disability living allowance, attendance allowance, constant attendance allowance, or an analogous benefit'. Again this is an inclusive rather than an exclusive definition (see para 7.005).

occupation, or such longer period as is considered reasonable (paragraph 7.006; Regulations Sch 4 para 16).

e) Local authorities have an overall discretion to disregard the capital value of premises, not covered by the above exceptions, in which a third party continues to live.[17] Paragraph 7.007 of CRAG suggests that:

> LAs will have to balance the use of this discretion with the need to ensure that residents with assets are not maintained at public expense. It may be reasonable, for example, to disregard a dwelling's value where it is the sole residence of someone who has given up their own home in order to care for the resident, or someone who is an elderly companion of the resident particularly if they have given up their own home.

Charges to enable the sale of property to be deferred

12.34 Health and Social Care Act (HSCA) 2001 ss53–55 introduced a 'deferred payments' scheme which enable a resident to enter into an agreement with the local authority whereby the value of his or her main home is disregarded when deciding whether or not that person needs 'care and attention which is not otherwise available'. In effect the council then pays the resident's care home fees (including any top-up – see para 7.89) and recovers these payments from the sale of the property after the resident's death. The scheme was implemented in England in 2001 and in Wales in 2003[18] and is the subject of guidance[19] that explains that its aim is to:

> ... allow people with property, but without income and other assets sufficient to meet their full assessed contribution, to have a legal charge placed on their property to meet any shortfall. Hence people will be able to keep their homes on admission to residential care and for the duration of the deferred payments agreement.

12.35 The Department of Health was sufficiently concerned about the low take up of deferred payments by local authorities that in LAC(2002) 15 it drew attention to CI(2002)12 in which the Chief Inspector of Social Services reminded them that they are expected to have a deferred payments scheme in place and that they 'could be challenged if they did not consider exercising their discretion to offer deferred payments in individual cases'.

12.36 The procedure for implementing a deferred payment arrangement is described by CRAG at para 7.018 which includes reference to a pro forma legal agreement (in respect of the legal charge – revised to take account of the Land Registration Act 2002) that councils may wish to use in such cases.[20] At para 7.019 it contrasts such agreements, with charges imposed

---

17 Regulations Sch 4 para 18.

18 The National Assistance (Residential Accommodation) (Relevant Contributions) (England) Regulations 2001 SI No 3069 and the National Assistance (Residential Accommodation) (Additional Payments, Relevant Contributions and Assessment of Resources)(Wales) Regulations 2003 SI No 391 and the National Assistance (Residential Accommodation) (Disregarding of Resources)(Wales) Regulations 2003 SI No 969.

19 LAC(2001)25 and LAC(2001)29 in England and NAFWC 21/2003 in Wales.

under Health and Social Services and Social Security Adjudications Act (HASSASSAA) 1983 s22 (see para 12.68 below) in the following terms:

> Councils should bear in mind that deferred payments under section 55 of the Health and Social Care Act 2001 are distinct from the pursuit of debt through section 22 of HASSASSAA 1983 . . . Deferred payments should be offered when individuals are willing to pay their assessed contribution but do not wish to do so immediately. Section 22 of HASSASSAA applies to situations where residents are unwilling to pay their assessed contribution, either now or in the future, and a debt arises.

Joint beneficial ownership of property

12.37   CRAG and the Regulations[21] deal with the procedure to be adopted in order to value property which is the subject of joint beneficial ownership. The general rule is that where a resident owns property, ie, he or she has the right to receive some of the proceeds of a sale, it is the resident's interest in the property which is to be valued as capital, and not the property itself. Although jointly owned property is deemed to be owned in equal shares, this presumption can be rebutted in relation to property owned as tenants in common – where clear evidence of a different sharing arrangement exists.[22] In *Kelly v Hammersmith LBC*[23] the resident had purchased her council house (exercising her right to buy) but her daughter had funded the entire purchase costs and mortgage repayments. The court nevertheless held that the local authority was entitled to maintain a caution on the property in the mother's name for outstanding residential home fees because the daughter was unable to adduce sufficient evidence to show that her mother had no beneficial interest in the property.

12.38   The value of the resident's interest in a jointly owned property is governed by:

a) the resident's ability to re-assign the beneficial interest to somebody else; and

b) there being a market, ie, the interest being such as to attract a willing buyer for the interest.

12.39   CRAG suggests that in most cases there is unlikely to be any legal impediment preventing a joint beneficial interest in a property being re-assigned. But the likelihood of there being a willing buyer will depend on the conditions in which the joint beneficial interest has arisen. It goes on to advise (at paras 7.012 onwards) that where an interest in property is beneficially shared between relatives:

> . . . the value of the resident's interest will be heavily influenced by the possibility of a market amongst his or her fellow beneficiaries. If no other

20   Accessible at www.dh.gov.uk/PolicyAndGuidance/OrganisationPolicy/ FinanceAndPlanning/ResidentialCare/fs/en.

21   Reg 27(2) and CRAG paras 7.012–7.016.

22   See for instance, *Hourigan v Secretary of State for Work and Pensions* [2002] EWCA Civ 1890; [2003] 1 WLR 608; [2003] 3 All ER 924.

23   26 January 2004 (unreported) – Wilson J.

relative is willing to buy the resident's interest, it is highly unlikely that any 'outsider' would be willing to buy into the property unless the financial advantages far outweighed the risks and limitations involved. The value of the interest, even to a willing buyer, could in such circumstances effectively be nil. If the local authority is unsure about the resident's share, or their valuation is disputed by the resident, again professional valuation should be obtained.

12.40   CRAG provides local authorities with further advice (including the example below) as to what action they should take in such situations (at para 7.014A):

> If ownership is disputed and a resident's interest is alleged to be less than seems apparent from the initial information, the local authority will need written evidence on any beneficial interest the resident, or other parties possess. Such evidence may include the person's understanding of events, including why and how the property came to be in the resident's name or possession. Where it is contended that the interest in the property is held for someone else, the local authority should require evidence of the arrangement, the origin of the arrangement and the intentions for its future use. The law of equity may operate to resolve doubts about beneficial ownership, by deciding what is reasonable by reference to the original intentions behind a person's action, rather than applying the strict letter of the law.

Example

The resident has a beneficial interest in a property worth £60,000. He shares the interest with two relatives. After deductions for an outstanding mortgage, the residual value is £30,000. One relative would be willing to buy the resident's interest for £5,000. Although the value of the resident's share of the property may be £10,000, if the property as a whole had been sold, the value of just his share is £5,000 as this is the sum he could obtain from a willing buyer. The resident's actual capital would be £4,500 because a further 10 per cent would be deducted from the value of his share to cover the cost of transferring the interest to the buyer.

Property owned but rented to tenants

12.41   CRAG provides (para 7.017) that where a resident owns property, the value of which takes the resident's total capital above the upper capital limit and the property is rented to tenants, the resident will be assessed as able to pay the standard charge for the accommodation (because of the level of capital). It will then be for the resident to agree to pay the rental income (along with any other income) to the local authority in order to reduce the accruing debt. In cases where no deferred payment arrangement has been agreed (as above) authorities may chose to place a legal charge on the property and wait until the tenant dies before enforcing payment of the accrued debt (plus interest from the date of death) against the estate,[24] but they are not obliged to take this course.

24 See HASSASSA 1983 ss22 and 24.

Trust funds

12.42   Section 10 of CRAG advises on the question of the assessment of trust funds from which a resident may benefit. In general the capital value of a discretionary trust is disregarded – whereas payments from the trust to the resident may be taken into account as income. CRAG advises that certain minimum information be obtained in all such cases, and accordingly parties should ensure this is made available – even if satisfied that the trust monies ought ultimately be disregarded for means testing purposes.

12.43   In respect of personal injury trusts Schedule 4 para 10 of the Regulations stipulate that their capital value and any right to receive income be fully disregarded.[25] In relation to actual income derived from such trusts, CRAG advises (para 10.026) that:

> The following periodical payments are disregarded:
> •   Payments from a trust whose funds are derived from a payment made in consequence of any personal injury.
> •   Payments under an annuity purchased pursuant to any agreement or court order to make payments, or from funds derived from such a payment, in consequence of any personal injury.
> •   Payments received by virtue of any agreement or court order to make payments to the resident in consequence of any personal injury.
> (The agreements mentioned above include out-of-court settlements.)
> ... [such payments] are fully disregarded if intended and used to pay for any item which was not taken into account when the standard rate was fixed for the accommodation provided. Otherwise, £20 is disregarded.

Deprivation of capital

12.44   Regulation 25(1) of the Regulations provides that:

> A resident may be treated as possessing actual capital of which he has deprived himself for the purpose of decreasing the amount that he may be liable to pay for his accommodation except –
> (a) where that capital is derived from a payment made in consequence of any personal injury and is placed on trust for the benefit of the resident; or
> (b) to the extent that the capital which he is treated as possessing is reduced in accordance with regulation 26 [the diminishing notional capital rule – see below]; or
> (c) any sum to which paragraph 4.4(a) or 45(a) of Schedule 10 to the Income Support Regulations[26] (disregard of compensation for personal injuries which is administered by the Court) refers [see para 12.43 above].

25 See the National Assistance (Assessment of Resources) (Amendment) (No 2) England Regulations 2002 SI No 2531 and generally LAC(2002)15 paras 4–7.

26 The Income Support (General) Regulations 1987 SI No1967 which provide for the disregard of capital administered on behalf of a person by the High Court or the County Court under Civil Procedure Rules 1998 r21.11(1) or the Court of Protection, where such sum derives from (a) an award of damages for a personal injury to that person; or (b) compensation for the death of one or both parents where the person concerned is under the age of 18.

12.45   In seeking to determine whether a deprivation has occurred para 10 of LAC(98)8 advised as follows:

> Much information can be verified by reference to recent documentation provided by the client such as bank statements and building society account books. Authorities should also make use of information available to them from other departments within the authority or District Councils to verify client details, for example council tax benefit and housing records. They should also, as appropriate and with the consent of the client, undertake checks with other agencies such as the Benefits Agency [social security office], banks and private pension firms. Obviously it is not necessary for all information to be verified, and it is for authorities themselves to determine the extent and circumstances for verifying information.

Notional capital

12.46   CRAG explains[27] the impact of the rule in regulation 25(1) – that where an authority feels that a resident has deliberately deprived himself or herself of a capital asset in order to reduce the accommodation charge it may treat the resident as still possessing the asset. CRAG provides further guidance in the following terms:

> 6.062   There may be more than one purpose for disposing of a capital asset, only one of which is to avoid a charge for accommodation. Avoiding the charge need not be the resident's main motive but it must be a significant one.

> 6.063   If, for example, a person has used capital to repay a debt, careful consideration should be given to whether there was a need for the debt to be repaid at that time. If it seems unreasonable for the resident to have repaid that debt at that time, it may be that the purpose was to avoid a charge for accommodation.

> *Examples [CRAG para 6.063]*
> [1] A person moves into residential accommodation and has a 50% interest in property which continues to be occupied by his spouse. The LA ignore the value of the resident's share in property while the spouse lives there but the spouse decides to move to smaller accommodation and so sells the former home. At the time the property is sold, the resident's 50% share of the proceeds could be taken into account in the charging assessment but, in order to enable the spouse to purchase the smaller property, the resident makes part of his share of the proceeds from the sale available to the spouse. In these circumstances, in the Department's view, it would not be reasonable to treat the resident as having deprived himself of capital in order to reduce his residential accommodation charge.

> [2] A person has £24,000 in the bank. He is about to move permanently to a residential care home, and before doing so, pays off £3,500 outstanding on a loan for home improvements. It would be reasonable in these circumstances not to treat him as having deprived himself of the £3,500 deliberately in order to reduce his residential accommodation charge.

> [3] A resident has £18,000 in a building society. Two weeks before

27 At paras 6.057 onwards.

entering the home, he bought a car for £10,500, which he gave to his son on entering the home. If the resident knew he was to be admitted permanently to a residential care home at the time he bought the car, it would be reasonable to treat this as deliberate deprivation. However, all the circumstances must be taken into account. If he was admitted as an emergency and had no reason to think he would not be in a position to drive the car at the time he bought it, it would not be reasonable to treat it as deliberate deprivation.

12.47   As there have been few reported decisions on the scope of regulation 25 reference is sometimes made to the larger body of commissioners' decisions concerning the meaning of the equivalent (but not identical) 'notional capital' rule for income support purposes.[28] While the deprivation must have been made with the purpose of obtaining increased benefits, this does not have to be the person's predominant purpose, provided it was a '*significant operative purpose*'.[29] The authority must establish that the resident actually knew of the capital limit rule[30] (or that given the person's background this can be inferred).

Timing of the disposal

12.48   The length of time between the disposal and the application for financial assistance will generally be relevant; the longer the time between the disposal of an asset and a person's liability for accommodation charges, the less likely it is that the obtaining of the financial advantage was a foreseeable consequence of the transaction. CRAG states (para 6.064):

> The timing of the disposal should be taken into account when considering the purpose of the disposal. It would be unreasonable to decide that a resident had disposed of an asset in order to reduce his charge for accommodation when the disposal took place at a time when he was fit and healthy and could not have foreseen the need for a move to residential accommodation.

12.49   The leading judgment concerning a deprivation under regulation 25 is that of the Scottish Court of Session (Extra Division) in *Yule v South Lanarkshire Council*[31] where it was held that a local authority was entitled to take account of the value of an elderly woman's home transferred to her daughter over 18 months before the woman entered residential care. The Court held that there was no time limit on local authorities when deciding whether a person had deprived themselves of assets for the purposes of avoiding residential care fees.

---

28   Income Support (General) Regulations 1987 reg 51, which commences: 'A claimant shall be treated as possessing capital of which he has deprived himself for the purpose of securing entitlement to income support or increasing the amount of that benefit ...' The applicability of the comparison between the two provisions should be treated with caution, in view of the comments made in *Yule v South Lanarkshire Council* (see para 12.50 below).

29   Commissioner's Decision R(SB) 40/85.

30   Commissioner's Decision CIS 124/1990.

31   (2001) 4 CCLR 383.

12.50   Richards J relied upon the following extract from the *Yule* judgment in the subsequent case of *R (Beeson) v Dorset CC*:[32]

> The process of assessment, therefore begins with the requirement for the resident or prospective resident to provide information to the local authority from which the local authority can be satisfied that he is unable to pay the standard charge for the accommodation. The local authority cannot be so satisfied if the capital, both actual and notional, exceeds the specified sum. In determining the matter of notional capital, the local authority can only proceed upon the material which is available to them either from their own sources or upon that material as supplemented by material from the applicant and from such other sources as the local authority can reasonably be expected to apply to. We agree with counsel for the petitioner that in considering whether there is notional capital to be added to the actual capital of an applicant, the local authority must look to the information before them to determine whether a purpose to the effect specified in the regulations can be deduced. But in our opinion, this is not a matter of onus of proof. Rather, before the local authority can reach such a view, it must have material before it from which it can be reasonably inferred that the deprivation of capital took place deliberately and with a purpose of the nature specified. The local authority cannot look into the mind of the person making the disposition of capital or of others who may be concerned in the transaction. It can only look at the nature of the disposal within the context of the time at which and the circumstances in which that disposal took place . . .
>
> . . . [W]e do not consider . . . that it is necessary that the claimant should know of 'the' capital limit above which, in terms of the relevant regulations applicable at the time, the local authority is bound to refuse the application, if it is a reasonable inference, looking to the transaction in the whole surrounding circumstances relating to the applicant, that it must have been a purpose of the transaction to avoid having to pay any charges in the event of becoming a resident in residential accommodation provided by the local authority. In this respect we consider that the 1992 Regulations have to be looked at in a different light to those concerned with provision for income related benefits, not least because the purpose of the individual may have formed possibly some time ahead of the prospect that he or she might require to enter such residential accommodation . . .

12.51   The Beeson proceedings concerned a challenge to a decision that B had deprived himself of his house for the purpose of decreasing his liability to residential care fees. B transferred his house to his son by deed of gift, his stated reason being that he wished to ensure his son had a home if he needed it following the breakdown of his marriage. B continued to live in the house for two years before finally being assessed by the council as being in need of residential care. B's wish had been to live at home as long as possible and to die there. He returned home after several spells in hospital and received home care. At the time of the transfer, social services had not mentioned the possibility of residential care being required, but the council took the view that residential care was an inevitability and that this

---

32   The extract from the *Yule* judgment is at (2001) 4 CCLR 383 at 395–396 being cited in the *Beeson* judgment at (2002) 5 CCLR 5 at [9].

was B's motive in making the transfer and accordingly it treated the house as notional capital for the purposes of regulation 25 of the regulations.

12.52 The Court of Appeal[33] upheld the first instance decision of Richards J concerning the relevant test for disposals of assets, as stated in *Yule v South Lanarkshire*. Richards J held that the local authority had shown no evidence that Mr Beeson had transferred the property with the intention of reducing his potential liability for care home charges – indeed the evidence was the other way. The council's decision was therefore quashed and had to be reconsidered.

Diminishing notional capital rule

12.53 Where a resident is deemed to possess notional capital (such that he or she is deemed liable to pay some or all of the standard rate for the residential accommodation), then the diminishing notional capital rule means that over time he or she may nevertheless qualify for financial assistance from the authority in meeting the accommodation charges. Regulation 26 provides that where a resident has been assessed as having notional capital, that capital will have to be reduced each week by the difference between the rate which he or she is paying for the accommodation and the rate he or she would have paid if he or she was not treated as possessing the notional capital. CRAG gives the following example of the workings of such a calculation (albeit based on out of date capital and income thresholds) (para 6.068):

> A resident is assessed as having notional capital of £14,250 plus actual capital of £6,000. This results in him having to pay the standard charge for the cost of the accommodation, eg, £250. If he did not possess the notional capital, his capital would not affect his ability to pay for the accommodation so, based on an income of £86 and a personal allowance of, for example, £16 he would be assessed as paying a charge of £70. The notional capital should be reduced by £180 per week, ie, the difference between the sum he has to pay because of the notional capital (£250) and the charge he would have had to pay if the notional capital did not exist (£70).

Local authority responses to deliberate deprivations

12.54 If an authority believes that a resident has disposed of capital in order to reduce the charge payable, it will have to decide whether to treat the resident as having the capital (notional capital) and assess the charge payable accordingly. It will then have to decide what if any action it should take. CRAG advises that there are two options, namely (para 6.067):

a) to recover the assessed charge from the resident; or

b) if the resident is unable to pay the assessed charge, to use the provisions of HASSASSAA 1983 s21 to transfer liability to the recipient of the asset for that part of the charges assessed as a result of the notional capital (see para 12.60 below).

12.55 In addition to their enforcement powers under HASSASSAA 1983 s21

---

33 *R (Beeson) v Dorset CC* [2002] EWCA Civ 1812; (2003) 6 CCLR 5.

authorities are able in certain situations to use powers provided by the Insolvency Act 1986. These options are considered below.

12.56　　Local authorities would also appear to have another effective response where it is believed that a deliberate deprivation has occurred. If the authority believes that in consequence the resident has notional capital in excess of the upper capital limit it may decide that it need not provide or fund the accommodation at all. Whether this is a lawful response, will almost certainly depend upon the context of any particular case. Thus (for instance) if the resident has sufficient mental capacity to make the arrangement, then it could be argued that the local authority has no continuing obligation (see in this respect para 7.16 above). However if he or she lacks the necessary capacity the situation may be otherwise. In *Robertson v Fife Council*[34] the House of Lords had to construe the Scottish legislation on this issue – which, although similar, is in key respects materially different from that in England.[35] Fife Council had assessed an applicant as having notional capital above the upper limit and then had refused to provide assistance on the above basis (that no continuing obligation existed under NAA 1948 s21). The House of Lords rejected this, holding:

> The assessment of need and decisions as to whether they call for the provision of any of the community care services comes first. The assessment of means, and the requirement to pay what a person can afford, comes afterwards.

12.57　A persuasive argument exists that the opposite conclusion would have been reached had the case been determined according to the legislative regime in England/Wales: namely that a person with full capacity who had notional capital above the upper limit might be owed no duty under NAA 1948 s21. This was referred to by the Court of Appeal in the *Beeson* judgment, where it was noted (but the question not determined) that it had been argued:

> That different amendments to the 1948 Act as between England and Scotland made all the difference; and if it had been an English appeal *Robertson* would have been decided the other way.[36]

34　[2002] UKHL 35; (2002) 5 CCLR 543 at [53].

35　The material difference between the two legislative frameworks being that unlike the situation in England and Wales – where the duty to assess is separate from the 'community care service' provision obligation – in Scotland the two functions are combined (in the Social Work (Scotland) Act 1968). The key provisions of the 1968 Act being (1) s12(1) (which is broadly equivalent to a hybrid version of NAA 1948 ss21/29 and CA 1989 s17) which places a general duty on local authorities to promote social welfare by making a variety of services available including residential (but not nursing care); (2) s12A (which is broadly the same wording NHSCCA 1990 s47(1)) creates the assessment obligation; and (3) s13A which has no English/Welsh equivalent, creates a specific duty to provide nursing home accommodation, where a person has been assessed as needing it. This obligation (nor that under s12(1) above) is not subject to a proviso (as in England/Wales under s21) that the duty only arises 'if the need for care and attention is not otherwise available'. Mrs Robertson was in need of nursing home accommodation.

36　*R (Beeson) v Dorset County Council* (2002) 5 CCLR 5 at 22D; see also in this respect *Ellis v CAO* (1997) *Times* 14 May; [1998] FLR 184; Independent Law Report 15 May 1997.

Enforcement powers

12.58   If the local authority decides to take action to recover the disposed property (or the proceeds of sale) it has a number of statutory provisions available to assist. It has also been suggested that authorities may be given extra powers to strengthen 'procedures to prevent and detect evasion of care charges'.[37]

12.59   Where the resident has transferred assets to other parties with the purpose of avoiding or reducing his or her liability for charges, then the options available to the authority will depend, in part, on when the transfer occurred.

12.60   *Transfers within six months of entering residential accommodation*
HASSASSAA 1983 s21(1) provides:

> (1) Subject to the following provisions of this section, where –
>   (a) a person avails himself of Part III accommodation; and
>   (b) that person knowingly and with the intention of avoiding charges for the accommodation –
>   (i) has transferred any asset to which this section applies to some other person or persons not more than six months before the date on which he begins to reside in such accommodation; or
>   (ii) transfers any such asset to some other person or persons while residing in the accommodation; and
>   (c) either –
>   (i) the consideration for the transfer is less than the value of the asset; or
>   (ii) there is no consideration for the transfer,
> the person or persons to whom the asset is transferred by the person availing himself of the accommodation shall be liable to pay the local authority providing the accommodation or arranging for its provision the difference between the amount assessed as due to be paid for the accommodation by the person availing himself of it and the amount which the local authority receive from him for it.

12.61   The effect of HASSASSAA 1983 s21 is that where a resident has transferred any asset to a third party at less than its full value, then the authority can take enforcement proceedings against the third party if:

a)   the transfer took place no more than six months before the resident entered local authority funded care home accommodation, and

b)   the authority can establish that the transfer was effected '*knowingly and with the intention of avoiding charges for the accommodation*'.

12.62   Although section 21 is differently worded to the notional capital rule under regulation 25 of the Regulations ('*knowingly and with the intention of*' rather than '*for the purpose of*'), it is difficult to see that any practical differences of interpretation emerge from the two phrases; where a deprivation of capital is assessed as having occurred, then it would seem that this is also sufficient for the purposes of section 21.

---

37   See *A New Partnership for Care in Old Age*, para 3.2; a government consultation paper on the future funding of long-term care (HMSO, May 1996).

12.63   *Transfers over six months before entering residential accommodation*
If an authority has determined that:

a) a resident has notional capital, and

b) the notional capital asset was transferred to a third party more than six months before the resident took up residence in the residential home, and

c) in order to recover its charges (or payments made on the resident's behalf) it needs to take proceedings to set aside the disposition of the notional capital asset,

then the authority has the option of using the enforcement procedures under the Insolvency Act 1986 by which the court is empowered in certain situations to set aside such transfers and restore the position to what it would have been if the resident had not entered into the transaction.

12.64   By virtue of Insolvency Act 1986 s339, where an individual is adjudged bankrupt and he or she has entered into a transaction at an undervalue, the trustee in bankruptcy may (subject to the following time limits) apply to the court for an order restoring the position to what it would have been had the transaction not occurred.[38] The relevant time limits are computed backwards from the day of presentation of the bankruptcy petition and are, in general:

5 years   if the individual was insolvent[39] at the time of the transaction, or became insolvent in consequence of the transaction; or

2 years   if the above criteria do not apply.

12.65   By virtue of Insolvency Act 1986 s423, where the court is satisfied that an individual entered into a transaction (among other things) at an undervalue for the purpose of putting assets beyond the reach of a creditor or future creditor, then it may make such order as it thinks fit (including an order restoring the position to what it would have been had the transaction not been entered into).

12.66   The powers available to the court under Insolvency Act 1986 s423 are without time limit and are exercisable without the need for bankruptcy proceedings[40] (or for the individual in question to be insolvent). In *Midland Bank v Wyatt*[41] the court held that for the purposes of section 423 proof of dishonesty was not a requirement 'merely proof of avoidance of creditors whether they be existing or future creditors': that the judge had to be 'fully satisfied as to the true nature or object of the transaction' and that:

38 The details given here are a simplified account of the actual provisions; 'transactions at an undervalue' are defined by Insolvency Act (IA) 1986 s339 and are contrasted with 'preferences' (IA 1986 s340), for which slightly different rules apply.

39 Insolvency Act 1986 s341(3) states that an individual is insolvent if he or she is unable to pay his or her debts as they fall due, or the value of his or her assets is less than the amount of his or her liabilities, taking into account contingent and prospective liabilities. Section 341(2) creates a rebuttable presumption that an individual is insolvent where he or she enters into a transaction at an undervalue with an associate – see IA 1986 s435.

40 See generally *Midland Bank v Wyatt* [1995] 1 FLR 697.

41 [1995] 1 FLR 697.

... if the purpose of the transaction can be shown to put assets beyond the reach of future creditors, section 423 will apply whether or not the transferor was about to enter into a hazardous business ... It is a question of proof of intention or purpose underlying the transaction. Clearly, the more hazardous the business being contemplated is, the more readily the court will be satisfied of the intention of the settlor or transferor.

The breadth of s423 has been explained thus:

While the burden of proof remains on the applicant, establishing the necessary purpose should be less difficult to achieve than proving intent to defraud under the previous law ... The inclusion of persons who 'may at some time claim' against the debtor envisages potential future creditors who, individually unknown to the debtor at the time of the transaction, become victims of a risky business enterprise against the consequences of failure of which the debtor seeks to protect himself at the outset. In extending the purposes of present or future claimants, the ambit of the section is made very wide ...[42]

12.67 Where the resident has transferred the capital asset using a firm or business which specifically markets schemes designed to avoid the value of the asset being taken into account for residential fee purposes, this may, perversely, be used as evidence to establish the purpose behind the transaction.[43]

12.68 *Registering of a charge or caution on any interest in land which the resident may have (under HASSASSAA 1983 s22)*[44]

Where a resident fails to pay an assessed charge for accommodation and has a beneficial interest in land, then HASSASSAA 1983 s22 enables the local authority to create a charge in its favour on that land.[45] CRAG advises that where a local authority is contemplating taking such a step, it should advise the resident to consult a solicitor about the procedure. Any charge so registered does not carry interest until the resident's death, when section 24 of the 1983 Act provides for interest from that date 'at a reasonable rate' (determined by the local authority). While local authorities have no statutory power to charge interest[46] there would appear to be nothing to prevent them suing on the accumulated arrears since such a judgment debt would normally then carry interest at the statutory rate.

12.69 Section 22 empowers, but does not oblige, local authorities to place charges on property. In certain situations authorities may consider that the possession of a valuable asset (such as a house) is such that the resident has no need of assistance. The basis for this view being that the resident has

---

42 Berry et al, *Personal Insolvency* (Butterworths, 1993).

43 See paras 3 and 12 in particular of the Law Society guidelines, *Gifts of Property: Guidelines for Solicitors* (September 1995) and see also *Barclays Bank v Eustice* [1995] 1 WLR 1238.

44 For guidance on the application of HASSASSAA 1983 s22 see CRAG Annex D.

45 If the land is jointly owned, then the local authority cannot create a charge, but can register a caution (CRAG Annex D para 3.5).

46 CRAG at Annex D para 3A specifically states that the general powers under Local Government Act 1972 s111 cannot be used for this purpose.

capital in excess of the upper capital limit (ie, the value of the house) and accordingly is able to pay their own way (by for instance, raising a commercial loan secured on the property, pending its sale). The authority then determine that the care and attention is 'otherwise available' and refuse to provide temporary financial support and to register a charge under HASSASSAA 1983 s22.

12.70   As section 22 is phrased in discretionary terms, authorities are in principle entitled, where the circumstances allow, to take such a course. Whether such a decision is reasonable in any particular situation will depend upon the relevant facts. In general, a suggestion that a person take out a commercial loan (or obtain a home's agreement to defer payment until the sale of a property) assumes (at a minimum):

- the need for accommodation does not arise in an emergency (ie, there is sufficient time to arrange a loan) and;
- that the person has sufficient mental capacity and experience to arrange such a loan; and
- that in all the circumstances, the taking of a commercial loan is something that it would be reasonable for the resident to do.

Less dependent residents

12.71   For the purposes of the charging rules[47] a 'less dependent resident' means:

> . . . a resident who is in, or for whom accommodation is proposed to be provided in, premises which are not an establishment which is carried on or managed by a person who is registered under Part II of the Care Standards Act 2000.

12.72   The charging rules allow for a difference in treatment, for charging purposes of 'less dependent' residents – especially in relation to the amount of their personal expenses allowance (see para 12.18 above).

12.73   Before April 1993, social services authorities had powers to arrange for the provision of residential accommodation under National Health Service Act (NHSA) 1977 Sch 8 as well as under National Assistance Act (NAA) 1948 Part III. The NHSA 1977 powers were mainly used to accommodate people who were able to live more independently than those accommodated under the 1948 Act, but who nevertheless required some degree of care and support (but not board) – generally (but not always) people under pension age. Authorities were empowered but not required to charge for accommodation provided under the NHSA 1977.[48] This meant that the money left with residents for their personal use was not limited to the prescribed amount for personal expenses allowed for people accommodated under the 1948 Act. The reason for this difference in treatment was to encourage less dependent residents to acquire independent living skills (such as purchasing their own food and paying for their expenses or travel

47 Regulation 2(1).
48 Using their discretionary powers under HASSASSAA 1983 s17.

to work) often with a view to eventually living independently in the community.

12.74   With the repeal, in April 1993, of the accommodation powers under NHSA 1977 Sch 8[49] adult care home placements made by social services authorities are now made under the NAA 1948 – even if the resident is 'less dependant'. Regulation 5 of the Regulations accordingly enables authorities to continue to treat 'less dependent' residents differently where they consider it reasonable in the circumstances to do so. It enables authorities to disregard the resources of such residents, taking into account:

- the resident's commitments, ie, costs of necessities such as food, fuel, and clothing,
- the degree of the resident's independence, ie, the extent to which he or she should be encouraged to take on expenditure commitments, and
- whether he or she needs a greater incentive to become more independent, eg, he or she may be encouraged to take on paid employment if most or all of the earnings are disregarded.

Temporary residents

12.75   As noted above (at para 10.118) residents placed in care home accommodation as part of a programme of intermediate care are entitled to that service free of charge. Additionally, NAA 1948 s22(5A) stipulates that authorities are not obliged to apply the charging rules to other temporary residents. The subsection provides:

> If they think fit, an authority managing premises in which accommodation is provided for a person shall have power on each occasion when they provide accommodation for him, irrespective of his means, to limit to such amount as appears to them reasonable for him to pay the payments required from him for his accommodation during a period commencing when they begin to provide the accommodation for him and ending not more than eight weeks after that.

12.76   CRAG advises that where the authority decides to make an assessment of ability to pay, then it should do so on the normal charging basis. Where it decides not to make such an assessment, then it is able to charge such amount as it considers reasonable for the resident to pay (para 3.005). CRAG additionally highlights the difficulties that may arise as a result of the different capital rules for income support/pension credit entitlement (paras 3.006A–B).

12.77   Where a resident aged under 60 enters residential accommodation for a temporary period Income Support is not payable if his capital exceeds £8,000 or £12,000 respectively. This may mean that, where the resident has capital of above £8,000 but not more than £19,500, the resident's contribution towards the cost of his or her accommodation will not include any Income Support.

---

49 The accommodation powers under NHSA 1977 were repealed by NHSCCA 1990 Sch 10.

12.78 Where a resident aged 60 or over enters residential accommodation for a temporary period, the calculation of Pension Credit, including deemed income from capital, will be the same as when he was in his own home, ie, the lower capital limit of £10,000 for permanent residents will not apply. This may mean that Pension Credit that would normally be payable to a permanent resident may not be payable at the same level.

Liable relatives

12.79 The Department of Health in its consultation papers on the April 2004 CRAG changes stated that it was 'planning to repeal the liable relatives' rules at the earliest opportunity'. The Welsh Assembly (in its consultation paper on the October 2003 changes) has stated that it was 'actively considering' the question of the continuance of the liable relative rule. The following section therefore continues to have relevance only until such time as the rule is repealed.

12.80 Married couples are liable to maintain each other under NAA 1948 s42 as they are under the social security legislation.[50] Section 42 provides:

> (1) For the purposes of this Act –
>   (a) a man shall be liable to maintain his wife and his children, and
>   (b) a woman shall be liable to maintain her husband and her children.
> (2) Any reference in subsection (1) of this section to a person's children shall be construed in accordance with section 1 of the Family Law Reform Act 1987.

12.81 NAA 1948 s43 makes provision for local authorities to recover payments from such liable relatives although CRAG advises that it is not worthwhile to pursue such payments where income support/pension credit is in payment to the resident (para 11.003). The government's intentions as to the future of the liable relative rule are unclear. In 2002 it stated that it was 'committed to more robust and fairer guidance on how and when councils should seek "liable relative contributions" from married partners when one of them enters residential care'[51] whereas in 2003 both the Department of Health and Welsh Assembly in their consultation papers on the annual CRAG changes stated that they were 'actively considering' the question of the continuance of the liable relative rule.

Seeking payments from liable relatives

12.82 Where it appears to an authority that it is appropriate to pursue a resident's spouse under NAA 1948 s42, CRAG gives advice as to the procedure to be followed:

> 11.005 ... LAs may ask a spouse to refund part or all of the authority's expenditure in providing residential accommodation for his/her husband or wife. LAs should note that this does not mean that an authority can

---

50 Social Security Administration Act 1992 ss78(6) and 105(3).
51 LAC(2002)11 Annex para 18.

demand that a spouse provide details of his/her resources. LAs should not use assessment forms for the resident which require information about the means of the spouse. LAs should use tact in explaining to residents and spouses the legal liability to maintain and point out that the extent of that liability is best considered in the light of the spouses' resources.

11.005A A council can negotiate a liable relative contribution even if the liable relative does not wish to supply details of his or her resources. In the absence of details councils should not charge the partner for any of the care unless negotiation has taken place.

11.006 In practical terms, LAs may wish to proceed as follows:
(i) assess the ability of the resident to pay based solely on his/her own resources. This establishes the charge the resident is able to pay without assistance from the liable relative;
(ii) if the resident is unable to pay for his/her accommodation at the standard rate, the LA decides whether it is worth pursuing the spouse for maintenance towards the shortfall;
(iii) if it is worth pursuing the spouse for maintenance, consider in each case what would be 'appropriate' for the spouse to pay by way of maintenance. This will involve discussion and negotiation with the spouse, and will be determined to a large extent by his/her financial circumstances in relation to his/her expenditure and normal standard of living. In the Department's view, it would not be appropriate, for example, to necessarily expect spouses to reduce their resources to Income Support/Pension Credit levels in order to pay maintenance;
(iv) ultimately, only the courts can decide what is an 'appropriate' amount of maintenance to pay. When negotiating maintenance payments with spouses the LA should therefore consider whether the amount being sought would be similar to that decided by the courts. Councils should consider court action as a last resort.

11.006A The assessment and discussions about a liable relative's contribution should be timely, and should not delay the resident's admission to residential care and immediate funding. If negotiation with the married partner is still continuing on admission of the resident, the council should make contributory payment in the interim. If appropriate, councils should secure retrospective contribution from the married partner.

Liable relative payments

12.83 Where a resident receives money from his or her spouse or former (divorced) spouse, then CRAG provides procedures for deciding whether these payments are to be treated as capital or income. The possible permutations for such payments are many, and the detailed guidance in CRAG should be referred to if such a problem is encountered (see paras 11.007–11.025).

Challenging charges

12.84 Complaints about the level of charges levied by an authority are subject to the usual social services complaints procedures; see chapter 19.

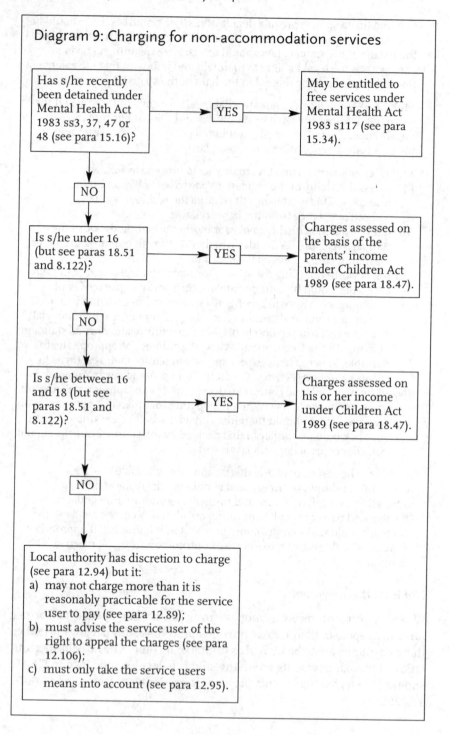

Diagram 9: Charging for non-accommodation services

Has s/he recently been detained under Mental Health Act 1983 ss3, 37, 47 or 48 (see para 15.16)?

YES → May be entitled to free services under Mental Health Act 1983 s117 (see para 15.34).

NO

Is s/he under 16 (but see paras 18.51 and 8.122)?

YES → Charges assessed on the basis of the parents' income under Children Act 1989 (see para 18.47).

NO

Is s/he between 16 and 18 (but see paras 18.51 and 8.122)?

YES → Charges assessed on his or her income under Children Act 1989 (see para 18.47).

NO

Local authority has discretion to charge (see para 12.94) but it:
a) may not charge more than it is reasonably practicable for the service user to pay (see para 12.89);
b) must advise the service user of the right to appeal the charges (see para 12.106);
c) must only take the service users means into account (see para 12.95).

Charges for non-accommodation services

12.85 The charging provisions for adult non-accommodation services differ in significant respects from those relating to residential accommodation:

a) social services authorities are under no obligation to charge for non-accommodation services; whereas they are obliged to charge for residential accommodation (with the exception of temporary residential accommodation);[52] and

b) there is no statutorily defined procedure for assessing non-accommodation charges.

12.86 Social services authorities have a discretionary power to charge for certain non-accommodation services. In relation to adult services the power presently[53] derives from Health and Social Services and Social Security Adjustments Act (HASSASSAA) 1983 s17 which provides as follows:

(1) Subject to subsection (3) below, an authority providing a service to which this section applies may recover such charge (if any) for it as they consider reasonable.

(2) This section applies to services provided under the following enactments:

(a) section 29 of the National Assistance Act 1948 (welfare arrangements for disabled persons);

(b) section 45(1) of the Health Services and Public Health Act 1968 (welfare of old people);

(c) Schedule 8 to the National Health Service Act 1977 (care of mothers and young children, prevention of illness and care and after-care and home help and laundry facilities);

(d) section 8 of the Residential Homes Act 1980[54] (meals and recreation for old people); and

(e) paragraph 1 of Part II of Schedule 9 to this Act, other than the provision of services for which payment may be required under section 22 or 26 of the National Assistance Act 1948.

(f) section 2 of the Carers and Disabled Children Act 2000.

(3) If a person –

(a) avails himself of a service to which this section applies, and

(b) satisfies the authority providing the service that his means are insufficient for it to be reasonably practicable for him to pay for the service the amount which he would otherwise be obliged to pay for it,

the authority shall not require him to pay more for it than it appears to them that it is reasonably practicable for him to pay.

(4) Any charge under this section may, without prejudice to any other method of recovery, be recovered summarily as a civil debt.

---

52 National Assistance Act 1948 s22(5A) – see above.

53 The power was formerly to be found under NAA 1948 s29(5) which provided that '[a] local authority may recover from persons availing themselves of any service provided under this section such charges (if any) as, having regard to the cost of the service, the authority may determine, whether generally or in the circumstances of any particular case'.

54 Repealed by HASSASSAA 1983 s 30 and Sch 10 Pt I.

12.87   Separate charging provision relate to services provided under Children Act (CA) 1989 Part III, and these are considered separately at para 18.47.

12.88   The Assembly in Wales is seeking to phase out charging for home care services. However, in England, authorities are under considerable pressure to operate home care charging schemes. The 1990 policy guidance states that it 'is expected that local authorities will institute arrangements so that users of services of all types pay what they can reasonably afford towards their costs', although it then adds, that the provision of services should 'not be related to the ability of the user or their families to meet the costs' and that 'the assessment of means should, therefore, follow the assessment of need and decisions about service provision' (at para 3.31). The pressure on authorities to levy charges is also evident from LAC(94)1, which explained the position thus:

> 17. . . . The Government's view . . . has consistently been that users who can pay for such services should be expected to do so taking account of their ability to pay. The White Paper and Policy Guidance also make it clear that ability to pay should not influence decisions on the services to be provided, and the assessment of financial means should therefore follow the care assessment.

> 18. Authorities are locally accountable for making sensible and constructive use of the discretionary powers they have, in order to prevent avoidable burdens falling on council and national taxpayers. Authorities are reminded that the standard spending assessment formula for domiciliary care for elderly people does not take account of the level of income from charges actually received by each authority. This means that any authority which recovers less revenue than its discretionary powers allow is placing an extra burden on the local population or is foregoing resources which could be used to the benefit of the service . . .

Not reasonably practicable

12.89   HASSASSAA 1983 s17 enables local authorities to make reasonable charges for non-residential services, but also requires that they have procedures for reducing or waiving the charge where it is not *'reasonably practicable'* for the user to pay the full charge.

12.90   The Local Government Ombudsman has held that it was maladministration for an authority to adopt a charging policy which only permitted exceptions if users provided 'proof of hardship'[55] since this was a materially more severe criterion than 'not reasonably practicable'. Likewise in *R v Calderdale DC ex p Houghton*[56] the local authority conceded that its procedures for assessing the reasonableness of its charges were unreasonably high: they required that applicants establish that their expenditure was so exceptional that it was not reasonable for the authority to charge the full amount.

12.91   The Ombudsman has further held that where a claimant had produced

---

55   Complaint Nos 99/C/02509 and 02624 against Gateshead.
56   Unreported but see (1999) 2 CCLR 119 – Community care law update.

evidence that her expenditure exceeds her income, then the authority cannot insist on her paying the full charge without providing cogent reasons why it considers her able to pay the amount claimed.[57]

12.92   While the onus is on service users to provide the necessary information in order that the amount of the charge can be reviewed,[58] there is an attendant obligation on the authority to ensure that it gives clients accurate information about the charges they will face and information as to how they can challenge those charges if they believe that they are unreasonable. Guidance issued by the Social Services Inspectorate in January 1994 (ostensibly as advice to its own officers – the '1994 SSI guidance') at para 28 stipulates:

> Good practice requires that users should be given an accurate indication of the charges that they will incur before they are required to commit themselves to a particular care plan. Only exceptional circumstances can justify not doing so. They also should be given a written statement of their financial liability at the earliest opportunity, with access to advice and explanation as required.

12.93   This advice was echoed in a 'Good Practice Handbook' issued in 1996 by the Association of County Councils and the Association of Metropolitan Authorities (and endorsed by the Local Government Ombudsman)[59] which states that authorities should ensure that:

- information about their charging policies for service users and carers is accurate, and that it contains a clear explanation of the law and the authority's 'discretion' (page 18);[60] and
- that copies of the financial information that the user has supplied should be made available to the user (page 32).

Services that must be provided free

12.94   Certain non-accommodation services must be provided free of charge, and these include:

- services under Mental Health Act 1983 s117 (see para 15.54 above); and
- intermediate care services, for instance intensive help at home (see para 10.118 above);
- (in England)[61] community equipment/minor adaptations where the cost is less than £1,000 (see para 8.107 above);

---

57   Complaint Nos 99/C/02509 and 02624 against Gateshead.

58   If the resident refuses to co-operate with the financial assessment, then the authority will be entitled to charge the full standard rate.

59   Para 153 Complaint 98/C/0911 and others against Stockton-on Tees Borough Council 29 July 1999.

60   The importance of this information being available in appropriate languages was noted by the Local Government Ombudsman in Complaint No 91A/3782 against Greenwich LBC (1993).

61   The Welsh Assembly has indicated that it has no intention of brining in Community Care (Delayed Discharge, etc) Act 2003 Part I into effect in Wales (the Part that deals with fines for delayed discharge). It has not however (as yet) indicated whether or not it will bring into effect the 'free service' provisions under Part II.

- services provided to persons suffering from any form of Creuzfeldt Jacob Disease (CJD), or payments to people who have been infected with hepatitis C as a result of NHS treatment with blood or blood products.[62]

Assessable income and assets

12.95   HASSASSAA 1983 s17(3) directs local authority attention to the question of whether a service user's means are sufficient for it to be reasonably practicable for him or her to pay for the service. It follows that the question concerns the service users means alone and that 'any means test must be confined to the means of the service user'.[63] The 2001 policy guidance on non-accommodation charging (see para 12.99 below) reinforces this advice stating:

> 62. Section 17 of the HASSASSAA 1983 envisages that councils will have regard only to an individual user's means in assessing ability to pay a charge.

> 63. This will mean that parents and other members of an adult user's family cannot be required to pay the charges, except in certain legal circumstances, for example, where a family member may be managing the user's own resources.

12.96   There will of course be situations where assets belonging to the service user are in fact held in the name of a third party, such as under a power of attorney, a receivership order or a simple trust arrangement. In such cases the assets, although administered by a third party, clearly belong to the service user and can be taken into account in the means test. In this respect the 2001 policy guidance advises:

> 64. Councils may wish to consider in individual cases whether a user's means may include resources not held in that person's name, but to which the user has a legal entitlement. The most likely instances of this kind will arise in relation to married or unmarried couples. In some circumstances, the user may have a legal right to a share in the value of an asset, for example a bank account, even if it is not in his or her name. In some circumstances, statutory provisions provide such a right. In other circumstances, what are known as 'equitable principles' may apply to give such a right, for example where there is an unwritten agreement between partners that they both own a property or an asset, even though the title is in only one of their names. If the council has some reason to believe that the user does have means other than those initially disclosed, a request may reasonably be made for the user to arrange for the partner to disclose his or relevant resources. If there is no such disclosure, the council may consider that it is not satisfied that the user has insufficient means to pay the charge for the service. It will be for the council to consider each case in the light of their own legal advice.

---

62   Para 75 'Fairer Charging Policies for Home Care and other non-residential Social Services' September 2003 accessible at www.doh.gov.uk/scg/homecarecharges/.

63   Social Services Inspectorate Guidance issued in January 1994 (ostensibly as advice to its own officers) para 12.

12.97 Certain income is excluded from the charging calculation. This includes any earnings, Working Tax Credit and Child Tax Credit and any mobility component of Disability Living Allowance (DLA),[64] any payments to people who have been infected with hepatitis C as a result of NHS treatment with blood products[65] and any income which is being received from the Independent Living (1993) Fund.[66] In *R v Coventry CC ex p Carton*[67] the local authority changed its non-residential care charges so that there was no automatic disregard for the night component of higher rate DLA for service users receiving day care only. The Administrative Court held that it was irrational, unlawful and unfair for the council to apply a charging policy which treated as income available for day care sums of DLA paid in respect of night care.

12.98 In *Avon CC v Hooper*[68] (an unusual fact case) the Court of Appeal held that a person's 'means' (for the purposes of HASSASSAA 1983 s17) were not limited to cash, but included other financial resources – for instance an expectation of compensation in legal proceedings such that a local authority could recover the care costs it had provided a person from his estate (in this case amounting to over £232,000). Hobhouse LJ court considered the interpretation of section 17(3) in the following terms:[69]

> If the local authority decides to charge and is acting reasonably [under section 17(1)] ... the person availing himself of the service has ... to satisfy the authority under subsection (3) that his means are insufficient for it to be reasonably practicable for him to pay the amount which he would otherwise be obliged to pay. It is for the recipient of the service to discharge this burden of persuasion. He must show that he has insufficient means. The time at which he has to do this is the time when the local authority is seeking to charge him for the services. If his means have been reduced, as might be the case with a business man whose business had run into difficulties after his being injured, the reduction in his means is something upon which he would be entitled to rely as making it impracticable for him to pay, even though at an earlier date he might have been better off. The consideration under subsection (3)(b) is the practical one: are his means such that it is not reasonably practicable for him to pay?
>
> This also bears on the alternative argument ... that only cash should be taken into account. This is too narrow a reading of subsection (3). As a matter of the ordinary use of English, the word 'means' refers to the financial resources of a person: his assets, his sources of income, his liabilities and expenses. If he has a realisable asset, that is part of his

---

64 Social Security Contributions and Benefits Act 1992 s73(14) requires this benefit to be disregarded in any charging scheme – see the 2003 policy guidance 'Fairer Charging Policies for Home Care and other non-residential Social Services' at para 30.

65 Announced in the 'consultation' paper preceding the April 2004 uprating: and to be included in CRAG guidance for April 2004.

66 2003 policy guidance 'Fairer Charging Policies for Home Care and other non-residential Social Services' at para 74

67 (2001) 4 CCLR 41

68 (1998) 1 CCLR 366.

69 (1998) 1 CCLR 366 at 371E–K.

means; he has the means to pay. The subject matter of paragraph (b) is the practicability of his paying. If he has an asset which he can reasonably be expected to realise and which will (after taking into account any other relevant factor) enable him to pay, his means make it practicable for him to pay.

Where the person has a right to be indemnified by another against the cost of the service, he has the means to pay. He can enforce his right and make the payment. There is nothing in any part of section 17 which suggests that it is intended that subsection (3) should have the effect of relieving those liable to indemnify the recipient of the service for the cost of the service from their liability. On the contrary, it is clear that the intention of the section is to enable the local authority to recover the cost save when it is unreasonable that it should do so or impracticable for the recipient to pay.

Policy guidance

12.99   Until 2001 no national policy guidance on charging for non-accommoda-
tion services existed, with the result that wide disparities existed in the charges levied by social services authorities. In its White Paper 'Modern-ising Social Services' (1998) the government acknowledged these local vari-ations and committed itself to establish greater consistency and fairness.[70] This was realised in November 2001 with the publication by the Depart-ment of Health of 'Fairer Charging Policies for Home Care and other non-residential Social Services' LAC (2001)32 and in July 2002 when the Welsh Assembly issued similar guidance[71] (both under LASSA 1970 s7). The current guidance in England was issued in September 2003 (to reflect the introduction of the Pension Credit)[72] and is referred to in this section as the '2003 Fairer Charging policy guidance'.

12.100   The key principles embodied in the English and Welsh policy guidance can be summarised as follows:

1) Councils are not obliged to charge for non-residential social services.

2) Flat-rate charges are acceptable only in limited circumstances (for instance where they are a substitute for ordinary living costs – such as for meals on wheels or meals at a day centre).

3) Net incomes should not be reduced below basic Income Support levels or the Guarantee Credit of Pension Credit, plus a buffer of 25%, Coun-cils should consider and specifically consult on the need to set a maxi-mum charge: 'basic levels' of Income Support includes the personal allowance and all premiums, but it 'need not include the Severe Dis-ability Premium' (para 19).

4) Where disability benefits are taken into account as income in assessing ability to pay a charge, councils should assess the individual user's

70 Cm 4169 at para 2.31.

71 The Labour party in its Welsh manifesto for the 2003 Assembly elections committed itself to 'eliminate all charges for home care services for disabled people in Wales'.

72 Accessible at www.dh.gov.uk/assetRoot/04/07/50/99/04075099.doc.

disability-related expenditure; councils should specifically consult on the need to assess disability-related expenditure for other users. It is not acceptable to make a charge on disability benefits without assessing the reasonableness of doing so for each user.

5) Councils should ensure that comprehensive benefits advice is provided to all users at the time of a charge assessment. Councils have a responsibility to seek to maximise the incomes of users, where they would be entitled to benefits, particularly where the user is asked to pay a charge.

6) As a minimum, the same savings limits as for residential care charges should be applied. Councils are free to operate more generous rules, as with other parts of the guidance.

7) 'To ensure that disabled people and their carers, who wish to do so, are able to enter and progress in work', the guidance requires earnings (including Working Families Tax Credit and Disabled Person's Tax Credit) to be disregarded in charge assessments.

12.101 Examples of the practical application of these principles, were provided in the September 2003 reissue of the Department of Health guidance[73] – including those in Table 8 on page 372.

Practice guidance

12.102 In August 2002 Practice Guidance concerning the home care charging policy was issued by the Department of Health.[74] The notable points in this important guidance include:

- It favours the creation of a specialist service, separating financial assessment from assessment of care needs (para 27); these financial assessments should normally be carried out by personal interview in the user's own home (para 40).

- Users who may be entitled to benefits which would bring them within charging, may be given an 'interim assessment' so that the local authority has the option of backdating the charge assessment against any backdated benefits award: however the guidance notes that this is 'an issue for local policy' (para 35).

- Spending not incurred, as an unmet need, should not be allowed (para 36). However where disability benefit has been newly awarded, an assessment should be capable of review to take account of the likelihood of the disabled person increasing his or her disability related expenditure due to the higher level of income (para 37).

- Research informing the practice guidance (undertaken in Torbay in 1999/2000) showed that 34 per cent of those assessed had disability related expenditure above £40 pw, and 49 per cent above £30 (para 44).

73   2003 Fairer Charging policy guidance Annex C.
74   2003 Fairer Charging policy guidance Annex C.

Table 8: Examples of the application of home care charging rules (the applicable rules being those for 2003/04)

All the examples detailed below relate to a hypothetical 66 year old single person, with disability-related benefits and £25 disability-related expenditure

Pension Credit only	Occupational pensioner	Occupational pensioner, higher income
Basic state pension £77.45 + Guarantee credit £24.65 + Additional amount for severe disability £42.95 + AA £38.30	Basic state pension £77.45 + occupational pension £102.00 + AA £38.30	Basic state pension £77.45 + occupational pension £400.00 + AA £38.30 + Savings £15,000, tariff income = £12.00
Assessable income £183.35	Assessable income £217.75	Assessable income £527.75
Deduct £102.10 + (25%) £25.53 £127.63 Deduct: Rent/housing Nil Council Tax Nil	Deduct £102.10 + (25%) £25.53 £127.63 Deduct: Rent/housing £42.00 Council Tax £15.00	Deduct £102.10 + (25%) £25.53 £127.63 Deduct: Rent/housing Nil Council Tax £15.00
Disability-related [£25.00] Dietary £6.00 Extra heating £7.00 Cleaner £7.00 Gardening services £5.00	Disability-related [£25.00] Dietary £6.00 Extra heating £7.00 Cleaner £7.00 Gardening services £5.00	Disability-related [£25.00] Dietary £6.00 Extra heating £7.00 Cleaner £7.00 Gardening services £5.00
Total deductions £152.63	Total deductions £209.63	Total deductions £167.63
Assessable income remaining = £30.72 Actual charge depends on hours of care, subject to assessable income remaining	Assessable income remaining = £8.12 Actual charge depends on hours of care, subject to assessable income remaining	Assessable income remaining = £360.12 Actual charge depends on hours of care, subject to assessable income remaining and any maximum

- Para 46 provides a detailed list of typical disability related expenditure, including:
  - Community alarm
  - Private care arrangements, including respite care
  - Specialist washing powders
  - Laundry
  - Specialist diets
  - Clothing/footwear
  - Additional bedding (eg, because of incontinence)
  - Extra heating or water (standard rates suggested for heating; and councils must ignore Winter Fuel/Cold Weather Payments)
  - Garden maintenance
  - Cleaning or domestic help – the cost of private cleaning services should be allowed when they are not provided through social services . . .; and 'consideration should be given to higher needs for cleaning as a consequence of disability and the needs of carers' . . .
  - Purchase, maintenance and repair of disability related equipment.
  - Personal assistance costs – eg, paying for the meals or transport costs for personal assistants or carers.
  - Other transport costs 'over and above the Mobility Component of DLA'.
  - It may be reasonable for a council not to allow costs where a reasonable alternative *is available* at lesser cost.
- Information about how to complain should be available as a matter of routine (para 64).
- '[T]he Department of Health is under no illusion that a considerable number of local councils will need to set up or strengthen resources to provide benefit advice and support with claims . . .'

Local charging schemes: the duty to consult

12.103 HASSASSAA 1983 s17(1) requires local authorities to set a rate that they consider 'reasonable'. This necessarily requires the consideration of a variety of factors – including the views of service users.[75]

12.104 The 1996 Good Practice Handbook (see para 12.93) stressed the importance of consultation with service users concerning the development and piloting of charging procedures and that a realistic timescale needed to be set for the consultation process before any changes took place. It noted that 'the experience of local authorities suggests that consultation will take months'.[76] The Local Government Ombudsman has been critical of charging schemes that have been introduced with undue haste, ie, before the procedures for its implementation were in place.[77] In *R v Coventry CC ex p Carton*[78] the local authority changed its non-residential care charges so that

---

75 See in this respect, 2003 Fairer Charging policy guidance paras 98–99.
76 At pages 16 and 25–27.
77 Complaint No 91A/3782 against Greenwich LBC (1993).
78 (2001) 4 CCLR 41.

(among other things) there was no automatic disregard for the night component of higher rate DLA for service users receiving day care only. The Administrative Court held that before fundamental changes of this nature could be made to a charging structure, there had to be proper consultation with users.

Challenging the assessed charge

12.105 Where a service user wishes to challenge a non-accommodation charge, the usual procedure will be to pursue the matter through the local authority's complaints procedures (see para 19.4).[79]

12.106   The Local Government Ombudsman has emphasised that service users should be given clear information as to the criteria for having charges reduced or waived, and of their right to a hearing before an appeal panel if their initial challenge was unsuccessful. He has also stressed the need for panel decisions to be as consistent as possible and that clear reasons for their decisions should be given so that appellants can then decide whether or not to pursue the matter further.[80]

12.107   At any hearing, the panel will need to bear in mind that an authority's power to reduce or waive charges is not limited to a consideration of the service user's financial means. As the authority has an overall discretion whether or not to levy any charges, it must retain discretion to waive or reduce charges on any ground. Such an overall discretion might be used where, for instance, the service user lacked mental capacity and the services were therefore being put in without consent, or where the service user is at risk of serious and immediate harm if the services are not provided, but refuses to have the services if he or she is charged for them.

12.108   The 1996 Good Practice Handbook states (at page 29) that 'the principle that service users should be enabled to seek independent advice and advocacy is one which needs to underpin any charging policy or procedure'. The Local Government Ombudsman has specifically criticised the lack of proper advocacy assistance to appellants during the appeals process.[81]

The consequences of non-payment

12.109 Where the community care service is provided by the authority in consequence of a statutory duty (for instance under Chronically Sick and Disabled Persons Act (CSDPA) 1970 s2), then the service cannot as a matter of law be withdrawn merely because the service user is refusing to pay for it. The Ombudsman has held, accordingly, that it is maladministration to allow a person to terminate their care services due to an inability to pay for

79 The omission of HASSASSA Act 1983 s17 from the list of social services 'functions' in LASSA 1970 Sch 1 was rectified via Care Standards Act 2000 s112; see also the 1990 Policy Guidance para 6.5.

80 Complaints Nos 90A/2675, 2075, 1705, 1228 and 1172 against Essex (1990).

81 Complaint Nos 98/C/0911, 1166, 1975, 1977 and 1978 against Stockton-on Tees Borough Council, 29 July 1999.

them, without advising that social services cannot withdraw services for non-payment.[82]

12.110　　The 1990 policy guidance extends this principle to all services, stating 'the provision of services, whether or not the local authority is under a duty to make provision, should not be related to the ability of the service user or their families to meet the costs . . . The assessment of financial means should, therefore, follow the assessment of need and decisions about service provision' (at para 3.31). In this respect the 1994 SSI guidance states, 'once someone has been assessed as needing a service, that service should not be withdrawn even if he or she refuses to pay the charge required. The authority should continue provision of the service while pursuing the debt, if necessary, through the magistrates' court' (at para 26).

12.111　　HASSASSAA 1983 s17(4) states that any charge levied 'may, without prejudice to any other method of recovery, be recovered summarily as a civil debt'. The use of the phrase 'summarily as a civil debt' is a reference to Magistrates' Courts Act 1980 s58(1). In principle it appears undesirable that such a procedure (normally reserved for the collection of overdue local taxes such as council tax) be used to collect such monies. A far more appropriate course would be the use of the small claims system in the county courts. It is unclear whether local authorities are able to use this option, although, as the magistrates' procedure is expressed as being 'without prejudice to any other method', it would in principle appear to be a possibility.[83] The advantage of the county court process is that the case will be considered by a judge familiar with such civil concepts of lack of mental capacity and its legal consequences (a problem which is frequently an issue with frail service users) and the civil courts have greater expertise in determining realistic debt repayment arrangements.

Charging for direct payments

12.112　The policy intention underlying the direct payments scheme (more generally considered at para 9.5 above) is that recipients be subject to the same charging regime as that which applies to other service users. Accordingly the 2003 Fairer Charging policy guidance (at para 87) advises:

> In considering whether, and if so how, to ask an individual to make a financial contribution to the cost of their care package, councils should treat people receiving direct payments as they would have treated them under the council's charging policy, if those people were receiving the equivalent services. Charges should be assessed and made in all respects in accordance with this guidance.

12.113　The legislative framework for direct payments adopts therefore the same phrasing as HASSASSAA 1983 s17. In England[84] the relevant provision is

---

82　Complaint No 99/C/1983 against Durham, 9 October 2000.

83　In *Avon CC v Hooper* (1998) 1 CCLR 366 – the proceedings took place in the High Court and the jurisdictional issue does not appear to have been raised.

84　In Wales the charging regime is still regulated by Community Care (Direct Payments) Act 1996 s1(2) which also adopts the same phrasing as HASSASSAA 1983 s17.

regulation 5 of the Community Care, Services for Carers and Children's Services (Direct Payments) (England) Regulations 2003,[85] which provides:

(1) Subject to paragraphs (3) and (4), a direct payment shall be made as a gross payment unless the responsible authority decide it shall be made as a net payment.

(2) For the purpose of making the payment referred to in paragraph (1), the responsible authority shall determine, having regard to the prescribed person's means, what amount or amounts (if any) it is reasonably practicable for him to pay towards securing the provision of the relevant service (whether by way of reimbursement as mentioned in section 57(4) of the 2001 Act or by way of a contribution as mentioned in section 57(5) of that Act).

(3) Where the relevant service is one which, apart from these Regulations, would be provided under section 117 of the 1983 Act (after-care) –
  (a) the payment shall be made at the rate mentioned in subsection (4)(a) of section 57 of the 2001 Act; and
  (b) subsection (4)(b) of that section shall not apply.

(4) Where a direct payment is made to a person falling within section 17A(5) of the 1989 Act –
  (a) the payment shall be made at the rate mentioned in subsection (4)(a) of section 57 of the 2001 Act; and
  (b) subsection (4)(b) of that section shall not apply.

(5) A direct payment may be paid to –
  (a) the prescribed person who falls within section 57(2) of the 2001 Act or section 17A(2) of the 1989 Act (as the case may be), or
  (b) a person nominated by the prescribed person to receive the payment on his behalf.

Services not directly provided by the social services authority

12.114　While the principles of charging for community care services are relatively straightforward in relation to services provided by a social services authority, they become relatively complex in the case of jointly supplied services, such as those provided by a jointly funded NHS/social services arrangement.[86] In this respect the 2003 Fairer Charging policy guidance advises:

> **Use of powers to transfer funds**
> 88. Local councils and health authorities may jointly commission social care services under section 28A of the NHS Act 1977. The details of any charges should be devised with advice from the local council's own lawyers. The council may recover from users up to the full cost of the social care service, even though the NHS may have met some or all of the cost of the social care service. Local councils must, however, bear in mind that section 17 of the HASSASSAA 1983 is not a provision designed to enable them to raise general revenue. If a council purchases social care and a health authority purchases health care services from the same

85　SI No 762.

86　As noted at para 10.197 in England the Health Act 1999 enables the social services charging function to be transferred to the NHS as part of a partnership scheme – the NHS Bodies and Local Authorities Partnership Arrangements (Amendment) (England) Regulations 2003 SI No 629.

provider, then charges to users may only be made for the social care element. Any services for which the NHS has underlying responsibility are automatically free at the point of use,[87] in whatever setting they are provided and whichever agencies provide or commission the service in practice.

Health Act 1999 partnerships

89. The Health Act 1999 did not alter the local authority powers to charge in the event of a partnership arrangement. In agreeing partnership arrangements, agencies will have to consider how best to manage charging (where local councils charge for services) and how to clarify the difference between charged-for and non-charged for services. There is no intention to increase or expand charging arrangements through the Partnership Arrangements. In entering into an arrangement, the partners will need to agree on the approach to be taken on charging.

90. Partners will need to bear in mind that, where charging is retained, the arrangements will need to be carefully explained to users of services, to avoid any misunderstanding that NHS services are being charged for, especially when an NHS Trust is providing a service, part of which is being charged for. It will be critical that charging arrangements are properly explained at the outset of the assessment process. See section XIX below. The existing charging review or appeals mechanisms should be made clear to the user.

91. The NHS Plan makes clear (in the Government's response to the Royal Commission on Long Term Care) that community equipment services should be integrated across health and social services by 2004, using the partnership flexibilities in the Health Act, 1999. Local councils will retain the right to charge for providing disability equipment, but will need to consider the cost-effectiveness of doing so within the new integrated community equipment services.

Intermediate care

92. Separate guidance has been issued about charging arrangements for intermediate care in HSC 2001/01; LAC 2001/01. Councils should have regard to that guidance where a time-limited package of intermediate care includes the provision of non-residential social services. In summary, HSC 2001/01; LAC/2001/01 requires that non-residential social services which are an integral part of a time-limited package of intermediate care, as defined in the circular, should be free at the point of use.

Charging for Mental Health Act 1983 services

12.115 Authorities are only empowered to charge for the community care services listed in HASSASSAA 1983 s17(2). This list does not mention the Mental Health Act (MHA) 1983.

---

87 Other than services for which specific charging powers exist, such as NHS prescription charges.

Services under MHA 1983 s117

12.116 In *R v Manchester CC ex p Stennett and others*[88] the House of Lords held that it was unlawful for local authorities to charge for services under MHA 1983 s117. The implications of this judgment are considered in further detail at para 15.34 below.

Guardianship under MHA 1983 s7

12.117 MHA 1983 ss7–9 of the 1983 Act provide for the making of Guardianship Orders and for the powers of Guardians. They do not however authorise or require the provision of any services. Accordingly where residential or domiciliary care services are provided for a person the subject of a Guardianship Order, these services are made available under other statutory provisions (ie, NAA 1948 s21, CSDPA 1970 s2, MHA 1983 s117, etc). Whether or not a charge can be levied for such a service depends, of course, upon whether charging is permitted under the statute in question. Thus if the user was formerly detained under MHA 1983 s3 or one of the criminal provisions of the 1983 Act, services will be provided under MHA 1983 s117 for which services a charge can not be made.

12.118 The Department of Health has expressed the opinion[89] that the right to free services under MHA 1983 s117 also applies to Guardianship. Most probably the Department was referring to Guardianship under MHA 1983 s19 (considered below), although it might be that the advice addresses the more general issue of the human rights predicament of users who are required by their guardian to live (against their wishes) at a residential or nursing home.

12.119 Such persons have no choice but to live at a specified address, and while this may not amount to a form of detention, it is clearly an infringement of the right to choose the type of home they live in. If the state is requiring them to live in more expensive accommodation (a registered care or nursing home rather than rented accommodation) then the added requirement that they pay the additional cost may be a violation of their rights under the European Convention on Human Rights to respect for their home (article 8) in combination with article 14 (non-discrimination). Some support for this line of reasoning was provided by the comments of Lord Steyn in the *ex p Stennett* judgment – which are considered at para 4.120 above.

12.120 Where however the guardianship order is pursuant to MHA 1983 s19, then, since the patient is in such circumstances also entitled to MHA 1983 s117 services, it follows that these services must be provided without charge to the user.

---

88 [2002] UKHL 34; [2002] 3 WLR 584; [2002] 4 All ER 124; (2002) 5 CCLR 500.

89 In a letter of 18 January 1995 to Oldham Social Services. The letter states that 'until recently it had been assumed that local authorities could use an implied power to charge based upon Local Government Act 1972 s111, if they wished to charge for any services where they had no express power to charge. Following the decision in *R v Richmond LBC ex p McCarthy* [1992] 2 AC 48, it is now clear that this is not the case . . .'

Charging for Chronically Sick and Disabled Persons Act 1970 s2 services

12.121   Notwithstanding that CSDPA 1970 s2 services are not listed in HASSASSAA 1983 s17(2), the 1994 SSI guidance advised that charges could be recovered for services provided under that section, as 'these services are arranged by local authorities in exercise of their functions under s29 of the 1948 Act'. This advice was upheld by the Court of Appeal, in *R v Powys CC ex p Hambidge*.[90] The relationship between CSDPA 1970 s2 and NAA 1948 s29 is however a difficult one. While the Court of Appeal decision confirms that local authorities are acting lawfully when they charge adults for the services they provide under CSDPA 1970 s2, the judgment does not address the problem of the different client groups covered by the two sections. If services, assessed as being necessary under section 2, are actually provided 'in exercise of functions under section 29', it begs the question of the authority for providing disabled children with such services; NAA 1948 s29 only applies to persons aged 18 or over. This question is considered at para 8.122 above.

90   (1998) 1 CCLR 458.

Charging for Chronically Ill and Disabled Persons Act 1970 Service

CHAPTER 13

Learning disability and mental capacity

Introduction

13.1   It is estimated that there are about 210,000 people with severe learning disabilities in England, and about 1.2 million with a mild or moderate disability. Annual health and social services expenditure on services for adults with learning disabilities amounts to approximately £3 billion.[1]

13.2   People with learning disabilities come within the definition of a 'disabled person' (see para 8.21 above) for the purposes of the primary community care statutes (ie, National Assistance Act (NAA) 1948 s21 and Chronically Sick and Disabled Persons Act (CSDPA) 1970 s2) as well as the Disability Discrimination Act 1995. It follows that they have an equal right to services under these statutes and that any difference in treatment, based upon a categorisation of 'learning disability', will require justification under the 1995 Act.

13.3   The service provision needs of people with learning disabilities are such that in a number of situations policy and practice guidance singles them out for specific mention. This can be seen, for instance, in relation to the obligations on the NHS to fund long-term support arrangements (see para 10.89) and in relation to the 'less dependent residents' provisions that apply to some people with learning disabilities receiving services under NAA 1948 s21 (see para 12.71).

13.4   In 2001 the Department of Health[2] published the white paper, *Valuing People: A New Strategy for Learning Disability for the 21st Century*,[3] which promised a number of new policy initiatives[4] concerning the rights of people with learning disabilities and undertook to ensure that four key principles would underpin all new proposals: 'Rights, Independence, Choice and Inclusion'.

13.5   In large measure the white paper sought to ensure that existing schemes (such as the Quality Protects programme,[5] the Schools Access Initiative

---

1   *Valuing People: A New Strategy for Learning Disability for the 21st Century*, p2; White Paper Secretary of State for Health, March 2001, Cm 5086.

2   No equivalent paper has been published in Wales. There is however an emerging programme being developed by the Learning Disability Advisory Group (whose reports can be accessed at www.wales.gov.uk/subisocialpolicy/topics-e.htm#learn); see also in this respect the report *Fulfilling the Promises* (2001) produced by All Wales People First and obtainable from Mencap Cymru, 31 Lambourne Crescent, Cardiff Business Park, Llanishen, Cardiff CF14 5GF.

3   March 2001, Cm 5086.

4   Including a new 'Learning Disability Development Fund' of £50 million per annum to support (among other things) the modernisation of day centres, enabling people to move from long-stay hospitals into the community, developing supported living schemes and specialist local services for people with severe challenging behaviour and developing integrated facilities for children with severe disabilities and complex needs. Additionally an 'Implementation Support Fund' of £2.3 million a year to fund advocacy programmes, a national information centre and help line.

5   The programme seeks to tackle the social exclusion of children looked after by councils; children in the child protection system; and other children in need – details at www.children.doh.gov.uk/qualityprotects/info/speeches/990607jh.htm.

and the Connexions Service)[6] were sensitive to the needs of people with learning disabilities.[7] It additionally committed the government to take measures to increase the potential for people with learning disabilities benefiting from direct payments, and improving their access to advocacy services.

13.6 The white paper proposed the development within each local authority area of Learning Disability Partnership Boards whose responsibility it would be to implement the adult aspects of the programme. Policy guidance in 2001[8] outlined the composition and responsibilities of these boards. This has since been followed up by more detailed practice guidance on implementation.[9]

Person-centred planning

13.7 A key phrase emerging from the white paper is that of a 'person-centred approach' to the needs of people with learning disabilities to enable them 'to have as much choice and control as possible over their lives'.

13.8 The need for such an approach is explained in at para 4.1 of the white paper in the following terms:

> People with learning disabilities currently have little control over their own lives, though almost all, including the most severely disabled, are capable of making choices and expressing their views and preferences. The current problems are:
> - services have been too slow to recognise that people with learning disabilities have rights like other citizens;
> - provision of advocacy services is patchy;
> - people with learning disabilities have little involvement in decision making;
> - few people with learning disabilities receive direct payments;
> - people with learning disabilities and their families are not central to the planning process;
> - not enough effort to communicate with people with learning disabilities in accessible ways.

6 The Connexions service offers a range of guidance and support for 13 to 19-year-olds to help make the transition to adult life a smooth one – details at www.connexions.gov.uk/partnerships/.

7 This aims to make mainstream schools more accessible to children with disabilities and special educational needs – details at www.teachernet.gov.uk/management/sen/schools/accessibility/sai/.

8 *Valuing People: a New Strategy for Learning Disability for the 21st Century: Implementation Guidance* HSC 2001/016; LAC(2001)23 (policy guidance for the purposes of LASSA 1970 s7 (see para 1.30 above)).

9 See generally the documentation at the Department of Health website accessible at www.dh.gov.uk/PolicyAndGuidance/HealthAndSocialCareTopics/LearningDisabilities/fs/en including *Planning with People Towards Person-centred Approaches – Guidance For Partnership Boards* December 2001; *Guidance For Implementation Groups and Planning with People Towards Person-centred Approaches – Guidance For Partnership Boards* December 2001.

13.9   Follow-up 2001 practice guidance[10] stipulated that the development of a person-centred approach in organisational cultures and practice was a priority for Partnership Boards who were required to produce a framework for implementation of this approach by April 2002. The guidance defined 'person-centred planning' as:[11]

> ... a *process* for continual listening and learning, focused on what is important to someone now and for the future, and acting upon this in alliance with family and friends. This listening and learning is used to understand a person's capacities and choices. Person-centred planning is a basis for problem solving and negotiation to mobilise the resources necessary to pursue the person's aspirations. These resources may be obtained from a person's personal network, from service agencies or from a range of non-specialist and non-service sources.

13.10   Although it has now become common to refer to the care plans for people with learning disabilities as 'Person-Centred Plans' – this is a misnomer. As the 2001 guidance explains:[12]

> Person-centred planning is not the same as assessment and care planning under section 47 of the National Health Service and Community Care Act 1990. Assessment and care planning should, however be undertaken using person-centred approaches and is greatly assisted by person-centred planning undertaken independently of it. Where services are required, formal assessment might well be triggered by person-centred planning. [Neither is it] the same as reviews of service provision. Person-centred planning should, however, make a significant contribution to reviews, ensuring that they are based on what matters to a person from their own perspective.

Advocacy and learning disability services

13.11   Independent advocacy services exist in most parts of England and Wales and have many different names and functions.[13] Broadly, however they can be divided into the following two general categories:

Citizen advocacy

13.12   Citizen advocacy involves the advocate developing a longer term relationship with the disabled person.[14] It is a form of advocacy where 'an ordinary citizen develops a relationship with another person who risks social exclu-

---

10 *Planning with People Towards Person-centred Approaches – Guidance For Partnership Boards* December 2001 (see note 9 above).

11 *Planning with People Towards Person-centred Approaches – Guidance For Partnership Boards* p2.

12 *Planning with People Towards Person-centred Approaches – Guidance For Partnership Boards* p4.

13 For a review of the role of advocacy see R Henderson and M Pochin, *A Right Result?* (Policy Press, 2001).

14 See for instance Dunning, *A Citizen Advocacy with Older People: a Code of Good Practice* (CPA, 1995).

sion or other unfair treatment because of a handicap. As the relationship develops, the advocate chooses ways to understand, respond to, and represent the other person's interests as if they were the advocate's own'.[15]

Crisis advocacy

13.13 Crisis advocacy is generally concerned with short-term interventions, most commonly in relation to a dispute or complaint. The following sections are primarily concerned with the provision of this form of advocacy support.

13.14 While the white paper 'Valuing People'[16] acknowledged that effective advocacy, including self-advocacy, had the ability to transform the lives of people with learning disabilities, it cautioned that:

> . . . both citizen advocacy and self-advocacy are unevenly developed across the country. Barriers to future development include: insecure funding; limited support for local groups; and potential for conflicts of interest with statutory agencies who provide funding. This must change.

13.15 In order to address the problem it committed the government to the (long-term) aim of 'developing a range of independent advocacy services available in each area so that people with learning disabilities can choose the one which best meets their needs' (para 4.9) and to invest £1.3 million per annum (until 2005) to establish 'a National Citizen Advocacy Network and to promote self-advocacy, both in partnership with the voluntary sector'; the aim being to ensure the establishment of at least one citizen advocacy group in each local authority area (para 4.9). Advocacy arrangements were accordingly made a high priority for the new Learning Disability Partnership Boards.[17]

Mental incapacity

13.16 The present state of our domestic law concerning the decision-making powers of third parties on behalf of people who lack the necessary mental capacity, is highly confused and inadequate. Substantial proposals for reform have been made and these are considered at para 13.69 below.

13.17 All adults are presumed to be capable of handling their own affairs unless the contrary is shown. The standard of proof is 'the balance of probabilities'. The fact that (for instance) a person has been detained under the Mental Health Act (MHA) 1983 does not affect this presumption.[18] In the

---

15 See B Sang and J O'Brien, *Advocacy: the United Kingdom and American experiences,* King's Fund Project paper No 51, 1984, p27.

16 *Valuing People: A New Strategy for Learning Disability for the 21st Century* para 4.7; Secretary of State for Health, March 2001, Cm 5086.

17 See LAC(2001) 23 para 27

18 The Mental Health Act 1983 is not primarily concerned with the needs of vulnerable adults: the central provision of the 1983 Act concern the detention and treatment of 'mentally disordered' persons. Part VII of the Act, however, concerns the power of the Court of Protection to manage the affairs of persons deemed 'incapable, by virtue of mental disorder, of managing and administering' their property (MHA 1983 s94(2)).

absence of proof to the contrary, such a person is assumed to retain their capacity to make informed decisions. Where an adult is deemed incapable of making an informed decision concerning a particular question, then a variety of legal provisions can apply.

13.18   The Court of Appeal in *Re MB (Caesarean section)*[19] defined incapacity (in the context of a medical treatment decision) as follows:

> A person lacks capacity if some impairment or disturbance of mental functioning renders the person unable to make a decision whether to consent to or refuse treatment. That will occur when:
>
> (a) the patient is unable to comprehend and retain information which is material to the decision, especially as to the likely consequences of having or not having the treatment in question;
>
> (b) the patient is unable to use the information and weigh it in the balance as part of the process of arriving at the decision.

13.19   The 'best interests' to be served by the intervention are those of the incapacitated person's alone. Thus in *Re Y (Mental incapacity: bone marrow transplant)*[20] the court held that the fact that the donation of bone marrow by a mentally incompetent woman to her sister could save the sister's life, was not relevant unless as a result of that donation the best interests of the donor were served. In relation to such medical treatment cases, permission for treatment will only be given by the court when the necessity for the treatment has been established 'convincingly'. This does not necessarily require a unanimity of view on the question in issue.[21]

The assessment of legal capacity

13.20   Whether, as a matter of law, a person has sufficient mental capacity to make a decision depends upon the decision that has to be made. Thus a person may have sufficient mental capacity to buy some clothes but insufficient to purchase a house. In the former case the issue is straight forward whereas in the latter the size and implications of the transaction (including the consequent legal responsibilities of a home owner) demand a greater comprehension. The legal principle has been expressed as follows:[22]

> . . . the mental capacity required by the law . . . is relative to the particular transaction which is being effected . . . and may be described as the capacity to understand the nature of that transaction when it is explained.

13.21   The legal test of capacity thus focuses on the issue of understanding and not the ability to make prudent or wise decisions,[23] or indeed the ability to personally comprehend the fine detail of the choice or question in issue.

19 [1997] 2 FLR 426; [1997] FCR 541; (1998) 38 BMLR 175.
20 [1997] 2 FCR 172.
21 *R v Dr M and others ex p N* [2002] EWCA Civ 1789; [2003] 1 WLR 562.
22 *Re Beaney (Deceased)* [1978] 1 WLR 770 at 774D; [1978] 2 All ER 595.
23 *Masterman-Lister v Jewell* [2002] EWCA Civ 1889 at [46]; (2004) 7 CCLR 5.

13.22   *White v Fell*[24] concerned the capacity of a disabled person to agree settlement terms in court proceedings. Boreham J considered that the assessment of capacity should be construed in a common sense way and observed:

> I have no doubt that the plaintiff is quite incapable of managing unaided a large sum of money such as the sort of sum that would be appropriate compensation for her injuries. That, however, is not conclusive. Few people have the capacity to manage all their affairs unaided . . . It may be that she would have chosen, and would choose now, not to take advice, but that is not the question. The question is: is she capable of doing so? To have that capacity she requires first the insight and understanding of the fact that she has a problem in respect of which she needs advice . . . Secondly, having identified the problem, it will be necessary for her to seek an appropriate adviser and to instruct him with sufficient clarity to enable him to understand the problem and to advise her appropriately . . . Finally, she needs sufficient mental capacity to understand and to make decisions based upon, or otherwise give effect to, such advice as she may receive.

In the judge's opinion it followed that:

> . . . the court should only take over the individual's function of decision making when it is shown on the balance of probabilities that such person does not have the capacity sufficiently to understand, absorb and retain information (including advice) relevant to the matters in question sufficiently to enable him or her to make decisions based upon such information.

13.23   Such a formulation of the legal position can have unusual consequences. *Re K (Enduring Powers of Attorney)*[25] concerned a refusal by the Court of Protection to register an enduring power of attorney. Within a few days of the power being signed, the attorney applied for its registration. The court initially refused to agree to the registration – on the basis that the short period between the signing and the registration suggested that the person lacked mental capacity at the time the document was signed. Allowing the appeal Hoffmann J held that there was no logical reason why a person who understood that something needed to be done, but who lacked the requisite understanding to do it personally, should not confer on another the power to do what needs to be done.[26] Accordingly, a person may have insufficient mental capacity to manage his or her affairs, but sufficient capacity to delegate this function to an attorney.

13.24   Where an issue arises as to the sufficiency of a person's mental capacity, the courts will almost invariably require medical evidence, although ultimately the decision is a legal one.[27] In this respect, Denzil Lush has

---

24 12 November 1987 (unreported), cited in *Masterman-Lister v Jewell* [2002] EWCA Civ 1889 at [18]–[20]; [2003] WLR 1511; (2004) 7 CCLR 5.

25 [1988] Ch 310.

26 [1988] Ch 310 at 315B–C; see also Chadwick LJ in *Masterman-Lister v Jewell* [2002] EWCA Civ 1889 at [83]; [2003] WLR 1511; [2003] 3 All ER 162; (2004) 7 CCLR 5.

27 *Masterman-Lister v Jewell* [2002] EWCA Civ 1889 at [34] and *Richmond v Richmond* (1914) 111 LT 273 at 274.

observed that[28] 'although the court attaches a great deal of weight to the evidence of a registered medical practitioner on questions of incapacity, it does not automatically prefer medical opinion to lay opinion'.[29]

13.25   Medical evidence will be of limited value unless it is demonstrated that the expert was aware of the relevant legal test for capacity – what it was that the person was required to comprehend. The courts have provided guidance on a wide range of capacity decisions (eg, the capacity to make a will; to marry; to have sexual relations; to vote; to make a gift; to litigate; to consent to medical treatment – and so on) and an analysis on the relevant criteria has been given by the British Medical Association and the Law Society.[30]

Decisions concerning 'property and affairs'

13.26 If a decision has to be made on behalf of a person who lacks mental capacity and that decision relates to the person's 'property' or 'affairs', then legal mechanisms such as Enduring Powers of Attorney or the Court of Protection are available. In this context however, the words 'property' and 'affairs' have been given a restrictive interpretation and in effect are limited to issues concerning 'business matters, legal transactions and other dealings of a similar kind'.[31]

13.27   Accordingly where the issue does not concern the 'property or affairs' of an adult, (for instance a decision has to be made where the person lives, or whether contact should be allowed with a third party) then the law is significantly deficient. If guardianship is not available, then generally all that can legally be done is to invoke the inherent jurisdiction of the High Court (considered below).

The Court of Protection

13.28 The Court of Protection is an Office of the Supreme Court governed by MHA 1983 Part VII. The court has power to 'do or secure the doing of all such things as appear necessary or expedient' concerning persons who lack mental capacity. The court can however only take action in relation to a person's property and affairs, and only after it has been satisfied (after considering medical evidence) of the necessary mental incapacity. The court can in particular take action:

28 'Elderly Clients' by Denzil Lush (Master of the Court of Protection) Jordans, 1996, p38 – including the following note.

29 In this respect, Denzil Lush states (at p38) 'see the discussion in *Birkin v Wing* (1890) 63 LT 80, at pp83 and 84, in which Kekewich J preferred the evidence of a solicitor as to his client's contractual capacity to a doctor's evidence alleging incapacity. In a Canadian case, *Re Price* [1994] 2 DLR 592, at p595, Laidlaw J stated that a judgment as to capacity 'is a practical question which may be answered by a layman of good sense with as much authority as a doctor'.

30 Assessment of mental capacity: guidance to doctors and lawyers (1995). A joint report by the BMA and Law Society, published and available from the BMA – currently being revised and updated.

31 *Re F (mental patient: sterilisation)* [1990] 2 AC 1, per Lord Brandon at 59E–H.

1) for the maintenance or other benefit of the patient;
2) for the maintenance or other benefit of the patient's family;
3) for making provision for other persons or purposes for whom or which the patient might be expected to provide if he were not mentally disordered, or;
4) otherwise, for administering the patient's affairs (MHA 1983 s95).

13.29   Generally the court will do this by appointing a 'receiver', although in certain situations, this is not necessary, for instance when the patient's only assets consist of:

1) social security benefits;
2) a pension or similar payment from a government department or local authority;
3) entitlement under a discretionary trust;
4) property which does not exceed £16,000 in value and there is no property to be sold. In such cases 'short order' can be made avoiding the necessity of a receiver. A short order may authorise the applicant to:
    - receive pensions or trust income;
    - receive some or all of the client's money that is held in bank or building society accounts;
    - pay nursing home fees or other charges, debts, expenses and any solicitor's costs; and
    - make sure documents and valuables, such as furniture and jewellery, are safely looked after.

13.30   Where a receivership order has been made, the incapacitated person is generally referred to as a 'patient' of the Court of Protection. A separate administrative agency exists to manage (or supervise the management of) the affairs of patients, known as the Public Guardianship Office.[32]

Powers of attorney

General powers

13.31   Individuals have always had the power to appoint another person to act as their agent in respect of their financial affairs. The so called 'power of attorney' may be in general terms (allowing the attorney to do anything that the 'donor' could do) or limited to specific acts (for instance, signing a contract for the sale of land). The law regulating such powers is presently contained in the Powers of Attorney Act 1971.

13.32   An ordinary power of attorney only authorises the attorney to do what the donor of the power could do; it follows that if the donor ceases to have mental capacity, then the attorney's authority also ceases.

---

32   Archway Tower, 2 Junction Road, London N19 5SZ; Tel 0845 330 2900; email: custserv@guardianship.gov.uk; Internet: www.guardianship.gov.uk; DX 141150 Archway 2.

Enduring powers

13.33   The Enduring Powers of Attorney Act 1985 enables an attorney to be appointed whose powers continue even after the donor has become mentally incapable.

13.34   As noted above, in *Re K (Enduring Powers of Attorney)*[33] it was held that only limited mental capacity is required in order to execute an enduring power of attorney. In the judge's opinion the donor needs to understand:[34]

> First (if such be the terms of the power) that the attorney will be able to assume complete authority over the donors affairs. Secondly (if such be the terms of the power) that the attorney will in general be able to do anything with the donors property which he himself could have done. Thirdly, that the authority will continue if the donor should be or become mentally incapable. Fourthly, that if he should be or become mentally incapable, the power will be irrevocable without confirmation by the court.

13.35   The procedure for creating such powers is straightforward. A pre-printed form is completed and signed by the donor and each attorney (their signatures are witnessed). The power can come into force immediately or once the donor loses his or her mental capacity.

13.36   The attorney is under a duty to apply to the Public Guardianship Office as soon as he or she has reason to believe that the donor is (or is becoming) mentally incapable. Before applying, the attorney must give notice of the intention to apply for registration of the enduring power, to the donor, the donor's relatives and any 'co-attorney'. At least three relatives must receive the notice (and the Act states the priority of relative). People served with these notices have the power to object to registration. Failing an objection, the registration takes effect (within about five weeks).

13.37   Attorneys acting under an enduring power are only authorised to make decisions concerning the donor's property and affairs. As noted above, they lack the power to make decisions on associated issues such as arrangements about health care matters or, where the person should live or with whom they should have contact, etc.

Social security agents and appointees

13.38   Social security claimants are able to nominate a person to collect their benefits for them when they are unable, due to illness or other circumstances, to collect the benefits personally. In such cases the person collecting the benefit is simply acting as an 'agent' for the claimant. Such agency arrangements can however only occur in respect of claimants who have the requisite mental capacity to manage their social security monies.

13.39   Social Security (Claims and Payments) Regulations 1987[35] reg 33 allows

---

33   [1988] Ch 310.
34   *Re K (Enduring Powers of Attorney)* [1988] Ch 310 at 316D–F.
35   SI No 1968.

for an appointee to be appointed where the claimant is 'unable for the time being to act'. The Department of Work and Pensions is the responsible authority for the appointment, supervision and revocation of appointee-ships. The appointee is personally responsible for ensuring that the social security monies are applied in the patient's interests.[36]

13.40 Standard 35 of the National Minimum Standards for Care Homes for Older People[37] states that the registered manager of a care home may only be appointed as agent for a service user where no other individual is available. In such cases the manager must ensure that the registration authority is notified of this arrangement and that records are kept of all incoming and outgoing payments. Additionally, if the manager is an appointee for social security purposes the [relevant social security office] must be notified. Age Concern has stated that 'although the home proprietor may be prepared to manage an individual's financial affairs and large groups of homes may have a specific Finance Department, it should be remembered that no available guidance recommends this. It should therefore be considered only as a last resort, and all the parties involved must ensure that the appropriate safeguards are observed'.[38]

13.41 Concern has also been expressed about the lack of protection for people subject to an appointeeship order[39] including the lack of any adequate appeal provision. At present all that an individual can do in such cases is to request that the secretary of state exercise his discretion to revoke such an order. It is arguable that this state of affairs conflicts with article 6(1) of the European Convention on Human Rights.

Guardianship

13.42 MHA 1983 s7 provides for the making of a guardianship order in relation to mentally disordered people (aged 16 or over) where 'it is necessary in the interests of the welfare of the patient or for the protection of other persons that'[40] such an order be made. It follows that mental incapacity is not a necessary pre-requisite for the making of a guardianship order. Where however the person has a learning disability, guardianship is not available unless the disability is associated with 'abnormally aggressive or seriously irresponsible conduct'.[41] In *Re F (Mental Health Act: Guardianship)*[42] the

---

36 See CIS/12022/96 which concerned an appointee's failure to notify the DSS about an increase in the disabled person's savings; the consequent over-payment was held to be recoverable from the appointee in addition to the claimant.

37 Department of Health, March 2001 issued under the Care Standards Act 2000 s23(1) (see para 7.69 above).

38 'Residents' Money', Age concern, 1996.

39 See for instance the Parliamentary Ombudsman annual report of July 2003 (Session 2002–2003; 5th report) case reference C1560/02 at http://www.ombudsman.org.uk/pca/document/par03/par03_c3.htm.

40 MHA 1983 s7(2)(b).

41 MHA 1983 ss7(2)(a) and 1(2).

42 [2000] 1 FLR 192.

Court of Appeal approved the Law Commission's interpretation of this requirement – that 'unless the meaning of these words is distorted, the vast majority of those with a learning disability (mental handicap) will be excluded from guardianship'.[43]

13.43   Under MHA 1983 s8 the guardian (normally a social services department) has three specific powers, namely:

1) the power to require the patient to reside at a place specified;
2) the power to require the patient to attend at places for medical treatment, occupation, education or training and;
3) the power to require access to the patient to be given.

Adult protection

13.44   In 2000 guidance was issued by both the Department of Health (*No Secrets*)[44] and the Welsh Assembly (*In Safe Hands*)[45] concerning the procedures local authorities should adopt to monitor and respond to concerns about adult abuse. The guidance is however process-orientated and contains no new powers to enable local authorities to protect the victims of abuse (short of criminal prosecution)[46] concentrating instead upon such issues as:

- the clarification of the roles and responsibilities of the relevant agencies (eg, social services, the police, NHS bodies);
- the development of multi-disciplinary procedures for responding to concerns and referrals, including joint protocols on such issues as information sharing;
- contract monitoring with independent providers;
- improvements to information for service users, carers and members of the public; and
- the development of monitoring systems and training strategies.

13.45   These processes, valuable as they may be,[47] are no substitute for a statutory

---

43 Law Commission report, Mental Incapacity (1995 Law Comm No 231) para 2.21.

44 Department of Health and the Home Office (2000) No Secrets: Guidance on developing and implementing multi-agency policies and procedures to protect vulnerable adults from abuse.

45 National Assembly for Wales (2000) 'In Safe Hands'.

46 In addition to the ordinary criminal investigative powers of the police, powers exist under the Mental Health Act 1983 enabling a magistrate to issue a warrant to authorise access by a police officer to premises where it is believed that a person suffering from a mental disorder is being ill-treated or neglected (MHA 1983 s135): such a warrant may also include a power of removal. Under MHA 1983 s127 it is an offence for anyone to (among other things) ill-treat or wilfully neglect a mentally disordered person who is in their custody or care. Local authorities also have limited powers under NAA 1948 s47 to remove vulnerable people who are not receiving proper care (see para 7.101 above).

47 There is indeed evidence to suggest that even the guidance has not been effectively implemented by social services – D Mathew, P Brown, C McCreadie, J Askham, 'The response to No Secrets' *The Journal of Adult Protection*, Vol 4, 1 (2002).

regime[48] that enables social services (where material evidence of abuse exists) to gain access to and effectively protect vulnerable adults.

The POVA list

13.46   The Care Standards Act 2000 provided for the establishment of a set of controls to prevent unsuitable persons from working with vulnerable adults in England and Wales. The controls revolve around the establishment of a list of persons who have been found to be unsuitable to work with vulnerable adults (the protection of vulnerable adults ('POVA') list). The Department of Health plans to partially implement these controls on 7 June 2004. In the first instance, the controls will only apply to persons working for, or providing, care homes and domiciliary care agencies (agencies supplying personal care to people in their own homes), including those provided by local authorities.[49]

Vulnerable witnesses

13.47   The report *Speaking Up For Justice* (Home Office, 1998) made a number of recommendations for encouraging and supporting vulnerable or intimidated witnesses to give their best evidence in criminal cases. Many of its provisions were enacted in the Youth Justice and Criminal Evidence Act 1999 Part II including the right of vulnerable witnesses to have the assistance of an intermediary when being interviewed or giving evidence (section 29). More detailed guidance is now provided in the January 2002, the Home Office Report 'Achieving Best Evidence: the interviewing of vulnerable and intimidated witnesses (including children) involved in criminal proceedings'.[50]

The High Court's inherent jurisdiction

13.48   The procedures outlined above, provide some protection for people who are deemed to lack the requisite degree of mental capacity. Where a person's property or financial affairs require protecting, then various mechanisms exist, including ultimately the Court of Protection. Where the protection that is required is personal rather than financial, then apart from the very limited scope of guardianship (limited in terms of the range of powers it provides and the range of people to whom it applies) there exist no formal statutory arrangements for the protection of vulnerable adults.

13.49   The failure of the law to address this issue has become more urgent with the enactment of the Human Rights Act (HRA) 1998. In *Z and others*

---

48   With the exception of guardianship powers – but these, as noted in para 13.42 above, apply to only a restricted range of people.

49   The proposals can be accessed at www.doh.gov.uk/vulnerableadults/index.htm.

50   Accessible at www.homeoffice.gov.uk/justice/legalprocess/witnesses/index.html, see also K Stone, Voice Box Community Care, 20–26 November 2003 p421.

v United Kingdom[51] the European Court of Human Rights found that there had been a violation of European Convention on Human Rights (ECHR) art 3 (degrading treatment) because a local authority 'had been aware of the serious ill-treatment . . . over a period of years . . . and failed to take any effective steps to bring it to an end'. In so deciding, the Court stated that the obligation under the ECHR (arts 1 and 3) required states:

> . . . to take measures designed to ensure that individuals . . . are not subjected to . . . degrading treatment . . . [which measures should] . . . provide effective protection, in particular, of children and other vulnerable persons and include reasonable steps to prevent ill-treatment of which the authorities had or ought to have had knowledge.

13.50   The implications of this judgment for vulnerable adults are considerable, given the widespread emotional, physical and sexual abuse they experience.[52] A major problem faced by social services departments and other public servants when confronted with evidence of adult abuse, has of course been the absence of legislation to facilitate effective action. Successive governments have failed to implement a statutory protection regime of the kind proposed by the Law Commission in its 1995 report 'Mental Incapacity'.[53]

13.51   Since the enactment of the HRA 1998, the higher courts have however dynamically developed a number of latent common law doctrines and mechanisms in an effort to provide some legal protection for vulnerable adults.

High Court – declaratory jurisdiction

13.52   The High Court has power (both inherent and statutory) to make a declaration as to whether an Act is lawful or not. The Law Commission, when reviewing this power commented as follows:[54]

> . . . a declaration by the High Court does not answer the question 'who decides?'. Nor does it answer the question 'what will be best?' It has been said that 'the essence of the jurisdiction is that the Court is like a camera photographing the relevant legal terrain. It registers what exists, and declares what it finds.

13.53   In spite of the fact that the declaration cannot change anything, the Court has expressed the view that certain serious issues should always be referred to it for a declaration in advance (ie, sterilisation/withdrawal of artificial feeding). It has also expressed a willingness to respond to new and difficult dilemmas, such as those that may arise where a dispute has arisen as to the

---

51 (2001) 34 EHRR 3.

52 Setting the Boundaries: Reforming the law on sex offences, Home Office, 2000 at para 0.17.

53 February 1995 No 231. Part II of the Draft Bill annexed to the report would have created a statutory regime by which applications could be made to the Court to obtain protection orders for 'vulnerable adults'.

54 Law Commission report, Mental Incapacity (1995 Law Comm No 231) para 2.25.

most appropriate place of residence of a person lacking sufficient mental capacity to make an informed decision on this question.

13.54 The declaration procedure has been used in cases concerning the cessation of artificial sustenance for a patient in persistent vegetative state[55] and to clarify the effect of purported refusals of treatment.[56] In *Re C (Mental patient: contact)*[57] it was invoked to determine a dispute concerning whether a disabled adult who lacked capacity should have contact with her mother. Although that case was settled prior to a full hearing, Eastham J accepted that there was jurisdiction in the High Court to make a declaration about such a matter. In *Re S*[58] declarations were sought as to whether a stroke victim should remain within the jurisdiction to receive treatment and care at his home in England.

13.55 *Re F (Adult: Court's jurisdiction)*[59] concerned a young adult who lacked sufficient mental capacity to make informed decisions as to where she should live or who posed a risk to her safety. As a minor she had been neglected and exposed to abuse while in the care of her parents and had accordingly been made a ward of court and placed in specialist accommodation. The wardship came to an end on her 18th birthday and the authority feared that without some form of court order her mother would seek her return home where she would be at risk of further abuse. As Dame Butler-Sloss observed:[60]

> There is an obvious gap in the framework of care for mentally incapacitated adults. If the court cannot act . . . this vulnerable young woman would be left at serious risk . . .

13.56 To fill this gap, the Court's solution was for it to 'grow' and 'shape'[61] the common law principle of 'necessity'; or as Sedley LJ expressed it, 'to speak where Parliament . . . was silent.'[62] In the Court's judgment, therefore, where a serious justiciable issue arose as to the best interests of an adult who lacks mental capacity, then it was able to grant declarations (in the exercise of its inherent jurisdiction) as to what would be in that person's best interests.[63]

13.57 Subsequent judgments have developed the principles established by the court in *Re F (Adult: Court's jurisdiction)*, notably *Re S (Adult Patient) (Inherent Jurisdiction: Family Life)*[64] and *A London Borough v BS and S: Re S (Adult's Lack of Capacity: Carer and Residence)*.[65] The facts of both cases

---

55 *Airedale NHS Trust v Bland* [1993] AC 789, HL.
56 *Re C (Adult: refusal of treatment)* [1994] 1 WLR 290.
57 [1993] 1 FLR 940.
58 [1995] 3 All ER 290.
59 (2000) 3 CCLR 210; [2000] 2 FLR 512.
60 (2000) 3 CCLR 210 at 219J.
61 (2000) 3 CCLR 210, per Sedley LJ at 227B.
62 (2000) 3 CCLR 210 at 226B.
63 (2000) 3 CCLR 210 at 218C–E.
64 [2002] EWHC 2278 (Fam); [2003] 1 FLR 292.
65 [2003] EWHC 1909 (Fam); [2003] 2 FLR 1235; (2004) 7 CCLR 132; but see also *A Local Authority v A Health Authority and A* [2003] EWHC Fam 2746; (2003) *Times* 5 December.

were similar; in that in each case a local authority considered that it was not in the best interests of the incapacitated adult to remain living with his or her parent. In both cases there had been allegations of abuse and in both cases a guardianship order was not possible because the incapacitated adult's learning disabilities were not associated with abnormally aggressive or seriously irresponsible conduct.

13.58   The courts in these cases have clarified the scope and availability of their declaratory jurisdiction, including:

Mental incapacity

13.59   It must be established that the person in question is incapable (by reason of mental incapacity) of making the relevant decision.

A serious justiciable issue

13.60   A 'serious justiciable issue' must exist which requires resolution. The courts have not sought to define precisely what is meant by this phrase. It will exist when the facts 'demonstrate a situation in which the doctrine of necessity might arise';[66] it is not the same as the threshold test for care proceedings under Children Act 1989 s31[67] and can arise even where there is no evidence of ill-treatment. In *A London Borough v BS and S*[67a] the 'significant issue' that had to be determined was where the incapacitated person should live. The local authority applied for a declaration, basing their application on evidence that the disabled person's father drank excessively and had assaulted her. The court rejected this evidence, but nevertheless considered that an order should be made. In this respect Wall J held:

> I agree that there must be good reason for local authority intervention in a case such as the present. Equally, if there are disputed issues of fact which go to the question of Mr S's capacity and suitability to care for S, the court may need to resolve them, if their resolution is necessary to the decision as to what is in S's best interests. Findings of fact against Mr S . . . would plainly reflect upon his capacity properly to care for S. But it does not follow, in my judgment, that the proceedings must be dismissed simply because the factual basis upon which the local authority instituted them turns out to be mistaken, or because it cannot be established on the balance of probabilities. What matters (assuming always that mental incapacity is made out) is which outcome will be in S's best interests. There will plainly be cases which are very fact specific. There will be others in which the principal concern is the future, and the relative suitability of the plans which each party can put forward for both the short and the long term care of the mentally incapable adult. The instant case, in my judgment, is one of the cases in the latter category.

66   *Re F (Adult: Court's jurisdiction)* (2000) 3 CCLR 210; [2000] 2 FLR 512 per Butler Sloss LJ.

67   *In Re S (Adult Patient) (Inherent Jurisdiction: Family Life)* [2002] EWHC 2278 (Fam); [2003] 1 FLR 292, per Munby J.

67a   (2004) 7 CCLR 132.

Best interests and the 'balance sheet' assessment

13.61 In *Re MB (Caesarean Section)*[68] the Court of Appeal held that a patient's best interests are not confined to their medical best interests and in *Re A (Medical treatment: Male Sterilisation)*[69] the High Court considered that they could encompass medical, emotional and all other welfare issues. The Law Commission in its 1995 report[70] suggested that in deciding what is in a person's best interests regard should be held to the following:

(a) so far as ascertainable, his past and present wishes and feelings and the factors which he would consider if he were able to do so;

(b) the need to permit and encourage that person to participate, or to improve his ability to participate, as fully as possible in anything done for and any decision affecting him;

(c) if it is practicable and appropriate to consult them, the views as to that person's wishes and feelings and as to what would be in his best interests of –

(i) any person named by him as someone to be consulted on those matters;

(ii) anyone (whether his spouse, a relative, friend or other person) engaged in caring for him or interested in his welfare;

(iii) the donee of any continuing power of attorney granted by him;

(iv) any manager appointed for him by the court;

(d) whether the purpose for which any action or decision is required can be as effectively achieved in a manner less restrictive of his freedom of action.

13.62 In deciding which outcome would best serve the interests of the disabled person, the courts require a 'balance sheet' to be drawn up listing the potential benefits and 'dis-benefits' that may flow from an intervention. This approach was identified by the Court of Appeal in *Re A (Medical Treatment: Male Sterilisation)*,[71] in the following terms:

Pending the enactment of a checklist or other statutory direction it seems to me that the first instance judge with the responsibility to make an evaluation of the best interests of a claimant lacking capacity should draw up a balance sheet. The first entry should be of any factor or factors of actual benefit . . . Then on the other sheet the judge should write any counter-balancing 'dis-benefits' to the applicant . . . Then the judge should enter on each sheet the potential gains and losses in each instance making some estimate of the extent of the possibility that the gain or loss might accrue. At the end of that exercise the judge should be better placed to strike a balance between the sum of the certain and possible gains against the sum of the certain and possible losses. Obviously only if the account is in relatively significant credit will the judge conclude that the application is likely to advance the best interests of the claimant.

13.63 In the *A London Borough v BS and S* proceedings Wall J considered that the

---

68 [1997] 2 FLR 426; [1997] FCR 541; (1998) 38 BMLR 175.

69 (2000) 53 BMLR 66 at 72.

70 Law Commission report, Mental Incapacity (1995 Law Comm No 231) at section 3 of the Draft Bill, p223.

71 [2000] 1FLR 560F–H.

benefits of the daughter remaining with her father included his love for, and strong sense of duty towards her and the fact that he had adequately provided for her in the recent past. The benefits of her moving to an independent residential care placement included the fact that her father (due to his age and poor health) would progressively find it difficult to care for her; that she could have contact with her siblings (who were not prepared to visit her at her father's house); the proposed care home would provide her with an opportunity for social contact with people of her own age group. In addition the court considered that the professional evidence was 'crucial': the social and health professionals were of the opinion that the care home placement was the better option. In the judge's opinion therefore, the balance sheet came down firmly in favour of the care home placement.

The proportionality of interventions

13.64   The 'benefits/disbenefits' assessment process will almost always relate to an issue of fundamental relevance to a disabled person's private and family life and their home – and thus require an examination of the proportionality of the proposed action from the perspective of ECHR art 8. In this context, it would appear that there are certain presumptions – for instance that the proposed interference will be the least restrictive and presumably that there should be no 'order' unless strictly necessary.[72]

13.65   In practice this aspect appears to have attracted surprisingly little attention. Thus in *Re S (Adult Patient) (Inherent Jurisdiction: Family Life)*,[73] the court held that the assessment exercise is not predicated on any formal presumptions (for instance of the type to be found in Part I of the Children Act 1989), nevertheless:

> ... whilst there was no presumption that mentally incapacitated adults would be better off if they lived with a family, rather than an institution, the burden was on a local authority to establish, if it sought to do so, that it was the more appropriate person to look after the mentally incapacitated adult than his own family.

13.66   Likewise in *Re A (Medical Treatment: Sterilisation)*[74] it was held:

> At the end of that exercise the judge should be better placed to strike a balance between the sum of the certain and possible gains against the sum of the certain and possible losses. Obviously only if the account is in relatively significant credit will the judge conclude that the application is likely to advance the best interests of the claimant.

The range of potential declarations

13.67   In the *A London Borough v BS and S* decision, Wall J made a declaration authorising the local authority to continue with the care home arrangement (with defined contact between the father and daughter). Additionally

---

72 In this context, see the approach to a not dissimilar balancing exercise taken by Munby J, in *R (A and B) v East Sussex CC (No 2)* [2003] EWHC 167 (Admin); (2003) 6 CCLR 194 at 226–232.

73 [2002] EWHC 2278 (Fam); [2003] 1 FLR 292.

74 (1999) 53 BMLR 66; [2000] 1 FLR 549, CA.

he declared that the authority was to consult her father about any future medical treatment/care arrangements she might require and that she be provided with an independent advocate.

13.68   Declarations can also be sought concerning future situations, provided they are rooted in a serious 'justiciable issue' and are not overly hypothetical.[75] In *Re S (Adult Patient) (Inherent Jurisdiction: Family Life)*[76] the local authority was concerned that it might have to return to the court – repeatedly – for additional declarations, given the difficult relationship that existed between it and the incapacitated person's father. The authority accordingly asked the court to declare that it had – in effect – proxy decision-making power on a range of social welfare questions. Munby J held as follows:

> The court has jurisdiction to grant whatever relief in declaratory form is necessary to safeguard and promote the incapable adult's welfare and interests. If the court thinks that his interests will be best served by a judicial identification of some third party (the local authority) as the most appropriate person to be responsible not merely for his care but also for taking the kind of decisions to which I have already referred . . . then, in my judgment, there can be no objection whatever to the court so declaring. Indeed were the court not to do so in an appropriate case, it would, as it seems to me, be failing in its duties under both the common law and the Convention. After all, to declare that some specified person who is, in the eyes of the court, the most appropriate person to assume responsibility for this aspect of a patient's care is also to be clothed with practical decision-making on behalf of the patient, is merely to state explicitly that he has those powers and responsibilities which would in any event be reposed in him by the doctrine of necessity. Moreover, some such mechanism is essential if those caring for the incapable are to be allowed to get on with their task without the need for endless reference to the court – something which . . . would serve neither the public interest nor the interests of the mentally incapacitated.
>
> So, subject always to being satisfied that this really is in the best interests of the mentally incapacitated person, the court has, and in my judgment always has had, power to declare that some specified person is to be, in relation to specified matters, what is, in effect, a surrogate decision-maker for the incapable adult.

Proposals for reform

13.69   In 1995 the Law Commission, in its report 'Mental Incapacity',[77] recommended a wholesale reform of the law as it applies to mentally incapacitated adults. The proposals covered a number of areas including the law concerning adult abuse and decision-making. In 1997 the government invited comments on law reform in its consultation paper *Who Decides?*[78]

75 See for instance *R v Portsmouth Hospitals NHS Trust ex p Glass* (1999) 2 FLR 905; (1999) 50 BMLR 269 where the court considered a dispute about a future treatment decision too hypothetical.

76 [2002] EWHC 2278 (Admin); [2003] 1 FLR 292.

77 February 1995 No 231.

78 Lord Chancellor's Department, Cm 3803, Dec 1997.

and in 1999 it published its conclusions as *Making Decisions*[79] followed in 2003 by a Draft Incapacity Bill[80] that was then scrutinised by a Joint Committee of the Houses of Parliament to whose recommendations the Department for Constitutional Affairs responded in February 2004.[81] It is anticipated that the Bill will be introduced during 2004.

13.70   The Bill adopts most of the provisions recommended by the Law Commission – with the exception of the adult abuse protection measures. The Bill in outline covers the following:

Definition (clauses 1 and 2)

It provides a statutory definition of incapacity namely (at clause1):

> . . . a person lacks capacity in relation to a matter if at the material time he is unable to make a decision for himself in relation to the matter because of an impairment of or a disturbance in the functioning of the mind or brain.

Best interests (clause 4)

It lists the criteria that are relevant in assessing what is in the best interests of someone who lacks capacity (again very much in line with the Law Commission proposals (noted above)).

General authority (clauses 6 and 7)

Also in line with the Law Commission proposals, it introduces the concept of a 'general authority to act' that clarifies in statute the circumstances in which decisions can be taken on behalf of others without the need for any formal authority.

Lasting powers of attorney (clauses 8–13)

It repeals (with transitional provisions) the Enduring Powders of Attorney Act 1985 and creates a new concept – Lasting Powers of Attorney which in effect provide for enduring attorneys also to have decision-making powers on healthcare and personal welfare matters.

Court of Protection (clauses 14–22)

It provides for the establishment of a new Court of Protection to resolve complex issues and to appoint deputies (instead of receivers): the deputies to have a full range of powers – ie, including in relation to healthcare and personal welfare matters. It also creates a new Office of the Public Guardian (to replace the Public Guardianship Office), to support the new Court of Protection.

Advance decisions (clauses 23–25)

It provides for patients to make advance decisions (sometimes called 'advanced directives') that enable them to give notice that if they lose their mental capacity they wish to refuse future specified medical treatment.

Code of practice (clause 30)

The legislation will be augmented by a detailed code of practice.

---

79 Lord Chancellor's Department, Cm 4465, Oct 1999.
80 Accessible at www.dca.gov.uk/menincap/meninc.pdf.
81 The Department for Constitutional Affairs response is accessible at www.dca.gov.uk/ pubs/reports/mental-incapacity.htm.

Older people's services

Introduction

14.1   Today a fifth of the population of the UK is over 60, and the proportion is growing – particularly in relation to people aged over 80. It is estimated that between 1995 and 2025 the numbers of people over 80 will increase by 50 per cent and the number of people over 90 will double. At present almost 40 per cent of the NHS's budget and nearly 50 per cent of the social services budget are spent on people aged over 65.[1] About 600,000 such older people receive domiciliary services from the local authority and about 480,000 are in care homes (about 1 in 20 of all elderly people).[2]

14.2   In response to the social and health care challenges posed by an ageing population, the government in England published in 2001 a *National Service Framework for Older People* (NSF).[3] The NSF sets out eight key standards, providing in each case guidance on the local action required to ensure these are implemented – with detailed timescales and 'milestones to ensure progress, with performance measures to support performance improvement'. The eight standards are as follows:

1. *Rooting out age discrimination*
    NHS services will be provided, regardless of age, on the basis of clinical need alone. Social care services will not use age in their eligibility criteria or policies, to restrict access to available services.

2. *Person-centred care*
    NHS and social care services treat older people as individuals and enable them to make choices about their own care. This is achieved through the single assessment process, integrated commissioning arrangements and integrated provision of services, including community equipment and continence services.

3. *Intermediate care*
    Older people will have access to a new range of intermediate care services at home or in designated care settings, to promote their independence by providing enhanced services from the NHS and councils to prevent unnecessary hospital admission and effective rehabilitation services to enable early discharge from hospital and to prevent premature or unnecessary admission to long-term residential care.

4. *General hospital care*
    Older people's care in hospital is delivered through appropriate specialist care and by hospital staff who have the right set of skills to meet their needs.

---

1   *National Service Framework for Older People*, Department of Health, March 2001, p1, accessible at www.dh.gov.uk/PolicyAndGuidance/HealthAndSocialCareTopics/ OlderPeoplesServices/fs/en.

2   Royal Commission on long-term care report *With Respect to old age* (1999): Cm 4192, The Stationery Office.

3   See para 4.51 above: in Wales the equivalent initiative is *The Strategy for Older People In Wales* (2003) accessible at www.wales.gov.uk/subisocialpolicy/content/older/older-people-final-e.pdf.

5. *Stroke*
   The NHS will take action to prevent strokes, working in partnership with other agencies where appropriate. People who are thought to have had a stroke have access to diagnostic services, are treated appropriately by a specialist stroke service, and subsequently, with their carers, participate in a multidisciplinary programme of secondary prevention and rehabilitation.

6. *Falls*
   The NHS, working in partnership with councils, takes action to prevent falls and reduce resultant fractures or other injuries in their populations of older people. Older people who have fallen receive effective treatment and, with their carers, receive advice on prevention through a specialised falls service.

7. *Mental health in older people*
   Older people who have mental health problems have access to integrated mental health services, provided by the NHS and councils to ensure effective diagnosis, treatment and support, for them and for their carers.

8. *The promotion of health and active life in older age*
   The health and well-being of older people is promoted through a co-ordinated programme of action led by the NHS with support from councils.

Older people and the Single Assessment Process

14.3 Standard two of the English NSF[4] outlined the Single Assessment Process (SAP) which had been first proposed in the *NHS Plan*.[5] The SAP for older people would (the NSF stated) ensure that (at para 2.27):

- a more standardised assessment process is in place across all areas and agencies;
- standards of assessment practice are raised;
- older people's needs are assessed in the round.

14.4 Guidance[6] on the SAP has been issued to health and social services bodies and requires that they have fully integrated commissioning arrangements and integrated provision of services including community services and continence services by April 2004.[7] In Wales the Unified and Fair System for Assessing and Managing Care (UFSAMC) 2002 policy guidance

---

4 *Strategy for Older People in Wales* (January 2003), para 33 confirms that the NSF for older people in Wales (when published) will build upon the unified assessment guidance already issued.

5 *The NHS Plan* white paper (July 2000) Secretary of State for Health, Cm 4818-I, para 7.3.

6 In particular HSC 2002/001 and LAC (2002)1 *Guidance on the Single Assessment Process for Older People*, January 2002. The guidance is also considered at para 4.53 above.

7 Updated implementation guidance and advice on 'off the shelf' assessment tools continues to be provided by the Department of Health accessible at www.dh.gov. uk/PolicyAndGuidance/HealthAndSocialCareTopics/SocialCare/SingleAssessmentProcess/fs/en.

constitutes the equivalent guidance (ie, effectively a combined Fair Access to Care Services (FACS) and SAP document).

14.5   The raison d'être of the process is both organisational – in compelling health and social services bodies to work together in the assessing and providing care services – and cultural – to provide what the guidance calls a 'person-centred approach'. The aim is to ensure that older people are not subjected to ineffective (and inefficient) multiple assessments: as the guidance explains:[8]

> ... many frail older people will have numerous separate assessments per year with the majority of the information being repeated on each assessment. The single assessment process will help to minimise this unnecessary duplication, while allowing a full assessment to be built up over time. It will also reduce paperwork by providing a single assessment summary (preferably based on electronic records) for health and social care.

14.6   Unlike the FACS guidance (see para 4.50 above) the SAP does not seek to impose a single prescribed assessment tool: individual authorities are free to develop their own processes. However these must satisfy rigorous criteria laid down in the policy guidance[9] and against which they will be evaluated. It is expected however that there will be, over time, a convergence of the assessment methods used.[10]

14.7   As noted above, the SAP 2002 policy guidance lists four types of assessment:[11]

- *Contact assessment*
  This refers to a contact between an older person and health and social services where significant needs are first described or suspected. The assessment consists of recoding relevant (but limited) information and then deciding whether the persons needs are straightforward and can be dealt with there and then (eg, provision of a Blue Parking Badge, or a grab rail or other equipment, etc). If this is not possible then there may be a need for a more in depth assessment (eg, of a type below). The collection/verification of the data for a contact assessment may be 'by trained, but not professionally qualified, staff. The exploration of the presenting and other needs should be undertaken by a trained and competent single professional, qualified or not, in any of the settings to which this guidance applies'.[12]

- *Overview assessment*
  Assessment of this type occurs when the 'individual's needs are such that a more rounded assessment should be undertaken'. It will involve

---

8   *The Single Assessment Process Guidance for Local Implementation* policy guidance at para 12.

9   HSC 2002/001; LAC (2002)1 Annex C.

10 *The Single Assessment Process Guidance for Local Implementation* policy guidance at para 12(IX).

11 UFSAMC 2002 policy guidance in Wales, Annex E p12; para 4.3.

12 UFSAMC 2002 policy guidance in Wales, Annex E p14; paras 4.15–4.24.

consideration of 'all or some of the domains of the single assessment process, such as "personal care and physical well-being", "senses" and "mental health"' (see p72 above). The guidance explains that such an assessment may be completed by a single professional from either the NHS or social services. This person need not be a 'qualified professional' but have competence to carry out the assessment.[13]

- *Specialist assessments*
  Whereas the overview assessment looks at a broad range of a persons needs, a specialist assessment focuses on specific needs – eg, a health condition or problem or a social care need. Such assessments should be administered by the appropriate qualified professional.[14]

- *Comprehensive assessment*
  This arises when the individual's needs are such that all or most of the SAP domains need consideration and some (or all) require specialist assessment in addition. Such assessments should be carried out 'where the level of support and treatment likely to be offered is intensive or prolonged, including permanent admission to a care home, intermediate care services, or substantial packages of care at home'. Such assessments will involve a range of different professionals or specialist teams'.[15]

14.8 Apart from the insistence on a joint health/social services assessment process the SAP guidance is in many respects a gloss on the FACS guidance and reference should be made to chapter 4 where this guidance is further considered. Such assessments cannot in fact be 'unified' in the legal sense, unless the agencies have entered into formal partnership arrangements under Health Act 2001 s31 (see para 10.196 above).

SAP and the care programme approach

14.9 The Department of Health has issued a clarification note *Care Management for Older People with Serious Mental Health Problems*[16] concerning the interface between these two assessment regimes (the care programme approach (CPA) process is considered at para 15.5 below). The guidance advises:

- The CPA should be applied to older people with severe mental illness due to schizophrenia or other psychoses. The assessment of their needs should be based on the SAP for older people.
- SAP, plus critical aspects of CPA, should be applied to other older people with severe functional or organic mental health problems, who were they younger would be provided for under CPA.
- When individuals subject to CPA reach old age, switches to SAP are not inevitable, and should only be made in the best interests of individuals and the continuity of their care.

---

13 UFSAMC 2002 policy guidance in Wales, Annex E pp14–16; paras 4.25–4.31.
14 UFSAMC 2002 policy guidance in Wales, Annex E p18; paras 4.32–4.35.
15 UFSAMC 2002 policy guidance in Wales, Annex E pp18–19; paras 4.36–4.42.
16 Accessible at www.doh.gov.uk/scg/sap/sapandcpa.htm.

Advocacy and older people

14.10   Increasing attention is being given to the important role that advocacy services can fulfil in ensuring that the needs of older people are properly addressed.[17] In this respect the SAP guidance advises:[18]

> Agencies should consider at the earliest opportunity whether older people might need, or benefit, from the assistance of advocates, interpreters and translators, and specific communication equipment, during the assessment process and subsequent aspects of care planning and service delivery. Where such a need exists, councils should either arrange for this support or facilitate access to it.
>
> As emphasised in the NSF for Older People, the contribution of trained bi- or multi-lingual co-workers can be important in this regard. It is the Department of Health's view that translation and interpretation is best provided by accredited professionals. The role of an advocate is a specialism in its own right, and should ideally be provided by professionals who are independent of both statutory agencies and the older person.

Community care services for older people

14.11   As noted above at para I.19 the community care legislation divides service users into three discrete (but largely artificial) categories: namely 'older people; disabled people and ill people' (see para 8.124). Not infrequently an individual will straddle all three categories – for instance an older person with dementia. However for some people, the need for services arises not because of illness or disability, but merely because the ageing process has made them frail – for instance through muscle wastage. Although such persons are entitled to accommodation services under National Assistance Act (NAA) 1948 s21 (see para 7.20) they are not eligible for domiciliary or community based services under NAA 1948 s29 or Chronically Sick and Disabled Persons Act (CSDPA) 1970 s2 – because they do not fall within the definition of a disabled person for the purposes of these sections (see para 8.24). Such persons are however entitled to care services under the Health Services and Public Health Act (HSPHA) 1968 s45.

Care services HSPHA 1968 s45

14.12   Section 45 of the HSPHA 1968 provides:

> (1) A local authority may with the approval of the secretary of state, and to such extent as he may direct, shall make arrangements for promoting the welfare of old people.

17 For details concerning advocacy initiatives on behalf of older people, see Older People's Advocacy Alliance (OPAAL (UK)), c/o Beth Johnson Foundation, Parkfield House, 64 Princes Road, Hartshill, Stoke-on-Trent, Staffordshire, ST4 7JL. Their web site being at www.opaal.org.uk/.

18 The Annex to HSC 2002/001 and LAC (2002)1 pp19–20: *Guidance on the Single Assessment Process for Older People*, January 2002.

14.13 Section 45 is drafted to the same pattern as NAA 1948 s29, in that it does not authorise the provision of any services but leaves to the secretary of state the power to specify in directions what services may and what services must be provided.

14.14 The only (and current) directions that have been issued are contained in DHSS Circular 19/71 (see below). The circular explains (at para 3) that the purpose of HSPHA 1968 s45 is to enable authorities to make approved arrangements for the elderly who are not substantially and permanently handicapped, and thus to promote the welfare of the elderly generally and so far as possible to prevent or postpone personal deterioration or breakdown.

Client group

Old people

14.15 HSPHA 1968 s45 services are available to old people. The phrase 'old people' is not defined, and probably needs no definition. If a person requires domiciliary services for any reason other than the fact that age has made him or her frail, then statutory provisions exist to enable that service to be provided.[19]

14.16 The circular guidance suggested however that in the early days of the power (ie, post-April 1971):

> ... it might prove desirable to start by identifying the needs of certain groups of the elderly who seem likely to be particularly vulnerable, eg, (a) elderly people, especially the more elderly, who are housebound or living alone or recently bereaved or about to be discharged from hospital, and (b) other persons over, say, 75 living in the community, particularly where there are high concentrations of very elderly people in particular districts.[20]

Ordinarily resident

14.17 Neither the Act nor the directions restrict HSPHA 1968 s45 services to persons 'ordinarily resident' in the local authority's area. This again is not strictly necessary, in that the directions have been limited to authorising (but not directing) the provision of such services. Accordingly social services authorities are entitled to reach a general policy decision (without fettering their individual discretion) to limit the use of their powers to elderly persons ordinarily resident within their area.

Services under HSPHA 1968 s45

14.18 The statutory framework for the provision of services under HSPHA 1968 s45 is similar to that under NAA 1948 s29. As with NAA 1948 s29, HSPHA

19 That is, under NAA 1948 s29, CSDPA 1970 s2, NHSA 1977 Sch 8 or MHA 1983 s117.
20 DHSS Circular 19/71 at para 7.

1968 s45 leaves to the secretary of state the power to determine the type of domiciliary services which can be provided. Section 45 services are subject to three basic limitations, namely:

1) that the purpose of the service must be the promotion of the welfare of elderly people;[21]

2) by virtue of section 45(4)(a) that the direct payment of money to 'old people' is not permitted (except if a payment for their 'work in accordance with the arrangements'. As noted, however, this restriction is now academic as a consequence of the direct payments legislation (see para 9.5 above); and

3) by virtue of section 45(4)(b) that no accommodation or services can be provided under section 45 if the accommodation or services could be provided under the National Health Service Act (NHSA) 1977.[22]

14.19   The secretary of state's only Direction in respect of HSPHA 1968 s45 services was issued in DHSS Circular 19/71 para 4, in March 1971. Although the wording of section 45 would allow the directions to place social services authorities under a duty to provide certain services, the direction merely empowers the provision of the specified services, without creating any obligation.

Powers to provide HSPHA 1968 s45 services

14.20   The directions give social services authorities the discretion to provide[23] the services specified below. Authorities may provide services over and above those actually specified in the directions if they first obtain the secretary of state's specific approval.[24]

'Meals and recreation in the home or elsewhere'

14.21   The guidance suggests that 'many of the elderly who are mobile or who can be transported will require social centres providing meals and opportunities for occupation as well as companionship and recreation. For the housebound and the frailer elderly meals-on-wheels will also need to be developed'.[25] The services available under this direction include the provision of 'recreation'. This would include day centres, outings; the provision of a television in the home and so on. District councils are empowered to provide similar services by virtue of Health and Social Services and Social Security Adjudications Act (HASSASSAA) 1983 Sch 9 (see para 14.30

---

21 The wording of HSPHA 1968 s45 is such that the service need not be provided *to* the disabled person; ie, a service provided to a carer may be 'an arrangement which promotes the welfare of an elderly person'.

22 See para 8.58 above.

23 The local authority may provide the services alone, or by employing independent or private providers – see HSPHA 1968 s45(3) and DHSS Circular 19/71 paras 5(b), 7 and 11 onwards.

24 DHSS Circular 19/71 at para 4.

25 DHSS Circular 19/71 at para 10.

below). The equivalent services for disabled people (under the CSDPA 1970 s2(1)(g) and 2(1)(c) respectively) are considered at paras 8.76 and 8.110 and for people who are, or have been, ill, under the NHSA 1977, at para 8.147.

Information on elderly services

14.22 'To inform the elderly of services available to them and to identify elderly people in need of services'. The guidance cautions against attempts to develop a comprehensive register of elderly people.[26] It emphasises however that 'good services together with wide and continuing publicity about them are a pre-requisite of any scheme for finding out needs. The elderly and those who know of them cannot be expected to come forward if they do not know of any reason for doing so'.[27] The more specific duty to inform under CSDPA 1970 s1 is considered at para 3.4 above.

Travel assistance to participate in HSPHA 1968 s45 services

14.23 'To provide facilities or assistance in travelling to and from the home for the purpose of participating in services provided by the authority or similar services'. The equivalent duty under the CSDPA 1970 is dealt with at para 8.82.

Assistance in finding boarding accommodation

14.24 'To assist in finding suitable households for boarding elderly persons'. Social services authorities are given the power to provide this service (and those detailed in 7 and 8 below) to meet the needs of elderly people, similar to the powers approved for disabled people under NAA 1948 s29 in LAC (93)10 appendix 2, para 3 (see para 8.53).

Social work support and advice

14.25 'To provide visiting and advisory services and social work support'. The guidance suggests that social visiting services should be given high priority and that they should be co-ordinated by local authorities but largely undertaken by voluntary workers or others after suitable preparatory training.[28]

Home help and home adaptations

14.26 'To provide practical assistance in the home, including assistance in the carrying out of any additional facilities designed to secure the greater safety, comfort or convenience'. The guidance states that 'home-help, including laundry services and other aids to independent living, should probably be high on any priority list'.[29] The equivalent (and more substantial) duties to

26 DHSS Circular 19/71 at para 6(a).
27 DHSS Circular 19/71 at para 6(b).
28 DHSS Circular 19/71 at para 10; and see also para 8.42 where the equivalent service under NAA 1948 s29 is considered.
29 DHSS Circular 19/71 at para 10.

provide such services under CSDPA 1970 s2 and under NHSA 1977 Sch 8 para 3 (home helps only) are dealt with at paras 8.87, 8.70 and 8.148 respectively.

Subsidy of warden costs

14.27 'To contribute towards the cost of employing a warden on welfare functions in warden-assisted housing schemes'. See the note to para 14.24 above.

Warden services

14.28 'To provide warden services for occupiers of private housing'. See the note to para 14.24 above.

Excluded groups

14.29 The effect of Immigration and Asylum Act 1999 s117, by amending HSPHA 1968 s45, is to exclude from services older people who are asylum-seekers and are in need of community care services solely on account of being 'destitute'[30] (see para 7.25 above).

Care services HASSASSAA 1983 Sch 9

14.30 The Health and Social Services and Social Security Adjudications Act 1983 Sch 9 Part II makes provision for district councils to provide 'meals and recreation for old people'. Schedule 9 para 1 states:

> A district council or Welsh county council or county borough council shall have power to make such arrangements as they may from time to time determine for providing meals and recreation for old people in their homes or elsewhere and may employ as their agent for the purpose of this paragraph any voluntary organisation whose activities consist in or include the provision of meals or recreation for old people.

14.31 In order to achieve these objectives para 2 of the schedule empowers such authorities to contribute to the funds of voluntary organisations, permit them to use their premises or furniture, vehicles or equipment (gift or loan or otherwise). Para 3 provides the secretary of state with regulation making powers – which have not as yet been exercised.

14.32 It appears that these powers are generally exercised by district councils in collaboration with social services authorities in respect of supported accommodation arrangements. The partnership arrangements under the Health Act 1999 s31 (see para 10.196) enable payments to be made by health bodies to district councils in relation to such arrangements.[31]

---

30 HSPHA 1968 s45(4A) as inserted by Immigration and Asylum Act 1999 s117.
31 Health Act 1999 s31(8).

Mental health service users

Introduction

15.1   At any one time, approximately one in six people of working age have a mental health problem (most often anxiety or depression) and one in 250 will have a psychotic illness such as schizophrenia or bipolar affective disorder (manic depression).[1]

15.2   In order to address the social and mental health needs of working age adults up to 65, in 1999 the government in England published a National Service Framework (NSF) for Mental Health.[2] The English NSF sets out seven key standards, providing in each case detailed guidance on the local action required to ensure these are implemented – with timescales and 'milestones to ensure progress, with performance measures to support performance improvement'. In Wales an equivalent NSF was published in April 2002, *Adult Mental Health Services: A National Service Framework for Wales*.[3] The seven English standards are as follows:

1. *Mental health promotion*
    Health and social services should:
    - promote mental health for all, working with individuals and communities;
    - combat discrimination against individuals and groups with mental health problems, and promote their social inclusion.

2. *Primary care and access to services*
    Any service user who contacts their primary health care team with a common mental health problem should:
    - have their mental health needs identified and assessed;
    - be offered effective treatments, including referral to specialist services for further assessment, treatment and care if they require it.

3. *Primary care and access to services*
    Any individual with a common mental health problem should:
    - be able to make contact round the clock with the local services necessary to meet their needs and receive adequate care;
    - be able to use NHS Direct, as it develops, for first-level advice and referral on to specialist helplines or to local services.

4. *Effective services for people with severe mental illness*
    All mental health service users on the Care Programme Approach (CPA) should:
    - receive care which optimises engagement, prevents or anticipates crisis, and reduces risk;

---

1   *A National Service Framework for Mental Health: Modern Standards and Service Models*, page 1. Department of Health; September 1999, accessible at www.publications. doh.gov.uk/nsf/mhexecsum.htm.

2   *A National Service Framework for Mental Health: Modern Standards and Service Models*.

3   Accessible at www.wales.gov.uk/subihealth/content/keypubs/pdf/adult-mental-nsf-e.pdf. The Welsh NSF has eight standards, namely (1) Promoting social inclusion; (2) Empowerment and support of service users and carers; (3) Promotion of opportunities for a normal pattern of daily life; (4) Commissioning equitable, accessible services; (5 and 6) Delivering responsive, comprehensive services; (7) Effective client assessment and care pathways and (8) Ensuring a well staffed, skilled and supported workforce.

- have a copy of a written care plan which:
  - includes the action to be taken in a crisis by service user, their carers, and their care co-ordinators;
  - advises the GP how they should respond if the service user needs additional help;
  - is regularly reviewed by the care co-ordinator;
- be able to access services 24 hours a day, 365 days a year.

5. *Effective services for people with severe mental illness*
   Each service user who is assessed as requiring a period of care away from their home should have:
   - timely access to an appropriate hospital bed or alternative bed or place, which is:
     - in the least restrictive environment consistent with the need to protect them and the public;
     - as close to home as possible;
   - a copy of a written after care plan agreed on discharge, which sets out the care and rehabilitation to be provided, identifies the care co-ordinator, and specifies the action to be taken in a crisis.

6. *Caring about carers*
   All individuals who provide regular and substantial care for a person on CPA should:
   - have an assessment of their caring, physical and mental health needs, repeated on at least an annual basis;
   - have their own written care plan, which is given to them and implemented in discussion with them.

7. *Preventing suicide*
   Local health and social care communities should prevent suicides by:
   - promoting mental health for all, working with individuals and communities (Standard one);
   - delivering high quality primary mental health care (Standard two);
   - ensuring that anyone with a mental health problem can contact local services via the primary care team, a helpline or an A and E department (Standard three);
   - ensuring that individuals with severe and enduring mental illness have a care plan which meets their specific needs, including access to services round the clock (Standard four);
   - providing safe hospital accommodation for individuals who need it (Standard five);
   - enabling individuals caring for someone with severe mental illness to receive the support which they need to continue to care (Standard six);
   - and in addition:
     - supporting local prison staff in preventing suicides among prisoners;
     - ensuring that staff are competent to assess the risk of suicide among individuals at greatest risk;
     - developing local systems for suicide audit to learn lessons and take any necessary action.

Assessment and care planning for mental health service users

15.3   Standard 2 of the NSF concerns the right of mental health service users to a needs assessment and standard 3 entitles them to 'round the clock' access to the local services necessary to meet their needs and to receive adequate care. Standard 4 elaborates upon the rights of mental health service users to be assessed using the Care Programme Approach.

15.4   People with mental health problems are entitled to receive care services under the National Assistance Act (NAA) 1948 and the Chronically Sick and Disabled Persons Act (CSDPA) 1970 as well as under the National Health Service Act (NHSA) 1977 sch 8 (see para 8.124). As such, therefore, they are entitled to a community care assessment under National Health Service and Community Care Act (NHSCCA) 1990 s47 (see para 4.14). In addition, however 'adults of working age in contact with the secondary mental health system'[4] are entitled to an integrated health and social care assessment under what is generally referred to as the 'care programme approach'.

The care programme approach

15.5   The care programme approach (CPA) was introduced by the joint health/social services Circular HC (90)23; LASSL (90)11. Health authorities were given lead responsibility for implementing the policy although there was an obligation on health and social services authorities to reach formal and detailed inter-agency agreements to ensure its full implementation.[5] The Department of Health has consistently stressed the importance it attaches to the CPA[6] and issued regular updating guidance: in May 1994 with the publication of *Guidance on the Discharge of Mentally Disordered People and their Continuing Care in the Community* as HSG (94)27; LASSL (94)4; in 1996 with an *Audit Pack for Monitoring the Care Programme Approach*[7] and most recently in England in October 1999[8] with *Effective care co-ordination in mental health services: modernising the care programme approach: a policy booklet.* This remains the current guidance in England and is referred to below as the '1999 CPA guidance'.

15.6   The relevant guidance in Wales was issued in February 2003 as *Mental*

---

4   'Effective care co-ordination in mental health services: Modernising the care programme approach – a policy booklet', Department of Health, October 1999, para 17 accessible at www.publications.doh.gov.uk/nsf/polbook.htm.

5   See *Social Services Departments and the Care Programme Approach: An SSI Inspection Report* (Department of Health 1995 para 4.3.11).

6   See *Care Management and Assessment: Managers' Guide* (HMSO 1991) p93; *Health of the Nation: Key Area Handbook: Mental Illness* (1993) Appendix 9.3; (1995) chapters 9 and 11.

7   Accessible at www.doh.gov.uk/mentalhealth/auditpack.pdf.

8   See note 4 above.

Health Policy Wales Implementation Guidance: The Care Programme Approach for Mental Health Service-users.[9] The guidance retains the CPA in Wales on broadly similar lines to that in England, although it seeks to integrate such assessments within the Unified Assessment Process (see para 4.51 above).

15.7   The care programme approach applies to all patients receiving care from the specialist psychiatric services[10] – ie, regardless of whether or not the patient has been detained under the MHA 1983. The four main elements of the CPA are:[11]

- systematic arrangements for assessing the health and social needs of people accepted into specialist mental health services;
- the formation of a care plan which identifies the health and social care required from a variety of providers;
- the appointment of a key-worker to keep in close touch with the service user and to monitor and co-ordinate care; and
- regular review and, where necessary, agreed changes to the care plan.

15.8   Although the CPA is specifically directed at 'the most needy of service users who require a complex care planning response',[12] it is also intended that all service users in contact with specialist psychiatric services are dealt with under the programme, albeit that in respect of such persons a less intensive/bureaucratic response is required from the relevant services. As the 1999 CPA guidance explains (para 18):

> ... The key principles of the CPA are applicable to all service users, even those who require only a uni-disciplinary intervention. They have the right to a thorough assessment of their needs, the development of a care plan and a review of that care by the professionals involved in their care. Indeed, this is good professional practice.

15.9   The guidance accordingly separates service users into two categories, those that require a 'standard CPA' and those that require a more intensive or 'enhanced CPA'.

Standard CPA

15.10   The 1999 CPA guidance para 57 suggests that the characteristics of people on standard CPA will include some of the following:

- they require the support or intervention of one agency or discipline or they require only low-key support from more than one agency or discipline;
- they are more able to self-manage their mental health problems;

---

9   Accessible at www.wales.gov.uk/subihealth/content/keypubs/pdf/mental-health-policy-imple-guide-e.pdf.

10 HSG(96)6. The spectrum of care: a summary of comprehensive local services for people with mental health problems 24-hour nursed beds for people with severe and enduring mental illness an audit pack for the care programme approach.

11 1999 CPA guidance para 4.

12 1999 CPA guidance para 18.

- they have an active informal support network;
- they pose little danger to themselves or others;
- they are more likely to maintain appropriate contact with services.

15.11　The guidance explains the nature of the Standard CPA as follows:

> 19. It is important to stress, however, that where the service user has standard needs and has contact with only one professional, that professional will in effect be the person who co-ordinates their care and any clinical or practice notes will constitute the care plan and record of review. Service users should be given the opportunity to sign the agreed care plan and then receive a copy. It is not necessary to engage in further bureaucracy for the care of such people. As a minimum, service providers must ensure that central records are maintained on all those in contact with services and that care planning and review take place regularly.

Enhanced CPA

15.12　The enhanced CPA is described by the 1999 guidance as being appropriate to service users who have some of the following characteristics (para 58):

- they have multiple care needs, including housing, employment, etc, requiring inter-agency co-ordination;
- they are only willing to co-operate with one professional or agency but they have multiple care needs;
- they may be in contact with a number of agencies (including the criminal justice system);
- they are likely to require more frequent and intensive interventions, perhaps with medication management;
- they are more likely to have mental health problems co-existing with other problems such as substance misuse;
- they are more likely to be at risk of harming themselves or others;
- they are more likely to disengage with services.

CPA and the Code of Practice Guidance to the Mental Health Act 1983

15.13　Mental Health Act (MHA) 1983 s118 requires the secretary of state to prepare a code of practice for the guidance of the relevant professionals on the application the Act. It has been held that the code is – in effect – strong policy guidance (see para 1.36 above) that should be followed unless in an individual case there is a good reason for departing from it.[13] At chapter 27 of the (April 1999) code, the objectives and requirements of the CPA are outlined as follows:

> 27.2 These objectives apply to all patients receiving treatment and care from the specialist psychiatric services, whether or not they are admitted to hospital and whether or not they are detained under the Act. They are

13　*Munjaz v Mersey Care NHS Trust and others* [2003] EWCA Civ 1036; [2003] 3 WLR 1505; (2003) 74 BMLR 178.

embodied in the Care Programme Approach (CPA) set out in Circular HC(90)23; LASSL(90)11, and in the Welsh Office Mental Illness Strategy (WHC(95)40).[14] The key elements of the CPA are:

- systematic arrangements for assessing people's health and social care needs;
- the formulation of a care plan which addresses those needs;
- the appointment of a key worker to keep in close touch with the patient and monitor care;
- regular review and if need be, agreed changes to the care plan.

. . .

27.4 NHS Managers and Directors of Social Services should ensure that all staff are aware of the CPA and related provisions. Further guidance on the discharge of mentally disordered people and their continuing care in the community is given in HSG(94)27; LASSL(94)4 and WHC(95)7 and WHC(96)26. The relationship between the CPA, section 117 after-care and local authority arrangements for care management is more fully explained in *Building Bridges – A Guide to arrangements for inter-agency working for the care and protection of severely mentally ill people (Department of Health 1995)*.

27.5 Before the decision is taken to discharge or grant leave to a patient, it is the responsibility of the [responsible medical officer] RMO to ensure, in consultation with the other professionals concerned, that the patient's needs for health and social care are fully assessed and the care plan addresses them. If the patient is being given leave for only a short period a less comprehensive review may suffice but the arrangements for the patient's care should still be properly recorded.

27.6 The RMO is also responsible for ensuring that:

- a proper assessment is made of risks to the patient or other people;
- in the case of offender patients, the circumstances of any victim and their families are taken into account;
- consideration is given to whether the patient meets the criteria for after-care under supervision, or under guardianship (see chapter 13 and 28); and
- consideration is given to whether the patient should be placed on the supervision register established in accordance with HSG(94)5.

Mental Health Review Tribunals and managers' hearings

27.7 The courts have ruled[15] that in order to fulfil their obligations under section 117 health authorities and local authority social services authorities must take reasonable steps to identify appropriate after-care facilities for a patient before his or her actual discharge from hospital. In view of this, some discussion of after-care needs, including social services and other relevant professionals and agencies, should take place before a patient has a Mental Health Review Tribunal or managers hearing, so that suitable after-care arrangements can be implemented in the event of his or her being discharged (see para 22.12).

14 WHC(95)40 was in fact a draft document and the correct reference should have been to WC19/96.
15 *R v Ealing District Health Authority ex p Fox* [1993] 3 All ER 170, QBD.

Who should be involved

27.8 Those who should be involved in consideration of the patient's after-care needs include:

- the patient, if he or she wishes and/or a nominated representative;
- the patient's RMO;
- a nurse involved in caring for the patient in hospital;
- a social worker/care manager specialising in mental health work;
- the GP and primary care team;
- a community psychiatric/mental health nurse;
- a representative of relevant voluntary organisations;
- in the case of a restricted patient, the probation service;
- subject to the patient's consent, any informal carer who will be involved in looking after him or her outside hospital;
- subject to the patient's consent, his or her nearest relative;[16]
- a representative of housing authorities, if accommodation is an issue.

27.9 It is important that those who are involved are able to take decisions regarding their own and as far as possible their agency's involvement. If approval for plans needs to be obtained from more senior levels (for example, for funding) it is important that this causes no delay to the implementation of the care plan.

Considerations for after-care

27.10 Those concerned must consider the following issues:

a. the patient's own wishes and needs, and those of any dependents;

b. the views of any relevant relative, friend or supporter of the patient;

c. the need for agreement with authorities and agencies in the area where the patient is to live;

d. in the case of offender patients, the circumstances of any victim and their families should be taken into account when deciding where the patient should live;

e. the possible involvement of other agencies, eg, probation, voluntary organisations;

f. the establishing of a care plan, based on proper assessment and clearly identified needs, including:

- day time activities or employment,
- appropriate accommodation,
- out-patient treatment,
- counselling, and personal support,
- assistance in welfare rights and managing finances,
- a contingency plan should the patient relapse.

g. the appointment of a key worker (see para 27.2) from either of the statutory agencies to monitor the care plan's implementation, liaise and co-ordinate where necessary and report to the senior officer in their agency any problems that arise which cannot be resolved through discussion;

h. the identification of any unmet need.

27.11 The professionals concerned should establish an agreed outline of the patient's needs, taking into account his or her social and cultural background, and agree a time-scale for the implementation of the various

---

16 There are special considerations governing consultation with the nearest relative of a patient subject to after-care under supervision; see chapter 28.

aspects of the plan. All key people with specific responsibilities with regard to the patient should be properly identified. Once plans are agreed it is essential that any changes are discussed with others involved with the patient before being implemented. The plan should be recorded in writing.

27.12 The care plan should be regularly reviewed. It will be the responsibility of the key worker to arrange reviews of the plan until it is agreed that it is no longer necessary. The senior officer in the key worker's agency responsible for after-care arrangements should ensure that all aspects of the procedure are followed.

CPA and community care assessments under NHSCCA 1990 s47

15.14   The relationship between the administrative obligation on joint NHS/ social services teams to prepare CPA assessments and the social services statutory duty to undertake community care assessments under National Health Service and Community Care Act (NHSCCA) s47 was considered in *R (HP and KP) v Islington LBC*.[17] The case concerned a patient being cared for at home by his family. He was assessed by the psychiatric services as suffering from a form of depression and at risk of severe neglect and 'vulnerable to deterioration in his mental state particularly if he stops taking his medication'. He was however considered not to have a 'severe and enduring mental illness' and deemed not eligible for CPA support. In view of this finding the local authority determined that he was not eligible for 'community care provision'. In quashing this decision, Munby J held that the authority had misunderstood the relationship between the CPA and the duty to assess under NHSCCA 1990 s47(1). The fact that the patient lacked a 'severe and enduring mental illness . . . was not determinative of whether he nonetheless had a need for generic health or social services community care'.[18] Accordingly, in the judge's opinion:

> In my judgment, Islington's demonstrable and serious error in its whole approach to the fundamental underlying questions must, in the circumstances, invalidate both parts of the process.[19] In my judgment there has never been a proper and comprehensive community care assessment of Mr P, only a CPA assessment. The process in relation to the community care assessment must start again.

CPA and the single assessment process

15.15   Guidance on the interface between the CPA and the single assessment process (SAP) is provided in a Department of Health clarification note *Care Management for Older People with Serious Mental Health Problems*[20] and is considered further at para 14.9 above.

---

17 [2004] EWHC 7 (Admin); 8 January 2004.

18 [2004] EWHC 7 (Admin) at [37].

19 The first being to undertake a 'needs assessment' and the second to arrive at a 'service provision decision' – see [2004] EWHC 7 (Admin) at [38].

20 Accessible at www.doh.gov.uk/scg/sap/sapandcpa.htm.

Services under Mental Health Act 1983 s117

15.16   Most non-accommodation services that authorities provide for people with a mental health difficulty are delivered under CSDPA 1970 s2. These services are available to persons 'who suffer from a mental disorder of any description'.[21] Likewise, most accommodation services that authorities provide for people with a mental health difficulty are delivered under NAA 1948 s21.

15.17   Only a small minority of people who receive community care services are entitled to their services under MHA 1983 s117. For such people, however, as section 117 services are virtually unlimited in nature (including where appropriate the provision of accommodation) and (potentially) give users specific individual legal rights the availability of those services under other Acts is in reality academic. From a service user's perspective, the receipt of services under MHA 1983 s117 has the added advantage that social services authorities are not empowered to charge for them (see para 15.34).

15.18   Mental Health Act 1983 s117 (as amended) reads as follows:

(1) This section applies to persons who are detained under section 3 above, or admitted to a hospital in pursuance of a hospital order made under section 37 above, or transferred to a hospital in pursuance of a hospital direction made under section 45A above or a transfer direction made under section 47 or 48 above, and then cease to be detained and (whether or not immediately after so ceasing) leave hospital.

(2) It shall be the duty of the Primary Care Trust or Health Authority[22] and of the local social services authority to provide, in co-operation with relevant voluntary agencies, after-care services for any person to whom this section applies until such time as the Primary Care Trust or Health Authority and the local social services authority are satisfied that the person concerned is no longer in need of such services but they shall not be so satisfied in the case of a patient who is subject to after-care under supervision at any time while he so remains subject.

(2A) It shall be the duty of the Primary Care Trust or Health Authority to secure that at all times while a patient is subject to after-care under supervision –

---

21 In addition, services are also available NHSA 1977 Sch 8 for (among others) persons who are, or have been, suffering from an illness.

22 Although the section has been amended (as a result of the demise of health authorities in England and Wales) to insert 'Primary Care Trusts' (National Health Service Reform and Health Care Professions Act 2002 Sch 2 (2) Para 56), no equivalent amendment has occurred in Wales – to insert the term 'Local Health Boards'. It appears however that this is not strictly necessary, as a result of a combination of Welsh Statutory Instrument the Health Authorities (Transfer of Functions, Staff, Property, Rights and Liabilities and Abolition) (Wales) Order 2003 SI No 813 (W98) – which transfers all functions of health authorities in Wales to the Assembly – and the Local Health Boards (Functions) (Wales) Regulations 2003 SI No 150 (W20) which provides (subject to exceptions) that functions that were exercised by Health Authorities and were transferred to the Assembly by SI No 2003/813 are to be exercised by Local Health Boards.

(a) a person who is a registered medical practitioner approved for the purposes of section 12 above by the secretary of state as having special experience in the diagnosis or treatment of mental disorder is in charge of the medical treatment provided for the patient as part of the after-care services provided for him under this section; and

(b) a person professionally concerned with any of the after-care services so provided is supervising him with a view to securing that he receives the after-care services so provided.

(2B) Section 32 above shall apply for the purposes of this section as it applies for the purposes of Part II of this Act.

(3) In this section 'the Primary Care Trust or Health Authority' means the Primary Care Trust or Health Authority and 'the local Social services authority' means the local social services authority for the area in which the person concerned is resident or to which he is sent on discharge by the hospital in which he was detained.

Reasons for detention

15.19   *Section 3.* Persons are detained under MHA 1983 s3 when admitted for treatment (as opposed to being detained under MHA 1983 s2 (admission for assessment, whether or not accompanied by any treatment)).

Section 37. Persons may only be detained under MHA 1983 s37 by order of a criminal court after being convicted of an offence (punishable by imprisonment) in criminal proceedings and the court being satisfied (among other things) that at the time of conviction the offender was suffering from a specific mental disorder.

Section 45A.[23] Under MHA 1983 s45A, and subject to certain restrictions, the Crown Court may, when sentencing a person who suffers from a psychopathic disorder to a term of imprisonment, direct that they be detained in a specified hospital.

Section 47. Persons may only be detained under MHA 1983 s47 if they are serving a sentence of imprisonment (in a prison) and the secretary of state is satisfied (among other things) that they are suffering from a specific mental disorder (ie, mental illness, psychopathic disorder, mental impairment or severe mental impairment) and should in consequences be removed and detained in a hospital.

Section 48. Detention under MHA 1983 s48 arises in the same circumstances as under MHA 1983 s47, except that section 48 applies to persons who, although detained, are not serving a sentence of imprisonment (eg, they are on remand pending trial, are civil prisoners or being detained under the Immigration Act 1971), and the person must be suffering from a mental illness of severe mental impairment.

---

23 Inserted by Crime (Sentences) Act 1997.

The nature of the section 117 duty

15.20   The duty to provide after-care services under MHA 1983 s117 crystallises when the person 'ceases to be detained'. The nature of the duty under section 117, and the meaning of the phrase 'ceases to be detained' has been considered in a number of diverse fact cases, including by the Court of Appeal in *R (K) v Camden and Islington Health Authority*[24] and the House of Lords in *R (IH) v Secretary of State for the Home Department and others*.[25] From these decisions, it appears that the MHA 1983 s117 duty:

1) only arises on the patient's discharge from hospital although the NHS body has the power to take preparatory steps prior to discharge;[26]

2) insofar as it relates to the provision of ordinary social care services – there is a specific duty (see para 1.5) to ensure that these services are made available;[27]

3) insofar as it relates to the provision of personal/professional services (most notably by the NHS in the form of securing a psychiatrist prepared to accept responsibility for the patient on discharge into the community), the duty is merely to 'use its best endeavours to procure' the services it deems necessary (or those specified by a mental health review tribunal).[28]

15.21   MHA 1983 s117 services are also available to patients on MHA 1983 s17 leave.[29] Section 17 provides that a 'responsible medical officer' can authorise leave of absence to patients detained under Part II of the Act (ie, under non-criminal detention).

15.22   This entitlement arises because MHA 1983 s117 services are provided to persons who are detained under (among others) section 3 'and then ceases to be detained and (whether or not immediately after so ceasing) leave hospital'. A person can therefore be entitled to services under MHA 1983 s117 even though still formally detained under section 3, since the crucial question is whether or not he or she is physically detained in a hospital rather than legally 'liable to be detained' under MHA 1983 s3.

District or area of residence

15.23   MHA 1983 s117(3) provides that services under that section are the responsibility of the social services/health body for the area in which 'the person concerned is resident or to which he is sent on discharge by the hospital in

---

24   [2001] EWCA Civ 240; [2002] QB 198; [2001] 3 WLR 553; (2001) 4 CCLR 170; (2001) 61 BMLR 173.

25   [2003] UKHL 59; [2003] 3 WLR 1278; (2004) 7 CCLR 147.

26   *R (K) v Camden and Islington Health Authority* [2001] EWCA Civ 240 at [20].

27   *R v Ealing District Health Authority ex p Fox* [1993] 3 All ER 170, QBD.

28   *R (IH) v Secretary of State for the Home Department and others* [2003] UKHL 59 at [29].

29   This entitlement, which is noted in the Code of Practice to the 1983 Act (paragraph 20.7 asserts that the 'duty to provide after-care under MHA 1983 s117 includes patients on leave of absence') was confirmed by Sullivan J, in *R v Richmond LBC and others ex p Watson and others* (1999) *Times* 15 October, see also para 15.28 below.

which he was detained'. The question of ordinary residence under section 117 is considered further at para 6.21 above.

Services

15.24   In *R v Mental Health Review Tribunal ex p Hall*[30] the Divisional Court held that the duty to provide after care services under MHA 1983 s117(2) was jointly shared by the health and social services authority in which the patient was resident at the time he was detained. It is therefore up to individual health body and social services authorities to decide among themselves as to how they will discharge these joint responsibilities. However, it would appear probable that most such patients, who are discharged to nursing care homes, would meet the continuing health care criteria (see para 10.87 above).

15.25   Section 117 places no restriction upon the type of services that can be provided.[31] All that is required is that the person concerned must need these services. 'After-care' services under MHA 1983 s117 include therefore all the traditional community care services such as advice, guidance and counselling; occupational, social, cultural or recreational activities as well as day centre and drop-in centre provision; domiciliary care[32] as well as laundry and other such services; residential care accommodation and so on.

15.26   Only limited guidance on the nature and extent of s117 services has been issued. The Code of Practice to the Mental Health Act (April 1999) at paragraph 27.1 notes, however that 'a central purpose of all treatment and care is to equip patients to cope with life outside hospital and function there successfully without danger to themselves or other people'. At paragraph 27.10 (f) it suggests that the user's care plan should identify, various needs, including, 'daytime activities or employment, appropriate accommodation, out-patient treatment, counselling and personal support and assistance in welfare rights and managing finances.

15.27   Guidance on the Mental Health (Patients in the Community) Act 1995 (see below) suggests that MHA 1983 s117 services may include[33] 'appropriate daytime activities, accommodation, treatment, personal and practical support, 24-hour emergency cover and assistance in welfare rights and financial advice' as well as 'support for informal carers'.

The duration of the duty

15.28   The services provided under MHA 1983 s117 must continue to be supplied until the authorities are satisfied that he or she is no longer in need of them. In *R v Richmond LBC and others ex p Watson and others*,[34] (a case concerning

---

30   [1999] 4 All ER 883; [2000] 1 WLR 1323.
31   In co-operation with the relevant voluntary agencies – MHA 1983 s117(2).
32   Including, for instance, such services as are detailed in Chronically Sick and Disabled Persons Act 1970 s2.
33   LAC (96)8/HSG (96)11, para 18.
34   (1999) *Times* 15 October.

the lawfulness of charging for services under MHA 1983 s117 – see para 15.34 below) Sullivan J held that after-care provision under section 117 does not have to continue indefinitely, although it must continue until such time as the health body and the local authority are satisfied that the individual is no longer in need of such services.

15.29   In his judgment he considered the following question: 'What are the local authorities' duties under MHA 1983 s117 towards a person, who because of old age, illness or other circumstances, has been provided with residential accommodation under National Assistance Act 1948 s21, then becomes mentally unwell, is detained under MHA 1983 s3, is discharged from hospital and returns to his or her former accommodation as part of their after care package?'

15.30   He held:

> I can see no reason why such a person should be in any worse position than the patient who has not previously been provided with accommodation under section 21. On leaving hospital, the local authority will owe them a duty under section 117. There may be cases where, in due course there will be no more need for after care services for the person's mental condition' but he or she will still need social services provision for other needs, for example, physical disability. Such cases will have to be examined individually on their facts, through the assessment process provided for by section 47. In a case . . . where the illness is dementia, it is difficult to see how such a situation could arise.

15.31   The issue was also considered by the Local Government Ombudsman in a complaint against Clwyd.[35] The facts being that the resident had been detained under MHA 1983 s3 from which she was discharged and eventually moved to an Elderly Mentally Ill (EMI) nursing home. Steps were then taken by the local authority to assess her liability for residential care charges and in due course the authority placed a charge on her home.

15.32   After the resident's daughter questioned the authority's power to levy such charges the hospital consultant met with the relevant social worker and purported to discharge the MHA 1983 s117 after care. Neither the resident or her daughter were aware of the discharge meeting or decision.

15.33   The Ombudsman considered all these matters, but in particular the decision to discharge the MHA 1983 s117 arrangements. In his decision he held:

> 1. The council had a duty to provide after-care services at no cost to the resident from the moment she was discharged from hospital until such time as it was satisfied that she was no longer in need of such services.
> 2. In deciding that she no longer needed after-care under MHA 1983 s117 the council had failed to address the relevant question which was whether she needed and whether she continued to need after-care services. The Ombudsman concluded that if the council had asked itself the relevant

35 Dated 19 September 1997, see (1998) 1 CCLR 546; and see also Report No 98/B/0341 from the English Local Ombudsman against Wiltshire where a similar finding was made coupled with a recommendation that the cases of other people who might have had to pay for services inappropriately also be reviewed.

question, it would have had to conclude that she was in need of the specialist care provided at a home for the elderly mentally infirm.

3. The Ombudsman concluded that the council's maladministration had been exacerbated by a number of factors including their failure to take account of the daughters views before ceasing to provide after-care services under MHA 1983 s117.

Charging for MHA 1983 s117 services

15.34   In *R v Manchester CC ex p Stennett and others*[36] the House of Lords held that it was unlawful for local authorities to charge for services under MHA 1983 s117. Although the judgment confirmed the consistent view of the Department of Health,[37] many local authorities had hitherto been charging for such services and accordingly a substantial number of claims were then made for reimbursement – many of which coming to the notice of the local government ombudsman. Accordingly in July 2003 a special report was issued by the three English Local Government Ombudsmen,[38] the key advice therein being summarised as follows:[39]

- That, in general, social services authorities (SSAs) should not carry out retrospective assessments purporting to remove a person from section 117 aftercare as from an earlier date.

- That SSAs should review any retrospective assessments that have so far been made.

- That, for the next 12 months at least, complaints made about previous assessments to end section 117 aftercare should not be rejected by SSAs as out of time.

- That where previous assessments to end section 117 aftercare were not properly made, then restitution will generally be appropriate until a proper assessment is devised.

- That people who have paid for section 117 aftercare should receive financial restitution with interest.

- That SSAs should now put mechanisms in place to identify those persons improperly charged, or improperly deprived of financial assistance, and establish arrangements for reimbursing them or their estates.

- That no generally applicable cut-off date should be used when calculating repayments. Cases where such cut-off dates have been applied should be reviewed.

---

36   [2002] 3 WLR 584; [2002] 4 All ER 124; (2002) 5 CCLR 500.

37   See for instance LAC(2000)3 (Feb 2000) *After-care under the Mental Health Act 1983: section 117 after-care services.*

38   July 2003 accessible www.lgo.org.uk/pdf/special-report-web.pdf. The report contains copies of the key reports: Clwyd, 19 September 1997; (1998) 1 CCLR 546; Wiltshire County Council, 14 December 1999; (2000) 3 CCLR 60, and Leicestershire, 25 October 2001; C00/B/08307.

39   July 2003 guidance (see note 38 above) at para 5.

Mental Health (Patients in the Community) Act 1995

15.35   The 1995 Act introduced the possibility of 'after-care under supervision' generally referred to as supervised discharge – its purpose has been described in the following terms:[40]

> After-care under supervision is an arrangement by which a patient who has been detained in hospital for treatment under the provisions of the Act may be subject to formal supervision after he or she is discharged. Its purpose is to help ensure that the patient receives the after-care services to be provided under section 117 of the Act. It is available for patients suffering from any of the four forms of mental disorder in the Act but is primarily intended for those with severe mental illness.

15.36   For such a supervised discharge to take place, it must be shown:

> (a) that unless aftercare services under s117 are provided there will be:
>   (i) a substantial risk of serious harm to the health or safety of the patient or the safety of others, or
>   (ii) a risk that the patient will be seriously exploited; and
> (b) in any event that placing the patient under supervised discharge is likely to help ensure that s/he will receive the relevant after-care services.

15.37   Guidance on the 1995 Act has been issued in the form of Circular LAC (96)8 / HSG (96)11,[41] which includes the following:

> 18.   The arrangements for after-care under supervision will need to be drawn up as part of the normal discharge planning process, following the principles of the Care Programme Approach in England and WHC (95)40[42] in Wales and in accordance with the formal consultation requirements in the Act (see below). Chapter 27 of the Code is also relevant. The professional team providing care in the community will need to consider and plan the services to be provided, including as may be appropriate daytime activities, accommodation, treatment, personal and practical support, 24-hour emergency cover and assistance in welfare rights and financial advice. They will also need to consider how often the patient is likely to need particular services. Support for informal carers should not be overlooked as the care plan may be to some degree dependent on their role.
>
> 19.   The Act defines requirements which may be imposed when a patient is subject to supervised discharge. These are:
> • that the patient should live in a particular place;
> • that the patient should attend a particular place at set times for medical treatment, occupation, education or training;
> • that the supervisor, or a person authorised by the supervisor, should be allowed access to the patient at his or her place of residence (see paragraph 51 below).

40   Code of Practice to the Mental Health Act (April 1999) at paragraph 28.2.
41   WHC(96)11 in Wales.
42   WHC(95) 40 was in fact a draft document and the correct reference should have been to WC 19/96.

The reasons for imposing requirements should be explained to the patient, and details of them should be included in the care plan. A requirement to attend for medical treatment does not carry with it any power to impose medication or other treatment against the patient's wishes.

MHA 1983 reform

15.38　The government has announced controversial proposals to reform the MHA 1983,[43] and has indicated that it proposes to publish a revised Bill in 2004. It is expected that the amended proposals will make material changes to the definition of a 'mental disorder' (in relation to which the detention and treatment provisions will then apply); will require all detention and compulsory treatment beyond 28 days to be sanctioned by a new Mental Health Tribunal; will provide for patients to be subject to community-based orders, and the provision of services under MHA 1983 s117 will be repealed.

43　See www.dh.gov.uk/PolicyAndGuidance/HealthAndSocialCareTopics/MentalHealth/ fs/en, generally for the draft 2002 Bill and explanatory notes and consultation documents.

Drug, alcohol and HIV/AIDS services

Introduction

16.1   It is thought that about four million people in England and Wales use at least one illicit drug each year, of which about one million use one of the most dangerous drugs (such as heroin and crack).[1] Approximately 250,000 such users develop serious drug problems and it is this group that is considered responsible for 99 per cent of the social and economic costs associated with misuse – which are thought to be in the region of £18 billion a year.[2]

16.2   In 1998 the government published a strategy paper, *Tackling Drugs To Build A Better Britain*,[3] in order to co-ordinate its 'combating misuse' policies. The policy was reviewed and revised in 2002 – when an updated strategy was published. The current programme targets those considered to have a serious drug problem, particularly the 50 per cent who are not in treatment. It aims to double the number of people in treatment by (among other things) increasing the availability of services, with the current expenditure on such treatment services of £450 million (2003–04) projected to increase to £573 million by 2005. There is some evidence that the programme is proving to be effective.[4]

16.3   The service provision strategy in England[5] is co-ordinated through the National Treatment Agency for Substance Misuse (NTA)[6] is a special health authority, created in 2001[7] to improve the availability, capacity and effectiveness of treatment for drug misuse in England. The NTA issues policy and practice guidance and distributes funding (via its nine regional offices) to the 149 Drug Action Teams (DATs) which cover all English local authorities. DATs are local consortia that include representatives of all the local agencies involved in tackling the misuse of drugs, including primary care trusts, local authorities, the police and probation service. It is the responsibility of DATs to provide drug misusers with access to advice and information, needle exchanges and counselling.

---

1   Updated Drug Strategy (Home Office, 2002) accessible at www.drugs.gov.uk/Home.

2   A government estimate – see www.drugs.gov.uk/NationalStrategy.

3   Cm 3945; a multi-departmental initiative, accessible at www.archive.official-documents.co.uk/document/cm39/3945/3945.htm.

4   The number of people receiving treatment for their drug problem appear to have increased by 41 per cent between 1998 and 2002 with an apparent two-thirds reduction in waiting times for treatment between December 2001 and October 2003.See http://www.nta.nhs.uk/ press release 11 December 2003.

5   In Wales, a similar programme exists, See *Welsh Assembly Government Wales Substance Misuse Services Review 2002/03 Final Report*: accessible at www.wales.gov.uk/subicrimeprevention/content/substance-misuse-report-e.htm.

6   Their web site is accessible at www.nta.nhs.uk/.

7   The National Treatment Agency (Establishment and Constitution) Order 2001 SI No 713.

Community care provision for drug and alcohol misusers

16.4 The white paper *Health of the Nation*[8] and the Policy Guidance confirm that an important objective of the community care reforms was to ensure that community care services were available to those whose need for them arose by reason of alcohol or drug misuse. The Policy Guidance (at para 8.4) emphasises the point thus:

> The government attaches a high priority[9] to tackling the problems associated with the misuse of alcohol and drugs, and to ensuring the provision of a comprehensive network of services for alcohol and drug misusers.

16.5 In similar vein, guidance on the housing/community care interface, LAC(92)12 makes the following point:

> Housing authorities will need to be aware that for some clients, such as alcohol and drug misusers, their care plan may include a planned progression from some form of residential care to a more independent lifestyle, possibly away from their original area of residence.[10]

16.6 The principal social services circular guidance concerning services for drug and alcohol misusers is LAC(93)2, which stresses the special circumstances surrounding the provision of services for this client group, and in particular comments:

> 12. Addressing the needs of people with alcohol and drug problems will present a particular challenge to LAs. The aim must be to respond effectively and to offer a programme of care that will help the misuser make positive changes to his or her life. LAs will need to bear in mind that people who misuse alcohol and drugs may:
> * present to LAs with problems other than alcohol and/or drug misuse. LAs will need to ensure that the possibility of alcohol and drug misuse is covered in essential procedures;
> * have particularly complex needs including urgent workplace or family crises or difficulties with child care, which may not have been revealed to LA services;
> * move between areas frequently, and a significant proportion will have no settled residence or be living away from their area of ordinary residence;
> * self-refer to agencies which are not in their home area, both because of their transient lifestyle and for therapeutic reasons, and many will need urgent help;
> * avoid contact with statutory services; drug misusers in particular may be reluctant to become involved with statutory agencies because of the illegal nature of their drug-related activities;

---

8 (1993) See for instance para D.17–D.18.
9 The point is also made in the white paper *Tackling Drugs Together* (Cm 2846, 1995) at para B.55.
10 At para 2 of the Annex to the circular.

- need to be provided with services several times before they succeed in controlling their alcohol or drug misuse;
- require residential treatment and rehabilitation as a positive treatment choice;
- sometimes behave unpredictably and may not fit easily into assessment and care management systems designed to meet the needs of other client groups.

Assessment procedures

16.7   Circular LAC(93)2 makes a number of important points concerning the need for authorities to adopt flexible assessment procedures in relation to people who misuse alcohol or drugs, and the related need in many cases to develop a close working relationship with the probation services.

> 13. People with serious and urgent alcohol and/or drug problems are likely to need a rapid response because of crises and to capture fluctuating motivation. Serious deterioration which may carry social, legal and care implications may ensue if there is delay before assessment or if assessment procedures are prolonged.
>
> *Eligibility for assessment*
> 14. LAs should ensure that any criteria they may develop governing eligibility for assessment are sensitive to the circumstances of alcohol and drug misusers. As with all other user groups, the LA should have criteria for determining the level of assessment that is appropriate to the severity or complexity of the need. LAs should ensure that:
> - arrangements have been agreed with all the agencies in their area to which misusers are likely to present for help, which will enable those agencies to initiate assessment procedures where in their view they are indicated;
> - arrangements are in place to facilitate the assessment of a person by another authority where that person is ordinarily resident in that other authority's area, for example by agreeing with another LA to undertake an assessment on that authority's behalf;
> - individuals who are of no settled residence are not excluded from assessment by means of eligibility criteria which require duration of residence. The Department proposes to issue guidance to LAs in 1993 about the resolution of disputes and the procedures to be adopted in the last resort where disputes cannot be resolved between the authorities concerned.[11] Disputes about ordinary residence should not prevent people receiving the care they need.
>
> *Adapting assessment to the special needs of alcohol and drug misusers*
> 15. LAs will need to ensure that their assessment systems take full account of the different ways in which alcohol and drug misusers present for services, their different characteristics and their particular needs:
> - standard LA assessment procedures and documentation should include consideration of substance misuse.
> - LA staff will need to be able to identify the indications of substance misuse so that specialist agencies can be involved where appropriate.

11   This was effected via LAC(93)7 Part II – see para 6.4 above.

Rapid assessment procedures ('fast-track' assessment)

16. There are a range of organisations and professionals who deal frequently with alcohol and drug misusers. A great many of the services, including virtually all residential services, are provided by the independent sector. There is, therefore, within the independent sector, a substantial reservoir of experienced professionals with skills to undertake assessment in this field. LAs should consider involving independent sector agencies in the assessment process. Practice guidance issued by the Department of Health Social Services Inspectorate[12] emphasises the importance of training to equip those people within LAs who undertake assessment with the necessary knowledge and skills. Policy guidance issued by the Department, 'Community Care in the Next Decade and Beyond'[13] states that where a specialist service – for example a drug and alcohol service – is provided by an independent agency under arrangements with a social services department, it will be possible to include assessment of needs in relation to such services in contract arrangements. In these circumstances LAs will need to ensure that the specialist agency is aware of other potential needs for which LAs have a responsibility.

17. Residential placements should not normally take place without a comprehensive needs assessment. Where assessment is contracted to an independent specialist agency, decisions to commit resources and ultimate responsibility for the assessment remains with the LA.

18. Because many alcohol and drug misusers present or are referred to services outside their area of ordinary residence LAs are encouraged to work together to identify systems so that they can feel confident about committing resources on the basis of an assessment undertaken in another LA. This may be facilitated by the development of standard and agreed assessment procedures and forms and networks of named responsible officers within LAs.

19. The Department is encouraging local authority associations to work with the independent sector to establish rapid assessment procedures for alcohol and drug misusers and good practice guidance in out of area referrals which they can commend to local authorities.

20. Individual LAs and independent service providers should, together, ensure that rapid assessment procedures meet the needs of alcohol and drug misusers. In order to do so LAs and providers may want to determine the pattern of referrals of their residents/clients in order to establish contact and set up appropriate arrangements where regular flows exist. LAs and independent sector service providers will together wish to have regard to the Department's study examining good practice in care management and assessment for alcohol and drug misusers which will be available to local authorities shortly.

Emergency action

21. LAs need to be aware that alcohol and drug misusers may sometimes be in such urgent need that residential care will need to be provided immediately. 'The Care Management and Assessment' practice guidance

---

12 *Care Management and Assessment: A Practitioners' Guide* (1991) see para 4.45 above.

13 Referred to in this text as the 1990 Policy Guidance; see para 1.33 above.

issued by the Department of Health covers the arrangements for urgent admission to both residential and nursing home care.[14]

22. LAs may contract with a provider to offer an emergency direct access service for people in urgent need, with assessment and a decision about longer term treatment following as soon as practicable. LAs may wish to contract with a voluntary organisation to provide direct access to residential care without assessment in these circumstances. In such cases of urgent need the area of ordinary residence of the person should not be a consideration.[15]

Out of area referrals

23. Because of the transient lifestyles of a significant proportion of drug and alcohol misusers LAs will be involved in negotiations about area of ordinary residence for people with alcohol and drug misuse problems to a greater extent than for others. Where people are ordinarily resident in the area of the LA undertaking the assessment, there may be therapeutic benefit in referring people to a residential service away from the area in which they are experiencing their alcohol and drug problems. LAs are reminded that the statutory direction on choice[16] of residential accommodation advises that people assessed as needing residential care should be able to exercise choice over the place where they receive that care. LAs should ensure that resources can be identified for out of area placements.

24. As should ensure that there are arrangements in place for responding to the following types of out of area referrals:
- where people are ordinarily resident outside the area of the LA undertaking the assessment, there will be a need to liaise with the LA in the area of ordinary residence to establish responsibility for funding the care package.
- where people are ordinarily resident outside the area of the LA but are in urgent need of residential care.[17]
- here it is impossible to identify a person's area of ordinary residence; in these circumstances the LA where they present for services should assume responsibility for arranging and providing the necessary services.[18]

Probation service

25. Some alcohol and/or drug misusing clients of the Probation Service will continue to seek access to residential and non-residential care, and LAs should liaise with probation services to ensure that these needs can be considered within the community care arrangements. Attention should be given to establishing joint assessment or common assessment procedures, such as those LAs have developed with other client groups. LAs will also need to be aware that there may be requests for resources to provide

---

14 Practice Guidance (1991) at para 4.45 for nursing homes and para 4.97 for residential homes.
15 National Assistance Act (NAA) 1948 s24(3).
16 National Assistance Act 1948 (Choice of Accommodation) Directions 1992; see para 7.84 and appendix B.
17 NAA 1948 s24(3)(b).
18 NAA 1948 ss24(3)(a) and 32.

residential and non-residential care for persons whose alcohol or drug misuse comes to light through offending, appearance in court and/or involvement with probation services. LAs are reminded that the Criminal Justice Act 1991 which came into force on 1 October 1992 emphasises that it is preferable for offenders who misuse alcohol or drugs to be dealt with in the community rather than in custody.[19]

16.8   In this respect, the Strategy Paper, '*Tackling Drugs To Build A Better Britain*' (1998)[20] also highlighted the crucial role of inter-disciplinary working (particularly between health, social services, housing , education and employment services).

Delegation of duty to assess

16.9   LAC(93)2 gives guidance on the use of third parties to assist the assessment process, including:

> 14. . . . LAs should ensure that:
> - arrangements have been agreed with all the agencies in their area to which misusers are likely to present for help, which will enable those agencies to initiate assessment procedures where in their view they are indicated;
> - arrangements are in place to facilitate the assessment of a person by another authority where that person is ordinarily resident in that other authority's area, for example by agreeing with another LA to undertake an assessment on that authority's behalf;
> - individuals who are of no settled residence are not excluded from assessment by means of eligibility criteria which require duration of residence . . .
>
> 25. Some alcohol and/or drug misusing clients of the Probation Service will continue to seek access to residential and non-residential care, and LAs should liaise with probation services to ensure that these needs can be considered within the community care arrangements. Attention should be given to establishing joint assessment or common assessment procedures, such as those LAs have developed with other client groups . . .
>
> 27. As with alcohol and drug misusers, LAs should have flexible systems of assessment and care management that allow such people [homeless people with other needs] access to the services they need in a way that meets their special circumstances. Their homelessness may in itself mean that an urgent response is called for. LAs will be aware that there are a wide variety of agencies which specialise in providing care for homeless people. As with specialist alcohol and drug providers, these agencies may be in a position to assist in assessment procedures.

---

19 See Powers of Criminal Courts Act 1973 Sch 1A.
20 Cm 3945, at page 23.

The provision and commissioning of services

16.10   Although the statutory responsibility for the provision of heath and social care services for drug and alcohol misusers rest with the NHS and social services authorities, in practice the assessment and service provision functions are discharged by DATs.[21]

16.11   Every DAT should have access to a range of services to cater for the assessed needs of misusers. These services are detailed in a 2002 NTA/Department of Health publication *Models of care*[22] which guidance is intended to have a 'similar status to a national service framework. All commissioners of drug treatment services will be expected to plan and commission services based on the system outlined in Models of care'.[23] This anticipates that a person may receive a number of different forms of treatment at the same time – for example someone may be receiving counselling as well as medication – or a sequence of treatment, for example as a hospital inpatient for a detoxification programme, followed by a residential rehabilitation service.

16.12   The NTA's formal definition of treatment is as follows:[24]

> The term 'treatment' describes a range of interventions which are intended to remedy an identified drug-related problem or condition relating to a person's physical, psychological or social (including legal) well-being.
>   Structured drug treatment follows assessment and is delivered according to a care plan, with clear goals, which is regularly reviewed with the client.

16.13   *Models of care* (chapter 4) requires that DATs ensure that users have access to four 'tiers' of service – made up of different types or modalities of treatment. The terms 'tiers' and 'modalities' are used (it explains) because they are the recognised way of referring to treatment in the NHS. The treatment tiers are summarised as follows:

Tier 1: Non-substance misuse services
Tier 1 services do not specialise in providing treatment for drug misuse, but because of the nature of their work, they do come into contact with drug misusers. Tier 1 services act as important gateway and referral routes to more specialised services.

Tier 2: Open access substance misuse services
Tier 2 services are specialist drug services, but they are open access services. People who want to use these services can access them very

---

21   For contact details of the local services, the NTA provides a link to a general search facility at www.drugscope.org.uk/drugbaseii/home.asp and a separate search engine for identifying residential services at www.nta.nhs.uk/residentialdirectory/index.html.

22   'Models of Care: for treatment of adult drug misusers. Framework for developing local systems of effective drug misuse treatment in England' (Parts 1 and 2) October 2002 accessible at NTA 'background' briefing statement at www.nta.nhs.uk/.

23   'Models of Care: for treatment of adult drug misusers. Framework for developing local systems of effective drug misuse treatment in England' para 2.1.

24   NTA 'Treatment modalities/services' briefing statement at www.nta.nhs.uk/.

easily, and can refer themselves. The aim of tier 2 services is to engage drug misusers in treatment and to reduce drug-related harm. Drug misusers often access other services through tier 2 services.

Tier 3: Structured community-based substance misuse services

Tier 3 services are specialist drug treatment services that are provided in a structured way in the community (ie, they do not require clients to stay in overnight accommodation).

Tier 4: Residential substance misuse services

Tier 4 services provide a residential element to their treatment where the client lives in a centre for a period of time. These types of services are very intensive and are aimed at people with high levels of need. There are two main types of tier 4 services:

Tier 4a: Residential services that deal specifically with drug misusers. This would include: inpatient drug detoxification or stabilisation services within hospitals; drug residential rehabilitation units; and residential drug crisis intervention centres.

Tier 4b: Highly-specialised residential services that have not been established to deal specifically with drug misusers, but because of the nature of their work, they often treat people with drug problems. This would include: specialist hospital liver units that treat liver diseases, including hepatitis which drug misusers can pick up through sharing injecting equipment; and forensic services for offenders with mental health problems – many of whom also have drug problems. Some of these services also provide support to the other tiers of treatment, (eg, specialist hepatitis nurses, HIV liaison clinics, genito-urinary medicine).

Service user failure

16.14   Drug and alcohol services can be relatively expensive, and the guidance (LAC(93)2 para 11) states, 'there is a comparatively rapid turnover' of such service users in residential accommodation due in part to the relatively high 'failure rate' experienced by people trying to rid themselves of an addiction. The NTA endorse this advice – that relapses are to be expected and planned for, stating that 'most drug misusers relapse and need to return to treatment a number of times before getting their habit under control'. It notes, however that 'around 50 per cent of those who do complete a comprehensive treatment programme are still drug-free after five years'.[25]

16.15   The importance of this factor was also stressed in *Purchasing Effective Treatment and Care for Drug Misusers* (March 1997) which stated (at para 1.7):

> Drug misusers suffer relapses, and may need several periods of treatment before they achieve the ultimate aim of 'abstinence'. 'Instant' cures are relatively rare, partly because drug misuse is closely associated with many other problems. These include unemployment, family break up, homelessness and crime. Tackling drug misuse effectively may therefore involve a range of interventions by several agencies, for people at different stages of their drug misusing careers. If these are not properly co-ordinated resources will be wasted.

25   NTA 'background' briefing statement at www.nta.nhs.uk/.

NHS obligations

16.16   The effects of alcohol/drug misuse can be life-threatening and frequently require specialist medical and nursing interventions. The NHS has a clear responsibility in this field, although it is, in relation to such matters as rehabilitation and recovery (see para 10.109), an overlapping responsibility with social services authorities. LAC(93)2 confirms[26] that 'the new community care arrangements do not affect health authorities' responsibilities for funding the healthcare element of any alcohol and drug service. LAs will need to consider and draw up agreements with health authorities covering arrangements for funding treatment and rehabilitation services for people with alcohol and/or drug problems'.

16.17   The white paper *Tackling Drugs Together*[27] in referring to the role of health care services stated:[28]

> The Government's aim is to provide a comprehensive range and choice of local services to help drug misusers give up drugs and maintain abstinence. Such services also promote better health and reduce the risks of drug misuse, including infections associated with sharing injecting equipment such as HIV and hepatitis. These services include residential detoxification and rehabilitation, community drug dependency services, needle and syringe exchange schemes, advice and counselling, and after-care and support services. Facilities are provided by both statutory and independent agencies. General practitioners are also encouraged to address the needs of drug misusers. Guidelines on clinical management, *Drug Misuse and Dependence*[29] were issued to all doctors in 1991. Guidelines for the clinical management of substance misusers in police custody[30] were issued in March 1995.

16.18   EL(95)114 required health authorities to review and report on their arrangements for 'shared care' of drug misusers. The outcome of this review and advice on general health authority commissioning is contained in the Department of Health publication *Purchasing Effective Treatment and Care for Drug Misusers* (March 1997), appendix C to which lists a number of specific health services that ought to be available for drug misusers. These include hospital drug detoxification units,[31] providing urgent assessment and acute care as well as support, counselling and rehabilitation; methadone reduction programmes, hospital outpatient and community-based clinics, general counselling as well as GP training and encouragement to 'identify drug misuse, promote harm minimisation and where appropriate refer to specialist services'. The publication expressed particular concern about failures of co-ordination between health and local authorities such that there

---

26 At para 7.
27 Cm 2846, HMSO, 1995.
28 At para B.49.
29 Department of Health, HMSO, 1991.
30 Substance Misuse Detainees in Police Custody: Guidelines on Clinical Management (Department of Health, 1995).
31 Or through specialist nursing home facilities.

were 'long waits for detoxification', noting that this may mean that drug misusers lose their motivation to continue with treatment (para 8.5).

Social services obligations

Accommodation

16.19 The duty to provide residential care or nursing home accommodation under National Assistance Act (NAA) 1948 s21 specifically includes a duty towards persons who are 'alcoholic or drug-dependent'.[32] The duties under NAA 1948 s21 are considered in detail in chapter 7.

16.20 The role of residential care facilities is the subject of guidance in LAC(93)2, which states:

> 10. Residential services are an important component of overall service provision for alcohol and drug misusers and have developed as a national network. There are many LAs without such an alcohol or drug service in their area. Residential services offer a number of different treatment approaches, and LAs will need to ensure that people are referred to a service best suited to their needs. LAs can obtain information about the network of residential service provision in publications from two national voluntary organisations, Alcohol Concern and SCODA.[33]

> 11. The length of treatment programmes in a residential setting varies between three and eighteen months. The comparatively rapid turnover of alcohol and drug clients in residential care mean that places will begin to become vacant on a relatively large scale after 1 April 1993. LAs will need to address issues of assessment and care management for these people now so that they are ready from 1 April 1993 to provide new applicants with the care they need.[34]

16.21 A Social Services Inspectorate report *Residential Care for People with Drug/ Alcohol Problems* (1994) made the following general comments concerning the accommodation needs of such people:

- Drug/alcohol misusers often have a range of problems which may contribute to, or be exacerbated by, substance misuse; residential care is only one part of a continuum of services.
- Residential care may be the preferred option most appropriate to meet individual need for one of the following reasons:
  - the service user may need 'time out' from an environment which is not conducive to cessation of drug/alcohol misuse;
  - the service user many have a number of complex and inter-related problems which can be addressed only in a residential environment.
- A primary and major need of people, in other client groups, requiring residential care is usually for supervised accommodation; for

---

32 LAC(93)10 appendix 1, para 2(6).

33 The Standing Conference on Drug Abuse, Waterbridge House, 32–36 Loman Street, London SE1 0EE. Tel: 020 7928 9500.

34 LAC(93)2 was issued in January 1993.

drug/alcohol misusers, accommodation is often only one of a range of needs which require intensive support.

- The characteristics and needs of drug/alcohol misusers are different in some ways from those of other client groups who require residential care because they are unable, or do not feel able, to live independently in their home environment. Many drug/alcohol misusers are in their early adult years and residential care is required as an appropriate temporary environment in which to provide intensive therapeutic care as well as physical and social care. Residential care is rarely provided for drug/alcohol misusers as a permanent home.

Non-accommodation obligations

16.22   Services under National Health Service Act (NHSA) 1977 Sch 8 para 2 are specifically available for persons who are 'alcoholic or drug-dependent' and these services are considered at paras 8.124 and 8.147g above. In general drug and alcohol misusers will only qualify for services under Chronically Sick and Disabled Persons Act (CSDPA) 1970 s2 where their addiction is such as to bring them within the criteria of being 'substantially and permanently handicapped'.[35]

16.23   The description of possible arrangements which can be made under NHSA 1977 Sch 8 para 2 is so widely drafted as to be capable of encompassing virtually all the traditional domiciliary and community care services. The inclusion in the directions (at appendix 3 to LAC(93)10) of a separate category of potential service 'specifically for persons who are alcoholic or drug-dependent', is clearly designed to ensure that authorities are empowered to provide all the relevant services which may be required by alcohol or drug misusers. The 1990 policy guidance (at para 8.6) states that the range of services local authorities will need to consider 'include prevention and harm minimisation, advice and counselling, day care and residential rehabilitation'.[36]

16.24   *Purchasing Effective Treatment and Care for Drug Misusers* (March 1997), gives commissioning advice on various community and residential based services, including outreach programmes and structured day care.[37] It however emphasised the central part played by counselling (both structured and general) in all drug misuse treatments (para 8.6) and the 'evidence that residential rehabilitation programmes can effectively help many drug misusers, particularly with chaotic lifestyles and severe problems related to their misuse (para 8.5).

---

35 This will be so even though such services are also available to persons suffering from a mental disorder of any description, since Mental Health Act 1983 s1(3) excludes persons whose disorder is solely attributable to dependence on alcohol or drugs.

36 See 'New Options: Changing residential and social care for drug users' (1997) SCODA (see note 33 above).

37 See also 'Structured Day Programmes: new options in community care for drug misusers' (1996) SCODA.

Dual diagnosis

16.25   Between a third to a half of people with severe mental health problems have substance misuse related problems.[38] In order to avoid such persons being 'shuttled between services, with a corresponding loss of continuity of care' attempts have been made to ensure that specialist mental health services and specialist substance abuse services co-operate closely. *Models of care*[39] for instance, at para 2.3 notes that 'mental health services should work closely together to meet the needs of drug misusers with dual diagnosis (psychiatric co-morbidity). In this instance, providers should have access to medical clinical leadership and/or advice from mental health specialists in line with good practice guidelines'.

16.26   The key 'good practice guideline' in this domain is a Department of Health publication *Mental Health Policy Implementation Guide Dual Diagnosis Good Practice Guide* (2002).[40] The document seeks to better integrate working between the specialist agencies – rather than create a separate organisation for 'dual diagnosis' users. In relation to the policy that should inform specialist units working in these fields, it summarises the key points of its advice, thus:

- Mainstream mental health services have a responsibility to address the needs of people with a dual diagnosis.

- Where they exist, specialist teams of dual diagnosis workers should provide support to mainstream mental health services.

- All staff in assertive outreach must be trained and equipped to work with dual diagnosis.

- Adequate numbers of staff in crisis resolution and early intervention teams, community mental health teams (CMHTs) and inpatient settings must also be so trained.

- They must be able to link up with each other and with specialist advice and support, including from drug and alcohol agencies.

- All local health and social care economies must map need including for those in prison.

- Project teams must be set up and must agree a local plan to meet need which must contain an agreed local focused definition, care pathways/care co-ordination protocols and clinical governance guidelines.

- All clients must be on the care programme approach (CPA) and must have a full risk assessment regardless of their location within services.

- Local implementation teams (LITs) should take the lead in implementing these guidelines ensuring that commissioning is co-ordinated across PCTs and DATs.

---

38 *Mental Health Policy Implementation Guide Dual Diagnosis Good Practice Guide*, Department of Health, 2002, para 1.3.1.

39 See para 16.11 above.

40 Accessible at www.dh.gov.uk/assetRoot/04/06/04/35/04060435.pdf.

16.27　It summarises the key points of its advice, concerning assessment and treatment approaches in the following terms:

- assessment of substance misuse forms an integral part of standard assessment procedures for mental health problems;

- services need to develop routine screening procedures and, where substance misuse is identified, the nature and severity of that misuse and its associated risks should be assessed;

- an awareness of specific groups for whom these dual conditions generate specific needs must inform the assessment process;

- treatments should be staged according to an individual's readiness for change and engagement with services;

- staff should avoid prematurely pushing clients towards abstinence but adopt a harm reduction approach;

- an optimistic and longitudinal perspective regarding the substance misuse problem and its treatment are necessary;

- a flexible and adaptive therapeutic response is important for the integrated management of these dual conditions;

- attention must be paid to social networks of clients, to meaningful daytime activity and to sound pharmacological management.

People with HIV/AIDS

16.28　In contrast to the requirements of people who abuse alcohol or drugs, the needs of people with HIV or AIDS are not specifically mentioned in the community care legislation or directions. However people with HIV/AIDS are potential (or actual) community care users and therefore entitled to an assessment and where appropriate, services. In general residential care or nursing home accommodation will be provided by social services departments under NAA 1948 s21 (see chapter 7 above) and by health authorities under the continuing care obligations (see para 10.87 above).

16.29　In relation to non-accommodation services, the social services' obligation under CSDPA 1970 s2 is owed to people who are already 'substantially and permanently handicapped'. These services are therefore only likely to be available for people who have developed the AIDS symptoms. In contrast the social services duties under NHSA 1977 Sch 8 are owed to people who have an illness (whether or not it is has already resulted in them becoming permanently and substantially handicapped) or for people who are recovering from an illness or in order to prevent illness. These services, which are of primary relevance to people with HIV, but who have not yet developed the AIDS symptoms are considered in detail at para 8.124 above.

16.30　The Department of Health has published guidance and issued a number of circulars concerning the social care needs of people with HIV infection and AIDS; these include:

1) HIV infection – The working interface between voluntary organisations and social services departments (1992).

2) Children and HIV – Guidance for local authorities (1992).

3) The health and social care of people with HIV infection and AIDS – Findings and good practice recommendations from research funded by the Department of Health 1986–1992 (1993).

4) Women and HIV (1993).

5) Inspection of local authority services for people affected by HIV/AIDS: Overview 1994.

6) Implementing Caring for People: Caring for People with HIV and AIDS (1994).

7) Support Grant for social services for people with AIDS 1998/99: LAC(98)9.

8) Better prevention: Better services: Better sexual health: The national strategy for sexual health and HIV Implementation action plan (June 2002).[41]

---

41 Department of Health accessible at www.dh.gov.uk/assetRoot/04/01/95/90/04019590.pdf.

Housing and community care

Introduction

17.1   Over 1.3 million tenants and owner-occupiers are beneficiaries of housing-related community care services and over £2 billion is spent each year on the housing aspects of community care.[1] Disabled people place a high value on appropriate accommodation. A Help the Aged 'Independent Living Survey' in 1995 identified aids and adaptations, such as stairlifts and wheelchair ramps as the most effective means to enable them to remain in their own homes and a 1998 Audit Commission report highlighted housing as the single most important service required by people with mental health problems to live independently in the community.[2]

17.2   The widespread neglect of housing in community care planning at local and central government level has been described in a Rowntree Foundation report in the following terms:

> Housing is more than a neglected dimension of community care. It is more, even, than a 'key component'. The logic of the 'new' community care entails the redefinition of housing as the basic requirement – the foundation – of community care. Anything less than this will reinforce past mistakes, expensive in human and financial terms, which have relegated so many people to less-than-ordinary lives in less-than-ordinary housing.[3]

17.3   While this chapter is primarily concerned with the obligations on housing authorities to provide disabled facilities grants and, to a lesser extent, the statutory obligations to house homeless people it must be appreciated that the issue of appropriate accommodation is a fundamental theme in relation to almost all community care services. As the Audit Commission has noted, 'it is not simply the provision of a roof over people's heads that makes housing's contribution so important, it is the personal support to help vulnerable people cope with everyday living – for example, negotiating the complexities of rent payments or resolving problems with water, gas and electricity suppliers – that makes the difference between life in the community and institutionalisation'.[4] Many aspects of the housing contribution to community care are therefore considered elsewhere in this book, most notably the provision of residential care accommodation (which may comprise nothing more than a simple tenancy), which is considered at para 7.53 above and home adaptations under Chronically Sick and Disabled Persons Act (CSDPA) 1970 s2(1)(e) is considered at para 8.87 above.

17.4   Housing authorities, in meeting their responsibilities under Housing Act 1985 s8 to consider housing conditions and provision in their area are

---

1   'Home Alone' report into the role of housing in community care, Audit Commission, 1998, paras 6 and 8.
2   'Home Alone', paras 6 and 8.
3   P Arnold, et al, *Community Care: The housing dimension* (Joseph Rowntree Foundation, 1993); and see also P Arnold and D Page, *Housing and Community Care* (University of Humberside, 1992).
4   'Home Alone', para 7.

required, by CSDPA 1970 s3, to have specific regard to the special needs of chronically sick and disabled persons, including the provision or adaptation of existing accommodation for their own disabled tenants. In this respect Department of the Environment guidance Circular 17/96 (Annex I para 2) reminds authorities of their 'wide responsibilities in identifying disabled people who need help with essential adaptations arising out of their disability' and that they should 'consider the needs of the disabled person in the context of their wider life-style and desired activities'.

17.5   The community care needs of disadvantaged people will not infrequently come to the notice of the courts by way of possession proceedings founded upon their failure to pay rent or their behaviour. In such cases the courts have power to adjourn to enable an urgent assessment of needs to be carried out. Such an assessment will inevitably involve the social services department liaising with the housing authority under National Health Service and Community Care Act (NHSCCA) 1990 s47(3) (see para 4.68 above). The courts have wide powers to adjourn possession proceedings in secure and assured tenancy cases,[5] however, in assured shorthold cases judges will need to rely on the power they have to adjourn under the Civil Procedure Rules 3.1 and 3. 2 in furtherance of the overriding objective in Rule 1 to enable the court to deal with the case 'justly'. Where the application for possession is brought by a housing department, a failure to liaise with the social services department and the absence of a full assessment will be relevant to the question of 'reasonableness'.

17.6   In *Croydon LBC v Moody*[6] the Court of Appeal concluded that in determining whether it was reasonable to make a possession order on the grounds of nuisance, relevant factors included the fact that the defendant suffered from a personality disorder that was amenable to treatment and that he had agreed to this treatment, as well as his likely fate in the event of an eviction order being made.

17.7   *North Devon Homes Ltd v Brazier*[7] concerned an application to evict a tenant with mental health problems who was causing 'annoyance, nuisance and inconvenience' to her neighbours. The court held that the tenant's 'bizarre and unwelcome behaviour' was attributable to her mental illness. In its view, it followed (by virtue of Disability Discrimination Act 1995 s22(3)(c))[8] that an eviction would amount to less favourable treatment on grounds of her disability and in the circumstances of the case, an eviction could not be justified. The court however noted[9] that:

> . . . unlawfulness under the 1995 Act would not necessarily be
> determinative of the application under the Housing Act . . . The Act
> does not bar evictions: only those which are not justified by the specific
> circumstances set out in section 24. The respondent, having adopted a

5   Housing Act 1985 s85 and Housing Act 1988 s9.
6   (1999) 2 CCLR 92.
7   [2003] EWHC 574 (QB); (2003) 6 CCLR 245; (2003) 22 EG 141.
8   Applying *Clark v TDG Ltd (T/A Novacold)* [1999] 2 All ER 977; (1998) 48 BMLR 1, CA.
9   [2003] EWHC 574 (QB) at [22].

proper review of the situation in accordance with the express terms of the Act, may conclude in the future that the health and safety of her neighbours are prejudiced and thus steps should be taken to evict the appellant. But this situation has not arisen.

17.8   In *R v Kensington and Chelsea RLBC ex p Kujtim*[10] the Court of Appeal held that the duty to provide accommodation (under National Assistance Act (NAA) 1948 s21 see para 7.44 above) can be treated as discharged if the applicant 'either unreasonably refuses to accept the accommodation provided or if, following its provision, by his conduct he manifests a persistent and unequivocal refusal to observe the reasonable requirements of the local authority in relation to the occupation of such accommodation'.

Collaboration in assessment and care planning

17.9   The need for housing and social services authorities to co-operate fully in the community care planning and assessment process is obvious and is itself a statutory obligation for county council social services authorities. NHSCCA 1990 s47(3) provides:

> If at any time during the assessment of the needs of any person under subsection (1)(a) above, it appears to a local authority –
> (a) that there may be a need for the provision to that person by such Primary Care Trust or Health Authority as may be determined in accordance with regulations of any services under the National Health Service Act 1977, or
> (b) that there may be the need for the provision to him of any services which fall within the functions of a local housing authority (within the meaning of the Housing Act 1985)[11] which is not the local authority carrying out the assessment,
> the local authority shall notify that Primary Care Trust or Health Authority or local housing authority and invite them to assist, to such extent as is reasonable in the circumstances, in the making of the assessment; and, in making their decision as to the provision of services needed for the person in question, the local authority shall take into account any services which are likely to be made available for him by that Primary Care Trust or Health Authority or local housing authority.

17.10   It follows that (in non-unitary authorities) where during the assessment process a housing need is disclosed, the assessing authority is obliged to notify the housing authority and at the same time to specify what assistance that authority is requested to provide in order to facilitate the assessment. Although the housing authority is not under any statutory duty to respond or co-operate,[12] where the assessing authority notifies the housing

---

10 (1999) 2 CCLR 340 at 354I.

11 A 'housing function' is defined by Housing Act 1985 ss228 onwards and covers the wide range of activities connected with the provision of housing.

12 Unlike under the Children Act 1989 s27: see *R v Northavon DC ex p Smith* [1994] 3 All ER 313, HL.

authority of a housing need, separate, parallel duties under the Housing Act 1996 may well be triggered. The housing authority will be under a duty to receive applications[13] and to make enquiries under Housing Act 1996 s184 in cases of homelessness and apparent priority need. As the application need not be in any particular form,[14] it may be argued in appropriate cases that notification of housing need amounts in itself to an application made on behalf of the assessed person.[15] Presumably, a housing authority's failure to respond – or failure to respond within a reasonable time or in a reasonable manner – would be vulnerable to challenge as maladministration. Likewise, there must be an administrative obligation within unitary authorities for the housing and social services departments to liaise, notwithstanding that this is not required by NHSCCA 1990 s47(3).[16] In *R v Lewisham LBC ex p Pinzon and Patino*[17] Laws J held that the recommendations in the circular guidance that housing and social services authorities work together does not in itself convert that obligation into a legally enforceable duty.

17.11   The duty to co-operate has been reinforced by joint guidance issued by the Departments of Health and the Environment in LAC(92)12; DOE Circular 10/92, which includes the following advice:

> 16. Social services authorities and housing should construct an individual's care plan with the objective of preserving or restoring non-institutional living as far as possible, and of securing the most appropriate and cost-effective package of care, housing and other services that meets the person's future needs. For some people the most appropriate package of care will be in a nursing or residential home, but in many cases this will be achieved by bringing in domiciliary support and making any necessary adaptations to the individual's existing home. The balance between these should be considered carefully. For example, where expensive or disruptive adaptations or improvements are being considered it may be more cost-effective to provide domiciliary care and support together with more minor works. In other cases adaptations or improvements (eg, to help people bathe or cook by themselves) may reduce or obviate the need for domiciliary support.
>
> . . . .
>
> 19. The new proposals will require effective relationships to be established and built upon between all parties involved. The aim should be to provide a seamless service for clients, with a mutual recognition of all authorities' responsibilities. This will require all the relevant agencies, including housing, health and social services authorities, to put an emphasis on

---

13 *R v Camden LBC ex p Gillan* (1988) *Independent* 13 October, DC.

14 *R v Chiltern DC ex p Roberts* (1990) 23 HLR 387, DC.

15 Disabled adults with insufficient mental capacity to make an application or authorise someone else to do so are not entitled to apply under Housing Act 1996 Part VII – see *R v Tower Hamlets LBC ex p Begum* (1993) 25 HLR 319, HL; however see also *R (Patrick) v Newham LBC* (2001) 4 CCLR 48 – considered at para 7.45 above.

16 In *R (Wahid) v Tower Hamlets LBC ex p* (2002) 5 CCLR 239 at p249J Hale LJ observed that it was 'obviously good practice . . . to involve the housing department where this is part of the same local authority'.

17 (1999) 2 CCLR 152.

discussion, understanding and agreement in the planning of services, rather than unilateral decision making. Joint working will be important to maximise the use of existing resources. Administrative systems will need to be developed, perhaps including joint planning structures, in order to monitor and plan effective use of services. Authorities may wish to set up pilot projects. In taking forward their role in community care, housing authorities in particular should have regard to the points made in the annex to this circular [which amongst other things expands upon what 'joint working' is likely to entail].

17.12   In relation to the processing of disabled facilities grants, (see below) Housing Grants, Construction and Regeneration Act 1996 s24(3) imposes a duty on local housing authorities to consult social services authorities in order to decide whether the proposed works are 'necessary' and 'appropriate' to meet the needs of the disabled occupant. In this respect the relevant guidance (Department of the Environment as Circular 17/96) states:

> 7.7.2 Within their statutory responsibilities, housing and social services authorities are expected to co-operate fully in carrying out the assessments under section 24(3) for the purposes of meeting the needs of disabled people in their area. In many areas, efficient and effective systems of consultation between the respective authorities have been developed locally in meeting these statutory responsibilities. This not only enables people needing help to receive the best possible service but also ensures that there are common practices for consultation with all those involved. It also ensures that there is wide consistency across the area covered by individual social services authorities.

Housing homeless persons overlap

17.13   The obligation to house homeless persons originated as NAA 1948 s21(1)(b) being a power to provide temporary accommodation for persons who were homeless in circumstances that could not have been foreseen. The power was repealed by the Housing (Homeless Persons) Act 1977, although the relic duty to provide residential accommodation for persons 'in urgent need' remains under NAA 1948 s21(1)(a) (see para 6.13). Likewise in relation to the needs of 'children in need' the Children Act 1989 empowers social services authorities to provide ordinary housing in appropriate circumstances, see para 18.32 below.

17.14   Disabled, elderly or ill people may however also come within the scope of the homelessness provisions of Housing Act 1996 Part VII since it provides that:

(a) a person is homeless for the purposes of the Act if s/he has no accommodation which it would be reasonable for him or her to occupy[18] (Housing Act 1996 s175(3)); and

18 Housing Act 1996 s175(3); which section 176 qualifies by stipulating that accommodation shall be treated as available for a person's occupation only if it is available for occupation by him or her together with any other person who normally resides with him or her as a member of the family, or any other person who might reasonably be expected to reside with him or her.

(b) a person is considered in priority need if he or she 'is vulnerable as a result of old age, mental illness or handicap or physical disability or other special reason, or is a person with whom such a person resides or might reasonably be expected to reside' (Housing Act 1996 s189(1)(c)).[19]

17.15 The relationship between the housing authority homelessness obligations under Housing Act 1996 Part VII and the community care obligations of social services authorities is considered at paras 3–4 (in particular) of the Annex to LAC(92)12:

> 3. Housing authorities should bear in mind their duties under the homelessness legislation to secure accommodation for applicant households who are unintentionally homeless and in priority need. Section 59(1) of the Housing Act 1985[20] defines priority need categories as including families with dependent children, households containing a pregnant woman, or people who are vulnerable through old age, mental illness or handicap or other special reasons.
>
> 4. Paragraph 6.11 of the Homelessness Code of Guidance (3rd edition) sets out the procedures to be followed in the case of those recently discharged, or about to be discharged, from psychiatric or learning difficulty (mental handicap) hospitals. In such cases, if the housing authority sees the need, they should establish whether the local social services authority has been involved and give consideration to referring cases for assessment if this seems appropriate.

17.16 This advice has been given statutory effect through Homelessness Act 2002 s1(2) which requires social services authorities to assist housing authorities in the formulation of their homelessness strategies. This obligation is explained in the Homelessness Code of Guidance for Local Authorities (July 2002)[21] as follows:

> 1.5. In non-unitary districts, where the social services authority and the housing authority are different authorities, section 1(2) requires the social services authority to give the housing authority such assistance as may be reasonably required in carrying out a homelessness review and formulating and publishing a homelessness strategy. Since a number of people who are homeless or at risk of homelessness will require social services support, it is unlikely that it would be possible for a housing authority to formulate an effective homelessness strategy without assistance from the social services authority. It will be necessary therefore in all cases for housing authorities to seek assistance from the social services authority. In unitary authorities, the authority will need to ensure that the social services department assist the housing department in carrying out homelessness reviews and formulating and publishing homelessness strategies.

17.17 The principal homelessness duties under Housing Act 1996 ss193 and 195 apply only to applicants who have a priority need for accommodation and

---

19 As a cautionary note, see *Ortiz v City of Westminster* (1995) 27 HLR 364.
20 Now Housing Act 1996 s189(1).
21 Office of the Deputy Prime Minister: Accessible at www.odpm.gov.uk.

by Housing Act 1996 s189(1)(c) this includes persons who are 'vulnerable as a result of old age, mental illness or handicap or physical disability or other special reason, or with whom such a person resides or might reasonably be expected to reside'. Para 8.13 of the 2002 Code of Guidance advises that the critical test of vulnerability for the applicant is:

> . . . whether, when homeless, the applicant would be less able to fend for himself than an ordinary homeless person so that he would be likely to suffer injury or detriment, in circumstances where a less vulnerable person would be able to cope without harmful effects.

17.18   It then provides guidance in relation to the specific classes of people deemed to be 'vulnerable' including:

Old age

8.14.   Old age alone is not sufficient for the applicant to be deemed vulnerable. However, it may be that as a result of old age the applicant would be less able to fend for him or herself as provided in paragraph 8.13, above. All applications from people aged over 60 need to be considered carefully, particularly where the applicant is leaving tied accommodation. However, housing authorities should not use 60 (or any other age) as a fixed age beyond which vulnerability occurs automatically (or below which it can be ruled out); each case will need to be considered in the light of the individual circumstances.

Mental illness, learning or physical disability

8.15.   Housing authorities should have regard to any medical advice or social services advice obtained, but the final decision on the question of vulnerability will rest with the housing authority. In considering whether such applicants are vulnerable, factors that a housing authority may wish to take into account are:

(i)   the nature and extent of the illness or disability which may render the applicant vulnerable; and

(ii) the relationship between the illness or disability and the individual's housing difficulties.

8.16.   Health authorities have an express duty to implement a specifically tailored care programme for all patients considered for discharge from psychiatric hospitals and all new patients accepted by the specialist psychiatric services (see Department of Health circulars HC(90)23, LASSL(90)11, HSG(94)27 and LASSL(94)4). People discharged from psychiatric hospitals and local authority hostels or people with mental health problems are likely to be vulnerable. Effective liaison between housing, social services and health authorities will be essential in such cases but authorities will also need to be sensitive to direct approaches from former patients who have been discharged and may be homeless.

8.17.   Physical disabilities or long-term acute illnesses, such as those defined by the Disability Discrimination Act 1995, which impinge on the applicant's housing situation and give rise to vulnerability may be readily discernible, but advice from health or social services staff should be sought, wherever necessary. As for all homelessness applicants, the decision on vulnerability rests with the housing authority.

. . .

Other special reason

8.28. Section 189(1)(c) provides that a person has a priority need for accommodation if he or she is vulnerable for an 'other special reason'. A person with whom such a vulnerable person normally lives or might reasonably be expected to live also has a priority need. The legislation envisages that vulnerability can arise because of factors that are not expressly provided for in statute. It does not permit housing authorities to predetermine that some groups can never be considered vulnerable for an 'other special reason'. Each application must be considered in the light of the facts and circumstances of the case. Moreover, other special reasons giving rise to vulnerability are not restricted to the physical or mental characteristics of a person. Other special reasons may include a combination of factors and circumstances that render a person less able than others to fend for him or herself when homeless. Where applicants have a need for support but have no family or friends on whom they can depend they may be vulnerable as a result of an other special reason.

8.29. Housing authorities must keep an open mind and should avoid blanket policies that assume that particular groups of applicants will, or will not, be vulnerable for an 'other special reason'. Where a housing authority consider that an applicant may be vulnerable, it will be important to make an in-depth assessment of the circumstances of the case. Guidance on certain categories of applicants who may be vulnerable as a result of an 'other special reason' is given below. The list below is not exhaustive and housing authorities must ensure that they give proper consideration to every application on the basis of the individual circumstances.

8.30. *Chronically sick people, including people with AIDS and HIV related illnesses.* People in this group may be vulnerable not only because their illness has progressed to the point of physical or mental disability (when they are likely to fall within one of the specified categories of priority need) but also because the manifestations or effects of their illness, or common attitudes to it, make it very difficult for them to find and maintain stable or suitable accommodation. Whilst this may be particularly true of people with AIDS, it could also apply in the case of people infected with HIV (who may not have any overt signs or symptoms) if the nature of their infection is known.

Joint working

17.19 The 2002 Code of Guidance places emphasis on the importance of joint working, noting that Homelessness Act 2002 s3(5) requires housing authorities to consider, among other things, the extent to which any of the strategy's objectives can be achieved through joint action involving two or more of the organisations. It suggests that this could include (at para 1.37):

> . . . the housing authority, the social services authority, neighbouring housing authorities and any other public authorities working to alleviate homelessness within the district, for example, the Probation Service. It might also include any other organisation or person whose activities could contribute to achieving the objectives of the homelessness strategy, for example, voluntary sector organisations working with homeless people,

registered social landlords, and private landlords. The most effective strategies will be those which harness the potential of all the organisations and persons working to prevent and alleviate homelessness in the district, and which ensure that all the activities concerned are consistent and complementary.

At para 1.38 it gives examples of the collaborative working envisaged, for instance:

- establishment of a multi-agency forum for practitioners and providers to share knowledge; information, ideas and complementary practices;
- protocols for the referral of clients between services and sharing information between services;
- joint assessment of certain homeless people by housing and social services authorities under [Housing Act 1996] Part VII, the Children Act 1989 and community care legislation;
- establishment of formal links with other services, (for example, reconciliation services for young people estranged from their family).

17.20   At para 1.40 it specifically refers to local authority powers under Local Government Act 2000 s2 (see para 1.46 above) suggesting that these provide substantial opportunity for 'cross boundary partnership working with other authorities and partners, such as the health and social services sectors'. In relation to health care, this will be of particular relevance in the context of hospital discharge, and the 2003 hospital discharge guidance[22] states that 'it is vital all hospitals consider the housing situation of patients to ensure that people are not discharged to inappropriate places, homeless or become homeless as a result of their stay in hospital'.

Disabled facilities grants

17.21   Disabled facilities grants (DFGs) are grants paid towards the cost of building works which are necessary in order to meet the needs of a disabled occupant. The housing authority is responsible for the administration and payment of the grant, although the original application may be instigated (and referred to it) by a social services authority after a community care assessment. The maximum mandatory grant is currently £25,000 in England[23] and £30,000 in Wales[24] although local authorities have the discretion to make higher awards. Special rules apply for minor adaptations under £1,000 (see para 12.9 above).

17.22   The grants are primarily for the purpose of:

- facilitating a disabled person's access to:
  - the dwelling;
  - a room usable as the principal family room, or for sleeping in;

---

22 *Discharge from hospital: pathway, process and practice* (2003) para A5.5.1 (see para 10.157 above) accessible at www.publications.doh.gov.uk/hospitaldischarge/index.htm.
23 The Disabled Facilities Grants and Home Repair Assistance (Maximum Amounts) (Amendment No 2) (England) Order 2001 SI No 4036.
24 The Disabled Facilities Grants and Home Repair Assistance (Maximum Amounts) (Amendment) (Wales) Order 2002 WSI No 837 (W99).

- a WC, bath, shower, etc (or the provision of a room for these facilities);
- facilitating the preparation of food by the disabled person;
- improving/providing a heating system to meet the disabled persons needs;
- facilitating the disabled person's use of a source of power;
- facilitating access and movement around the home to enable the disabled person to care for someone dependent upon them;
- making the dwelling safe for the disabled person and others residing with him or her.

Eligibility

17.23　The grant is subject to a means test (see para 17.49 below) and is only payable in respect of disabled occupants; ie, persons who are 'substantially and permanently handicapped' within the meaning of NAA 1948 s29 (see para 8.21). It is not therefore available for persons whose need arises solely through age or temporary illness.[25]

17.24　All owner-occupiers, tenants (both council, housing association and private) and licensees[26] are potentially eligible to apply for disabled facilities grants as are landlords on behalf of disabled tenants. The guidance advises that where a 'council tenant is seeking help with adaptations, it is for the authority to decide whether to carry out the works under its own resources for capital works or to advise the applicant to apply for a DFG. If the local authority decides to undertake the works from their own resources they should be carried out on the same terms as if a DFG has been awarded'.[27] Accordingly any material difference in treatment of council and non-council tenants, it will constitute maladministration.[28] In such cases the ombudsman has held that 'any delay beyond six months' (from the social services referral to the execution of the works) will generally be considered unjustified and constitute maladministration.[29]

17.25　The Local Government Ombudsman has highlighted a problem with the DFG scheme in that it only applies to existing tenants (Housing Grants, Construction and Regeneration Act (HGCRA) 1996 s24(2)).[30] Accordingly where it is proposed that a disabled person move to new tenancy and that

---

25　Other housing grants are available from housing authorities for renovation and minor repairs and these are available to non-disabled people as well as disabled people (and can for instance be used to carry out renovation work in addition to the installation of disabled facilities, etc) These grants are, discretionary and subject the priorities set by each local authority.

26　HGCRA 1996 s19(5) extends eligibility for a DFG to a range of licensees, for example, secure or introductory tenants who are licensees, agricultural workers, and service employees such as publicans.

27　DoE Circular 10/90 Annex I para 11 and see also para 8.7.4–8.7.5.

28　See the report and further report of Complaint No 99/B/00012 against North Warwickshire District Council, 15 May 2000 and 30 November 2000 respectively.

29　Complaint No 02/C/08679 against Bolsover Distrct Council, 30 September 2003.

30　In *R v Bradford MDC ex p Pickering* (2000) Lawtel 19 September 2000, Munby J held that a purchaser under an (uncompleted) rental purchase agreement had a sufficient 'owner's interest' for the purposes of the grant.

tenancy be adapted prior to the move, then in order to obtain the grant, it will be necessary to take on the new tenancy. During this period the applicant will have the cost of two tenancies and accordingly there is a need for such works to be done as quickly as possible and without any unnecessary delays.[31]

Mobile homes and houseboats

17.26   The DFG scheme was extended in 2003[32] to persons living in mobile homes and houseboats. However only mobile home owners living in a 'qualifying park home' were covered, ie, people on a protected site within the meaning of the Mobile Homes Act 1983. As a result of representations made concerning the discriminatory effect of this measure (Gypsies living on local authority sites do not come within the scope of the provision) it is proposed that such grants will be extended to cover all people living in a caravan as their only or main dwelling. This amendment is to be effected via the Housing Bill (introduced into Parliament on 8 December 2003) clause 167.

The statutory scheme

17.27   The relevant statutory provision regulating the availability of DFGs is the Housing Grants, Construction and Regeneration Act (HGCRA) 1996 Part I. Detailed guidance on the scheme has been issued by the Department of the Environment as Circular 17/96. As has been noted above (at para 8.90) there is considerable overlap between the duties of the housing authority to process these grants, and the duties owed by social services authorities to facilitate such adaptations. Unfortunately this complex interplay of duties has not been simplified by the existence of separate guidance from the Department of Health on the social services responsibilities, as LAC(90)7.[33] All references to paragraphs in the following section are references to paragraphs of Circular 17/96 unless otherwise stated.

17.28   HGCRA 1996 s23 provides:

> *Disabled facilities grants: purposes for which grant must or may be given*
> 23(1) The purposes for which an application for a grant must be approved, subject to the provisions of this Chapter, are the following –
> (a) facilitating access by the disabled occupant to and from –
>   (i) the dwelling, qualifying houseboat or qualifying park home, or
>   (ii) the building in which the dwelling or, as the case may be, flat is situated;
> (b) making –
>   (i) the dwelling, qualifying houseboat or qualifying park home, or
>   (ii) the building, safe for the disabled occupant and other persons residing with him;

---

31 Complaint No 00/C/19154 against Birmingham, 19 March 2002.

32 This has been amended by virtue of an amendment to HGCRA 1996 s23 via the Regulatory Reform (Housing Assistance) (England and Wales) Order 2002 art 2.

33 LAC(90)7 was issued jointly as Department of the Environment Circular 10/90. While DoE Circular 10/90 has been withdrawn (and superseded by new guidance, Circular 17/96) LAC(90)7 remains in force (see DoE 4/98 and LASSL(99)21).

(c) facilitating access by the disabled occupant to a room used or usable as the principal family room;

(d) facilitating access by the disabled occupant to, or providing for the disabled occupant, a room used or usable for sleeping;

(e) facilitating access by the disabled occupant to, or providing for the disabled occupant, a room in which there is a lavatory, or facilitating the use by the disabled occupant of such a facility;

(f) facilitating access by the disabled occupant to, or providing for the disabled occupant, a room in which there is a bath or shower (or both), or facilitating the use by the disabled occupant of such a facility;

(g) facilitating access by the disabled occupant to, or providing for the disabled occupant, a room in which there is a washhand basin, or facilitating the use by the disabled occupant of such a facility;

(h) facilitating the preparation and cooking of food by the disabled occupant;

(i) improving any heating system in the dwelling, qualifying houseboat or qualifying park home to meet the needs of the disabled occupant or, if there is no existing heating system there or any such system is unsuitable for use by the disabled occupant, providing a heating system suitable to meet his needs;

(j) facilitating the use by the disabled occupant of a source of power, light or heat by altering the position of one or more means of access to or control of that source or by providing additional means of control;

(k) facilitating access and movement by the disabled occupant around the dwelling, qualifying houseboat or qualifying park home in order to enable him to care for a person who is normally resident there and is in need of such care;

(l) such other purposes as may be specified by order of the Secretary of State.

. . .

(3) If in the opinion of the local housing authority the relevant works are more or less extensive than is necessary to achieve any of the purposes set out in subsection (1), they may, with the consent of the applicant, treat the application as varied so that the relevant works are limited to or, as the case may be, include such works as seem to the authority to be necessary for that purpose.

Role of the housing authority

17.29 The housing authority is responsible for the administration of the disabled facilities grant, through all stages from initial enquiry (or referral by the social services authority) to post-completion approval. This requirement stems from HGCRA 1996 s24(3):

A local housing authority shall not approve an application for a grant unless they are satisfied –

(a) that the relevant works are necessary and appropriate to meet the needs of the disabled occupant, and

(b) that it is reasonable and practicable to carry out the relevant works having regard to the age and condition of –
   (i) the dwelling, qualifying houseboat or qualifying park home, or
   (ii) the building.
In considering the matters mentioned in paragraph (a) a local housing authority which is not itself a social services authority shall consult the social services authority.

17.30   Although the Act specifically requires housing authorities to consult with social services authorities over whether the proposed works are necessary and appropriate, it is nevertheless for housing authorities to decide in any particular case whether or not to approve a grant; they are not bound to follow the social services authority's advice – although the guidance suggests that this should in general be a rare occurrence (Annex I para 4).

Reasonable and practicable

17.31   HGCRA 1996 s24(3)(b) charges the housing authority with the duty of deciding whether it is reasonable and practicable to carry out the proposed adaptation works. In making its assessment, a housing authority is specifically required to have regard to the age and condition of the dwelling or building. While section 24(4) of the Act permits grants to be made even where on completion of the works the property would remain unfit for human habitation the guidance advises as to what alternatives should be offered by the housing and social services departments to the disabled person if the final 'unfitness' of the property is considered such that it renders the proposed works unreasonable and impractical (Annex I para 51).[34] In determining whether the work is reasonable and practicable, the guidance refers to other relevant considerations, including the architectural and structural characteristics of the property, conservation considerations, the practicalities of carrying out work on smaller properties or older properties with limited access and the impact on other occupants of the proposed works[35] (Annex I para 52).

Necessary and appropriate

17.32   In deciding whether the proposed works are necessary and appropriate to meet the needs of the disabled occupant, the housing authority must consult the social services authority. On this aspect Annex I to the guidance makes the following points:[36]

34 Including the possibility of obtaining a discretionary renovation grant, reducing the amount of DFG work, and the possibility of re-housing the disabled person.
35 That is, if the works would lead to substantial disruption to other tenants (eg, the noise of an air-compressor, in *R v Kirklees MBC ex p Daykin* (1998) 1 CCLR 512, or alternatively be of indirect benefit to neighbours as in *R v Kirklees MBC ex p Good* (1998) 1 CCLR 506).
36 Separate and at times slightly divergent guidance is given to social services in LAC(90)7 para 36 onwards; but since final responsibility rests with the housing authority, the DoE guidance is of more weight.

47. The housing authority must satisfy itself that the works are necessary and appropriate to meet the needs if the disabled person under section 24(3)(a), and in doing so should consult the social services authority. They need to consider a number of factors. In particular whether the proposed adaptations or improvements:

- are needed to provide for a care plan to be implemented which will enable the disabled occupant to remain living in their existing home as independently as possible;
- would meet, as far as possible, the assessed needs of the disabled person taking into account both their medical and physical needs; and
- distinguish between what is desirable and possibly legitimate aspirations of the disabled person, and what is actually needed and for which grant support is fully justified.

48. In determining the needs of the disabled person consideration should be given to the particular household group in which the disabled occupant resides so that any adaptations being contemplated do not cause strain on the household which may lead to a breakdown of the present care arrangements. For instance, a relevant factor might be the continued privacy of the disabled person or carer following completion of works.

49. DFGs are designed to give the disabled person a degree of independence in the home. Consideration therefore needs to be given to the impact of adaptations on the level of care given to the disabled person and whether those tasks will be reduced or eased. Adaptation works would not have achieved their objective within a care package if the disabled person does not gain an acceptable degree of independence, where possible, or, where the disabled person remains dependent upon the care of others, where the adaptation does not significantly ease the burden of the carer.

17.33 The consideration of what 'meets' the assessed needs of a disabled person, can take into account the issue of cost, where there are alternative ways of meeting the need. Thus in *R v Kirklees MBC ex p Daykin*[37] the disabled person was assessed as needing to be able to get into and out of his council flat. Collins J held that it was reasonable for the authority to decide that this need could either be met by the provision of a stair lift, or by re-housing and for it to take into account the respective costs of both options, in deciding which was to be preferred.

17.34 *R (B) v Calderdale MBC*[38] the Court of Appeal considered the interplay between HGCRA 1996 ss23 and 24(3), commenting as follows:

28. ... What ... the local authority has ... failed to do ... [is] to segregate the section 24(3) question from the section 23(1) question, and to answer it in the light of the fact that the claimant has established his grant-eligibility in principle under [section 23(1)]. The council must now decide whether it is satisfied that a loft conversion is necessary and appropriate to meet D's particular needs, which include the need not to harm his brother. This is a

37 (1998) 1 CCLR 512.
38 [2004] EWCA Civ 134; (2004) *Times* 26 February.

matter for the council's considered judgment. Unless it is so satisfied it cannot pay the grant.

29. One has no wish to be critical of non-lawyers who have to apply this difficult and sensitive legislation not in the calm of a courtroom but in the course of a pressured day's work in the office. But one straightforward guideline is that section 23(1) and section 24(3) should be applied sequentially. A lot of the difficulty in the present case arose from decision-makers running the two together. Section 23(1) is a gateway provision. Section 24(3) is a control for those applications which get through the gateway. In a suitable case, no doubt, it may be legitimate to decide that, even assuming that the application passes the section 23(1) threshold, the work cannot be regarded as necessary or as appropriate. But that too is sequential reasoning. What is not permissible is to decide the section 23(1) issue by reference to the section 24(3) criteria.

Grant-eligible works

Mandatory grants

17.35   Section 23(1) details the purposes for which mandatory grants may be awarded. The guidance (at para 7.5.2) explains that:

> . . . the prominent purpose for which mandatory disabled facilities grant is given is that of access and provision: this includes access into and around the dwelling, to essential facilities and amenities within the dwelling and the provision of certain facilities within the dwelling, such as a making the building safe, where this is the only or most suitable option.

17.36   The duty is not a 'resource' dependent duty (see para 4.92 above); thus in *R v Birmingham CC ex p Taj Mohammed*[39] Dyson J held that housing author-ities were not entitled to take resources into account when deciding whether or not to approve a disabled facilities grant. The work will gener-ally be within a dwelling but may in certain situations be elsewhere, for instance, in the common parts of a building containing flats (Annex I para 30). The works eligible for mandatory grant support can be conveniently grouped as follows.

Making the dwelling safe

17.37   Annex I para 17 of the guidance explains that works under this heading may include 'the provision of lighting where safety is an issue of adapta-tions designed to minimise the risk of danger where a disabled person has behavioural problems which cause him to act occasionally or regularly in a boisterous or violent manner damaging the house, himself and perhaps other people'. It may also include enhanced alarm systems for people with hearing difficulties.

39   (1998) 1 CCLR 441.

17.38   In *R (B) v Calderdale MBC*[40] Sedley LJ (at para 24) considered that a grant to make a dwelling safe (under HGCRA 1996 s23(1)(b)) required that:

> ... the proposed works must be such as to minimise the material risk, that is to say to reduce it so far as is reasonably practicable, assuming that it cannot be eliminated.

Facilitating access and provision

17.39   Annex I para 15 of the guidance explains that this includes works which remove or help overcome any obstacles which prevent the disabled person from moving freely into and around the dwelling and enjoying the use of the dwelling and the facilities or amenities within it. In particular this includes works which enable the disabled person to prepare and cook food as well as facilitating access to and from the dwelling and to the following:

- the principal family room;
- a room used for sleeping (or providing such a room);
- a room in which there is a lavatory, a bath or shower and a washbasin (or providing such a room).

Room usable for sleeping

17.40   Annex I para 20 of the guidance advises that the building of a new room 'usable for sleeping' should only be grant funded if the housing authority is satisfied that the adaptation of an existing room (or access to that room) is not a suitable option. It states, however, that where the disabled person shares a bedroom grant funding may be given to provide a room of sufficient size 'so that the normal sleeping arrangements can be maintained'.

Bathroom

17.41   The guidance explains (Annex I para 21) that the Act separates the provision of a lavatory and washing, bathing and showering facilities, in order to clarify that a grant support is available to ensure that the disabled person has access to each of these facilities (as well as facilitating their use).

Facilitating preparation and cooking of food

17.42   Eligible works under this heading include the rearrangement or enlargement of a kitchen to ease manoeuvrability of a wheelchair and specially modified or designed storage units, gas, electricity and plumbing installations to enable the disabled person to use these facilities independently (Annex I para 22). The guidance advises, however, that a full adaptation of a kitchen would not generally be appropriate where most of the cooking and preparation is done by another household member.

---

40 [2004] EWCA Civ 134; (2004) *Times* 26 February.

Heating, lighting and power

17.43   The guidance (Annex I para 24) advises that although grant support may be made in order to provide (or improve, or replace) a heating system, this should only extend to rooms normally used by the disabled person and central heating should only be funded 'where the wellbeing and mobility of the disabled person would be otherwise adversely affected'. Works in relation to lighting and power may include the relocation of power points and the provision of suitably adapted controls.

Dependent residents

17.44   Grant support is available to cover work which improves a disabled person's access and movement around a dwelling in order to care for another person who normally resides there (HGCRA 1996 s23(1)(k)). The guidance makes it clear that the dependent being cared for need not be a disabled person and need not be a relation.

Discretionary grants

17.45   Prior to July 2003, the HGCRA 1996 provided for discretionary grants (under section 23(2)) to be made in certain situations. Although this provision has been repealed[41] local authorities continue to have power to provide assistance with such adaptations or to help the occupant to move to alternative accommodation.[42] The assistance may be paid in addition, or as an alternative to the grant, and there is no restriction on the amount of assistance that may be given – it may, for instance, cover such matters as:

- the provision of small adaptations that are either not covered by the grant or to deliver remedies for urgent adaptations quicker;
- a top-up to the grant because the work is particularly expensive or the applicant cannot afford the contribution or some work required is not eligible for the grant;
- assisting the disabled person to move to a more suitable property where it is more cost effective than adapting the current home of a disabled person to make it suitable for his or her needs, even though the new property may need some adaptations.

Ineligibility for grant and the social services overlap

17.46   Cases arise where the social services authority assesses a need for the adaptation, but the housing authority refuses or is unable to approve the grant. This may occur because the works in question do not come under the

---

41 By the Regulatory Reform (Housing Assistance)(England and Wales) Order 2002 SI No 1860.
42 2002 SI No 1860 art 3.

mandatory scheme, or because the housing authority does not consider the proposed works to be reasonable or practicable or because the applicant fails the means test.[43] In such situations the failure of the DFG application does not absolve the social services authority of their duty to meet an assessed need. This overlapping responsibility is considered at para 8.90 above and addressed in the guidance (Annex I) as follows:

> 5. Social services authorities' responsibilities under section 2 of the Chronically Sick and Disabled Persons Act 1970 to make arrangements for home adaptations are not affected by the grants legislation. Where an application for DFG has been made, those authorities may be called upon to meet this duty in two ways:
>
> (a) where the assessed needs of a disabled person exceeds the scope for provision by the housing authority under section 23 of the 1996 Act; and
>
> (b) where an applicant for DFG has difficulty in meeting his assessed contribution determined by the means test and seeks financial assistance from the authority.
>
> 6. In such cases, where the social services authority determine that the need has been established, it remains their duty to assist even where the local housing authority either refuse or are unable to approve an application. Social services authorities may also consider using their powers under section 17 of the Health and Social Services and Social Security Adjudications Act 1983 to charge for their services where appropriate.

17.47   In such situations the guidance reminds of the duties of social services authorities, namely:

> 7.4.1 The existing statutory duties of social services departments under section 2(1)(e) of Chronically Sick and Disabled Persons Act 1970 to provide assistance to disabled people needing home adaptations and other facilities designed to secure the greater safety, comfort and convenience of a disabled person, remain. Such help is normally available in the form of financial assistance, including loans, to assist with equipment in the home but, under these powers, social services authorities have a duty to assist disabled people who, because of their particular circumstances, cannot afford the assessed contribution towards the cost of works for which a DFG has been approved by the housing authority. Resources are also available to fund adaptation work either from housing associations or from the Housing Corporation where the adaptation is required for a property in that sector and local authorities may wish, where appropriate, to ensure that this option is considered.

---

43 Research suggests that one in three families who, as a result of the means test, were assessed as needing to make a contribution towards an adaptation to their home for their children's needs, could not afford to do so. It is estimated that the removal of the means test for DFGs for disabled children would cost the government in England between £10 and £20 million a year – House of Lords, Hansard Parliamentary Questions – Baroness Wilkins 5 January 2004: Column 2.

Fixtures and fittings

17.48   While disabled facilities grants are available to cover (among other things) adaptations to the fabric of a building, questions do arise as to whether items of specialist equipment, etc, come within the scheme. In this respect the guidance advises:

> 7.6.1   Under arrangements agreed between the Secretaries of State for Health and the Environment, help with equipment which can be easily installed and removed with little or no modification to the dwelling, is normally the responsibility of the social services authority under its responsibilities under the 1970 Act with larger adaptations requiring structural modification of a dwelling normally coming within the scope of a disabled facilities grant. However, it is for housing authorities and social services authorities between them to decide how the particular adaptation needs of a disabled person should be funded. In taking such decisions authorities should not forget that the needs of the disabled occupant *are paramount within the framework of what can be offered.*

> 7.6.2   Close co-operation between the respective authorities is vital to ensure that those requiring help in paying for works for essential adaptations to meet their special needs, are given the most efficient and effective support.

Additional advice in the guidance, at Annex I states:

> 7.   It is for housing authorities and social services authorities between them to decide how particular adaptations should be funded either through CSDPA 1970 or through a DFG.

> 8.   However, since DFGs were introduced in 1990 under the Local Government and Housing Act 1989, it has been common practice that equipment which can be installed and removed fairly easily with little or no structural modification of the dwelling is normally the responsibility of the social services authority.

> 9.   For larger items such as *stairlifts* and *through floor lifts* which require such structural works to the property, help is normally provided by housing authorities through DFG. However, some routine installations may not involve structural work. To ensure that such adaptations are progressed quickly, the respective authorities should jointly agree a standard line on the installation of lifts which will apply unless there are exceptional circumstances. Authorities will wish to include arrangements for routine servicing, maintenance, removal and possible re-use.

Means testing

17.49   Section 30 of the Housing Grants, Construction and Regeneration Act 1996 provides that eligibility for a disabled facilities grant is subject to a means test. Only the financial circumstances of the disabled occupant[44] and their partner are assessed and not to other members of the household. In the case of adaptations for a disabled child (ie, under 18) the test takes

---

44   The disabled occupant may or may not be the applicant.

into account the resources of the parents (or the 'relevant person' where the child does not live with his parents).[45]

17.50   The details of the means test are determined by regulations,[46] are relatively complex and set out in detail in the guidance (Annex J2). In many instances the calculation adopts housing benefit principles; thus the value of a person's savings is determined in the same way as for housing benefit and a tariff income of £1 per £250 (per £500 if aged over 60) is applied to any capital in excess of £6,000 (there is no upper capital limit).

17.51   Income is also assessed on basic housing benefit principles and the person's relevant 'applicable amount' is the current housing benefit sum. Where the financial resources do not exceed the relevant applicable amount plus a 'grant premium' of £51.60 (or £67.08 for disabled children) the disabled facilities grant will be the cost of the approved works. Where the financial resources are greater than the applicable amount, a staggered taper is applied to the surplus, designed to produce what the regulations term an 'affordable loan' (regulation 10). The idea being that the contribution made by the applicant constitutes 'an affordable loan that could be raised based on the current standard national rate of interest, over repayment periods of 10 years for owner-occupiers and 5 years for tenants' (Annex J2, para 17).

Timescales and loan deferment

17.52   Under HGCRA 1996 s34, the housing authority must approve or refuse a grant application as soon as reasonably practicable and in any event not later than six months after the date of application. It is therefore essential that the completed application be lodged with the housing authority at the earliest opportunity, as time runs from that date. The guidance stresses that 'local authorities should not use pre-application tests as a way of delaying applications or avoiding their statutory duty to process applications within six months' (Annex I para 45). Notwithstanding this advice, there is substantial evidence of delay (the subject of frequent comment by the Local Government Ombudsman – see para 8.96 above) particularly pre-application delays (ie, resulting from a prolonged wait for an occupational therapist (OT) assessment, or the provision of building tenders, etc). The government has indicated that it will strengthen the guidance in this respect (ie, that delays should only occur in 'exceptional circumstances' – see below) and the relevant minister has stated that 'waiting times for any adaptation of more than 250 working days, from the point of initial inquiry

---

45 The relevant person is the parent of the disabled child or the person who has made a claim for child benefit on the child's behalf or 'in any other case the person who has the primary responsibility for' the child – but subject to exceptions in relation to children placed by local authorities under (among other provisions) Children Act 1989 s23. Housing Renewal Grants Regulations 1996 SI No 2890, regs 5, 8 and 9 as amended.

46 The Housing Renewal Grants Regulations 1996 SI No 2890 subject to annual amendment, most recently to the Housing Renewal Grants (Amendment) (England) Regulations 2003 SI No 2504.

to completion, are unacceptable'.[47] In this vein, the draft guidance issued to local authorities jointly by the Department of Health and the Office of the Deputy Prime Minister (for consultation) includes:

> ... target times for the complete delivery process including needs assessment, processing of the application and the completion of building works. These target times will depend on the complexity of, and priority attached to, individual cases but the guidance suggests that the maximum target time for the entire process should in any event be no more than 260 working days and only 80 working days in high priority cases. The [two departments are] currently considering responses to this consultation and hope to issue final guidance to local housing and social service authorities early next year [ie, 2004].[48]

17.53   The Local Government Ombudsman has criticised on numerous occasions the failure of councils to prioritise referrals (to ensure that those in greatest need have their grant processed with expedition) and the failure of district and county councils to have agreed protocols to ensure that the processing of DFG applications are not delayed (by, for instance, avoiding the need to queue twice – once for the social services input and then again for the housing authority determination).[49]

17.54   HGCRA 1996 s36 provides local authorities with a discretion to notify the grant applicant that payment of their mandatory disabled facilities grant will not be made until a date not more than 12 months following the date of the application. The guidance (at para 7.5.4) states that this:

> ... should enable authorities to manage their resources better between financial years by prioritising cases. However, this power should be used only in exceptional circumstances and not where the applicant would suffer undue hardship. There is no expectation that the contractor would complete the work in advance of the date the grant has been scheduled for payment. The 12 month period for completion of grant assisted works is not affected although the date from which this runs will be the date in the notification of the authority's decision.[50]

Supporting People programme

17.55   In an effort to streamline the housing benefit scheme, the costs attributable to various housing support services required by vulnerable people, have been transferred to a separate budget – the 'supporting people programme'. People who need these support services are no longer eligible for

---

47   House of Commons, Hansard, 27 January 2003: Column 696. The Parliamentary Under-Secretary of State, Office of the Deputy Prime Minister (Mr Tony McNulty).

48   Keith Hill, Minister for Local Housing and Planning, House of Commons Written Answers, 17 November 2003, Column 533W in response to a question tabled by Sandra Gidley MP.

49   See for instance Complaint No 02/C/04897 against Morpeth BC and Northumberland CC, 27 November 2003.

50   Further guidance on this issue being given in Annex I.

enhanced rates of housing benefit, but instead seek assistance with the costs from the authority that administers these monies (generally the local social services authority).[51]

17.56   The services funded under the programme are not 'community care services', and accordingly subject to a distinct assessment and charging regime. Although the programme does not affect the responsibility of social services authorities to meet the assessed needs of service users, the funds it makes available do enable local authorities to provide a greater breadth of housing related solutions in any particular case. Thus instead of providing a person with a care home or home help services, the local authority could utilise the supporting people's monies to fund a warden service[52] in a sheltered housing scheme or provide support for a person with learning disabilities or mental health problems in moving into more independent living (for instance by providing help in making rent payments and ensuring windows are locked at night and that other housing related obligations are discharged).

17.57   The key documentation governing the programme in England[53] can be accessed at the Supporting People website;[54] the principal materials being:

- the Supporting People (England) Directions 2003;
- the Supporting People Programme Grant and Grant Conditions (the 2003 Grant Conditions);[55]
- the Supporting People Grant (England) Guidance 2003 (the 2003 Guidance);[56] and
- the Local Authorities (Charges for Specified Welfare Services) (England) Regulations 2003.[57]

---

51 Technically the local authority only administers the scheme – which it does on behalf of its partners in the programme – eg, health trusts, probation services and the housing authority (if a different authority to the social services authority).

52 This might be a 'floating' warden service, where wardens visit a number of different homes or as an on-site warden.

53 In Wales there are currently two grant schemes – Supporting People Revenue Grant (SPRG) (paid by the Welsh Assembly Government), and Supporting People Grant (SPG) (paid by local authorities). The key documents can be accessed at www.housing.wales.gov.uk/index.asp?task=content&a=k1. The principal guidance being 'Guidance to Local Authorities on the Arrangements for the Implementation and Administration of Supporting People in Wales' (Feb 2003).

54 www.spkweb.org.uk/.

55 Two sets of conditions have been imposed; one for 'excellent' authorities (which provides only a light [regulatory] touch' and one for 'non-excellent authorities'. Both were issued in September 2003 and reference in the following text is made to the guidance for non-excellent authorities.

56 The Guidance is issued under Local Government Act 2000 s93(8) guidance which provides a local authority must have regard to any guidance issued by the secretary of state 'with respect to the administration and application of grants under this section which are paid to them'. The guidance can be accessed at www.spkweb.org.uk/Evolution/5.1.1DocumentDetail.asp?Doc_ID=13493.

57 SI No 907.

Services under the Supporting People programme

17.58   The directions and guidance detail the services that can be funded under the scheme – and those that cannot.

Eligible services

17.59   Eligible services are defined in the Schedule to the 2003 Grant conditions. Such a service must fulfil the following criteria:

1. It must be a housing-related support service

17.60   A 'housing-related service' is one whose purpose is to develop or sustain an individual's capacity to live independently in accommodation. Para 2 of the Grant Conditions makes it clear that such services cannot be general health, social services, or statutory personal care services, but rather a service whose aim is to support more independent living arrangements.

17.61   The 2003 Guidance (at para 50) advises that where there is doubt as to whether a services is eligible:

> . . . it may be helpful to ask the question 'would this person be unable to move to more independent housing, or be at risk of losing their home and moving to less independent care, if this housing related support was not provided?' That is, is the primary purpose of the service to enable the person to live in more independent accommodation than they otherwise might, or to prevent the loss of this independent accommodation. For example, the service may provide help with life skills such cooking or budgeting, which are an integral part of living independently in accommodation; or an elderly person may need the general support of a visiting support worker to give them the confidence to sustain their own home. Other health or statutory care services may be provided alongside but the basic objective is to enable or sustain independent living.

2. It must be provided as part of an agreed package of support services

17.62   In this respect the 2003 guidance at para 52 explains:

> This means that services of an ad hoc nature providing general advice (such as occasional advice on housing management issues provided on demand, or drop in services for the public) are not eligible services. The exception to this are 'occasional welfare services' which are provided on an ad hoc basis and directly enable an aspect of an agreed package of support to be delivered . . .

17.63   The scheme aims not to be overly prescriptive, and accordingly services that do not fit exactly within the detailed definitions may still be eligible for grant support. Para 1(4) of the 2003 Grant Conditions for instance, allows for payments to be made with respect to *'occasional welfare services'*. As the 2003 Guidance explains (paras 53–55) these may be:

> . . . welfare services provided on an ad hoc basis and considered by the Administering Authority to be ancillary to housing-related support services . . .

and that

> This provision is intended to cover services that it may be necessary from time to time to provide in order for the main package of support to be delivered to the service recipient.

17.64   The guidance[58] gives as examples of such a service 'arrangements for tidying the garden for an elderly person perhaps to allow support workers to access the property to deliver support (though as with handy-person schemes, the payment for the work itself would not be eligible, just the arranging of the work)'.

3. It must be provided to people with vulnerabilities in need of support services

17.65   Services under the programme are for people who are at risk of losing their home 'due to an inability to cope with the demands and requirements of living independently' (para 50 of 2003 Guidance). In this context the guidance states that service users with 'any of the following vulnerabilities' are potentially eligible for support:[59]

- previous homelessness or rough sleeping;
- previous imprisonment, or at risk of re-offending;
- mental health problems;
- learning difficulties;
- being at risk of domestic violence;
- teenage pregnancy;
- vulnerability due to age, including both older vulnerable people having difficulty coping (or anticipating having difficulty coping) and young people at risk;
- drug and alcohol problems;
- physical and sensory disability;
- having HIV or AIDS;
- being a refugee;
- a previous history of repeated and unplanned loss of tenancy;
- travellers.

Excluded services

17.66   Certain services are explicitly excluded from the programme, and these are detailed in 2003 Guidance para 59, and include:

- *Services provided at a residential care establishment (unless the establishment was in receipt of legacy funding).*
- *Services that are of a nature such that they are required to be provided by a registered care provider.*
  The 2003 guidance explains (para 59) that this provision:

  > . . . acknowledges that some registered care providers also provide services that are not required to be delivered by a registered care

---

58   2003 Guidance, para 54.
59   2003 Guidance, para 52.

provider. Such additional or separate services are eligible, but not the services for which registration is required.

- *Personal or nursing care.*
- *Services that are provided in satisfaction of a statutory duty.*
  The 2003 Guidance emphasises at para 59 that Supporting People monies are not to be used for support services that local authorities have a statutory duty to provide. However:

  > ... housing-related support services may be provided under one contract to a range of people, some of whom may have a statutory right to receive support while others do not. As long as administrative arrangements allow for the separation of Supporting People grant from payment from other funding sources, there should be no impediment to funding such a mix of clients within a single service.

- *Building works other than the provision of advice and personal support services.*
- *Provision of equipment* (for example stair-lifts or specialist adaptations).
- *Psychological therapy or programmes of therapeutic counselling.*
  The 2003 Guidance explains (para 59) that:

  > ... providing housing-related support is an activity of advice and counselling, but what is excluded here is specialist counselling. An example of a counselling activity that would be ineligible might be counselling as part of a drug or alcohol rehabilitation project delivered by specialist accredited therapeutic counsellors. The intention of Supporting People is to enable or sustain independent living, and the elements of counselling have this as its specific purpose can be funded through the Supporting People grant. This is not to say that an individual should not benefit from a package of support, care and counselling – simply that it is only the housing-related support element of this package that should be funded by Supporting People.

- *Services to enforce specific requirements imposed by a court of law.*
- *General housing management services.*

Charging for Supporting People services

17.67   The 2003 Directions and 2003 Grant Conditions require local authorities to develop charging schemes for recipients of Supporting People monies. The provisions are relatively complex – largely due to the cohort of Supporting People grant recipients that were previously in receipt of Transitional Housing Benefit. However the stated aim of the guidance is that over time the charging rules will harmonise with the 'Fairer Charging' arrangements for users of domiciliary care services (see para 12.99 above).

17.68   Paragraph 7 of the 2003 Grant Conditions and para 26 of the 2003 Guidance set out principal requirements for any charging scheme including:

- Transitional protection is to be provided for people who were previously in receipt of Transitional Housing Benefit, or who were previously in local authority services with pooled costs: such persons 'should not suffer financially from the move to the new administrative arrangements'.

- People receiving Housing Benefit are exempt from charging.
- People in 'short-term services' are exempt from charging: a 'short-term services' is defined[60] as a services which:
    - (a) aims to bring about independent living within two years (disregarding practical delays in securing move-on accommodation) following resolution of a specific need or needs which the supported living arrangement aims to remedy, or following completion of a time-limited programme of support of under two years intended duration; or
    - (b) aims to increase the capacity for independent living (even if fully independent living may not be likely) through a package of time-limited housing related support under these directions, which package has an intended duration of under two years.

A service is not short term if it aims to maintain a limited degree of independent living which is not expected to increase, and may diminish over time, as part of a permanent or open-ended arrangement.

---

60 2003 Guidance, para 42.

Children Act 1989 duties to children in need

Introduction

18.1   The Children Act (CA) 1989 is widely regarded as a statute that both radically reformed and simplified UK child care law. While this was undoubtedly the case for child protection proceedings this was not so in relation to the provision of services for disabled children. In this respect the Act complicated matters; creating new rights and duties which apply alongside and overlap with the pre-existing legislation. As a consequence disabled children and their carers have rights to child and family support services both under the CA 1989 and under the community care and carers' legislation.[1] In general, however, it will be appropriate for disabled children to be assessed under the CA 1989 regime – even if the services that are subsequently provided derive from another statute.

Disabled parents

18.2   As noted at para 4.51 above (and para 18.30 below) the Social Services Inspectorate report *A Jigsaw of Services* (2000) sought to evaluate (and make recommendations) concerning the way in which local authorities (and other agencies) managed and planned support services for disabled adults. The report highlighted the community care responsibilities of social services in this domain. These obligations are additionally stressed by the FACS 2002 Policy Guidance (see para 4.50 above) which states that 'in the course of assessing an individual's needs, councils should recognise that adults, who have parenting responsibilities for a child under 18 years, may require help with these responsibilities' (para 9). The FACS 2003 Practice Guidance (see para 4.50 above) provides additional detail on the social services obligation, including that the assessment process must cover the assistance required to carry out 'family and other social roles and responsibilities' and that 'family responsibilities' include 'parenting roles and responsibilities' (Q4.1 onwards).[2]

Disabled children and the Children Act 1989

18.3   Children Act 1989 s17(1) places a general duty on social services authorities to safeguard and promote the interests of children 'in need' and in furtherance of this duty they are empowered to provide a wide range of services.

18.4   CA 1989 s17(10) provides that a child shall be taken to be 'in need' if:

---

1   As has already been noted, disabled children have rights to services under (for instance) National Health Service Act (NHSA) 1977 Sch 8 para 3 (see para 8.128 above) and Chronically Sick and Disabled Persons Act (CSDPA) 1970 s2 (see para 8.67 above). As a consequence they are entitled to be assessed under National Health Service and Community Care Act (NHSCCA) 1990 s47 (see para 4.14 above).

2   In Wales the relevant guidance is to be found in the Unified and Fair System for Assessing and Managing Care (UFSAMC) 2002 guidance at p65 (see para 4.77 above).

(a) he is unlikely to achieve or maintain, or to have the opportunity of achieving or maintaining, a reasonable standard of health or development without the provision for him of services by a local authority . . .; or

(b) his health or development is likely to be significantly impaired, or further impaired, without the provision for him of such services; or

(c) he is disabled.

18.5   The definition of a disabled child (which closely follows the definition of a disabled adult in National Assistance Act (NAA) 1948 s29) is contained in CA 1989 s17(11), namely:

> For the purposes of this Part, a child is disabled if he is blind, deaf or dumb or suffers from mental disorder of any kind or is substantially and permanently handicapped by illness, injury or congenital deformity or such other disability as may be prescribed; and in this Part –
> 'development' means physical, intellectual, emotional, social or behavioural development; and
> 'health' means physical or mental health.

18.6   A child who is not 'substantially and permanently handicapped' may nevertheless be a child in need by virtue of CA 1989 s17(10)(a) or (b) and therefore entitled to assistance (see para 11.61 where this question is considered in detail in relation to young carers). Having identified the potential recipients of assistance under section 17, the Act then follows a similar route to the community care legislation, namely an assessment of needs followed by a decision on whether services are called for.

18.7   The Children Act 1989 also follows NAA 1948 s29 by requiring social services authorities to maintain a register of disabled children (under Sch 2 Part I para 2).

Disabled children's register

18.8   Social services departments are obliged to keep a register of children with disabilities,[3] as part of their duty to safeguard and promote the interests of disabled children. Volume 6 of the Children Act Guidance (Children with Disabilities) makes the following comments on the role of registers:

> 4.2 . . . There is no duty on parents to agree to registration (which is a voluntary procedure) and services are not dependent upon registration. Registration can contribute positively to coherent planning of service provision for children with disabilities under the Children Act . . .

> 4.3 [Social services departments] SSDs . . . will need to liaise with their education and health counterparts to achieve an understanding of disability which permits early identification; which facilitates joint working; which encourages parents to agree to registration and which is meaningful in terms of planning services for the children in question and children in general. The creation of a joint register of children with disabilities between health, education and social services would greatly

---

3   CA 1989 Sch 2 para 2; and see also para 4.2 of volume 6 of the Children Act Guidance (Children with Disabilities).

facilitate collaboration in identification and a co-ordinated provision of services under the Act . . .

4.4 Whichever agency is the first to identify a child as having a disability whether it is the [local education authority] LEA, SSD or child health services they should initiate discussions with the parents about services or procedures which might be beneficial to the child and family. This should include an explanation of what other agencies can provide and information about the register. The registration of children with disabilities will be effective and productive only if parents and children are regarded as partners in the assessment process and as experts in their own right, from whom professionals may have much to learn.

The assessment of children in need

18.9 There is no duty to assess under the CA 1989 equivalent to that found in NHSCCA 1990 s47. However, in *R (G) v Barnet LBC and others*[4] Lord Hope expressed the view that there was a specific law obligation to assess under the 1989 Act, observing:

77. My noble and learned friend Lord Nicholls has said that, on the respondents' approach to the construction of section 17(1), it follows that a local authority is not under a duty to assess the needs of a child in need under section 17(1) and that this would go far to stultify the purpose of Part III of the Act. I . . . am unable to agree that this conclusion follows from the respondents' argument. Section 17(2) provides that, for the purpose of facilitating the discharge of the general duty under that section, every local authority shall have the specific duties and powers set out in Part I of Schedule 2. The duty of the local authority to take reasonable steps to identify the extent to which there are children in need in their area is to be found in paragraph 1 of the Schedule. That will involve assessing the needs of each child who is found to be in need in their area as paragraph 3 makes clear.

18.10 The assessment obligation is strongly reinforced by policy guidance and given the alternative rights of disabled children to an assessment under the community care legislation the CA 1989 assessment obligation must in most cases be tantamount to a public law duty.

18.11   The original CA 1989 policy guidance[5] concerning assessments states as follows:

2.7 Good practice requires that the assessment of need should be undertaken in an open way and should involve those caring for the child, the child and other significant persons. Families with a child in need, whether the need results from family difficulties or the child's circumstances, have the right to receive sympathetic support and sensitive intervention in their family's life . . .

---

4   [2003] UKHL 57; [2003] 3 WLR 1194; (2003) 6 CCLR 500. Lord Scott (also part of the majority) was of the opinion that at the very least it was 'implicit in this provision that the local authority will assess the actual needs of a child in need whenever it appears necessary to do so' – at [117].

5   Guidance to the Children Act 1989 Volume 2 (Family Support) para 2.7.

2.8 In making an assessment, the local authority should take account of the particular needs of the child – that is in relation to health, development, disability, education, religious persuasion, racial origin, cultural and linguistic background, the degree (if any) to which these needs are being met by existing services to the family or the child and which agencies' services are best suited to the child's needs.

18.12   The English[6] 2000 policy guidance, the *Framework for the Assessment of Children in Need and their Families*[7] describes the social services response to an initial contact or a referral requesting help as 'critically important' (para 3.3) and lays down a timetable for the assessment process, in the following terms:

3.8 There is an expectation that **within one working day** of a referral being received or new information coming to or from within a social services department about an open case, there will be a decision about what response is required. A referral is defined as a request for services to be provided by the social services department. The response may include no action, but that is itself a decision and should be made promptly and recorded. The referrer should be informed of the decision and its rationale, as well as the parents or caregivers and the child, if appropriate.

3.9 A decision to gather more information constitutes an initial assessment. An initial assessment is defined as a brief assessment of each child referred to social services with a request for services to be provided. This should be undertaken **within a maximum of 7 working days** but could be very brief depending on the child's circumstances. It should address the dimensions of the Assessment Framework, determining whether the child is in need, the nature of any services required, from where and within what timescales, and whether a further, more detailed core assessment should be undertaken. An initial assessment is deemed to have commenced at the point of referral to the social services department or when new information on an open case indicates an initial assessment should be repeated. All staff responding to referrals and undertaking initial assessments should address the dimensions which constitute the Assessment Framework . . .

3.10 Depending on the child's circumstances, an initial assessment may include some or all of the following:
- interviews with child and family members, as appropriate;
- involvement of other agencies in gathering and providing information, as appropriate;
- consultation with supervisor/manager;
- record of initial analysis;
- decisions on further action/no action;
- record of decisions/rationale with family/agencies;
- informing other agencies of the decisions;
- statement to the family of decisions made and, if a child is in need, the plan for providing support.

6   In Wales equivalent guidance has been published in very similar terms (2001) Stationery Office; accessible at www.wales.gov.uk/subichildren/content/ framework-m/framework-m.pdf.

7   Stationery Office, 2000; accessible at www.dh.gov.uk/assetRoot/04/01/44/30/ 04014430.pdf.

As part of any initial assessment, the child should be seen. This includes observation and talking with the child in an age appropriate manner . . .

3.11 **A core assessment** is defined as an in-depth assessment which addresses the central or most important aspects of the needs of a child and the capacity of his or her parents or caregivers to respond appropriately to these needs within the wider family and community context. While this assessment is led by social services, it will invariably involve other agencies or independent professionals, who will either provide information they hold about the child or parents, contribute specialist knowledge or advice to social services or undertake specialist assessments. Specific assessments of the child and/or family members may have already been undertaken prior to referral to the social services department. The findings from these should inform this assessment. At the conclusion of this phase of assessment, there should be an analysis of the findings which will provide an understanding of the child's circumstances and inform planning, case objectives and the nature of service provision. The timescale for completion of the core assessment is a **maximum of 35 working days**. A core assessment is deemed to have commenced at the point the initial assessment ended, or a strategy discussion decided to initiate enquiries under Section 47, or new information obtained on an open case indicates a core assessment should be undertaken. Where specialist assessments have been commissioned by social services from other agencies or independent professionals, it is recognised that they will not necessarily be completed within the 35 working day period. Appropriate services should be provided whilst awaiting the completion of the specialist assessment.

18.13   In *R (AB and SB) v Nottingham CC*[8] Richards J described the assessment process detailed in the policy guidance in the following terms:

There should be a systematic assessment of needs which takes into account the three domains (child's developmental needs, parenting capacity, family and environmental factors) and involves collaboration between all relevant agencies so as to achieve a full understanding of the child in his or her family and community context. It is important, moreover, to be clear about the three-stage process: identification of needs, production of a care plan, and provision of the identified services. It seems to me that where an authority follows a path that does not involve the preparation of a core assessment as such, it must nevertheless adopt a similarly systematic approach with a view to achievement of the same objectives. Failure to do so without good cause will constitute an impermissible departure from the guidance.

18.14   Although the policy guidance accepts that in some situations this may not lead to a full assessment – this is unlikely to be the case in relation to disabled children. The guidance applies to all 'children in need' and is primarily framed to address issues that arise in the context of the child protection process. The accompanying 2000 practice guidance *Assessing Children in*

---

8   [20001] EWHC Admin 235; (2001) 4 CCLR 294 at 306G–I. See also *R (J) v Newham LBC* [2001] EWHC Admin 992; (2002) 5 CCLR 302 where a similar mandatory order to undertake a CA 1989 assessment was made.

Need and their Families: Practice Guidance[9] contains a specific section (chapter 3) dealing with the assessment of disabled children, which includes the observation that:

> While disabled children's basic needs are the same as all children's needs, impairments may create additional needs. Disabled children are also likely to face additional disabling barriers which inhibit or prevent their inclusion in society.

Services for disabled children

18.15 Following an assessment, a wide spectrum of services can be made available to disabled children. These services may be home, community or institutionally based and may derive from a variety of legislative provisions, although the primary statutes are the Chronically Sick and Disabled Persons Act (CSDPA) 1970 and the CA 1989.

Services for disabled children under the CSDPA 1970

18.16 As noted at para 8.67 above, by virtue of CSDPA 1970 s28A, section 2 services are available to disabled children within the meaning of CA 1989 s17(11). The range of services available under the 1970 Act are considered at para 8.69 above. These services are also capable of being provided under the CA 1989 and in *R v Bexley LBC ex p B*[10] the court had to determine under which statute services were being provided to the disabled child. This is not an entirely academic question, since the duty under the 1970 Act is a specific law duty (see para 1.5 above) whereas the nature of the duty under the 1989 Act is uncertain (and in relation to some services only a target duty – see para 18.20 below). The case concerned the provision of care services for a severely disabled boy of 10 years old. The respondent council sought to argue (among other things) that his home care services were being provided under CA 1989 rather than under CSDPA 1970 s2. Latham J rejected the argument, reasoning as follows:

> The relationship between the Children Act 1989 and the Chronically Sick and Disabled Persons Act 1970 is an uneasy one. The provisions of the Children Act 1989 are in general terms; and the duties are of a type which Woolf LJ described as 'target duties' in *R v Inner London Education Authority ex p Ali* (1990) 2 Admin LR 822. An assessment of a disabled child's needs pursuant to paragraph 3 of Schedule 2 to the Act does not appear to give rise to any specific duty pursuant to the Act itself, which is the point made by the respondents. They accept, however, that section 2(1) of the Chronically Sick and Disabled Persons Act 1970 will impose a specific duty to provide, for example, practical assistance for a disabled person in his home, if they are satisfied that it is necessary to provide that in order to meet his needs. But, as I have already said, their argument is that no such assessment was made because there was no request for such

9 Stationery Office, 2000; accessible at www.asylumsupport.info/publications/doh/practiceguidance.pdf.

10 (2000) 3 CCLR 15.

an assessment. If this is a proper analysis, it would result in an Authority being able to avoid the specific duty under the Chronically Sick and Disabled Persons Act 1970 by purporting to act simply under the Children Act 1989. The same problem does not arise in relation to adults. Section 47 of the National Health Service and Community Care Act 1990 provides that an Authority is under an obligation to carry out an assessment of a person's needs wherever it appears to the Authority that he may be in need of community care services, and if it concludes that the person is a disabled person, it is under obligation to make a decision as to what services, if any, he requires under section 2(1) of the Chronically Sick and Disabled Persons Act 1970. This section does not apply to children because services provided pursuant to the Children Act 1989 are not community health services for the purposes of the Act.[11]

Authorities are, however, under an obligation to make provision under the Chronically Sick and Disabled Persons Act 1970 whenever they are satisfied that the relevant conditions have been met. A request by or on behalf of a disabled person is not one of those conditions. It seems to me that the Court should look at the reality of the situation. In the present case, although no formal request was made by the applicant's mother for an assessment of the applicant's needs, that was the effect of what happened in the early months of 1994. As a result, it seems to me that the respondents were satisfied that it was necessary to provide practical assistance for him in the house in order to meet his needs. [The social worker] clearly decided that to expect his mother to go on meeting those needs without further help would be to the applicant's disadvantage. He had a need for full time care of a quality which one person could not be expected to continue to provide in the way the applicant's mother was then providing it. The only conclusion which a reasonable Authority could reach in that situation was that it was under a duty pursuant to section 2(1) of the Chronically Sick and Disabled Persons Act 1970 to provide practical assistance in his home. The respondents, in so far as they considered that they were simply exercising their general duties pursuant to the Children Act 1989, were wrong, and in breach of their duty under the Chronically Sick and Disabled Persons Act 1970.[12]

Services for disabled children under the CA 1989

18.17   Once a child has been accepted as being 'in need', and that need identified by an assessment or otherwise, then the CA 1989 specifies that a range of support services be made available. Section 17(1) provides:

It shall be the general duty of every local authority (in addition to the other duties imposed on them by this Part) –

11   The phrase used here, 'community health services', is clearly a mistake, and should read 'community care services'. The judge is also mistaken in relation to the ambit of NHSCCA 1990 s47. As detailed at para 8.128 the duty to assess under NHSCCA 1990 s47(1) is activated when (among other things) an authority is aware of a potential service user possibly being in need of community care services. The definition of community care services under NHSCCA 1990 s46 includes services under NHSA 1977 Sch 8; home help services under para 3 of which can be supplied to disabled adults or disabled children; thus the assessment duty under NHSCCA 1990 s47(1) will generally be triggered for all disabled people regardless of age.

12   (2000) 3 CCLR 15 at 22E–23C.

(a) to safeguard and promote the welfare of children within their area who are in need; and

(b) so far as is consistent with that duty, to promote the upbringing of such children by their families,

by providing a range of services appropriate to those children's needs.

18.18 In *R (G) v Barnet LBC and others*[13] (which involved a number of consolidated appeals) the House of Lords had to determine (among other things) whether the obligation to provide services under the 1989 Act, was a target or specific law duty. The case was unusual in that the CA 1989 service sought by the appellants was the provision of housing. In a split 3:2 judgment, the majority held that although there was an obligation under the CA 1989 to provide accommodation (once it had been identified in an assessment as a 'need') this was a target duty rather than a specific law duty (see para 1.5 above).

18.19 As noted above (at para 18.9) Lord Hope (and the other two majority judgments)[14] was nevertheless of the opinion that the effect of CA 1989 s17(2) was to create specific duties and powers in relation to those services itemised in Part I of Schedule 2 of the Act – the relevant service provision paragraphs of which comprise:

Paragraph 5: Provision for disabled children
Every local authority shall provide services designed –
(a) to minimise the effect on disabled children within their area of their disabilities; and
(b) to give such children the opportunity to lead lives which are as normal as possible.

Paragraph 8: Provision for children living with their families
Every local authority shall make such provision as they consider appropriate for the following services to be available with respect to children in need within their area while they are living with their families –
(a) advice, guidance and counselling;
(b) occupational, social, cultural or recreational activities;
(c) home help (which may include laundry facilities);
(d) facilities for, or assistance with, travelling to and from home for the purpose of taking advantage of any other service provided under this Act or of any similar service;
(e) assistance to enable the child concerned and his family to have a holiday.

18.20 It is unclear however, the extent to which the Lords were of the view that there were 'specific law duties' to provide services under Part I of Schedule 2 once an assessment had identified them as necessary. Lord Hope stated:

80. An examination of the range of duties mentioned elsewhere in Part III of the Act and Part I of Schedule 2 tends to support the view that section 17(1) is concerned with general principles and is not designed to confer

---

13 [2003] UKHL 57; [2003] 3 WLR 1194; (2003) 6 CCLR 500.

14 Lord Millett expressed agreement with the judgement of Lord Hope and Lord Scott at [117] stating that 'Part I of Schedule 2 to the Act, as section 17(2) has led one to expect, imposes specific duties and confers specific powers on local authorities'.

absolute rights on individuals. These other duties appear to have been carefully framed so as to confer a discretion on the local social services authority as to how it should meet the needs of each individual child in need.

and

82. The discretion which is given by these provisions to the local authority is framed in various ways, but the result is the same in each case. Where a discretion is given, the child in need does not have an absolute right to the provision of any of these services.

18.21   It is also unclear what the extent is of the public law duty on a local authority once an assessment has disclosed a need for services under the CA 1989. Frequently this will be academic, since the services will be capable of being provided under the CSDPA 1970, for which the statutory duty is 'specific' and enforceable (see para 1.5). However if the need identified does not fall into the category of services that could be delivered under the 1970 Act, then the Lords' judgment suggests that the public law obligation is imperfect. The *Barnet* judgment is, however, probably best viewed as one that is fact specific, in that it concerned a service that could not be provided under CA 1989 Sch 2 Part I, and had not been assessed as necessary by the local authority. If a local authority assesses it necessary to provide a disabled child with a service of a nature covered by Part I of Schedule 2 (but not falling under the 1970 Act) then the public law obligation to make that service available will be considerable – even if not 'absolute'. An additional factor in any such analysis will concern the extent to which a failure to make the service available would impact on the authority's positive obligations under article 8 of the European Convention on Human Rights[15] (see para 19.187).

18.22   The guidance to the CA 1989 conveniently summarises the breadth of powers available to social services authorities in such cases:[16]

This general duty is supported by other specific duties and powers such as the facilitation of 'the provision by others, including in particular voluntary organisations of services' (section 17(5) and Schedule 2). These provisions encourage SSDs to provide day and domiciliary services, guidance and counselling, respite care and a range of other services as a means of supporting children in need (including children with disabilities) within their families. The Act recognises that sometimes a child can only be helped by providing services for other members of his family (section 17(3)) 'if it [the service] is provided with a view to safeguarding or promoting the child's welfare' . . . The SSD may make such arrangements as they see fit for any person to provide services and support 'may include giving assistance in kind, or in exceptional circumstances in cash' (section 17(6)).[17] However, where it is the SSD's view that a child's welfare is adequately provided for and no unmet need exists, they need not act.

18.23   The general public law principles relevant to the provision of services to adults are applicable to those for disabled children. Accordingly a failure by a service provider (for instance in relation to respite care) does not negate

15 For an analysis of this question, see The Journal of Community Care Law and Practice, Issue 10, February 2004 pp2–12 (Arden Davies Publishing).

16 Guidance Volume 6 para 3.3.

the obligation on the local authority to ensure a similar service is made available (see para 5.32 above). Likewise an apparently 'harsh' assessment decision – which appears to have the hallmarks of a 'budget led' assessment – will also be susceptible to traditional administrative law challenge (see para 4.141 above).

18.24 Not infrequently however, the service difficulty encountered is that of a dearth of service providers available to meet an assessed need – for instance a need for respite or short-break care. It may be that there is no approved service provider in the locality capable of providing the assessed need. In such situations it may be that the parents of the disabled child could make the necessary arrangements themselves if they had 'direct payments – for instance by arranging for one of their acquaintances or relations to make provide the service.

Direct payments

18.25 The Carers and Disabled Children Act 2000 s7 inserted a new provision into the CA 1989 – section 17A – empowering local authorities to provide direct payments (in lieu of CA 1989 services) to people with parental responsibility for a disabled child or the disabled child itself if aged 16 or 17.

18.26 Section 17A has been amended in England (but not as yet in Wales – see para 9.5 above) by the Health and Social Care Act (HSCA) 2001 s58. This extends the categories of person entitled to direct payments in relation to CA 1989 services to include persons with parental responsibility for a disabled child, and provides the secretary of state with regulatory powers. Regulations have now been issued under HSCA 2001 s58 and reference should be made to chapter 9 where these are further considered.

18.27 People with parental responsibility for a disabled child are entitled to an assessment under Carers (Recognition and Services) Act (C(RS)A) 1995 s1(2) and Carers and Disabled Children Act (CDCA) 2000 s6. In general however, a separate assessment under one or both of these Acts should be unnecessary – since a holistic assessment under the CA 1989 should fully address their needs.[18] There may, however, be instances where a parent carer might insist upon a separate carer's assessment. This might, for example occur where a local authority was proving reluctant to provide services which would enable a parent carer to return to work or maintain employment. If he or she sought an assessment under the 2000 Act reliance could be placed upon the guidance which stresses the benefits of supporting parents in such situations (see para 11.47 above).

18.28 Detailed practice guidance has now been issued by the Department of Health[19] concerning the new direct payments regime. This is considered in

17 Subsequent to this guidance the CA 1989 was amended to insert an additional right to direct payments – see para 18.25 below).

18 *A Practitioner's Guide to Carers Assessments under the Carers and Disabled Children Act 2000*, para 10.

19 'Direct Payment Guidance. Community Care, Services for Carers and Children's Services (Direct Payments) Guidance England 2003' (September 2003) accessible at www.dh.gov.uk/assetRoot/04/06/92/62/04069262.pdf.

general terms at para 9.6 above. In relation to the potential risk of disabled children being exposed to abuse by third parties, the guidance advises:

> *Disabled children (paras 104–106)*
> The Protection of Children Act 1999 enables a person who is considering employing an individual to care for their child, or a disabled 16- or 17-year-old who is considering employing a care worker themselves to ask the local council to carry out checks under the Protection of Children Act 1999 through the Criminal Records Bureau (CRB). When the person with parental responsibility or the disabled young person requests such a check the local council has a duty to comply.
>
> Councils should work in partnership with parents to help them make arrangements that are designed to safeguard and promote the welfare of the child. The majority of parents will be both willing and able to do this, but local councils should only arrange a direct payment for a parent of a disabled child when they are satisfied this is the case.
>
> Local councils may want to clarify with those who request a CRB check the council's responsibility for child protection, and the implications should a parent insist on employing an individual who has been found to be unsuitable following such a check.

18.29   The direct payment regulations restrict the ability of the recipients of direct payments to use the monies to purchase care services from their close relatives or partners.[20] As noted at paras 9.20–9.22 above, these restrictions are considerably less onerous than those that previously applied under the Community Care (Direct Payments) Act (CC(DP)A) 1996. Where the payment is made to the parent of a disabled child then it can used to purchase services from a close relative (regulation 6(1)(b)) – see para 9.18 above).

18.30   In relation to the general use of direct payments for the CA 1989 services, the guidance advises:

> *Direct payments to disabled parents with parental responsibility for a child*
> 113. The Social Services Inspectorate report *A Jigsaw of Services*[21] found that many disabled parents had difficulties accessing appropriate support to enable them to look after their children. Councils should ensure that needs assessments for disabled adults include parenting responsibilities.
>
> 114. Disabled people who are parents could be assessed as needing services under both community care legislation and/or the 1989 Act to assist them in their parenting role. This means that direct payments can be used to meet the social care needs of them, their children or their family that arise from their disability. It is important that the needs of the disabled person and their family are looked at holistically, bearing in mind that specific duties may arise under particular legislation. In the interest of the family and to avoid duplication, local councils should ensure the assessment process is streamlined and co-ordinated between adult and children's services and other relevant departments such as education.
>
> 115. Where there is a disabled parent, the local council may be under a

20 The Community Care, Services for Carers and Children's Services (Direct Payments)(England) Regulations 2003 SI 2003 No 762, reg 6.
21 Department of Health, March 2001 (CI (2000)6) accessible at www.dh.gov.uk/assetRoot/04/05/75/42/04057542.pdf.

duty to assist the family if they are assessed as needing help in bringing up their child.

Direct payments to a parent with parental responsibility for a disabled child
116. In this section, 'parent' and 'parents' refers to those with parental responsibility for a disabled child.

117. Where a parent opts for direct payments, councils retain their responsibilities under the 1989 Act to assess and review the needs of disabled children and their families in the normal way.

118. In considering direct payments some parents will require advice about their child's need for additional support or protection. Other parents need support and sometimes permission to let their disabled child take risks in their everyday lives. This may include allowing their 16- or 17-year-old to manage their own support through a direct payment.

119. Local councils should make clear the steps that people with parental responsibility for a disabled child ought to take to satisfy themselves that the person offering help with the care of their child is a suitable person. (*'The available UK evidence on the extent of abuse among disabled children suggests that disabled children are at increased risk of abuse.'*)[22] It is important that people with parental responsibility for disabled children are fully alerted to any risks of abuse and provided with advice to minimise those risks.

120. The responsibilities of people with parental responsibility for disabled children are often made more arduous by the difficulty of accessing mainstream services such as childcare, after school clubs and leisure activities. Families with disabled children may not think existing services provided or commissioned by their local council are suitable for their child and may well be able to make more appropriate arrangements for themselves. Direct payments can enable parents with parental responsibility for a disabled child to make such arrangements.

121. Parents should be encouraged and supported to use direct payments with a view to enabling their disabled children to access the same kinds of opportunities and activities as their non-disabled peers. Direct payments to people with parental responsibility for a disabled child are provided within the framework of Part III of the 1989 Act which requires local councils to provide a range of services to safeguard and promote the welfare of children in need.

Intimate care for a disabled child using direct payments
122. Parents may use direct payments to purchase services of an intimate nature to meet the assessed needs of their disabled children. However, as children mature parents should be encouraged to give greater weight to the child's views about how their intimate care needs are to be met. Particular care should be taken to ascertain the child's wishes when they have a cognitive and/or communication impairment.

Childminding
123. Local councils may make available the list of registered child minders and other registered providers of childcare in the area. The local council may consider that a direct payments support service is also well placed to provide such information and support.

22 *Working Together to Safeguard Children*, Department of Health et al, 1999, para. 6.27.

124. Section 79D of the 1989 Act states that anyone caring for a child under eight for over two hours a day and for payment in their own home has to be registered as a childminder. Parents of disabled children should be aware of this requirement, designed to safeguard the welfare of young children, when purchasing support via a direct payment.

125. A checklist such as that available on www.childcarelink.gov.uk that enables parents to select safe childcare may be helpful.

Education

126. Social services departments are encouraged to develop appropriate links with educational services and with the Connexions service. Connexions make available a network of personal advisers to 13- to19-year-olds to ensure that the needs of young people are met in an integrated and co-ordinated manner. They have specific responsibilities towards disabled young people and where necessary can continue working with disabled young people until the age of 25. They should inform disabled young people about direct payments.

Transition: young person into adulthood

127. Parents often face challenges or problems in supporting and preparing their children for an independent adult life. The transition to financial independence and independent living is not usually a single event, nor does it happen quickly. Families with disabled children often face additional challenges that may delay or limit the children's move towards independence. For any young person (with or without a disability) the process of growing up involves the gradual taking on of more and more responsibility for himself or herself.

128. In some cases the young disabled person at age 16 or 17 may wish, as part of the transition to adulthood, to take control of parts or all of the direct payment that has to date been managed by the person with parental responsibility. This can allow them to gain experience of managing direct payments in a gradual way prior to reaching adulthood.

129. Whatever decisions are made when the disabled child reaches age 16 or 17, people with parental responsibility for a disabled child may not continue to receive direct payments to purchase services that meet the needs of that child once the child reaches his or her majority. However, if they are going to continue in their caring role, such carers may be entitled to receive direct payments as an alternative to local council directly provided carers' services under section 2 of the Carers and Disabled Children Act 2000. Carers' services would be to support the parent carer in their caring role and to help them maintain their own health and wellbeing.

130. It will be important for local councils to recognise and respect the views of parents who have been managing the delivery of support for their child in setting in place any new arrangements once the young person reaches his or her majority. The parents would, for example, normally be involved in setting up and running a user-controlled trust.

131. Disabled 16- and 17-year-olds are entitled to take advantage of the flexibility of direct payments where this will safeguard and promote their welfare. Direct payments enable them to make more decisions for themselves and to provide opportunities for them to have more control over their lives.

132. Some disabled 16-and 17-year-olds may have previous experience of direct payments because their parents are receiving them to meet the family's needs. However, many disabled 16- and 17-year-olds' parents will have been receiving services direct from their council.

133. A way to develop a young person's ability to manage the direct payment can be to put in place transitional arrangements, initially set up with the young person managing only a proportion of their support with a direct payment. This proportion could increase as the young person matures, with the objective of full management of the support package at age.

134. Young disabled people may receive assistance with managing the direct payment, just as any other direct payment recipient may do. Where that assistance takes the form of a user-controlled trust or similar arrangement, it should be set up in the knowledge of the views of those people with parental responsibility. Their ability to exercise their views should not be undermined by the arrangement.

135. The above case study highlights how services and direct payments can be used imaginatively by seeking to overcome disabling barriers that prevent the child from accessing social and leisure opportunities available to non-disabled peers. It also shows the importance of linking the different agencies that support disabled children.[23]

Vouchers in lieu of CA 1989 services

18.31 CA 1989 s17B (inserted by CDCA 2000 s7) makes provision for vouchers to be provided to people with parental responsibility for disabled children in relation to respite care services. The operation of voucher schemes is considered further at para 11.53 above.

Housing and residential care services

18.32 In *R v Tower Hamlets LBC ex p Bradford*[24] the court considered the housing and community care needs of a family which included a severely disabled mother and an 11-year-old son with special educational needs. Although the family members experienced particularly unpleasant harassment from their neighbours their 'housing points' were insufficient to make them an 'overriding priority' for re-housing. A judicial review challenging this decision was adjourned on grounds that the authority undertook various assessments, including under Children Act 1989 Part III. When considering its duty to provide accommodation under the Act, the authority effectively confined its attention to CA 1989 s20, the cross-heading to which section states '*provision of accommodation for children: general*'. This section (which is in effect what, prior to 1989, used to be called 'voluntary care') only arises where there is no one with parental responsibility, or where the child is lost or abandoned or where the parents are prevented from

---

23 See *Assessing Children in Need and their Families, Practice Guidance*, Department of Health et al, 2000, para 3.70.

24 (1998) 1 CCLR 294.

providing suitable accommodation or care. Since these factors were not present, the authority declined to provide accommodation under Part III of the Act. Dyson J held that the authority had fundamentally misunderstood its accommodation powers under the Act; in that any housing would be provided under CA 1989 s17 (and not CA 1989 s20). Section 17 enables authorities to provide an almost unlimited range of services including, in appropriate cases, housing.

18.33   Subsequent to the *ex p Bradford* decision, considerable controversy arose concerning the extent of the housing obligation under the CA 1989 s17, culminating in the House of Lords judgment in *R (G) v Barnet LBC and others*,[25] where the majority concluded that there was only a target duty under CA 1989 s17 to provide this service. The position has now been put beyond doubt, by the amending of section 17(6)[26] to expressly include the provision of 'accommodation' as one of the general services that may be provided (and section 22 amended so as to exclude children provided with accommodation under s17). Guidance on these amendments has been provided in England in LAC(2003)13 which includes the following:

> The amendment to section 17 did not affect the duties and powers of local authorities to provide accommodation for lone children under section 20 of the Children Act 1989, or under a care order. Accordingly, the power to provide accommodation under section 17 will almost always concern children needing to be accommodated with their families. However, there may be cases where a lone child who needs help with accommodation, but does not need to be looked after, might appropriately be assisted under section 17.

Homelessness

18.34   Housing Act 1996 s213A (inserted by the Homelessness Act 2002 s12) states that where a housing authority has reason to believe that an applicant with whom a person under the age of 18 normally resides, or might reasonably be expected to reside may be ineligible for housing assistance or intentionally homeless or threatened with homelessness intentionally, then that authority should seek to obtain the applicant's permission to refer his or her case to the relevant social services authority. In relation to this provision, para 10.7 of the Homelessness Code of Guidance for Local Authorities (July 2002)[27] advises:

> Where a social services authority have been made aware of a homelessness family likely to be found ineligible for assistance or intentionally homeless by the housing authority, and they consider the needs of a child or children could best be met by helping the family to obtain accommodation, they can request the housing authority to provide them with such advice and assistance as is reasonable in the circumstances. By section 213A(5), the housing authority must comply with such a request. Advice and assistance as is reasonable in the circumstances might include, for example, help

---

25 [2003] UKHL 57; [2003] 3 WLR 1194; (2003) 6 CCLR 500.
26 Through Adoption and Children Act 2002 s116.
27 Office of the Deputy Prime Minister: accessible at www.odpm.gov.uk.

with locating suitable accommodation and making an inspection of the property to ensure that it meets adequate standards of fitness and safety. However, the duty does not extend to a requirement on the housing authority to provide accommodation for the family.

18.35   The 2002 Code of Guidance advises that homeless applicants with dependent children should be treated as being in priority need for housing (para 8.6). Additionally the Housing Act 1996 s175 states that a person is homeless if he or she has no accommodation which is available for his or her occupation and Housing Act 1996 s176 provides that accommodation shall be treated as available for a person's occupation only if it is available for occupation by him or her together with any other person who normally resides with him or her as a member of the family, or any other person who might reasonably be expected to reside with him or her. This would for instance include a disabled child for whom the present accommodation was unsuitable.

Housing and asylum-seekers with disabled children

18.36   As noted at para 7.27 above, the Immigration and Asylum Act (IAA) 1999 s95 empowers the Home Secretary (who acts through the National Asylum Support Service (NASS)) to provide 'support' for adult asylum-seekers who are destitute or likely to become destitute'. However by IAA 1999 s122, there is a duty on NASS to support destitute asylum-seekers with dependent children, and in particular under section 122(3) to make available 'adequate accommodation for the child'. In *R (A) v NASS and Waltham Forest LBC*[28] the Court of Appeal held that the accommodation of families with disabled children who fell within the provisions of IAA 1999 s122 was the sole responsibly of NASS, although in discharging this duty NASS could seek assistance from a local authority under IAA 1999 s100 (and in such cases the authority must assist so far as is 'reasonable in the circumstances').

NHS services for disabled children

18.37   The NHS has, as noted in chapter 10, important responsibilities for the health and social care of disabled people, including disabled children. The guidance on the continuing health care responsibilities of the NHS (HSC 2001/015; LAC (2001)18 – see para 10.88 above) only applies to adults (para 8) but it must be the case that children who fall within the *Coughlan* criteria (see para 10.75 above) must be entitled to their care services free from the NHS – namely children whose care needs cannot be described as:

- merely incidental or ancillary to the provision of the accommodation which a local authority is under a duty to provide to the category of persons to whom section 21 refers; and

28 [2003] EWCA Civ 1473; [2004] 1 All ER 15; (2003) 6 CCLR 538 – see also *R (O) v Haringey LBC* [2003] EWHC 2798 (Admin) where it was held that NASS had responsibility even where there were disabled adult family members.

- of a nature which it can be expected that an authority whose primary responsibility is to provide social services can be expected to provide, then they can be provided under section 21.

18.38   The responsibility of the NHS to fund (or contribute towards the funding of) a care package includes respite care (see para 10.20 above) as well as more long term arrangements. This responsibility may arise – in relation to children with learning disabilities – even where the need is primarily social as opposed to health care (see para 10.89 above).

18.39   At present there is no current NHS guidance in relation to children's services – though this should emerge as a component in the National Service Framework for Children (when published).[29] However the April 2004 NHS guidance relating to children 'Standard for Hospital Services' [30] includes the following statement:

> 4.52 Disabled children have the same right to high quality services as any other child, though evidence suggests many are excluded from mainstream services . . . As more disabled children with complex needs survive for longer, they make up an increasing part of the work of children's hospital services. Hospitals need to recognise and meet the very particular needs of this group of patients and involve them and their parents in the planning of services.
> . . .
>
> 4.55 There should be a multi-agency plan, developed and agreed with the disabled young person and their parents, and updated as needed . . . It should say who does what – GP, hospital, social services, therapy services, school, and respite setting.

The transition into adulthood[31]

18.40   It is tempting to see community care law as synonymous with 'adult care law' and the CA 1989 as the statute which provides for the community care needs of disabled children. Many social services authorities divide their services for disabled people into 'adult care' and 'child care' services. While there may be good social work practice reasons for this division (eg, the need of disabled children for a 'childhood' and to share in the common development experiences of their peers), there is no significant justification for it at law.

18.41   Although, in general, services for disabled children under the CA 1989 cease to be available when they reach the age of 18,[32] their entitlement to

29 Details of which can be accessed at www.dh.gov.uk/PolicyAndGuidance/ HealthAndSocialCareTopics/ChildrenServices/ChildrenServicesInformation/fs/en.

30 Accessible at www.dh.gov.uk/assetRoot/04/06/72/51/04067251.pdf.

31 For a detailed consideration of these issues, see J Read and L Clements 'Disabled Children, the Law and Good Practice' (Jessica Kingsley, 2000).

32 Now subject to important exceptions, notably as a consequence of the Children (Leaving Care) Act 2000.

services under CSDPA 1970 s2 and under NHSA 1977 Sch 8 para 3 remain. The practical effect of the judgment in *R v Bexley LBC ex p B*[33] (as discussed at para 18.16) is to confirm that most home care services provided to disabled children are done so under the CSDPA 1970 rather than the CA 1989.

18.42   There are of course dangers in separating adult and child care services and these often surface when care responsibilities are being transferred from the child to the adult social work team. All too often at this stage the quality of the services deteriorates significantly or the child is effectively lost to the system and ceases to receive any continuing care. Such a transfer of responsibility often occurs when the young person's special education provision is also coming to an end.

18.43   Statutory provisions exist which endeavour to ensure that there is a smooth hand-over of responsibility from the education department (responsible for special education provision) to the social services department. The Disabled Persons (Services, Consultation and Representation) Act 1986 ss5 and 6 require education authorities to consult social services authorities to establish whether a child over the age of 14 who has been 'statemented' under Education Act 1996 Part IV, is likely to require support from the social services department when he or she leaves school. This duty has been reinforced by the Education (Special Educational Needs) (England) (Consolidation) Regulations 2001[34] reg 21 of which requires the contribution of social services departments and others to a transitional plan which the education department is required to prepare on the annual review of a statement made when the student attains the age of 14. The essential aim of such a plan is to ensure a smooth transition for the young person into adult life.

18.44   The CA 1989 guidance also stresses the social services' obligation to ensure such a smooth transition, stating:[35]

> The SSD's provision of services to children with disabilities should involve an initial assessment of need, a continuing process of reassessment and review of the plan for the child. Continuity should not be broken for reasons which concern organisational or administrative convenience rather than the welfare of the child or young person. A smooth transition, when the young person reaches 18 . . . should be the objective.

18.45   Paragraph 55 of the FACS (2002) policy guidance (see para 4.50 above) additionally states:

> Councils should have in place arrangements to identify individuals who, as they move from youth to adulthood and then into older age, may need different kinds of service. In these situations, councils may wish to reassess their needs, but in responding should note that marked changes in the type, level and location of support are usually not in service users' best interests.

---

33   (2000) 3 CCLR 15, QBD.
34   SI No 3455.
35   Paragraph 5.4 volume 6 of the Children Act Guidance (Children with Disabilities).

18.46   The *Special Educational Needs Code Of Practice 2001* issued by the Department for Education and Skills (2002)[36] provides detailed guidance on the education and social services department responsibilities in developing and progressing the Transitional Plan of disabled pupils (paras 9.51–9.64).

Charging for children's services

Charging for domiciliary and community based services

18.47   As with most statutory adult care services, local authorities are empowered to charge for the services they provide under the CA 1989. The Act's charging provisions differ in a number of respects from those for adult service users (see para 12.3 above) most obviously in the fact that it is generally the carer's (ie, the parent's) means which are assessed rather than the service user's.

18.48   CA 1989 s29(1) empowers the authority to recover 'such charge as they consider appropriate'. This is subject to the following restrictions:

a) that no person can be charged while in receipt of income support, or of any element of child tax credit (other than the family element) or working tax credit or of an income-based jobseeker's allowance. (s29(3)); and

b) that where the authority is satisfied that a person's means are insufficient for it to be reasonably practicable for him or her to pay the charge, the authority cannot require him or her to pay more than he or she can reasonably be expected to pay (s29(2)). This provision follows closely the wording found in Health and Social Services and Social Security Adjudications Act 1983 s17, and reference should be made to paras 12.86 onwards where the issues of charge reduction or waiver are considered in detail.

18.49   The persons who can be charged are specified in CA 1989 s29(4), namely:

(a) where the service is provided for a child under 16, each of his parents;
(b) where it is provided for a child who has reached the age of 16, the child himself; and
(c) where it is provided for a member of the child's family, that member.

18.50   As with charges for adult non-accommodation services, authorities are empowered to recover outstanding charges 'summarily as a civil debt'[37] and where a service is assessed as being required, the authority must provide it even if the liable person refuses to pay the assessed charge.

---

36 Accessible at www.dfes.gov.uk/sen/documents/SENCodeOfPractice.pdf in Wales the equivalent (and very similar) code (Special Educational Needs Code of Practice for Wales is accessible at www.wales.gov.uk/subieducationtraining/content/senforwales-e.pdf).

37 Children Act 1989 s29(5).

Charging for services under the Chronically Sick and Disabled Persons Act 1970

18.51 As noted at para 8.122 above, it is questionable whether social services departments are able to charge for any services provided under CSDPA 1970 s2 and in general few attempt to do so.

Charging for accommodation services under the Children Act 1989

18.52 Children Act 1989 Sch 2 part III empowers (but does not oblige) local authorities to charge for the cost of accommodating children. The rules are the same as for non-accommodation services, save only that (in addition):

1) the local authority cannot charge a sum greater than 'they would normally be prepared to pay if they had placed a similar child with local authority foster parents; and

2) provision is made for the local authority to serve what is known as a 'contribution notice' which they are able to enforce through the magistrates court if necessary; which court can also arbitrate on any dispute as to the reasonableness of such a notice.

CHAPTER 19

Remedies

continued

Introduction

19.1 Frequently the most effective way of resolving a community care dispute will be through informal contact with the local authority or NHS body or an MP or a local councillor; indeed contact with the local media can also be a very effective way of remedying a problem. The law however provides six principal procedures by which a failure in the provision of community care services may be challenged. These are:

1) a complaint to the responsible local authority;
2) a complaint to the responsible NHS body;
3) a complaint to the local government ombudsman or health service commissioner;
4) an application to the High Court for judicial review;
5) an application to the Secretary of State for Health or Wales to use his or her default powers under Local Authority Social Services Act 1970 s7D.
6) an ordinary court application under Human Rights Act 1998 s7.

19.2 Other procedures or remedies may be available in certain specific cases. Mentally disordered people and their carers continue to have direct access to the Commission for Healthcare Audit and Inspection (CHAI),[1] and individuals continue to have access to their elected representatives for assistance in any particular case.[2] In addition it should be noted that where judicial review proceedings fail to provide an adequate remedy, there remains the option of an application to the European Commission of Human Rights (this potential remedy is considered below in the judicial review section).

19.3 A complainant will generally be expected to give the local authority or NHS body the opportunity to remedy the problem before the court, ombudsman or secretary of state concerned will be prepared to consider a complaint. In certain situations the ombudsman or court will accept an application without the complaints process being utilised: these circumstances are discussed in the relevant sections below.

Local authority complaints procedures

19.4 Local Authority Social Services Act (LASSA) 1970 s7B gives to the secretary of state the power to require social services authorities to establish a complaints procedure.[3] This power was exercised through the Local Authority Social Services (Complaints Procedure) Order 1990,[4] which required each such authority to have in place a complaints system by 1 April 1991. The

---

1 The 1990 policy guidance para 6.35 refers to the Mental Health Commission whose functions transferred to CHAI with the enactment of the Health and Social Care (Community Health and Standards) Act 2003, see para 19.99 below.
2 1990 policy guidance para 6.34.
3 Section 7B was inserted by National Health Service and Community Care Act 1990 s50.
4 SI No 2244.

Diagram 10: Complaints flow diagram

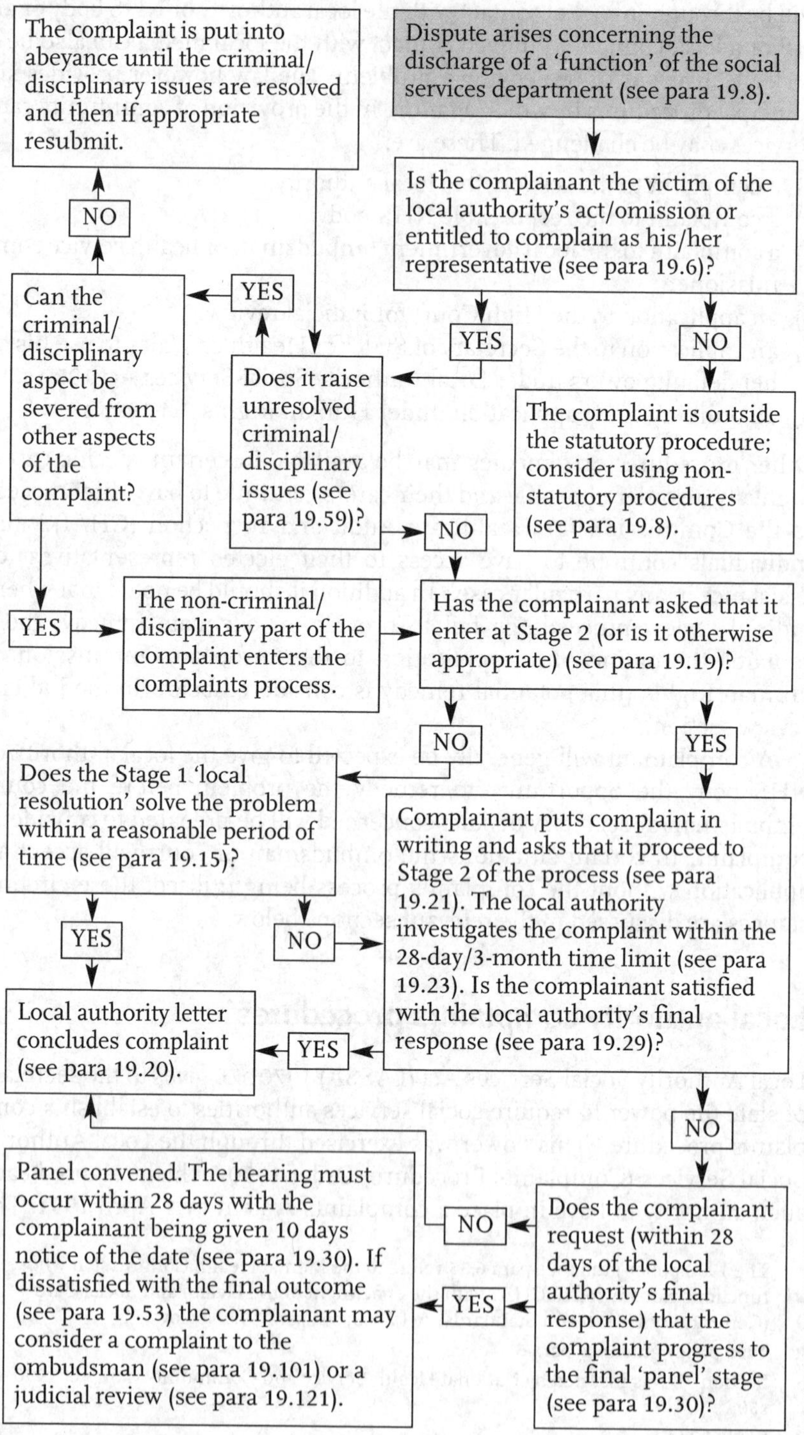

The complaint is put into abeyance until the criminal/ disciplinary issues are resolved and then if appropriate resubmit.

Dispute arises concerning the discharge of a 'function' of the social services department (see para 19.8).

NO

Is the complainant the victim of the local authority's act/omission or entitled to complain as his/her representative (see para 19.6)?

Can the criminal/ disciplinary aspect be severed from other aspects of the complaint?

YES

YES

NO

Does it raise unresolved criminal/ disciplinary issues (see para 19.59)?

The complaint is outside the statutory procedure; consider using non-statutory procedures (see para 19.8).

YES

NO

The non-criminal/ disciplinary part of the complaint enters the complaints process.

Has the complainant asked that it enter at Stage 2 (or is it otherwise appropriate) (see para 19.19)?

NO

YES

Does the Stage 1 'local resolution' solve the problem within a reasonable period of time (see para 19.15)?

YES

NO

Complainant puts complaint in writing and asks that it proceed to Stage 2 of the process (see para 19.21). The local authority investigates the complaint within the 28-day/3-month time limit (see para 19.23). Is the complainant satisfied with the local authority's final response (see para 19.29)?

Local authority letter concludes complaint (see para 19.20).

YES

NO

Panel convened. The hearing must occur within 28 days with the complainant being given 10 days notice of the date (see para 19.30). If dissatisfied with the final outcome (see para 19.53) the complainant may consider a complaint to the ombudsman (see para 19.101) or a judicial review (see para 19.121).

NO

YES

Does the complainant request (within 28 days of the local authority's final response) that the complaint progress to the final 'panel' stage (see para 19.30)?

secretary of state has directed the form and the procedures which must be adopted by each authority, by issuing the Complaints Procedure Directions 1990 (the full text of which is at appendix B) and by including a chapter of guidance in the 1990 policy guidance. Additionally the Department of Health has issued guidance on good practice, *The Right to Complain*.[5] The Social Services Inspectorate (SSI) has issued to all social services complaints officers *Notes on Good Practice* (1995). A separate complaints procedure exists in relation to children's services under the Children Act (CA) 1989. The process is very similar to that required by the Local Authority Social Services (Complaints Procedure) Order 1990 – and is considered at para 19.66 below.

19.5   The social services complaints procedures will undergo reform when Chapter 9 of the Health and Social Care (Community Health and Standards) Act 2003 comes into effect (most probably in April 2005). The proposed reforms are considered at para 19.62 below.

Who can complain?

19.6   LASSA 1970 s7B(2) stipulates that a person is a 'qualifying individual' (and thus entitled to make a complaint) if the authority has a power or a duty to secure the provision of services for him or her and the person's needs or possible needs for such a service have (by whatever means) come to the attention of the authority.

19.7   The breadth of this provision is emphasised by the 1990 policy guidance, which explains that the intention of the Act is to allow access to the complaints process by anyone who is likely to want to make representations, including complaints about actions, decisions or apparent failings of a social services department; and to allow any other person to act on behalf of the individual concerned. The procedure excludes only those for whom the authority has no power or duty to provide a service (para 6.5).

19.8   In order for a complaint to be valid, the complainant must not only be a 'qualifying individual', but the complaint must also (by virtue of LASSA 1970 s7B(1)) relate to a social services authority's discharge of (or failure to discharge) any of its social services functions in respect of that individual. The 1990 policy guidance suggests that in consequence 'complaints of a general nature which are not concerned with an individual case are also likely to fall outside the statutory definition, as are anonymous complaints (para 6.5)'. Whether such a conclusion flows from a reading of LASSA 1970 s7B is perhaps debatable – and will inevitably depend upon the particular facts of each case. The guidance however goes on to state that authorities will in any event be able (at their discretion) to deal with a complaint not covered by LASSA 1970 s7B (para 6.5). This point has also been made by the local government ombudsman in a case where she accepted that although the complainant was not a qualifying individual, it was nevertheless important that her 'complaints were still given full and proper consideration in a

5   HMSO 1991.

way which equated to the standard of service a complainant would have received under the council's formal complaints procedure'.[6]

Representatives

19.9 Research highlights the importance of service users being supported in making complaints; that 'fear of the consequences' was by far the most commonly cited reason for service users not making formal complaints – fear of retaliatory action by the authority (for instance the withdrawal of discretionary services).[7]

19.10 The 1990 policy guidance (at para 6.10) requires local authorities to ensure that their procedures 'provide an effective means of allowing service users or their representatives to complain about the quality or nature of services'. The guidance is, however silent on who may or may not be a representative, albeit that separate guidance exists concerning the importance of independent advocacy in such cases (see for example paras 13.13 and 14.10 above). As a general principle, however it must be the case that local authorities should be slow to question the good faith or 'standing' of a representative, particularly if the issue raised is one of importance.

The structure of the complaints system

19.11 The structure and key timescales of the complaints system are outlined in the Complaints Procedure Directions 1990. Authorities must designate an officer to assist in the co-ordination of all aspects of the consideration of complaints.[8] The investigating officer must not have any conflict of interest in the investigation.[9] The 1990 policy guidance suggests that the designated officer should be a senior officer of the department and that the post may also combine responsibility for the Children Act 1989 complaints procedures.[10] The local government ombudsman has stated that such a system can only function properly if the designated officer is of sufficient seniority to run the complaints system and to ensure that complaints are dealt with,

6 The complaint in fact concerned the Children Act 1989 complaint procedures, but is nevertheless of no less relevance: see Report No 94/C/2959 against Nottingham City Council, 28 November 1994. See also Local Government Ombudsman Complaint No 97/C/1614 against Bury MBC (1999) where the ombudsman accepted that part of the complaint lay outside the statutory complaints process but nevertheless warranted investigation, and commented 'it is hard to identify any aspect of the council's handling of Mr Redfern's complaints which was in the proper manner or in full accordance with the statutory complaints procedure and/or the council's own written complaints procedure.

7 K Simons, *I'm Not Complaining, but . . .*, (Joseph Rowntree Foundation, 1995).

8 Direction 4(1); the 1990 policy guidance paras 6.15 omwards; *The Right to Complain* para 3.4.

9 Local Government Ombudsman Complaint No 97/C/1614 against Bury MBC (1999), where the investigator was a line manager of the officer whose actions were the subject of the complaint.

10 The 1990 policy guidance at paras 6.15–6.16; see also *The Right to Complain* at para 3.3.

not only within the statutory times, but also with sufficient commitment[11] and has commented in one report as follows:

> In my view the council's procedures for dealing with complaints are seriously flawed. There seems to be no officer of sufficient seniority to run the complaints system and to ensure that complaints are dealt with, not only within the statutory times, but also with sufficient commitment.[12]

19.12 The directions require that the basic structure of all such complaints procedures be made up of three distinct stages:

1) the informal or problem-solving stage (direction 5(1));
2) the formal or registration stage (direction 6(1));
3) the review stage (direction 7(2)).

19.13 While authorities have no discretion in respect of the basic framework of the process, nevertheless the 1990 policy guidance stresses that 'an inflexible application of the complaints procedure in all cases would clearly be inappropriate. There will be cases where the earlier stages of the procedure should be bypassed; or an entirely different route taken.'[13]

19.14 Inevitably there will be certain types of complaint which raise particular problems requiring that they be subject to different procedures (such as complaints which involve an NHS-social services overlap of responsibilities or those which concern the discharge by a private operator of a community care function, or complaints which concern discretionary charging policies or which raise disciplinary questions). These are discussed below under the heading of 'special cases'.

Stage one: the informal or problem-solving stage

19.15 Direction 5(1) states that where a local authority receives representations from any complainant, it must attempt to resolve the matter informally. At this stage there is no requirement that the complaint be in writing (1990 policy guidance para 6.17). *The Right to Complain*[14] explains that:

> ... normal good practice should sort out, to the user's satisfaction, the queries and grumbles which are part of a social work department's daily workload. Stage 1 then alerts the relevant worker, supervisor or manager to the fact that there is a more fundamental problem, as perceived by the user or her or his representative. It gives users the right to decide whether or not to pursue the issue and ensures that it is taken seriously and not dismissed by busy staff. The fact, however, that this stage is not 'formal' does not mean that it is 'casual'.[15]

19.16 At the first stage, a complaint does not have to be registered (although many authorities do keep a written record of these):[16] It is simply an opportunity

---

11 Complaint No 92/A/3725 against Haringey LBC.
12 Report No 94/C/2659 against Nottingham City Council.
13 The 1990 policy guidance para 6.30.
14 Para 4.3.
15 *The Right to Complain* para 4.2–4.3.
16 *The Right to Complain* para 4.32.

for the local authority to attempt 'problem-solving, conciliation and negotiation'.[17] The local government ombudsman has been critical of councils who have arbitrarily decided that a complaint is not a complaint but an 'issue' or some such other grumble which it could then ignore.[18] Although in general the ombudsman has considered offers of mediation to be 'positive', she has held them to be premature if made before basic facts had been established.[19]

19.17   A significant defect with the informal first stage (as opposed to the next two stages) is the lack of any statutory timescale for its completion. In practice most authorities specify in their local procedures maximum periods for this phase (often in the region of one to four weeks).

19.18   Local authorities should provide complainants with a simple explanation of how the complaints process works and the relevant timescales. The provision of a leaflet with this information does not obviate the need to advise complainants (in correspondence at the appropriate times) of their rights at subsequent stages (ie, of the right to seek a panel hearing if dissatisfied with a stage 2 report, etc).[20] It will also be maladministration to fail to make it clear to a complainant at which particular stage of the process the complaint is currently being considered.[21]

Stage two: the formal stage

19.19   This stage involves the formal registration of the complaint. A complainant is entitled to go straight to this stage (omitting the informal stage) if he or she so wishes.[22] Given the flexibility permitted by the guidance, it must follow that where a local authority considers it appropriate it too may skip the first 'informal' stage.[23]

19.20   Complaints Procedure Directions 1990 direction 5(2) states that if the complaint cannot be resolved to the satisfaction of the complainant at the first (informal) stage, then the local authority shall give or send to the complainant an explanation of the complaints procedure and ask the complainant to submit a written representation if he or she wishes to proceed. Direction 5(3) requires authorities to offer assistance and guidance to the complainant on the use of the procedure (or an explanation as to where this assistance can be obtained). This point is amplified in *The Right to Complain*, which states that it is good practice to provide help to those who wish

---

17   *The Right to Complain* para 4.4.
18   Local Government Ombudsman Annual Report 1997/98 p10.
19   Complaint No 02/C/16768 against Bradford MDC, 4 November 2003.
20   Local Government Ombudsman Complaint No 97/A/2464 against Waltham Forest LBC (1998).
21   Local Government Ombudsman Complaint No 96/B/4438 against Devon (1998).
22   *The Right to Complain* para 4.9.
23   *The Right to Complain* para 4.9 and para 6.30 of the 1990 policy guidance: especially if the complaint is serious – see for instance Complaint No 98/B/4580 against Staffordshire which concerned a death in residential care.

to make a complaint and stresses the importance of an advocacy service in this respect.[24]

19.21 *The Right to Complain* (at para 4.10) explains that at the second stage the complaint will need to be put in writing, either by the individual concerned or someone else on their behalf to the designated complaints officer; and that:

> ... many people will need support and advice from someone they trust either from within or outside the department. Some people will need help in writing and sometimes formulating a complaint. Those who give help in writing down the complaint must ensure that it fully reflects what the complainant wishes to say and ask the complainant to sign it.

19.22 The mere fact that a complaint has progressed to the formal stage does not absolve the authority from its duty to try and resolve the problem.[25]

19.23 Direction 6(1) directs the social services authority to consider the complaint and then formulate a response within 28 days of its receipt. If for any reason it is not possible to comply with the 28-day period, the authority must (within that period) explain to the complainant why this is so, and explain when the response will be given. In any event, the response must be forthcoming within three months.

19.24 Authorities have considerable latitude in how they investigate complaints at this stage although the investigation should adhere to the principles of 'natural justice, expedition, competence and commitment' expounded by the SSI in their Notes of Good Practice (1995). Authorities may, if the need arises, appoint an independent person[26] at this stage to oversee the investigation (along the same lines as is required in the Children Act 1989 complaints procedures).[27] *The Right to Complain* explains that the significance of this stage of the complaints process is that other people (apart from the relevant worker, the supervisor or manager and the complainant) are involved in the consideration, discussion and possibly, investigation of the complaint.[28]

19.25 *The Right to Complain* recommends that the designated complaints officer be given the power to postpone or stop decisions which are the subject-matter of the complaint (para 3.10). It also draws attention to the need in some investigations for 'expert advice' to be obtained (para 3.16).

19.26 While the Directions are phrased in mandatory terms as to the maximum length of the stage two investigation process (a response must be made within 28 days if possible, and if not, within three months),

---

24 See para 6.9 of the 1990 policy guidance and the Practice Guidance which also refers to the role of advocacy.

25 Local Government Ombudsman Complaint No 98/C/3591 against Liverpool (1999).

26 *The Right to Complain* para 4.12.

27 See Representations Procedure (Children) Regulations 1991 SI No 894 regs 5 and 6 and Children Act 1989 Guidance Volume 3 paras 10.33 onwards. Considered at para 19.66 below.

28 *The Right to Complain* para 4.11.

frequently this may prove to be an unreasonably short period[29] – particularly where the complaint involves a number of matters and its investigation requires several persons to be interviewed. Not unusually the complainant will (when clarifying the nature of the grievance) articulate what are in reality separate complaints; obviously the time for the investigation of these new matters runs from the date on which they were first articulated. While it has been suggested that a breach of the time limits alone may justify an application for judicial review,[30] it would have to be an extreme case for such action to serve any useful purpose (given the inherent delay involved in such proceedings). In general, authorities should be reminded of the time limits and asked to explain any failure to comply with them; provided the investigation is being conducted diligently, it is unlikely to be criticised either by the courts or the ombudsman.

19.27   Direction 7(1) requires the authority to notify the complainant in writing of the result of its investigation. In addition notification must also be sent to the person on whose behalf the complaint was made (unless the authority considers that that person is not able to understand it or it would cause him or her unnecessary distress). The authority should also notify any other person whom it considers to have sufficient interest in the case.[31] Complaints investigators should generally give complainants the opportunity to comment upon a draft of the investigator's report[32] (particularly in relation to any counter-allegations that may have been made)[33] prior to producing a final report.

19.28   Where possible, the investigator's report should distinguish between fact and conclusion, and 'all matters put forward as issues by the complainant should be dealt with: if they are considered unfounded or insignificant, the report should explain this'.[34]

19.29   There is no requirement at this stage for the authority to give reasons for its decision. As the Directions and 1990 policy guidance specifically require reasons to be given at the next stage, it may be argued that in general there is no enforceable obligation on the authority to give reasons at this point (unless there is something peculiar to the decision which in fair-

---

29 See for instance K Simons, *I'm Not Complaining but . . .* (Joseph Rowntree, 1995) p23 concerning a prevalent view among social services authorities that the timescales are unrealistic 'even in the most straightforward of cases'. See, however, Complaint No 98/C/1088 against Bolton MBC in which the ombudsman acknowledged this problem, but stressed the need for councils to endeavour to meet the timescales and provide full explanations when this proved impossible; and Complaint No 01/C/16105 against Bradford CC where the ombudsman stated that 'the law imposes very tight timescales for the investigations of social services complaints, which, in some cases, will be wholly unrealistic'.

30 See R Gordon, *Community Care Assessments* (Longman, 1993) at p50.

31 Para 6.19 of the 1990 policy guidance suggests that the aim should be to keep the number of those informed to an essential minimum.

32 Local Government Ombudsman Complaint No 97/C/4618 against Cheshire (1999).

33 Local Government Ombudsman report No 98/C/1294 against Calderdale MBC.

34 Local Government Ombudsman Complaint No 97/C/4618 against Cheshire (1999).

ness calls for reasons to be given).[35] There is also no requirement that a copy of the investigator's report (if any) be made available to the complainant. If, however, he or she takes the complaint to the next stage, it is difficult to see how the report can be kept confidential; it could not as a matter of natural justice be considered by the panel without being available to the complainant. The ombudsman has noted that if the report is not disclosed, complainants may feel at a disadvantage;[36] investigators should therefore ensure that they compile their reports in such a way as to facilitate early disclosure.

Stage three: the review stage

19.30   The complainant may (if dissatisfied), within 28 days of receiving the decision, request that the complaint be referred to a panel for review (direction 7(2)). Such a request must be made in writing. In such cases the local authority is required to convene a panel hearing within 28 days of receipt of the complainant's request (direction 7(3)). The 1990 policy guidance requires that the complainant be notified in writing at least 10 days beforehand of the time and place of the panel hearing, and be invited to attend.[37] Direction 2(1) requires the panel to comprise three persons, at least one of whom (the chairman)[38] must be an independent person, and direction 2(3) defines an 'independent person' as someone who is neither a member nor an officer of the authority, nor, where, the authority has delegated any of its functions to an organisation, a person who is a member of or employed by that organisation, nor the spouse of any such person.

19.31   Complainants should be advised of the name and status of the panel members. There is no requirement that the wing members[39] be independent; the 1990 policy guidance suggests that they may be independent persons or councillors or other persons whom the authority considers suitable,[40] although it stresses that where possible the persons appointed to the panel should have experience relevant to the subject-matter of the complaint.[41] In most cases authorities tend to appoint a councillor as one wing member and an officer as the other; obviously in such cases the panel is not 'independent', but this is an arrangement referred to without criticism by *The Right to Complain*[42] and in *R (Beeson) v Dorset CC*[43] the Court of Appeal

---

35 See for instance *R v Higher Education Funding Council ex p Institute of Dental Surgery* [1994] 1 All ER 651, QBD at 667C; and compare *R v Bristol CC ex p Bailey and Bailey* (1995) 27 HLR 307, QBD.
36 Complaint No 94/A/3636 against Lambeth LBC, 21 October 1996.
37 Annex A para 5.
38 Annex A para 2.
39 Those who sit either side of the chairman.
40 Annex A para 3.
41 Annex A para 2, and see also *The Right to Complain* para 4.23: 'If a particular disability or minority group is involved, the panel should be convened so that the complainant's concerns are responded to sensitively and appropriately.'
42 At para 4.24.
43 [2002] EWCA Civ 1812; (2002) 6 CCLR 5.

has held that such an arrangement did not contravene the fair trial requirements of article 6(1) of the European Convention on Human Rights (see para 19.185 below).

19.32   As soon as a complaint is referred to a panel, a complainant should ensure that sufficient details of the independent person are provided to establish his or her independence.[44] The independence of such a person may be compromised for many reasons – for instance, he or she may be a past employee of the authority or have a connection with some other body (such as a health authority or local health trust) which has close contractual relations with the authority.

Panel hearings

19.33   The basic procedure to be followed by the panel is detailed in the 1990 policy guidance (Annex A paras 5–7). Complainants should be told in advance which officers of the authority will be present. Complainants are entitled to make written submissions to the panel before the meeting and to make oral submissions at the meeting. They are entitled to be accompanied by another person who is entitled to be present at the whole meeting and to speak on their behalf. The guidance states that this person should not be a barrister or solicitor acting in a professional capacity.[45] Natural justice dictates that if the applicant is not entitled to have legal representation at a panel hearing, then the same applies to the local authority, and accordingly the local ombudsman has criticised the presence of a local authority's solicitor at a hearing, stating:

> I find it hard to see how a solicitor employed by the council could be seen as an 'unbiased observer' and consider the way he joined at the outset in the in camera deliberations of the panel to be unwise at the very least.[46]

19.34   The 1990 policy guidance requires that the panel:

> . . . meeting should be conducted as informally as possible. The chairperson of the panel should open the meeting by explaining its purpose and the proposed procedure to be adopted for the hearing. In addition the participants should be reminded that the hearing is in private and of the need to respect the rules of confidentiality. The complainant (or a person accompanying him or her) should be given an opportunity to make an oral submission before the authority's representative does. Other people may attend the meeting to make oral submissions if requested to do so by the complainant, subject to the consent of the panel, but will normally only be allowed to be present for that part of the meeting (chapter 6 Annex A para 6).

44   The 1990 policy guidance merely requires that 'complainants be informed of the name and status of the panel members' – chapter 6 Annex A para 5.

45   The 1990 policy guidance uses the word 'should' rather than 'cannot'; in certain instances legal representation may be desirable (as indeed occurred at the panel hearing the subject-matter of the judicial review in *R v Avon CC ex p M* [1994] 2 FLR 1006); if there is no lawyer present for the complainant, natural justice requires that this is also the case for the authority (see note 54 below, where the ombudsman came to such a conclusion).

46   Complaint No 92/C/1042 against Cleveland County Council.

19.35 The panel hearing must follow the rules of natural justice. If the complainant and/or his or her representative attend the hearing, the panel members should not talk to (or have lunch with) one party in the absence of the other.[47] The panel is however entitled to set reasonable time limits on the oral submissions to be made by the parties, provided these are used as 'guidelines rather than guillotines'.[48]

19.36 The local government ombudsman has made a number of criticisms about the conduct of panel hearings, including:

- A failure to ensure that key witnesses attended the panel hearing.[49]
- The panel interviewing witnesses at an adjourned hearing, in the absence of the complainant.[50]
- The failure of the local authority to ensure that the panel had clerical assistance: 'the job entrusted to panels is complex and stressful enough and they need adequate administrative support to be able to perform efficiently and effectively'.[51]
- The introduction of new material by the local authority at the hearing.[52]
- The need for independent advocates to assist complainants when the complaint is serious or particularly distressing (for instance involving bereavement).[53]
- The presence of a senior social services officer throughout a panel hearing as this may have 'inhibited junior staff from saying all they felt to be pertinent'.[54]
- The interviewing of several members of staff, at different levels of seniority, simultaneously.[55]
- Failing to give clear reasons for their recommendations.[56]
- Failing to provide sufficient training.[57]

47 Local Government Ombudsman Complaint No 96/B/4438 against Devon (1998).
48 Complaint No 96/B/4438.
49 Local Government Ombudsman Complaint No 97/B/2441 against Hampshire (1999).
50 Complaint No 97/B/2441.
51 Complaint No 97/B/2441.
52 See for instance Complaint No 96/B/4438 against Devon (1998) and Complaint No 99/A/00988 against Southwark LBC (2001) where the local authority produced a chronology at a panel hearing which it had not previously disclosed to the complainant. However, it will amount to serious maladministration for the local authority to suggest that evidence put forward by a complainant at a panel hearing is 'new material' when it is not, Local Government Ombudsman Complaint No 97/C/1614 against Bury MBC (1999).
53 Local Government Ombudsman Complaint No 97/C/4618 against Cheshire (1999).
54 Complaint No 97/C/4618.
55 Complaint No 97/C/4618.
56 Complaint No 99/B/3078 against Kent (2001) at para 106.
57 Complaint No 01/C/09018 against Wolverhampton CC (2002) where the ombudsman found 'most disturbing' that the chairperson had not understood the 'extent of his responsibility as an independent Chair' and 'did not know he had the power to reject an investigation report, to ask for a fresh investigation, or even ask for additional investigation of specific matters' concluding that such a process was 'very far from the robust and "arms length" complaints procedure that the legislation requires' and that the failure to provide the panel with 'proper support, guidance and training to enable them to carry out their responsibilities properly' was maladministration.

19.37   If possible, the panel should have read key papers (and submissions) before the hearing. If on reading these the panel requires further information (for instance, a copy of a relevant assessment or details of the authority's eligibility criteria, etc), it should endeavour to obtain this before the hearing if at all possible. Likewise any possible conflict on legal interpretation should be resolved before any hearing, as the panel is not qualified to make such determinations: ultimately, if the conflict persists, it will have little option other than to accept the local authority's view on such issues. A problem that has been identified on a number of occasions relates to the complainant's access to his or her social services file. The law allows 40 days for files to be prepared (see para 3.46 above), whereas the Directions require that a panel meet within 28 days; the local ombudsman has noted this problem and a possible solution, namely that 'information should be given about rights of access and timescales at the first stage of the procedure'.[58]

19.38   The role of the panel is to consider all the relevant evidence, weigh it up, and recommend a particular outcome. It is the panel's job to re-examine the previous decision;[59] it is the 'body entrusted with the basic fact-finding exercise under the complaints procedure'.[60]

19.39   Within 24 hours of the review hearing, the panel must reach a decision in writing and forward its recommendations (and reasons) to the local authority, the complainant (and his or her representative) and any other person who is considered to have sufficient interest (direction 8(1) and (2)). The 1990 policy guidance para 6.22 suggests that members of the local authority staff with a direct interest in the complaint should receive an explanation of the outcome of the review. If a panel member disagrees with the majority recommendation, the decision letter should also record that member's view, and the reasons for it.[61]

19.40   A panel's recommendations can fall into four broad categories, namely:

1)   recommendations of a factual nature;
2)   recommendations concerning compensation;
3)   recommendations of a policy nature;
4)   recommendations of a legal nature.

Factual recommendations

19.41   The panel is, as stated above, the basic fact-finding body in the complaints process. Its task is to weigh up the evidence, evaluate witnesses, consider all the relevant facts, ignore irrelevant factors and apply these considerations reasonably in order to reach its recommendations. The panel should concentrate on resolving the complaint and endeavour to ensure (if appropriate) that any issues of wider significance arising out of the complaint are

---

58   Complaint No 93/A/3007 against Hounslow LBC, 10 October 1995; and see also Complaint No 97/A/1082 where the need for local authority files to be made available, promptly, for inspection be complainants was emphasised.

59   *The Right to Complain* para 4.16.

60   *R v Avon CC ex p M* [1994] 2 FLR 1006.

61   The 1990 policy guidance chapter 6 Annex A.

made known to the senior management of the authority (via the panel's recommendations). A panel's recommendations may be wide-ranging. The local ombudsman has, for instance, commented favourably on a panel's decision which (among other things) recommended that the local authority prepare a report 'in a year's time or earlier if appropriate, on what action had been taken [on the broad policy implications arising out of their findings]; and that a copy of the report be sent to the complainants'.[62]

19.42   The local government ombudsman expects local authorities to act on practical recommendations made by panels, and has noted that 'it is no use having a complaints procedure which provides for a thorough investigation but where no one acts upon its recommendations'.[63]

Compensation

19.43   One of the defects of many local authority complaints procedures is their disinclination to award compensation. Historically this stemmed from a belief that this was permitted by law. However as a result of pressure from the ombudsman[64] the government have legislated to put this point beyond doubt. The Local Government Act (LGA) 2000 s92 provides that:

(1) Where a relevant authority consider –
   (a) that action taken by or on behalf of the authority in the exercise of their functions amounts to, or may amount to, maladministration, and
   (b) that a person has been, or may have been, adversely affected by that action,
   the authority may, if they think appropriate, make a payment to, or provide some other benefit for, that person.
(2) Any function which is conferred on the Greater London Authority under this section is to be exercisable by the Mayor of London and the London Assembly acting jointly on behalf of the Authority.
(3) In this section –
   'action' includes failure to act,
   'relevant authority' has the same meaning as in Part III of this Act.

19.44   The local government ombudsman has stressed that the possibility of compensation should be an element in a good complaints procedure[65] and expressed irritation with authorities who do not, in appropriate cases, offer to pay complainants compensation (or some other appropriate recompense) as part of their settlement.[66] He has emphasised that this is particularly important in relation to complaints panel recommendations.[67]

---

62 Complaint No 93/A/3007 against Hounslow LBC, 10 October 1995.
63 Local Government Ombudsman Digest of Cases 1996 p112; and see also similar criticism at p112 of the 1998 Digest of Cases.
64 Annual Report 1998/99 p7.
65 Appendix 2 to Guidance on Good Practice 1: 'Devising a Complaints System', February 1992.
66 Local Government Ombudsman Annual Report 1996/97 p11.
67 Local Government Ombudsman Annual Report 1998/99 p11. This is particularly so if the complaint concerns a failure to provide adequate (or any services) see Complaint No 00/B/09315 against Hertfordshire.

Accordingly good practice guidance has been issued, aimed at promoting greater consistency in the remedies recommended by local authorities.[68]

19.45   The guidance noted that an appropriate remedy may require a number of separate elements, including recommendations as to specific action that should be taken and as to an apology. As a general principle the remedy needs to be 'appropriate and proportionate to the injustice. It should, as far as possible, put the complainant in the position he or she would have been in but for the maladministration' and that where 'this cannot be achieved because of the passage of time or of events which have occurred . . . financial compensation may be the only available approach'.[69]

19.46   On the question of compensation, however, it states that 'financial compensation may be appropriate, for example, if the council has taken the appropriate action but has delayed in doing so and the delay has caused injustice; or if there is no practical action which would provide a full and appropriate remedy; or if the complainant has sustained loss and suffering'. The guidance suggests that the calculation of what is appropriate may include consideration of:

- The effect of the complainant's own action.
- Reimbursement to the complainant of any money which is owing but unpaid (ie, unpaid housing benefit).
- Quantifiable loss; ie, 'paying for the additional help the parents procured for a child with special educational needs because the council delayed in drawing up a statutory statement or providing the help'.
- Loss of a non-monetary benefit; ie, 'a council tenant has been unable to use one of the rooms in his or her flat for a period because of lack of repair'.
- Loss of value; where something owned by the complainant has lost value.
- Lost opportunity; 'compensation for a lost opportunity may sometimes be a fairly small sum, because it is only the loss or opportunity which is certain and the actual outcome which would have obtained cannot be known'.
- Distress 'including stress, anxiety, frustration, uncertainty, worry, inconvenience or outrage'. 'This element may be a moderate sum of no more than a few hundred pounds or less but in cases where the distress has been severe and/or prolonged, a more substantial sum may be justified'. The guidance suggests that generally it will be 'in the range of £500 to £2,000 for a year, with broadly pro rata sums for shorter or longer periods'.[70]
- Professional fees in pursuing the dispute; while the guidance advises that complainants usually do not need a solicitor or other professional

---

68 Guidance on good practice, 6 'Remedies' March 2003 (replacing the previous guidance of September 1996) accessible at www.lgo.org.uk/pdf/remedies.pdf.
69 Guidance on good practice p3.
70 Guidance on good practice p21.

to help them make a complaint, it may sometimes be appropriate. In such cases the recommendation may be for a contribution to costs rather than reimbursement of the whole of the expenditure.[71]

- Time and trouble in pursuing the complaint (but this should not be confused with the question of distress (as above)). The guidance suggests that generally it will be in the range of £25 to £250.[72]
- Offsetting compensation; in circumstances where the complainant owes money to the council (eg, rent arrears) 'it would usually be appropriate for the compensation to be offset against the debt'.
- Interest.
- Formula; the guidance advises that 'sometimes it may be appropriate to express a remedy, not as a sum of money, but as a formula which sets out how the council should itself calculate the requisite sum of money. Where relevant, this needs to include reference to any continuing problem so that the formula is designed to encompass the future as well as the past'.

Policy recommendations

19.47 Panels will need to know (preferably before any hearing) the status of any policy matters relevant to the hearing (eg, eligibility criteria or charging policies and whether they are in draft form, approved or in the process of revision). Panels should be wary of making any recommendations which would be contrary to such general policies if they have been formulated and approved by the elected members (and especially if this was after the policies were the subject of proper consultation). The risk in such cases is of course that the panel is attempting to usurp the democratic community role of the council.

19.48 The local government ombudsman's guidance on good practice suggests, however, that in suitable cases the panel's recommendation can include advice that the authority review its practices, procedures or policies or give consideration to particular suggestions for improvements that have come to its notice.

Legal recommendations

19.49 Where there is a straightforward disagreement between the complainant and the local authority about the law, then it is doubtful that the panel can do anything other than accept the authority's interpretation. While in such cases a complainant can use the complaints process, it is difficult to see that it can produce anything of value; the appropriate remedy in such a case is by way of a judicial review in order that the court can decide (see also para 19.121 below).

71 However, where an accountant acting under an Enduring Power of Attorney pursued a complaint the ombudsman held that he was entitled to be paid at his professional rate, and recommended over £16,000 for this item alone: Complaint No 00/C/03176 against Nottingham County and City Councils (2002).
72 Guidance on good practice p31.

19.50   The panel must restrict itself to the relevant factors in the complaint and ignore the irrelevant. In a complaint to the local ombudsman involving East Sussex County Council[73] the panel had decided that because a council officer had given misleading advice (that the complainants were not eligible for certain benefits when they were), the complainants lost £4,220 in benefits. The panel recommended that they receive an ex gratia payment of £750, holding that it was not appropriate for the council to reimburse the unpaid benefit, as it was not the council's responsibility to issue such benefits but that of the Department of Social Security (DSS). The local government ombudsman held that the panel had considered an irrelevant factor, stating:

> The consequence of the misleading advice . . . was that they did not take up their entitlement to benefits. Accordingly, whether or not the Department itself was responsible for such benefits was not relevant to the panel's consideration.

19.51   The ombudsman held that the full sum of unpaid benefit be paid by the council (plus £250 for the complainants 'time and trouble' in making the complaint).

19.52   The panel is required to give reasons for its recommendation (direction 8(3)). The extent of this obligation is discussed below (in that the same obligation rests with the local authority when deciding its response to the recommendations).

Subsequent action

19.53   The local authority has 28 days from the date of the panel's recommendations to decide what action should be taken. It must notify in writing all the persons who received copies of the panel's recommendations; the notification must detail not only the authority's decision but also its reasons for taking that decision and of any action which it has in consequence taken (or which it proposes to take) (direction 8(4)).

19.54   While a local authority is not bound to accept a panel's recommendation, it will in practice have to have extremely cogent reasons for deciding differently. Sedley J held in *R v Islington LBC ex p Rixon*[74] 'a failure to comply with a review panel's recommendations is not by itself a breach of law; but the greater the departure, the greater the need for cogent articulated reasons if the court is not to infer that the panel's recommendations have been overlooked'.

19.55   The case of *R v Avon CC ex p M*[75] concerned the failure of a social services department to comply with the findings of its complaints review panel. Henry J held:

> I would be reluctant to hold (and do not) that in no circumstances whatsoever could the Social Services Committee have overruled the

---

73   Local Government Ombudsman Complaint No 93/A/3738 against East Sussex CC.
74   (1998) 1 CCLR 119.
75   (1999) 2 CCLR 185; [1994] 2 FLR 1006, QBD.

Review Panel's recommendation in the exercise of their legal right and duty to consider it. Caution normally requires the Court not to say 'never' in any obiter dictum pronouncement. But I have no hesitation in finding that they could not overrule that decision without a substantial reason and without having given that recommendation the weight it required. It was a decision taken by a body entrusted with the basic fact-finding exercise under the complaints procedure. It was arrived at after a convincing examination of the evidence, particularly the expert evidence. The evidence before them had, as to the practicalities, been largely one way. The Panel had directed themselves properly, in law, and had arrived at a decision in line with the strength of the evidence before them. They had given clear reasons and they had raised the crucial factual question with the parties before arriving at their conclusion . . . It seems to me that anybody required, at law, to give their reasons for reconsidering and changing such a decision must have good reasons for doing so, and must show that they gave that decision sufficient weight and, in my judgment, it failed to do. Their decision must be quashed.

19.56 The case was, however, distinguished by Dyson J in *R v North Yorkshire CC ex p Hargreaves*,[76] where he stated:

All that Henry J was saying was that where a panel has given a carefully reasoned decision adverse to the local authority on the subject of a complaint and the local authority rejects the panel's recommendation without itself giving a rational reason for doing so, then there is a strong prima facie case for quashing the local authority's decision as unlawful.

19.57 The local authority is (like the panel) required to give reasons for its decision. Such reasons must be 'proper, adequate and intelligible' and must deal with the substantial points raised by the complainant.[77] An unparticularised assertion that 'on the evidence' the panel makes certain findings and 'recommends . . . ' will be considered inadequate.[78]

Special cases

19.58 Certain complaints will inevitably require a different investigative or review procedure by virtue of their particular facts or the nature of the subject-matter.

Disciplinary or grievance procedures

19.59 The 1990 policy guidance (at para 6.12) stresses the importance of keeping complaints procedures separate from grievance procedures (which concern staff issues, ie, conditions of service) and disciplinary procedures (which apply to the actions of staff in relation to failures to comply with codes of conduct, etc).

19.60 Where serious allegations are made, senior staff will need to be involved

---

76 (1994) 30 September, CO/878/94 (unreported).
77 *Westminster CC v Great Portland Estates Plc* [1985] 1 AC 661 at 673, HL and *In re Poyser and Mills' Arbitration* [1964] 2 QB 467 at 478.
78 *R v Secretary of State for Transport ex p Cumbria CC* [1983] RTR 129, QBD.

at the outset. Where such allegations suggest that a criminal offence may have been committed, the relevant local procedure, which may be contained in the authority's standing orders, should be followed. Where the allegation is serious and substantial, the police must be notified immediately.[79]

NHS overlap

19.61   The NHS complaints procedures, both in relation to general complaints and in respect of the specific procedure for challenging a discharge from NHS care, (considered in detail in chapter 10 above) are quite separate from those applied by social services authorities. Occasionally, however, a complaint will concern a matter which is an overlapping responsibility of both authorities. The 1990 policy guidance suggests that in such cases it will   be necessary to decide quickly which authority should deal with the complaint, and that the complainant should be informed at once when a complaint is transferred to the NHS system, together with an explanation of the reason for the transfer and details of the person who will then be dealing with it (para 6.33). Where the complaint is lodged by a person being cared for in a nursing home under the terms of a contractual arrangement made between the home and a local authority, the 1990 policy guidance (para 6.32) advises that the complaint should initially be referred to the health authority registration officer responsible for registration and inspection of the home.[80] With the demise of health authorities and their registration role, this should presumably now be taken as meaning a referral to the National Care Standards Commission in England or the Care Standards Inspectorate for Wales in Wales.

19.62   As noted immediately below the reforms proposed to the complaints process will oblige health and social services authorities to co-operate with each other where complaints raise questions concerning both their actions. However, until these reforms come into effect, in such cases, it will remain necessary to make separate complaints to each body. If for instance the complaint concerns a faulty hospital discharge it may be necessary to make complaint to the social services department, the NHS trust and to the PCT. Thus (and absurdly) a complainant may need to maintain three separate complaints merely to remedy an injustice which may have arisen because the three bodies have failed to work with each other appropriately. However social services authorities have the power to agree with respective NHS bodies to pursue a joint investigation and this approach has been approved by the ombudsman – who has also criticised authorities that insist on complainants having to make separate NHS/social services complaints when they concern the same factual matrix.[81]

79 The 1990 policy guidance para 6.30 and see *The Right to Complain* paras 7.1 onwards.

80 Although ultimately it may be the local authority's duty to investigate the complaint, see Complaint No 97/A/4002 against Bexley LBC.

81 See Complaint No 97/A/4002 against Bexley LBC – where the ombudsman also stated (at para 134) that it was unreasonable to expect complainants to have to pursue

Proposed reforms

19.63 As noted (see para 19.5 above) major reform of the social services complaints procedure will occur when chapter 9 of the Health and Social Care (Community Health and Standards) Act (HSC(CHS)A) 2003 comes into effect. The main change being that the panel stage of the process will (in England only) become the responsibility of new Commission for Social Care Inspection (CSCI). The CSCI has absorbed the functions of the Social Services Inspectorate (SSI), the Joint Review team of the SSI/Audit Commission and the functions of the National Care Standards Commission in relation to social care (see para 7.69 above).

19.64 The HSC(CHS)A 2003 provides the Secretary of State (the Assembly in Wales) with power to make regulations providing for a two-stage process for representations and complaints dealing with local authority social services. In relation to complaints concerning adults this is achieved by section 114 and in relation to children, by section 116 (which inserts a new section section 26ZA, after CA 1989 s26). It is envisaged that the first stage will comprise the informal and formal/registered stages of the current process and these will remain the responsibility of the local social services authority concerned. If this fails then the CSCI will be responsible for the final stage (the present panel stage). The government in England has stated that the social services reforms will be implemented in April 2005 and draft regulations will be issued 'later in 2004'. It appears likely that in the reformed complaints process the CSCI will fulfil functions similar to that proposed for CHAI (see para 19.100 below).

Independent and private sector providers

19.65 The 1990 policy guidance states that, wherever possible, the service provider should handle complaints about care services provided in the voluntary and private sector with financial support from the local authority. Complainants who remain dissatisfied with the response to their complaints by the service provider may nevertheless choose to refer the matter to the social services department. Complaints received in such circumstances should be treated as registered complaints (para 6.31). Registered residential care homes are required by law to have a procedure for investigating complaints.[82] The Care Homes Regulations 2001, regulation 22 requires care homes to have an appropriate complaints procedure, that operates within a 28-day investigation period. It must be provided in writing to any service user who requests a copy (in an acceptable format where possible – ie, Braille). Further specific requirements are detailed in regulation 20 and the appropriate National Minimum Standards (see para 7.81).

separate complaints against each authority; and complaint 99/C/1276 against Northumberland CC where she approved a joint NHS/social services investigation (at para 61).

82 Residential Care Homes Regulations 1984 SI No 1345 reg 17.

Children procedures

19.66   Complaints concerning the discharge by an authority of any of its functions under Children Act 1989 Part III (services for children 'in need',
including disabled children – see para 18.3) are dealt with under similar
but separate procedures (which are also to be reformed – see para 19.64
above).[83] The most significant difference between the two procedures is
that at the equivalent (second) stage of the children's complaints procedure
an independent person must be involved. The Health and Social Care
(Community Health and Standards) Act 2003 s116 will amend the
Children Act 1989 complaints procedures (see para 19.62 above). These
have already been amended in relation to children leaving care to introduce
a 14-day time limit for the informal resolution stage of the complaints
process.[84]

Overlap with education and housing

19.67   The statutory procedures for social services complaints (described above)
are not applicable to complaints concerning education or housing (or
indeed any other local authority function). It follows that local authorities
have greater latitude in the arrangements they have for such complaints.
Good administration requires, however, that any complaints process must
incorporate the principles outlined in the local ombudsman's guidance to
local authorities on how such complaints procedures should be operated.[85]

Housing

19.68   Not infrequently it may be unclear whether a complaint relates to a housing or social services function: for instance a dispute concerning adaptations funded through a disabled facilities grant – or the provision of a
house identified as needed in a care plan. The local government ombudsman has considered a number of such cases. In a complaint against
Kirklees Metropolitan Council[86] she concluded:

> There was confusion within the Council as to whether [the] complaint
> should be considered by the Housing or Social Services Department. From

---

83   See Representations Procedure (Children) Regulations 1991 SI No 894 regs 5 and 6
and Children Act 1989 Guidance Volume 3 paras 10.33 onwards.

84   See the Children (Leaving Care) (England) Regulations 2001 SI No 2874, reg 13
[Children (Leaving Care) (Wales) Regulations 2001 SI No 2189 (W151)].

85   Good Practice 1: 'Devising a Complaints System'. Local Government Ombudsman,
February 1992; see also Local Government Ombudsman Complaint No 94/C/2959
against Nottingham City Council 28 November 1994; see also Local Government
Ombudsman Complaint No 97/C/1614 against Bury MBC (1999) where the
ombudsman accepted that part of the complaint lay outside the statutory complaints
process but nevertheless warranted investigation, and commented 'it is hard to
identify any aspect of the council's handling of Mr Redfern's complaints which was
in the proper manner or in full accordance with the statutory complaints procedure
and/or the council's own written complaints procedure.

86   Complaint No 01/C/00627, 28 January 2003, at para 68.

[the complainant's] point of view this was irrelevant, they simply wanted the complaint to be considered thoroughly and promptly. The Council should have been able to do that. Although officers say they made internal changes as a result of the complaint no remedy was offered to [the complainant] for the Council's acknowledged failings.

19.69 Likewise in a complaint against Sunderland City Council[87] she concluded:

I consider that [the complainant's] complaint about the failure to rehouse his family should also have been dealt with under the Social Services Statutory Complaints Procedure as the application arose out of a stated need in a care plan. The failure to consider the complaint under the statutory procedure was maladministration. This has caused injustice as it denied [the complainant] the opportunity of having his complaints properly addresses at an earlier date.

Education

19.70 With the exception of complaints concerning the provision of national curriculum[88] information, there is no statutory complaints process for parental/student disputes with the local education authority (LEA) or school governors.

19.71 In 1989 the Department of Education issued guidance on the need for complaints procedures (Circular 1/89) and as a consequence most local authorities have adopted a model complaints code formulated jointly by the Associations of Metropolitan and County Councils. This involves a phased response, commencing at the first stage with local resolution via teacher and parent, followed by formal complaint to the governors and then to the LEA. The LEA stage provides for a 'designated officer' to investigate and for the results of the investigation to be considered by a panel of three LEA members.

NHS complaints

19.72 The legal basis for the NHS complaints system stems from directions[89] issued by the secretary of state. Guidance has been issued[90] on the working of the scheme, particularly as a Department of Health booklet 'Complaints Listening, Acting, Improving: Guidance on implementation of the NHS

---

87 Complaint Nos 00/C/12118 and 00/C/12621, 21 August 2002 at para 252.
88 Curriculum/information disputes are subject to the provisions of Education Act 1996 s409 (and if the local resolution of such a complaint fails, provision exists for them to be made directly to the secretary of state under ss496–497 of the 1996 Act).
89 Directions to NHS Trusts, Health Authorities and Special Health Authorities for Special Hospitals on Hospital Complaints Procedures 1996; Miscellaneous Directions to Health Authorities for Dealing with Complaints 1996; given under National Health Service Act 1977 s17, National Health Service and Community Care Act 1990 Sch 2 para 6(2)(a) and the NHS (Functions of Health Authorities) (Complaints) Regulations 1996 SI No 669.
90 Guidance EL(95)121; EL(96)19; EL(96)58.

Complaints Procedure' (March 1996) and in the remainder of this section any paragraph reference is a reference to this document, and any direction reference refers to the 1996 Directions to NHS Trusts.[91]

19.73   There are many parallels between the NHS and social services complaints procedures, the most significant difference being that the NHS system has only two stages – and the complainant has no automatic entitlement to progress from the first to the second stage. Considerable concern has been expressed about the performance of the present NHS complaints process[92] and major change will take place when the Health and Social Care (Community Health and Standards) Act 2003 comes into force (expected in April 2005) see para 19.99 below.

Patient Advice and Liaison Service

19.74   'The NHS Plan' announced the commitment to establish a Patient Advice and Liaison Service (PALS) in every NHS trust by 2002.[93] PALS area non-statutory advice service that 'do not replace existing specialist advocacy services, such as mental health and learning disability advocacy. Rather, they are complementary to existing services. Providing information and on the spot help for patients, their families and carers, they are powerful lever for change and improvement'.[94] PALS are regulated by a Department of Health 'Standards and Evaluation Framework' 2003[95] and their core functions include:

- Being accessible to patients, their careers, friends and families.

- Providing on the spot help in every Trust with the power to negotiate immediate solutions or speedy resolutions of problems. PALS will listen and provide the relevant information and support to help resolve service users' concerns quickly and efficiently. They will liaise with staff and managers, and, where appropriate, with other PALS services, health and related organisations, to facilitate a resolution.

- Acting as a gateway to appropriate independent advocacy services, including the Independent Complaints Advocacy Services (see below).

- Providing accurate information to patients, carers and families.

---

91   See note 89 above.

92   For an analysis of the fragmented nature of the current health service complaints process see S Kerrison and A Pollock *Complaints as Accountability? The Case of Health Care in the United Kingdom* [2001] PL 115–133.

93   The NHS Plan, para 10.17. Department of Health, The Stationery Office, July 2001, Cm 4818-I.

94   Department of Health notice accessible at www.dh.gov.uk/PolicyAndGuidance/ PatientChoice/PatientAdviceAndLiaisonServices/fs/en.

95   Accessible at www.dh.gov.uk/PolicyAndGuidance/PatientChoice/ PatientAdviceAndLiaisonServices/fs/en.

Independent Complaints Advocacy Service

19.75   HSCA 2001 s12 obliges the secretary of state to 'arrange, to such extent as he considers necessary to meet all reasonable requirements' for the provision of an Independent Complaints Advocacy Service (ICAS) to assist individuals making complaints against the NHS. ICAS replaced the service previously provided by Community Health Councils in England. As at April 2004, the service is largely provided by offices attached to Citizens Advice Bureau and its development has encountered significant problems. Patients who want to complain about NHS services can approach ICAS directly (or directed there by the PALS). Complaints managers at trust level are also expected to advise patients of the availability of this service and assist them in making contact. The Commission for Patient and Public Involvement in Health acts as Department of Health's agent in managing the contracts with individual ICAS providers and in this capacity develops the quality standards for the service. Further information on the service can be accessed from the Department of Health website.[96]

Who may complain?

19.76   Complaints may be made by existing or former users of NHS trust services. People may complain on behalf of existing or former users where the trust (usually through its complaints manager) or the convener at the independent review stage, accepts them as a suitable representative (para 4.7 and direction 11).

19.77   In relation to GPs the complainants may be existing or former patients, or people who have received services from that GP (para 4.8).

Time limits

19.78   The guidance states that a complaint should be made within six months of the event giving rise to it (or of the patient becoming aware of that event). There is, however, a discretion to extend the time limit where it would be unreasonable in the circumstances of a particular case for the complaint to have been made earlier and where it is still possible to investigate the facts of the case (para 4.11 and direction 10).

19.79   It is suggested (at para 4.12) that this power to vary the time limit should be used with flexibility and sensitivity.

Complaints personnel

Complaints manager

19.80   The complaints manager is the person in the GP's practice, the trust or health authority who is responsible for ensuring complaints are responded to and that the first-stage process is properly discharged. Such managers

96 www.dh.gov.uk/PolicyAndGuidance/OrganisationPolicy/ComplaintsPolicy/fs/en.

must be readily accessible to the public and the complaints managers for trusts and health authorities should not only have access to all relevant records; they should also be directly accountable to the chief executive (paras 4.16–4.18).

Convener

19.81   A convener must be appointed by each trust or health authority. The convener must be a non-executive director and his or her function is to consider (and determine) requests made by complainants for their complaints to be referred to the independent review panel. Although not independent, he or she is advised to distance him or herself from those involved in the complaint and ensure that it is dealt with impartially (paras 4.22–4.24).

Excluded matters

19.82   The procedure is concerned with resolving complaints and not with investigating disciplinary matters or criminal offences (paras 4.27 onwards) and the guidance gives advice on the procedure to be followed when a trust or health authority receives a complaint which raises such questions. If a complaint raises issues of negligence, the guidance states that the complaints procedure should not cease unless the complainant explicitly indicates an intention to take legal action in respect of the complaint (para 4.37 and direction 7(1)(a)). The mere fact that a complainant is seeking compensation in a complaint, does not however exclude it from the scheme. This point has been confirmed by the NHS Executive, stating:

> There is nothing in the guidance or Directions to prevent a health authority (or NHS trust) from making an ex gratia payment as part of the resolution of a complaint if it is deemed appropriate. Similarly, an independent review panel could recommend an ex gratia payment in a report but it would be for the health authority (or NHS trust) to agree to this and to decide what amount would be paid.[97]

19.83   A separate process exists for patients who are challenging their discharge from hospital and/or seeking continuing health care funding from the NHS and this is considered at para 10.187 above.

Stage one

Trusts and health authorities

19.84   The first stage of the complaints procedure requires that trusts and health authorities establish a clear local resolution process, whose 'primary objective . . . is to provide the fullest possible opportunity for investigation and resolution of the complaint, as quickly as is sensible in the circumstances, aiming to satisfy the patient, while being scrupulously fair to staff' (para

---

97   Private correspondence with the Complaints and Clinical Negligence Policy Unit, 28 September 1999.

5.2). The guidance makes the following points concerning the stage 1 process:

> 5.2 ... The process should encourage communication on all sides. The aim should be to resolve complaints at this stage, and many should be capable of resolution orally. Local resolution should not be seen simply as a run-up process to independent review: its primary purpose is to provide a comprehensive response that satisfies the complainant. Rigid, bureaucratic, and legalistic approaches should be avoided at all stages of the procedure, but particularly during local resolution.
> ...
>
> 5.7 When deciding whether or not to pass the complainant on to the complaints manager, front-line staff, for example in trusts, will need to take into account the seriousness of the complaint and the possible need for more independent investigation and assessment. While an important role of the complaints manager is to investigate written complaints and to satisfy complainants, this must not preclude the complaints manager from advising front-line and other staff in the resolution of complaints.
> ...
>
> 5.10 The Patient's Charter gives patients the right to a written reply from the relevant trust/health authority chief executive in response to a written complaint. The ombudsman has criticised chief executives of NHS bodies for failure to sign written responses to complainants who have made written complaints, and the Chief Executive of the NHS has reaffirmed the importance which he and Ministers attach to performance in this area (see EL(95)136). The reply might take the form of a full personally signed response or shorter letter covering a full report from another member of staff, which the chief executive has reviewed and is content with. Some oral complaints are sufficiently serious, or difficult to resolve, that they should be recorded in writing by the complaints manager. These complaints ought also receive a written from the chief executive.

GP complaints

19.85 The GP service obligations (see para 10.45 above) require that they have in place practice-based complaints procedures which comply with minimal national criteria; they are that:

- practices must give the procedures publicity;
- practices must ensure it is clear how to lodge a complaint and to whom;
- an initial response should normally be made within two working days;
- the person nominated to investigate the complaint should make all necessary inquiries such as interviews, if appropriate, of the complainant, GPs and practice staff; and
- an explanation should normally be provided within two weeks (ie, 10 working days).

The guidance states that health authorities will have a role to play in the stage 1 process for GPs by, for instance, having lay conciliators where for some reason the complainant does not wish the complaint to be dealt with by the practice (para 5.14). Detailed advice as to how GPs should organise their complaints systems has been issued by the NHS Executive as *Practice-Based Complaints Procedures* (January 1996).

Financial redress

19.86   Many NHS bodies refuse to pay complainants compensation – even when making a finding of fault and where that fault has led to the complainant incurring costs (or losing the benefit of services, etc). The Health Service Commissioner has been critical of this failure to offer financial redress – stating:

> I see no reason why the NHS should not follow the lead of central and local government and offer some form of financial redress for justified complaints when circumstances warrant it.[98]

Completion of stage 1 procedure

19.87   The entire stage 1 process may be conducted orally. The guidance (at para 5.18 and direction 13) states, however, that where the complainant is dissatisfied with the oral response, or that he or she wishes to take the matter further, then:

> . . . it is recommended that local resolution be best rounded off with a letter to the complainant. Any letter concluding the local resolution stage (whether signed by the Chief Executive because it is a written complaint, or by some other appropriate person) should indicate the right of the complainant to seek an independent review of the complaint, or any aspect of the response to it with which the complainant remains dissatisfied, and that the complainant has twenty-eight days from the date of the letter to make such a request.

Stage two: the independent review panel

19.88   Any request for an independent review panel hearing (whether made orally or in writing) must be passed to the convener within 28 days (direction 15(2)). The convener must acknowledge receipt in writing, and then:

> . . . before deciding whether to convene a panel, the convener must obtain a signed statement signed by the complainant setting out their remaining grievances and why they are dissatisfied with the outcome of local resolution (para 6.4).

19.89   Before deciding whether to convene the panel the convener must:

- decide whether all opportunities for satisfying the complaint at stage 1 have been explored and fully exhausted (para 6.8);
- consult with one of the independent lay chairmen (ideally not the one who will actually chair the panel) in order to obtain an 'external independent view', although ultimately the decision to recommend the convening of a panel is the convener's alone (para 6.9);

98   Health Service Commissioner's 1st Report – Session 2003–2004; 16 Dec 2003 page v (HC 119) accessible at: www.ombudsman.org.uk/hsc/document/hicas03/hicas03.pdf.

- take appropriate clinical advice (if any question of clinical judgment is involved in the complaint – para 6.15). Detailed guidance is given on this aspect of complaints and from whom such advice should be sought.

19.90 The cost of convening a panel is an irrelevant consideration in this decision (para 6.14). Paragraph 6.20 advises that conveners should not recommend the setting up of a panel where:

- any legal proceedings have been commenced, or there is an explicit indication of the intention to make a legal claim;
- they consider that all practical action has already been taken and that a panel would add no further value to the process;
- there is still further scope for action at the stage 1 process.

19.91 The complainant must be informed in writing of the convener's decision and reasons must be given if he or she decides to advise that a panel should not be set up. In such cases the complainant must be advised of the right to complain to the ombudsman. The decision whether or not to convene a panel should be determined within 20 working days of the date the convener first received the complainant's request (para 6.29).

19.92 Good practice guidance has been issued to conveners as HSC 1999/193. In addition the NHS Ombudsman has issued a number of critical reports concerning the actions of conveners[99] and in his Annual Report 1997–98 he highlighted a number of the common problems, the most common of which being a failure to obtain appropriate clinical advice. However, even when clinical advice was taken, he found that some conveners and clinical advisers misunderstood the purpose of clinical advice at this stage of the complaints procedure: it being to assess the adequacy of the response to the clinical aspects of the complaint at the local resolution stage, and not to reassess the clinical events themselves. He also stressed that it was not appropriate for conveners to investigate the complaint themselves: their role is to consider whether it has been adequately answered locally, whether further local resolution is needed, or whether it should proceed to independent review.

19.93 He found a number of failings in relation to the letters of determination sent by conveners, most frequently their failure to address all the issues fully and a failure to provide an adequate explanation of why he or she had decided against holding an independent review. Other areas of difficulty included:

- conveners failing to identify and refer matters back for local resolution;
- unreasonable delay in the convening process;
- failure to explain time limits (such as the requirement that a request for an independent review should be made within 28 days of the conclusion of independent resolution) or to exercise reasonable discretion in applying them;

99 See for instance E859/96–97 and E918/96–97 Annual Report 1996–97; the general comments at piii the Report of Selected Investigations April–September 1996 and generally in his Annual Report 1996–97.

- conveners failing to consult lay chairs;
- conveners unreasonably prejudging the effectiveness of independent review or misunderstanding the role of review panels;
- conveners making unreasonable assumptions about a complainant's intention to resort to the law; and
- conveners failing to explain complainants' right of recourse to the NHS Ombudsman.

The panel

19.94　The panel will comprise:

a) an independent chairman who must not be a present or past employee of the NHS or a member of any clinical profession nor have any previous formal links with the trust or health authority (para 7.2);

b) the convener; and

c) either:

　　i) in the case of a trust panel, a representative of the purchaser;

　　ii) in the case of a health authority, another independent person.

19.95　If the convener considers the complaint to be a clinical complaint, then the panel will be advised by at least two independent clinical assessors (para 7.2). The guidance lays down detailed procedures for their selection, the submission of reports and the procedures to be followed if the panel disagrees with their reports. The panel should be convened within four weeks of the convener's decision to convene, and it should complete its work within 12 weeks (para 7.51). Its process should be informal, flexible and non-adversarial (para 7.9). No legal representation is permitted, although the complainant may be accompanied by a person of his or her choosing (para 7.10). A draft of the panel's report should be sent to the relevant parties (to check its accuracy) 14 days before it is formally issued (para 7.30). The report is confidential, and should set out the results of the panel's investigations, outlining its conclusions with any appropriate comments or suggestions (para 7.32). Following receipt of the panel's report, the chief executive must write to the complainant informing him or her of any action the trust or health authority is taking as a result of the panel's deliberations and of the right of the complainant to take his or her grievance to the Ombudsman if he or she remains dissatisfied (para 7.35).

19.96　　In his Annual Report 1997–98 the NHS Ombudsman made a number of comments concerning investigations into flawed panel hearings. While he noted that the directions/guidance gave considerable discretion as to the conduct of the panel stage and as to how evidence was taken, he stressed that the underlying principle was the need for panels to adopt procedures that enabled the facts to be examined fully and fairly. He specifically criticised panels whose decisions on procedure contributed to a failure to fulfil these essential functions, for example by:

- failing to identify and take evidence from key witnesses or others able to assist the panel in reaching its conclusions;

- failing to take evidence from the parties to the complaint; and
- taking evidence of a clinical nature in the absence of one or more of the clinical assessors.

19.97 The NHS Ombudsman also reminded panel chairpersons that they are required to report their findings in writing, and that their reports must include:

- findings of fact relevant to the complaint;
- the opinion of the panel on the complaint having regard to the findings of fact;
- the reasons for the panel's opinion;
- the report of the assessors and the panel's reasons for any disagreement with it.

19.98 Reports must additionally advise complainants that if they are dissatisfied with the outcome of the panel hearing, that they have a right to take their complaint to the NHS Ombudsman – and this process is considered at para 19.118 below.

NHS complaints reforms

19.99 As noted above, major reform of the NHS complaints process is proposed when chapter 9 of the Health and Social Care (Community Health and Standards) Act (HSC(CHS)A) 2003 comes into effect. The main change being that the panel stage of the process will become the responsibility of a new Commission for Healthcare Audit and Inspection (CHAI). CHAI (which covers both England and Wales) has absorbed the functions of the Commission for Health Improvement, the Mental Health Act Commission, the national NHS value for money work of the Audit Commission and the independent healthcare work of the National Care Standards Commission.

19.100 HSC(CHS)A 2003 s113 gives the secretary of state (the Assembly in Wales) power to make regulations concerning the structure of the NHS complaints procedure. Draft regulations have been issued in England (the National Health Service (Complaints) Regulations 2004) that leave NHS bodies responsible for the first 'local resolution' stage of the complaints procedure and CHAI which is responsible for the second 'independent review' stage. It has not yet been confirmed, as to precisely when the new system will come into force. The new elements in the draft Regulations (ie, those materially different from the existing scheme) include:

- They make provision for 'complex complaints' (ie, those that involve more than one body (ie, more than one NHS body or one involving an NHS body and a local authority) and place an obligation on these authorities to co-operate each with each other in the investigation of any complaint.
- The complaints manager must acknowledge the complaint (in writing).

- The letter of acknowledgement must also include information about the right to advocacy assistance under HSCA 2001 s12 (see para 19.75 above).

- The complaints manager must investigate the complaint – obtaining all the relevant information (reg 20) and provide a written and reasoned response 'as soon as possible and in any event within 25 working days.

- If the complainant is dissatisfied with the outcome of the first stage process he or she can ask CHAI to investigate. CHAI must then decide whether to:
  a) to take no further action (in which case the complainant must be advised of his or her right to complaint to the NHS Ombudsman);
  b) to refer the complaint back to the NHS body with recommendations as to what action might be taken to resolve it;
  c) to investigate the complaint further itself;
  d) to refer the complaint to a panel (with the complainants consent);
  e) to consider the subject matter of the complaint as part of or in conjunction with any other investigation which it is conducting or proposes to conduct;
  f) to refer the complaint to a health regulatory body;
  g) to refer the complaint to a local authority;
  h) to refer the complaint to the NHS Ombudsman

- CHAI is required to maintain a list of people who are suitable to be members of an independent lay panel. Individual panels consist of three such persons.

Local government ombudsman procedures

19.101 The Commissioners for Local Administration in England and Wales (generally known as the Local Government Ombudsmen) were established by (and in England[100] remain governed by) Local Government Act (LGA) 1974 Part III. By virtue of LGA 1974 s25 they are empowered to investigate (among other things) any local authority. Section 26 stipulates that all complaints must be in writing and made by members of the public who claim to have sustained injustice in consequence of maladministration in connection with action taken by or on behalf of an authority. Complaints no longer have to be introduced by a local councillor, although this remains advisable where possible.

19.102   In *R v Commissioner for Local Administration ex p Eastleigh BC*[101] Lord Donaldson MR commented:

---

100 The Local Government Ombudsman is governed by the provisions of the LGA 2000 Part III and The Commission for Local Administration in Wales and Local Commissioner in Wales (Functions and Expenses) Regulations 2001 SI No 2275 (W165).

101 [1988] 3 All ER 151, CA.

Maladministration is not defined in the 1974 Act, but its meaning was considered in *R v Local Commissioner for Administration for the North and East Area of England ex p Bradford MCC* [1979] 2 All ER 881. All three judges (Lord Denning MR, Eveleigh LJ and Sir David Cairns) expressed themselves differently, but in substance each was saying the same thing, namely that administration and maladministration, in the context of a local authority, is concerned with the *manner* in which decisions by the authority are reached and the *manner* in which they are or are not implemented.

19.103 The Health Service Ombudsman in his annual report for 1993–94 (para 1.4) commented on the nature of maladministration in the following terms:

The terms given by Mr Richard Crossman in 1966 were 'bias, neglect, inattention, delay, incompetence, ineptitude, perversity, turpitude, arbitrariness and so on'. I have added:
- rudeness (though that is a matter of degree);
- unwillingness to treat the complainant as a person with rights;
- refusal to answer reasonable questions;
- neglecting to inform a complainant on request of his or her rights or entitlement;
- knowingly giving advice which is misleading or inadequate;
- ignoring valid advice or overruling considerations which would produce an uncomfortable result for the overruler;
- offering no redress or manifestly disproportionate redress;
- showing bias whether because of colour, sex or any other grounds;
- omission to notify those who thereby lose a right of appeal;
- refusal to inform adequately of the right of appeal;
- faulty procedures; failure by management to monitor compliance with adequate procedures;
- cavalier disregard of guidance which is intended to be followed in the interest of equitable treatment of those who use the service;
- partiality; and
- failure to mitigate the effects of rigid adherence to the letter of the law where that produces manifestly inequitable treatment.

19.104 Complaints must in general be made to the local ombudsman (or the local councillor) within 12 months from the date on which the person aggrieved first had notice of the matters alleged in the complaint, although the local ombudsman has an overall discretion to extend time if he or she considers it reasonable to do so (LGA 1974 s26(4)).

19.105 The local ombudsman cannot investigate a complaint unless it has first been drawn to the attention of the local authority in question, and that authority has been afforded an opportunity to investigate and reply to the complaint (LGA 1970 s26(5)).

19.106 Unless the local ombudsman is satisfied that in the particular circumstances it is not reasonable to expect the aggrieved person to resort to such a remedy, complaints cannot be entertained where there exists an alternative remedy, for instance a right of appeal to a tribunal or to a minister of the Crown or a remedy by way of court proceedings. However, in general, relatively few complaints are rejected by the local ombudsman on these grounds (5 per cent in 1998–99).

19.107   Only about 3 per cent of all complaints result in the local ombudsman preparing a final report; the most significant reasons for a complaint not resulting in a report being: (1) it discloses no maladministration; (2) the complaint is premature; (3) a local settlement results; and (4) the complaint is outside the ombudsman's jurisdiction.

19.108   An increasing (although still small) number of complaints are being received by the local ombudsman concerning the actions of social services authorities. In 2002–03 they amounted to 7 per cent of all complaints,[102] 1,201 in all (of which 593 concerned services for adults, 489 services for children, 14 registered homes and 105 'other'). Only 20 full investigation reports (concerning social services) were produced by the ombudsman during the period.[103]

19.109   LGA 1974 s26(5) requires complainants to bring complaints to the notice of the local authority first before the local ombudsman will consider them. In general the ombudsman requires complainants to use the authority's complaints procedures before he or she will be prepared to investigate the matter. However, if the complaint is not investigated properly by the authority (for instance, if there was an unjustified breach of the timescales or a serious breach of the rules of natural justice), then the local ombudsman may be prepared to accept the complaint even though it has not traversed the local authority's entire complaints process.

19.110   In his annual report for 1992–93 the local ombudsman, Mr G F Laws, commented on his general approach in this area:

> The recommendations of a statutory complaints panel to a director of social services are not binding. In assessing complaints that have been through the procedure and have then been rejected, I have looked at the investigation process; if it has been satisfactory, I have often adopted the recommendations of the panel and attempted to settle the matter. In this way I have been able to avoid the need for a further lengthy and costly investigation by my office.

19.111   As complaints to the local ombudsman are only (in general) accepted if no effective legal remedy is available, the judicial review and ombudsman procedures are distinct and not 'alternative options'.[104] In *R v Commissioner for Local Administration ex p PH*[105] an applicant commenced judicial review proceedings against a local authority on the grounds that it had delayed in carrying out a special educational needs assessment. As a consequence such an assessment took place. Subsequently she complained to the ombudsman seeking compensation for the effect of the council's delay. The ombudsman decided, under LGA 1974 s26(6) that the complaint was outside his jurisdiction because the complainant had already sought a

---

102 The total number of complaints (ie, including all categories) amounted to 18,376.

103 Annual Report 2002–03.

104 Ombudsman decisions are, however, susceptible to judicial review; see for instance, *R v Parliamentary Commissioner ex p Dyer* (1993) *Times* 27 October and *R v Parliamentary Commissioner ex p Balchin* (1999) EGCS 78.

105 (1999) COD 382, as cited in the Annual Report 1998–99 p7.

judicial review of the council's actions. In upholding the ombudsman's decision, Turner J held:

> It can hardly have been the intention of Parliament to have provided two remedies, one substantive by way of judicial review and one compensatory by way of the Local Commissioner ... where a party has ventilated a grievance by way of judicial review it was not contemplated that they should enjoy an alternative, let alone an additional right by way of complaint to a local commissioner.

19.112 The fact that lawyers are involved and threatening legal action does not of itself make the ombudsman process unavailable. A 2001 report concerned a council that delayed the provision of (assessed) services until threatened with a judicial review. A subsequent complaint concerning the delay was upheld and a compensation recommendation made by the ombudsman.[106]

19.113 There are many advantages to a complainant in using the local ombudsman procedures. They are free to the complainant, they can result in the award of significant sums in compensation and the authority is required to publicise the ombudsman's report (LGA 1974 s30). The ombudsman has access to all the relevant files and other records; can require the authority to furnish additional information and has the same powers as the High Court in respect of the attendance and examination of witnesses/the production of documents (LGA 1974 s29). Complaints to the local ombudsman are not subject to the such short time limits as in judicial review.

19.114 The disadvantages include the apparent reluctance of the local ombudsman to accept many complaints, the fact that less than 5 per cent of all complaints actually result in a final report, and the length of time taken to complete the investigations (although this has shown recent improvement, with more than half of all complaints being resolved within 52 weeks.[107]

19.115 The local ombudsman's internet sites contains copies of the complaint forms (which can also be obtained from Citizen's Advice Bureaux), previous relevant reports, publications and key addresses.

19.116 The regional offices of the local ombudsman are as follows (in England the office to use is generally the one closest to the relevant authority):

England

21 Queen Anne's Gate, London SW1H 9BU
Tel: 020 7222 5622.

The Oaks, Westwood Way, Westwood Business Park, Coventry CV4 8JB
Tel: 01203 695999.

Beverley House, 17 Shipton Road, York YO3 6FZ
Tel: 01904 630151.
Web address: www.open.gov.uk/lgo/index.htm.

---

106 Complaint No 99/B/04621 against Cambridgeshire, 29 January 2001.
107 Annual Report 2002–03, p5.

Wales

Derwen House, Court Road, Bridgend, Mid-Glamorgan CF31 1BN
Tel: 01656 661325.
Web address: www.ombwdsman-cymru.org/.

19.117   Full copies of all the local ombudsman's reports in England can be obtained from the London office (21 Queen Anne's Gate, London SW1H 9BU). For a modest annual fee a subscription can be taken out to receive all copies of social services complaints reports.

Health Service Ombudsman

19.118   The Health Service Commissioner (generally called the NHS (or Health Service) Ombudsman) now has wide powers to investigate complaints concerning GPs, trusts and health authorities, including clinical practice. In general he cannot consider a complaint until the relevant NHS complaints procedures have been exhausted. He has however stated that:[108]

> In considering whether to investigate, I consider, case by case, what is the most appropriate way to resolve the particular complaint. If there is still scope for it to be done locally, then I shall continue to favour that. If, however, there is evidence of a breakdown of trust between the complainant and the NHS body, or if I believe that further local action would not satisfy the complainant, I may use my discretion to investigate the substance of the complaint when the matter first comes to me, even though it has not gone through all the possible stages of the NHS procedure.

19.119   Complaints should be made within one year of the date when the action complained about occurred. Complaints must concern issues of maladministration.

19.120   As noted above the ombudsman has issued various important reports concerning the NHS's continuing care obligations (see paras 10.70 and 10.82); recent English reports are now available on the internet (see below). The ombudsman's addresses in England and Wales are as follows:

Full details can be obtained from:
The Health Service Commissioner for England
Millbank Tower, Millbank, London SW1P 4QP
Tel: 0845 0154033
web address: www.ombudsman.org.uk/.

The Health Service Commissioner for Wales
5th Floor, Capital Tower House, Greyfriars Road, Cardiff CF1 3AG
Telephone: 029 394621
web address: www.ombudsman.org.uk/hse/welsh/make_complaint.html.

---

108   Health Service Commissioner – Annual Report 1997–98, chapter 3.

Judicial review

19.121 Judicial review is a procedure by which the High Court reviews the lawfulness of decisions made by public bodies, such as the departments of state, local authorities and NHS bodies.

19.122   In general the law allows private individuals or businesses to behave unreasonably or make capricious decisions; public bodies however have no such freedom. They must act reasonably in reaching decisions, and (since October 2000) must not act in any way which is incompatible with the European Convention on Human Rights (ECHR).[109] If they fail to act in such a way, and significant injustice results, then the High Court may be prepared to quash the decision and require that it be considered again without the contaminant of unfairness.

19.123   What is 'reasonable' depends upon the nature of the decision and the context in which it is to be made. It will invariably require that in reaching a decision all relevant matters be considered; that all irrelevant matters are disregarded; that the body correctly applies the relevant law (including that it has the power to make the decision). In certain situations reasonableness may require that prior to making a decision consultation take place with persons who are likely to be affected. Likewise reasonableness may require that a particular decision-making procedure be followed, if affected parties have a 'legitimate expectation' that this will occur. Even if a public body adheres to all these principles, its ultimate decision will be capable of judicial challenge if it bears no sensible relationship to the material facts on which it was based (if it in essence 'defies logic') or if the decision amounts to an abuse of power.

19.124   The High Court, through the use of judicial review, seeks to improve the way public bodies make decisions and thus contribute to a fairer and more open administrative system. It does not seek to usurp the powers of these bodies. It follows therefore that the court will only get involved if the aggrieved party acts swiftly and produces significant evidence, not only of a 'flawed' decision-making process but also that as a consequence a real risk of injustice may result.

19.125   While decisions made by private or voluntary providers (such as independent nursing homes or voluntary sector day centres, etc) are not susceptible to judicial review (unless adopted by a responsible public body), they may constitute a breach of private law rights (eg, a breach of a contract with a nursing home).

Complaint to local authority monitoring officer

19.126 Where judicial review proceedings are contemplated, it is often advisable, as a preliminary step, to make a formal complaint to the local authority monitoring officer requesting that the impugned decision be reviewed. This may be in the form of (and constitute) the letter before action in

---

109 Human Rights Act (HRA) 1998 s6.

appropriate cases. In general, the monitoring officer will be the chief executive or senior legal officer of the authority.

19.127   The duties of the monitoring officer are set out in Local Government and Housing Act 1989 s5.[110] Section 5(2) provides that if at any time it appears to the monitoring officer that 'any proposal, decision or omission by the authority' (or any officer or committee of the authority) is likely to be unlawful or amount to maladministration then he or she must investigate and prepare a report on the issue in question.

19.128   The monitoring officers' functions have been extended by the LGA 2000, to include consideration of allegations of misconduct against members and former members of the local authority which have been investigated by the authority's ethical standards officer (LGA 2000 ss59, 60 and 64). Under LGA 2000 s66 the secretary of state has power to make regulations to determine the way in which such matters should be dealt with.

Sufficient standing

19.129 In order to apply for judicial review, an applicant must have a sufficient interest in the matter to which the application relates.

19.130   In *R v Gloucestershire CC ex p RADAR*[111] Carnwath J considered an application by the Royal Association for Disability and Rehabilitation (RADAR) for judicial review of a decision made by Gloucestershire County Council relating to a general procedure which the council had adopted for the reassessment of the community care needs of disabled people. Having considered the relevant authorities (such as *R v Foreign Secretary ex p World Development Movement*)[112] he held:

> . . . the general principle, that the Authority is obliged to go through a process of reassessment in respect of all those affected by the 1994 decision [consequent on the decision in *R v Gloucestershire County Council ex p Mahfood*[113]] is one which can, in my view, properly and conveniently be asserted by a body such as RADAR. It cannot be in anyone's interests that it should be left to each individual separately to assert that right. No doubt other individual test cases can be brought, but there is always a risk that if the particular individual loses his direct interest, either because his circumstances change or because the Authority carry out a reassessment, then the proceedings will prove abortive. In my view, RADAR has a sufficient interest to entitle it to a declaration as to the position as I have outlined it.

19.131 Carnwath J, however, went on to suggest that it would 'be very rare that it would be appropriate for a coercive order such as an order for mandamus, to be granted to a body like RADAR'.

---

110 As amended by the Local Government Act 2003 s113.
111 (1998) 1 CCLR 476
112 [1995] 1 All ER 611, QBD.
113 (1997) 1 CCLR 7; 94 LGR 593.

An alternative remedy?

19.132 Judicial review is not available where the applicant has failed to pursue an equally convenient, expeditious and effective remedy. This will mean that, in the absence of cogent reasons, an applicant should first utilise the complaints procedures. As a general rule disputes which are primarily factual are best suited to the complaints process and disputes which concern the interpretation of directions or guidance are suited to resolution via the default procedures.[114]

19.133 The court may be prepared to entertain a judicial review, notwithstanding that the applicant has not attempted to use the complaints or default procedures, if it can be shown that there are substantial reasons for believing that these remedies are not 'equally convenient, expeditious and effective'. Frequently this will be the case where:

a) the matter in issue is a clear-cut dispute of a legal definition;
b) what is in issue is a blanket practice or fixed policy;
c) there is an urgent need for the service (ie, a requirement for 'interim relief') or it can be otherwise shown that the complaints procedure would be incapable of adequately resolving the dispute.[115]

19.134 In *R v Gloucestershire CC ex p RADAR*[116] it was unsuccessfully argued that an application for judicial review could not be made until the alternative remedy of a local authority complaint under Local Authority Social Services Act 1970 s7B had been pursued. Carnwath J held that in certain cases such a remedy might be appropriate, especially:

> . . . where individual relief is being sought. However, in relation to a general issue of principle as to the authority's obligations in law . . . I do not think that can be regarded as a suitable or alternative remedy to the procedure of judicial review.[117]

19.135 Likewise, in *R v Devon CC ex p Baker and others*[118] such an argument (not only that an alternative remedy via the complaints procedure existed, but also that under LASSA 1970 s7D the applicants should first have asked the secretary of state to use her default powers, see para 19.167 below), was rejected on the grounds that:

> . . . as the issue is entirely one in law in a developing field which is peculiarly appropriate for decisions by the court rather than by the secretary of state, I would hold that the applicants in the Durham case were not precluded from making their application for judicial review by the availability of another remedy; the case is one which it is proper for this court to entertain.[119]

114 *R v Westminster CC ex p P and others* (1998) 1 CCLR 486 and see also *R v Kirklees MBC ex p Good* (1998) 1 CCLR 506.
115 See Richard Gordon, *Community Care Assessments* (Longman 1993) pp61 onwards.
116 (1998) 1 CCLR 476.
117 *See also Secretary of State for Education and Science v Tameside MBC ex p Ellerton* [1985] 1 WLR 749, and *R v Kent CC ex p Bruce* (1996) *Times* 8 February.
118 [1995] 1 All ER 73.
119 Per Dillon LJ at p87; and see also *R v Brent LBC ex p Sawyers* [1994] 1 FLR 203, CA.

19.136 In *Cowl and others v Plymouth CC*[120] the Court of Appeal spoke of the heavy obligation on lawyers in such disputes to resort to litigation only if it is really unavoidable and in *R (Lloyd) v Barking and Dagenham LBC*[121] the Court of Appeal held that it was not an appropriate organ to prescribe the degree of detail that should go into a care plan or the amount of consultation to be carried out with a patient's advisers.

Grounds for judicial review

19.137 As noted above, judicial review generally concerns a challenge to the decision-making process (ie, the procedure followed in coming to the decision) rather than to the decision itself. In such 'procedural' challenges, applicants are required to show some substantial flaw in the process by which the public body reached its decision. In certain cases, however, the court will entertain a 'substantive' challenge to the actual decision itself; for instance on the basis that (given the process followed) the impugned decision is so absurd that in reaching it, the local authority must 'have taken leave of [its] senses'.[122]

19.138   The principles underlying judicial review are sophisticated and multifaceted and are continually being refined and developed by the judiciary.

19.139   Thus, when in *Kruse v Johnson*[123] the High Court indicated that it would be prepared to set aside local authority decisions which were 'manifestly unjust, partial, made in bad faith or so gratuitous and oppressive that no reasonable person could think them justified' it was merely outlining the type of situation which might provoke judicial intervention, not making any definitive statement of the potential grounds for review. Likewise, 50 years later, in *Associated Provincial Picture Houses v Wednesbury Corporation*[124] when Lord Greene described what are now the classic '*Wednesbury*' principles, he was again only sketching out examples of administrative behaviour which might attract judicial censure, not seeking to compile an exhaustive list. In his judgment he instanced the following behaviour as being potentially justiciable:

- contravention of the law;
- a fettering of a discretion;
- unreasonableness in the sense of bad faith or dishonesty;
- failing to consider 'matters which he is bound to consider';
- failing to exclude matters which are irrelevant;
- reaching a decision that is 'so absurd that no sensible person could even dream that it lay within the powers of the authority'.

120 [2001] EWCA Civ 1935; (2002) 5 CCLR 42 at [27]. Views reiterated by Maurice Kay J in *R (Dudley and Whitbread and others) v East Sussex CC* [2003] EWHC 1093 Admin, 16 April 2003.
121 [2001] EWCA Civ 533; (2001) 4 CCLR 196 at [27].
122 *R v Secretary of State for the Environment ex p Nottinghamshire CC* [1986] AC 240, HL at 247.
123 (1898) 2 QB 91.
124 [1948] 1 KB 223.

19.140 With the enactment of the Human Rights Act (HRA) 1998, the courts have accepted that their traditional approach to administrative scrutiny may no longer be sufficient. In *R (Daly) v Secretary of State for the Home Department*[125] Lord Steyn contrasted the traditional *Wednesbury* approach with the requirements of 'proportionality' – when a decision potentially engaged considerations of fundamental human rights. In his view there was considerable overlap between the two approaches and in most cases the same decision would be reached whichever approach was adopted. However in at least three ways, the procedures differed, such that in certain situations they were liable to 'yield different results':

> First, the doctrine of proportionality may require the reviewing court to assess the balance which the decision-maker has struck, not merely whether it is within the range of rational or reasonable decisions. Secondly, the proportionality test may go further than the traditional grounds of review inasmuch as it may require attention to be directed to the relative weight accorded to interests and considerations. Thirdly, even the heightened scrutiny test developed in *R v Ministry of Defence ex p Smith* [1996] QB 517, 554 is not necessarily appropriate to the protection of human rights. It will be recalled that in *Smith* the Court of Appeal reluctantly felt compelled to reject a limitation on homosexuals in the army. The challenge based on article 8 of the Convention for the Protection of Human Rights and Fundamental Freedoms (the right to respect for private and family life) foundered on the threshold required even by the anxious scrutiny test. The European Court of Human Rights came to the opposite conclusion: *Smith and Grady v United Kingdom* (1999) 29 EHRR 493. The court concluded, at p543, para 138:
>
> > '... the threshold at which the High Court and the Court of Appeal could find the Ministry of Defence policy irrational was placed so high that it effectively excluded any consideration by the domestic courts of the question of whether the interference with the applicants' rights answered a pressing social need or was proportionate to the national security and public order aims pursued, principles which lie at the heart of the court's analysis of complaints under article 8 of the Convention.'

19.141 The following sub-headings list some of the main principles which today are used by the courts, to test the validity of public law decisions. As indicated above, the labelling of these principles is not a taxonomic science, but merely an attempt to illustrate some of the more obvious characteristics of the jurisprudence in this field.

Illegality

19.142 A judicial review challenge on the grounds of illegality is based upon the notion that a 'decision-maker must understand correctly the law that regulates his decision-making power and give effect to it'.[126] Professor de

---

125 [2001] UKHL 26; [2001] 2 WLR 1622; [2001] 3 All ER 433 at paras [27]–[28].
126 *Council of Civil Service Unions v Minister for the Civil Service* [1985] AC 374, HL at 410.

Smith[127] separates administrative decisions which are flawed for illegality into those which are either beyond the power which authorises the making of the decision, or those which pursue an objective other than that for which the power to make the decision was conferred. Illegality may present itself in a number of guises, for instance action by an authority which although within its power, has and ulterior and improper motive,[128] such as action designed to frustrate the purpose of a statute. Common examples are outlined below.

Ultra vires[129]

19.143 Social services and NHS bodies are statutory creatures and only able to act in accordance with the powers they have been given by statute (although as noted at para 1.46 above social services authorities' powers are now particularly wide). Accordingly it is unlawful for a public body to act beyond its powers (ultra vires).

19.144   By way of example, certain actions are well established as being in general outside social services authority powers; for instance, the provision of healthcare services or assistance to some asylum-seekers. Certain areas, however, are less clear; for instance, it has been argued that local authorities are not empowered to change the address of adult persons who lack mental capacity, without authority of the High Court (and in situations where the person is not subject to a guardianship order under Mental Health Act 1983 s7).[130]

Misdirection of law

19.145 A decision may be challenged by way of judicial review if the authority can be shown to have misunderstood the relevant law in reaching its decision,[131] although the mere existence of a mistake of law does not vitiate the impugned decision unless it 'is a relevant error of law, ie, an error in the actual making of the decision which affected the decision itself'.

19.146   Given the confusing and complex nature of community care law, there is clearly wide scope for local authority decisions to be challenged on this ground; for instance, in *R v Tower Hamlets LBC ex p Bradford*[132] the court held that the authority had fundamentally misunderstood its powers under Children Act 1989 Part III and so quashed the decision it had reached.

19.147   An authority may make an error of law by misunderstanding the nature of its statutory obligation; it may, for instance, consider its obligation to be discretionary when it is in fact mandatory.

127 De Smith, Woolf and Jowell, *Judicial Review of Administrative Action* (Sweet & Maxwell, 5th edn, 1995).

128 De Smith et al, *Judicial Review of Administrative Action* p330, note 69.

129 Action which is outside the public body's legal powers.

130 See for instance *Mental Incapacity*, Law Commission Paper No 231, 28 February 1995, para 2.23 and *Re F (Mental Patient: Sterilisation)* [1990] 2 AC 1, HL; and *Re S (Hospital Patient: Court's Jurisdiction)* [1995] 3 All ER 29.

131 *R v Hull University Visitor ex p Page* [1993] AC 682, HL at 701–702.

132 (1998) 1 CCLR 294; see para 18.32 above.

Decision not made in accordance with the facts

19.148 The decision made by the authority must be in accordance with (and supported by) the evidence. Authorities cannot simply 'go through the motions' by paying lip service to the evidence but in reality having no regard to the individual merits of the case.[133] Accordingly in *R v Avon CC ex p M*[134] Henry J overruled a decision by the social services authority which directly conflicted with a recommendation made by the panel. In so doing, he stated:

> The evidence before [the panel] had, as to the practicalities, been largely one way. The panel had directed themselves properly at law, and had arrived at a decision in line with the strength of the evidence before them ... the strength, coherence and apparent persuasiveness of that decision had to be addressed head-on if it were to be set aside and not followed. These difficulties were not faced either by the respondent's officers in their paper to the social services committee or by the social services committee themselves. Not to face them was either unintentional perversity on their part or showed a wrong appreciation of the legal standing of that decision. It seems to me that you do not properly reconsider a decision when, on the evidence, it is not seen that the decision was given the weight it deserved.

Relevant and irrelevant considerations

19.149 A basic tenet of the *Wednesbury* decision is that a decision-maker must take into account all relevant considerations before making his or her decision and must ignore the irrelevant. In *R v Avon County Council ex p M* the court found that the authority, in deciding which residential placement to support, had ignored the applicant's psychological needs. In so doing it failed to take account of a relevant (and in the court's view a 'crucial') consideration. In addition, the authority had decided that the applicant's preferred home should not be funded because (among other reasons) such a funding decision would 'set a precedent'. In this context the judge held that this was a misleading consideration; essentially whether or not the decision set a precedent was an irrelevant consideration. The same principle applies to the local ombudsman's finding[135] in a complaint against East Sussex County Council. The complaint concerned a panel's refusal to recommend the payment of compensation for benefits a service user lost as a result of wrong advice he received from the social services department. The ombudsman held that the refusal was based upon an irrelevant consideration (namely that it was the Benefits Agency, not the local authority, which was responsible for the payment of such benefits).

19.150 A further aspect of this decision-making principle is illustrated in the case of *R v Gloucestershire CC ex p Mahfood*.[136] In this case, the respondent

---

133 *Hemns v Wheller* [1948] 2 KB 61 and *Sagnata Investments v Norwich Corporation* [1971] 2 QB 614, CA.

134 [1994] 2 FLR 1006; (1999) 2 CCLR 185.

135 No 93/A/3738; see para 19.50 above.

136 (1997) 1 CCLR 7; 94 LGR 53.

council withdrew services to various disabled people solely because the council's resources had been cut. McCowan LJ considered that this was making one consideration determinative (ie, at the cost of and overruling all others) and in his view, 'this amounted to treating the cut in resources as the sole factor to be taken into account, and that was, in my judgment, unlawful'.

Fettering of discretion

19.151   While an authority 'charged with exercising an administrative discretion is entitled to promulgate a policy or guidelines as an indication of a norm which is intended to be followed',[137] it is not entitled to fetter its discretion by approaching a decision with a pre-determined policy as to how all cases falling within a particular class will be treated. Accordingly in *R v Ealing LBC ex p Leaman*[138] Mann J held that where a disabled person had applied to a local authority under Chronically Sick and Disabled Persons Act 1970 s2(1)(f) for financial assistance in taking a privately arranged holiday, it was an error of law for the authority to decline to consider the application on the ground that it would only grant such assistance for holidays which it itself had arranged or sponsored (as the Act specifically allows for the support of holidays 'provided under arrangements made by the authority or otherwise'). On this principle, it would also be unlawful for an authority to have a fixed policy that it will not fund home help which consists solely of cleaning a house or ironing, etc (as no such limitation is imposed by s2(1)(a) of the 1970 Act); likewise fixed policies by health or local authorities in relation to drug rehabilitation, which either confine such rehabilitation solely to funding detoxification (as opposed to harm minimisation or stabilisation) or where there is a fixed policy only to fund detoxification for a fixed and limited period, would again amount to a fettering of discretion (given again, that no such limitations are imposed by the primary legislation).[139]

19.152   In *R v North West Lancashire Health Authority ex p A*[140] the Court of Appeal held that the respondent's policy of not providing treatment for gender reassignment 'save in cases of overriding clinical need, was 'nonsense' since the authority considered that there was no effective treatment for the condition, and accordingly an 'overriding clinical need' could not therefore arise. Auld LJ held:

> . . . the stance of the authority, coupled with the near uniformity of its reasons for rejecting each of the respondent's requests for funding was not a genuine application of a policy subject to individually determined exceptions of the sort considered acceptable by Lord Scarman in *Findlay*.[141]

---

137 See *R v Eastleigh BC ex p Betts* [1983] 2 AC 613, HL.
138 (1984) *Times* 10 February.
139 National Assistance Act 1948 s21, subject to the directions in LAC(93)10 Appendix 1 para 2(6) and under National Health Service Act 1977 Sch 8 para 2, subject to the secretary of state's directions in LAC(93)10 Appendix 3 para 3(3)(g).
140 (1999) *Times* 24 August.
141 *In re Findlay* [1985] 1 AC 318.

It is similar to the over-rigid application of the neat 'blanket policy' questioned by Judge J in *R v Warwickshire CC ex p Collymore* [1995] ELR 217, at 224 onwards:

'which while in theory admitting exceptions, may not, in reality result in the proper consideration of each individual case on its merits'.

19.153 The court also made reference to *R v Bexley LBC ex p Jones*[142] where Leggatt LJ held:

It is . . . legitimate for a statutory body . . . to adopt a policy designed to ensure a rational and consistent approach to the exercise of a statutory discretion in particular types of case. But it can only do so provided that the policy fairly admits of exceptions to it. In my judgment, the respondents effectively disabled themselves from considering individual cases and there has been no convincing evidence that at any material time they had an exceptions procedure worth the name. There is no indication that there was a genuine willingness to consider individual cases.

Unlawful delegation or dictation

19.154 Decision-makers cannot avoid their duties by allowing themselves to be dictated to by, or simply accepting the decision of, another body. Further, decision-makers may not delegate their decisions to others unless they have specific power to do so and have done so properly.[143]

19.155 An example of this difficulty arises in relation to the duty on social services authorities to provide assistance for works of adaptation in a house, or the provision of additional facilities in the home (Chronically Sick and Disabled Persons Act (CSDPA) 1970 s2(1)(e)). Not infrequently social services authorities allow their decision whether or not to provide assistance with such adaptations to be determined solely by whether the disabled person obtains a grant under Housing Grants, Construction and Regeneration Act 1996 s23 (a disabled facilities grant). In fact, the responsibility on the social services authority under CSDPA 1970 s2 is independent of the question of whether or not a disabled facilities grant is awarded (although the award or refusal of a grant is a relevant consideration).[144]

Procedural impropriety

19.156 Procedural impropriety embraces a number of issues of natural justice.

The duty to act fairly

19.157 Decision-makers must act fairly, must not be biased, must allow a party time to prepare his or her case, must ensure that a party has a proper opportunity to be heard, and in appropriate situations, must give reasons for their decisions.

---

142 [1995] ELR 42 at 55. In this context see para 5.25 above.
143 J Manning, *Judicial Review Proceedings* (Legal Action Group, 2nd edition, 2004) at para 6.78.
144 DoE Circular 10/90 para 15, see paras 8.95 and 17.27 above.

19.158   Natural justice will most obviously come to the fore when authorities are discharging their duties to assess under National Health Service and Community Care Act 1990 s47(1) and during the complaints process, particularly at panel hearings. The complaints process specifically requires reasons to be given for the panel's recommendation and the local authority's subsequent decision (see para 19.53 above).

Legitimate expectation and the abuse of power

19.159   Initially the courts developed the notion of 'legitimate expectation', as a facet of 'procedural impropriety' or the requirement of administrative fairness. As will be noted below, in relation to the *Coughlan* decision, the Court of Appeal has now signalled that the doctrine may also be of relevance in substantive challenges. The basic principle however, requires that no decision should be taken which will adversely affect an individual, without that person being given an opportunity of making representations as to why the particular benefit or advantage should not be withdrawn.[145] Local authority eligibility criteria will probably fall into this category; so that an individual would have the legitimate expectation that authorities would not depart from these criteria.

19.160   In *R v North and East Devon Health Authority ex p Coughlan*[146] the Court of Appeal reviewed the development of the doctrine which it considered had 'emerged as a distinct application of the concept of abuse of power in relation to substantive as well as procedural benefits'. The Court continued:

> Legitimate expectation may play different parts in different aspects of public law. The limits to its role have yet to be finally determined by the courts. Its application is still being developed on a case by case basis. Even where it reflects procedural expectations, for example concerning consultation, it may be affected by an overriding public interest. It may operate as an aspect of good administration, qualifying the intrinsic rationality of policy choices. And without injury to the *Wednesbury* doctrine it may furnish a proper basis for the application of the new established concept of abuse of power.[147]

and

> . . . in relation to this category of legitimate expectation, we do not consider it necessary to explain the modern doctrine in *Wednesbury* terms, helpful though this is in terms of received jurisprudence . . . We would prefer to regard the *Wednesbury* categories themselves as the major instances (not necessarily the sole ones . . .) of how public power may be misused. Once it is recognised that conduct which is an abuse of power is contrary to law its existence must be for the court to determine.[148]

145 *Council of Civil Service Unions v Minister for the Civil Service* [1985] AC 374, HL.
146 (1999) 2 CCLR 285, CA.
147 (1999) 2 CCLR 285 at p311.
148 (1999) 2 CCLR 285 at p315.

19.161   An example of legitimate expectation is found in *R (Theophilus) v Lewisham LBC*.[149] The claimant accepted a place to study law at a college in Dublin, after the authority informed her that she would receive student support provided she studied anywhere in the European Union. The authority subsequently informed her that it had made an error and she was not entitled to support under the Education (Student Support) Regulations 2001.[150] This was correct, but the local authority continued to have power to fund the placement under the Local Government Act 2000 s2. On the basis of the legitimate expectation, created by the promise of grant support, the authority was held obliged to use its powers under the 2000 Act.

The duty to consult

19.162   The principle of procedural propriety also appears, in certain situations, as a duty to consult. In *R v Devon CC and Durham CC ex p Baker et al*[151] it was stated that the duty:

> ... encompasses those cases in which it is held that a particular procedure, not otherwise required by law in the protection of an interest, must be followed consequent upon some specific promise or practice. Fairness requires that the public authority be held to it.

19.163   In this case, the court quashed a decision by Durham County Council to close various residential care homes because the authority had not properly consulted (see para 7.113 above). The court approved an earlier judgment[152] where the duty to consult was formulated as consisting of four parts, the requirements being:

> First that the consultation must be at a time when proposals are still at a formative stage. Second that the proposer must give sufficient reasons for any proposal to permit of intelligent consideration and response. Third ... that adequate time must be given for consideration and response and, finally, fourth, that the product of consultation must be conscientiously taken into account in finalising any statutory proposals.[153]

19.164   In general consultations should conform to the Cabinet Office's 'Code of Practice on Written Consultation'[154] which states that 12 weeks should be 'standard minimum period' for a consultation exercise. It also states that the:

> Timing of consultation should be built into the planning process for a policy (including legislation) or service from the start so that it has the best prospect of improving the proposals concerned, and so that sufficient time is left for it at each stage.

---

149   [2002] EWHC 1371 (Admin); [2002] 3 All ER 851.
150   SI No 951.
151   [1995] 1 All ER 89, QBD.
152   *R v Brent LBC ex p Gunning* (1986) 84 LGR 168.
153   [1995] 1 All ER 89 at p91.
154   Code of Practice on Written Consultation, Cabinet Office (2004) accessible at www.dh. gov.uk/PolicyAndGuidance/PatientChoice/PatientAdviceAndLiaisonServices/fs/en.

The duty to act in accordance with mandatory or directory requirements

19.165 A further requirement of the duty to act fairly is that the decision-maker must comply with procedures laid down by parliament. This is sometimes known as the duty to act in accordance with 'mandatory or directory requirements'. In *R v North Yorkshire CC ex p Hargreaves*[155] it was accepted that the respondent authority, in assessing the applicant's sister's needs, failed to take into account the preferences of the sister, contrary to the mandatory (or directory) requirements set out in the 1990 policy guidance.[156] As the Guidance was made under Local Authority Social Services Act 1970 s7(1) requiring authorities to act *under* such guidance, a failure to do so rendered the decision unlawful. Dyson J held that the requirements of the 1990 policy guidance were mandatory and that the decision should, therefore, be quashed. See also *Secretary of State for Trade and Industry v Langridge*[157] where guidance was given on the principles to be applied in deciding whether a particular duty is mandatory or directory.

The duty to give reasons

19.166 Although there is no general duty on authorities to give reasons for their decisions, where the relevant statute, regulation or direction stipulates that reasons should be given, then the reasons must be 'proper, adequate and intelligible' and must deal with the substantial points raised by the complainant. An unparticularised assertion that 'on the evidence' the decision-maker makes certain findings 'and recommends . . . ' will be considered inadequate.[158] An express duty to give reasons exists, for instance, in the Complaints Procedure Directions (see para 19.53 above). In the absence of an express provision requiring the giving of reasons, they may nevertheless be required, if, for instance, the decision would otherwise be unintelligible, or would contravene the minimum standards of fairness.[159]

Default procedures

19.167 Local Authority Social Services Act 1970 s7D[160] provides:

(1) If the Secretary of State is satisfied that any local authority have failed without reasonable excuse, to comply with any of their duties which are social services functions[161] (other than a duty imposed by or under the

---

155 (1994) 30 September QBD, CO/878/94.

156 Paras 3.16 and 3.25; and see also *R v Islington LBC ex p Rixon* (1998) 1 CCLR 119.

157 [1991] 3 All ER 591.

158 See paras 19.36 and 19.57 above.

159 *R v Secretary of State for Home Department ex p Doody* [1993] 3 WLR 154, HL.

160 Inserted by National Health Service and Community Care Act 1990 s50 and replacing an equivalent provision under National Assistance Act 1948 s36(1).

161 A function set out in Local Authority Social Services Act 1970 Sch 1 other than a duty imposed by or under the Children Act 1989.

Children Act 1989,[162] he may make an order declaring that authority to be in default with respect to the duty in question.

(2) An order under subsection (1) may contain such directions for the purpose of ensuring that the duty is complied with within such period as may be specified in the order as appear to the Secretary of State to be necessary.

(3) Any such direction shall, on the application of the Secretary of State, be enforceable by mandamus.

19.168 On the face of it, a person aggrieved by a local authority decision, may seek redress by making formal request to the secretary of state that he or she use this default power to remedy the particular injustice. In reality such executive powers are rarely if ever exercised. The power under LASSA 1970 s7D is no exception; it appears that it has never been used, and it is highly unlikely that in anything but the most extreme of situations that it would be so exercised. The power can only be used where the authority has failed to exercise a 'duty' (rather than a 'power'); it only arises if the local authority has 'no reasonable excuse' for its failure; the secretary of state has to be 'satisfied' about the lack of any reasonable excuse; and even then s/he has wide discretion whether or not to take any such action.

19.169 In practice, when a complainant writes to the Department of Health referring to an apparent failure by an authority to comply with its statutory duty, the Department writes to the authority seeking an explanation. There is some evidence that this action in itself may lead to a resolution of the problem.[163]

19.170 In *R v Kent CC ex p Bruce*[164] it was held that the secretary of state was not a 'tribunal of fact' and in considering whether to exercise the default procedure 'must properly be concerned with whether the local authority had misdirected itself in law or formed an irrational view of the facts'. In *R v Devon CC ex p Baker and others*[165] an argument that the existence of the default procedure constituted an alternative remedy which thereby excluded the use of judicial review was, in this particular case, rejected.

19.171 In *R v Westminster CC ex p P and others*[166] four destitute asylum-seekers challenged the policy of various London Boroughs to accommodate them outside London. Simon Brown LJ, in rejecting the application (on grounds that there was an alternative remedy, see para 19.132 above) held as follows:

> For my part I have reached the clear conclusion that the more 'convenient, expeditious and effective' course here is indeed that of applying to the secretary of state to exercise his default powers under section 7D. This is par excellence an area of administration in which the secretary of state rather than the courts should be closely involved. In the first place it is the

---

162 An equivalent default power is found in Children Act 1989 s84.

163 See for instance pp5 onwards of 'Putting Teeth into the Act', a report produced by RADAR on attempts made between 1970–81 to enforce Chronically Sick and Disabled Persons Act 1970 s2.

164 (1986) *Times* 8 February.

165 [1985] 1 All ER 73.

166 (1998) 1 CCLR 486 and see also *R v Kirklees MBC ex p Good* (1998) 1 CCLR 506.

secretary of state who funds the housing of asylum-seekers under s21 of the 1948 Act. Secondly, it is the proper construction and application of his own Directions and Guidance which lie at the heart of the dispute. Thirdly, it was at the secretary of state's insistence that the appeal from the Court of Appeal's decision in *R v Westminster CC ex p M*,[167] which was to be heard by the House of Lords last month, was adjourned, specifically because the Government are currently conducting a review of the treatment of asylum-seekers and did not wish to risk a final judgment depriving asylum-seekers of all protection until a decision had been made as to what (if any) alternative arrangements should be made.

The European Convention on Human Rights

19.172   The following section makes numerous reference to the case law of the European Court of Human Rights. All judgments of the court are accessible on the Council of Europe website.[167a]

19.173   The Human Rights Act (HRA) 1998 came into force in 2000. HRA 1998 s6 makes it unlawful for a public body to act in such a way as to violate a person's 'Convention rights' (and an 'act' for the purposes of section 6 includes 'a failure to act' (HRA 1998 s6(6)). Where a violation of such a right is alleged to have occurred, an individual can take proceedings (under HRA 1998 s7) for (among other things) compensation (HRA 1988 s8).

19.174   In *R (Bernard) v Enfield LBC*[168] (discussed below) the court considered that the appropriate level of damages for violations of the 1998 Act was that awarded by the local government ombudsman. However in *Anufrijeva and others v Southwark LBC and others*[169] the Court of Appeal held:

> Where an infringement of an individual's human rights has occurred, the concern will usually be to bring the infringement to an end and any question of compensation will be of secondary, if any, importance. This is reflected in the fact that, when it is necessary to resort to the courts to uphold and protect human rights, the remedies that are most frequently sought are the orders which are the descendents of the historic prerogative orders or declaratory judgments. The orders enable the court to order a public body to refrain from or to take action, or to quash an offending administrative decision of a public body. Declaratory judgments usually resolve disputes as to what is the correct answer in law to a dispute. This means that it is often procedurally convenient for actions concerning human rights to be heard on an application for judicial review in the Administrative Court. That court does not normally concern itself with issues of disputed fact or with issues as to damages. However, it is well placed to take action expeditiously when this is appropriate.

---

167   *R v Westminster CC ex p M* (1997) 1 CCLR 85.
167a   www.dhcour.coe.int/hudoc/.
168   [2002] EWHC 2282 (Admin); (2002) 5 CCLR 577.
169   [2003] EWCA Civ 1406; (2003) 6 CCLR 415 at [53].

Convention rights

19.175 The Convention rights of most relevance in the context of community care law are articles 2, 3 5, 6, 8 and 14 of the European Convention on Human Rights (ECHR). These are briefly considered below – but reference should be made to one of the many specialist text on this subject.[170]

Article 2

19.176 Article 2 places a positive obligation on the state to protect life.[171] Cases are likely to occur concerning actions by health and social services authorities which might be harmful, such as the closure of dementia wards or residential care homes (see para 7.124 above) as well as decisions not to provide treatment for people with serious illness, such as the decision in *R v Cambridge Health Authority ex p B*[172] considered at para 10.20 above).

19.177 Violations of the obligations under article 2 have been found in cases such as the failure to protect a vulnerable prisoner from a dangerous cellmate.[173] The Court has accepted that positive obligations require special measures to be taken to protect potentially suicidal patients[174] and may require individuals exposed to be warned if exposed to any serious environmental or health risks.[175] The Commission has likewise considered the extent of the state's obligation to reduce the risks of a vaccination programme [176] or to fund a health service.[177] There are however limits to the obligation under article 2; it cannot for instance be construed to provide a right for an incapacitated adult to have another assist her in dying (*Pretty v United Kingdom*).[178]

Article 3

19.178 Article 3 prohibits torture inhuman and degrading treatment and places a positive obligation on the state to take reasonable measures to ensure no one is subjected to such treatment.

19.179 The Court has emphasised that for treatment to be 'degrading' it must reach a minimum threshold of severity;[179] although it has indicated that

---

170 See for instance, L Clements and J Read, *Disabled People and European Human Rights*, Policy Press, 2003.

171 *Osman v United Kingdom* (1998) EHRR 245 at 305.

172 [1995] 2 All ER 129, CA.

173 *Edwards v United Kingdom* (2002) *Times* 1 April.

174 *Keenan v United Kingdom* (2001) 33 EHRR 38, (2001) *Times* 18 April.

175 *LCB v United Kingdom* (1998) 27 EHRR 212.

176 *Association X v United Kingdom* DR 14/31.

177 *Osman v United Kingdom* (1998) 29 EHRR 245; [1999] Crim LR 82; (1998) *Times* 5 November.

178 (2002) 35 EHRR 1; and see also domestic proceedings at [2001] 3 WLR 1598; [2002] 1 All ER 1.

179 *Costello-Roberts v United Kingdom* (1993) 19 EHRR 105.

this may be significantly lower for disabled[180] and elderly people.[181] Arbitrary and gross acts of discrimination may exceptionally be considered to violate article 3, even in the absence of actual physical or mental harm.[182] The negative obligations under article 3 are engaged by detention conditions,[183] corporal punishment[184] and poor prison conditions.[185] Extradition may violate article 3 if the expelled person is thereby put at risk of degrading treatment (even if solely a consequence of inadequate medical treatment in the receiving country).[186]

19.180   As noted above (at para 7.35) article 3 has been construed as creating a positive obligation on states to ensure that no one suffers from degrading treatment, and in this respect eligibility criteria cannot exclude services from persons at 'significant risk of harm'. The case law on article 3 has established that the courts and social services are obliged to use their powers to protect children[187] and vulnerable adults[188] from abuse. Where credible evidence exists that an individual has suffered abuse whilst in the care of a public authority, a positive obligation arises under article 3 for an independent and open investigation to be convened.[189]

19.181   *Price v United Kingdom*[190] concerned a Thalidomide impaired applicant who in the course of debt recovery proceedings refused to answer questions put to her and was committed to prison for seven days for contempt of court. She alleged that she suffered degrading treatment as a result of the prison's inadequate facilities, but the UK government argued that any discomfort she experienced had not reached the minimum level of severity required by article 3. The Court however considered that the threshold depended 'on all the circumstances of the case, such as the duration of the treatment, its physical and mental effects and, in some cases, the sex, age and state of health of the victim', and after a thorough review it concluded:

> . . . that to detain a severely disabled person in conditions where she is dangerously cold, risks developing sores because her bed is too hard or unreachable, and is unable to go to the toilet or keep clean without the greatest of difficulty, constitutes degrading treatment contrary to article 3.

19.182   Of particular interest was the concurring opinion of Judge Greve, in which he stated:

180 *Price v United Kingdom* (2001) 34 EHRR 1285; (2002) 5 CCLR 306; (2001) *Times* 13 August.

181 See *Papon v France* 7 June 2001 an inadmissibility decision.

182 See *Cyprus v Turkey* (2002) No 25781/94 and *Patel v United Kingdom* (the *East African Asians* case) 3 EHRR 76.

183 *McGlinchley v United Kingdom* (2003) 50390/99; 29 April 2003.

184 *Campbell and Cosans v United Kingdom* (1982) 2 EHRR 293.

185 *Napier v Scottish Minister* (2001) *Times* 15 November and see also *Price v United Kingdom* (2001) 34 EHRR 1285; (2002) 5 CCLR 306; (2001) *Times* 13 August.

186 *D v United Kingdom* (1997) 24 EHRR 423.

187 *Z and others v United Kingdom* (2002) 34 EHRR 3; (2001) *Times* 31 May.

188 *In re F (Adult: Court's Jurisdiction)* (2000) 3 CCLR 210; (2000) *Times* 25 July.

189 *Assenov v Bulgaria* (1998) 28 EHRR 652; see also *Labita v Italy* 6 April 2000.

190 (2001) 34 EHRR 1285; (2002) 5 CCLR 306; (2001) *Times* 13 August.

It is obvious that restraining any non-disabled person to the applicant's level of ability to move and assist herself, for even a limited period of time, would amount to inhuman and degrading treatment – possibly torture. In a civilised country like the United Kingdom, society considers it not only appropriate but a basic humane concern to try to ameliorate and compensate for the disabilities faced by a person in the applicant's situation. In my opinion, these compensatory measures come to form part of the disabled person's bodily integrity.

Article 5

19.183 Article 5(1) places a total prohibition upon a state's power to detain people except in six clearly defined instances, including under article 5(1)(e) 'the lawful detention of persons for the prevention of the spreading of infectious diseases, of persons of unsound mind, alcoholics or drug addicts or vagrants'. A substantial body of case law exists concerning the Convention requirements that must be satisfied before a mental health service user can be legally detained, and the Mental Health Act 1983 was largely a response to a number of adverse Strasbourg judgments.[191] Increasingly the court is requiring detention under this ground to be accompanied by a suitably therapeutic environment.[192]

19.184   In *Winterwerp v Netherlands*[193] and a series of subsequent cases,[194] the Court has laid down a number of factors which must be satisfied before the detention of a person of unsound mind is lawful within the meaning of the Convention including:

1) The mental disorder must be reliably established by objective medical expertise.

2) The nature or degree of the disorder must be sufficiently extreme to justify the detention.

3) The detention should only last as long as the medical disorder (and its required severity) persists.

4) If the detention is potentially indefinite, then there must be a system of periodic reviews by a tribunal that has power to discharge.

5) The detention must be in a hospital, clinic or other appropriate institution authorised for the detention of such persons.[195]

---

191 See, for instance, *X v United Kingdom* (1981) 4 EHRR 188; and *Ashingdane v United Kingdom* (1985) 7 EHRR 528 and *Winterwerp v Netherlands* (1979) 2 EHRR 387.

192 *Michel Aerts v Belgium* (1998) 29 EHRR 50.

193 (1979) 2 EHRR 387; 24 October 1979, Series A No 33.

194 See for instance, X v *United Kingdom* (1981) 4 EHRR 188; 24 October 1981, Series A No 46 and *Ashingdane v United Kingdom* (1985) 7 EHRR 528; 28 May 1985, Series A No 93.

195 *Ashingdane v United Kingdom*, Series A No 93 at paragraph 44. In the case of *Michel Aerts v Belgium*, the Commission found a violation of article 5(1) in relation to the detention of the applicant in the psychiatric wing of a prison which was not an 'appropriate establishment' in view of the lack of qualified personnel. Commission Report adopted on 20 May 1997. Pending before the Court. The failure to provide medical treatment to a person in detention under article 5(1)(e) could amount to inhuman treatment contrary to article 3.

Article 6

19.185   Article 6(1) entrenches the right of parties to a fair hearing when their civil rights are affected (or when charged with a criminal offence). It requires hearings to be before an 'independent and impartial tribunal' and to be held within a 'reasonable time' which has in certain situations has been held to require 'exceptional diligence' to ensure their early listing.[196] A difficulty experienced with the application of article 6(1) concerns the way the European Court of Human Rights has interpreted the phrase 'civil rights'. Put simply it covers the laws of a particular country which are neither criminal nor administrative/public law rights. In general civil rights are 'private law' rights, concerned with such matters as employment, property and commercial law. A 'civil' dispute must generally be something that could be the subject of proceedings in the county court, or before the relevant social security or planning or employment tribunal. Thus a dispute concerning a child's education is not considered a civil dispute[197] (although it engages a Convention right – article 2 of the First Protocol), whereas a dispute about social security benefits is considered civil.[198]

19.186   A problem arises in relation to the statutory social services[199] and NHS complaints procedures.[200] In the majority of cases the statutory procedures will not engage the article 6 obligation to provide 'independent and impartial' tribunals since the subject matter of the complaint will not be 'civil' within the meaning of article 6. In *R (Beeson) v Dorset CC and Secretary of State for Health*[201] (a case that concerned a challenge to a decision that B had deprived himself of his house for the purpose of decreasing his liability to residential care fees – see para 12.51 above) it was argued that the local authority complaints process was in breach of article 6(1) of the Convention. The Court of Appeal held (reversing the High Court judgment) that although the complaints panel was considering a civil right within the scope of article 6(1), the independent element in the panel, plus the scope for judicial review, satisfied the requirements of article 6(1).

Article 8

19.187   The court has consistently defined article 8 as positive in nature.[202] This arises out of the presence of the word 'respect': rather than obliging states 'not to interfere' with private and family life article 8(1) provides that 'every-

---

196   *H v United Kingdom* 10 EHRR 95; see also *P and D v United Kingdom* [1996] EHRLR 526.

197   *R v Alperton Community School and others ex p B and others* (2001) *Times* 8 June.

198   *Schuler-Zgraggen v Switzerland* (1995) 16 EHRR 405.

199   Under Local Authority Social Services Act 1970 s7B and Representations Procedure (Children) Regulations 1991 SI No 894.

200   Under Directions to NHS Trusts, Health Authorities and Special Health Authorities for Special Hospitals on Hospital Complaints Procedures 1996; Miscellaneous Directions to Health Authorities for Dealing with Complaints 1996; given under NHSA 1977 s17, NHSCCA 1990 Sch 2 para 6(2)(a) and the NHS (Functions of Health Authorities) (Complaints) Regulations 1996 SI No 669.

201   [2002] EWCA Civ 1812; [2002] HRLR 15; (2002) 5 CCLR 5.

202   *Marckx v Belgium* (1979) 2 EHRR 330.

one has the right to respect for his private and family life, his home and his correspondence'. The demonstration of 'respect' is inherently positive in nature.

19.188 While family life, the home and correspondence have been given their everyday meanings, the concept of 'private life' has acquired an altogether more expansive interpretation, including a 'person's physical and psychological integrity' for which respect is due in order to 'ensure the development, without outside interference, of the personality of each individual in his relations with other human beings'.[203] Thus issues of sexual rights,[204] environmental pollution,[205] physical barriers to movement,[206] access to files[207] and information about one's illness[208] have been held to come within its reach.

19.189 Article 8 is a 'qualified right' in that state interfere with the right is permitted, but only where the interference is 'lawful' and is done in a proportionate way in pursuance of a legitimate aim. Although article 8(2) provides an exhaustive list of six legitimate aims, these are so widely drawn (including for example action which protects the rights and freedoms of others, action for economic reasons, or to protect morals or to prevent crime) that in general the court will have little difficulty in finding any 'interference' with article 8(1) pursues a legitimate aim.

19.190 It is however in respect of the second limb of the test that public bodies have most difficulty. They must establish that what they did, had not only a legitimate aim, but also that it was 'proportionate'. Although there is substantial jurisprudence concerning the of concept of 'proportionality' – the key principles of most relevance in a social welfare context concern the need for the action to be 'the least restrictive interference' commensurate with the legitimate aim pursued, and also that overall the action be 'balanced'.

19.191 In *Gaskin v United Kingdom*[209] the applicant sought access to his social services records. The request was refused in part on the ground that some of the information had originally been given in confidence and the law at that time did not permit disclosure of information where such third parties had not provided their consent to the disclosure. The information was important to Mr Gaskin as he had spent almost all his life in care and he wanted it for identity purposes. His was a legitimate claim, as indeed was the refusal to divulge the information, which had been given to the local authority in confidence.

19.192 The Court considered that the refusal to disclose pursued a legitimate aim (that of protecting the rights and freedoms of others) but was disproportionate. It was not the 'least restrictive interference'. The Court

---

203 *Botta v Italy* (1998) 153/1996/772/973 24 February 1998.
204 *Norris v Ireland* 13 EHRR 186 (1988).
205 *Hatton v United Kingdom* (2001) 34 EHRR 1.
206 *Botta v Italy* (1998) 153/1996/772/973 24 February 1998.
207 *Gaskin v United Kingdom* (1989) 12 EHRR 36.
208 *McGinley and Egan v United Kingdom* (1998) 27 EHRR 1; and *LCB v United Kingdom* (1998) 27 EHRR 212.
209 (1989) 12 EHRR 36.

considered that some of the 'third party' material could be disclosed without prejudicing their rights – for instance if the person who had given the information had since died, or could not be traced, or if anyone reading the information would be unable to identity its author. It also considered that the blanket refusal was not 'balanced' since it meant that in such cases Mr Gaskin's claim always failed – and the concept of 'balance' requires that in certain situations the balance of interest might come down in favour of the person seeking disclosure. It was as a consequence of the *Gaskin* judgment that the changes in the Data Protection Act 1998 to accessing social services files were introduced (see paras 3.34 and 3.68 above).

19.193   For many disabled people, their home is (in one form or another) in an institutional setting. Provided the stay has been for a reasonable length of time[210] the care home or hospital ward, etc, will be deemed the person's 'home' for the purposes of article 8. Accordingly any attempt to move the resident, will have to be justified as being proportionate. *R v North and East Devon Health Authority ex p Coughlan*[211] concerned an attempt by a health authority to move the applicant from her specialist NHS unit where she had lived for six years. Having regard to all the circumstances (which included the health authority's desire to close the facility for budgetary reasons) the Court considered that the authority had failed to establish that such an interference with the applicant's article 8 right was justified.

19.194   *R (Bernard) v Enfield LBC*[212] concerned a disabled applicant and her family who through the local authorities failure to properly assess her community care needs, and then provide the necessary services, had been forced to live in 'deplorable conditions' for over 20 months.

19.195   The Court held that this level of suffering had not attained the threshold required by article 3. It relied upon the fact that the treatment, unlike in *Price v United Kingdom*[213] (see para 19.181 above) was not deliberate but due to 'corporate neglect'. However it considered that the council's failure to act on its assessments had the effect of condemning the applicant and her family to live in conditions which made it virtually impossible for them to have any meaningful private or family – and on the facts found a violation of article 8.

19.196   In deciding what level of damages were appropriate under HRA 1998 s8, the court was guided by community care maladministration awards made by the Local Government Ombudsman. This was viewed as a severe case of maladministration and the applicant was accordingly awarded £8,000 and the husband £2,000. The court also ordered that Enfield must not 'claw-back' these sums when assessing the claimants' liability to contribute towards the cost of the accommodation.

---

210 In *O'Rourke v United Kingdom* (1999) 26 June 2001 No 39022/97, the Court doubted that occupation of a hotel room for one month was sufficient and continuous enough to make it his 'home' for the purposes of article 8.

211 (1999) 2 CCLR 285.

212 (2002) 5 CCLR 577.

213 (2001) 34 EHRR 1285; (2002) 5 CCLR 306; (2001) *Times* 13 August.

Article 14

19.197 Article 14 can only be invoked in relation to one of the substantive rights set out in articles 2–12 of the Convention and the Protocols. Article 14 requires that in the delivery of the substantive rights, there be no discrimination. Discrimination is permissible under article 14, if it is established that the measure has an objective and reasonable justification and is 'proportionate'.

19.198 Thus a violation of article 14 can only occur in combination with another article;[214] for instance the inferior inheritance rights of illegitimate children in Belgium (compared to legitimate children) were held to violate article 14 in conjunction with article 8[215] (right to family life). The court has been particularly forthright on the issue of sex discrimination, holding that '[t]he advancement of the equality of the sexes is today a major goal in the member-States of the Council of Europe and very weighty reasons would have to be put forward before such a difference of Treatment could be regarded as compatible with the Convention'.[216]

European Court of Human Rights

19.199 A complaint can only be made to the European Court of Human Rights once all domestic remedies have been exhausted. The complainant must be an individual who claims to have actually suffered as a result of the measure in issue, and the complaint must be made within six months of the exhaustion of the last domestic remedy. The complaint must allege a violation of at least one of the principal articles of the European Convention on Human rights (or the first protocol thereto).[217]

---

214 It may be that major improvement in this field will more likely flow from EU law, ie, the Amsterdam Treaty amendments.

215 *Marckx v Belgium* (1979) 2 EHRR 330.

216 *Schuler-Zgraggen v Switzerland* (1995) 16 EHRR 405.

217 For detailed consideration of the law and procedures, see L Clements, *European Human Rights: Taking a Case Under the Convention*, Sweet & Maxwell, 2nd edition, 1999.

APPENDICES

Legislation: key provisions

NATIONAL ASSISTANCE ACT 1948 ss21–33
Duty of local authorities to provide accommodation

21 (1) Subject to and in accordance with the provisions of this Part of this Act, a local authority may with the approval of the Secretary of State, and to such extent as he may direct shall, make arrangements for providing:

(a) residential accommodation for persons aged eighteen or over who by reason of age, illness, disability or any other circumstances are in need of care and attention which is not otherwise available to them and

(aa) residential accommodation for expectant and nursing mothers who are in need of care and attention which is not otherwise available to them.

(1A) A person to whom section 115 of the Immigration and Asylum Act 1999 (exclusion from benefits) applies may not be provided with residential accommodation under subsection (1)(a) if his need for care and attention has arisen solely –

(a) because he is destitute; or

(b) because of the physical effects, or anticipated physical effects, of his being destitute.

(1B) Subsections (3) and (5) to (8) of section 95 of the Immigration and Asylum Act 1999, and paragraph 2 of Schedule 8 to that Act, apply for the purposes of subsection (1a) as they apply for the purposes of that section, but for the references in subsections (5) and (7) of that section and in that paragraph to the Secretary of State substitute references to a local authority.

(2) In making any such arrangements a local authority shall have regard to the welfare of all persons for whom accommodation is provided, and in particular to the need for providing accommodation of different descriptions suited to different descriptions of such persons as are mentioned in the last foregoing subsection.

(2A) In determining for the purposes of paragraph (a) or (aa) of subsection (1) of this section whether care and attention are otherwise available to a person, a local authority shall disregard so much of the person's resources as may be specified in, or determined in accordance with, regulations made by the Secretary of State for the purposes of this subsection.

(2B) In subsection (2A) of this section the reference to a person's resources is a reference to his resources within the meaning of regulations made for the purposes of this subsection.

(3) [*Repealed*]

(4) Subject to section 26 of this Act, accommodation provided by a local authority in the exercise of their functions under this section shall be provided in premises managed by the authority or, to such extent as may be determined in accordance with the arrangements under this section, in such premises managed by another local authority as may be agreed between the two authorities and on such terms as to the reimbursement of expenditure incurred by the said other authority, as may be so agreed.

(5) References in this Act to accommodation provided under this Part thereof shall be construed as references to accommodation provided in accordance with this and the five next following sections, and as including references to board and other services, amenities and requisites provided in connection with the accommodation except where in the opinion of the authority managing the premises their provision is unnecessary.

(6) References in this Act to a local authority providing accommodation shall be construed, in any case where a local authority agree with another local authority for the provision of accommodation in premises managed by the said other authority, as references to the first-mentioned local authority.

(7) Without prejudice to the generality of the foregoing provisions of this section, a local authority may –

(a) provide, in such cases as they may consider appropriate, for the conveyance of persons to and from premises in which accommodation is provided for them under this Part of the Act;

(b) make arrangements for the provision on the premises in which accommodation is being provided of such other services as appear to the authority to be required.

(8) Nothing in this section shall authorise or require a local authority to make any provision authorised or required to be made (whether by that or by any other authority) by or under any enactment not contained in this Part of this Act, or authorised or required to be provided under the National Health Service Act 1977.

Charges to be made for accommodation

22 (1) Subject to section 26 of this Act, where a person is provided with accommodation under this Part of this Act the local authority providing the accommodation shall recover from him the amount of the payment which he is liable to make in accordance with the following provisions of this section.

(2) Subject to the following provisions of this section, the payment which a person is liable to make for any such accommodation shall be in accordance with a standard rate fixed for that accommodation by the authority managing the premises in which it is provided and that standard rate shall represent the full cost to the authority of providing that accommodation.

(3) Where a person for whom accommodation in premises managed by any local authority is provided, or proposed to be provided, under this Part of this Act satisfies the local authority that he is unable to pay therefor at the standard rate, the authority shall assess his ability to pay, and accordingly determine at what lower rate he shall be liable to pay for the accommodation.

(4) In assessing for the purposes of the last foregoing subsection a person's ability to pay, a local authority shall assume that he will need for his personal requirements such sum per week as may be prescribed by the Minister, or such other sum as in special circumstances the authority may consider appropriate.

(4A) Regulations made for the purposes of subsection (4) of this section may prescribe different sums for different circumstances.

(5) In assessing as aforesaid a person's ability to pay, a local authority shall give effect to regulations made by the Secretary of State for the purposes of this subsection except that, until the first such regulations come into force, a local authority shall give effect to Part III of Schedule 1 to the Supplementary Benefits Act 1976, as it had effect immediately before the amendments made by Schedule 2 to the Social Security Act 1980.

(5A) If they think fit, an authority managing premises in which accommodation is provided for a person shall have power on each occasion when they provide accommodation for him, irrespective of his means, to limit to such amount as appears to them reasonable for him to pay the payments required from him for his accommodation during a period commencing when they begin to provide the accommodation for him and ending not more than eight weeks after that.

(6) [*Repealed*]

(7) [*Repealed*]

(8) Where accommodation is provided by a local authority in premises managed by another local authority, the payment therefor under this section shall be made to the authority managing the premises and not to the authority providing the accommodation, but the authority managing the premises shall account for the payment to the authority providing the accommodation.

(8A) This section shall have effect subject to any regulations under section 15 of the Community Care (Delayed Discharges, etc) Act 2003 (power to require certain community care services and services for carers to be provided free of charge).

(9) [*Repealed*]

Management of premises in which accommodation provided

23 (1) Subject to the provisions of this Part of this Act, a local authority may make rules as to the conduct of premises under their management in which accommodation is provided under this Part of this Act and as to the preservation of order in the premises.

(2) Rules under this section may provide that where by reason of any change in a person's circumstances he is no longer qualified to receive accommodation under this Part of this Act or where a person has otherwise become unsuitable therefor, he may be required by the local authority managing the premises to leave the premises in which the accommodation is provided.

(3) Rules under this section may provide for the waiving of part of the payments due under the last foregoing section where in compliance with the rules ersons for whom accommodation is provided assist in the running of the premises.

Authority liable for provision of accommodation

24 (1) The local authority empowered under this Part of this Act to provide residential accommodation for any person shall subject to the following provisions of this Part of this Act be the authority in whose area the person is ordinarily resident.

(2) [*Repealed*]

(3) Where a person in the area of a local authority –

(a) is a person with no settled residence, or

(b) not being ordinarily resident in the area of the local authority, is in urgent need of residential accommodation under this Part of this Act,

the authority shall have the like power to provide residential accommodation for him as if he were ordinarily resident in their area.

(4) Subject to and in accordance with the arrangements under section twenty-one of this Act, a local authority shall have power, as respects a person ordinarily resident in the area of another local authority, with the consent of that other local authority to provide residential accommodation for him in any case where the authority would have a duty to provide such accommodation if he were ordinarily resident in their area.

(5) Where a person is provided with residential accommodation under this Part of this Act, he shall be deemed for the purposes of this Act to continue to be ordinarily resident in the area in which he was ordinarily resident immediately before the residential accommodation was provided for him.

(6) For the purposes of the provision of residential accommodation under this Part of this Act, a patient in a hospital vested in the Secretary of State or an NHS trust shall be deemed to be ordinarily resident in the area, if any, in which he was ordinarily resident immediately before he was admitted as a patient to the hospital, whether or not he in fact continues to be ordinarily resident in that area.

(7) In subsection (6) above 'NHS trust' means a National Health Service trust established under Part I of the National Health Service and Community Care Act 1990 or under the National Health Service (Scotland) Act 1978 and 'Primary Care Trust' means a Primary Care Trust established under section 16A of the National Health Service Act 1977.

25   [*Repealed*]

Provision of accommodation in premises maintained by voluntary organisations

26 (1) Subject to subsections (1A) and (1C) below, arrangements under section 21 of this Act may include arrangements made with a voluntary organisation or with any other person who is not a local authority where –

(a) that organisation or person manages premises which provide for reward accommodation falling within subsection (1)(a) or (aa) of that section, and

(b) the arrangements are for the provision of such accommodation in those premises.

(1A) Arrangements must not be made by virtue of this section for the provision of accommodation together with nursing or personal care for persons such as are mentioned in section 3(2) of the Care Standards Act 2000 (care homes) unless –

(a) the accommodation is to be provided, under the arrangements, in a care home (within the meaning of that Act) which is managed by the organisation or person in question; and

(b) that organisation or person is registered under Part II of that Act in respect of the home.

. . .

(1C) Subject to subsection (1D) below, no arrangements may be made by virtue of this section for the provision of accommodation together with nursing without the consent of such Primary Care Trust or Health Authority as may be determined in accordance with regulations.

(1D) Subsection (1C) above does not apply to the making by an authority of temporary arrangements for the accommodation of any person as a matter of urgency; but, as soon as practicable after any such temporary arrangements have been made, the authority shall seek the consent required by subsection (1C) above to the making of appropriate arrangements for the accommodation of the person concerned.

(1E) . . .

(2) Any arrangements made by virtue of this section shall provide for the making by the local authority to the other party thereto of payments in respect of the accommodation provided at such rates as may be determined by or under the arrangements and subject to subsection (3a) below the local authority shall recover from each person for whom accommodation is provided under the arrangements the amount of the refund which he is liable to make in accordance with the following provisions of this section.

(3) Subject to subsection (3A) below, a person for whom accommodation is provided under any such arrangements shall, in lieu of being liable to make payment therefor in accordance with section twenty-two of this Act, refund to the local authority any payments made in respect of him under the last foregoing subsection:

Provided that where a person for whom accommodation is provided, or proposed to be provided, under any such arrangements satisfies the local authority that he is unable to make refund at the full rate determined under that subsection, subsections (3) to (5) of section twenty-two of this Act shall, with the necessary modifications, apply as they apply where a person satisfies the local authority of his inability to pay at the standard rate as mentioned in the said subsection (3).

(3A) Where accommodation in any premises is provided for any person under any arrangements made by virtue of this section and the local authority, the person concerned and the voluntary organisation or the other person managing the premises (in this subsection referred to as 'the provider') agree that this section shall apply –

(a) so long as the person concerned makes the payments for which he is liable under paragraph (b) below, he shall not be liable to make any refund under subsection (3) above and the local authority shall not be liable to make any payment under subsection (2) above in respect of the accommodation provided for him;

(b) the person concerned shall be liable to pay to the provider such sums as he would otherwise (under subsection (3) above) be liable to pay by way of refund to the local authority; and

(c) the local authority shall be liable to pay to the provider the difference between the sums paid by virtue of paragraph (b) above and the payments which, but for paragraph (a) above, the authority would be liable to pay under subsection (2) above.

(4) Subsections (5a), (7) and (9) of the said section twenty-two shall, with the necessary modifications, apply for the purposes of the last foregoing subsection as they apply for the purposes of the said section twenty-two.

(4AA) Subsections (2) to (4) shall have effect subject to any regulations under section 15 of the Community Care (Delayed Discharges, etc) Act 2003 (power to require certain community care services and services for carers to be free of charge).

(4A) Section 21(5) of this Act shall have effect as respects accommodation provided under arrangements made by virtue of this section with the substitution for the references to the authority managing the premises of a reference to the authority making the arrangements.

(5) Where in any premises accommodation is being provided under this section in accordance with arrangements made by any local authority, any person authorised in that behalf by the authority may at all reasonable times enter and inspect the premises

(6) [*Repealed*]

(7) In this section the expression 'voluntary organisation' includes any association which is a housing association for the purposes of the Housing Act 1936 and 'exempt body' means an authority or body constituted by an Act of Parliament or incorporated by Royal Charter.

27 [*Repealed*]

28 [*Repealed*]

Welfare arrangements for blind, deaf, dumb and crippled persons, etc

29 (1) A local authority may, with the approval of the Secretary of State, and to such extent as he may direct in relation to persons ordinarily resident in the area of the local authority shall make arrangements for promoting the welfare of persons to whom this section applies, that is to say persons aged eighteen or over who are blind, deaf or dumb or who suffer from mental disorder of any description, and other persons aged eighteen or over who are substantially and permanently handicapped by illness, injury, or congenital deformity or such other disabilities as may be prescribed by the Minister.

(2) [*Repealed*]

(3) [*Repealed*]

(4) Without prejudice to the generality of the provisions of subsection (1) of this section, arrangements may be made thereunder –

(a) for informing persons to whom arrangements under that subsection relate of the services available for them thereunder;

(b) for giving such persons instruction in their own homes or elsewhere in methods of overcoming the effects of their disabilities;

(c) for providing workshops where such persons may be engaged (whether under a contract of service or otherwise) in suitable work, and hostels where persons engaged in the workshops, and other persons to whom arrangements under subsection (1) of this section relate and for whom work or training is being provided in pursuance of the Disabled Persons (Employment) Act 1944 or the Employment and Training Act 1973 may live;

(d) for providing persons to whom arrangements under subsection (1) of this section relate with suitable work (whether under a contract of service or otherwise) in their own homes or elsewhere;

(e) for helping such persons in disposing of the produce of their work;

(f) for providing such persons with recreational facilities in their own homes or elsewhere;

(g) for compiling and maintaining classified registers of the persons to whom arrangements under subsection (1) of this section relate.

(4A) Where accommodation in a hostel is provided under paragraph (c) of subsection (4) of this section –

(a) if the hostel is managed by a local authority, section 22 of this Act shall apply as it applies where accommodation is provided under section 21;

(b) if the accommodation is provided in a hostel managed by a person other than a local authority under arrangements made with that person, subsections (2) to (4A) of section 26 of this Act shall apply as they apply where accommodation is provided under arrangements made by virtue of that section; and

(c) sections 32 and 43 of this Act shall apply as they apply where accommodation is provided under sections 21 to 26;

and in this subsection references to 'accommodation' include references to board and other services, amenities and requisites provided in connection with the accommodation, except where in the opinion of the authority managing the premises or, in the case mentioned in paragraph (b) above, the authority making the arrangements their provision is unnecessary.

(5) [*Repealed*]

(6) Nothing in the foregoing provisions of this section shall authorise or require –

(a) the payment of money to persons to whom this section applies, other than persons for whom work is provided under arrangements made by virtue of paragraph (c) or paragraph (d) of subsection (4) of this section or who are engaged in work which they are enabled to perform in consequence of anything done in pursuance of arrangements made under this section; or

(b) the provision of any accommodation or services required to be provided under the National Health Service Act 1977.

(7) A person engaged in work in a workshop provided under paragraph (c) of subsection (4) of this section, or a person in receipt of a superannuation allowance granted on his retirement from engagement in any such workshop, shall be deemed for the purposes of this Act to continue to be ordinarily resident in the area in which he was ordinarily resident immediately before he was accepted for work in that workshop; and for the purposes of this subsection a course of training in such workshop shall be deemed to be work in that workshop.

Voluntary organisations for disabled persons' welfare

30 (1) A local authority may, in accordance with arrangements made under section 29 of this Act, employ as their agent for the purposes of that section [any voluntary organisation or any person carrying on, professionally or by way of trade or business, activities which consist of or include the provision of services for any of the persons to whom section 29 above applies, being an organisation or person appearing to the authority to be capable of providing the service to which the arrangements apply.

(2) [*Repealed*]

(3) [*Repealed*]

Research

30A   Without prejudice to any powers conferred on them by any other Act, –

    (a) the Secretary of State may promote research into any matter relating to the functions of local authorities under this Part of this Act, and, in particular, may participate with or assist other persons in conducting such research; and

    (b) a local authority may conduct or assist other persons in conducting research into any matter relating to the functions of local authorities under this Part of this Act.

31   [*Repealed*]

FINANCIAL ADJUSTMENTS BETWEEN LOCAL AUTHORITIES
Adjustments between authority providing accommodation, etc, and authority of area of residence

32 (1) Any expenditure which apart from this section would fall to be borne by a local authority –

    (a) in the provision under this Part of this Act of accommodation for a person ordinarily resident in the area of another local authority, or

    (b) in the provision under section twenty-nine of this Act of services for a person ordinarily so resident, or

    (c) in providing under paragraph (a) of subsection (7) of section twenty-one of this Act for the conveyance of a person ordinarily resident as aforesaid,

shall be recoverable from the said other local authority, and in this subsection any reference to another local authority includes a reference to a local authority in Scotland.

  (2) For the purposes of paragraph (a) of the last foregoing subsection it shall be assumed that the expenditure incurred by a local authority in providing accommodation for any person is, as respects accommodation provided in premises managed by a local authority, at the rate for the time being fixed for that accommodation under subsection (2) of section twenty-two of this Act, and, as respects accommodation provided pursuant to an arrangement made under section twenty-six of this Act, at the rate referred to in subsection (2) of that section.

  (3) Any question arising under this Part of this Act as to the ordinary residence of a person shall be determined by the Minister.

LOCAL AND CENTRAL AUTHORITIES
Local Authorities for purposes of Part III

33 (1) In this Part of this Act the expression 'local authority' means a council which is a local authority for the purposes of the Local Authority Social Services Act 1970 in England or Wales, and a council constituted under section 2 of the Local Government etc (Scotland) Act 1994 in Scotland.

  (2) [*Repealed*]

HEALTH SERVICES AND PUBLIC HEALTH ACT 1968 s45
Promotion, by local authorities, of the welfare of old people

45 (1) A local authority may with the approval of the Secretary of State, and to such extent as he may direct shall, make arrangements for promoting the welfare of old people.

(2) [*Repealed*]

(3) A local authority may employ as their agent for the purposes of this section any voluntary organisation or any person carrying on, professionally or by way of trade or business, activities which consist of or include the provision of services for old people, being an organisation or person appearing to the authority to be capable of promoting the welfare of old people.

(4) No arrangements under this section shall provide –

   (a) for the payment of money to old people except in so far as the arrangements may provide for the remuneration of old people engaged in suitable work in accordance with the arrangements;

   (b) for making available any accommodation or services required to be provided under the National Health Service Act 1977.

(4a) No arrangements under this section may be given effect to in relation to a person to whom section 115 of the Immigration and Asylum Act 1999 (exclusion from benefits) applies solely –

   (a) because he is destitute; or

   (b) because of the physical effects, or anticipated physical effects, of his being destitute.

(4b) Subsections (3) and (5) to (8) of section 95 of the Immigration and Asylum Act 1999, and paragraph 2 of Schedule 8 to that Act, apply for the purposes of subsection (4a) as they apply for the purposes of that section, but for the references in subsections (5) and (7) of that section and in that paragraph to the Secretary of State substitute references to a local authority.

[*section continues*]

CHRONICALLY SICK AND DISABLED PERSONS ACT 1970 ss1 and 2
Information as to need for and existence of welfare services

1 (1) It shall be the duty of every local authority having functions under section 29 of the National Assistance Act 1948 to inform themselves of the number of persons to whom that section applies within their area and of the need for the making by the authority of arrangements under that section for such persons.

(2) Every such local authority –
(a) shall cause to be published from time to time at such times and in such manner as they consider appropriate general information as to the services provided under arrangements made by the authority under the said section 29 which are for the time being available in the area; and
(b) shall ensure that any such person as aforesaid who uses any of those services is informed of any other service provided by the authority (whether under any such arrangements or not) which in the opinion of the authority is relevant to his needs and of any service provided by any other authority or organisation which in the opinion of the authority is so relevant and of which particulars are in the authorities' possession.

Provision of welfare services

2 (1) Where a local authority having functions under s29 National Assistance Act 1948 are satisfied in the case of any person to whom that section applies who is ordinarily resident in their area that it is necessary in order to meet the needs of that person for that authority to make arrangements for all or any of the following matters, namely –
(a) the provision of practical assistance for that person in his home;
(b) the provision for that person of, or assistance to that person in obtaining, wireless, television, library or similar recreational facilities;
(c) the provision for that person of lectures, games, outings or other recreational facilities outside his home or assistance to that person in taking advantage of educational facilities available to him;
(d) the provision for that person of facilities for, or assistance in, travelling to and from his home for the purpose of participating in any services provided under arrangements made by the authority under the said section 29 or, with the approval of the authority, in any services provided otherwise than as aforesaid which are similar to services which could be provided under such arrangements;
(e) the provision of assistance for that person in arranging for the carrying out of any works of adaptation in his home or the provision of any additional facilities designed to secure his greater safety, comfort or convenience;
(f) facilitating the taking of holidays by that person, whether at holiday homes or otherwise and whether provided under arrangements made by the authority or otherwise;
(g) the provision of meals for that person whether in his home or elsewhere;
(h) the provision for that person of, or assistance to that person in obtaining, a telephone and any special equipment necessary to enable him to use a telephone,
then, subject to the provisions of section 7(1) of the Local Authority Social Services Act 1970 (which requires local authorities in the exercise of certain functions, including functions under the said section 29, to act under the general guidance of the Secretary of State) and to the provisions of section 7A of that Act (which requires local authorities to exercise their social services functions in accordance with directions given by the Secretary of State) it shall be the duty of that Authority to make those arrangements in exercise of their functions under the said section 29.

LOCAL AUTHORITY SOCIAL SERVICES ACT 1970 ss6, 7, 7A–E
The director of social services

6 (1) A local authority shall appoint an officer, to be known as the director of social services, for the purposes of their social services functions.

(2) Two or more local authorities may, if they consider that the same person can efficiently discharge, for both or all of them, the functions of director of social services for both or all of those authorities, concur in the appointment of a person as director of social services for both or all of those authorities.

(3), (4) & (5) [*Repealed*]

(6) A local authority which has appointed, or concurred in the appointment of, a director of social services, shall secure the provision of adequate staff for assisting him in the exercise of his functions.

Local authorities to exercise social services functions under guidance of Secretary of State

7 (1) Local authorities shall, in the exercise of their social services functions, including the exercise of any discretion conferred by any relevant enactment, act under the general guidance of the Secretary of State.

Directions by the Secretary of State as to exercise of social services functions

7A(1) Without prejudice to section 7 of this Act, every local authority shall exercise their social services functions in accordance with such directions as may be given to them under this section by the Secretary of State.

(2) Directions under this section –

(a) shall be given in writing; and

(b) may be given to a particular authority, or to authorities of a particular class, or to authorities generally.

Complaints procedure

7B(1) The Secretary of State may by order require local authorities to establish a procedure for considering any representations (including any complaints) which are made to them by a qualifying individual, or anyone acting on his behalf, in relation to the discharge of, or any failure to discharge, any of their social services functions in respect of that individual.

(2) In relation to a particular local authority, an individual is a qualifying individual for the purposes of subsection (1) above if –

(a) the authority have a power or a duty to provide, or to secure the provision of, a service for him; and

(b) his need or possible need for such a service has (by whatever means) come to the attention of the authority or if he is in receipt of payment from the authority under the Community Care (Direct Payments) Act 1996.

(3) A local authority shall comply with any directions given by the Secretary of State as to the procedure to be adopted in considering representations made as mentioned in subsection (1) above and as to the taking of such action as may be necessary in consequence of such representations.

(4) Local authorities shall give such publicity to any procedure established pursuant to this section as they consider appropriate.

Inquiries

7C(1) The Secretary of State may cause an inquiry to be held in any case where, whether on representations made to him or otherwise, he considers it advisable to do so in connection with the exercise by any local authority of any of their social services functions (except in so far as those functions relate to persons under the age of eighteen).

(2) Subsections (2) to (5) of section 250 of the Local Government Act 1972 (powers in relation to local inquiries) shall apply in relation to an inquiry under this section as they apply in relation to an inquiry under that section.

Default powers of Secretary of State as respects social services functions of local authorities

7D(1) If the Secretary of State is satisfied that any local authority have failed, without reasonable excuse, to comply with any of their duties which are social services functions (other than a duty imposed by or under the Children Act 1989), he may make an order declaring that authority to be in default with respect to the duty in question.

(2) An order under subsection (1) may contain such directions for the purpose of ensuring that the duty is complied with within such period as may be specified in the order as appear to the Secretary of State to be necessary.

(3) Any such direction shall, on the application of the Secretary of State, be enforceable by mandamus.

Grants to local authorities in respect of social services for the mentally ill

7E The Secretary of State may, with the approval of the Treasury, make grants out of money provided by Parliament towards any expenses of local authorities incurred in connection with the exercise of their social services functions in relation to persons suffering from mental illness.

NATIONAL HEALTH SERVICE ACT 1977 ss1–3, 21, 22, 28, Sch 8 paras 1–3

Secretary of State's duty as to health service

1 (1) It is the Secretary of State's duty to continue the promotion in England and Wales of a comprehensive health service designed to secure improvement –

   (a) in the physical and mental health of the people of those countries; and

   (b) in the prevention, diagnosis and treatment of illness,

   and for that purpose to provide or secure the effective provision of services in accordance with this Act.

   (2) The services so provided shall be free of charge except in so far as the making and recovery of charges is expressly provided for by or under any enactment, whenever passed.

Secretary of State's general power as to services

2   Without prejudice to the Secretary of state's powers apart from this section, he has power –

   (a) to provide such services as he considers appropriate for the purpose of discharging any duty imposed on him by this Act; and

   (b) to do any other thing whatsoever which is calculated to facilitate, or is conducive or incidental to, the discharge of such a duty.

   This section is subject to section 3(3) below.

Services generally

3 (1) It is the Secretary of State's duty to provide throughout England and Wales, to such extent as he considers necessary to meet all reasonable requirements –

   (a) hospital accommodation;

   (b) other accommodation for the purpose of any service provided under this Act;

   (c) medical, dental, nursing and ambulance services;

   (d) such other facilities for the care of expectant mothers and young children as he considers are appropriate as part of the health service;

   (e) such facilities for the prevention of illness, the care of persons suffering from illness and the after care of persons who have suffered from illness as he considers are appropriate as part of the health service;

   (f) such other services as are required for the diagnosis and treatment of illness.

   (1A) The Secretary of State may provide or secure the provision of anything mentioned in subsection (1) above outside England and Wales.

   (2) Where any hospital provided by the Secretary of State in accordance with this Act was a voluntary hospital transferred by virtue of the National Health Service Act 1946, and –

   (a) the character and associations of that hospital before its transfer were such as to link it with a particular religious denomination, then

   (b) regard shall be had in the general administration of the hospital to the preservation of that character and those associations.

   (3) Nothing in section 2 above or in this section affects the provisions of Part II of this Act (which relates to arrangements with practitioners for the provision of medical, dental, ophthalmic and pharmaceutical services).

   (4) For the purposes of the duty in subsection (1), services provided under –

   (a) section 16CA(2) or 16CC(2) below, or

   (b) a general medical services contract or a general dental services contract,

   are to be regarded as provided by the Secretary of State.

CO-OPERATION AND ASSISTANCE
Local social services authorities

21 (1) Subject to paragraphs (d) and (e) of section 3(1) above, the services described in Schedule 8 to this Act in relation to –

(a) care of mothers,

(b) prevention, care and after care,

(c) home help and laundry facilities,

are functions exercisable by local social services authorities, and that Schedule has effect accordingly.

(2) A local social services authority who provide premises, furniture or equipment for any of the purposes of this Act may permit the use of the premises, furniture or equipment –

(a) by any other social services authority, or

(b) by any of the bodies constituted under this Act, or

(c) by a local education authority.

This permission may be on such terms (including terms with respect to the services of any staff employed by the authority giving permission) as may be agreed.

(3) A local social services authority may provide (or improve or furnish) residential accommodation –

(a) for officers employed by them for the purposes of any of their functions as a local social services authority, or

(b) for officers employed by a voluntary organisation for the purposes of any services provided under this section and Schedule 8.

Co-operation between health authorities and local authorities

22 (1) In exercising their respective functions NHS bodies (on the one hand) and local authorities (on the other) shall co-operate with one another in order to secure and advance the health and welfare of the people of England and Wales.

(1A) In this section 'NHS body' means –

(za) a Strategic Health Authority;

(a) a Health Authority;

(b) a Special Health Authority;

(c) a Primary Care Trust;

(cc) a Local Health Board;

(d) an NHS trust;

. . .

Supply of goods and services by local authorities

28 (1) In the Local Authorities (Goods and Services) Act 1970 the expression 'public body' includes any Strategic Health Authority, Health Authority and Special Health Authority, Primary Care Trust or Local Health Board and so far as relates to his functions under this Act includes the Secretary of State.

(2) The provisions of subsection (1) above have effect as if made by an order under section 1(5) of that Act of 1970, and accordingly may be varied or revoked by such an order.

(3) Every local authority shall make available to Strategic Health Authorities, Health Authorities, Special Health Authorities, Primary Care Trusts, Local Health Boards and NHS trusts acting in the area of the local authority the services of persons employed by the local authority for the purposes of the local authority's functions under the Local Authorities Social Services Act 1970 so far as is reasonably necessary and practicable to enable Strategic Health Authorities, Health Authorities, Special Health Authorities, Primary Care Trusts, Local Health Boards and NHS trusts

to discharge their functions under this Act and the National Health Service and Community Care Act 1990.

(4) . . .

SCHEDULE 8: LOCAL SERVICES AUTHORITIES
Care of mothers and young children

1 (1) A local social services authority may, with the Secretary of State's approval, and to such extent as he may direct shall, make arrangements for the care of expectant and nursing mothers (other than for the provision of residential accommodation for them).

Prevention, care and after-care

2 (1) A local social services authority may, with the Secretary of State's approval, and to such extent as he may direct shall, make arrangements for the purpose of the prevention of illness and for the care of persons suffering from illness and for the after-care of persons who have been suffering and in particular for –

(a) [*Repealed*]

(b) the provision for persons whose care is undertaken with a view to preventing them from becoming ill, persons suffering from illness and persons who have been so suffering, of centres or other facilities for training them or keeping them suitably occupied and the equipment and maintenance of such centres;

(c) the provision, for the benefit of such persons as are mentioned in paragraph (b) above, of ancillary or supplemental services; and

(d) for the exercise of the functions of the Authority in respect of persons suffering from mental disorder who are received into the guardianship under Part II or III of the Mental Health Act 1983 (whether the guardianship of the local social services authority or of other persons).

Such an authority shall neither have the power nor be subject to a duty to make under this paragraph arrangements to provide facilities for any of the purposes mentioned in section 15(1) of the Disabled Persons (Employment) Act 1944.

(2) No arrangements under this paragraph shall provide for the payment of money to persons for whose benefit they are made except –

(a) in so far as they may provide for the remuneration of such persons engaged in suitable work in accordance with the arrangements, of such amounts as the local social services authority think fit in respect of their occasional personal expenses where it appears to that authority that no such payment would otherwise be made.

(2A) No arrangements under this paragraph may be given effect to in relation to a person to whom section 115 of the Immigration and Asylum Act 1999 (exclusion from benefits) applies solely –

(a) because he is destitute; or

(b) because of the physical effects, or anticipated physical effects, of his being destitute.

(2B) Subsections (3) and (5) to (8) of section 95 of the Immigration and Asylum Act 1999, and paragraph 2 of Schedule 8 to that Act, apply for the purposes of subsection (2a) as they apply for the purposes of that section, but for the references in subsections (5) and (7) of that section and in that paragraph to the Secretary of State substitute references to a local social services authority.

(3) The Secretary of State may make regulations as to the conduct of premises in which, in pursuance of arrangements made under this paragraph, are provided for persons whose care is undertaken with a view to preventing them from becoming sufferers from mental disorder within the meaning of that Act of 1983 or who are, or have been, so suffering, facilities for training them or keeping them suitably occupied.

(4A) This paragraph does not apply in relation to persons under the age of 18.

(4AA) No authority is authorised or may be required under this paragraph to provide residential accommodation for any person.

Home help and laundry facilities

3 (1) It is the duty of every local social services authority to provide on such a scale as is adequate for the needs of their area, or to arrange for the provision on such a scale as is so adequate, of home help for households where such help is required owing to the presence of a person who is suffering from illness, lying-in, an expectant mother, aged, handicapped as a result of having suffered from illness or by congenital deformity,and every such authority has power to provide or arrange for the provision of laundry facilities for households for which home help is being, or can be, provided under this sub-paragraph.

MENTAL HEALTH ACT 1983 s117
After-care

117 (1) This section applies to persons who are detained under section 3 above, or admitted to a hospital in pursuance of a hospital order made under section 37 above, or transferred to a hospital in pursuance of a hospital direction made under section 45A above or a transfer direction made under section 47 or 48 above, and then cease to be detained and (whether or not immediately after so ceasing) leave hospital.

(2) It shall be the duty of the Primary Care Trust or Health Authority and of the local social services authority to provide, in co-operation with relevant voluntary agencies, after-care services for any person to whom this section applies until such time as the Primary Care Trust or Health Authority and the local social services authority are satisfied that the person concerned is no longer in need of such services but they shall not be so satisfied in the case of a patient who is subject to after-care under supervision at any time while he so remains subject.

(2A) It shall be the duty of the Primary Care Trust or Health Authority to secure that at all times while a patient is subject to after-care under supervision –

(a) a person who is a registered medical practitioner approved for the purposes of section 12 above by the Secretary of State as having special experience in the diagnosis or treatment of mental disorder is in charge of the medical treatment provided for the patient as part of the after-care services provided for him under this section; and

(b) a person professionally concerned with any of the after-care services so provided is supervising him with a view to securing that he receives the after-care services so provided.

(2B) Section 32 above shall apply for the purposes of this section as it applies for the purposes of Part II of this Act.

(3) In this section 'the Primary Care Trust or Health Authority' means the Primary Care Trust or Health Authority and 'the local social services authority' means the local social services authority for the area in which the person concerned is resident or to which he is sent on discharge by the hospital in which he was detained.

HEALTH AND SOCIAL SERVICES AND SOCIAL SECURITY ADJUDICATIONS ACT 1983 ss17, 21, 22, 24 and Sch 9 Pt II
Charges for local authority services in England and Wales

17 (1) Subject to subsection (3) below, an authority providing a service to which this section applies may recover such charge (if any) for it as they consider reasonable.

(2) This section applies to services provided under the following enactments –

(a) section 29 of the National Assistance Act 1948 (welfare arrangements for blind, deaf, dumb and crippled persons etc.);

(b) section 45(1) of the Health Services and Public Health Act 1968 (welfare of old people);

(c) Schedule 8 to the National Health Service Act 1977 (care of mothers and young children, prevention of illness and care and after-care and home help and laundry facilities);

(d) section 8 of the Residential Homes Act 1980 (meals and recreation for old people); and

(e) paragraph 1 of Part II of Schedule 9 to this Act other than the provision of services for which payment may be required under section 22 or 26 of the National Assistance Act 1948;

(f) section 2 of the Carers and Disabled Children Act 2000.

(3) If a person –

(a) avails himself of a service to which this section applies, and

(b) satisfies the authority providing the service that his means are insufficient for it to be reasonably practicable for him to pay for the service the amount which he would otherwise be obliged to pay for it,

the authority shall not require him to pay more for it than it appears to them that it is reasonably practicable for him to pay.

(4) Any charge under this section may, without prejudice to any other method of recovery, be recovered summarily as a civil debt.

(5) This section has effect subject to any regulations under section 15 of the Community Care (Delayed Discharges, etc) Act 2003 (power to require certain community care services and services for carers to be free of charge).

Recovery of sums due to local authority where persons in residential accommodation have disposed of assets

21 (1) Subject to the following provisions of this section, where –

(a) a person avails himself of Part III accommodation; and

(b) that person knowingly and with the intention of avoiding charges for the accommodation –

(i) has transferred any asset to which this section applies to some other person or persons not more than six months before the date on which he begins to reside in such accommodation; or

(ii) transfers any such asset to some other person or persons while residing in the accommodation; and

(c) either –

(i) the consideration for the transfer is less than the value of the asset; or

(ii) there is no consideration for the transfer,

the person or persons to whom the asset is transferred by the person availing himself of the accommodation shall be liable to pay to the local authority providing the accommodation or arranging for its provision the difference between the amount assessed as due to be paid for the accommodation by the person availing himself of it and the amount which the local authority receive from him for it.

(2) This section applies to cash and any other asset which falls to be taken into account

for the purpose of assessing under section 22 of the National Assistance Act 1948 the ability to pay for the accommodation of the person availing himself of it.

(3) Subsection 1(1) above shall have effect in relation to a transfer by a person who leaves Part III accommodation and subsequently resumes residence in such accommodation as if the period of six months mentioned in paragraph (b)(i) were a period of six months before the date on which he resumed residence in such accommodation.

(3A) If the Secretary of State so directs, subsection (1) above shall not apply in such cases as may be specified in the direction.

(4) Where a person has transferred an asset to which this section applies to more than one person, the liability of each of the persons to whom it was transferred shall be in proportion to the benefit accruing to him from the transfer.

(5) A person's liability under this section shall not exceed the benefit accruing to him from the transfer.

(6) Subject to subsection (7) below, the value of any asset to which this section applies, other than cash, which has been transferred shall be taken to be the amount of the consideration which would have been realised for it if it had been sold on the open market by a willing seller at the time of the transfer.

(7) For the purpose of calculating the value of an asset under subsection (6) above there shall be deducted from the amount of the consideration –

(a) the amount of any incumbrance on the asset; and

(b) a reasonable amount in respect of the expenses of the sale .

(8) In this Part of this Act 'Part III accommodation' means accommodation provided under sections 21 to 26 of the National Assistance Act 1948, and, in the application of this Part of this Act to Scotland, means accommodation provided under the Social Work (Scotland) Act 1968 or section 7 (functions of local authorities) of the Mental Health (Scotland) Act 1984.

Arrears of contributions charged on interest in land in England and Wales

22 (1) Subject to subsection (2) below, where a person who avails himself of Part III accommodation provided by a local authority in England, Wales or Scotland –

(a) fails to pay any sum assessed as due to be paid by him for the accommodation; and

(b) has a beneficial interest in land in England and Wales,

the local authority may create a charge in their favour on his interest in the land.

(2) In the case of a person who has interests in more than one parcel of land the charge under this section shall be upon his interest in such one of the parcels as the local authority may determine.

(2A) In determining whether to exercise their power under subsection (1) above and in making any determination under subsection (2) above, the local authority shall comply with any directions given to them by the Secretary of State as to the exercise of those functions.

(3) [*Repealed*].

(4) Subject to subsection (5) below, a charge under this section shall be in respect of any amount assessed as due to be paid which is outstanding from time to time.

(5) The charge on the interest of an equitable joint tenant in land shall be in respect of an amount not exceeding the value of the interest that he would enjoy in the land if the joint tenancy were severed but the creation of such a charge shall not sever the joint tenancy.

(6) On the death of an equitable joint tenant in land whose interest in the land is subject to a charge under this section –

(a) if there are surviving joint tenants, their interests in the land; and

(b) if the land vests in one person, or one person is entitled to have it vested in him, his interest in it,

shall become subject to a charge for an amount not exceeding the amount of the charge to which the interest of the deceased joint tenant was subject by virtue of subsection (5) above.

(7) A charge under this section shall be created by a declaration in writing made by the local authority.

(8) Any such charge, other than a charge on the interest of an equitable joint tenant in land, shall in the case of unregistered land be a land charge of Class B within the meaning of section 2 of the Land Charges Act 1972 and in the case of registered land be a registrable charge taking effect as a charge by way of legal mortgage.

Interest on sums charged on or secured over interest in land

24 (1) Any sum charged on or secured over an interest in land under this Part of this Act shall bear interest from the day after that on which the person for whom the local authority provided the accommodation dies.

(2) The rate of interest shall be such reasonable rate as the Secretary of State may direct or, if no such direction is given, as the local authority may determine.

Schedule 9, Part II: Meals and recreation for old people

1 A district council or Welsh county council or county borough council shall have power to make such arrangements as they may from time to time determine for providing meals and recreation for old people in their homes or elsewhere and may employ as their agent for the purpose of this paragraph any voluntary organisation whose activities consist in or include the provision of meals or recreation for old people.

2 A district council or Welsh county council or county borough council may assist any such organisation as is referred to in paragraph 1 above to provide meals or recreation for old people –

(a) by contributing to the funds of the organisation;

(b) by permitting them to use premises belonging to the council on such terms as may be agreed; and

(c) by making available furniture, vehicles or equipment (whether by way of gift or loan or otherwise) and the services of any staff who are employed by the council in connection with the premises or other things which they permit the organisation to use.

3 (1) District councils or Welsh county councils or county borough councils shall exercise their functions under this Part of this Schedule (including any discretion conferred on them under it) in accordance with the provisions of any regulations of the Secretary of State made for the purposes of this paragraph; and without prejudice to the generality of this paragraph, regulations under this paragraph –

(a) may provide for conferring on officers of the Secretary of State authorised under the regulations such powers of inspection as may be prescribed in relation to the exercise of functions under this Part of this Schedule by or by arrangement with or on behalf of district councils; and

(b) may make provision with respect to the qualifications of officers employed by district councils for the purposes of this Part of this Schedule or by voluntary organisations acting under arrangements with or on behalf of district councils for those purposes.

(2) The power to make regulations under this paragraph shall be exercisable by statutory instrument which shall be subject to annulment in pursuance of a resolution of either House of Parliament.

DISABLED PERSONS (SERVICES, CONSULTATION AND REPRESENTATION) ACT 1986 ss4, 8 and 16

Services under s2 of the 1970 Act: duty to consider needs of disabled persons

4   When requested to do so by –

(a) a disabled person

(b) by his authorised representative, or

(c) any person who provides care for him in the circumstances mentioned in section 8,

a local authority shall decide whether the needs of the disabled person call for the provision by the authority of any services in accordance with section 2(1) of the 1970 Act (provision for welfare services).

Duty of local authority to take into account abilities of carer

8 (1) Where –

(a) a disabled person is living at home and receiving a substantial amount of care on a regular basis from another person (who is not a person employed to provide such care by any body in the exercise of its functions under any enactment), and

(b) it falls to a local authority to decide whether the disabled person's needs call for the provision by them of any services for him under any of the welfare enactments,

the local authority shall, in deciding that question, have regard to the ability of that other person to continue to provide such care on a regular basis.

(2) Where that other person is unable to communicate, or (as the case may be) be communicated with, orally or in writing (or in each of those ways) by reason of any mental or physical incapacity, the local authority shall provide such services as, in their opinion, are necessary to ensure that any such incapacity does not prevent the authority from being properly informed as to the ability of that person to continue to provide care as mentioned in subsection (1).

(3) Section 3(7) shall apply for the purposes of subsection (2) above as it applies for the purposes of section 3(6), but as if any reference to the disabled person or his authorised representative were a reference to the person mentioned in subsection (2).

Interpretation

16 (1) In this Act –

'the 1948 Act' means the National Assistance Act 1948;

'the 1968 Act' means the Social Work (Scotland) Act 1968;

'the 1970 Act' means the Chronically Sick and Disabled Persons Act 1970;

'the 1977 Act' means the National Health Service Act 1977;

'the 1978 Act' means the National Health Service (Scotland) Act 1978;

'the 1980 Act' means the Education (Scotland) Act 1980;

'the 1983 Act' means the Mental Health Act 1983;

'the 1984 Act' means the Mental Health (Scotland) Act 1984;

'authorised representative' has the meaning given by section 1(1) above;

'disabled person'—

(a) in relation to England and Wales, means –

(i) in the case of a person aged eighteen or over, a person to whom section 29 of the 1948 Act applies, and

(ii) in the case of a person under the age of eighteen, a person who is disabled within the meaning of Part III of the Children Act 1989; and

(b) in relation to Scotland, means –

(i) in the case of a person aged eighteen or over, one chronically sick or disabled or one suffering from mental disorder (being, in either case, a relevant person for the purposes of section 12 of the Social Work (Scotland) Act 1968); and

(ii) in any other case, a disabled child ('disabled child' being construed in accordance with Chapter 1 of Part II of the Children (Scotland) Act 1995);

'guardian' (except in section 1(6)) –

(a), (b)

'Health Authority' means a Health Authority established under section 8 of the 1977 Act;

'Health Board' means a Health Board within the meaning of the 1978 Act;

'hospital' –

(a) in relation to England and Wales, means –
  (i) a health service hospital within the meaning of the 1977 Act, or
  (ii) any accommodation provided by any person pursuant to arrangements made under section 23(1) of that Act (voluntary organisations and other bodies) and used as a hospital; and

(b) in relation to Scotland, means a health service hospital within the meaning of the 1978 Act;

'local authority' (except in section 2(7)) –

(a) in relation to England and Wales, means a council which is a local authority for the purposes of the Local Authority Social Services Act 1970 or, so long as an order under section 12 of that Act is in force, the Council of the Isles of Scilly; and

(b) in relation to Scotland, means a council constituted under section 2 of the Local Government, etc (Scotland) Act 1994 on whom functions are imposed by section 1 of the 1968 Act or any of the enactments mentioned in section 5(1B) of that Act;

'mental disorder' –

(a) in relation to England and Wales, has the meaning given by section 1 of the 1983 Act; and

(b) in relation to Scotland, has the meaning given by section 1(2) of the 1984 Act;

'modifications' includes additions, omissions and amendments;

'parent' –

(a) in relation to England and Wales, means, in the case of a child who is illegitimate, his mother, to the exclusion of his father; and

(b) in relation to Scotland, means, in the case of a child whose father is not married to the mother, his mother, to the exclusion of his father;

'parental responsibility' has the same meaning as in the Children Act 1989;

'Primary Care Trust' means a Primary Care Trust established under section 16A of the National Health Service Act 1977;

'services' includes facilities;

'Special Health Authority' means a Special Health Authority established under section 11 of the 1977 Act;

'State hospital' means a State hospital within the meaning of the 1984 Act;

'statutory services' –

(a) in relation to England and Wales, means services under any arrangements which a local authority are required to make by virtue of any of the welfare enactments, and

(b) in relation to Scotland, means services which a local authority find it necessary to provide themselves or by arrangement with another local authority, or with any voluntary or other body, in connection with the performance of the local authority's functions under the welfare enactments;

'Strategic Health Authority' means a Strategic Health Authority established under section 8 of the 1977 Act;

'voluntary organisation' means a body the activities of which are carried on otherwise than for profit, but does not include any public or local authority;

'the welfare enactments' means Part III of the 1948 Act, section 2 of the 1970 Act and –

(a) in relation to England and Wales, Schedule 8 to the 1977 Act and Part III of the Children Act 1989, and

(b) in relation to Scotland, section 27 of the National Health Service (Scotland) Act 1947, the 1968 Act, sections 7 and 8 of the 1984 Act and Chapter 1 of Part II of the Children (Scotland) Act 1995.

(2) In this Act any reference to a child who is looked after by a local authority has the same meaning as in the Children Act 1989.

(2A) In this Act as it applies in relation to Scotland, any reference to a child who is looked after by a local authority shall be construed in accordance with section 17(6) of the Children (Scotland) Act 1995.

CHILDREN ACT 1989 ss17–29
Provision of services for children in need, their families and others

17 (1) It shall be the general duty of every local authority (in addition to the other duties imposed upon them by this Part) –

    (a) to safeguard and promote the welfare of children within their area who are in need; and

    (b) so far as is consistent with that duty to promote the upbringing of such children by their families,

by providing a range and level of services appropriate to those children's needs.

(2) For the purpose principally of facilitating the discharge of their general duty under this section, every local authority shall have the specific duties and powers set out in Part I of Schedule 2.

(3) Any service provided by an authority in the exercise of functions conferred on them by this section may be provided for the family of a particular child in need or for any member of his family, if it is provided with a view to safeguarding or promoting the child's welfare.

(4) The Secretary of State may by order amend any provision of Part I of Schedule 2 or add any further duty or power to those for the tune being mentioned there.

(5) Every local authority –

    (a) shall facilitate the provision by others (including in particular voluntary organisations) of services which the authority have power to provide by virtue of this section, or section 18, 20, 23, 23B to 23D, 24A or 24B; and

    (b) may make such arrangements as they see fit for any person to act on their behalf in the provision of any such service.

(6) The services provided by a local authority in the exercise of functions conferred on them by this section may include providing accommodation and giving assistance in kind or, in exceptional circumstances, in cash.

(7) Assistance may be unconditional or subject to conditions as to the repayment of the assistance or of its value (in whole or in part).

(8) Before giving any assistance or imposing any conditions, a local authority shall have regard to the means of the child concerned and of each of his parents.

(9) No person shall be liable to make any repayment of assistance or of its value at any time when he is in receipt of income support under Part VII of the Social Security Contributions and Benefits Act 1992, of any element of child tax credit other than the family element, of working tax credit or of an income-based jobseeker's allowance.

(10) For the purposes of this Part a child shall be taken to be in need if –

    (a) he is unlikely to achieve or maintain, or to have the opportunity of achieving or maintaining, a reasonable standard of health or development without the provision for him of services by a local authority under this Part;

    (b) his health or development is likely to be significantly impaired, or further impaired, without the provision for him of such services; or

    (c) he is disabled,

and 'family', in relation to such a child, includes any person who has parental responsibility for the child and any other person with whom he has been living.

(11) For the purposes of this Part, a child is disabled if he is blind, deaf or dumb or suffers from mental disorder of any kind or is substantially and permanently handicapped by illness, injury or congenital deformity or such other disability as may be prescribed; and in this Part –

'development' means physical, intellectual, emotional, social or behavioural development; and

'health' means physical or mental health.

(12) The Treasury may by regulations prescribe circumstances in which a person is to be treated for the purposes of this Part (or for such of those purposes as are prescribed) as in receipt of any element of child tax credit other than the family element or of working tax credit.

Direct payments

17A(1) The Secretary of State may by regulations make provision for and in connection with requiring or authorising the responsible authority in the case of a person of a prescribed description who falls within subsection (2) to make, with that person's consent, such payments to him as they may determine in accordance with the regulations in respect of his securing the provision of the service mentioned in that subsection.

(2) A person falls within this subsection if he is –
(a) a person with parental responsibility for a disabled child,
(b) a disabled person with parental responsibility for a child, or
(c) a disabled child aged 16 or 17,
and a local authority ('the responsible authority') have decided for the purposes of section 17 that the child's needs (or, if he is such a disabled child, his needs) call for the provision by them of a service in exercise of functions conferred on them under that section.

(3) Subsections (3) to (5) and (7) of section 57 of the 2001 Act shall apply, with any necessary modifications, in relation to regulations under this section as they apply in relation to regulations under that section.

(4) Regulations under this section shall provide that, where payments are made under the regulations to a person falling within subsection (5) –
(a) the payments shall be made at the rate mentioned in subsection (4)(a) of section 57 of the 2001 Act (as applied by subsection (3)); and
(b) subsection (4)(b) of that section shall not apply.

(5) A person falls within this subsection if he is –
(a) a person falling within subsection (2)(a) or (b) and the child in question is aged 16 or 17, or
(b) a person who is in receipt of income support under Part 7 of the Social Security Contributions and Benefits Act 1992, of any element of child tax credit other than the family element, of working tax credit or of an income-based jobseeker's allowance.

(6) In this section –
'the 2001 Act' means the Health and Social Care Act 2001;
'disabled' in relation to an adult has the same meaning as that given by section 17(11) in relation to a child;
'prescribed' means specified in or determined in accordance with regulations under this section (and has the same meaning in the provisions of the 2001 Act mentioned in subsection (3) as they apply by virtue of that subsection).

Vouchers for persons with parental responsibility for disabled children

17B(1) The Secretary of State may by regulations make provision for the issue by a local authority of vouchers to a person with parental responsibility for a disabled child.

(2) 'Voucher' means a document whereby, if the local authority agrees with the person with parental responsibility that it would help him care for the child if the person with parental responsibility had a break from caring, that person may secure the temporary provision of services for the child under section 17.

(3) The regulations may, in particular, provide –
(a) for the value of a voucher to be expressed in terms of money, or of the delivery of a service for a period of time, or both;

(b) for the person who supplies a service against a voucher, or for the arrangement under which it is supplied, to be approved by the local authority;

(c) for a maximum period during which a service (or a service of a prescribed description) can be provided against a voucher.

Day care for pre-school and other children

18 (1) Every local authority shall provide such day care for children in need within their area who are –

(a) aged five or under; and

(b) not yet attending schools,

as is appropriate.

(2) A local authority may provide day care for children within their area who satisfy the conditions mentioned in subsection (1)(a) and (b) even though they are not in need.

(3) A local authority may provide facilities (including training, advice, guidance and counselling) for those –

(a) caring for children in day care; or

(b) who at any time accompany such children while they are in day care.

(4) In this section 'day care' means any form of care or supervised activity provided for children during the day (whether or not it is provided on a regular basis).

(5) Every local authority shall provide for children in need within their area who are attending any school such care or supervised activities as is appropriate –

(a) outside school hours; or

(b) during school holidays.

(6) A local authority may provide such care or supervised activities for children within their area who are attending any school even though those children are not in need.

(7) In this section 'supervised activity' means an activity supervised by a responsible person.

19 [*Repealed*]

Provision of accommodation for children
Provision of accommodation for children: general

20 (1) Every local authority shall provide accommodation for any child in need within their area who appears to them to require accommodation as a result of –

(a) there being no person who has parental responsibility for him;

(b) his being lost or having been abandoned; or

(c) the person who has been caring for him being prevented (whether or not permanently, and for whatever reason) from providing him with suitable accommodation or care.

(2) Where a local authority provide accommodation under subsection (1) for a child who is ordinarily resident in the area of another local authority, that other local authority may take over the provision of accommodation for the child within –

(a) three months of being notified in writing that the child is being provided with accommodation; or

(b) such other longer period as may be prescribed.

(3) Every local authority shall provide accommodation for any child in need within their area who has reached the age of sixteen and whose welfare the authority consider is likely to be seriously prejudiced if they do not provide him with accommodation.

(4) A local authority may provide accommodation for any child within their area (even though a person who has parental responsibility for him is able to provide him with accommodation) if they consider that to do so would safeguard or promote the child's welfare.

(5) A local authority may provide accommodation for any person who has reached the age of sixteen but is under twenty-one in any community home which takes

children who have reached the age of sixteen if they consider that to do so would safeguard or promote his welfare.

(6) Before providing accommodation under this section, a local authority shall, so far as is reasonably practicable and consistent with the child's welfare –

    (a) ascertain the child's wishes regarding the provision of accommodation; and

    (b) give due consideration (having regard to his age and understanding) to such wishes of the child as they have been able to ascertain.

(7) A local authority may not provide accommodation under this section for any child if any person who –

    (a) has parental responsibility for him; and

    (b) is willing and able to –

        (i) provide accommodation for him; or

        (ii) arrange for accommodation to be provided for him,

objects.

(8) Any person who has parental responsibility for a child may at any time remove the child from accommodation provided by or on behalf of the local authority under this section.

(9) Subsections (7) and (8) do not apply while any person –

    (a) in whose favour a residence order is in force with respect to the child; or

    (aa) who is a special guardian of the child; or

    (b) who has care of the child by virtue of an order made in the exercise of the High Court's inherent jurisdiction with respect to children,

agrees to the child being looked after in accommodation provided by or on behalf of the local authority.

(10) Where there is more than one such person as is mentioned in subsection (9), all of them must agree.

(11) Subsections (7) and (8) do not apply where a child who has reached the age of sixteen agrees to being provided with accommodation under this section.

Provision for accommodation for children in police protection or detention or on remand, etc

21 (1) Every local authority shall make provision for the reception and accommodation of children who are removed or kept away from home under Part V.

(2) Every local authority shall receive, and provide accommodation for, children –

    (a) in police protection whom they are requested to receive under section 46(3)(f);

    (b) whom they are requested to receive under section 38(6) of the Police and Criminal Evidence Act 1984;

    (c) who are –

        (i) on remand under paragraph 7(5) of Schedule 7 to the Powers of Criminal Courts (Sentencing) Act 2000 or section] 23(1) of the Children and Young Persons Act 1969; or

        (ii) the subject of a supervision order imposing a local authority residence requirement under paragraph 5 of Schedule 6 to that Act of 2000,

and with respect to whom they are the designated authority.

(3) Where a child has been –

    (a) removed under Part V; or

    (b) detained under section 38 of the Police and Criminal Evidence Act 1984,

and he is not being provided with accommodation by a local authority or in a hospital vested in the Secretary of State or a Primary Care Trust, or otherwise made available pursuant to arrangements made by a Health Authority or a Primary Care Trust, any reasonable expenses of accommodating him shall be recoverable from the local authority in whose area he is ordinarily resident.

Duties of local authorities in relation to children looked after by them

General duty of local authority in relation to children looked after by them

22 (1) In this Act, any reference to a child who is looked after by a local authority is a reference to a child who is –

(a) in their care; or

(b) provided with accommodation by the authority in the exercise of any functions (in particular those under this Act) which are social services functions within the meaning of the Local Authority Social Services Act 1970, apart from functions under sections 17, 23B and 24B.

(2) In subsection (1) 'accommodation' means accommodation which is provided for a continuous period of more than 24 hours.

(3) It shall be the duty of a local authority looking after any child –

(a) to safeguard and promote his welfare; and

(b) to make such use of services available for children cared for by their own parents as appears to the authority reasonable in his case.

(4) Before making any decision with respect to a child whom they are looking after, or proposing to look after, a local authority shall, so far as is reasonably practicable, ascertain the wishes and feelings of –

(a) the child;

(b) his parents;

(c) any person who is not a parent of his but who has parental responsibility for him; and

(d) any other person whose wishes and feelings the authority consider to be relevant,

regarding the matter to be decided.

(5) In making any such decision a local authority shall give due consideration –

(a) having regard to his age and understanding, to such wishes and feelings of the child as they have been able to ascertain;

(b) to such wishes and feelings of any person mentioned in subsection (4)(b) to (d) as they have been able to ascertain; and

(c) to the child's religious persuasion, racial origin and cultural and linguistic background.

(6) If it appears to a local authority that it is necessary, for the purpose of protecting members of the public from serious injury, to exercise their powers with respect to a child whom they are looking after in a manner which may not be consistent with their duties under this section, they may do so.

(7) If the Secretary of State considers it necessary, for the purpose of protecting members of the public from serious injury, to give directions to a local authority with respect to the exercise of their powers with respect to a child whom they are looking after, he may give such directions to the authority.

(8) Where any such directions are given to an authority they shall comply with them even though doing so is inconsistent with their duties under this section.

Provision of accommodation and maintenance by local authority for children whom they are looking after

23 (1) It shall be the duty of any local authority looking after a child –

(a) when he is in their care, to provide accommodation for him; and

(b) to maintain him in other respects apart from providing accommodation for him.

(2) A local authority shall provide accommodation and maintenance for any child whom they are looking after by –

(a) placing him (subject to subsection (5) and any regulations made by the Secretary of State) with –

      (i) a family;

      (ii) a relative of his; or

      (iii) any other suitable person,

on such terms as to payment by the authority and otherwise as the authority may determine;

(aa) maintaining him in an appropriate children's home; or

(f) making such other arrangements as –

      (i)   seem appropriate to them; and

      (ii) comply with any regulations made by the Secretary of State.

(2A) Where under subsection (2)(aa) a local authority maintains a child in a home provided, equipped and maintained by the Secretary of State under section 82(5), it shall do so on such terms as the Secretary of State may from time to time determine.

(3) Any person with whom a child has been placed under subsection (2)(a) is referred to in this Act as a local authority foster parent unless he falls within subsection (4).

(4) A person falls within this subsection if he is –

(a) a parent of the child;

(b) a person who is not a parent of the child but who has parental responsibility for him; or

(c) where the child is in care and there was a residence order in force with respect to him immediately before the care order was made, a person in whose favour the residence order was made.

(5) Where a child is in the care of a local authority, the authority may only allow him to live with a person who falls within subsection (4) in accordance with regulations made by the Secretary of State.

(5A) For the purposes of subsection (5) a child shall be regarded as living with a person if he stays with that person for a continuous period of more than 24 hours.

(6) Subject to any regulations made by the Secretary of State for the purposes of this subsection, any local authority looking after a child shall make arrangements to enable him to live with –

(a) a person falling within subsection (4); or

(b) a relative, friend or other person connected with him,

unless that would not be reasonably practicable or consistent with his welfare.

(7) Where a local authority provide accommodation for a child whom they are looking after, they shall, subject to the provisions of this Part and so far as is reasonably practicable and consistent with his welfare, secure that –

(a) the accommodation is near his home; and

(b) where the authority are also providing accommodation for a sibling of his, they are accommodated together.

(8) Where a local authority provide accommodation for a child whom they are looking after and who is disabled, they shall, so far as is reasonably practicable, secure that the accommodation is not unsuitable to his particular needs.

(9) Part II of Schedule 2 shall have effect for the purposes of making further provision as to children looked after by local authorities and in particular as to the regulations that may be made under subsections (2)(a) and (f) and (5).

(10) In this Act –

'appropriate children's home' means a children's home in respect of which a person is registered under Part II of the Care Standards Act 2000; and

'children's home' has the same meaning as in that Act.

The responsible authority and relevant children

23A(1) The responsible local authority shall have the functions set out in section 23B in respect of a relevant child.

(2) In subsection (1) 'relevant child' means (subject to subsection (3)) a child who –
  (a) is not being looked after by any local authority;
  (b) was, before last ceasing to be looked after, an eligible child for the purposes of paragraph 19B of Schedule 2; and
  (c) is aged sixteen or seventeen.
(3) The Secretary of State may prescribe –
  (a) additional categories of relevant children; and
  (b) categories of children who are not to be relevant children despite falling within subsection (2).
(4) In subsection (1) the 'responsible local authority' is the one which last looked after the child.
(5) If under subsection (3)(a) the Secretary of State prescribes a category of relevant children which includes children who do not fall within subsection (2)(b) (for example, because they were being looked after by a local authority in Scotland), he may in the regulations also provide for which local authority is to be the responsible local authority for those children.

Additional functions of the responsible authority in respect of relevant children

23B(1) It is the duty of each local authority to take reasonable steps to keep in touch with a relevant child for whom they are the responsible authority, whether he is within their area or not.
  (2) It is the duty of each local authority to appoint a personal adviser for each relevant child (if they have not already done so under paragraph 19C of Schedule 2).
  (3) It is the duty of each local authority, in relation to any relevant child who does not already have a pathway plan prepared for the purposes of paragraph 19B of Schedule 2 –
    (a) to carry out an assessment of his needs with a view to determining what advice, assistance and support it would be appropriate for them to provide him under this Part; and
    (b) to prepare a pathway plan for him.
  (4) The local authority may carry out such an assessment at the same time as any assessment of his needs is made under any enactment referred to in sub-paragraphs (a) to (c) of paragraph 3 of Schedule 2, or under any other enactment.
  (5) The Secretary of State may by regulations make provision as to assessments for the purposes of subsection (3).
  (6) The regulations may in particular make provision about –
    (a) who is to be consulted in relation to an assessment;
    (b) the way in which an assessment is to be carried out, by whom and when;
    (c) the recording of the results of an assessment;
    (d) the considerations to which the local authority are to have regard in carrying out an assessment.
  (7) The authority shall keep the pathway plan under regular review.
  (8) The responsible local authority shall safeguard and promote the child's welfare and, unless they are satisfied that his welfare does not require it, support him by –
    (a) maintaining him;
    (b) providing him with or maintaining him in suitable accommodation; and
    (c) providing support of such other descriptions as may be prescribed.
  (9) Support under subsection (8) may be in cash.
  (10) The Secretary of State may by regulations make provision about the meaning of 'suitable accommodation' and in particular about the suitability of landlords or other providers of accommodation.

(11) If the local authority have lost touch with a relevant child, despite taking reasonable steps to keep in touch, they must without delay –
   (a) consider how to re-establish contact; and
   (b) take reasonable steps to do so,
and while the child is still a relevant child must continue to take such steps until they succeed.

(12) Subsections (7) to (9) of section 17 apply in relation to support given under this section as they apply in relation to assistance given under that section.

(13) Subsections (4) and (5) of section 22 apply in relation to any decision by a local authority for the purposes of this section as they apply in relation to the decisions referred to in that section.

Continuing functions in respect of former relevant children

23C(1) Each local authority shall have the duties provided for in this section towards –
   (a) a person who has been a relevant child for the purposes of section 23A (and would be one if he were under eighteen), and in relation to whom they were the last responsible authority; and
   (b) a person who was being looked after by them when he attained the age of eighteen, and immediately before ceasing to be looked after was an eligible child,
and in this section such a person is referred to as a 'former relevant child'.

(2) It is the duty of the local authority to take reasonable steps –
   (a) to keep in touch with a former relevant child whether he is within their area or not; and
   (b) if they lose touch with him, to re-establish contact.

(3) It is the duty of the local authority –
   (a) to continue the appointment of a personal adviser for a former relevant child; and
   (b) to continue to keep his pathway plan under regular review.

(4) It is the duty of the local authority to give a former relevant child –
   (a) assistance of the kind referred to in section 24B(1), to the extent that his welfare requires it;
   (b) assistance of the kind referred to in section 24B(2), to the extent that his welfare and his educational or training needs require it;
   (c) other assistance, to the extent that his welfare requires it.

(5) The assistance given under subsection (4)(c) may be in kind or, in exceptional circumstances, in cash.

(6) Subject to subsection (7), the duties set out in subsections (2), (3) and (4) subsist until the former relevant child reaches the age of twenty-one.

(7) If the former relevant child's pathway plan sets out a programme of education or training which extends beyond his twenty-first birthday –
   (a) the duty set out in subsection (4)(b) continues to subsist for so long as the former relevant child continues to pursue that programme; and
   (b) the duties set out in subsections (2) and (3) continue to subsist concurrently with that duty.

(8) For the purposes of subsection (7)(a) there shall be disregarded any interruption in a former relevant child's pursuance of a programme of education or training if the local authority are satisfied that he will resume it as soon as is reasonably practicable.

(9) Section 24B(5) applies in relation to a person being given assistance under subsection (4)(b) as it applies in relation to a person to whom section 24B(3) applies.

(10) Subsections (7) to (9) of section 17 apply in relation to assistance given under this section as they apply in relation to assistance given under that section.

Personal advisers

23D(1) The Secretary of State may by regulations require local authorities to appoint a personal adviser for children or young persons of a prescribed description who have reached the age of sixteen but not the age of twenty-one who are not –

  (a) children who are relevant children for the purposes of section 23A;

  (b) the young persons referred to in section 23C; or

  (c) the children referred to in paragraph 19C of Schedule 2.

  (2) Personal advisers appointed under or by virtue of this Part shall (in addition to any other functions) have such functions as the Secretary of State prescribes.

Pathway plans

23E(1) In this Part, a reference to a 'pathway plan' is to a plan setting out –

  (a) in the case of a plan prepared under paragraph 19B of Schedule 2 –

   (i) the advice, assistance and support which the local authority intend to provide a child under this Part, both while they are looking after him and later; and

   (ii) when they might cease to look after him; and

  (b) in the case of a plan prepared under section 23B, the advice, assistance and support which the local authority intend to provide under this Part,

  and dealing with such other matters (if any) as may be prescribed.

  (2) The Secretary of State may by regulations make provision about pathway plans and their review.

Persons qualifying for advice and assistance

24 (1) In this Part 'a person qualifying for advice and assistance' means a person who –

  (a) is under twenty-one; and

  (b) at any time after reaching the age of sixteen but while still a child was, but is no longer, looked after, accommodated or fostered.

  (2) In subsection (1)(b), 'looked after, accommodated or fostered' means –

  (a) looked after by a local authority;

  (b) accommodated by or on behalf of a voluntary organisation;

  (c) accommodated in a private children's home;

  (d) accommodated for a consecutive period of at least three months –

   (i) by any Health Authority, Special Health Authority, Primary Care Trust or local education authority, or

   (ii) in any care home or independent hospital or in any accommodation provided by a National Health Service trust; or

  (e) privately fostered.

  (3) Subsection (2)(d) applies even if the period of three months mentioned there began before the child reached the age of sixteen.

  (4) In the case of a person qualifying for advice and assistance by virtue of subsection (2)(a), it is the duty of the local authority which last looked after him to take such steps as they think appropriate to contact him at such times as they think appropriate with a view to discharging their functions under sections 24A and 24B.

  (5) In each of sections 24A and 24B, the local authority under the duty or having the power mentioned there ('the relevant authority') is –

  (a) in the case of a person qualifying for advice and assistance by virtue of subsection (2)(a), the local authority which last looked after him; or

  (b) in the case of any other person qualifying for advice and assistance, the local authority within whose area the person is (if he has asked for help of a kind which can be given under section 24A or 24B).

Advice and assistance

24A(1) The relevant authority shall consider whether the conditions in subsection (2) are satisfied in relation to a person qualifying for advice and assistance.

(2) The conditions are that –

(a) he needs help of a kind which they can give under this section or section 24B; and

(b) in the case of a person who was not being looked after by any local authority, they are satisfied that the person by whom he was being looked after does not have the necessary facilities for advising or befriending him.

(3) If the conditions are satisfied –

(a) they shall advise and befriend him if he was being looked after by a local authority or was accommodated by or on behalf of a voluntary organisation; and

(b) in any other case they may do so.

(4) Where as a result of this section a local authority are under a duty, or are empowered, to advise and befriend a person, they may also give him assistance.

(5) The assistance may be in kind [and, in exceptional circumstances, assistance may be given –

(a) by providing accommodation, if in the circumstances assistance may not be given in respect of the accommodation under section 24B, or

(b) in cash.

(6) Subsections (7) to (9) of section 17 apply in relation to assistance given under this section or section 24B as they apply in relation to assistance given under that section.

Employment, education and training

24B(1) The relevant local authority may give assistance to any person who qualifies for advice and assistance by virtue of section 24(2)(a) by contributing to expenses incurred by him in living near the place where he is, or will be, employed or seeking employment.

(2) The relevant local authority may give assistance to a person to whom subsection (3) applies by –

(a) contributing to expenses incurred by the person in question in living near the place where he is, or will be, receiving education or training; or

(b) making a grant to enable him to meet expenses connected with his education or training.

(3) This subsection applies to any person who –

(a) is under twenty-four; and

(b) qualifies for advice and assistance by virtue of section 24(2)(a), or would have done so if he were under twenty-one.

(4) Where a local authority are assisting a person under subsection (2) they may disregard any interruption in his attendance on the course if he resumes it as soon as is reasonably practicable.

(5) Where the local authority are satisfied that a person to whom subsection (3) applies who is in full-time further or higher education needs accommodation during a vacation because his term-time accommodation is not available to him then, they shall give him assistance by –

(a) providing him with suitable accommodation during the vacation; or

(b) paying him enough to enable him to secure such accommodation himself.

(6) The Secretary of State may prescribe the meaning of 'full-time', 'further education', 'higher education' and 'vacation' for the purposes of subsection (5).

Information

24 (1) Where it appears to a local authority that a person –

   (a) with whom they are under a duty to keep in touch under section 23B, 23C or 24; or

   (b) whom they have been advising and befriending under section 24A; or

   (c) to whom they have been giving assistance under section 24B,

proposes to live, or is living, in the area of another local authority, they must inform that other authority.

(2) Where a child who is accommodated –

   (a) by a voluntary organisation or in a private children's home;

   (b) by any Health Authority, Special Health Authority, Primary Care Trust or local education authority; or

   (c) in any care home or independent hospital or any accommodation provided by a National Health Service trust or an NHS foundation trust,

ceases to be so accommodated, after reaching the age of sixteen, the organisation, authority or (as the case may be) person carrying on the home shall inform the local authority within whose area the child proposes to live.

(3) Subsection (2) only applies, by virtue of paragraph (b) or (c), if the accommodation has been provided for a consecutive period of at least three months.

Representations: sections 23A to 24B

24D(1) Every local authority shall establish a procedure for considering representations (including complaints) made to them by –

   (a) a relevant child for the purposes of section 23A or a young person falling within section 23C;

   (b) a person qualifying for advice and assistance; or

   (c) a person falling within section 24B(2),

about the discharge of their functions under this Part in relation to him.

(2) In considering representations under subsection (1), a local authority shall comply with regulations (if any) made by the Secretary of State for the purposes of this subsection.

Secure accommodation

Use of accommodation for restricting liberty

25 (1) Subject to the following provisions of this section, a child who is being looked after by a local authority may not be placed, and, if placed, may not be kept, in accommodation provided for the purpose of restricting liberty ('secure accommodation') unless it appears –

   (a) that –

     (i) he has a history of absconding and is likely to abscond from any other description of accommodation; and

     (ii) if he absconds, he is likely to suffer significant harm; or

   (b) that if he is kept in any other description of accommodation he is likely to injure himself or other persons.

(2) The Secretary of State may by regulations –

   (a) specify a maximum period –

     (i) beyond which a child may not be kept in secure accommodation without the authority of the court; and

     (ii) for which the court may authorise a child to be kept in secure accommodation;

   (b) empower the court from time to time to authorise a child to be kept in secure accommodation for such further period as the regulations may specify; and

   (c) provide that applications to the court under this section shall be made only by local authorities.

(3) It shall be the duty of a court hearing an application under this section to determine whether any relevant criteria for keeping a child in secure accommodation are satisfied in his case.

(4) If a court determines that any such criteria are satisfied, it shall make an order authorising the child to be kept in secure accommodation and specifying the maximum period for which he may be so kept.

(5) On any adjournment of the hearing of an application under this section, a court may make an interim order permitting the child to be kept during the period of the adjournment in secure accommodation.

(6) No court shall exercise the powers conferred by this section in respect of a child who is not legally represented in that court unless, having been informed of his right to apply for representation funded by the Legal Services Commission as part of the Community Legal Service or Criminal Defence Service and having had the opportunity to do so, he refused or failed to apply.

(7) The Secretary of State may by regulations provide that –

   (a) this section shall or shall not apply to any description of children specified in the regulations;

   (b) this section shall have effect in relation to children of a description specified in the regulations subject to such modifications as may be so specified;

   (c) such other provisions as may be so specified shall have effect for the purpose of determining whether a child of a description specified in the regulations may be placed or kept in secure accommodation.

(8) The giving of an authorisation under this section shall not prejudice any power of any court in England and Wales or Scotland to give directions relating to the child to whom the authorisation relates.

(9) This section is subject to section 20(8).

Supplemental
Review of cases and inquiries into representations

26 (1) The Secretary of State may make regulations requiring the case of each child who is being looked after by a local authority to be reviewed in accordance with the provisions of the regulations.

(2) The regulations may, in particular, make provision –

   (a) as to the manner in which each case is to be reviewed;

   (b) as to the considerations to which the local authority are to have regard in reviewing each case;

   (c) as to the time when each case is first to be reviewed and the frequency of subsequent reviews;

   (d) requiring the authority, before conducting any review, to seek the views of –

      (i) the child;

      (ii) his parents;

      (iii) any person who is not a parent of his but who has parental responsibility for him; and

      (iv) any other person whose views the authority consider to be relevant,

     including, in particular, the views of those persons in relation to any particular matter which is to be considered in the course of the review;

   (e) requiring the authority to consider, in the case of a child who is in their care whether an application should be made to discharge the care order;

   (f) requiring the authority to consider, in the case of a child in accommodation provided by the authority, whether the accommodation accords with the requirements of this Part;

   (g) requiring the authority to inform the child, so far as is reasonably practicable, of any steps he may take under this Act;

(h) requiring the authority to make arrangements, including arrangements with such other bodies providing services as it considers appropriate, to implement any decision which they propose to make in the course, or as a result, of the review;

(i) requiring the authority to notify details of the result of the review and of any decision taken by them in consequence of the review to –

   (i) the child;

   (ii) his parents;

   (iii) any person who is not a parent of his but who has parental responsibility for him; and

   (iv) any other person whom they consider ought to be notified;

(j) requiring the authority to monitor the arrangements which they have made with a view to ensuring that they comply with the regulations;

(3) Every local authority shall establish a procedure for considering any representations (including any complaint) made to them by –

   (a) any child who is being looked after by them or who is not being looked after by them but is in need;

   (b) a parent of his;

   (c) any person who is not a parent of his but who has parental responsibility for him;

   (d) any local authority foster parent;

   (e) such other person as the authority consider has a sufficient interest in the child's welfare to warrant his representations being considered by them,

about the discharge by the authority of any of their functions under this Part in relation to the child.

(3C) The duty under subsection (3) extends to any representations (including complaints) which are made to the authority by –

   (a) a child with respect to whom a special guardianship order is in force,

   (b) a special guardian or a parent of such a child,

   (c) any other person the authority consider has a sufficient interest in the welfare of such a child to warrant his representations being considered by them, or

   (d) any person who has applied for an assessment under section 14F(3) or (4),

   about the discharge by the authority of such functions under section 14F as may be specified by the Secretary of State in regulations.

(4) The procedure shall ensure that at least one person who is not a member or officer of the authority takes part in –

   (a) the consideration; and

   (b) any discussions which are held by the authority about the action (if any) to be taken in relation to the child in the light of the consideration,

(5) In carrying out any consideration of representations under this section a local authority shall comply with any regulations made by the Secretary of State for the purpose of regulating the procedure to be followed.

(6) The Secretary of State may make regulations requiring local authorities to monitor the arrangements that they have made with a view to ensuring that they comply with any regulations made for the purposes of subsection (5).

(7) Where any representation has been considered under the procedure established by a local authority under this section, the authority shall –

   (a) have due regard to the findings of those considering the representation; and

   (b) take such steps as are reasonably practicable to notify (in writing) –

      (i) the person making the representation;

      (ii) the child (if the authority consider that he has sufficient understanding); and

(iii) such other persons (if any) as appear to the authority to be likely to be affected,

of the authority's decision in the matter and their reasons for taking that decision and of any action which they have taken, or propose to take.

(8) Every local authority shall give such publicity to their procedure for considering representations under this section as they consider appropriate.

Representations: further consideration

26ZA(1) The Secretary of State may by regulations make provision for the further consideration of representations which have been considered by a local authority in England under section 24D or section 26.

(2) The regulations may in particular make provision –

(a) for the further consideration of a representation by the Commission for Social Care Inspection ('the CSCI');

(b) for a representation to be referred by the CSCI for further consideration by an independent panel established under the regulations;

(c) about the procedure to be followed on the further consideration of a representation;

(d) for the making of recommendations about the action to be taken as the result of a representation;

(e) about the making of reports about a representation;

(f) about the action to be taken by the local authority concerned as a result of the further consideration of a representation;

(g) for a representation to be referred by the CSCI back to the local authority concerned for reconsideration by the authority;

(h) for a representation or any matter raised by the representation to be referred by the CSCI –

(i) to a Local Commissioner in England for him to consider whether to investigate the representation or matter under Part 3 of the Local Government Act 1974 as if it were a complaint duly made under section 26 of that Act; or

(ii) to any other person or body for him or it to consider whether to take any action otherwise than under the regulations.

(3) The regulations may require –

(a) the making of a payment, in relation to the further consideration of a representation under this section, by any local authority in respect of whose functions the representation is made;

(b) any such payment to be –

(i) made to such person or body as may be specified in the regulations;

(ii) of such amount as may be specified in, or calculated or determined under, the regulations;

(c) an independent panel to review the amount chargeable under paragraph (a) in any particular case and, if the panel thinks fit, to substitute a lesser amount.

(4) The regulations may also –

(a) provide for different parts or aspects of a representation to be treated differently;

(b) require the production of information or documents in order to enable a representation to be properly considered;

(c) authorise the disclosure of information or documents relevant to a representation –

(i) to a person or body who is further considering a representation under the regulations; or

(ii) to a Local Commissioner in England (when a representation is referred to him under the regulations);

and any such disclosure may be authorised notwithstanding any rule of common law that would otherwise prohibit or restrict the disclosure.

(5) In this section, 'Local Commissioner in England' means a Local Commissioner under Part 3 of the Local Government Act 1974 (c 7), who is a member of the Commission for Local Administration in England.

Representations: further consideration (Wales)

26ZB (1) The Secretary of State may by regulations make provision for the further consideration of representations which have been considered by a local authority in Wales under section 24D or section 26.

(2) The regulations may in particular make provision –

   (a) for the further consideration of a representation by an independent panel established under the regulations;

   (b) about the procedure to be followed on the further consideration of a representation;

   (c) for the making of recommendations about the action to be taken as the result of a representation;

   (d) about the making of reports about a representation;

   (e) about the action to be taken by the local authority concerned as a result of the further consideration of a representation;

   (f) for a representation to be referred back to the local authority concerned for reconsideration by the authority.

(3) The regulations may require –

   (a) the making of a payment, in relation to the further consideration of a representation under this section, by any local authority in respect of whose functions the representation is made;

   (b) any such payment to be –

      (i) made to such person or body as may be specified in the regulations;

      (ii) of such amount as may be specified in, or calculated or determined under, the regulations; and

   (c) for an independent panel to review the amount chargeable under paragraph (a) in any particular case and, if the panel thinks fit, to substitute a lesser amount.

(4) The regulations may also –

   (a) provide for different parts or aspects of a representation to be treated differently;

   (b) require the production of information or documents in order to enable a representation to be properly considered;

   (c) authorise the disclosure of information or documents relevant to a representation to a person or body who is further considering a representation under the regulations;

and any such disclosure may be authorised notwithstanding any rule of common law that would otherwise prohibit or restrict the disclosure.

Advocacy services

26A (1) Every local authority shall make arrangements for the provision of assistance to –

   (a) persons who make or intend to make representations under section 24D; and

   (b) children who make or intend to make representations under section 26.

(2) The assistance provided under the arrangements shall include assistance by way of representation.

(3) The arrangements –

   (a) shall secure that a person may not provide assistance if he is a person who is prevented from doing so by regulations made by the Secretary of State; and

   (b) shall comply with any other provision made by the regulations in relation to the arrangements.

(4) The Secretary of State may make regulations requiring local authorities to monitor the steps that they have taken with a view to ensuring that they comply with regulations made for the purposes of subsection (3).

(5) Every local authority shall give such publicity to their arrangements for the provision of assistance under this section as they consider appropriate.

Co-operation between authorities

27 (1) Where it appears to a local authority that any authority . . . mentioned in subsection (3) could, by taking any specified action, help in the exercise of any of their functions under this Part, they may request the help of that other authority . . . , specifying the action in question.

(2) An authority whose help is so requested shall comply with the request if it is compatible with their own statutory or other duties and obligations and does not unduly prejudice the discharge of any of their functions.

(3) The authorities are –
   (a) any local authority;
   (b) any local education authority;
   (c) any local housing authority;
   (d) any Health Authority, Special Health Authority, Primary Care Trust or National Health Service trust; and
   (e) any person authorised by the Secretary of State for the purposes of this section.

(4) [Repealed]

Consultation with local education authorities

28 (1) Where –
   (a) a child is being looked after by a local authority; and
   (b) the authority propose to provide accommodation for him in an establishment at which education is provided for children who are accommodated there,

   they shall, so far as is reasonably practicable, consult the appropriate local education authority before doing so.

(2) Where any such proposal is carried out, the local authority shall, as soon as is reasonably practicable, inform the appropriate local education authority of the arrangements that have been made for the child's accommodation.

(3) Where the child ceases to be accommodated as mentioned in subsection (1)(b), the local authority shall inform the appropriate local education authority.

(4) In this section 'the appropriate local education authority' means –
   (a) the local education authority within whose area the local authority's area falls; or,
   (b) where the child has special educational needs and a statement of his needs is maintained under Part IV of the Education Act 1996, the local education authority who maintain the statement.

Recoupment of cost of providing services etc

29 (1) Where a local authority provide any service under section 17 or 18, other than advice, guidance or counselling, they may recover from a person specified in subsection (4) such charge for the service as they consider reasonable.

(2) Where the authority are satisfied that that person's means are insufficient for it to be reasonably practicable for him to pay the charge, they shall not require him to pay more than he can reasonably be expected to pay.

(3) No person shall be liable to pay any charge under subsection (1) for a service provided under section 17 or section 18(1) or (5) at any time when he is in receipt of income support under Part VII of the Social Security Contributions and Benefits Act 1992, of any element of child tax credit other than the family element, of working tax credit or of an income-based jobseeker's allowance.

(3A) No person shall be liable to pay any charge under subsection (1) for a service provided under section 18(2) or (6) at any time when he is in receipt of income support under Part VII of the Social Security Contributions and Benefits Act 1992 or of an income-based jobseeker's allowance.

(3B) No person shall be liable to pay any charge under subsection (1) for a service provided under section 18(2) or (6) at any time when –

  (a) he is in receipt of guarantee state pension credit under section 1(3)(a) of the State Pension Credit Act 2002, or

  (b) he is a member of a married or unmarried couple (within the meaning of that Act) the other member of which is in receipt of guarantee state pension credit.

(4) The persons are –

  (a) where the service is provided for a child under sixteen, each of his parents;

  (b) where it is provided for a child who has reached the age of sixteen, the child himself; and

  (c) where it is provided for a member of the child's family, that member.

(5) Any charge under subsection (1) may, without prejudice to any other method of recovery, be recovered summarily as a civil debt.

(6) Part III of Schedule 2 makes provision in connection with contributions towards the maintenance of children who are being looked after by local authorities and consists of the re-enactment with modifications of provisions in Part V of the Child Care Act 1980.

(7) Where a local authority provide any accommodation under section 20(1) for a child who was (immediately before they began to look after him) ordinarily resident within the area of another local authority, they may recover from that other authority any reasonable expenses incurred by them in providing the accommodation and maintaining him.

(8) Where a local authority provide accommodation under section 21(1) or (2)(a) or (b) for a child who is ordinarily resident within the area of another local authority and they are not maintaining him in –

  (a) a community home provided by them;

  (b) a controlled community home; or

  (c) a hospital vested in the Secretary of State or a Primary Care Trust, or any other hospital made available pursuant to arrangements made by a Strategic Health Authority, a Health Authority or a Primary Care Trust,

  they may recover from that other authority any reasonable expenses incurred by them in providing the accommodation and maintaining him.

(9) Except where subsection (10) applies, where a local authority comply with any request under section 27(2) in relation to a child or other person who is not ordinarily resident within their area, they may recover from the local authority in whose area the child or person is ordinarily resident any reasonable expenses incurred by them in respect of that person.

(10) Where a local authority ('authority A') comply with any request under section 27(2) from another local authority ('authority B') in relation to a child or other person –

  (a) whose responsible authority is authority B for the purposes of section 23B or 23C; or

  (b) whom authority B are advising or befriending or to whom they are giving assistance by virtue of section 24(5)(a),

  authority A may recover from authority B any reasonable expenses incurred by them in respect of that person.

NATIONAL HEALTH SERVICE AND COMMUNITY CARE ACT 1990
ss46–47
Local authority plans for community care services

46 (1) Each local authority –

    (a) shall, within such period after the day appointed for the coming into force of this section as the Secretary of State may direct, prepare and publish a plan for the provision of community care services in their area;

    (b) shall keep the plan prepared by them under paragraph (a) above and any further plans prepared by them under this section under review; and

    (c) shall, at such intervals as the Secretary of State may direct, prepare and publish modifications to the current plan, or if the case requires, a new plan.

  (2) In carrying out any of their functions under paragraphs (a) to (c) of subsection (1) above, a local authority shall consult –

    (a) any Health Authority and any Local Health Board the whole or any part of whose area lies within the area of the local authority;

    (b) [*Repealed*]

    (c) in so far as any proposed plan, review or modifications of a plan may affect or be affected by the provision or availability of housing and the local authority is not itself a local housing authority, within the meaning of the Housing Act 1985, every such local housing authority whose area is within the area of the local authority;

    (d) such voluntary organisations as appear to the authority to represent the interests of persons who use or are likely to use any community care services within the area of the authority or the interests of private carers who, within that area, provide care to persons for whom, in the exercise of their social services functions, the local authority have a power or a duty to provide a service;

    (e) such voluntary housing agencies and other bodies as appear to the local authority to provide housing or community care services in their area; and

    (f) such other persons as the Secretary of State may direct.

  (3) In this section –

'local authority' means the council of a county, a county borough, a metropolitan district or a London borough or the Common Council of the City of London;

'community care services' means services which a local authority may provide or arrange to be provided under any of the following provisions –

    (a) Part III of the National Assistance Act 1948;

    (b) section 45 of the Health Services and Public Health Act 1968;

    (c) section 21 of and Schedule 8 to the National Health Service Act 1977; and

    (d) section 117 of the Mental Health Act 1983; and

'private carer' means a person who is not employed to provide the care in question by any body in the exercise of its function under any enactment.

Assessment of needs for community care services

47 (1) Subject to subsections (5) and (6) below, where it appears to a local authority that any person for whom they may provide or arrange for the provision of community care services may be in need of any such services, the authority –

    (a) shall carry out an assessment of his needs for those services; and

    (b) having regard to the results of that assessment, shall then decide whether his needs call for the provision by them of any such services.

  (2) If at any time during the assessment of the needs of any person under subsection (1)(a) above it appears to a local authority that he is a disabled person, the authority –

    (a) shall proceed to make such a decision as to the services he requires as is mentioned in section 4 of the Disabled Persons (Services, Consultation and Representation) Act 1986 without his requesting them to do so under that section; and

(b) shall inform him that they will be doing so and of his rights under that Act.

(3) If at any time during the assessment of the needs of any person under subsection (1)(a) above, it appears to a local authority –

(a) that there may be a need for the provision to that person by such Primary Care Trust or Health Authority as may be determined in accordance with regulations of any services under the National Health Service Act 1977, or

(b) that there may be the need for the provision to him of any services which fall within the functions of a local housing authority (within the meaning of the Housing Act 1985) which is not the local authority carrying out the assessment,

the local authority shall notify that Primary Care Trust, Health Authority or local housing authority and invite them to assist, to such extent as is reasonable in the circumstances, in the making of the assessment; and, in making their decision as to the provision of services needed for the person in question, the local authority shall take into account any services which are likely to be made available for him by that Primary Care Trust, Health Authority or local housing authority.

(4) The Secretary of State may give directions as to the manner in which an assessment under this section is to be carried out or the form it is to take but, subject to any such directions and to subsection (7) below, it shall be carried out in such manner and take such form as the local authority consider appropriate.

(5) Nothing in this section shall prevent a local authority from temporarily providing or arranging for the provision of community care services for any person without carrying out a prior assessment of his needs in accordance with the preceding provisions of this section if, in the opinion of the authority, the condition of that person is such that he requires those services as a matter of urgency.

(6) If, by virtue of subsection (5) above, community care services have been provided temporarily for any person as a matter of urgency, then, as soon as practicable thereafter, an assessment of his needs shall be made in accordance with the preceding provisions of this section . . .

CARERS (RECOGNITION AND SERVICES) ACT 1995 s1
Assessment of ability of carers to provide care: England and Wales

1 (1) Subject to subsection (3) below, in any case where –

   (a) a local authority carry out an assessment under section 47(1)(a) of the National Health Service and Community Care Act 1990 of the needs of a person ('the relevant person') for community care services, and

   (b) an individual ('the carer') provides or intends to provide a substantial amount of care on a regular basis for the relevant person,

   the carer may request the local authority, before they make their decision as to whether the needs of the relevant person call for the provision of any services, to carry out an assessment of his ability to provide and continue to provide care for the relevant person; and if he makes such a request, the local authority shall carry out such an assessment and shall take into account the results of that assessment in making that decision.

  (2) Subject to subsection (3) below, in any case where –

   (a) a local authority assess the needs of a disabled child for the purpose of Part III of the Children Act 1989 or section 2 of the Chronically Sick and Disabled Persons Act 1970, and

   (b) an individual ('the carer') provides or intends to provide a substantial amount of care on a regular basis for the disabled child,

   the carer may request the local authority, before they make their decision as to whether the needs of the disabled child call for the provision of any services, to carry out an assessment of his ability to provide and continue to provide care for the disabled child; and if he makes such a request, the local authority shall carry out such an assessment and shall take into account the results of that assessment in making that decision.

(2A) For the purposes of an assessment under subsection (1) or (2), the local authority may take into account, so far as it considers it to be material, an assessment under section 1 or 6 of the Carers and Disabled Children Act 2000.

  (3) No request may be made under subsection (1) or (2) above by an individual who provides or will provide the care in question –

   (a) by virtue of a contract of employment or other contract with any person; or

   (b) as a volunteer for a voluntary organisation . . .

  (4) The Secretary of State may give directions as to the manner in which an assessment under subsection (1) or (2) above is to be carried out or the form it is to take but, subject to any such directions, it shall be carried out in such manner and take such form as the local authority consider appropriate.

  (5) Section 8 of the Disabled Persons (Services, Consultation and Representation) Act 1986 (duty of local authority to take into account ability of carers) shall not apply in any case where –

   (a) an assessment is made under subsection (1) above in respect of an individual who provides the care in question for a disabled person; or

   (b) an assessment is made under subsection (2) above.

  (6) In this section –

   'community care services' has the meaning given by section 46(3) of the National Health Service and Community Care Act 1990;

   'child' means a person under the age of eighteen;

   'disabled child' means a child who is disabled within the meaning of Part III of the Children Act 1989;

   'disabled person' means a person to whom section 29 of the National Assistance Act 1948 applies;

   'local authority' has the meaning given by section 46(3) of the National Health Service and Community Care Act 1990; and 'voluntary organisation' has the same meaning as in the National Assistance Act 1948.

(7) [*Repealed*]

HOUSING GRANTS, CONSTRUCTION AND REGENERATION ACT 1996 ss23–24

Grants: purposes for which grant must or may be given

23 (1) The purposes for which an application for a grant must be approved, subject to the provisions of this Chapter, are the following –

    (a) facilitating access by the disabled occupant to and from
        (i) the dwelling, qualifying houseboat or qualifying park home, or
        (ii) the building in which the dwelling or, as the case may be, flat is situated;

    (b) making
        (i) the dwelling, qualifying houseboat or qualifying park home, or
        (ii) the building,
    safe for the disabled occupant and other persons residing with him;

    (c) facilitating access by the disabled occupant to a room used or usable as the principal family room;

    (d) facilitating access by the disabled occupant to, or providing for the disabled occupant, a room used or usable for sleeping;

    (e) facilitating access by the disabled occupant to, or providing for the disabled occupant, a room in which there is a lavatory, or facilitating the use by the disabled occupant of such a facility;

    (f) facilitating access by the disabled occupant to, or providing for the disabled occupant, a room in which there is a bath or shower (or both), or facilitating the use by the disabled occupant of such a facility;

    (g) facilitating access by the disabled occupant to, or providing for the disabled occupant, a room in which there is a washhand basin, or facilitating the use by the disabled occupant of such a facility;

    (h) facilitating the preparation and cooking of food by the disabled occupant;

    (i) improving any heating system in the dwelling, qualifying houseboat or qualifying park home to meet the needs of the disabled occupant or, if there is no existing heating system there or any such system is unsuitable for use by the disabled occupant, providing a heating system suitable to meet his needs;

    (j) facilitating the use by the disabled occupant of a source of power, light or heat by altering the position of one or more means of access to or control of that source or by providing additional means of control;

    (k) facilitating access and movement by the disabled occupant around the dwelling, qualifying houseboat or qualifying park home in order to enable him to care for a person who is normally resident there and is in need of such care;

    (l) such other purposes as may be specified by order of the Secretary of State.

(2) [Repealed]

(3) If in the opinion of the local housing authority the relevant works are more or less extensive than is necessary to achieve any of the purposes set out in subsection (1), they may, with the consent of the applicant, treat the application as varied so that the relevant works are limited to or, as the case may be, include such works as seem to the authority to be necessary for that purpose.

Grants: approval of application

24 (1) The local housing authority shall approve an application for a grant for purposes within section 23(1), subject to the following provisions.

(2) Where an authority entertain an owner's application for a grant made by a person who proposes to acquire a qualifying owner's interest, they shall not approve the application until they are satisfied that he has done so.

(3) A local housing authority shall not approve an application for a grant unless they are satisfied –

    (a) that the relevant works are necessary and appropriate to meet the needs of the disabled occupant, and

    (b) that it is reasonable and practicable to carry out the relevant works having regard to the age and condition of

        (i)   the dwelling, qualifying houseboat or qualifying park home, or

        (ii) the building.

In considering the matters mentioned in paragraph (a) a local housing authority which is not itself a social services authority shall consult the social services authority.

(4) An authority proposing to approve an application for a grant shall consider –

    (a) in the case of an application in respect of works to a dwelling, whether the dwelling is fit for human habitation;

    (b) in the case of a common parts application, whether the building meets the requirements in section 604(2) of the Housing Act 1985,

and the authority shall take that into account in deciding whether it is reasonable and practicable to carry out the relevant works.

(5) A local housing authority shall not approve a common parts application for a grant unless they are satisfied that the applicant has a power or is under a duty to carry out the relevant works.

CARERS AND DISABLED CHILDREN ACT 2000 ss1–4
Right of carers to assessment

1 (1) If an individual aged 16 or over ('the carer') –

(a) provides or intends to provide a substantial amount of care on a regular basis for another individual aged 18 or over ('the person cared for'); and

(b) asks a local authority to carry out an assessment of his ability to provide and to continue to provide care for the person cared for,

the local authority must carry out such an assessment if it is satisfied that the person cared for is someone for whom it may provide or arrange for the provision of community care services.

(2) For the purposes of such an assessment, the local authority may take into account, so far as it considers it to be material, an assessment under section 1(1) of the Carers (Recognition and Services) Act 1995.

(3) Subsection (1) does not apply if the individual provides or will provide the care in question –

(a) by virtue of a contract of employment or other contract with any person; or

(b) as a volunteer for a voluntary organisation.

(4) The Secretary of State (or, in relation to Wales, the National Assembly for Wales) may give directions as to the manner in which an assessment under subsection (1) is to be carried out or the form it is to take.

(5) Subject to any such directions, it is to be carried out in such manner, and is to take such form, as the local authority considers appropriate.

(6) In this section, 'voluntary organisation' has the same meaning as in the National Assistance Act 1948.

Services for carers

2 (1) The local authority must consider the assessment and decide –

(a) whether the carer has needs in relation to the care which he provides or intends to provide;

(b) if so, whether they could be satisfied (wholly or partly) by services which the local authority may provide; and

(c) if they could be so satisfied, whether or not to provide services to the carer.

(2) The services referred to are any services which –

(a) the local authority sees fit to provide; and

(b) will in the local authority's view help the carer care for the person cared for,

and may take the form of physical help or other forms of support.

(3) A service, although provided to the carer –

(a) may take the form of a service delivered to the person cared for if it is one which, if provided to him instead of to the carer, could fall within community care services and they both agree it is to be so delivered; but

(b) if a service is delivered to the person cared for it may not, except in prescribed circumstances, include anything of an intimate nature.

(4) Regulations may make provision about what is, or is not, of an intimate nature for the purposes of subsection (3).

Vouchers

3 (1) Regulations may make provision for the issue of vouchers by local authorities.

(2) 'Voucher' means a document whereby, if the local authority agrees with the carer that it would help him care for the person cared for if the carer had a break from caring, the person cared for may secure that services in lieu of the care which would otherwise have been provided to him by the carer are delivered temporarily to him by another person by way of community care services.

(3) The regulations may, in particular, provide –

(a) for the value of a voucher to be expressed in terms of money, or of the delivery of a service for a period of time, or both;

(b) for the person who supplies a service against a voucher, or for the arrangement under which it is supplied, to be approved by the local authority;

(c) for vouchers to be issued to the carer or to the person cared for;

(d) for a maximum period during which a service (or a service of a prescribed description) can be provided against a voucher.

Assessments and services for both carer and person cared for

4 (1) In section 1 of the Carers (Recognition and Services) Act 1995 (which provides for carers to be assessed as to their ability to care in connection with an assessment of the needs of the individual cared for), after subsection (2) insert –

'(2A) For the purposes of an assessment under subsection (1) or (2), the local authority may take into account, so far as it considers it to be material, an assessment under section 1 or 6 of the Carers and Disabled Children Act 2000.'

(2) Subsection (4) applies if the local authority –

(a) is either providing services under this Act to the carer, or is providing community care services to or in respect of the person cared for (but not both); and

(b) proposes to provide another service to (or in respect of) the one who is not receiving any such service,

and the new service, or any service already being provided, is one which could be provided either under this Act, or by way of community care services.

(3) Subsection (4) also applies if –

(a) the local authority is not providing services to the carer (under this Act) or to the person cared for (by way of community care services), but proposes to provide services to each of them following an assessment under section 1 and under section 47 of the National Health Service and Community Care Act 1990; or

(b) the local authority is providing services both to the carer (under this Act) and to the person cared for (by way of community care services), and proposes to provide to either of them a new service,

and (in a paragraph (a) case) any of the services, or (in a paragraph (b) case) the new service, is one which could be provided either under this Act, or by way of community care services.

(4) In the case of each such service, the local authority must decide whether the service is, or is in future, to be provided under this Act, or by way of community care services (and hence whether it is, or is in future, to be provided to the carer, or to the person cared for).

(5) The local authority's decision under subsection (4) is to be made without regard to the means of the carer or of the person cared for.

LOCAL GOVERNMENT ACT 2000 ss2, 3 and 92

Promotion of well-being
Promotion of well-being

2 (1) Every local authority are to have power to do anything which they consider is likely to achieve any one or more of the following objects –
  (a) the promotion or improvement of the economic well-being of their area;
  (b) the promotion or improvement of the social well-being of their area, and
  (c) the promotion or improvement of the environmental well-being of their area.
  (2) The power under subsection (1) may be exercised in relation to or for the benefit of –
  (a) the whole or any part of a local authority's area, or
  (b) all or any persons resident or present in a local authority's area.
  (3) In determining whether or how to exercise the power under subsection (1), a local authority must have regard to their strategy under section 4.
  (4) The power under subsection (1) includes power for a local authority to –
  (a) incur expenditure,
  (b) give financial assistance to any person,
  (c) enter into arrangements or agreements with any person,
  (d) co-operate with, or facilitate or co-ordinate the activities of, any person,
  (e) exercise on behalf of any person any functions of that person, and
  (f) provide staff, goods, services or accommodation to any person.
  (5) The power under subsection (1) includes power for a local authority to do anything in relation to, or for the benefit of, any person or area situated outside their area if they consider that it is likely to achieve any one or more of the objects in that sub-section.
  (6) Nothing in subsection (4) or (5) affects the generality of the power under subsection (1).

Limits on power to promote well-being

3 (1) The power under section 2(1) does not enable a local authority to do anything which they are unable to do by virtue of any prohibition, restriction or limitation on their powers which is contained in any enactment (whenever passed or made).
  (2) The power under section 2(1) does not enable a local authority to raise money (whether by precepts, borrowing or otherwise).
  (3) The Secretary of State may by order make provision preventing local authorities from doing, by virtue of section 2(1), anything which is specified, or is of a descrip-tion specified, in the order.
  (4) Before making an order under subsection (3), the Secretary of State must consult such representatives of local government and such other persons (if any) as he con-siders appropriate.
  (5) Before exercising the power under section 2(1), a local authority must have regard to any guidance for the time being issued by the Secretary of State about the exercise of that power.
  (6) Before issuing any guidance under subsection (5), the Secretary of State must con-sult such representatives of local government and such other persons (if any) as he considers appropriate.
  (7) In its application to Wales, this section has effect as if for any reference to the Sec-retary of State there were substituted a reference to the National Assembly for Wales.
  (8) In this section 'enactment' includes an enactment comprised in subordinate legis-lation (within the meaning of the Interpretation Act 1978).

Maladministration, etc

Payments in cases of maladministration, etc

92 (1) Where a relevant authority consider –

    (a) that action taken by or on behalf of the authority in the exercise of their functions amounts to, or may amount to, maladministration, and

    (b) that a person has been, or may have been, adversely affected by that action,

the authority may, if they think appropriate, make a payment to, or provide some other benefit for, that person.

(2) Any function which is conferred on the Greater London Authority under this section is to be exercisable by the Mayor of London and the London Assembly acting jointly on behalf of the Authority.

(3) In this section –

'action' includes failure to act,

'relevant authority' has the same meaning as in Part III of this Act.

HEALTH AND SOCIAL CARE ACT 2001 ss49, 53–58

Nursing care
Exclusion of nursing care from community care services

49 (1) Nothing in the enactments relating to the provision of community care services shall authorise or require a local authority, in or in connection with the provision of any such services, to –

(a) provide for any person, or

(b) arrange for any person to be provided with,

nursing care by a registered nurse.

(2) In this section 'nursing care by a registered nurse' means any services provided by a registered nurse and involving –

(a) the provision of care, or

(b) the planning, supervision or delegation of the provision of care,

other than any services which, having regard to their nature and the circumstances in which they are provided, do not need to be provided by a registered nurse.

Measures to increase availability of Part 3 accommodation
Disregarding of resources when determining need for residential accommodation

53 In section 21 of the 1948 Act (duties of local authorities to provide accommodation), for subsections (2A) and (2B) there shall be substituted –

'(2A) In determining for the purposes of paragraph (a) or (aa) of subsection (1) of this section whether care and attention are otherwise available to a person, a local authority shall disregard so much of the person's resources as may be specified in, or determined in accordance with, regulations made by the Secretary of State for the purposes of this subsection.

(2B) In subsection (2A) of this section the reference to a person's resources is a reference to his resources within the meaning of regulations made for the purposes of that subsection.'

Funding by resident etc of more expensive accommodation

54 (1) Regulations may make provision for and in connection with the making, in respect of the provision of Part 3 accommodation, of additional payments –

(a) by persons for whom such accommodation is provided ('residents'); or

(b) by other persons (including persons liable to maintain residents by virtue of section 42 of the 1948 Act).

(2) In this section 'additional payments', in relation to a resident, means payments which –

(a) are made for the purpose of meeting all or part of the difference between the actual cost of his Part 3 accommodation and the amount that the local authority providing it would usually expect to pay in order to provide Part 3 accommodation suitable for a person with the assessed needs of the resident; and

(b) (in the case of additional payments by the resident) are made out of such of his resources as may be specified in, or determined in accordance with, regulations under subsection (1);

and for this purpose 'resources' has the meaning given by such regulations.

(3) In this Part 'Part 3 accommodation' means accommodation provided under sections 21 to 26 of the 1948 Act.

Power for local authorities to take charges on land instead of contributions

55 (1) Where a person ('the resident') –

(a) is availing himself of Part 3 accommodation provided by a local authority, or is proposing to do so, and

(b) is liable, or would be liable, to pay for the accommodation (whether at the full standard rate determined in accordance with section 22(2) or 26(2) of the 1948 Act or at any lower rate),

the local authority may enter into a deferred payment agreement with the resident.

(2) The relevant authority may by directions require local authorities, where –

(a) they provide or are to provide Part 3 accommodation for a person falling within subsection (1) ('the resident'), and

(b) any conditions specified in the directions are satisfied,

to enter into a deferred payment agreement with the resident.

(3) A 'deferred payment agreement' is an agreement whereby –

(a) during the exempt period the resident will not be required to make payment to the authority of any relevant contributions in respect of periods (or parts of periods) falling within the exempt period, but

(b) the total amount of the relevant contributions shall become payable to the authority on the day after the date on which the exempt period ends, and

(c) the resident will grant the authority a charge in their favour in respect of any land specified in the agreement in which he has a beneficial interest (whether legal or equitable) for the purpose of securing the payment to the authority of the total amount payable to them as mentioned in paragraph (b).

(4) 'The exempt period', in relation to a deferred payment agreement, is the period beginning with the time when the agreement takes effect and ending –

(a) 56 days after the date of the resident's death, or

(b) with any earlier date which, in accordance with the agreement, the resident has specified in a notice given by him to the authority for the purposes of subsection (5)(b).

(5) The provisions of any deferred payment agreement and any such charge as is mentioned in subsection (3)(c) –

(a) shall be determined by the authority in accordance with any directions given by the relevant authority; but

(b) shall secure that the agreement and any such charge may be terminated by notice given to the authority by the resident on payment of the full amount which he is liable to pay as mentioned in subsection (3)(a) down to the date of the payment.

(6) Where a deferred payment agreement is in force in respect of the resident –

(a) no interest shall accrue at any time on or before the date on which the exempt period ends in respect of any sum which he is liable to pay as mentioned in subsection (3)(a); but

(b) as from the day after that date, any such sum shall bear interest at such reasonable rate as the relevant authority may direct or, if no such directions are given, as the authority may determine;

and accordingly any charge granted in pursuance of subsection (3)(c) shall secure payment to the authority of any interest falling due by virtue of paragraph (b) above.

(7) Any reference in this section to relevant contributions is a reference to so much of the payments which the resident is liable to pay to an authority for Part 3 accommodation (including any payments which are additional payments for the purpose of section 54) as may be specified, or determined in accordance with, regulations made for the purposes of this subsection.

(8) Any directions given by the relevant authority under this section shall be given to local authorities generally.

Cross-border placements

56 (1) Regulations may make provision for and in connection with authorising a local authority to make arrangements under section 21 of the 1948 Act for a person to be

provided with residential accommodation in Scotland, Northern Ireland, any of the Channel Islands or the Isle of Man.

(2) Regulations under this section may, in particular, make provision –

(a) specifying conditions which must be satisfied before a local authority make any arrangements in pursuance of the regulations in respect of a person;

(b) for the application of provisions of the 1948 Act in relation to –

(i) any such arrangements, or

(ii) the person in respect of whom any such arrangements are made,

with or without modifications.

Direct payments
Direct payments

57 (1) Regulations may make provision for and in connection with requiring or authorising the responsible authority in the case of a person of a prescribed description who falls within subsection (2) to make, with that person's consent, such payments to him as they may determine in accordance with the regulations in respect of his securing the provision of the service mentioned in paragraph (a) or (b) of that subsection.

(2) A person falls within this subsection if a local authority ('the responsible authority') have decided –

(a) under section 47 of the 1990 Act (assessment by local authorities of needs for community care services) that his needs call for the provision by them of a particular community care service (within the meaning of section 46 of that Act), or

(b) under section 2(1) of the Carers and Disabled Children Act 2000 (c 16) (services for carers) to provide him with a particular service under that Act.

(3) Regulations under this section may, in particular, make provision –

(a) specifying circumstances in which the responsible authority are not required or authorised to make any payments under the regulations to a person, whether those circumstances relate to the person in question or to the particular service mentioned in paragraph (a) or (b) of subsection (2);

(b) for any payments required or authorised by the regulations to be made to a person by the responsible authority ('direct payments') to be made to that person ('the payee') as gross payments or alternatively as net payments;

(c) for the responsible authority to make for the purposes of subsection (4) or (5) such determination as to –

(i) the payee's means, and

(ii) the amount (if any) which it would be reasonably practicable for him to pay to the authority by way of reimbursement or contribution,

as may be prescribed;

(d) as to the conditions falling to be complied with by the payee which must or may be imposed by the responsible authority in relation to the direct payments (and any conditions which may not be so imposed);

(e) specifying circumstances in which the responsible authority –

(i) may or must terminate the making of direct payments,

(ii) may require repayment (whether by the payee or otherwise) of the whole or part of the direct payments;

(f) for any sum falling to be paid or repaid to the responsible authority by virtue of any condition or other requirement imposed in pursuance of the regulations to be recoverable as a debt due to the authority;

(g) displacing functions or obligations of the responsible authority with respect to the provision of the service mentioned in subsection (2)(a) or (b) only to such extent, and subject to such conditions, as may be prescribed;

    (h) authorising direct payments to be made to any prescribed person on behalf of the payee.

(4) For the purposes of subsection (3)(b) 'gross payments' means payments –

    (a) which are made at such a rate as the authority estimate to be equivalent to the reasonable cost of securing the provision of the service concerned; but

    (b) which may be made subject to the condition that the payee pays to the responsible authority, by way of reimbursement, an amount or amounts determined under the regulations.

(5) For the purposes of subsection (3)(b) 'net payments' means payments –

    (a) which are made on the basis that the payee will himself pay an amount or amounts determined under the regulations by way of contribution towards the cost of securing the provision of the service concerned; and

    (b) which are accordingly made at such a rate below that mentioned in subsection (4)(a) as reflects any such contribution by the payee.

(6) Regulations under this section shall provide that, where direct payments are made in respect of a service which, apart from the regulations, would be provided under section 117 of the Mental Health Act 1983 (c 20) (after-care) –

    (a) the payments shall be made at the rate mentioned in subsection (4)(a); and

    (b) subsection (4)(b) shall not apply.

(7) Regulations made for the purposes of subsection (3)(a) may provide that direct payments shall not be made in respect of the provision of residential accommodation for any person for a period in excess of a prescribed period.

(8) In this section 'prescribed' means specified in or determined in accordance with regulations under this section.

Direct payments in respect of children

58   For section 17A of the Children Act 1989 (c 41) there shall be substituted –

'17A Direct payments

(1) The Secretary of State may by regulations make provision for and in connection with requiring or authorising the responsible authority in the case of a person of a prescribed description who falls within subsection (2) to make, with that person's consent, such payments to him as they may determine in accordance with the regulations in respect of his securing the provision of the service mentioned in that subsection.

(2) A person falls within this subsection if he is –

    (a) a person with parental responsibility for a disabled child,

    (b) a disabled person with parental responsibility for a child, or

    (c) a disabled child aged 16 or 17,

and a local authority ('the responsible authority') have decided for the purposes of section 17 that the child's needs (or, if he is such a disabled child, his needs) call for the provision by them of a service in exercise of functions conferred on them under that section.

(3) Subsections (3) to (5) and (7) of section 57 of the 2001 Act shall apply, with any necessary modifications, in relation to regulations under this section as they apply in relation to regulations under that section.

(4) Regulations under this section shall provide that, where payments are made under the regulations to a person falling within subsection (5) –

    (a) the payments shall be made at the rate mentioned in subsection (4)(a) of section 57 of the 2001 Act (as applied by subsection (3)); and

    (b) subsection (4)(b) of that section shall not apply.

(5) A person falls within this subsection if he is –

(a) a person falling within subsection (2)(a) or (b) and the child in question is aged 16 or 17, or

(b) a person who is in receipt of income support, working families' tax credit or disabled person's tax credit under Part 7 of the Social Security Contributions and Benefits Act 1992 (c 4) or of an income-based jobseeker's allowance.

(6) In this section –

'the 2001 Act' means the Health and Social Care Act 2001;

'disabled' in relation to an adult has the same meaning as that given by section 17(11) in relation to a child;

'prescribed' means specified in or determined in accordance with regulations under this section (and has the same meaning in the provisions of the 2001 Act mentioned in subsection (3) as they apply by virtue of that subsection).'

Regulations and directions

SECRETARY OF STATE'S APPROVALS AND DIRECTIONS UNDER SECTION 21(1) OF THE NATIONAL ASSISTANCE ACT 1948 (LAC(93)10 Appendix 1)

The Secretary of State for Health, in exercise of the powers conferred on her by section 21(1) of the National Assistance Act 1948, hereby makes the following Approvals and Directions –

Commencement, interpretation and extent

1 (1) These Approvals and Directions shall come into force on 1st April 1993.

(2) In these Approvals and Directions, unless the context otherwise requires, 'the Act' means the National Assistance Act 1948.

(3) The Interpretation Act 1978 applies to these Approvals and Direction as it applies to an Act of Parliament.

(4) These Approvals and Directions shall apply only to England and Wales.

Residential accommodation for persons in need of care and attention

2 (1) The Secretary of State hereby –

(a) approves the making by local authorities of arrangements under section 21(1)(a) of the Act in relation to persons with no settled residence and, to such extent as the authority may consider desirable, in relation to persons who are ordinarily resident in the area of another local authority, with the consent of that other authority; and

(b) directs local authorities to make arrangements under section 21(1)(a) of the Act in relation to persons who are ordinarily resident in their area and other persons who are in urgent need thereof,

to provide residential accommodation for persons aged 18 or over who by reason of age, illness, disability or any other circumstance are in need of care and attention not otherwise available to them.

(2) Without prejudice to the generality of sub-paragraph (1), the Secretary of State hereby directs local authorities to make arrangements under section 21(1)(a) of the Act to provide temporary accommodation for persons who are in urgent need thereof in circumstances where the need for that accommodation could not reasonably have been foreseen.

(3) Without prejudice to the generality of sub-paragraph (1), the Secretary of State hereby directs local authorities to make arrangements under section 21(1)(a) of the Act to provide accommodation –

(a) in relation to persons who are or have been suffering from mental disorder, or

(b) for the purposes of the prevention of mental disorder, for persons who are ordinarily resident in their area and for persons with no settled residence who are in the authority's area.

(4) Without prejudice to the generality of sub-paragraph (1) and subject to section 24(4) of the Act, the Secretary of State hereby approves the making by local authorities of

arrangements under section 21(1)(a) of the Act to provide residential accommodation –

(a) in relation to persons who are or have been suffering from mental disorder; or

(b) for the purposes of the prevention of mental disorder,

for persons who are ordinarily resident in the area of another local authority but who following discharge from hospital have become resident in the authority's area.

(5) Without prejudice to the generality of sub-paragraph (1), the Secretary of State hereby approves the making by local authorities of arrangements under section 21(1)(a) of the Act to provide accommodation to meet the needs of persons for –

(a) the prevention of illness;

(b) the care of those suffering from illness; and

(c) the aftercare of those so suffering.

(6) Without prejudice to the generality of sub-paragraph (1), the Secretary of State hereby approves the making by local authorities of arrangements under section 21(1)(a) of the Act specifically for persons who are alcoholic or drug-dependent.

Residential accommodation for expectant and nursing mothers

3   The Secretary of State hereby approves the making by local authorities of arrangements under section 21(1)(aa) of the Act to provide residential accommodation (in particular mother and baby homes) for expectant and nursing mothers (of any age) who are in need of care and attention which is not otherwise available to them.

Arrangements to provide services for residents

4   The Secretary of State hereby directs local authorities to make arrangements in relation to persons provided with accommodation under section 21(1) of the Act for all or any of the following purposes –

(a) for the welfare of all persons for whom accommodation is provided;

(b) for the supervision of the hygiene of the accommodation so provided;

(c) to enable persons for whom accommodation is provided to obtain –

   (i)   medical attention,

   (ii) nursing attention during illnesses of a kind which are ordinarily nursed at home, and

   (iii) the benefit of any services provided by the National Health Service of which they may from time to time be in need,

   but nothing in this paragraph shall require a local authority to make any provision authorised or required to be provided under the National Health Service Act 1977;

(d) for the provision of board and such other services, amenities and requisites provided in connection with the accommodation, except where in the opinion of the authority managing the premises their provision is unnecessary;

(e) to review regularly the provision made under the arrangements and to make such improvements as the authority considers necessary.

Arrangements for the conveyance of residents

5   The Secretary of State hereby approves the making by local authorities of arrangements under section 21(1) of the Act to provide, in such cases as the authority considers appropriate, for the conveyance of persons to and from premises in which accommodation is provided for them under Part III of the Act.

Duties in respect of residents in transferred accommodation

6 (1) Where a person is provided with accommodation pursuant to section 21(1) of the Act, and –

(a) the residential accommodation is local authority accommodation provided pursuant to section 21(4) of the 1948 Act; and

(b) the local authority transfer the management of the residential accommodation to a voluntary organisation who –
  (i) manages it as a residential care home within the meaning of Part I of the Registered Homes Act 1984, and
  (ii) is registered under that Part or is not required to be so registered by virtue of being an exempt body; and
(c) the person is accommodated in the residential accommodation immediately before and after the transfer,

while that person remains accommodated in that residential accommodation, the local authority shall remain under a duty to make arrangements to provide accommodation for him after any transfer to which paragraph (b) of this sub-paragraph refers.

(2) For the purposes of paragraph (c) of sub-paragraph (1), a person shall be regarded as accommodated in residential accommodation if –
  (a) he is temporarily absent from such accommodation (including circumstances in which he is in hospital or on holiday);
  (b) before 1st April 1993, that accommodation was provided under paragraph 2(1) of Schedule 8 to the National Health Service Act 1977.

(3) Where immediately before these Approvals and Directions come into force a local authority was under a duty to provide a person with accommodation by virtue of –
  (a) the Secretary of State's former Directions under section 21(1) of the National Assistance Act 1948 contained in Annex 1 of Department of Health Circular LAC(91)12; or
  (b) the Secretary of State's former Directions under paragraph 2 of Schedule 8 to the National Health Service Act 1977 contained in Annex 2 of Department of Health Circular LAC(91)12,

while that person remains accommodated in that residential accommodation, the local authority shall remain under a duty to make arrangements to provide that person with accommodation from the date on which these Directions come into force.

Powers to make arrangements with other local authorities and voluntary organisations, etc

7   For the avoidance of doubt, these Approvals and Directions are without prejudice to any of the powers conferred on local authorities by section 21(4) and section 26(1) of the Act (arrangements with voluntary organisations, etc).

Dated 17/2/1993

SECRETARY OF STATE'S APPROVALS AND DIRECTIONS UNDER SECTION 29(1) OF THE NATIONAL ASSISTANCE ACT 1948 (LAC(93)10 Appendix 2)

The Secretary of State for Health, in exercise of the powers conferred on her by section 29(1) of the National Assistance Act 1948, hereby makes the following Approvals and Directions: –

Commencement, interpretation and extent

1 (1) These Approvals and Directions shall come into force on 1st April 1993.

(2) In these Approvals and Directions, unless the context otherwise requires, 'the Act' means the National Assistance Act 1948.

(3) The Interpretation Act 1978 applies to these Approvals and Directions as it applies to an Act of Parliament.

(4) These Approvals and Directions shall apply only to England and Wales.

Powers and duties to make welfare arrangements

2 (1) The Secretary of State hereby approves the making by local authorities of arrangements under section 29(1) of the Act for all persons to whom that subsection applies and directs local authorities to make arrangements under section 29(1) of the Act in relation to persons who are ordinarily resident in their area for all or any of the following purposes –

(a) to provide a social work service and such advice and support as may be needed for people in their own homes or elsewhere;

(b) to provide, whether at centres or elsewhere, facilities for social rehabilitation and adjustment to disability including assistance in overcoming limitations of mobility or communication;

(c) to provide, whether at centres or elsewhere, facilities for occupational, social, cultural and recreational activities and, where appropriate, the making of payments to persons for work undertaken by them.

(2) The Secretary of State hereby directs local authorities to make the arrangements referred to in section 29(4)(g) of the Act (compiling and maintaining registers) in relation to persons who are ordinarily resident in their area.

(3) The Secretary of State hereby approves the making by local authorities of arrangements under section 29(1) of the Act for all persons to whom that subsection applies for the following purposes –

(a) to provide holiday homes;

(b) to provide free or subsidised travel for all or any persons who do not otherwise qualify for travel concessions, but only in respect of travel arrangements for which concessions are available;

(c) to assist a person in finding accommodation which will enable him to take advantage of any arrangements made under section 29(1) of the Act;

(d) to contribute to the cost of employing a warden on welfare functions in warden assisted housing schemes;

(e) to provide warden services for occupiers of private housing.

(4) Save as is otherwise provided for under this paragraph, the Secretary of State hereby approves the making by local authorities of all or any of the arrangements referred to in section 29(4) of the Act (welfare arrangements, etc.) for all persons to whom section 29(1) applies.

Welfare arrangements with another local authority

3 The Secretary of State hereby approves the making by local authorities of arrangements under section 29(1) of the Act, where appropriate, with another local authority for the provision of any of the services referred to in these Approvals and Directions.

Welfare arrangements with voluntary organisations and otherwise

4   For the avoidance of doubt, these Approvals and Directions are without prejudice to the powers conferred on local authorities by section 30(1) of the Act (voluntary organisations for disabled persons' welfare).

Dated 17/3/1993

SECRETARY OF STATE'S APPROVALS AND DIRECTIONS UNDER PARAGRAPHS 1 AND 2 OF SCHEDULE 8 TO THE NATIONAL HEALTH SERVICE ACT 1977
(LAC(93)10 Appendix 3)

The Secretary of State for Health, in exercise of the powers conferred on her by paragraphs 1(1) and 2(1) of Schedule 8 to the National Health Service Act 1977, hereby makes the following Approvals and Directions –

Commencement, interpretation and extent

1 (1) These Approvals and Directions shall come into force on 1st April 1993.

(2) In these Approvals and Directions, unless the context otherwise requires, 'the Act' means the National Health Service Act 1977.

(3) The Interpretation Act 1978 applies to these Approvals and Directions as it applies to an Act of Parliament.

(4) For the avoidance of doubt, these Approvals and Directions apply only to England and Wales.

Services for expectant and nursing mothers

2   The Secretary of state hereby approves the making of arrangements under paragraph 1(1) of Schedule 8 to the Act for the care of expectant and nursing mothers (of any age) other than the provision of residential accommodation for them (services for the purpose of the prevention of illness etc.).

3 (1) The Secretary of State hereby approves the making by local authorities of arrangements under paragraph 2(1) of Schedule 8 to the Act for the purpose of the prevention of illness, and the care of persons suffering from illness and for the aftercare of persons who have been so suffering and in particular for –

(a) the provision, for persons whose care is undertaken with a view to preventing them becoming ill, persons suffering from illness and persons who have been so suffering, of centres or other facilities for training them or keeping them suitably occupied and the equipment and maintenance of such centres;

(b) the provision, for the benefit of such persons as are mentioned in paragraph (a) above, of ancillary or supplemental services.

(2) The Secretary of State hereby directs local authorities to make arrangements under paragraph 2(1) of Schedule 8 to the Act for the purposes of the prevention of mental disorder, or in relation to persons who are or who have been suffering from mental disorder –

(a) for the provision of centres (including training centres and day centres) or other facilities (including domiciliary facilities), whether in premises managed by the local authority or otherwise, for training or occupation of such persons;

(b) for the appointment of sufficient social workers in their area to act as approved social workers for the purposes of the Mental Health Act 1983;

(c) for the exercise of the functions of the authority in respect of persons suffering from mental disorder who are received into guardianship under Part II or III of the Mental Health Act 1983 (whether the guardianship of the local social services authority or of other persons);

(d) for the provision of social work and related services to help in the identification, diagnosis, assessment and social treatment of mental disorder and to provide social work support and other domiciliary and care services to people living in their homes and elsewhere.

(3) Without prejudice to the generality of sub-paragraph (1), the Secretary of State hereby approves the making by local authorities of arrangements under paragraph 2(1) of Schedule 8 to the Act for the provision of –

(a) meals to be served at the centres or other facilities referred to in sub-paragraphs (1)(a) and (2)(a) above and meals-on-wheels for house-bound people not provided for –

(i) under section 45(1) of the Health Services and Public Health Act 1968(a), or

(ii) by a district council under paragraph 1 of Part II of Schedule 9 to the Health and Social Services and Social Security Adjudications Act 1983;

(b) remuneration for persons engaged in suitable work at the centres or other facilities referred to in sub-paragraphs (1)(a) and (2)(a) above, subject to paragraph 2(2)(a) of Schedule 8 to the Act;

(c) social services (including advice and support) for the purposes of preventing the impairment of physical or mental health of adults in families where such impairment is likely, and for the purposes of preventing the break-up of such families, or for assisting in their rehabilitation;

(d) night-sitter services;

(e) recuperative holidays;

(f) facilities for social and recreational activities;

(g) services specifically for persons who are alcoholic or drug-dependent.

Services made available by another local authority etc.

4 For the purposes of any arrangements made under these Approvals and Directions, the Secretary of State hereby approves the use by local authorities of services or facilities made available by another authority, voluntary body or person on such conditions as may be agreed, but in making such arrangements, a local authority shall have regard to the importance of services being provided as near to a person's home as is practicable.

Dated 17/3/1993
Signed on behalf of the Secretary of State for Health

COMPLAINTS PROCEDURE DIRECTIONS 1990

4 (1) The local authority shall appoint one of their officers to assist the authority in the co-ordination of all aspects of their consideration of the representations.

 (2) The local authority shall ensure that all the members or officers involved in the handling of representations under s7B(1) are familiar with the procedures set out in these Directions.

5 (1) Where a local authority receives representations from any complainant they shall attempt to resolve the matter informally.

 (2) If the matter cannot be resolved to the satisfaction of the complainant, the local authority shall give or send to him an explanation of the procedures set out in these Directions and ask him to submit a written representation if he wishes to proceed.

 (3) The local authority shall offer assistance and guidance to the complainant on the use of this procedure, or give advice on where he may obtain it.

6 (1) The local authority shall consider the representations and formulate a response within 28 days of their receipt, or if this is not possible, explain to the complainant within that period why it is not possible and tell him when he can expect a response, which shall in any event be within three calendar months of receipt of the representations.

 (2) The representations may be withdrawn at any stage by the complainant, in which case the procedures set out in these Directions (other than direction 9 and 11) shall no longer apply to that case.

7 (1) The local authority shall notify in writing the result of their consideration to –

 (a) the complainant;

 (b) the person on whose behalf the representations were made, unless the local authority consider that person is unable to understand it or it would cause him unnecessary distress;

 (c) any other person who the local authority considers has sufficient interest in the case.

 (2) If the complainant informs the local authority in writing within 28 days of the date on which the notification mentioned in paragraph (1) is sent to him that he is dissatisfied with that result and wishes the matter to be referred to a panel for review, the local authority shall appoint a panel (including any independent person) to consider the matter which the local authority shall refer to it.

 (3) The panel shall meet within 28 days of the receipt of the complainant's request for review by the local authority to consider the matter together with any oral or written submissions as the complainant or the local authority wish the panel to consider.

8 (1) Where a panel meets under direction 7, it shall decide on its recommendations and record them in writing within 24 hours of the end of the meeting.

 (2) The panel shall send written copies of their recommendations to –

 (a) the local authority,

 (b) the complainant,

 (c) if appropriate, the person on whose behalf the representations were made, and

 (d) any other person who the local authority considers has sufficient interest in the case.

 (3) The panel shall record the reasons for their recommendations in writing.

 (4) The local authority shall consider what action they ought to take, and notify in writing the persons specified in paragraph (1)(b), (c) and (d) of the local authority's decision and of their reasons for taking that decision and of any action which they may have taken or propose to take within 28 days of the date of the panel's recommendation.

9 The local authority shall keep a record of each representation received, the outcome of each representation, and whether there was compliance with the time limits specified in directions 6(1), 7(3), and 8(1) and 8(4).

NATIONAL ASSISTANCE ACT 1948 (CHOICE OF ACCOMMODATION) DIRECTIONS 1992

The Secretary of State in exercise of the powers conferred by section 7A of the Local Authority Social Services Act 1970 and of all other powers enabling her in that behalf hereby makes the following Directions –

Citation, commencement and extent

1 (1) These Directions may be cited as the National Assistance Act 1948 (Choice of Accommodation) Directions 1992 and shall come into force on 1st April 1993.

(2) These Directions extend only to England.

Local authorities to provide preferred accommodation

2 Where a local authority have assessed a person under section 47 of the National Health Service and Community Care Act 1990 (assessment) and have decided that accommodation should be provided pursuant to section 21 of the National Assistance Act 1948 (provision of residential accommodation) the local authority shall, subject to paragraph 3 of these Directions, make arrangements for accommodation pursuant to section 21 for that person at the place of his choice within England and Wales (in these Directions called 'preferred accommodation') if he has indicated that he wishes to be accommodated in preferred accommodation.

Conditions for provision of preferred accommodation

3 Subject to paragraph 4 of these Directions the local authority shall only be required to make or continue to make arrangements for a person to be accommodated in his preferred accommodation if –

(a) the preferred accommodation appears to the authority to be suitable in relation to his needs as assessed by them;

(b) the cost of making arrangements for him at his preferred accommodation would not require the authority to pay more than they would usually expect to pay having regard to his assessed needs;

(c) the preferred accommodation is available;

(d) the persons in charge of the preferred accommodation provide it subject to the authority's usual terms and conditions, having regard to the nature of the accommodation, for providing accommodation for such a person under Part III of the National Assistance Act 1948.

GUIDANCE ON NATIONAL ASSISTANCE ACT 1948 (CHOICE OF ACCOMMODATION) DIRECTIONS 1992

NATIONAL ASSISTANCE (RESIDENTIAL ACCOMMODATION) (ADDITIONAL PAYMENTS AND ASSESSMENT OF RESOURCES) (AMENDMENT) (ENGLAND) REGULATIONS 2001

1 Purpose

1.1 This guidance updates the guidance that accompanied the Choice of Accommodation Directions 1992 ('the Directions'), and the further guidance included in LAC(2001)29 to take account of the National Assistance Act 1948 (Choice of Accommodation) (Amendment) (England) Directions 2001 and the National Assistance (Additional Payments and Assessment of Resources) (Amendment) (England) Regulations 2001 ('the Regulations').

1.2 The Directions are intended to ensure that when councils with social services responsibilities ('councils') make placements in care homes or care homes providing nursing care, that, within reason, individuals are able to exercise genuine choice over where they live.

1.3 The Regulations give individuals the right to enter into more expensive accommodation than they would otherwise have been offered in certain circumstances, these are outlined below in paragraph 4.

1.4 The guidance sets out what individuals should be able to expect from the council that is responsible for funding their care, subject to the individual's means, when arranging a care home place for them. The guidance is intended to describe the minimum amount of choice that councils should offer individuals. Even where not required to act in a certain way by the Directions or the Regulations, councils should make all reasonable efforts to maximise choice as far as possible within available resources and the law.

2 Summary

2.1 If, after an assessment of need, made in accordance with the General Principles of Assessment in LAC(2002)13 *Fair Access to Care Services*,[1] and discussion with the individual and their carers, a council decides to provide residential accommodation under section 21 of the National Assistance Act 1948 either permanently or temporarily (intermediate care or short term break or any interim care arrangement), it will make a placement on behalf of the individual in suitable accommodation. Nearly all placements under section 21 of the National Assistance Act 1948 are made in registered care homes. Some adults are placed in unregistered settings where they need neither nursing care or personal care While the detail of this guidance applies to registered care homes, the principles apply to adults placed in unregistered settings.

2.2 When the term 'residential care' is used in this guidance, it covers placements made on both a long-term and a temporary basis to care homes, whether they provide nursing care or not.

2.3 If the individual concerned expresses a preference for particular accommodation ('preferred accommodation') within England and Wales, the council must arrange for care in that accommodation, provided:

- The accommodation is suitable in relation to the individual's assessed needs (see paragraphs 3.5.1 to 3.5.3).
- To do so would not cost the council more than what it would usually expect to pay for accommodation for someone with the individual's assessed needs see paragraphs 3.5.4 to 3.5.8). This is referred to throughout this guidance as the usual cost.

---

1   www.doh.gov.uk/publications/coinh.html.

- The accommodation is available (see paragraphs 3.5.9 and 3.5.15).
- The person in charge of the accommodation is willing to provide accommodation subject to the council's usual terms and conditions for such accommodation (see paragraphs 3.5.16 to 3.5.17).

2.4 If an individual requests it, the council must also arrange for care in accommodation more expensive than it would usually fund provided a third party or, in certain circumstances, the resident, is willing and able to pay the difference between the cost the council would usually expect to pay and the actual cost of the accommodation, (see paragraph 4).

3   Preferred Accommodation

3.1 As with all aspects of service provision, there should be a general presumption in favour of individuals being able to exercise reasonable choice over the service they receive. The limitations on councils' obligation to provide preferred accommodation set out in the Directions and the Regulations are not intended to deny individuals reasonable freedom of choice, but to ensure that councils are able to fulfil their obligations for the quality of service provided and for value for money. The terms of the Directions and the Regulations are explained more fully below. Where, for any reason, a council decides not to arrange a place for someone in their preferred accommodation it must have a clear and reasonable justification for that decision which relates to the criteria of the Directions and is not in breach of the Regulations.

3.2 Arrangements under section 26(3A) of the National Assistance Act 1948 require the agreement of all parties. Individuals should not be refused their preferred accommodation without a full explanation from councils, in writing, of their reasons to do so.

3.3 The location of the preferred accommodation need not be limited by the boundaries of the funding council. Councils are obliged to cater for placements falling within the Directions or the Regulations in any permitted care home within England or Wales. Any extension to this beyond England and Wales is subject to any future regulations governing cross-border placements (but see LAC(93)18 in respect of placements involving Scotland and the Department of Health/Welsh Assembly protocol on free nursing care for cross border placements).[2]

3.4 Funding councils may refer to their own usual costs when making placements in another council's area. However, because costs vary from area to area, if in order to meet a resident's assessed need it is necessary to place an individual in another area at a higher rate than the funding council's usual costs, that council should meet the additional cost itself.

3.5 The Directions state that a council must arrange for care in an individual's preferred accommodation subject to four considerations:

(a) Suitability of accommodation

3.5.1 Suitability will depend on the council's assessment of individual need. Each case must be considered on its merits.

3.5.2 Accommodation provided in a care home will not necessarily be suitable for the individual's needs simply because it satisfies registration standards. On the other hand, accommodation will not necessarily be unsuitable simply because it fails to conform to the council's preferred model of provision, or to meet to the letter a standard service specification laid down by the council.

3.5.3 The Directions and Regulations do not affect Section 26(1A) of the National Assistance Act 1948 as amended by the Care Standards Act 2000. Arrangements should not be made for the provision of accommodation together with nursing or personal care in a care home unless the accommodation to be provided is managed by an organisation or person who is registered under Part II

---

2   At www.doh.giv.uk/jointunit/nhsfundednursingcare.htm.

of the Care Standards Act. Similarly, the Directions and the Regulations do not require a council to contract with any accommodation where for any other reason it is prevented by law from doing so.

(b) Cost

3.5.4   One of the conditions associated with the provision of preferred accommodation is that such accommodation should not require the council to pay more than they would usually expect to pay, having regard to assessed needs (the 'usual cost'). This cost should be set by councils at the start of a financial or other planning period, or in response to significant changes in the cost of providing care, to be sufficient to meet the assessed care needs of supported residents in residential accommodation. A council should set more than one usual cost where the cost of providing residential accommodation to specific groups is different. In setting and reviewing their usual costs, councils should have due regard to the actual costs of providing care and other local factors.

3.5.5   Individual residents should not be asked to pay more towards their accommodation because of market inadequacies or commissioning failures. For example, where an individual has not expressed a preference for more expensive accommodation, but there are not sufficient places at a given time at the council's usual cost, the council should make a placement in more expensive accommodation and meet the cost difference itself. Only when an individual has expressed a preference for more expensive accommodation than a council would usually expect to pay, can a third party or the resident be asked for a top up (see paragraph 4.1). From time to time, due to unforeseen circumstance, there may be insufficient care home places available to councils (at the usual cost) to meet the current assessed care needs of supported residents. In these circumstances, neither the resident nor a third party should be asked to contribute more than the resident would normally be expected to contribute. That is, in these circumstances, councils should make up the difference between the resident's assessed contribution and the actual care home fees. Costs of accommodation should be compared on the basis of gross costs before income from charging. Given the different amounts that councils will recover from individuals by ways of charges, it would not be appropriate for a council to determine a usual net cost that it would expect to pay.

3.5.6   For the cost of placements in other councils' areas see paragraph 3.3.

3.5.7   Councils should not set arbitrary ceilings on the amount they expect to pay for an individual's residential care. Residents and third parties should not routinely be required to make up the difference between what the council will pay and the actual fees of a home. Councils should provide residents with the level of service they could expect if the possibility of resident and third party contributions did not exist.

3.5.8   Costs can vary according to the type of care provided. For example, the cost a council might usually expect to pay for short-term care might be different from its usual cost for long-term care. There are also a number of situations where there may be higher costs incurred in providing residential care, be it long or short-term. Examples include specialist care for specific user groups with high levels of need or where necessary to prepare special diets and provide additional facilities for medical or cultural reasons. Councils should be prepared to meet these higher costs in order to ensure an individual's needs are appropriately met.

(c) Availability

3.5.9   Generally, good commissioning by councils should ensure there is sufficient capacity so individuals should not have to wait for their assessed (that is, eligible) needs to be met. However, waiting is occasionally inevitable, particularly when individuals have expressed a preference towards a particular care home where there are no current vacancies. Where individuals may need to wait, their access to the most appropriate (and possibly, preferred) service should be based solely on their assessed need, and councils should ensure that in the interim adequate alternative services are provided. Waiting for the preferred care home should not mean that the person's care needs are not met in the interim or that they wait in a setting unsuitable for their assessed needs, and this includes an acute hospital bed, until the most suitable or preferred accommodation becomes available. In view of the Community Care (Delayed Discharges etc.) Act 2003,[3] councils should have contingency arrangements in place, that address the likelihood that an individual's preferred accommodation will not always be readily available. These arrangements should meet the needs of the individual and sustain or improve their level of independence. For some, the appropriate interim arrangement could be an enhanced care package at home.

3.5.10 Councils should give individuals an indication of the likely duration of the interim arrangement. Councils should place the individual on the waiting list of the preferred accommodation and aim to move them into that accommodation as soon as possible. Information about how the waiting list is handled should be clear and the individual should be kept informed of progress. If the duration of the interim arrangement exceeds a reasonable time period, eg, 12 weeks, the individual should be reassessed to ensure that the interim and preferred accommodation, are still able to meet the individual's assessed needs and to prevent any unnecessary moves between care homes that are unable to meet the individual's assessed needs.

3.5.11 Councils should ensure that while waiting in temporary residential accommodation, if an individual has to contribute towards their care costs it is in accordance with the National Assistance (Assessment of Resources) Regulations 1992. Individuals who are waiting in these circumstances should not be asked to pay more than their assessed financial contribution to meet the costs of these residential care services which have been arranged or suggested by the council to temporarily meet their assessed needs.

3.5.12 Councils should take all reasonable steps to gain an individual's agreement to an interim care home or care package. Councils should make reasonable efforts to take account of the individual's desires and preferences. In doing this, councils should ascertain all relevant facts and take into account all the circumstances relevant to the person, and ensure that the individual (and their family or carers) understands the consequences of failing to come to an agreement. Where patients have been assessed as no longer requiring NHS continuing inpatient care, they do not have the right to occupy indefinitely an NHS bed. If an individual continues to unreasonably refuse the interim care home or care package, the council is entitled to consider that it has fulfilled its statutory duty to assess and offer services, and may then inform the individual, in writing, they will need to make their own arrangements. This position also applies to the unreasonable refusal of a permanent care home, not just the interim care home or care package. If at a later date further contact is made with social services regarding the individual, the council should re-open the care planning process, if it is satisfied that the individual's needs remain such to justify the provision of services and there is no longer reason to think that the individual will persist in refusing such services unreasonably. Councils may wish to take their own legal advice in such circumstances.

---

3   At www.legislation.hmso.gov.uk/acts/acts2003/20030005.htm.

3.5.13 In all but a very small number of cases where an individual is being placed under Part II of the Mental Health Act 1983, individuals have the right to refuse to enter a care home. This includes patients who are awaiting discharge from hospital. In such cases the social services department should work with the person, his or her family and carers, and NHS partners, (and potentially housing partners), to explore alternative options, including a package of health and social care in the person's own home or suitable alternative accommodation.

3.5.14 In some cases, individuals who move into a care home for an interim period may choose to remain there, even if a place in their original preferred accommodation becomes available. If the care home is able to accept the individual on a long-term basis, they should be taken off the waiting list of their original preferred accommodation. If the cost of the interim care home is higher than the usual cost the council would expect to pay for their assessed need, upon making the choice to remain in that home, a third party or the resident could be approached for the total difference between the two rates. This should be clearly explained to individuals before they enter the home. See paragraph 4.2 for fuller details.

3.5.15 The Directions only apply to individuals whose care is being arranged by a council under Part 3 of the National Assistance Act 1948. For example, where hospital patients need to move to a different type of care, and social services are not involved, this is a matter for the NHS and the individual patient and the Directions do not apply. For good practice on handling these situations, see the Hospital Discharge Workbook.[4]

(d) Terms and conditions

3.5.16 In order to ensure that they are able to exercise proper control over the use of their funds, councils need to be able to impose certain contractual conditions, for example, in relation to payment regimes, review, access, monitoring, audit, record keeping, information sharing, insurance, sub-contracting, etc.

3.5.17 The contractual conditions required of preferred accommodation should be broadly the same as those councils would impose on any other similar operation. Stricter conditions should never be used as a way of avoiding or deterring a placement. As with suitability, account should be taken of the nature and location of the accommodation. There may be occasions where it would be unreasonable for a council not to adapt its standard conditions and others where it would be unreasonable to expect it to do so. For example, councils should take into account the fact that care homes in other areas, or those that take residents from many areas, may have geared themselves to the normal requirements of other councils. Councils should be flexible in such circumstances and avoid adding to the administrative burden of care homes.

4   More expensive accommodation

4.1 The guidance set out in paragraphs 4.2 to 4.5.11, applies only where a resident explicitly chooses to enter accommodation other than that which the council offers them, and where that preferred accommodation is more expensive than the council would usually expect to pay.

4.2 In certain circumstances, councils can make placements in more expensive accommodation than they would usually expect to pay for, provided a resident or a third party is able and willing to make up the difference (to 'top up'). Residents that are subject to the 12 week property disregard or have agreed a deferred payments agreement with the council may make top-ups from specified resources on their

---

4   At www.doh.gov/uk/hospitaldischarge/index.htm.

own behalf. These are the only situations where the resident may top up. The most common arrangement is that a third party is providing the top-up. A third party in this case might be a relative, a friend, or any other source. For liable relatives see paragraph 4.5.10.

4.3 When setting its usual cost(s) a council should be able to demonstrate that this cost is sufficient to allow it to provide residents with the level of care services that they could reasonably expect to receive if the possibility of resident and third party contributions did not exist.

4.4 Councils should not seek resident or third party contributions in cases where the council itself decides to offer someone a place in more expensive accommodation in order to meet assessed needs, or for other reasons. Where there are no placements at the council's usual rate, councils should not leave individuals to make their own arrangements having determined that they need to enter residential accommodation and do not have care and attention otherwise available to them. In these instances, councils should make suitable alternative arrangements and seek no contribution from the individual other than their contribution as assessed under the National Assistance (Assessment of Resources) Regulations 1992. Councils must never encourage or otherwise imply that care home providers can or should seek further contributions from individuals in order to meet assessed needs.

4.5 This paragraph deals with considerations that apply where either residents or third parties are making further contributions to costs over and above the resident's assessed contribution under the National Assistance (Assessment of Resources) Regulations 1992.

(a) Responsibility for costs of accommodation

4.5.1 When making arrangements for residential care for an individual under the National Assistance Act 1948, a council is responsible for the full cost of that accommodation. Therefore, where a council places someone in more expensive accommodation, it must contract to pay the accommodation's fees in full. The resident's or the third party's contribution will be treated as part of the resident's income for charging purposes and the council will be able to recover it in that way. However, under a deferred payments agreement, where the resident is topping up against the value of their home, their top-up contribution is added to their deferred contribution.

4.5.2 Councils will be aware that under section 26(3A) of the National Assistance Act 1948 (as inserted by the NHS and Community Care Act 1990), it is open to them to agree with both the resident and the person in charge of their accommodation that, instead of paying a contribution to the council, the resident may pay the same amount direct to the accommodation, with the council paying the difference. In such a case, the third party would also pay the accommodation direct on behalf of the resident. However, it should be noted that even where there is such an agreement for the resident to make payments direct to the accommodation, the council continues to be liable to pay the full costs of the accommodation should either the resident or relative fail to pay the required amount.

4.5.3 Where top-ups are required from a resident or third party, the resident will therefore need to demonstrate that either they or the third party is able and willing to pay the difference between the council's usual rate and the accommodation's actual fees.

4.5.4 In order to safeguard both residents and councils from entering into top-up arrangements that are likely to fail, the resident or the third party must reasonably be expected to be able to continue to make top-up payments for the duration of the arrangements. Councils should, therefore, assure themselves that residents or third parties will have the resources to continue to make the required top-up payments. Councils should seek similar assurances when residents top-up against the value of their home when the home is subject to a deferred payments agreement. When the home is eventually sold, it should be possible for the resident or their estate to pay back the deferred contribution including the resident top-ups.

(b) The amount of the resident or third party top-up

4.5.5 The amount of resident or third party top-up payments should be the difference between the actual fee for the accommodation and the amount that otherwise the council would usually have expected to pay for someone with the individual's assessed needs. In determining the precise amounts in individual cases, the council will take account of the guidance give in paragraphs 3.5.4 to 3.5.8 above.

4.5.6 The amount of the resident or third party top-up should be calculated on gross costs; that is, the difference between the preferred accommodation's fees and the fees that a council would usually expect to pay. The fact that a resident might not have been able to meet the full cost of the accommodation that the council would otherwise have arranged does not affect their ability to benefit from the additional top-up payments.

(c) Price increases

4.5.7 Arrangements between the council, resident and third party will need to be reviewed from time to time to take account of changes to accommodation fees. There will also be changes to the council's usual cost, which should be reasonable and set in accordance with paragraphs 3.5.4 to 3.5.8. However, fees and usual costs may not change at the same rate, and residents and third parties should be told that there cannot be a guarantee that any increases in the accommodation's fees will automatically be shared evenly between the council and/or the resident or third party, should the particular accommodation's fees rise more quickly than the costs the council would usually expect to pay for similar individuals. A council may find it useful to agree with the resident (or third party) that the resident's (or third party's) contribution will be reviewed on a regular basis on the understanding that clear explanations for proposed increases are given. It is also important that individuals know when, and in what circumstances, the fees for their accommodation will be reviewed.

(d) Responsibilities of residents and third parties

4.5.8 Councils should make clear to residents and third parties, in writing, the basis on which arrangements are to be made when they seek to exercise their right to more expensive preferred accommodation. It should be clear from the outset to the resident, third party and person providing the accommodation that:

- failure to keep up top-up payments will normally result in the resident having to move to other accommodation, subject to a full community care assessment of the resident's needs. Where a resident's top-ups are being made against the value of property subject to a deferred payments agreement, a council will have
- assured itself from the outset that top-up payments are viable and recoverable when the home is sold;
- an increase in the resident's income will not necessarily lessen the need for a top-up contribution, since the resident's own income will be subject to means testing by the council in the normal way;
- a rise in the accommodation's fees will not automatically be shared equally between council, resident (if making a top-up), and third party.

(e) Suitability and Conditions

4.5.9   With reference to paragraphs 3.5.1 to 3.5.3 and 3.5.16 to 3.5.17 above, the criteria of suitability and willingness to provide on the basis of normal conditions should be applied in the same way as for other preferred accommodation. An exception to this is that it would be reasonable to expect providers entering this kind of arrangement to agree to do so on the basis that the council has the right, subject to notice, to terminate the contract should the resident's or third party's top-up payments cease to be adequate.

(f) Liable relatives

4.5.10   Liable relatives who are making maintenance contributions cannot act as third parties for the care of the relative to whose care they are already contributing under section 42 of the National Assistance Act 1948. This limitation does not apply to top-up arrangements agreed prior to 1 October 2001 with liable relatives. Neither does the limitation apply to liable relatives who are not making contributions under section 42 of the 1948 Act.

5   Individuals already resident in residential care

5.1   Individuals already placed by a council in residential accommodation, and those already in residential accommodation as self-funders but who, because of diminishing resources, are on the verge of needing council support, have the same rights under these Directions as those who have yet to be placed by the council. Any such individual who wishes to move to different or more expensive accommodation may seek to do so on the same basis as anyone about to enter residential care for the first time. Should a self-funder who is resident in a care home that is more expensive than a council would usually expect to pay later become the responsibility of the council due to diminishing funds, they should not be asked for a top-up or be expected to move from the care home, unless, after a care and risk assessment, they are deemed able to move to alternative accommodation.

6   Individuals who are unable to make their own choices

6.1   There will be cases in which prospective residents are unable to express a preference for themselves. It would be reasonable to expect councils to act on the preferences expressed by their advocate, carer or legal guardian in the same way that they would on the resident's own wishes, unless that would in the council's opinion be against the best interests of the resident.

7   Effect on contracting

7.1   Any block contract or other form of contract that a council may have with a provider should not serve to limit choice. An individual should not be limited to care homes that hold such contracts with the funding council, or cares homes that are run by councils. It would not be reasonable for a council to use as a test for the suitability of accommodation, its presence or absence from a previously compiled list of preferred suppliers. The Directions and Regulations do not, however, prevent an authority having a list of preferred providers with which it will contract where a potential resident expresses no preference for particular accommodation, nor from recommending such providers to prospective residents.

8   Information

8.1   Individuals, and/or those who represent them, need information on the options open to them if they are to be able to exercise genuine choice. They should be given fair and balanced information with which to make the best choice of accommodation for them. Councils should explain to individuals their rights under the Directions and the Regulations. Councils should also consider providing material in a range of forms including written leaflets in local community languages, Braille, on audio tape and in accessible language, eg, easy words, short sentences, large print and pictures (for those with learning disabilities). Councils should supply copies of the Directions and this guidance if requested in appropriate forms. They should work with local hospitals to provide clear information to hospital patients as early as possible in their stay about what the council will be able to provide should they require short or long-term residential care at the end of their hospital stay. Individuals should be told explicitly that:

- they are free to choose any accommodation that is likely to meet their needs subject to the constraints set out in the Directions and the Regulations.
- they may allow the council to make a placement decision on their behalf; and
- they may choose from a preferred list (if the authority operates such a system).

8.2 Individuals should also be told what will happen if the preferred accommodation is not available. Councils may also wish to cover the matters described in paragraph 3.5.12. Wherever possible, the individual should be encouraged to have a relative, carer or advocate present during the conversation. A written record of the conversation should be kept, in particular, recording any decisions taken or preferences expressed by the individual. This record should be shared with the individual.

9   Complaints

9.1 Complaints about the application of the Directions and the Regulations and decisions taken in individual cases will fall within the scope of councils' statutory complaints procedure. As in all aspects of their activity, councils should ensure that prospective residents are aware of and understand the existence of the complaints procedure and their rights under it.

Department of Health
September 2003

Precedents

PRECEDENT 1
COMMUNITY CARE ASSESSMENT REQUEST

To: Director of Social Services / Health Authority / NHS Trust, etc
[address]

From: Applicant's name
[address]

Date

Dear Director of Social Services

Community Care Assessment
Mr Albert Smith [address]

I am the [solicitor/carer/agent/advocate] for the above named who has asked that I assist him in obtaining an assessment of his needs for community care services under National Health Service and Community Care Act 1990 s47.

Mr Smith is [insert] years of age being born on [insert if known] and is a [disabled/ elderly/ill] person, in that he

[here detail as precisely as possible the impairments which have resulted in the applicant needing community care services].

The help that Mr Smith currently envisages as being necessary, is
[here detail if possible the services which are required].

I understand that your care manager will wish to contact Mr Smith in order to investigate this complaint. He suggests that this be done by [here give a telephone contact number and the time/days the client or carer, etc, are usually available or some other convenient way that contact can be made]

Yours sincerely

PRECEDENT 2
ACCESS TO INFORMATION LETTER

To: Director of Social Services / Health Authority / NHS Trust, etc
[address]

From: *Applicant's name*
[address]

Date

Access to Personal Information
Data Protection Act 1998

REQUEST FOR INFORMATION

I formally request that you give me access to the personal information held by your authority relating to my personal circumstances, by copying the relevant information to [me] [my agent, namely . .] at [insert address].

The information I require to be disclosed is all personal information which your authority holds which relates to myself. [*If possible describe as precisely as possible the information that is sought, including for instance where the information is likely to be located, the nature of the information and the dates between which it was collected*].

I understand that I am entitled to receive this information within 40 days. I also understand that you may wish me to pay a fee for the processing and copying of this information and

[I confirm that I am willing to pay such reasonable sum as you may require (subject to the statutory maximum)] or

[in order to expedite matters I enclose a cheque in the sum of £10, being the statutory maximum, and would be grateful if you could refund to me, if appropriate, any excess[1]]

Please confirm receipt of this request.

....

---

1   The 40-day period runs from the date of receipt of the request and any necessary fee. Accordingly, provision should be expedited if the fee is actually enclosed.

PRECEDENT 3
FORMAL COMPLAINT LETTER

To: Director of Social Services
[*address*]

From: *Applicant's name*
[*address*]

Date

Dear Director of Social Services

Formal Complaint
Complaints Procedure Directions 1990[1]

I ask that you treat this letter as a formal complaint concerning the discharge by your authority of its functions in respect of [*myself*] [*the person for whom I care – Mr/Mrs/Ms etc . . .*]

I require the complaint to be investigated under Stage 2 of the Complaints process in accordance with direction 6(1) of the above directions and paragraph 4.9 of 'The Right to Complain' (HMSO, 1991).[2]

My complaint is:
[*here set out as precisely as possible:*

a) *what it is that is being complained about;*
b) *the names of the key social workers whom the complaints investigator will need to speak to;*
c) *the dates of the relevant acts/omissions.*

If possible also enclose copies of any relevant papers.]

What I want to achieve by making this complaint is
[*here set out as precisely as possible what you want to be the result of your complaint: ie, an apology, a changed service provision, an alteration to practice, compensation, etc*]

I understand that your complaints receiving officer will wish to contact me in order to investigate this complaint. I suggest that this be done by [*here give a telephone contact number and the time/days you are normally available or some other convenient way you can be contacted*]

....

---

1 This reference will need amending once the relevant provisions of the Health and Social Care (Community Health and Standards) Act 2003 have come into effect – see para 19.62 above.
2 See note 1 above.

Index